Minorities and Representation in American Politics

To

Lori, Neal,

and

Reece Franklin

Minorities and Representation in American Politics

Rebekah Herrick

Oklahoma State University

Los Angeles | London | New Delhi
Singapore | Washington DC | Melbourne

FOR INFORMATION:

CQ Press
An Imprint of SAGE Publications, Inc.
2455 Teller Road
Thousand Oaks, California 91320
E-mail: order@sagepub.com

SAGE Publications Ltd.
1 Oliver's Yard
55 City Road
London EC1Y 1SP
United Kingdom

SAGE Publications India Pvt. Ltd.
B 1/I 1 Mohan Cooperative Industrial Area
Mathura Road, New Delhi 110 044
India

SAGE Publications Asia-Pacific Pte. Ltd.
3 Church Street
#10-04 Samsung Hub
Singapore 049483

Senior Acquisitions Editor: Michael Kerns
Development Editor: Nancy Matuszak
eLearning Editor: Allison Hughes
Production Editor: Tracy Buyan
Copy Editor: Kristin Bergstad
Typesetter: Hurix Systems Pvt. Ltd.
Proofreader: Jan Wickline
Indexer: Virgil Diodato
Cover Designer: Karine Hovsepian
Marketing Manager: Amy Whitaker

Printed in the United States of America

Library of Congress Cataloging-in-Publication Data

Names: Herrick, Rebekah, 1960– author.

Title: Minorities and representation in American politics / Rebekah Herrick, Oklahoma State University, Stillwater, OK.

Description: Thousand Oaks: SAGE/CQ Press, 2017. | Includes bibliographical references and index.

Identifiers: LCCN 2015039009 | ISBN 9781483386836 (pbk. : alk. paper)

Subjects: LCSH: Political participation—United States. | Representative government and representation—United States. | Minorities—Political activity—United States. | Sexual minorities—Political activity—United States. | Women—Political activity—United States.

Classification: LCC JK1764. H46 2017 | DDC 323.173—dc23 LC record available at http://lccn.loc.gov/2015039009

This book is printed on acid-free paper.

16 17 18 19 20 10 9 8 7 6 5 4 3 2 1

Brief Contents

Detailed Contents

List of Spotlights, Tables, Figures, and Maps

Spotlights

Tables

Figures

Maps

Preface

The United States is rapidly diversifying. Current predictions suggest that in about one generation, whites will no longer be the majority of Americans.[1] Not only are there a greater number of racial and ethnic minorities, but each minority group is diversifying as well. The increase in the number of first-generation blacks from Africa and the Caribbean is diversifying the African American community, Hispanic immigrants from Central and South America are diversifying the Hispanic community, and southern and southeastern Asian immigrants are diversifying the Asian American community. In addition to ethnic and racial diversification, there is growing recognition of diversity with regard to sex and gender. There are people who identify as straight men, straight women, gay men, lesbian, asexual, pansexual, bisexual, transgender, and transsexual, as well as people who are intersex.

Unfortunately, the way textbooks tend to approach minorities and politics is to examine groups in isolation. While examining race, ethnicity, or gender in isolation allows for great detailed understanding of individual groups, it misses the importance of understanding the similarities and differences in the politics between the different minority groups, and the dynamic interfaces of multiple groups. For example, the effects of electoral systems vary by minority groups. Candidates of minority groups such as African Americans who still see significant levels of segregation benefit from single-member districts; however, minority groups that are not segregated, such as women, do not benefit from a district with a single member. However, changes in Americans' attitudes toward race, ethnicity, and gender have had universally positive effects, improving the electoral prospects of all minority groups.

Examining multiple groups in one text also facilitates greater discussion of intersectionality and intergroup cooperation. Intersectionality suggests there is a matrix, such that each combination of race, gender, class, and ethnicity offers people unique experiences and sources of power and domination.[2] For example, non-Hispanic white men have different political interests than African American or Hispanic men or white women. Intergroup cooperation concerns the degree to which different groups work together for shared goals. Finally, a book that integrates race, ethnicity, and gender is more efficient since teachers will only have one textbook and the different minority groups will be examined in a similar fashion. A key goal of the textbook is to systematically examine the politics of several minority groups.

The main minority groups discussed in the book are women; gay, lesbian, bisexual, and transgender (LGBT) Americans; Hispanics; American Indians; Asian Americans; and African Americans. This is not a complete list of important minority groups but includes the groups that have received the most attention by scholars and results in a manageable number of groups to examine.

In order to integrate the discussion of the different groups, I use a representational framework; this is particularly appealing because political minorities are often defined as groups who are underrepresented. Thus, exploring their levels of representation and what affects representation is to explore the essence of minority politics. Additionally, it helps facilitate a discussion of the main topics concerning minorities in American politics: political participation, public policy, identity, public opinion, elite behavior in all three branches of government, court cases, and elections.

The representation of minorities is multifaceted. Not only are there numerous minority groups, but representation also has many forms and meanings.[3] Representation can involve electing representatives who look like America, having representatives who work to advance constituents' interests, having a system designed to give constituents a voice, or ensuring the people believe the government serves their interests.

Given the complexity of minorities and representation, a goal of this text is to try to digest what is known about how minorities are represented in a way that is simple enough that undergraduates can understand minority representation and what affects it, yet thorough enough to offer a fairly complete picture. In doing so, students should get a sense of the differences and similarities between the different minority groups. What factors have similar effects on the representation of African Americans, Asian Americans, American Indians, Hispanics, women, and LGBT (lesbian, gay men, bisexual, and transgender) individuals? How do these groups differ in their levels of these factors? And what factors have different effects on these groups?

Taxonomists, scientists who categorize groups, can be broken into two categories: lumpers and splitters. A lumper is known for "submerging many minor varieties under a single name, whereas a splitter does the opposite, naming the varieties as subspecies or even full species."[4] As students read the book, they may want to consider whether lumping minorities together or splitting them into categories is more appropriate. Do we learn more about minorities in American politics by examining them as several distinct groups who share underrepresentation or as one group with individuals who have more in common than not? This book does not purport to answer the question but leaves it up to students to decide for themselves.

Since much research on minorities in America has been multidisciplinary in focus, this book draws on theories outside of mainstream political science. However, this book is decidedly a book on politics. Of interest are topics such as the frequency of and importance of minority office holders, whether policies reflect minority interests, minority voting behavior, and what affects these phenomena. Of less interest are broader societal implications or less direct influences on minority political behavior. After the introductory chapter, the book explores levels of representation for each minority group, and what affects those levels. The next section explores in more detail the factors that affect representation, such as resources; group assimilation, consciousness, and cohesion; public opinion; political behavior; and social movements.

The book uses "Spotlight" boxes to explore some specific issues related to each chapter's topic. While many of these boxes focus on minority representation outside of the United States and biographies of key minority political figures, some boxes are designed to illustrate key points or discuss methodological issues. The biographical boxes examine people who are important symbols of minorities in American politics and whose lives illustrate what it takes for minorities to increase their representation. The international boxes indicate to students that minorities around the world face many of the same challenges that are faced by minorities in the United States.

This book was written with the aid of many people, and I would like to thank them here. The feedback I received from those who reviewed this book's proposal and early manuscript proved invaluable: Linda Beail, Point Loma Nazarene University; Monique Bruner, Rose State College; Deirdre Condit, Virginia Commonwealth University; Kenneth Fernandez, Elon University; Brian Frederick Bridgewater State University; Ewa Golebiowska, Wayne State University; Eduardo Magalhães, Simpson College; Karen Own, Reinhardt University; Sandra Pavelka, Florida Gulf Coast University, and especially David Wilkins, University of Minnesota. I would like to thank Anthony Gonzalez, who helped me gather much of the information on descriptive and policy representation, and Grant Armstrong, who helped me collect information on interest groups. I also want to thank Oklahoma State University for helping to fund these research assistants. I also want to thank Leslie Baker, Ravi Perry, Erica Townsend-Bell, Eve Ringsmuth, Lori Franklin, Elizabeth Herrick, and Emily Herrick, who looked at various drafts of the manuscript. Their comments and help were critical. The book could not have been completed without the editors who have helped me through the various stages of the process: Sarah Calabi, Nancy Matuszak, Raquel Christie, Tracy Buyan, Kristin Bergstad, Amy Whitaker, and Allison Hughes—a special thanks to them. Finally, I want to thank the anonymous reviewers whose comments helped greatly improve the book.

About the Author

Rebekah Herrick is a professor of political science at Oklahoma State University. Her research interests focus on issues of representation, particularly as they relate to gender and LGBT Americans. Her teaching interests concern U.S. elections, minorities, and legislatures. Her recent books include: *Representation and Institutional Design* and *Representing America: The Citizen and Professional Legislator in the House of Representatives*. Her research has appeared in *Journal of Politics, Legislative Studies Quarterly, Social Science Quarterly, American Politics Research,* and *State Politics and Policy Quarterly*.

CQ Press, an imprint of SAGE, is the leading publisher of books, periodicals, and electronic products on American government and international affairs. CQ Press consistently ranks among the top commercial publishers in terms of quality, as evidenced by the numerous awards its products have won over the years. CQ Press owes its existence to Nelson Poynter, former publisher of the *St. Petersburg Times,* and his wife Henrietta, with whom he founded Congressional Quarterly in 1945. Poynter established CQ with the mission of promoting democracy through education and in 1975 founded the Modern Media Institute, renamed The Poynter Institute for Media Studies after his death. The Poynter Institute *www.poynter .org* is a nonprofit organization dedicated to training journalists and media leaders.

In 2008, CQ Press was acquired by SAGE, a leading international publisher of journals, books, and electronic media for academic, educational, and professional markets. Since 1965, SAGE has helped inform and educate a global community of scholars, practitioners, researchers, and students spanning a wide range of subject areas, including business, humanities, social sciences, and science, technology, and medicine. A privately owned corporation, SAGE has offices in Los Angeles, London, New Delhi, and Singapore, in addition to the Washington DC office of CQ Press.

Chapter 1

Minorities and Representation

The first woman to make a serious run for president was not Hillary Clinton, and the first African American was not Barack Obama. Rather, the first woman and the first African American to toss her hat into the ring was Rep. Shirley Chisholm (D, NY) who did so in 1972. Although she was never favored to win, she did get 430,000 primary votes and 151 convention delegates by building a coalition of women and African American voters.[1] Her race for president and her congressional career were structured by her race and gender and the interplay of the two. Although she was African American, many African leaders did not back her campaign because they felt it was time for a black man and she was too tied to gender concerns. In addition, many women's groups did not support her because they did not think an African American woman could win.[2] In her elections prior to 1972, her race and gender played a role as well. In her first bid for Congress in 1968, she faced James Farmer, who had been head of the civil rights organization Congress for Racial Equality and who made her gender an issue in the campaign.[3] Of her election for the New York State Assembly four years earlier she said:

> I met with hostility because of my sex from the start of my first campaign. Even some women would greet me, "You ought to be home, not out here." . . . one man about seventy lit into me. "Young woman, what are you doing out here in this cold? Did you get your husband's breakfast this morning? Did you straighten up your house? What are you doing running for office? This is something for men."[4]

In office, she was an advocate for women, African Americans, and other minorities. She started by hiring only women staffers, half African American and half white,[5] and was a founding member of the Congressional Black Caucus. She fought for greater access for minorities to attend college, increased social service spending, was against apartheid in South Africa, against the war in Vietnam, and for abortion rights. She also had to deal with colleagues who told racist and sexist jokes. To demonstrate that she was not wanted in Congress, she was assigned to the Committee on Agriculture, since it would not help her represent her Brooklyn district.[6]

Rep. Chisholm's political career cannot be understood simply by knowing she is African American nor can it be understood simply by knowing she is female. As one biographer stated, today "Chisholm would be considered a womanist politician, meaning that for her, feminist politics were tridimensional. They were driven by the need to eradicate a sexism that was inextricably bound by racism and classism."[7] Yet most minority and politics textbooks and classes examine groups in isolation. They examine gender and politics, Hispanics and politics, African Americans and politics, and so on. While this approach has the advantage of allowing for a great understanding of each minority group, it makes it difficult to see the broader picture of what might unify minority groups or what

Shirley Chisholm's portrait is unveiled in the Cannon caucus room. Attending are Congressional Black Caucus Chairwoman Barbara Lee (D, CA), House Speaker Nancy Pelosi (D, CA), Rep. Donna Edwards (D, MD), and Rep. Maxine Waters (D, CA). Chisholm was the first African American woman to be elected to the U.S. Congress, and the first to run for president. The portrait was painted by Kadir Nelson. (*Scott J. Ferrell/Congressional Quarterly/Getty Images*)

might make each group's experiences and power sources unique. For example, although minorities in the United States are united by having faced discrimination, the nature of that discrimination varies. African American men did not get the right to vote until 1870 with the ratification of the Fifteenth Amendment, and women did not get the right to vote until 1920 with the ratification of the Nineteenth Amendment. Although the Constitution gave African American men the right to vote before it gave women the right, most African Americans were effectively disenfranchised by state voting laws designed to deny them the right to vote until the 1960s. Other groups too were affected by many of these and other laws. In addition, Asian Americans' and American Indians' voting rights have been affected by laws and Supreme Court decisions barring them from becoming citizens and, along with Hispanics, English-only ballots. Yet, while most groups have been denied voting rights at some point, no laws or court decisions have directly denied lesbians, gays, bisexuals, and transgender people (LGBT) voting rights, although as women, lesbians were denied the franchise until 1920. Thus, while minorities, with the exception of white gay men, have been denied their right to vote, the process and timing of their disenfranchisement has varied.

Examining each group individually also complicates examining **intersectionality**. Intersectionality suggests there is a matrix, such that each combination of race, gender, class, and ethnicity offers people unique experiences and sources of power and domination.[8] For example, women of color who are victims of sexual violence are treated differently from white women by social services, the judicial processes, feminist groups, and antiracism groups.[9] For example, compared to non-Hispanic white women, women of color often have a more difficult time contacting the authorities for protection because of cultural, economic, language, or trust of police issues, and when they do, they often find fewer services or protection due to language or racial stereotypes. The specific racial, ethnic, and gender mix of an individual can even influence the effects of electoral systems on the electability of candidates. It is likely that African American men candidates are advantaged where cities or states are broken into districts, and that white women benefit from at-large systems, but that Hispanics and African American women are less affected by the electoral system.[10]

To understand the political experiences and power of minorities, this book focuses on several complicated questions concerning political representation. It focuses on governments and asks questions such as: To what degree have minorities gained positions in power? To what degree does the government serve minority interests? What affects whether the government serves minority interests? What is the likelihood of multiminority coalitions? And what are the prospects for the future of minority representation?

The answers to these questions are only going to become more important in the years to come as the United States is rapidly diversifying. Current predictions suggest in about a generation non-Hispanic whites will no longer be a majority in the United States.[11] Not only are there more racial and ethnic minorities, but each group is diversifying as well. The increase in the number of first-generation blacks from Africa and the Caribbean is diversifying the African American community, Hispanics from central and South America are diversifying the Hispanic community, and southern and southeastern Asians are diversifying the Asian American community. Moreover, there is a growing recognition of diversity with regard to sex, gender, and sexual orientation (see Spotlight 1.1). There are people who identify as straight men, straight women, gay men, lesbians, as well as transgender and transsexual men and women and gender nonconformists. The diversity and intersectionality of these groups mean the issues of minorities in politics become even more complicated. In order to understand representation of the numerous minority groups, it is important to know what the terms *political minorities* and *representation* mean. This chapter offers an overview of key minority groups and representation.

Spotlight 1.1

Facebook Has at Least Fifty-six Gender Categories

In February 2014, Facebook expanded the gender options its users can check in their profile or timeline to at least fifty-six.[12] While the two categories of male and female may seem sufficient to a majority of Americans, it is insufficient to fully match the array of genders possessed by all Americans. The computer developer responsible for the change, who identifies as transwoman (transitioning from man to woman) said, "All too often transgender people like myself and other gender nonconforming people are given this binary option, do you want to be male or female? What is your gender? And it's kind of disheartening because none of those let us tell others who we really are. . . . This really changes that, and for the first time I get to go to the site and specify to all the people I know what my gender is."[13] The change received much support from LGBT groups, but was seen as unnecessary by others who believe that there are only two sexes or genders. To select one of the new categories, Facebook users need to type an option under the custom category, and Facebook will accept certain options. Although Facebook did not release the different options, Oreums of Slate discovered 56: agender, androgyne, androgynous, bigender, cis, cisgender, cis female, cis male, cis

man, cis woman, cisgender female, cisgender male, cisgender man, cisgender woman, female to male, FTM, gender fluid, gender nonconforming, gender questioning, gender variant, genderqueer, intersex, male to female, MTF, neither, neutrois, non-binary, other, pangender, trans, trans*, trans female, trans male, trans* male, trans man, trans* man, trans person, trans*person, trans woman, trans* woman, transfeminine, transgender, transgender female, transgender male, transgender man, transgender person, transgender woman, transmasculine, transsexual, transsexual female, transsexual male, transsexual man, transsexual person, transsexual woman, and two-spirit.

Many of these terms are synonyms, such as *Trans man,* compared to *Trans* man,* or *transgender man.* Others terms may seem like synonyms but have important distinctions. For example, *Ciswoman,* which means that a person was born female and identifies as a woman, differs from *woman* in that it is an effort to relate to transgender individuals. Although the fifty-six gender options may have some redundancy and overstate the point, they emphasize that there are many ways that individuals can identify with a sex or gender.

Who Are Minorities? Race as a Category

Minorities are defined as groups of people who are underrepresented in and by the government in that they lack power and do not have adequate access to decision makers. A group is a collection of people who share an interest, ancestry, language, culture, or other trait. Groups are not the same as organizations. Organizations have a structure, such as leadership, headquarters, or membership, while groups are collections of people who share a trait. Although minority groups are often thought of in terms of having small numbers of people, the key distinguishing trait is that they have inadequate political power for their interests to be reflected in governmental policy.[14] While there are countless minority

Spotlight 1.2

Minorities around the World

The United States is not the only nation that has treated minorities poorly and struggles with how to ensure their rights. South Africa had a brutal system of apartheid that separated black and white South Africans, allowing whites to have significantly more power and wealth. Today, many countries in Africa have significant conflict between tribes or groups of people, many of which have resulted in genocide and civil wars, such as those in Rwanda, Sudan, and Ethiopia. In Latin America, the indigenous people often have lower socioeconomic status and have limited say in decisions affecting their communities.[15] In several Latin American countries, there are also sizable black populations. Although Latin American countries tend to have interracial mingling and have had less of a history of legal discrimination than the United States, black Latin Americans' lives are shaped by race.[16] In Asia as well there are minority groups with similar issues. For example, in China there are several ethnic minorities, best known may be the Tibetans, Uighur, and Mongols. These people have rebelled against the Chinese government because of loss of culture, and economic and power concerns.[17]

Many European countries are made up of people with different ethnic heritages and languages. In Belgium, for example, the nation is divided between Dutch-speaking Flanders in the North and French-speaking Wallonia in the South. The tensions between the two can be severe at times. At the beginning of the twenty-first century, the conflict between the two sides delayed the formation of a government for months.[18] Mayors have been prevented from taking office because they have campaigned using French, schools have been segregated by language, and many feel greater identity to Flanders or Wallonia than Belgium.[19] Language is also related to a conflict in Spain between Catalans and the government in Madrid. Catalonia is on the northeastern part of Spain, and residents there speak Catalan as their native language. Catalans believe that they send more money to Madrid than they get in return and want a greater say in how taxes are raised and spent. The tensions are severe enough that there are calls for an Independent Catalonia. In a nonbinding referendum on November 9, 2014, a supermajority of Catalans voted to leave Spain.[20] The Catalans are not the only minority group wanting to leave Spain. There has been a militant group working on Basque independence. The issues of Spain, the United Kingdom, and Belgium are just the tip of the iceberg. If all the separatist movements in Europe were successful, there would be close to thirty-five new nations.[21]

groups, some are more important politically in that their shared interests are affected by governmental policy.

The most common minority groups can be distinguished by race (African Americans, American Indians, and Asian Americans), ethnicity (Hispanics), gender (women), and sexual orientation (lesbians, gays, and bisexual). In addition to these groups there are people of different religions, including atheists or Muslims, or economic minorities such as the poor, who share some of the characteristics of racial, ethnic, gender, and sexual minorities. Every part of the world faces problems of affording limited rights and powers to minorities (see Spotlights 1.2 and 1.3). However, to make the text manageable, it focuses on minorities that have received the greatest scholarly attention: those characterized by race, ethnicity, gender, and sexual orientation. Within these categories the greatest attention will be paid to African Americans, Hispanics, women, and gays and lesbians for similar reasons, but where information is available, Asian Americans, American Indians, and transgender individuals will also be discussed.

Race is a way to categorize individuals by physical traits (often color of skin) attributed to a shared ancestry. Throughout U.S. history different categories of people have been defined by race. For example, at one time being Jewish

Spotlight 1.3

Immigrants in Europe

Immigrants form an important minority group in Europe. Many European countries have had an influx of immigrants seeking greater freedoms and economic security in the past decades. About 16% of Austria; 15% of Sweden, Belgium, and Spain; 13% of Germany; and 12% of Norway, the United Kingdom, and France are foreign born.[22] Many of the immigrants were recruited to Europe from North Africa, South Asia, and the Caribbean during the boom years following World War II; but by the 1970s with a slowing economy there was a trend in Europe to stop the flow of immigration.[23] However, since most states continued to allow family members of immigrants to migrate, immigration has continued. These new groups have brought different cultural traditions and languages and often are concentrated in lower economic groups. This has led to some conflicts and the rise of some nationalist parties. For example, in 2012 France's National Front

Party, headed by Marine Le Pen, garnered 18% of the vote for president, its most.[24] The National Front Party is clearly anti-immigration, supporting legislation on strict immigration limits and that discriminates against non-nationals.

Although there is considerable variation by nation, Europeans generally have a negative view about immigration. For example, 70% of people in Greece believe that immigrants are a burden on their nation and take jobs and social benefits.[25] This compares to 60% of Italians, 52% of Poles and French, 46% of Spaniards, 37% of the British, and only 29% of Germans. Similarly, a significant percentage of Greeks and Italians want less immigration, 86% and 80%, respectively. A smaller percentage of people from other European nations want less immigration: 57% of the French, 55% of the British, 47% of the Spaniards, 44% of Germans, and 40% of Poles.

was considered a race. However, today few Americans would include Jewish people as a group to be protected by race-based laws. Because racial classifications and how society reacts to a group change with time, they should be considered **social constructs**. A social construct is a category that has meaning because society treats those in that category uniquely, but the category lacks any intrinsic meaning. For example, Americans who are African American are thought by many to have traits and a subculture that differ in some ways from those of the dominant white race. Thus, society often treats African Americans and whites differently. But the differences are not the results of genetic or biological markers, but rather peoples' perceptions of a difference. Thus, if a society treats a group of people with a shared inherited physical trait differently, it becomes a race. The racial categories used by the U.S. census, as well as most political scientists, include white, African American or black, American Indian or Alaska Native, Asian, and native Hawaiian or other Pacific Islander. The last three groups, native Hawaiians and other Pacific Islanders and Asians, are often placed in the category of Asian American.

There is a movement among some native Hawaiians to be included under laws protecting indigenous people or American Indians.[26] The Hawaiian movement has its roots in the 1970s efforts to protect the land but has grown to a larger movement to recognize the native Hawaiian language, culture, and sovereignty. Since the United States started occupying Hawaii in 1898, there has been little recognition of the culture and rights of native Hawaiians. The movement is an effort to regain a culture and sovereignty. There are divisions in the movement as to whether to work within the current power structure and remain part of the United States or to try to have independence.

A challenge today as well as in the past is determining who fits into a racial category. Although the United States is not the ideal melting pot, many Americans are of multiple races. For example, Tiger Woods, the professional golfer, has a mother of mixed ancestry but is primarily Thai. His father too is of mixed ancestry but is primarily African American and white. Thus, he cannot simply be categorized as one race. Similarly, although President Barack Obama identifies as African American, his mother was white, and his mother and maternal grandparents raised him.

Historically, a person's race was often determined with a **blood quantum** approach. This means the government determined a person's race based on the percentage of her ancestry that was of a minority race. For example, individuals with African American mothers and Asian American fathers would be 50% African American and 50% Asian American. This method was used extensively for determining who was African American. The percentage of blood that was needed for an individual to be classified as African American varied from state to state, but individuals would be considered African American for purposes of Jim Crow laws or antimiscegenation laws if one-quarter to one-sixteenth of their ancestry was African American.[27] **Jim Crow laws** were laws found predominantly in the South during the early to mid-1900s that segregated the races in schools, transportation, and other public places. A series of Supreme Court cases declared these laws unconstitutional. One of the best known cases in this area is ***Brown v. Board of Education of Topeka* (1954)**, which ruled segregated schools violated the equal protection clause of the Fourteenth Amendment (see Chapter 3 for a discussion of the equal protection clause). Antimiscegenation laws are laws that prevent people of different races from marrying. These laws have not been allowed since the Supreme Court ruled in ***Loving v. Virginia* (1967)** that they violate the equal protection clause of the Constitution. Today the most common approach used by the census and researchers to determine an individual's race is self-identification. Individuals who claim to be white are considered white; those who claim to be African American are African American, and so on. With the recent censuses, individuals have been able to indicate that they have a multiracial ancestry or identification. As a consequence, the census makes a distinction between people who list one race as their only race and those who list one race as one of more than one race.

African Americans

African Americans or blacks are people of non-Caucasian African[28] descent. The terms *black* and *African American* can be used interchangeably, unless referring to blacks who are not American or who identify more with the Caribbean. These individuals either do not identify as Americans or Africans. A recent Gallup survey indicated that most African Americans (61%) do not have a preference between the terms, but among those who do, most prefer African American (24%) to black (13%).[29] Since the term *African American* is preferred by those who have a preference, the term *African American* will be used in this book.

African Americans first arrived in the Americas in 1619 as indentured servants, but the slave trade quickly resulted in many more African Americans arriving in the Americas. Although in the United States we think of African American slaves arriving in the U.S. colonies, many African slaves also arrived in Latin America. For example, people of African descent are the dominant race in Haiti and Jamaica and make a sizeable minority in the Dominican Republic.[30] Although most African Americans in the United States are descendants of slaves who arrived on the continent, there are a growing number of African Americans who came to the United States from Caribbean nations and have the double minority status of being African American and Hispanic; about 4.5% of African Americans in the United States are Hispanic.[31] Not all Caribbean people are Hispanic, as the French or British settled some islands. For example, Shirley Chisholm's parents immigrated to New York from the Caribbean, and she spent a few childhood years in Barbados, which is English speaking, with her grandparents. There are also many African Americans who were born in Africa. These blacks started immigrating to the United States in earnest in the last half of the twentieth century. In the 1990s alone, 900,000 black people came to the United States from the Caribbean and 400,000 from Africa.[32] By 2007 almost three million of the thirty-seven million African Americans were foreign born.[33] Although the frequency of foreign-born African Americans has risen dramatically, the growth in the percentage of Americans who are African American has seen more modest gains. According to the 1990 census, 12.1% of Americans identified as African American, in 2000 the number was 12.9%,[34] and by the 2010 census 13.6% of Americans were African American.[35]

Asian Americans

Although Asian Americans only make up about 5.6% of the U.S. population, they are the fastest growing minority group.[36] Between 2000 and 2010, the U.S. Asian population grew 45.6%.[37] Even though African Americans are diversifying with the growing number of first- and second-generation Americans, the diversity among Asian Americans is even greater. *Asian Americans* include people whose ancestors come from nations as diverse as India, Vietnam, China, Japan, Pakistan, Sri Lanka, Thailand, and the Philippines. Table 1.1 presents population size by the different Asian nationalities. Although Americans with ancestry from these nationalities are categorized as Asian American, these individuals do not share a common culture, language, religion, or history in the United States.

The first Asian nationality to arrive in the United States in large numbers was the Chinese, who in the mid-1800s were recruited to provide cheap labor to work in gold mines and build railroads. The Japanese came later, first to Hawaii and then the west coast to work in agriculture. Both groups tended to prosper but faced discrimination.[38] For example, neither group could become naturalized citizens until the mid-1900s. In 1943, Congress passed the Magnuson Act allowing Chinese settlers to become naturalized citizens, and in 1952 Congress passed the Walter McCarran Act that allowed Japanese and other Asian immigrants to become naturalized U.S. citizens. During World War II, Japanese Americans were also forced to live in internment camps, which resulted in many Japanese Americans losing their property and freedom.[39] Starting in the mid-twentieth century, Asians from more diverse nations started to come to the United States in larger numbers. Asians from Southeast Asia, such as Vietnamese, Laotian, and Hmong, came to the United States in fairly large numbers following the Vietnam War, which lasted roughly from 1960 to 1975. Southern Asians, such as Indians, have also started to come to the United States in greater numbers in recent years. They differ from other Asians in appearance, looking more similar to Caucasians than other Asians but with darker skin.[40] While Asians as a group increased their numbers about 45% between the 2000 and 2010 census, the number of Asian Indians increased almost 70%.[41]

American Indians

There are many terms used to refer to people indigenous to the United States: American Indians, Native Americans, First People, Native nations, and Indigenous peoples. Although any of these, or several other terms, can be used to

TABLE 1.1 Breakdown of Asian Americans by Nationality (in Thousands)

Nationality	Number claiming nationality	Nationality	Number claiming nationality
Asian Indian	2,844	Laotian	191
Bangladeshi	129	Malaysian	16
Bhutanese	15	Maldivian	<1
Burmese	91	Mongolian	14
Cambodian	232	Nepalese	52
Chinese	3,347	Okinawan	3
Filipino	2,256	Pakistani	364
Hmong	248	Singaporean	3
Indonesian	63	Sri Lankan	39
Iwo Jiman	<1	Thai	167
Japanese	763	Vietnamese	1,548
Korean	2,424	Other	219

Source: Data from http://www.census.gov/prod/cen2010/briefs/c2010br-11.pdf, Table 5. Based on respondents who listed just one race and nationality.

describe individuals, different scholars, tribes, the government, and the people prefer specific terms for different reasons. Instead of participating in the debate of which term is best, this text will simply use the term *American Indians* since survey data suggest it is the preferred term.[42]

American Indians include people who lived in what is now the United States when Europeans first started to settle in the Americas and comprise only about 1.7% of the U.S. population.[43] The small number of American Indians depresses their political power, as does their diversity. There are well over 500 different tribes recognized by the federal government, making American Indians a very diverse group. The cultures and languages of Midwestern Sioux or Lakota, southwestern Navajo, southeastern Cherokee, or northeastern Iroquois are all very different. In addition, they differ in the degree to which they are recognized by the federal government, Congress, the courts, and the Bureau of Indian Affairs (BIA). Each has its own way to recognize American Indians and their tribes. The BIA is responsible for implementing many federal policies concerning American Indians. In addition, some tribes are recognized by states, and others have no governmental recognition. There is also variation as to whether or not they live on or have ties to a reservation. American Indians do, however, share a history of their lands being taken over by the U.S. government. There is also a special relationship between the federal government and American Indians referred to as the "Trust Responsibility."[44] In essence, the U.S. government is obligated, through treaties where tribes gave land to the United States, to protect tribes, ensure their well-being, and respect tribal sovereignty and lands. Many American Indian peoples and cultures also suffered from forced assimilation policies. These policies were designed to make American Indians lose their cultures and adopt the European influenced American culture. Starting in the middle of the nineteenth century, many American Indian children were taken from their homes and forced to attend boarding schools in order to lose their Indian language and culture. During the mid-1900s, the Urban Relocation Program provided money to American Indians to encourage them to leave reservations and move to cities, where it was thought they would fully assimilate into the dominant U.S. culture and society. While many participated in this program, others chose to remain on reservations. But what may have had the most significant negative effect on American Indian cultures was the allotment of private land to American Indians.[45] Such policies destroyed the collective nature of their cultures.

The story of American Indians and U.S. citizenship is complex. Although U.S. citizenship afforded American Indian men the possibility of the vote during the nineteenth century, it often came at a cost. American Indians were seen as citizens of tribes or nations that the United States saw as sovereign. Thus, to become a U.S. citizen they would have to give up their tribal membership and property. For some it would also involve giving up their culture. For example, some native nations were given the opportunity to become U.S. citizens on the condition they learned English and adopted Euro-American customs.[46] Citizenship was usually given to American Indians who participated in the allotment programs. The Fourteenth Amendment's citizenship clause that affords citizenship to anyone born in the United States would seem to give American Indians citizenship. However, the Court ruled in *Elk v. Wilkins* (1884) that even American Indians who had left their nation were not citizens because they were still subjects of their tribe. Citizenship was, finally, afforded all American Indians born in the United States with the 1924 Indian Citizenship Act. However, several nations, including the Five Civilized Tribes, initially refused membership.[47] As Wilkins and Stark note,

> This is one of the unique realities, that tribal members are citizens of three polities—their nations, the United States, the state—that make the study of indigenous people such a dynamic pursuit. For if a native person's tribal citizenship is an active one and he or she resides on or near Indian Country, he or she has rights as an Indian that may be adversely affected by federal plenary power. At the same time, such Indians enjoy certain protections, services, and, benefits because of their treaty or trust relationship with the federal government that are unavailable to other individuals or racial or ethnic groups in the nation.[48]

However, even after citizenship was granted questions about whether American Indians could vote remained, and many states with large populations of American Indians set up roadblocks to their enfranchisement.[49]

Many American Indian children were sent to boarding schools to become assimilated. This photo is of the Carlisle Indian School, Carlisle, Pennsylvania. (© *CORBIS*)

Being American Indian is not only a racial classification, but for many it represents a social and cultural way of life, often including membership in a particular tribe. Tribes have sovereignty in their territories, which means they have their own laws and tribal governments that are not subject to U.S. federal laws in the way that U.S. cities and states are. Although some tribal nations increase their budget through casino revenues, and some tribes possess lucrative mineral rights to their land, many tribes and their members lack financial resources.

Questions over who is a member of a tribe are not without debate. One way to determine tribal membership is through the Dawes Roll. Between 1898 and 1914, individuals who met certain requirements that proved their membership in one of the Five Civilized Tribes (Cherokees, Creeks, Choctaws, Chickasaws, and Seminoles) could sign the Dawes Roll and receive an allotment of land. Although the purpose of the allotment was to help assimilate American Indians by destroying their communal cultures, today it enables individuals who can trace their lineage to this roll to claim membership to one of these tribes. In the Hawaiian movement there is an effort to create a roll so that indigenous Hawaiians can create a governing body similar to American Indian tribes.[50] In many cases the tribe determines membership, and there can be controversies over who is a member. A continuing controversy among American Indians exists over tribal membership for the Freedmen.[51] The Freedmen are decedents of African American slaves who were owned by the Cherokee and later became free and full members of the tribe. According to treaties, they are entitled to Cherokee membership. However, in 2011 the Cherokee voted to amend their constitution and removed the Freedmen from their membership rolls.[52] After legal proceedings, the Freedmen's Cherokee citizenship was restored, but their status remains controversial.

Wilkins and Stark identify four ways American Indians differ from other minority groups.[53] First, they are indigenous to the United States and, as a consequence, make up nations. Second, and relatedly, the government has had to negotiate with tribes as sovereign entities. As a consequence of this, tribal rights are not based on the Constitution but on treaties, so in many ways their relationship is extra-constitutional. Third is the trust relationship or doctrine noted earlier. Finally, there is congressional plenary power. This means that the federal government, not the states, can negotiate treaties and that Congress has absolute powers to affect American Indians. These differences have had some benefits in that they allowed the government to make special programs for Indians, such as Indian health care, education, housing, and taxation, and allowed BIA to give preferential hiring to American Indians. It has also had negative effects in that it allows the government to prevent some American Indians from doing things other Americans can do, such as sell land.

Who Are Minorities? Ethnicity as a Category

Whereas race concerns physical traits from biology, **ethnicity** concerns categories of people based on shared cultural traits, such as language or religion. People who share a race often share an ethnicity in that they share a religion and language, and people who share an ethnicity are often of the same race. However, the terms *race* and *ethnicity* are distinct. For example, Hispanics are people in the United States who come from Spanish-speaking nations, such as Mexico, Spain, and many nations in the Caribbean and Central and South America. These include several races: African American (particularly from the Caribbean), American Indian, and white. In fact, most people from Latin America are Mestizo, meaning they are of a European and American Indian heritage. Even though race and ethnicity are separate concepts, ethnic minorities and racial minorities are similar in that they are treated differently by society in negative ways, such as inadequate education, job discrimination, and powerlessness. Although several ethnic groups have faced discrimination at some point in U.S. history, such as the Irish, Polish, or Italians,[54] today Hispanics are the dominant minority ethnicity.

Hispanics in America

Hispanics[55] or Latinos are individuals who speak Spanish as their native language or are of a nationality that speaks Spanish. Although the terms *Hispanic* and *Latino* are often used as synonyms, some people have strong preferences for one term or other. However, surveys tend to suggest that neither term is preferred by most Hispanics or Latinos. A 2012 survey of Hispanics and Latinos indicated that 51% of respondents had no preference between the terms

Hispanic or *Latino*, 33% prefer *Hispanic*, and 14% prefer *Latino*.[56] Since *Hispanic* is the term preferred by those who have a preference, Hispanic will be used in this book. According to the 2010 census, Hispanics make up 16.3% of the U.S. population; this is a larger group than African Americans, Asian Americans, or American Indians.[57] Not only is the Hispanic population large, but it grew dramatically in the first decade of the twenty-first century. Between the 2000 census and the 2010 census, the Hispanic population grew 43%.[58] Although the Hispanic population continues to grow, the rate of growth has declined since the recession that began in 2008. By 2013 the Hispanic population was estimated to be 17.1%, about a 0.5% increase in three years.[59] As with Asian Americans, Hispanics come from diverse nationalities. Table 1.2 lists the population size of the different nationalities classified as Hispanic by the U.S. census. People from these nations have had different experiences in the United States.

Prior to 1848 and the Treaty of Guadalupe Hidalgo, which ended the Mexican-American War, much of the Southwestern and lower Midwestern parts of the United States were Mexican territory. With the treaty, Mexicans living in what is now the United States were given the opportunity at the time to become U.S. citizens. Unfortunately, many who opted to become U.S. citizens lost their property and faced discrimination when many states did not recognize them as citizens and failed to protect their property.[60] As will be discussed in later chapters, Mexicans who have immigrated to the United States have continued to face discrimination and segregation.

Although Central and South Americans first immigrated to the United States in the 1800s, they started to arrive in larger numbers in the late twentieth century. Many of these people fled their homelands because of political instability, such as civil wars and political persecution. There are strict limits to the number of immigrants that can come to the United States, and many Mexicans and Central and South Americans choose to do so illegally. Although some Central and South Americans could apply for political asylum, many come illegally, since it is difficult to prove the need for asylum. An issue with classifying individuals as Hispanic is that Spanish is not the national language in all Latin American nations. For example, people who live in Brazil speak Portuguese and those in Belize speak English, yet have much in common with others living in Central and South America. As a result, some definitions include Brazilians and Belizeans as Hispanic, and some do not.

Gaining legal immigration status is easier for Cubans and is not an issue for Puerto Ricans. Cubans, who first arrived in large numbers in the United States following Fidel Castro's takeover of Cuba, have faced few obstacles once on U.S. soil. These refugees by and large have been welcomed in the United States For example, the United States has a "wet foot, dry foot" policy.[61] If Cubans make it to dry land, they can stay in the United States legally, but if they are found in the ocean, they will be deported to Cuba. Puerto Rico has been part of U.S. territory since the 1890s, and people born in Puerto Rico have been citizens since 1917. Nevertheless, they face discrimination similar to other Hispanics when on the mainland. For example, Puerto Ricans report similar rates of discrimination as other Hispanics.[62]

TABLE 1.2   Breakdown of Hispanic Americans by Nationality (in Thousands)

Nationality	Number claiming nationality	Nationality	Number claiming nationality
Argentinean	101	Nicaraguan	178
Bolivian	42	Other Central American	104
Chilean	69	Other South American	58
Colombian	471	Panamanian	92
Costa Rican	69	Paraguayan	9
Cuban	1,415	Peruvian	234
Dominican	765	Puerto Rican	4,624
Ecuadorian	261	Salvadoran	655
Guatemalan	372	Spaniards	100
Honduran	218	Uruguayan	19
Mexican	31,798	Venezuelan	92

Source: Data from Table 1 in Ennis, Rios-Vargas, and Albert, Hispanic Population: 2010, http://www.census.gov/prod/cen2010/briefs/c2010br-04.pdf, accessed September 26, 2014.

Whites in America

Racial and ethnic minority groups are often compared to whites, Caucasians or Anglos. The term *white* refers to people of European and Middle Eastern ancestry. The terms *white* and *Caucasian* are usually used when referring to race. Since many Hispanics are white, the term *Anglo* is often used to refer to whites who are not Hispanic. Thus, throughout this book the term *whites* will be used when examining race, and *Anglos* when looking at ethnicity. When comparing Hispanics, African Americans, Asian Americans, and American Indians, the terms *Anglos* and *non-Hispanic whites* will be used.

Although today we tend to treat whites as a monolithic group, there is diversity among non-Hispanic whites that has severely divided them in the past. In Colonial America, for example, Rhode Island was founded when Roger Williams fled religious persecution in the Massachusetts colony. Starting in the 1800s and continuing until the mid-1900s, the Irish, Italian, Greek, and Polish experienced large-scale discrimination.[63] For example, when the potato famine hit Ireland in the mid-1800s and the Irish fled in large numbers to the United States, they were not welcomed with open arms by the dominant ethnic group, British. Businesses advertised that they would not hire Irish, and they had very difficult times finding employment.[64] Resentment toward the largely Catholic Irish led to segregation, whose effects can still be found in large cities. To deal with discrimination, they became active in the labor movement, created Irish organizations, and eventually grew ties with the Democratic Party.[65] Their political power was strongest in areas with large Irish communities, but eventually Irish were seen less as an immigrant minority and more as a part of America. However, even when John F. Kennedy ran for president, his Irish roots affected some voters. Although each European group shared the experience of trying to survive in a new land that was unwelcoming, they did not share religion, language, or history, and Americans with European ancestry have not always been seen as a homogeneous group. Today these ethnic groups are largely treated as a single group, and many, if not most, white Americans' lineage includes multiple European ethnicities. Nevertheless, Anglos, as well as racial and ethnic groups, differ in many important ways such as gender, gender identity, and sexual orientation. These differences affect their political experiences and power, and will be the topic of the next section.

Who Are Minorities? Gender and Sexual Minorities

Although the terms *gender* and *sex* are used interchangeably in common language, they do not mean the same thing. **Sex** refers to the biological differences between males and females. The terms *male* and *female* are used to refer to an individual's sex. Females tend to have two X chromosomes and can give birth, whereas males tend to have one X and one Y chromosome, and produce sperm. Although sex is often treated as a dichotomous trait (having only two categories), there is variation among males and females. For example, some people who are otherwise male have an X chromosome. In addition, some people are intersexed. *Intersexed* individuals are born with both male and female reproductive organs. Although we will not be discussing the representation of intersexed people, there are organizations created to advocate on their behalf, such as the Intersex Society of North America or Advocates for Informed Choice.[66] **Gender**, on the other hand, is less concerned with biological differences and is more concerned with how men and women differ due to societal pressure or socialization. Thus, that women are more likely than men to be bank tellers has little to do with biological differences between men and women but is the result of a variety of societal and environmental forces, as well as job hierarchies.[67]

Gender, like race, is a social construct. Some feminists argue individuals are trained how to act as men and women in society and reinforce gender differences by "doing gender," or acting consistent with societal expectations, and if individuals did not perform their gender, gender differences would diminish or disappear altogether.[68] When referring to gender, the norm is to use the terms *men* and *women*. The key gender minority is women. Some may also consider lesbian, gays, bisexual, and transgender as gender minorities, but to emphasize the uniqueness of these groups, they will be discussed separately as sexual and gender identity minorities.

Women

According to the 2010 census, women make up 50.8% of the population.[69] Thus they are not a numeric minority, though they are a political minority, since women have faced discrimination and are not represented as well as men in government. For example, women make up about 20% of Congress, no woman has ever been president, and like racial and ethnic minorities, many issues important to women get little attention from policymakers. For much of U.S. history women could not vote, own property, initiate a divorce, attend many schools, or hold certain jobs. Further, women were seen as property of their husbands, and men could do as they wished with their property. As a consequence, marital rape and domestic violence were not crimes. Today conditions for women are much better, but women are still underrepresented. For example, although wives are no longer their husbands' property, they can own property, can vote, and there are laws against overt discrimination, few women are in the state legislatures that are passing laws regulating their health care and reproductive choices. In addition, the sexual assault of women in the military is a significant problem that has only recently received much attention.

Making up just over half of the population, women are a very diverse group of people. They come from all races, ethnicities, sexual orientations, economic situations, and so on. These traits tend to interact, such that each mix of gender, race, and class has unique experiences and politics. Edith Barrett finds that although African American women state legislators share some issue concerns with African American men and share others with white women, they have a unique, and unified, set of issue priorities.[70] For example, she found that while about 74% of African American women prioritized health care and education, fewer than 64% of legislators who were white women and men or were African American men prioritized education, and less than 56% of the other groups prioritized health care. Hispanic women legislators also approach legislating differently from Hispanic men.[71] For example, Fraga, Lopez, Martinez-Ebers, and Ramirez find that Hispanic women legislators are more likely than their male counterparts to prioritize representing the interests of minority groups, building consensus, and resolving conflict. As will become clear throughout this book, African American women are unique in their high levels of civic engagement and political participation (see Chapter 2). Women of different minority groups also differ some in policy concerns. For example, American Indian women are significantly more likely to be raped than other women, and their rapes are less likely to be prosecuted, in part because tribal governments have no authority over nontribal members. Thus, future chapters will note racial and ethnic differences among women and men where appropriate.

Gender Identity: Transgenderism and Nonconformity

Related to gender is gender identity. **Gender identity** refers to the sex individuals identify with and act as in society. As a political concept, it concerns transgender individuals. *Transgender* is an umbrella term for individuals who do not identify with their birth sex, and transsexuals are people who specifically wish to be of the other sex. Whereas transsexuals wish to be of their nonbirth sex, transgender people may or may not wish to transform their bodies to be of the other sex; the defining trait is that they do not follow the gender norms of their birth sex. Although many transsexual people have surgery to change their appearance to better reflect who they feel they are, sexual reassignment surgery is not needed to be transsexual. The percentage of transgender people is unknown, but Gallup estimates 0.3% of Americans are transgender.[72] A related term is *gender nonconformity*. **Gender nonconformity** refers to not identifying or presenting oneself as any one gender or sex. For example, someone who is androgynous would be considered a gender nonconformist. Although transgender individuals can be seen as a gender minority, they usually organize with gays, lesbians, and bisexuals for political reasons and will be discussed more in the section on sexual orientation.

Sexual Orientation

In addition to race, ethnicity, and gender minorities, another group of minorities is based on sexual orientation. Related to gender and sex is sexuality. *Sexuality* refers to "desire, emotional involvement, and fantasy, as enacted in a variety of long- and short-term intimate relationships."[73] Some people are attracted to individuals of their own sex, some people are attracted to individuals of the other sex, and some people are attracted to both or all sexes. When discussing the primary sex of an individual's attraction, the term *sexual orientation* is used. **Sexual orientation** refers to whether individuals are romantically attracted to people of their own sex, people of the other sex, both sexes, or neither sex. Non-gays and non-lesbians, or straight people, are attracted to people of the opposite sex. Gay men are attracted to men; lesbians are women attracted to women, and bisexuals are attracted to men and women. In addition, individuals who are asexual are not interested in having sex with others, and people who are pansexual are attracted to people of a variety of sexes and gender identities. Although theorists differ as to whether or not individuals' sexual orientation should be determined by behavior or identity,[74] it is common to rely on self-identification. That is, it is common to categorize people as gay, lesbian, or straight exclusively on whether they claim to be gay, lesbian, or straight. However, some people who are attracted to or have relationships with others of the same sex do not identify as gay, lesbian, or bisexual, and vice versa.

In reference to gays, lesbians, and bisexuals, it is common to use the acronym LGBT. The T in the acronym stands for transgender. Other acronyms are used that are more expansive. For example, LGBTQIA stands for lesbian, gay, bisexual, transgender, queer or questioning, intersex, and ally. Since transgender politics are usually discussed with gay and lesbian politics, this text will do so as well.

As with the other minority groups, LGBT have suffered and continue to suffer from discrimination. Although there have not been organized efforts to prevent LGBT Americans from voting, laws have discriminated against LGBT. Prior to the late twentieth and early twenty-first centuries, gays and lesbians were denied basic rights: gays, lesbians, and transgender Americans could be fired, assaulted, or denied services with no legal protection. Homosexual behavior was even punishable by prison. It has only been since 2012 that gays and lesbians could serve openly in the military, and in 2015 President Obama's administration began plans to allow transgender individuals to serve. LGBT still lack protection from employment discrimination in most states.

Although transgender people are placed in the same category as gays and lesbians, their issues and concerns differ. For example, key issues for transgender people are being able to change their sex on government documents, intersex restrooms, having insurance cover hormone therapy or reassignment surgery, police harassment, or laws based on gender identity as opposed to sexual orientation.[75] For example, some states' antidiscrimination laws cover sexual orientation but not gender identity. In these states, gay and lesbian workers are protected, but transgender workers are not. Research, too, finds that transgender people are not highly likely to be gay or lesbian.[76] Transgender people may also be among the most underrepresented groups as there are only a handful of transgender elected representatives, and there are few groups that speak only for their interests.

The percentage of LGBT Americans is difficult to pin down, but a recent Gallup poll estimated that about 3.5% of Americans identify as gay, lesbian, bisexual, or transgender.[77] This figure is similar to other recent estimates.[78] However, surveys likely underestimate the number of LGBT Americans due to respondents being unwilling to disclose their sexual orientation to survey interviewers.[79] A recent experiment that used a procedure to make it virtually impossible to know how an individual respondent answered a question on sexual orientation found a 65% increase in the number of respondents saying they were not heterosexual.[80]

Racial, ethnic, and gender minorities and LGBT are similar in that they share a history of discrimination, share many interests, and share the resistance or ambivalence of the majority of Americans to the expansion of policies, such as affirmative action, that are beneficial to their interests. They also share some similarities in the factors that affect their representation. For example, they all tend to have a greater number of representatives where voters support Democratic candidates. However, there are some very clear differences. For example, different minority groups have different strengths, such as Asian Americans tend to benefit from having high levels of socioeconomic status (high levels of education and income), but African Americans tend to have high levels of group consciousness and voter turnout. In addition, being LGBT, and to a lesser extent being Hispanic, is less visible than sex or race. Thus, it may be easier for individuals in these groups to blend into the larger political, social, or economic landscape. Also, since Hispanic and Asians Americans are more likely to be immigrants, they face unique challenges, such as voting ineligibility, lower levels of acculturation, and group cohesion and consciousness. In addition, other Americans may see them as a greater threat to the American way of life.

Representation

If minorities are defined as groups of individuals lacking adequate representation, we should ask, what is representation? Representation, according to Hanna Pitkin, means bringing present something that otherwise is not present.[81] This definition is too abstract to be very helpful in understanding minorities, and Pitkin offers much refinement. She notes that representation really has four meanings or types: descriptive, formalistic, symbolic, and substantive.[82]

Descriptive representation concerns whether representative bodies resemble the people they are to represent in that their membership corresponds to the demographic makeup of the people. Pitkin quotes John Adams, who stated that a representative legislature "should be an exact portrait, in miniature, of the people at large as it should think, feel, reason and act like them."[83] It is likely impossible for U.S. legislatures, city councils, or similar bodies to be perfect mirrors, and it would not be a good thing if they were. Good policy would not likely come from a legislature that has proportional numbers of ill-informed, disinterested, or apathetic people. However, few would argue that racial, ethnic, gender, and sexual minorities do not need to be in positions of power for them to increase their substantive representation. Jane Mansbridge suggests that descriptive representation is needed for a group when it does not trust that others can represent its interests, and policies do not reflect its interests. This would tend to include the minorities discussed in this text.[84] There are debates as well as to how many minorities are needed in a legislative body for a group to be represented. It is likely that the answer depends on the diversity of that group.[85] Women, who make up over 50% of the population and have lower levels of cohesion than the other minority groups, may need more members to fully represent their interests than a more homogeneous group.

Descriptive representation has been examined from a minority politics perspective asking: to what degree are individuals of minority groups in decision-making positions, what affects the degree of descriptive representation, and what difference does it make to policy representation? Indeed, much research suggests that descriptive representation is a key ingredient to the creation of policies beneficial to minorities.[86] Generally, though, it is thought that descriptive representation is important for minorities since (1) it provides role models that can empower other minority individuals, (2) it can help compensate for past and present violations, (3) it helps make sure minority interests will be heard, and (4) it can make democracy stronger.[87] Since descriptive representation is important to minorities' rights and political power, it is critical to understand what affects it. Much more will be said about this in the following chapters, but levels of descriptive representation are affected by district traits, such as racial makeup, ideological and partisan leanings, and socioeconomic status;[88] resources of minority groups, such as organizations and money; voters' views of minorities;[89] and candidates' decisions.[90]

Formalistic representation also affects descriptive representation. It concerns how representatives get their authority to make decisions and how they are held accountable.[91] In a democracy, formalistic representation is closely related to elections. Some of the most notorious laws that limit minority descriptive and policy representation include those preventing minorities from voting. As noted earlier, prior to the 1900s, most minorities could not become naturalized citizens and/or vote. Even after the federal law or Constitution gave minorities the right to vote, many states enacted laws to effectively disenfranchise them. These laws included not allowing American Indians living on reservations to vote, white primaries, grandfather clauses, and literacy tests (Chapter 3 will discuss these in more detail). States have also effectively limited descriptive and substantive representation through gerrymandering: drawing districts to either pack their vote (over-concentrate minorities in one district) or crack their vote (divide the minority vote into so many districts that it has little influence in any district). Many today believe that efforts to require government-issued photo IDs or laws that ban felons from voting disproportionately disenfranchise racial minorities.[92]

Substantive representation, also called **policy representation,** concerns whether representatives or the government act in a manner that affects their constituents' interests. To examine minorities' policy/substantive representation, one approach is to focus on what increases the likelihood that policies thought to be beneficial to minorities become law. It is difficult to determine whether a policy is in a group's interest or not. One approach to estimating a minority group's interests is to rely on the policies supported by organizations advocating on behalf of the group. For example, Rodney E. Hero and Caroline Tolbert, who were interested in determining whether Hispanic legislators were more likely to support legislation important to Hispanics, operationalized[93] Hispanic legislation as legislation supported by the Southwest Voter Research Institute (see Chapter 12 for a description of this group).[94] Another common approach to operationalizing, or measuring, minorities' interests is for researchers to use their expertise to develop a definition that reflects a group's interests and then use that definition to determine which legislation or policies are beneficial to a minority's interests. For example, Michelle Swers defines women's issue as "issues that are particularly salient to women because they seek to achieve equality for women; they address women's special needs, such as women's health concerns or child care; or they confront issues with which women have traditionally been concerned in their role as caregivers, such as education or the protection of children."[95] She then examined individual bills introduced in Congress and determined whether they were "particularly salient to women because they seek to achieve equality for women" in the ways specified by her definition. What is less common is to ask minorities their policy preferences. However, Katherine Tate used such an approach when she matched African American members of Congress's votes on legislation with the results of a survey of African American voters.[96]

The fourth type of representation is *symbolic* or *"stand for" representation.*[97] It focuses on how people, places, and things can "stand for" or be a symbol of something else such as a rainbow has come to represent LGBT rights, or a black fist the power of African Americans. The power of symbols is their ability to "evoke feeling or attitudes."[98] Since **symbolic representation** concerns how people feel about or react to the government, some research on minorities' symbolic representation has focused on minorities' attitudes toward the government and policymakers.[99] To get a sense of how minorities perceive the government and its officials, Chapter 5 examines how individuals of different minority groups evaluate the government and their members of Congress. Later chapters will also examine whether minorities' attitudes about government and politics are affected by descriptive representation.

Schwindt-Bayer and Mishler note that Pitkin expected the four types of representation to fit together.[100] Formalistic representation, the rules of the game, can make it easier or harder for minorities to participate and affect their descriptive, policy, and symbolic representation. Descriptive representation increases policy and symbolic representation, as having minority policymakers at the table helps their interests be heard. In addition, minorities who believe their interests are being represented are likely to feel better about the nation and have higher levels of symbolic representation. To test Pitkin's model, Schwindt-Bayer and Mishler examined women's representation in thirty-one nations in the mid-1990s. They found that the model generally works well, particularly as it relates to descriptive representation.

Overview of the Book

Pitkin's treatment of representation, which sees representation as multifaceted, including descriptive, formalistic, substantive, and symbolic representation, is used to organize this book. The next six chapters focus on minorities' levels of representation. It examines the level of descriptive representation in elected offices, particularly legislatures, and the immediate factors affecting these levels. It examines formalistic representation, or how gerrymandering, voting laws, and electoral systems can affect the ability of minorities to vote, as well as affect the electability of minority candidates. In addition, it examines the Fourteenth Amendment's equal protection clause, which is the backbone of many protections held by minorities. Chapter 4 also explores the policy or substantive representation of racial, ethnic, and gender minorities, and LGBT. It identifies the key policy concerns of minorities and how descriptive representation and other factors affect policy representation. This section also explores symbolic representation by examining minority individuals' support for the government and its symbols. Since some of the issues of minority representation are unique to the judicial branch and the bureaucracy, separate chapters will examine issues of representation in these branches.

Chapters 8 through 12 examine the conditions that affect minority representation. The first section notes that public opinion, the characteristics of minority groups, and interest groups affect the degree to which minorities have descriptive and policy representation, but it does not explore public opinion, the characteristics of minorities, or interest groups per se; these are examined in the second section. It explores Americans' attitudes toward minorities and policies that affect their interests, such as affirmative action, immigration, and same-sex marriage. Chapter 9 explores the resources or conditions held by each group that can influence its levels of representation, such as population size, population distribution, rates of citizenship, age, and socioeconomic status of individuals within a group. This section also explores the civic engagement of individuals in minority groups, as that also affects groups' political power. The ability of minority groups to mobilize these resources depends on the cohesiveness of the people within each group. And this will be explored by examining the degree to which individuals of each minority group hold similar beliefs, values, and attitudes, such as party identification and ideology, as well as their sense of shared fate. The extent to which people of the different minority groups are politically active is also explored, since their political participation affects their representation. Since interest groups are critical for any group to influence policy, Chapter 12 examines key interest groups and movements that have worked on minority rights. The concluding chapter examines the likelihood that the different minority groups will see greater representation in the future. It brings together implications of the earlier chapters and indicates what public opinion, interest groups, and the minority group resources suggest about the prospects for minorities' voices being heard in the future. Relatedly, it explores the likelihood that multiminority coalitions, which can benefit minorities collectively, will be formed. Finally, although the book focuses on racial, ethnic, and gender minorities, and LGBT, the concluding chapter also looks at three other minority groups that are becoming more significant: Muslims, atheists, and the poor.

Conclusion: Similarities, Differences, and Intersectionality in Representation

This chapter introduced readers to minorities and representation. Minorities are individuals who make up groups of people who are underrepresented. The key minority groups in the United States are based on race (African Americans, Asian Americans, and American Indians), ethnicity (Hispanics), gender (women), and sexual orientation (gays and lesbians). Although these groups differ in many fundamental ways, they share a history of discrimination and lack a voice in public policy. These similarities and differences help structure their political demands. For example, that members of each minority group have experienced discrimination in education has resulted in each group being particularly concerned about access to a good quality education. Yet there are some differences in their concerns for education. For Asian Americans and Hispanics there is often a language component to the concerns, and LGBT students are often afforded less legal protection from bullying than others (see Chapter 4). Among Hispanics there are differences too. Some Hispanic nationalities have large numbers of members who came to the United States without documents and are concerned about access to public schools, while Cubans and Puerto Ricans, who have legal status, are less affected by policies denying education and services to undocumented immigrants.

It is also important to remember that individuals have a gender, a race, an ethnicity, and a sexual orientation, and the collection of traits individuals possess affects their political power. The experiences of women of color with the government often differ from that of white women, whether these women are public officials, bureaucrats, or citizens requesting governmental services. While this intersectionality is a theme that will be explored throughout the book, a couple of examples at this point will help illustrate this point. Women who are not proficient in English will undoubtedly have a more difficult time getting governmental services, particularly if they speak a less common language. Racial stereotypes of African Americans can also make it difficult for them to win sexual assault cases.[101] Elected officials who are also women of color are also often ignored or excluded from proceedings.[102] Mary Hawkesworth notes that in Congress there is an

> ongoing racing-gendering in the institutional practices of Congress and in the interpersonal interactions among members of Congress. Through tactics such as silencing, stereotyping, enforced invisibility, exclusion, marginalization, challenges to epistemic authority, refusals to hear, legislative topic extinctions, and pendejo games, Congresswomen of color are constituted as "other." In committee operations, floor debates, and interpersonal interactions, they are treated as less than equals in various ways that carry palpable consequences for their identities and their policy priorities. They are forced to deal with institutional dynamics and interpersonal relations that constitute them as subordinate.[103]

These examples concern women of color, but white men, too, have a race and gender that interact to affect their power, albeit resulting in their power being greater than if they were women or not white. In addition, sexual orientation and social class interact with race and gender to affect individuals' power and representation. White men who are poor or gay are likely to have less power and privilege than white men who are wealthy and straight. Nevertheless, to keep this book manageable, this text will focus more on the intersection of race/ethnicity and gender than the intersections involving class and sexual orientation.

To provide some structure to understanding the role of the politics of the many types of minorities and their intersectionality in the United States, this book examines representation. *Representation* is a broad term that has four key forms: descriptive, formalistic, substantive/policy, and symbolic. This book is designed to help the reader understand the degree to which each minority group has representation, what affects their levels of representation, and what the prospects are for greater representation. The various minority groups share some aspects of representation but not others. As will be discussed in later chapters, while all the minority groups discussed here lack proportional numbers in our political institutions, women, LGBT, and African Americans tend to vote at similar or higher rates than Anglo men, but Asian Americans and Hispanics tend to vote at lower rates because large percentages of these groups have recently immigrated to the

United States. The next chapter will explore descriptive representation, what are the current levels of descriptive representation for each minority group, and what are the immediate conditions that affect it.

KEY TERMS

Blood quantum   (p. 8)
Brown v. Board of Education of Topeka (1954)   (p. 9)
Descriptive representation   (p. 21)
Ethnicity   (p. 14)
Formalistic representation   (p. 21)
Gender   (p. 17)

Gender identity   (p. 18)
Gender nonconformity   (p. 19)
Intersectionality   (p. 4)
Jim Crow Laws   (p. 8)
Loving v. Virginia (1967)   (p. 9)
Minorities   (p. 6)
Race   (p. 7)

Sex   (p. 17)
Sexual orientation   (p. 19)
Social constructs   (p. 8)
Substantive representation/policy representation   (p. 22)
Symbolic representation   (p. 22)

Chapter 2

Descriptive Representation and Minorities

Legislatures and Other Elective Offices

In 2013, the Senate, with its record twenty women members, passed long overdue legislation to help address the issue of sexual assault in the military. The U.S. military has been unable to effectively prohibit sexual assault in its ranks and hold offenders accountable. An Air Force lieutenant colonel who led a program on the military's response to sexual assault was accused of groping a woman, a pilot's conviction of aggravated sexual assault was overturned by a fellow pilot, and a 2012 survey indicated 26,000 troops had received "unwanted sexual contact."[1]

In the defense authorization bill, which allows the military to spend money, women senators worked hard to create policies to eliminate sexual assault in the military. Sen. Kirsten Gillibrand (D, NY) took a lead in proposing the most significant changes.[2] Her proposal would have removed commanders from playing a direct role in deciding whether to prosecute. Since commanders are often sympathetic toward their troops, it can be difficult for them to prosecute the accused. Her proposal had the support of several veterans' groups, women's groups, some key Republicans, such as Sens. Rand Paul and Ted Cruz, and most women senators. However, the Pentagon opposed it.[3] When the Senate voted on her proposal, it garnered fifty-five votes, which although a majority was not the sixty votes needed to withstand a filibuster.

The proposal that eventually won was introduced by Sen. Claire McCaskill (D, MO) and co-sponsored by Sens. Kelly Ayotte (R, NH) and Deb Fischer (R, NE). This bill did not interrupt the chain of command but allowed an outside civilian review if the commander and prosecutor disagree on whether to bring charges.[4] It also eliminated the good soldier defense, which allowed the accused to use his good record in the military in a case against him.

Even women senators not drafting their own proposals were active in efforts to reduce sexual assault in the military.[5] Many women senators spoke on the floor of the Senate about the problem: Barbara A. Mikulski (D, MD), Susan Collins (R, ME), Maria Cantwell (D, WA), Lisa Murkowski (R, AL), Amy Klobuchar (D, MN), Tammy Baldwin (D, WI), Patty Murray (D, WA), and Elizabeth Warren (D, MA).

That the women senators took the lead in congressional efforts to limit sexual assault in the military was not by happenstance.[6] In early summer 2013,

These sixty-five House Democratic women participate in a photo opportunity for their swearing in to the 114th Congress on the east steps of the Capitol in Washington, D.C., January 7, 2015. (© GARY CAMERON/Reuters/Corbis)

all twenty women senators met to discuss the issue and proposals to address it. Sen. Gillibrand's proposal got the greatest support from the women (sixteen out of twenty), but they agreed to focus more on the similarities than the differences of the bills as the debates moved forward. The women met again in November to discuss how to highlight the significance of the changes in both amendments and to maximize the number of women speaking on behalf of the changes.

The above story indicates the importance of minorities having descriptive representation. Descriptive representation concerns the degree to which the government resembles the demographic characteristics of the people. Without a significant number of women senators working together across party lines, it is unclear whether change would have been possible. This chapter explores the general levels of descriptive representation for elected offices, particularly legislative offices, as well as what affects minorities' levels of descriptive representation. Four key ideas you should take from this chapter are (1) minorities have low but increasing levels of descriptive representation; (2) although there are significant differences in what affects the descriptive representation of minority groups, descriptive representation is influenced by voters, context, and candidates; (3) minority women have higher levels of descriptive representation than Anglo women, and are increasing their numbers at a higher rate than minority men; and (4) descriptive representation alone will not ensure that minority interests will be fully heard.

Levels of Descriptive Representation in Legislatures

Although minorities do not have proportional representation, their representation has improved over the past fifty years. As a point of illustration, Figure 2.1 depicts the percentage of members in the House of Representative who are women, African American, or Hispanic since 1869, and Figure 2.2 depicts the percentages of these minority groups in the Senate. In looking at the House of Representatives, it is apparent that no woman served in Congress prior to the 1916 elections. In that year, Jeannette Rankin (R, MT) was elected to the House of Representatives and became the first congresswoman (see Spotlight 2.1). Since her election, the number of women has had a fairly consistent upward trend. Twenty years after her election, in the 75th Congress (1937–1939), there were six women in the House. In the 85th Congress (1957–1959), there were fifteen, and in the 95th Congress there were eighteen. The largest jump in the number of congresswomen, however, occurred following the 1992 elections. In 1992, forty-seven women won seats in the House. Nineteen-ninety-two was touted as the **year of the woman** because of the large number of women who ran and won. Several factors likely contributed to the increase, such as a scandal-ridden Congress, large turnover, and the televised **Clarence Thomas hearings.** During his confirmation hearing, Clarence Thomas was plagued by allegations of sexual harassment. The fact that no women served on the Senate Judiciary Committee, which held the hearings,

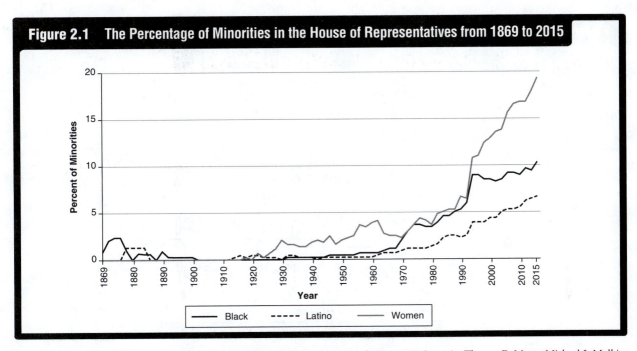

Figure 2.1   The Percentage of Minorities in the House of Representatives from 1869 to 2015

Sources: Data from http://www.cawp.rutgers.edu/history-women-us-congress and Norman J. Ornstein, Thomas E. Mann, Michael J. Malbin, Andrew Rugg, and Raffaela Wakeman, "Vital Statistics on Congress," April 7, 2014, www.brookings.edu/vitalstats, tables 1–16, 1–17, 1–18; and CQ Roll Call, "Updated Guide to the New Congress," November 5, 2014, http://info.cqrollcall.com, 58.

was used to bring out the gender inequality in Congress.[7] Following the historic 1992 elections, the number of women in the House has continued to grow. In the 108th Congress (2003–2004), there were sixty women in the House, and in the 113th Congress (2013–2014), there were seventy-nine.[8] Following the 2014 elections, there was an increase of five women House members.

The rise of women in the Senate was slower to start, but today the percentage of women in the Senate is similar to that of the House. The first woman senator, Rebecca Latimer Felton (D, GA), was appointed in 1922 and served for just one day. It would then be almost ten years before the next woman served in the Senate. Hattie Wyatt Caraway (D, AR) was appointed to fill her husband's seat in 1931 to give other Democratic candidates time to forge a campaign, but she surprised many when she ran and won in the special election to fill the seat. She then went on to serve two more terms. While in office she was a supporter of the New Deal, particularly as it helped agriculture, Prohibition, and an equal rights amendment for women and veterans but opposed civil rights for African Americans.[9] Women replacing their husbands in office offered a common way for women to enter Congress until the late twentieth century. This phenomenon is often referred to as the **widow effect.** Although there are only two women in Congress today who replaced their husbands, there have been a total of forty-seven widowed Congresswomen who followed their husbands into office.[10] Between

Figure 2.2   The Percentage of Minorities in the Senate from 1869 to 2015

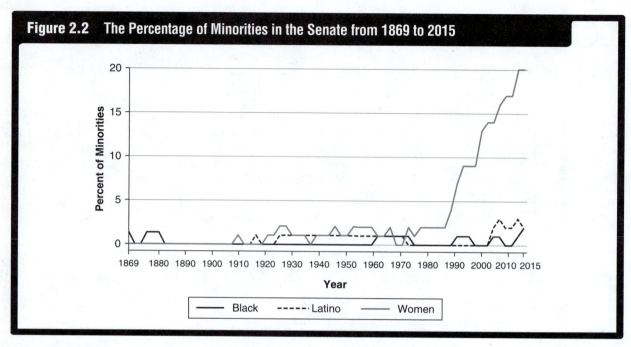

Sources: Data from http://www.cawp.rutgers.edu/history-women-us-congress and Norman J. Ornstein, Thomas E. Mann, Michael J. Malbin, Andrew Rugg and Raffaela Wakeman, "Vital Statistics on Congress," April 7, 2014, www.brookings.edu/vitalstats, tables 1–16, 1–17, 1–18; and CQ Roll Call, "Updated Guide to the New Congress," November 5, 2014, http://info.cqrollcall.com, 58.

Caraway's appointment and the 1990s, the number of women senators never exceeded two. Although the number jumped to four in 1991, the real growth occurred in the year of the woman, 1992, which saw the number of women senators rise to seven. Since then, there has been continued growth and the number of women in the 114th Congress stands at twenty.

Figures 2.1 and 2.2 depict the percentages of Congress members who are African American. Unlike women in Congress, the first African American member of Congress was seated as a senator, not a representative. In the 41st Congress (1869–1871) Sen. Hiram Rhodes Revels (R, MS) became the first African American member of Congress and the first African American senator (see Spotlight 2.2). In addition to being African American, he also was Scottish and Croatan Indian. Thus, he may have been one of the earliest American Indians in the Senate as well, although his Indian heritage was not a significant part of his identity, and he is not listed as one of the few American Indian senators.[11] This helps demonstrate the difficulty in determining individuals' race and ethnicity. Revels was appointed to finish a term and served only two years. The next African American senator, Blanche Bruce (R, MS), was elected in 1874 and served only one term. It would be close to ninety years before the next African American was elected to the Senate, when Edward Brooke (R, MA) was elected in 1966. Since then, the number of African American senators has fluctuated between zero and two, and currently stands at two.

Spotlight 2.1

Representative Jeannette Rankin

Rep. Jeannette Rankin (R, MT) is best known for two things: being the first woman in Congress and voting against U.S. entry to World War I and World War II. Although she was a trained social worker, she quickly left that work to become a suffragette. In 1916, the first year women could vote in Montana, she won a U.S. House seat. She served only one term before making an unsuccessful bid for the Senate. Roughly fifteen years later, she was elected to another term in the House (1941–1943).

Rep. Rankin's life work focused on social welfare, pacifism, and suffrage.[12] For example, during her first campaign for Congress, she noted that the government spent "$300,000 to study hog feed, and only $30,000 to study the needs of children."[13] She also was outspoken and worked on issues important to labor interests, often at the expensive of the powerful mining interests in Montana. She was a known pacifist, and her first vote in Congress was against entry into World War I, a vote that led to criticism from the leadership of the National American Women's Suffrage Association (NAWSA), her party, and many in the press. The NAWSA leaders feared people would interpret her vote as evidence women were not fit for office. Although forty-nine Congressmen voted alongside her, she received more negative publicity for the vote because of her novelty as a Congresswoman. What caused her greater criticism, however, was her lone vote in opposition to U.S. entry into WWII in 1941.

The other cause important to Rep. Rankin was suffrage. She was instrumental in women getting the right to vote in Montana, and suffrage was one of her motivations to run for Congress. As a Representative, she drafted a resolution calling for a women's suffrage amendment and served on the House Suffrage Committee. On the floor she spoke on its behalf, "'How shall we answer the challenge, gentleman?' she asked, 'How shall we explain to them the meaning of democracy if the same Congress that voted to make the world safe for democracy refuses to give this small measure of democracy to the women of our country?'"[14]

Rep. Rankin was aware that her performance in office would be used to judge the abilities of women in office and took pains to perform well and not be seen as a flirt. "She was the member from Montana and she intended to function in that role, not play the part of a fainthearted female who had strayed by chance into the council of men."[15] After leaving office, she continued her work as an advocate for peace and social justice. In 1973 she died at the age of ninety-two.

Source: The information for this Spotlight comes from the U.S. House webpage, http://history.house .gov/People/Listing/R/RANKIN,-Jeannette-(R000055)/; Norma Smith, *Jeannette Rankin: America's Conscience* (Helena, MT: Montana Historical Society Press, 2002); Hannah Josephson, *Jeannette Rankin* (Indianapolis, IN: Bobbs-Merrill, 1974).

In the House, two African American members served in the same Congress as Sen. Revels. This was during **Reconstruction,** when the federal government oversaw the treatment of the African Americans in the South following the Civil War. During Reconstruction there were as many as eight African American House members at one time.[16] However, after federal control over southern elections ended, the ability of African Americans to get elected diminished quickly, and no African American members served between 1901 and 1929. Although a handful of African American members served in the next four decades, it was not until the 1970s that there were very many African American members of Congress. In 1973, there were fifteen African American members, and in 1983 there were twenty-one. The real growth occurred with the 1992 elections. During the 103rd Congress (1993–1995), there were forty African American House members. The growth in the number of African American members is attributed to the creation of **majority-minority districts.** These districts have a majority of racial or ethnic minority voters and were created to increase the number of minority members. Since 1993, the number of African American members has been fairly stable. In the 108th Congress (2003–2005), there were thirty-seven African American members, and in the 113th (2013–2015), there were forty-three.[17] Following the election of 2014, there were forty-four African American members in the House and two in the Senate. The number of African Americans in the House is much more proportional than in the Senate. In the 114th Congress, about 10% of the House of Representatives and 2% of the Senate are African American. Remember, about 13% of the U.S. population is African American.

Spotlight 2.2

Senator Hiram Rhodes Revels

In 1869, Hiram Rhodes Revels became the first African American in Congress. Although he was born in 1827, he was born a free man and was able to get an education and attended seminary. After ordination he traveled to Indiana, Illinois, Kansas, Kentucky, and Tennessee preaching and educating African Americans. Eventually, he settled in Missouri, even though the state prohibited free African Americans from living there. In 1854, he was arrested for preaching to slaves. During the Civil War he recruited African American soldiers and served as a chaplain for part of the war. After the war, he settled in Mississippi, where he became active in the Republican Party and in 1869 was one of thirty African Americans to be seated in the 140-member state senate.[18]

One of the first tasks of the state legislature was to fill two U.S. Senate seats that were vacant. The radical Republicans wanted to fill one of the seats with an African American to help improve race relations. A deal was made with the Democrats where one of the seats would be filled by an African American man and the other by a white man. Since Revels had given a stirring prayer before the Senate, he was selected to have the seat whose term expired in 1871, and a white man got the seat whose term expired in 1875. When Revels arrived on Capitol Hill, there was an effort to block his appointment, but on February 25, 1870, Revels was seated as a U.S. senator.

In the short time Revels was in the Senate, he represented the interests of African Americans. Many African Americans not living in Mississippi saw him has their representative and contacted his office. He also defended the seating of African American legislators from Georgia, tried to get an African American into West Point, and helped African American mechanics gain employment in a navy work yard. Nevertheless, he was a moderate and also supported amnesty for former Confederates, and although he opposed legal segregation, he also opposed forced integration.

After leaving the Senate, Revels returned to Mississippi as president of Alcorn University. He later became interim secretary of the state of Mississippi before returning to preaching.

Figures 2.1 and 2.2 also illustrate the percentage of Hispanics in the House and Senate. Although the proportionality of Hispanics' descriptive representation is lower than that of African Americans, until recently the trends have been similar.[19] The first Hispanic House members served in the 1870s, and their numbers were very small until recently. The first Hispanic to serve as a regular member of Congress was Rep. Romualdo Pacheco (R, CA), who served from 1877 to 1878 and 1879 to 1883. He was of Californio descent (Hispanic born while California was a Spanish colony).[20] His election in 1876 was highly contested, and he was not seated; the Democratically controlled House replaced him with his opponent in the middle of the term. He ran again in 1878 and 1880, winning both times. Although he became a Republican prior to the Civil War because he opposed slavery, his first speech in Congress was to limit Asian immigration, and he focused on economic development of California while in office.[21] Following Rep. Pacheco, the number of Hispanics in the House never exceeded one until the 1960s, and remained in the single digits until the 1980s. The largest growth in the number of Hispanic House members followed the 1992 elections with the creation of majority-minority districts. Unlike African Americans, however, Hispanic members have continued to see their numbers in the House grow. In the 103rd Congress there were seventeen Hispanics in the House, and by the 113th Congress there were twenty-eight. Following the 2014 elections the number of Hispanics in the House rose by one, to twenty-nine. In the Senate, the number of Hispanics never exceeded one until the 2000s. In the 109th Congress (2005–2006) there were two Hispanic senators and in the 113th (2013–2014) and 114th (2015–2016) there were three.[22] A likely reason their numbers continue to increase is that the size of the Hispanic population has grown dramatically. Although the numbers have grown, with 3% in the Senate and 6.4% in the House, Hispanics, who make up about 17% of Americans, are still greatly underrepresented.

Asian Americans also remain underrepresented. Although prior to statehood Hawaii did have nonvoting members of Congress who were Asian, the first Asian American to serve as a regular member of the House was Dalip Singh Saund (D, CA), who was also a religious minority (Sikh); he served from 1957 to 1963.[23] Rep. Saund was born in India and immigrated to the United States to study food preservation, and eventually became a citizen and a judge. While in Congress he was most known for his work trying to ease U.S.-Asian relations.[24] The first Asian senator, Hiram Leon Fong (R, HI), became a senator when Hawaii gained statehood. The number of Asians in Congress, too, has increased, and in the 113th Congress there were eleven Asians: one in the Senate, and ten in the House.[25] One Asian, Rep. Bobby Scott (D, VA) who is Filipino, is also African American.

In the 114th Congress, there were two American Indians (Markwayne Mullins [R, OK] and Tom Cole [R, OK]), but there were no American Indian senators. There have been nine American Indians in the House of Representatives.[26] The first American Indian in Congress is usually identified as Charles Curtis (R, KS), who served in the House from 1893 to 1907. In 1907 he entered the Senate and served until 1913 and then again from 1915 to 1929. In the Senate, Curtis focused on American Indian issues and agriculture and became the first Senate majority leader. In 1928 he won the vice presidency alongside Herbert Hoover, the presidential candidate.[27] Demonstrating the difficulty in determining racial and ethnic membership, there are inconsistent lists of American Indians in the U.S. Senate. The Senate lists only three American Indian senators: Charles Curtis (R, KS), Robert L. Owens (D, OK), and Ben Nighthorse Campbell (D & R, CO); McClain and Stewart also include Matthew Stanley Quay (R, PA).[28] In addition, Sen. Revels may have been part Croatan Indian (see Spotlight 2.2). The most recent American Indian senator was Ben Nighthorse Campbell, who served from 1993 to 2005.

LGBT Americans have been the most recent minority group to be represented in Congress. Although several closeted LGBT members have served in Congress throughout its history, it wasn't until 1988 that Rep. Barney Frank (D, MA) became the first LGBT member of Congress to be elected after voluntarily disclosing his sexual orientation (see Spotlight 2.3 for more on Barney Frank). Barney Frank saw the number of "out" LGBT House members rise throughout his tenure. He retired at the end of the 112th Congress, and the 113th Congress had seven

Spotlight 2.3

Representative Barney Frank

"I'm used to being in the minority. I'm a left-handed gay Jew. I've never felt, automatically, a member of any majority." —Barney Frank[29]

Barney Frank has been politically active throughout his life. While attending Harvard he helped organize the 1964 Freedom Summer. After Harvard, he worked as a staffer for the Boston mayor and in Congress, then as a state legislator, before entering Congress in 1981. Throughout his career, he was a consistent liberal voice supporting women's and LGBT rights.[30] However, it was not until 1987, after the death of Congressman Stewart B. McKinney (D, CT) of AIDS and the outing of fellow Massachusetts congressman Gerry Studds, that Rep. Frank announced he was gay.[31] He said, "I have nothing to hide, nothing to advertise," and "If you asked the direct question 'Are you gay?' the answer is Yes. . . . So What?'"[32] Following his disclosure and until he announced his retirement in 2011, he won reelection fairly easily. Throughout his career, he was a strong supporter of minority rights. In his last Congress, he scored a 100% on the following interest groups' scorecards: NAACP,[33] HRC,[34] AAUW,[35] and the National Hispanic Leadership Agenda.[36]

Frank was known for his deal-making abilities and as a practical politician willing to make compromises.

However, this pragmatism has resulted in criticism from LGBT groups. During debates over the Employment Nondiscrimination Act in 2007, Frank proposed a bill that would extend protection based on sexual orientation, but not gender identity, meaning transgender workers would not be protected. He did so to increase the chance of the bill passing. Although the Human Rights Campaign did not directly oppose the bill, 280 gay rights groups opposed the bill for being discriminatory.[37]

LGBT rights were not Frank's only legislative concerns. He was an advocate for decreasing defense spending, helping the economically disadvantaged, and he helped co-author the Dodd-Frank bill that overhauled the banking system after the 2008 recession.[38]

Frank's career was not without scandal. In 1989, he was reprimanded for reflecting "discredit upon the House."[39] A reprimand is less than a censure or expulsion, but is a serious punishment. The reprimand came from his fixing several parking tickets and writing "misleading memoranda" for a male prostitute.[40] He survived the scandal and remained a powerful member until his retirement.

After retiring, Rep. Barney Frank publicly disclosed he was an atheist.

out members. The first LGBT senator, Tammy Baldwin (D, WI), was elected in 2012, and to date she is the only LGBT senator to have served. In 1998 she also became the first nonincumbent LGBT candidate to win a House seat. No transgender individuals have served in Congress.

To more fully understand the levels of descriptive representation, it is instructive to look at levels of representation broken down by gender and race/ethnicity. Doing so indicates that there is a higher percentage of minority women than one would expect by looking at the percentage of minorities and women independently. In the 114th Congress, 16% of Anglo members were women, 39% of African Americans were women, 28% of Hispanic members were women, and about 60% of Asian American members were women.[41] Looking at the percentage of women who are of color, 17% are African American, 6% are Asian American, and 9% are Hispanic.

Descriptive Representation in Congressional Leadership

Having minorities in Congress is helpful for minority policy representation, but so, too, is having those members in powerful positions. One set of powerful positions is party leadership. Party leaders help persuade their caucus (members of their party in their chamber) to vote on legislation supported by the party, and have several legislative resources, such as control of committee assignments and the agenda, that they can use to affect congressional action. Thus, if minorities are left out of leadership positions, their representation may be less than their numbers suggest. In terms of gaining leadership positions, congresswomen have done well in the twenty-first century. Nancy Pelosi (D, CA) became Speaker of the House in 2006. This is the most powerful position in the House and third in line to be president. Since the Democrats are no longer the majority party and able to select the Speaker, Rep. Pelosi is the minority leader, or leader of the Democratic Party in the House in the 114th Congress. Also in the 114th Congress, Rep. Cathy McMorris Rodgers (R, WA) was Republican Conference chair. Several women have also been secretary of their party's caucus.

Other minorities have also gained top Democratic leadership positions in the House. Rep. James Clyburn (D, SC), who is African American, was majority whip in the 110th and 111th Congresses and was assistant minority leader, most powerful next to minority whip, in the 114th Congress. In addition, in the

Rep. Barney Frank (D, MA) was the first openly gay member of Congress to win election. Here he is announcing his decision not to seek reelection, U.S. Capitol in Washington, D.C.
(© Benjamin J. Myers/Corbis)

114th Congress Rep. Xavier Becerra (D, CA), who is Hispanic, is Democratic Caucus chair. Since there are few Republican racial minorities in Congress, few minorities have held leadership positions in the Republican Party. Rep. J. C. Watts (R, OK), who was chair of the Republican Conference from 1999 to 2002, is the only African American Republican to obtain a high-ranking leadership position in the House. In the Senate, minorities have been less successful gaining top leadership positions. The Republican Party is the majority party in the 114th Congress (2015–2017), and it has no women or minorities on its current leadership team. The Democrats do only slightly better. In the 114th Congress, Sen. Patty Murray (D, WA) is the Democratic Party Conference secretary, the fourth most powerful position in the Democratic Party in the Senate. In addition, women chair several lesser party committees, and a leadership position was created for Sen. Elizabeth Warren as a liaison to liberal groups.

Another powerful position for members of Congress is committee chair. Congress has been referred to as "government by committee" to demonstrate the importance of committees. After bills are introduced in Congress, they are referred to committees. Committee action determines the fate of the vast majority of bills. In the 114th Congress, one woman and no racial/ethnic minorities chaired a House committee. Part of the reason for the lack of minority committee chairs in the 114th Congress was that few minority members were Republicans, and the Republican Party, as the majority party, determined committee chairs. In the 111th Congress (2009–2011), the last Congress with a Democratic majority, there were three women and four African American committee chairs, including Rep. Charles Rangel (D, NY), who controlled the powerful Ways and Means Committee. When the Democratic Party was the majority party in the House, African Americans, but not Hispanics, tended to gain committee chairs more quickly than Anglos, presumably because they were seated on less prestigious committees where it was easier to become a leader.[42] During the 114th Congress, the only minority committee chairs in the Senate were Sen. Susan Collins (R, ME), chair of the Special Committee on Aging, and Sen. Lisa Murkowski (R, AK), chair of Energy and Natural Resources. During the 113th Congress, the Democratic Party was the majority party, and there were seven women[43] and one Hispanic man as committee chairs.

Another way that minority groups can be descriptively represented in committees is to testify at hearings. During congressional hearings, experts from inside and outside of government testify before committees about policies and important issues of the day. They offer members an opportunity to collect information and persuade colleagues. Unfortunately there are biases in the types of people who testify at hearings. For example, the Sunlight Foundation recently reported that only 23% of those who testify are women.[44]

State Legislatures

Examining the descriptive representation of minorities in state legislatures in 2014 also indicates much underrepresentation. Table 2.1 gives the ratio of the

TABLE 2.1 Ratio of Percentage of Minorities in State to Percentage of Minorities in State Legislatures in 2013

	African Americans[af]	Hispanics[bg]	Asians Americans[ae]	American Indians[aj]	Women[ch]	LGBT[di]
Alabama	0.86 (23)	.00 (0)	0.00 (0)	0.00 (0)	.26 (13.3)	0.25 (0.7)
Alaska	0.21 (1)	0.00 (0)	0.00 (0)	0.81(12)	.60 (28.3)	0.00 (0)
Arkansas	0.68 (11)	0.00 (0)	0.00 (0)	0.00 (0)	.20 (17.0)	0.00 (0)
Arizona	0.4 (2)	0.64 (18.9)	0.00 (0)	0.57 (3)	.71 (35.6)	0.56 (2.2)
California	0.69 (5)	0.58 (22)	0.2 (3)	0.59 (1)	.53 (26.7)	1.68 (6.7)
Colorado	0.6 (3)	0.68 (14)	0.00 (0)	3.75 (6)	.84 (42.0)	2.50 (8.0)
Connecticut	0.71 (8)	0 .44 (6)	0.22 (1)	0.00 (0)	.57 (29.4)	0.32 (1.1)
Delaware	0.35 (8)	0.39 (3.2)	0.00 (0)	0.00 (0)	.50 (25.8)	0.47 (1.6)
Florida	1.1 (18)	0.47 (11)	0.00 (0)	0.00 (0)	.49 (25.0)	0.37 (1.3)
Georgia	0.67 (21)	0.09 (1)	0.00 (0)	0.00 (0)	.45 (22.9)	0.37 (1.3)
Hawaii	0.00 (0)	0.29 (2.6)	1.25 (72)	20.0 (8)	.63 (31.6)	0.25 (1.3)
Idaho	0.00 (0)	0.00 (0)	0.00 (0)	0.00 (0)	.52 (25.7)	0.00 (0)
Illinois	1.1 (17)	0.46 (7.3)	0.00 (0)	1.67 (1)	.63 (32.2)	0.61 (2.3)
Indiana	0.79 (8)	0.00 (0)	0.00 (0)	0.00 (0)	.41 (20.7)	0.00 (0)
Iowa	0.81 (3)	0.00 (0)	0.00 (0)	0.00 (0)	.46 (23.3)	0.46 (1.3)
Kansas	0.7 (5)	0.34 (3.6)	0.00 (0)	0.00 (0)	.47 (23.6)	0.00 (0)
Kentucky	0.34 (3)	0.00 (0)	0.00 (0)	3.33 (1)	.36 (18.1)	0.00 (0)
Louisiana	0.61 (20)	0.17 (.7)	0.00 (0)	0.00 (0)	.23 (11.8)	0.00 (0)
Maine	0.00 (0)	0.38 (.5)	0.00 (0)	1.43 (1)	.57 (29.0)	0.56 (2.7)
Maryland	0.55 (17)	0.13 (1.1)	0.00 (0)	2.0 (1)	.59 (30.3)	1.30 (4.3)
Massachusetts	0.38 (3)	0.31 (3)	0.00 (0)	0.00 (0)	.49 (25.5)	0.80 (3.5)
Michigan	0.72 (11)	0.32 (1.4)	1.00 (3)	0.00 (0)	.37 (18.9)	0.00 (0)
Minnesota	0.16 (1)	0.32 (1.5)	0.21 (2)	0.00 (0)	.67 (33.8)	0.52 (1.5)
Mississippi	0.56 (21)	0.00 (0)	0.00 (0)	0.00 (0)	.35 (17.8)	0.00 (0)
Missouri	0.72 (9)	0.29 (1)	0.00 (0)	0.00 (0)	.43 (21.8)	0.30 (1.0)
Montana	0.00 (0)	0.00 (0)	0.00 (0)	0.46 (3)	.57 (28.0)	0.50 (1.3)
Nebraska	0.74 (4)	0.00 (0)	0.00 (0)	0.00 (0)	.41 (20.4)	0.00 (0)
Nevada	1.5 (14)	0.42 (11)	0.00 (0)	1.25 (2)	.58 (28.6)	1.88 (7.9)
New Hampshire	N/A	0.25 (.7)	N/A	N/A	.65 (33.0)	0.19 (0.7)
New Jersey	0.88 (13)	0.33 (6)	0.00 (0)	0.00 (0)	.57 (29.2)	0.22 (0.8)

(Continued)

TABLE 2.1 (Continued)

	African Americans[af]	Hispanics[bg]	Asians Americans[ae]	American Indians[aj]	Women[ch]	LGBT[di]
New Mexico	0.00 (0)	0.93 (43)	0.00 (0)	0.49 (5)	.55 (27.7)	0.31 (0.9)
New York	1.0 (18)	0.53 (9)	0.00 (0)	0.00 (0)	.42 (21.6)	0.74 (2.8)
North Carolina	0.80 (18)	0.06 (.5)	0.00 (0)	0.33 (.5)	.42 (21.8)	0.18 (0.6)
North Dakota	0.00 (0)	0.00 (0)	0.00 (0)	0.18 (1)	.34 (17.0)	0.41 0.7
Ohio	1.12 (15)	0.48 (2)	0.00 (0)	0.00 (0)	.46 (23.5)	0.42 (1.5)
Oregon	0.38 (1)	0.19 (2)	0.00 (0)	0.00 (0)	.57 (28.9)	0.22 (1.1)
Oklahoma	0.46 (4)	0.08 (1)	0.00 (0)	1.8 (16)	.27 (13.4)	0.38 (1.3)
Pennsylvania	0.67 (8)	0.14 (1)	0.63 (2)	0.00 (0)	.35 (17.8)	0.30 (0.8)
Rhode Island	0.41 (3)	0.28 (4)	0.00 (0)	0.00 (0)	.53 (27.4)	0.78 (3.5)
South Carolina	0.59 (17)	0.00 (0)	0.00 (0)	0.00 (0)	.25 (12.9)	0.00 (0)
South Dakota	0.00 (0)	0.00 (0)	0.00 (0)	0.34 (3)	.44 (21.9)	0.23 (1.0)
Tennessee	0.34 (6)	0.00 (0)	0.00 (0)	0.00 (0)	.33 (16.7)	0.00 (0)
Texas	0.24 (3)	0.59 (22)	0.00 (0)	0.00 (0)	.42 (21.0)	0.18 0.6
Utah	0.00 (0)	0.29 (4)	0.36 (1)	0.00 (0)	.33 (16.3)	0.00 (0)
Vermont	2.0 (3)	0.4 (1)	0.00 (0)	0.00 (0)	.80 (40.6)	0.67 (3.3)
Virginia	0.62 (13)	0.09 (1)	0.15 (1)	0.00 (0)	.35 (17.9)	0.24 (0.7)
Washington	0.42 (2)	0.06 (1)	0.56 (5)	0.56 (1)	.61 (30.6)	1.03 (4.1)
West Virginia	0.24 (1)	0.00 (0)	0.00 (0)	0.00 (0)	.32 (16.4)	0.23 (0.7)
Wisconsin	0.85 (6)	0.14 (1)	0.00 (0)	0.00 (0)	.50 (25.0)	0.54 (1.5)
Wyoming	0.00 (0)	0.12 (1)	0.00 (0)	0.00 (0)	.34 (16.7)	0.38 (1.1)
Average	0.55 (7.5)	0.23 (3.8)	0.32 (1.8)	0.76 (1.3)	.46 (24.2)	0.43 (1.6)

Sources: [a] National Conference on State Legislatures.

[b] National Directory of Hispanic Elected Officials produced by the NALEO Education Fund.

[c] Center on American Women in Politics.

[d] Gay & Lesbian Victory Institute Listing of Out Officials.

[e] Elizabeth M, Hoeffel, Sonya Rastogi, Myong Ouk Kim, and Hasan Shahid, "The Asian Population: 2010: 2010 Census Briefs," March 2012, http://www.census.gov/prod/cen2010/briefs/c2010br-11.pdf.

[f] Sonya Rastogi, Tallese D. Johnson, Elizabeth M. Hoeffel, and Malcolm P. Drewery, Jr., "The Black Population: 2010: 2010 Census Briefs," September 2011, http://www.census.gov/prod/cen2010/briefs/c2010br-06.pdf.

[g] Sharon R. Ennis, Merarys Rios-Vergas, and Nora G. Albert, "Hispanic Population: Census Brief 2010," May 2011, http://www.census.gov/prod/cen2010/briefs/c2010br-04.pdf.

[h] http://www.indexmundi.com/facts/united-states/quick-facts/all-states/female-population-percentage#table.

[i] Gary Gates, and Frank Newport, "LGBT Percentage Highest in D.C., Lowest in North Dakota," February 15, 2013, http://www.gallup.com/poll/160517/lgbt-percentage-highest-lowest-north-dakota.aspx.

[j] http://www.indexmundi.com/facts/united-states/quick-facts/all-states/american-indian-and-alaskan-native-population-percentage#map.

Note: Numbers in parentheses are percentages of minorities in state legislature.

percentage of minority state legislators to minority population percentage in each state. For example, if 50% of the state is African American and 50% of the state legislators are African American, the state would have a ratio of 1.00. However, if only 25% of the state legislators are African American, the ratio would be .50. The ratio is given since descriptive representation is less concerned with the total number of minority legislators than with their proportionality to the people of each group. Table 2.1 also presents the percentage of each minority in the legislature. This demonstrates the importance of looking at the ratio instead of the actual percentage. For example, Mississippi's state legislature has one of the largest percentages of African American state legislators (21%), but since about 37% of Mississippians[45] are African American, African Americans remain severely underrepresented there. Conversely, only 3% of Vermont's legislature is African American,[46] but since less than 2% of Vermonters are African American, African Americans have disproportionately large levels of descriptive representation in Vermont. The actual number, though, can also be important, since the size of a group in a legislature indicates its potential to become a significant voting bloc and its potential to affect policy.

The first column indicates that African Americans remained severely underrepresented in many state legislatures in 2014. The average state has a ratio of only .55, meaning for every percentage of African Americans in the population, only 0.55% were African American state legislators. Part of the reason for this is the cumulative effect of states with very low percentages of African American citizens that had no African American legislators. For example, less than 3% of the populations of Hawaii, Idaho, Maine, Montana, New Mexico, North Dakota, South Dakota, Utah, and Wyoming were African American, and they had no African American, state legislators and consequently a ratio of 0. Another reason is that four states with large African American populations (20% or more) had a disproportionately small percentage of African American state legislators: Delaware, Maryland, South Carolina, and Mississippi. However, the low levels of African American representation in state legislators was not uniform. In six states the ratio was greater than 1.0.

Levels of Hispanic representation in state legislatures were lower than those of African Americans in 2014. The average state had a ratio of only 0.23, and eleven states had a ratio of 0, indicating they did not have a single Hispanic representative. Two of these states, Nebraska and Idaho, had fairly large Hispanic populations, around 10%. Only in one state did Hispanic representation even come close to proportionality. In New Mexico, for each 1% of Hispanics in the population, 0.9 of the legislators were Hispanic. A likely reason for the low levels for Hispanics was that many Hispanics were noncitizens and therefore unable to vote or hold office.

Another minority group with a large percentage of noncitizens and low levels of representation is Asian Americans. The ratio of the percentage of Asian American residents to the percentage of Asian American legislators in 2014 was 0.32. Again, the cumulative effects of states without any legislators of a minority group can depress the average ratio. Well over half of the states did not have any Asian state legislators. In two states, Hawaii and Michigan, Asian American representation was proportional: the ratio was at least 1.00.

The racial/ethnic group with the most proportional representation in 2014 was American Indians, with a ratio of 0.76. One reason for the higher levels of representation was that several states had a disproportionately large percentage of American Indian legislators: Colorado, Hawaii, Illinois, Kentucky, Maine, Maryland, Nevada, and Oklahoma. In addition, the percentage of American Indians was so small that the proportions are not likely to be stable, as having only one American Indian legislator could yield overrepresentation, or a ratio greater than 1.00.

The next to the last column in Table 2.1 presents the descriptive representation of women in state legislatures. It indicates that, like racial and ethnic minorities, gender minorities were underrepresented in the states and varied dramatically from state to state. The average state has a ratio of about .46 of women legislators to women in the population. In addition, in no state did women have proportional representation: a ratio of one or more. The states that came the closest were Colorado and Vermont; both had ratios of at least 0.80. Although all states had at least one woman state legislator, three states had ratios below 0.25: Arkansas, Louisiana, and South Carolina. Though it is not clear from this table, research finds that women of color were found in state legislatures at higher proportions than white women. Scola found that in 2004 whereas about 21% of white state legislators were women, about 35% of African American state legislators, 29% of Hispanic legislators, 31% of Asian American, and 24% of American Indian legislators were women.[47]

The last column in Table 2.1 presents the descriptive representation of LGBT in state legislatures. As with the other minority groups, the representation of LGBT Americans was low but varied by state. The average state's ratio was 0.43. Although LGBT citizens lacked any representatives in thirteen state legislatures, in four state legislatures, Colorado, California, Maryland, and Nevada, LGBT were overrepresented. However, none of the state legislators are transgender.

In the past fifty years or so, there have been four trends in reference to the descriptive representation of minorities in legislatures. One is the growth in the number of each of the minority groups. Some of this was caused by changes in Americans' attitudes, some by institutional changes such as majority-minority districts, and some by demographic changes such as the increase in the number of Hispanics. Another trend is that there is considerable variation across the states in the degree of minority representation. States like Illinois tend to have more descriptive legislatures than states like Mississippi. The third trend is that women of color tend to have higher levels of descriptive representation than Anglo women. Although it is not typical worldwide for minority women to outpace majority women in representation, the United States is not the only nation with this trend. Spotlight 2.4 discusses the representation of minority women in legislatures around the world. Another trend that has not been noted earlier is that there has been a change in the party identification of minority representatives. Most of the first minorities elected to Congress, Rankin, Revels, Curtis, and Fong, were Republicans. Yet by the end of the twentieth century, most minority members were Democrats. In the 113th Congress, twenty-three of the twenty-eight Hispanic House members, sixty of the seventy-nine women House members, and all African American House members were Democrats.[48] This was caused by a shift in the national parties' positions related to minorities in the last half of the twentieth century.[49] The national Democratic Party leaders during the 1950s and 1960s took actions, such as support for the Civil Rights Act and the Voting Rights Act, that alienated white southerners and gained the support of minorities, while the Republican Party, in an effort to gain white southern votes, distanced itself from the civil rights agenda. Recently, however, there has been an increase in the number of minority representatives who are Republican. Two of the three Hispanic members of the Senate are Republicans. In addition, in 2014, there were two very visible Republican African Americans elected to Congress. Sen. Tim Scott (R, SC), who had been appointed to replace Sen. Jim DeMint who stepped down in 2013, won a special election. He is the first Republican African American senator since Reconstruction. The other visible Republican African American elected in 2014 was Mia Love (R, UT). She is the first Republican congresswoman who is black (Haitian) and the first woman who is Mormon.

Spotlight 2.4

Descriptive Representation of Minority Women outside of the United States

Minority women are grossly underrepresented across the globe. Melanie Hughes created an index for eighty-one nations in the world to measure the levels of representation minority women have in national legislatures: The Minority Women Legislative Index.[50] Minorities are defined by Hughes as groups who are discriminated against and/or marginalized by society. The index compares the percentage of minority women in the legislature to that of the population, such that a score of 50 means that minority women are half way to reaching proportional representation based on population. The U.S. scored a 27.4 and the average was 16.9. Two nations had scores over 100, Finland and Burundi, and thirty-four nations scored zero. Hughes's research also finds that about 2% of national legislators are minority women, 11% are minority men, 15% are majority women, and the remaining 72% are majority men. This is despite 11% of these nations' populations being minority women, 11% minority men, 40% majority women, and 39% majority men.

Hughes has some interesting findings when breaking her analysis down by region of the world. African nations have "the highest average MWLI score (46.2) followed by the west (24.4). . . . Comparing average MWLI scores, Asia (14.6), Eastern Europe (11.0) and Latin American (9.8) fall in the middle. The Middle East (2.9) has by far the lowest MWLI score. . . ."[51] Her research, too, finds that the United States is not unique in the "puzzle of representation"; minority women in several nations have higher levels of representation than majority women.

Levels of Descriptive Representation in Executive Positions

Minorities are also underrepresented when it comes to elected executive positions. No woman has been president or even won the nomination of a major U.S. party. Two women, Geraldine Ferraro and Sarah Palin, have been nominees for vice president but did not win. Geraldine Ferraro was Vice President Walter Mondale's running mate in the 1984 presidential race against President Ronald Reagan. At the time, she was a third-term House member from New York. Sarah Palin was Sen. John McCain's running mate in the 2008 presidential race against Barack Obama. When she was nominated, she was in her first term as Alaska's governor. A handful of women, including Hillary Rodham Clinton, Shirley Chisholm, and Elizabeth Dole, have been unsuccessful candidates for their party's nomination. The woman coming closest to the White House was Hillary Rodham Clinton in 2008, who was a second-term senator from New York at the time and former First Lady. She lost in a close primary battle with Barack Obama, who later appointed her as Secretary of State. She is also a front-runner for the 2016 Democratic nomination. It should be noted that as with legislatures there has been a disproportionate number of women racial minorities who have run for president. Although there have only been a handful of women candidates, two have been African American: Shirley Chisholm, who, against the advice of many minority organizations for fear she would not do well, ran in the 1972 Democratic Primary and received 151 delegate votes at the Democratic convention. At the time, she was a congresswoman from New York. Also, Sen. Carol Moseley Braun, who had been a senator from Illinois, ran in 2004 but dropped out early.

Women have done somewhat better in mayoral and gubernatorial races than presidential races. In 1925, Nellie Tayloe Ross (D, WY) became the first woman elected as governor. She won a special election to replace her husband, who had been governor when he died months earlier. As governor she worked on many of the progressive reforms supported by her husband, such as Prohibition, spending cuts, and aid to farmers.[52] In 1926, she ran for but lost reelection in the highly Republican state. The next woman governor took office fifteen days after Gov. Nellie Tayloe Ross; Gov. Miriam "Ma" Ferguson (D, TX). She, too, replaced her husband.[53] But her husband, James Ferguson, did not die; he was impeached and removed from office. In office, she tried to defend her husband against ethics charges, was anti-Prohibition, and anti-Ku Klux Klan, and issued an unusually large number of pardons.[54] She lost reelection but was elected governor again in 1932. Since then, there have been thirty-four additional women governors, most serving since the 1980s. In 2015, there were six women governors: Gina Raimondo (D, RI), Jan Brewer (R, AZ), Mary Fallin (R, OK), Nikki Haley (R, SC), Maggie Hassan (D, NH), Susana Martinez (R, NM), and Kate Brown (D, OR).[55] However, the underrepresentation of women may vary by race and ethnicity, as two of the six women governors are a racial/ethnic minority: Gov. Nikki Haley is Asian Indian, and Gov. Susana Martinez is Hispanic.

Although the first woman mayor served in the mid-1880s—Susan Madora Salter was mayor of Argonia, Kansas, in 1886—a small percentage of mayors have been women.[56] For example, in 2014, 18.4% of mayors in cities over 30,000 were women.[57] Women were less likely to be mayors in larger cities. In 2012, only ten women were mayors in the 100 largest cities.[58] Thus, women remain underrepresented at the executive level in the local, as well as at the state and federal levels.

LGBT Americans, too, are underrepresented in executive positions. No LGBT, at least none that have disclosed such status, have been president, vice president, or a major party nominee for such positions in the United States. There have been two LGBT governors, although neither was elected governor as an out LGBT candidate. The first was Jim McGreevey (D, NJ). However, he did not come out until shortly before resigning and served less than two years. In 2015, Kate Brown, who is bisexual, became governor of Oregon when Gov. John Kitzhaber (D) resigned amid ethics allegations. She would need to win a special election in 2016 to keep the governorship. In 2014, Rep. Mike Michaud, who came out in 2013, was the Democratic nominee for governor of Maine but lost in a close election. Additionally, few LGBT have been mayors. In 2014, there were only thirty-six LGBT mayors.[59]

Compared to women and LGBT Americans, African Americans have more proportional representation when it comes to federal elected executive positions: President Barack Obama is African American. No other African American has received a major party's nomination for president, but several have run in primaries. Some of the more notable African American candidates for the Democratic nomination have been: Rep. Shirley Chisholm in 1972; Rev. Jesse Jackson in 1984, 1988; Gov. Douglas Wilder in 1992; former Sen. Carol Moseley Braun in 2004; and Al Sharpton in 2004. Three African Americans have sought the Republican nomination: Alan Keyes in 1992, 1994, 1998, 2004, and 2008; Herman Cain in 2008; and Dr. Ben Carson in 2016.

African Americans have been even less successful than women in gaining gubernatorial or mayoral positions. The first African American elected as governor was Douglas Wilder (D, VA), and he was not elected until 1990.[60] Although polls prior to Election Day showed Wilder easily ahead of his opponent, he just eked out a victory with less than 1% point. His term in office was dominated by economic crisis and budget cuts.[61] Due to term limits, he could not seek reelection, and he spent some time while in office making an unsuccessful bid for the White House. Since then, there have been only two African American governors: David Paterson (D, NY, 2008–2010) and Deval Patrick (D, MA; 2007–2015).[62] In terms of mayors, in 2011, only about 7% of mayors in cities with populations over 50,000 were African American.[63]

To date, no Asian American or Hispanic presidential or vice presidential candidate has won a major party nomination,[64] though two Hispanic senators were competing for the 2016 Republican presidential nomination: Ted Cruz (R, TX) and Marco Rubio (R, FL). Although there have not been any Asian American or Hispanic presidents or vice presidents, there has been one American Indian vice president: Charles Curtis (R, KS), who was one-eighth Kaw.

Asian Americans and Hispanics have done well at gaining gubernatorial positions because of their large concentration in a handful of states. Hawaii has had three Asian governors. The first was George Ariyoshi (D, 1974–1986), who was of Japanese descent. Not only was Gov. Ariyoshi Hawaii's first Asian American governor, he was the first Asian American governor in the United States. Asian American governors have also served in Washington, South Carolina, and Louisiana. Of the Asian Americans who have been governor, two were in office at the end of 2015: Nikki Haley (R, SC) and Bobby Jindal (R, LA), both of Indian descent. There have been ten Hispanic governors of states.[65] The first Hispanic was Romualdo Pacheco (R, CA) in 1875; he was also the first Hispanic U.S. senator. However, most Hispanic governors have served since the 1970s (eight), and most came from New Mexico (six).[66] Currently, there are two Hispanic governors: Susana Martinez (R, NM) and Brian Sandoval (R, NV). There have been relatively few Hispanic mayors as well. Of the thousands of mayors in 2013, only 238 were Hispanic.[67]

What Affects Levels of Descriptive Representation?

Three key factors that affect the ability of minorities to win elections are voters, context, and candidates. The stereotypes voters have of minority candidates and their willingness to vote for minority candidates can have a significant effect on the likelihood minority candidates will hold office, particularly if the district is not majority-minority. The context, too, can have a considerable effect on descriptive representation as minority candidates are more likely to win in some types of districts and under certain circumstances. But minorities as candidates can also affect their electability. For example, if potential minority candidates choose not to run for office, there will be few minorities in office. In addition, their strategic decisions can affect their electability. While these three factors affect descriptive election, the particular aspects of these factors that are helpful vary from one minority group to the other. The rest of this section discusses how voters, context, and candidates affect descriptive representation of African Americans, Hispanics, Asian Americans, women, and LGBT.

Voters

Historically, voters were reluctant to vote for minority candidates, but this is changing. Since the 1950s, Gallup has been asking respondents about their willingness to vote for a qualified presidential candidate of their own party who happens to be a woman or African American. Figure 2.3, which depicts the results of these Gallup surveys, demonstrates the rise in Americans' willingness to vote for African American and women presidential candidates.[68] Figure 2.3 indicates that it was not until the 1960s that even half of American voters would support an African American or woman candidate for president. But by the 1980s, the vast majority

Figure 2.3   Percentage Who Will Vote for Minority Candidates

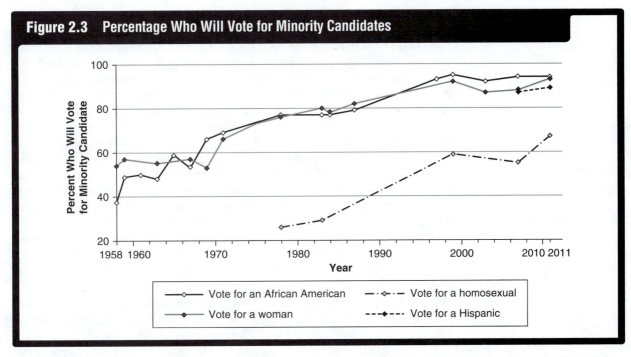

Sources: Jeffrey M. Jones, "Some Americans Reluctant to Vote for Mormon, 72 Year-Old Presidential Candidates: Strong for Black, Women, Catholic Candidates," February 20, 2007, http://www.gallup.com/poll/26611/Some-Americans-Reluctant-Vote-Mormon-72YearOld-Presidential-Candidates.aspx#2; Lydia Saad, "In U.S., 22% Are Hesitant to Support a Mormon in 2012," June 20, 2011, http://www.gallup.com/poll/148100/Hesitant-Support-Mormon-2012.aspx.

of Americans reported that they would vote for a qualified African American or woman candidate, and by 2011, 94% said they would vote for an African American presidential candidate, and 93% a woman presidential candidate.

In the 1970s, Gallup started asking respondents about their willingness to vote for a gay or lesbian presidential candidate. Figure 2.3 also depicts these results. They demonstrate an increased willingness of Americans to vote for gay and lesbian candidates, but they also demonstrate that Americans are significantly less likely to vote for these candidates than for African American or women candidates. Although there has been a dramatic increase in Americans' willingness to vote for gay and lesbian candidates, even as recently as 2011, almost a third said they would not vote for a gay or lesbian presidential candidate.

Only recently has Gallup asked respondents about their willingness to vote for a Hispanic presidential candidate. These data, also depicted in Figure 2.3, demonstrate that by 2011, 89% of the respondents said they would vote for a qualified presidential candidate of their party who was Hispanic.

Although Figure 2.3 offers some good news for most minority candidates, there are a couple of caveats. First, even a small percentage of voters can sway an election. At least at the presidential level, elections tend to be close, with less than

5% separating the winner from the loser. Thus, if a candidate loses 5% of her own party's vote because of her race or gender, it could cause her to lose the election. This problem may be greatest for Republican candidates, since Republican voters are less likely than Democratic voters to vote for minority candidates.[69]

A second caveat is that these figures may overestimate the willingness of voters to vote for minority candidates. Respondents to surveys may be reluctant to say they would not vote for someone because of race, ethnicity, or gender because it would violate social norms. Most people do not want to admit that they harbor racist or sexist feelings. The **Bradley Effect** refers to a problem often faced by minority candidates: they tend to poll better in surveys than on Election Day. The term comes from the 1982 California gubernatorial race where polls indicated that Tom Bradley, who was African American, was going to win easily, but he ended up losing. The common wisdom was that many voters, not wanting to appear prejudiced, overestimated the likelihood they would vote for Bradley when surveyed, and in the privacy of the voting booth, they could not bring themselves to vote for an African American governor.[70] Since Gov. Wilder had a similar experience, sometimes it is also referred to as the Wilder Effect.[71] However, things may be changing. Research suggests the Bradley Effect is much weaker in the twenty-first century.[72] There is little evidence of a Bradley Effect in President Obama's presidential elections as polls were fairly accurate in predicting the outcome of Obama's presidential runs.[73] There is also little evidence of a Bradley Effect for women candidates.[74]

To try to get around this common problem with surveys, other approaches have been used to examine the willingness of Americans to vote for minority candidates. An approach common in the women and politics field is to use experiments. In these experiments, one group of subjects is given one description of a hypothetical candidate, and another group is given a description of a slightly different hypothetical candidate. The only difference between the descriptions is that one candidate has a female first name and the other a male first name. Researchers can then compare subjects' views of candidates who are identical except for their sex. This literature suggests voters will vote for women but do not think they are viable.[75] If voters do not think women are likely to win, then they may be less willing to invest in a woman candidate by volunteering or giving her campaign donations. Experimental designs have also been used to estimate the electability of gays and lesbians, with somewhat more negative results. Voters see gay and lesbian candidates as less electable and judge them more negatively.[76] The effects of sexual orientation may be complex, however. The candidates' levels of masculinity or femininity[77] and whether they have publicly acknowledged their sexual orientation[78] also affect voters' evaluation of gay and lesbian candidates. Experimental research examining whites' willingness to vote for African American candidates has been mixed, but Highton finds little evidence of whites not voting for African American congressional candidates in real elections.[79]

Another approach is to try to estimate people's implicit prejudice and whether individuals' levels of implicit prejudice affect their voting. **Implicit prejudice** is less visible than explicit prejudice. Payne, Krosnick, Pasek, Lelkes, Akhtar, and Thompson used the **affect misattribution procedure** to measure implicit prejudice.[80]

Here subjects in an experiment are shown Chinese characters (i.e., writing) and asked to evaluate them. Just before each character, subjects were shown a photo of either an African American man or a white man so quickly they were barely aware that they saw it. Subjects with greater levels of implicit prejudice toward African Americans rated Chinese characters more negatively following the photo of the African American man. Research finds that those who scored high on implicit prejudice also scored high on explicit prejudice and were less likely to vote for Barack Obama. Kam used a similar approach to examine the electability of Hispanic candidates and found that voters with high levels of implicit and explicit prejudice toward Hispanics were not likely to vote for Hispanic candidates.[81]

Another issue with voters is that they tend to use race and gender stereotypes to estimate candidates' issues positions. Voters often lack critical information about the candidates and use **voting cues,** such as race, ethnicity, and gender, to guess at the candidates' traits and issue positions. Much research finds that women candidates are stereotyped as competent on issues related to women, health care, and education, while men are stereotyped as competent on issues related to agriculture, crime, the economy, and defense.[82] Gay men and lesbians are stereotyped as more supportive of LGBT issues.[83] African American politicians, compared to white politicians, are stereotyped as having survived adversity; being more vocal and passionate; having more integrity and empathy; and being better with issues associated with African Americans, such as civil rights and affirmative action.[84] There is also an ideological component to candidates' stereotypes, with women and African American candidates being stereotyped as liberal.[85] Although the use of stereotypes normally has a negative connotation, there are debates about whether they harm the electability of minority candidates. It is most likely that the degree to which stereotypes hurt minority candidates is contextual, depending on what voters in a particular location and time want from their politicians. For example, given the stereotypes of women candidates, women candidates may be advantaged when campaigns center on the need for domestic programs, and disadvantaged when campaigns center on war or the economy.

Context

The context of elections also influences the electability of minority candidates. The specific traits of the context vary by each minority group; but minority candidates tend to do better in some districts than others. Palmer and Simon coined the term **women friendly districts** to label the type of districts that are more likely to have women candidates and officials.[86] These districts tend to be in northern and western states, in nontraditional political cultures (see below), in urban areas, where voters have high levels of SES (socioeconomic status), where women do well in the labor force, and where there are large numbers of minorities.[87] Many of these factors overlap, such as in urban areas, which often have large minority populations. LGBT candidates tend to do well in districts where voters are well educated, Democratic, and less religious and where there are more LGBT voters.[88] Table 2.1 lists the percentage of women and LGBT in the different state legislatures. It demonstrates that less-urban states have smaller numbers of women and LGBT members in their legislatures. For example, while the populous states of California (26.7% women and 6.7% LGBT) and New York (21.6% and 2.8%, respectively) have relatively high levels of women and LGBT legislators, the less populous states of North Dakota (17% and 0.7%) and Wyoming (16.7% and 1.1%) have relatively low levels.

A state's political culture can also affect its level of descriptive representation. Although there are several different ways states can be classified by political culture, Elazar provides the best known typology of political culture in the states.[89] He suggests there are three main political cultures. The **traditionalistic culture** is concentrated in the South and is associated with a belief that the government exists to maintain order. States with traditionalistic cultures also tend to have less participation by the masses and an elite group that controls the government. In the **moralistic culture,** people see government as a social good and associate it with high levels of participation by the masses. Finally, there is the **individualistic culture** that is associated with more government corruption and the idea that government is there to foster private interests. Generally, the traditionalistic political culture is associated with less representation for minorities. And clearly, Southern states, with their traditional political culture, have a smaller percentage of women and LGBT representatives than other states. For example, Alabama has 13.3% women and 0.7% LGBT in its legislature. For Mississippi, the percentages are 17.8 and 0, and for South Carolina, the figures are 12.9% and 0. These states also have low ratios between racial and ethnic minority representatives and minority populations.

Rodney Hero created a political culture typology[90] that is particularly relevant to minority and politics because it is based on the racial and ethnic distributions. According to Hero, there are homogeneous states where a large majority of people have northern and western European ancestry; heterogeneous states that have large percentages of people from southern and eastern European ancestry and moderate percentages of minorities (African Americans, Asians, and Hispanics) and other Europeans; and bifurcated states that have large percentages of northern and western Europeans and minorities. Bifurcated states tend to be similar to those with a traditional political culture, with minorities being underrepresented in these states.

The key context for racial and ethnic minorities concerns the minority makeup of their districts.[91] Casellas examined Hispanic and African American candidates for the U.S. House and for state legislatures, and found the strongest influence on the electability of these candidates was the racial/ethnic makeup of the district.[92] Hispanic candidates won where the Hispanic population was large, and African American candidates won where the African American population was large. However, Hispanic candidates were not likely to be elected in majority African American districts and vice versa.[93] Since the United States is still segregated by race and ethnicity, it is possible to create majority-minority districts to help increase the electability of these groups. However, since there is less segregation by gender and sexual orientation than by race and ethnicity, majority-minority districts are less helpful for these groups. Although LGBT legislators are found in districts with larger LGBT populations,[94] this is more likely to be caused by LGBT individuals living in similar neighborhoods than by legislatures creating majority LGBT districts. In addition, LGBT voters do not make up the majority of voters in districts for high level offices. See Table 2.2 for the percentage of each minority in districts with minority Congress members in the 113th Congress.[95] It demonstrates that the average racial or ethnic minority member has a district that is largely comprised of similar voters. However, minority members do not serve districts with large percentages of constituents with a minority status not shared by the member. Women and LGBT members have higher than average racial and ethnic minority populations in their districts, but they do not tend to be majority-minority districts.

Although the percentage of women does not vary enough to help explain the descriptive representation of women, Smith, Reingold, and Owens note that women's descriptive representation in cities is affected by women's resources.[96] Women are more likely to be mayors where there are strong women's organizations. Additionally, women are more likely to serve on city councils in cities where women have high socioeconomic status.

Another way context has different effects on the frequency of different minority groups in elected office concerns socioeconomic status. Women, LGBT, and Asian American representatives tend to represent wealthier districts than do African American and Hispanic representatives.[97] To help demonstrate this, I calculated average median household incomes for minority Congress members in the 113th Congress. The average household income for districts represented by congresswomen was about $53,000; for districts represented by LGBT, it was $54,300; and for Asian Americans, it was about $59,200. For districts represented by African American members, the average median household income was $41,700, and for Hispanic members, it was $46,100.[98] As a point of reference, the national median household income for 2013 was $52,250.[99] Thus, African American and Hispanic members come from poorer than average districts, and

TABLE 2.2   Demographic Traits of Congress Members' Districts by Minority Status of Member

	% African American	% Hispanic	% Asian American
Woman	14.6	21.9	8.2
LGBT	6.3	21.7	3.4
African American	44.5	17.3	4.2
Hispanic	5.8	56.7	5.8
Average nationwide	13.6	16.3	5.6

Source: Percentages were calculated for type of legislator using 2010 census data by congressional district.

women, LGBT, and Asian American members come from wealthier than average districts. The low level of wealth in districts with African American and Hispanic members is easy to explain: African Americans and Hispanic Americans tend to be poorer than other Americans, and African American and Hispanic representatives tend to represent majority-minority districts.

Another part of context is media coverage. A significant body of research that has examined TV news coverage as well as print media over a variety of types of elections has found that the media coverage minority candidates receive differs from that of Anglos' and men's coverage.[100] This research tends to rely on content analysis. With content analysis, researchers devise a systematic method to observe the content of newspaper articles, TV news, and so on. For example, they might count the number of sentences, words, or articles that are positive or negative, or discuss a particular trait or issue. Research using content analysis tends to find that the tone of articles is more negative for minorities, that is, it uses more negative than positive adjectives and presents minority candidates as less electable. This research also suggests a different set of issues are covered for minority than nonminority candidates. For women, the coverage often focuses more on women's issues. For racial and ethnic minority candidates, the coverage often focuses more on the candidate's race and ethnicity. Analysis of the 2004 elections found that when white candidates ran against each other, race was mentioned only 3% of the time; when African Americans ran against each other, it was mentioned 57%; and when whites ran against African Americans, race was mentioned 23% of the time. In this last group, the race of the white candidate was mentioned just 4% of the time compared to 23% of the time for African American candidates.[101] A similar pattern was found among Hispanic candidates' media coverage.[102] The media can also bring up race, ethnicity, gender, or sexual orientation in subtle ways. For example, during the 2008 elections, the media's discussion of whether or not the Bradley Effect would undermine the accuracy of polling figures made race an issue in the campaign. Women too often receive more coverage about their family and appearance. There is also evidence that women and racial/ethnic minorities receive less media coverage. These biases may be weakening as some research suggests that the media coverage might be more equitable in recent elections than in the past.[103]

The race, ethnic, and gender biases in the media may be particularly damaging for minority women. Recent work finds significant differences in the press coverage of Anglo, African American, and Hispanic congresswomen. In looking at newspaper coverage, Gershon found that in the 2006 midterm elections, there were about twenty-two articles on the average Anglo woman's campaign, but only about eleven on the average African American, and five on the average Hispanic congresswoman's campaign.[104] Anglo women's names were also mentioned more: about eighty-six times compared to nineteen times for African American women, and only eight times for Hispanic women. Although there were not significant differences in the likelihood that Anglo, African American, and Hispanic women were endorsed by the newspapers, Anglo women received more compliments, three on average compared to almost two for African American women, and about 0.14 for Hispanic women. Anglo women also averaged more criticisms. There were also some noticeable differences in issue coverage. The issue receiving the most coverage for Anglo women candidates was defense, for African American women candidates, it was health care, and for Hispanic women candidates, it was immigration.

There are several reasons why the media may cover minority candidates differently than nonminority candidates. First, minority candidates may differ from nonminority candidates in their campaigns. The media may just be reflecting the issues important to the candidates. However, the evidence is mixed as to how much minority and nonminority candidates differ in their campaign issues.[105] In addition, Kahn found that the media tend to focus more on the campaign issues addressed by men's campaigns than women's campaigns. Second, reporters may be reacting to voters' assumptions about the candidates and offer coverage that they think voters want. Since voters stereotype candidates, the reporting may reflect these stereotypes. Another reason is that the reporters and editors may share the biases and stereotypes held by other Americans since they are members of the same society. Just as the rest of the population holds stereotypical views of minority candidates, reporters may as well. Another reason may concern differences in the context of elections. Minority candidates are more likely found in urban areas. Urban areas often have lots of campaigns to cover and so the local newspaper cannot adequately follow them all. Also, since minority candidates often run in majority-minority districts that are highly Democratic, they are less competitive, and noncompetitive campaigns are seen as less newsworthy.

Bias in media coverage is potentially damaging since it affects campaigns. Much of what voters know about the candidates they learn from the media. Researchers have found that the media affect voters' knowledge of candidates, how much they like a candidate, candidate viability, and if they are likely to vote for the candidate.[106] The more exposure voters have to television news, the more favorable they feel toward men, but not women candidates. For example, Gershon, using an experiment, found that candidates who had issue content similar to that received by Hispanic women candidates (see above) received less support than candidates whose coverage was similar to that of African American or Anglo candidates.[107] In addition the media can frame campaigns in ways that might be more favorable to some candidates than others. For example, if campaigns are framed as referenda on defense policy, men candidates may be advantaged, but if they are framed as referenda on education, women be advantaged.

Candidates

Besides voters and context, minority candidates themselves can affect the likelihood that they win elections. First, minority candidates have to run for office, and run where they have a fighting chance of winning in order to be elected. Knowing whether minority candidates are incumbents or challengers is needed to accurately assess their relative electability. Since the vast majority of incumbent legislators (in the neighborhood of 80%–90%, depending on office) win reelection, minority candidates who are not incumbents may have low election rates, but it is their challenger status not their minority status that affects their electability. Therefore, to estimate the electability of minority candidates, their incumbent/challenger status needs to be considered. When doing so, it is evident that minorities who run for office are as likely to win as their counterparts. According to Herrick and Mendez, "Between 1992 and 2010, among candidates who ran against a major party challenger, 93.4 % of women incumbents seeking reelection to the House won compared to 94.1% of men incumbents. Among challengers, 5.7% of women won and 5.7% of men won their races."[108] In 2012, there were seventy-six African American House candidates, forty-one (54%) won; only one African American member of Congress lost reelection.[109]

One reason minority candidates do well when they run is that they run where conditions are favorable. For example, Orndercin and Welch found that women candidates were more likely to run where women had held office in the past.[110] Haider-Markel also found that LGBT state legislative candidates did well on Election Day because they were selective about where they ran,[111] running where they had the best chance of winning: northern, urban, and Democratic districts. African American and Hispanic candidates, too, tend to be strategic, running in districts with large minority populations, for municipal offices and for seats previously held by minorities.[112] It is likely that if minorities were not selective in where they ran, their election rates would tumble.

Because women do well when they run, a common explanation for the underrepresentation of women is that they are unlikely to toss their hat in the ring. Even though there was a record number of women running for Congress in 2014, only 18.6% of possible House candidates and 27% of Senate candidates were women.[113] Part of the reason women are less likely to run is because women are less likely to come from the **"eligibility pool."**[114] In the United States, candidates tend to have certain traits, such as being successful businesspeople, lawyers, having military experience or previous electoral experience. Yet, only about 20% of law partners are women, and only fifty-one women are CEOs in Fortune's 1000 firms.[115] That relatively few women are in these categories is a likely cause for the low levels of descriptive representation for women. However, even within this pool, women are less likely to have considered or ran for office.[116] A couple of key reasons are: they see themselves as less qualified (even if they are not), and they are less likely to be recruited.[117] Another reason women may be reluctant to run for office is that they are primary caregivers of their children. Often women wait until their children have grown before they seek office, limiting the number of potential women candidates at any one time.

The lack of candidates may help explain the dearth of other minorities as well. In 2012, there was a shortage of racial and ethnic minority and LGBT candidates for Congress. There were only eight out LGBT congressional candidates, twenty-five Asian American, fifty-four Hispanic, and seventy-six African American candidates out of a possible 870 House and seventy-two Senate slots.[118] Racial and ethnic minorities, too, are less likely to come from the "eligibility pool," that is, less likely to be successful businesspeople or lawyers. But there are other reasons African Americans may be reluctant to run. In examining the decision of African American House members to run for the Senate, Johnson, Oppenheimer, and Selin found African American members were less likely to run: 4.35% of African American members compared to 9.45% of nonwhite members.[119] However, they found that race per se was not what discouraged them from running; what discouraged them from running was that they tended to be too liberal and too underfunded to win a higher level office. Additionally, they came from large states that have a large pool of potential challengers, which means the odds of winning were small.

Even if candidates run, they may not have the resources needed to win. One of the most critical resources is money. Not only does money help candidates get their message out, it is also a good indicator of the quality of candidates: whether the candidate has qualities like experience and name recognition needed to do well on Election Day. It is also a good indicator that the candidate has a good chance of winning because donors are more likely to give money to candidates who are likely to win. The evidence suggests that while African American and Hispanic candidates raise less campaign money than other candidates, women and gay and lesbian candidates raise as much. For example, looking at House incumbents between the 102nd (1991–1993) and 110th (2007–2009) Congresses, Johnson and colleagues find African American incumbents raised $300,000 less than other members of the House.[120] Similarly, women are found to raise more money than their male counterparts.[121] For example, during the 2012 elections, the average woman House candidate who won spent about $1.8 million, the average LGBT winning House candidate spent $1.7 million, but the average winning Hispanic candidate spent $1.1 million, and the average winning African American candidate spent only 0.9 million.[122] It is likely that the difference in fund-raising can be attributed to differences in the nature of their districts. African American and Hispanic members tend to come from poorer districts than women and LGBT candidates. African American and Hispanic members also tend to represent majority-minority districts that are heavily Democratic, so their elections tend to be less competitive and consequently less expensive. However, African American women candidates report difficulty raising money.[123] Thus, the lower levels of funds may be a combination of the districts they run in and the reluctance of large donors to contribute to their campaigns.

How candidates campaign, too, can affect their electability. Common wisdom for minority candidates is to limit discussions related to their minority status.[124] The term **deracialization** is often used for this phenomenon, but women and LGBT are also often counseled to avoid dwelling on issues related to their minority status. Although race surfaced in Barack Obama's presidential elections, candidate Obama was reluctant to discuss race, and certainly his campaign did not focus on race-based themes. However, he did not ignore race and often would incorporate race into discussions of policies with universal interests, such as jobs and health care.[125] There is evidence, too, that more recently mayoral candidates are using a similar approach, which has been dubbed targeted universalistic rhetoric.[126] The research on whether women are more likely to campaign on women's issues is mixed. Most likely the degree to which men's and women's campaigns differ depends on time and level of office. For example, while Dolan found women and men running for Congress discussed very similar issues on their webpages, Kahn found greater difference in the 1980s.[127] There is some evidence too that LGBT who run for state offices are more likely to campaign on LGBT issues than their straight counterparts.[128]

Although the common wisdom is to run a deracialized, degendered, or desexualorientation campaign, there are situations where it may make sense to run a raced or gendered campaign. Women may want to stress their gender when gender stereotypes match with the concerns of the day. David Canon's research, too, indicates that African American candidates running in majority-minority districts against an African American will do well to run a campaign running on themes common to all races, so that the candidate can pick up nonminority as well as minority votes. But if running against a white candidate in a majority-minority district, the candidate will do well to focus on themes of difference.[129]

The Election of Minority Women

As pointed out throughout this chapter, minority women tend to come closer to proportional representation than white women. It is likely that this will continue. The number of African American and Hispanic women elected officials is growing at a faster rate than that of their male counterparts or Anglo women.[130] In the 2014 congressional elections, four out of the five new African American Congress members were women. That minority women's descriptive representation outpaces that of white women is somewhat surprising since women of color have a double marginal status. Similarly, since voters and media stereotype minorities and women, one might think that minority women would suffer even more from stereotypes. However, that women of color have high levels of representation has been known for twenty years.[131] Several reasons have been offered for their high rates of representation: they appeal to a broad range of voters, they can do well without strong party support, training workshops designed for women of color help them build contacts and strategies, and sista' networks enable African American women to balance family and work.[132] A sista' network is an "Organization of supportive African American women who advance the political aspirations of other African American women. Coined by Tuesday Cooper, sista' networks refer to the networking and familial relationships between professional Black women which facilitate the procurement of unwritten practices and rule within various professions."[133] Relatedly, Philpot and Walton found that not only can qualified African American women candidates get the support of white women and men voters, African American women offered extremely high levels of support for African American women candidates. "Black women have created an identity that is greater than the sum of its parts. This, in turn, guides their political decision making whereby they evaluate candidates based on the potential benefit yielded to black women rather than blacks and or women."[134]

Descriptive Representation Is Not Sufficient

Scola suggests another reason minority women may outpace white women in levels of descriptive representation is that different conditions affect the electability of white and minority women.[135] She found that minority women state legislators were more likely to serve in wealthier states, those with traditionalistic political culture, large minority populations, and multimember districts, and white women were more likely to serve in states with moralistic cultures, liberal voters, a large percentage of professionalized women, and small minority populations. In essence she notes that minority women are more likely to serve in states that are raced. Another reason may be that minority women have high levels of political ambition. At least for African American women, this seems likely. African American women stand out in the high levels of civic engagement (volunteering and activity in religious organizations), high levels of group consciousness, high levels of civic duty, and ultimately high levels of voting.[136]

Descriptive Representation Is Not Sufficient

Although descriptive representation is important, few would argue that descriptive representation is sufficient for the full representation of minorities. Political institutions, such as Congress, state legislatures, the presidency, the courts, electoral system, and so on, were created by white heterosexual men with their lives, values, and interests in mind. As a consequence, many scholars believe that political institutions have a gender and race[137] in that they are biased toward the interests and lives of white heterosexual males. The terms used to describe this phenomenon are **gendered institutions** or **raced institutions**. Acker writes, "The term 'gendered institutions' means that gender is present in the processes, practices, images and ideologies, and distributions of power in the various sectors of social life."[138] As a consequence, the norms (informal unwritten guidelines as to how to behave), the rules, and structures have race and gender biases.

Kenney says if an institution has gender, individuals in it have a gender, are treated based on that gender, and that the institution produces, reproduces, and subverts gender.[139] The same could be said for race: institutions have race if individuals have race, are treated based on their race, and that the institution produces, reproduces, and subverts race. Remember that race and gender are social constructs whose meanings can change. Additionally, Kenney states: "To say that an institution is gendered, then, is to recognize that construction of masculinity and femininity are intertwined in the daily culture of an institution rather than existing out in society or fixed within individuals which they bring whole to the institution."[140] For example, most Americans' perceptions of political leaders are masculine.[141]

Women candidates, as well as men candidates, who are feminine are seen as less fit for office. A candidate who cries is somehow less fit for office than others. In 1987, when Rep. Patricia Schroeder (D, CO) announced she would not run for president, she cried, and women's groups were mortified, fearing that would be interpreted to mean women are not fit for office.[142] But there really is no reason why crying is a sign that someone is not fit for office, except that politics is gendered. Our political system is also hierarchical and based more on conflict between two competing sides, whether they are prosecutors and defendants in the courts or individuals on campaign trails and parties in capitol buildings, than it is on cooperation. Conflict and hierarchy, according to feminist theorists, are masculine.[143] These theories suggest that women are more focused on maintaining relationships and see the interconnectedness of ideas and things. As a consequence, women are less comfortable with conflict that might harm relationships or strict hierarchical levels of command. In addition, individuals with a stay-at-home spouse or who are single without children are better able to navigate the responsibilities we place on our representatives, who have irregular and demanding schedules. As Hawkesworth points out, if our governing institutions were not gendered or raced, then women and men and people of color and whites should hold equal positions, and they do not: minority women are often silenced, stereotyped, and excluded because they do not fit with the biases of the institution.[144]

Although individuals often behave in ways that reinforce the gendered or raced nature of institutions, notions of gendered or raced institutions tend to downplay or depersonalize actions. It is the institution, not that individual in the institution, that limits the role of women and other minorities in the institution. For example, in the fall of 2014 the press picked up on comments that Sen. Kirsten Gillibrand (D, NY) made in her book regarding sexist comments made to her by other senators, such as "Don't lose too much weight now, I like my girls chubby."[145] When asked to disclose who made the comments, she refused because the issue is how women are treated in the workplace, not the behavior of certain individuals.[146] Because political institutions are raced and gendered, for racial, ethnic, and gender minorities to be fully represented, the institutions themselves have to change.

Another reason simply having proportional numbers of women, African Americans, Hispanics, Asian Americans, American Indians, and LGBT Americans is not enough is that minority representatives may not have much in common with minority citizens. For example, although President Obama is African American, he has a law degree from Harvard, and in 2012 reported an income of over $600,000.[147] This is hardly the norm for people of color. Not only is the president wealthier and better educated than most minorities, but officials also generally tend to be better educated and wealthier than most minorities. Even the poorest members of Congress have salaries of $174,000 and opportunities to make even larger salaries when they leave office. Virtually all members of Congress, regardless of race, ethnicity, or gender, have college degrees; many have professional or advanced degrees, and many of these degrees are from prestigious universities.[148] The limited education and economic diversity of minority policymakers in nonelective offices may be even greater. For example, twenty-two out of Obama's first thirty-five top picks for administrative posts had degrees from Ivy League schools, or the Massachusetts Institute of Technology, Stanford University, University of Chicago, or an elite British university.[149] Similarly, all members of the Supreme Court have Ivy League degrees.

Minority representatives, too, may not be advocates for minority interests. For example, Rep. J. C. Watts (R, OK) may not be considered a good descriptive representative of African Americans. Watts represented a white conservative district, the African American community did not embrace him, and he scored a

20 on the NAACP's legislative scorecard (the range was 0–100) in the 104th Congress.[150] Rocha, Sanchez, and Uscinski, too, suggest that some Hispanic representatives do a better job representing Hispanic interests.[151] Many women activists also think that women representatives who do not support reproductive choice are not representing women's interests. And some women members score poorly on interest group scorecards put out by women's groups. For example, in the 113th Congress, Sen. Lisa Murkowitz (R, AK) received a 40 from the American Association of University Women (AAUW).[152] Canon's examination of members of Congress found that members who campaigned on themes related to differences between the races were more likely to work on minority interest policies and work in symbolic ways to represent African Americans, such as hiring African American staff while in office, than those who ran on themes of commonality.[153] Relatedly, African American mayors who have a more radical ideology are more responsive to minority interests than more moderate African American mayors.[154]

Another issue that indicates proportionality may be insufficient is that minority groups are diverse. Not only is there the intersectionality of race, ethnicity, gender, and sexual orientation, but within each category there is variation. As noted in Chapter 1, American Indians, Asian Americans, and Hispanics come from numerous tribes or nationalities that have unique histories and cultures. For example, an American of Mexican heritage living in Texas may not see a Cuban senator from Florida as being a descriptive representative. Added to this are the disagreements inside of groups as to what is good policy. For example, women are divided. Women are pro-life, pro-choice, liberal, conservative, Democratic, and Republican. Thus, having all congresswomen voting AAUW preferences would deny many women a meaningful descriptive representative.

One approach to this issue is to have diversity within the delegations of each minority group. For example, the recent election of Rep. Mia Love (R, UT) offers descriptive representation to African American Republican women. However, since a Congress made up of all the combinations of Americans may be impractical, Dovi offers another solution.[155] She argues that for representatives to offer descriptive representation, they should have "strong *mutual* relationships with *dispossessed subgroups*. This criterion is composed of two aspects. First preferable descriptive representatives should possess a particular kind of relationship (mutual) and second; they should have this kind of relationship *with* certain subgroups of historically disadvantaged groups (dispossessed)."[156]

Conclusion: Similarities, Differences, and Intersectionality in Descriptive Representation

This chapter demonstrates that in the big picture, minorities are similar in their descriptive representation, but when looking at the specifics, there are many differences. Each minority group has seen significant improvements in its levels of representation in the past fifty years, each remains underrepresented, and the pace of the improvement varies. The growth of LGBT representation was delayed until the end of the twentieth century. Congress has seen considerable growth in the number of Hispanic members, but this growth has not kept up with the growth in the number of Hispanic Americans. Hispanics and LGBT Americans also remain more severely underrepresented than African Americans, even though there has been little growth in the number of African Americans in Congress since the 1992 elections. Women, too, saw significant growth in their numbers in Congress following the 1992 elections, albeit for different reasons, and continue to see fairly steady growth.

Minorities also share the basic, but not always specific, factors affecting their descriptive representation, the voters (willingness to vote for minorities and stereotypes of minorities), context (the size of the minority population, and political culture), and the candidates (the decision to run and their resources). Although descriptive representation is affected by voters, context, and candidates, the specifics vary by minority group. That racial and ethnic minorities are more segregated than the gender minorities means the racial makeup of the district has a significant effect on racial minorities but not on women and LGBT. All minority groups have a shortage of candidates and tend to run campaigns that de-emphasize their minority status. Voters, too, report being more likely to vote for racial minorities and women than for LGBT. Although campaign resources are not a significant problem for women, LGBT, and Asian American candidates, Hispanic and African American candidates may have fewer financial resources.

This chapter also demonstrates the importance of considering the intersectionality of race and gender. The representation of racial and ethnic minority women is not the additive effect of the biases against women candidates plus the biases against racial and ethnic minorities. Instead, racial and ethnic minority women may be faring better than white women or racial and ethnic minority men, as there are more minority women in office than predicated by their separate levels of racial, ethnic, and gender representation. This may be because they get higher levels of support from other minority women, are likely to do better in different types of states than white women, or because they have higher levels of political ambition.

Besides voters, context, and candidates, descriptive representation can be affected by the rules of the game, or formalistic representation. Chapter 3 explores how electoral and institutional rules can affect the descriptive representation of minorities.

KEY TERMS

Affect misattribution procedure (p. 48)
Bradley Effect (p. 48)
Clarence Thomas hearings (p. 30)
Deracialization (p. 55)
Eligibility pool (p. 54)

Gendered institutions (p. 57)
Implicit prejudice (p. 48)
Individualistic culture (p. 50)
Majority-minority districts (p. 34)
Moralistic culture (p. 50)
Raced institutions (p. 57)

Reconstruction (p. 33)
Traditionalistic culture (p. 50)
Voting cues (p. 49)
Widow effect (p. 31)
Women friendly districts (p. 49)
Year of the woman (p. 30)

Chapter 3

Minorities and Formalistic Representation

Laws, Institutional Design, and Elections

On February 21, 1965, twenty-six-year-old Jimmie Lee Jackson lay in the hospital with a head injury and a gunshot wound; he died five days later. Also in the hospital were his mother and eighty-two-year-old grandfather Cager Lee, a retired farmer, both of whom had a broken scalp and bruises they received from Alabama state troopers.[1] They were attacked for marching out of Zion Chapel Methodist Church to protest the lack of voting rights. "Voting is what all this is about," Cager Lee told reporters.[2] Mr. Lee was not a registered voter because every time he had tried, he had been turned down.

Mr. Lee and his family were part of a series of actions in Selma, Alabama, to change laws so that African Americans could register and vote. Alabama had enacted voter registration requirements designed and enforced in ways to make it difficult for African Americans to register. The last time Mr. Lee had tried to register, the registrant read the questions so fast he couldn't understand what was said.[3]

Early in 1965, Martin Luther King Jr. called for a series of actions in Selma to try to change the laws. The most famous of the actions involved efforts to march fifty-four miles from Selma to Montgomery. Although the march was finally completed in March, it had faced brutal attacks by troopers at the Edmund Pettis Bridge. These actions led to thousands of arrests, hundreds injured, and two dead. People were willing to sacrifice for the vote because of its importance to policy representation. As Dr. King said in Selma: "If Negros could vote. . . . There would be no Jim Crows, there would be no oppressive poverty directed toward the Negros, our children would not be crippled by segregated schools, and the whole community might live together in harmony."[4]

That historically Americans have sacrificed much to try to gain the right to vote demonstrates the importance of formalistic representation. Formalistic representation concerns the formal arrangements that give representatives the authority to act for the represented or to hold representatives accountable (representatives can be removed by voters) to the represented.[5] In most democracies, the formal arrangements concern elections. Representatives are given authority

Jimmy Lee Jackson was shot and killed by a state trooper in Selma, Alabama, during a voting rights march in 1965. His death helped ignite the Selma actions of 1965. (© Jo Freeman, www.jofreeman.com)

by winning elections and are held accountable by facing the electorate periodically, or given authority by being appointed by elected officials who can hold them accountable. After reading this chapter, students should be familiar with laws affecting the ability of minorities to participate in elections by voting: the Fifteenth, Nineteenth, and Twenty-Fourth Amendments, the Voting Rights Act, and devices such as white primaries, literacy tests, and poll taxes. Also after reading the chapter, students should be familiar with how redistricting, electoral systems, and institutional designs affect the ability of minorities to win elections. The chapter ends with a discussion of the Fourteenth Amendment's equal protection clause and how the Supreme Court has used the rational basis, strict scrutiny, and heightened scrutiny tests to enforce it.

Formalistic Representation and the Right to Vote

Laws that affect minority Americans' right to vote affect their descriptive and policy representation. Groups who are disenfranchised have little ability to affect who represents them or to influence their behavior in office. Each minority group has a unique history with regard to the vote. For example, there have not been any laws that single out LGBT Americans for disenfranchisement, and women were late in getting the right to vote. Although a handful of states (Wyoming, Montana, Colorado, Utah, Idaho, Washington, and Illinois) gave women the right to vote prior to the ratification of the Nineteenth Amendment in 1920, the amendment was not followed by systematic efforts to block women from voting in the way states blocked racial and ethnic minorities from voting.

African Americans and other racial minorities would appear to be guaranteed the right to vote in 1870 with the ratification of the Fifteenth Amendment. Section 1 of the amendment states: "The right of citizens of the United States to vote shall not be denied or abridged by the United States or by any state on account of race, color, or previous condition of servitude." However, the effects of the amendment were limited. Voting was still limited to citizens, and nonwhite immigrants could not become naturalized citizens until the mid–twentieth century, and American Indians' citizenship was in flux until 1924. Another issue for many citizens is having ballots or voting materials in languages other than English. Some Asian Americans, Hispanics, and American Indians who are citizens speak English as a second language and need ballots and other voter materials in their native tongue to cast meaningful votes. Additionally, many states passed laws designed to disenfranchise African Americans and other minorities.

One type of law passed by states to limit African Americans' ability to vote was the **poll tax**. Poll taxes required people to pay a fee or tax before they could vote. Often the tax was retroactive, meaning voters would have to pay the tax for each previous election cycle in which they failed to pay it. Given minorities' low-income levels, the poll tax effectively prevented many minority citizens from voting. Many of these laws singled out newly enfranchised groups, as several states' poll tax laws contained grandfather clauses. **Grandfather clauses** meant the law only applied to individuals whose grandfathers could not vote. Grandfather clauses were ruled unconstitutional in 1915.[6] But the poll tax remained on the books for almost another fifty years. In 1964, the Twenty-Fourth Amendment, which outlawed poll taxes for federal elections, became law, and a year later the Voting Rights Act outlawed them for other elections. Another type of law passed in southern states created **white primaries**. Since southern states were one-party Democratic states, candidates who won their state's Democratic primary were virtually assured victory. Thus, if African Americans were prevented from voting in primaries, they were effectively denied a meaningful vote. The legal argument for the laws was that they complied with the Fifteenth Amendment because primaries were party actions, not state actions (the Fifteenth Amendment only limits governmental actions). After fifty years of white primaries, the Supreme Court eventually ruled otherwise, and in 1944, it stated that white primaries violated the Fifteenth Amendment.[7]

Another common device used to disenfranchise African Americans was a *literacy test*. **Literacy tests** required would-be voters to pass an exam before they could register to vote. These tests often required the would-be voter to interpret sections of the Constitution or answer questions that were difficult to answer (see Spotlight 3.1 for examples of questions from the Alabama literacy test). The administration of these laws was often biased and capricious.[8] In some locations, African Americans would be told they failed even if they answered questions correctly. The Voting Rights Act prohibited literacy tests.

African Americans were not the only minority group that states tried to bar from voting, and some of the devices used to deny African Americans the right to vote, such as poll taxes and literacy tests, were used on American Indians and on Mexicans and other Hispanics.[9] In addition, registration laws that made it hard for migrants also limited the Hispanic vote.[10] American Indians also faced state laws that barred American Indians living on reservations from voting or holding office; some required American Indians to give up their tribal relations or be taxed.[11] Many treaties prevent tribal members from paying some state taxes.

The **Voting Rights Act** of 1965 (VRA) is a key piece of legislation concerning minority voting rights. As already noted, this law prohibited literacy tests and poll taxes, and as important as these changes were, the law went even further. The law has been amended and expanded several times and prevents states and local governments from having voting requirements that deny or limit voting on account of race. The VRA prevents laws that have the effect of disproportionately limiting one race's right to vote regardless of the law's intention. A 1995 amendment to the VRA (section 203) requires that voting information be made available in a non-English language if needed for a significant number of voters. This is particularly significant for Hispanic and Asian Americans who are less likely to be native English speakers. American Indians also often need voting information in their native language to vote. For example, in 2014, a judge ruled that Alaska had to start offering voting information in Yupik and Gwich'in. This judgment required the government to provide information in these languages

Spotlight 3.1

Ten Questions from the 1965 Alabama Literacy Test

1. Which of the following is a right guaranteed by the Bill of Rights?
   _____ Public Education
   _____ Employment
   _____ Trial by Jury
   _____ Voting

2. The federal census of population is taken every five years.
   _____ True _____ False

3. If a person is indicted for a crime, name two rights which he has.
   _____ _____

4. A U.S. senator elected at the general election in November takes office the following year on what date?
   _____

5. A President elected at the general election in November takes office the following year on what date?
   _____

6. Which definition applies to the word "amendment?"
   _____ Proposed change, as in a Constitution
   _____ Make of peace between nationals at war
   _____ A part of the government

7. A person appointed to the U.S. Supreme Court is appointed for a term of
   _____

8. When the Constitution was approved by the original colonies, how many states had to ratify it in order for it to be in effect?
   _____

9. Does enumeration affect the income tax levied on citizens in various states?
   _____

10. Person opposed to swearing in an oath may say, instead (solemnly):
    _____

Answer key: 1. Trial by Jury only; 2. False (every 10 years); 3. Habeas Corpus (immediate presentation of charges); lawyer; speedy trial; 4. January 3; 5. January 20; 6. Proposed change, as in a Constitution; 7. Life (with good behavior); 8. Nine; 9. Yes; 10. Affirm.

Source: "1965 Alabama Literacy Test," Rufus A. Lewis Collection, H. Councill Trenholm State Technical College Archives.

on how to vote.[12] Sections 4 and 5 of the VRA required states with a history of low rates of African American voter registration and voting and a history of discriminatory voting laws to get preclearance from the federal government before they could create new laws regarding voting. Section 4, which specified the preclearance requirements, was ruled unconstitutional in a 2013 controversial Supreme Court decision, *Shelby County v. Holder,*[13] when the Court ruled that the requirements put on the states to avoid preclearance were an overreach of the federal government. This ruling ultimately negated both sections 4 and 5. Since it negated the requirements for preclearance, no state or local government could be subject to preclearance. Section 4 could be reinstated if Congress acts to amend the section.

The VRA, the Twenty-Fourth Amendment, and similar efforts were effective in increasing the voting rate of African Americans. According to American National Election Studies (ANES)[14] data, in the 1940s and 1950s less than 40% of African Americans voted in most elections, but by the 1980s, one half to two-thirds of African Americans reported voting, and today African Americans vote at similar levels as whites.[15] McCool, Olson, and Robinson looked at the effects of court cases based on the VRA involving American Indians and found significant increases in voter turnout and descriptive representation following the lawsuits.[16]

Hispanics, American Indians, and African Americans have also suffered from **voter dilution**.[17] This involves efforts to minimize the impact of minority voters. The clearest examples of voter dilution stem from redistricting. After the census, which occurs every ten years, states must redraw their legislative boundaries to ensure proportionality between districts; that is, each district should have the same number of residents. Redrawing of boundary lines is not politically neutral because how boundaries are drawn can affect a group's political power. When boundary lines are drawn to aid or harm groups of individuals it is called *gerrymandering*. Gerrymandering can involve "cracking" or placing minorities in so many districts that they are such a small percentage of voters in each district that they are unlikely to affect who wins; or gerrymandering can involve over-packing minorities into a small number of districts so that they only have influence in one or two districts instead of several. Prior to the 1980s, efforts such as these were common. However, during the 1990s, following a series of decisions by the judiciary, states started to pack African American and Hispanic voters into majority-minority districts to maximize, not minimize, their voting power. As was noted in Chapter 2, this resulted in a dramatic increase in the number of minority members of the House of Representatives. The creation of majority-minority districts to help American Indians is less common. In addition, there is still cracking to minimizing minority voting power.[18]

In order to maximize the number of majority-minority districts, several states made oddly shaped districts. In North Carolina, one district was held together by an interstate that meandered through the state. This same district resulted in a Supreme Court case, *Shaw v. Reno*[19] (1993). In the case, five white residents of the district sued, claiming it violated the Fourteenth Amendment's equal protection clause because it made white citizens' voting power weaker than that of other citizens. In a 5–4 decision, the Court ruled that district boundaries drawn based on race were unconstitutional. The Court has heard several cases since *Shaw* that have reinforced the idea that race should not be used in drawing lines.

Another problem with majority-minority districts is that they may actually have decreased the amount of influence minorities have.[20] Prior to the creation of majority-minority districts, minority members often comprised a sizeable percentage in several districts within a state, whereby minority constituents had some influence over their representatives. However, after the creation of majority-minority districts, minority constituents were packed into only a few districts. Thus, the overall influence of minority voters decreased. Let me give a simplistic example. Let's say there were three districts in a state in 1990, each with a one-third African American population. Since the size of the minority population was significant, the Congress members could not ignore African American voters and be confident of reelection. But after the creation of majority-minority districts, almost all African American voters lived in one district, and the other two districts were virtually all white (bleached districts). In this situation, there was only one representative to speak on behalf of minority concerns. As a consequence of these issues, many supporters of minority rights advocate for **influence districts** where minorities may not be a majority but either: "(a) Cast a decisive vote, or be expected to cast such a vote, for their choice among the candidates. (b) cast enough votes, or be expected to cast enough votes, for their choice among the candidates contesting the seat to constitute at least half of the margin of votes by which the candidate wins."[21] In these districts, a minority group would significantly influence which candidates win. As a consequence, candidates and officials wanting to be reelected would feel a need to listen to their interests.

Today one of the issues for minority suffrage, particularly racial and ethnic minorities, is that felons in most states cannot vote. Each state has its own laws regarding the voting rights of people who are convicted of felonies; however, all but two states restrict felons' voting rights, at least to some degree. Maine and Vermont allow felons to vote, even while in prison; fifteen states allow felons to vote after being released from incarceration; four states, Florida, Iowa, Kentucky, and Virginia, have lifetime bans; and the remaining states require convicted felons to finish parole or wait a period of time before voting.[22] The disenfranchisement of felons has a disproportional effect on African Americans and other minorities. The Sentencing Project estimates that one in thirteen African Americans cannot vote due to these laws, and in three states (Florida, Kentucky, and Virginia), one

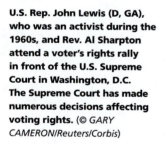

U.S. Rep. John Lewis (D, GA), who was an activist during the 1960s, and Rev. Al Sharpton attend a voter's rights rally in front of the U.S. Supreme Court in Washington, D.C. The Supreme Court has made numerous decisions affecting voting rights. (© GARY CAMERON/Reuters/Corbis)

in five African Americans is disenfranchised by these laws.[23] These laws have also been found to have indirect effects, depressing the vote of others in communities with a large number of minority felons.[24] One reason these laws disproportionately affect minorities is that there are some racial biases in laws and some police practices result in minorities being more likely to be convicted of felonies.[25] Some seemingly race neutral policies disproportionately affect racial and ethnic minorities. For example, laws increasing sentences near schools disproportionately affect racial and ethnic minorities who live in high-density locations where it is difficult to be far from a school.[26] Other causes are: resource allocations such as limited funding for public defenders, socioeconomic inequalities, and implicit racial prejudice held by many Americans.[27]

An issue of particular importance to Hispanic voting power is citizenship (see Chapters 9 and 11). In order to vote in U.S. elections, individuals have to be citizens, and about one-quarter of Hispanics in the United States are not U.S. citizens.[28] And indeed, areas with large Hispanic populations with voting rights are more likely to have Hispanic descriptive representation.[29] One of the issues with Hispanic citizenship is that many Hispanics came here illegally and are not able to become citizens. It is estimated that there are 11.7 million unauthorized immigrants, about 6 million of which came from Mexico.[30] If these individuals could become citizens and vote, it would have a dramatic effect on the Hispanic share of voters. Since Hispanics have become more Democratic in recent elections, and Republicans want to increase their share of the Hispanic vote, this issue will likely be on both parties' agendas in the next few years. Citizenship is an issue as well for Asian Americans, but they are more likely to be able to become citizens since they came here legally.

Although Puerto Ricans are U.S. citizens, their voting power is limited if they live on the island. Only states are afforded voting members of Congress and electoral votes. Thus, Puerto Ricans living in Puerto Rico, a U.S. territory, are effectively disenfranchised in national elections. As a consequence, there is a statehood movement in Puerto Rico. Although the District of Columbia has electoral votes,[31] it does not have any voting members of Congress; thus, residents of the District, who are heavily African American and LGBT,[32] have limited power to affect federal policies. Delegate Eleanor Holmes Norton, who is a nonvoting member of Congress representing the nation's capital and has introduced a bill for D.C. statehood for over twenty years, said citizens living in D.C. "are the only taxpaying Americans who are not treated as full and equal citizens. The only way for them to obtain the citizenship rights they are entitled to is through the same statehood used by other Americans."[33]

Another contemporary issue involving the enfranchisement of minorities is **voter ID laws**: laws requiring voters to show some form of identification before casting their votes. As of 2013, thirty-three states had passed some type of voter ID law.[34] These laws vary from requiring a government-issued photo ID before submitting a ballot, to requiring voters to present any type of identification. Supporters of the law indicate they want to prevent voter fraud, and opponents say these are veiled attempts to depress the voting of minorities and the poor. It is feared that the poor, elderly, and minorities will be disproportionately affected since they are less likely to have government-issued identification, such as a driver's license. Since these laws are new, research examining their effects has been limited and mixed. Recently, for example, Hood and Bullock's examination of the Georgia law found it depressed turnout of people lacking ID, but it did not depress minority voter turnout, per se.[35]

Other governmental action that affects minority voting concerns infrastructure. Since minority citizens tend to be poorer than nonminority citizens, they often vote in counties with fewer resources to hold elections. As a consequence, they tend to have to wait longer on Election Day and to cast ballots using antiquated machines that can result in unreadable or mismarked ballots. Charles Stewart found that in 2012, African Americans waited on average twenty-three minutes, compared to nineteen minutes for Hispanics and twelve for Anglos.[36] These long waits increase the costs of voting, which ultimately decreases the rationality or willingness of people to vote. There is research as well that demonstrates that administration of elections affects residual votes (votes that cannot be read).[37] This research finds that minority voters tend to have higher rates of residual voting. However, research also notes that it is unlikely that the administration of elections solely affects the high rates of residual votes by minorities.

The Electoral College may also affect the representation of minorities. The Electoral College is very complicated since each state determines the specifics of how it selects delegates. Presidents are selected by electors. Each state gets a number of electors equal to the number in its congressional delegation (number of Senators + number of House members) and determines how its electors are chosen.[38] With the exception of Nebraska and Maine, the electors are chosen through winner-take-all elections. That is, all of a state's electors are expected to vote for the candidate who won the state's election. This means if a majority of Wyoming voters vote for the Republican candidate, regardless of the margin of victory, all of its three electors will be chosen by the Republican Party. It also means that if a candidate wins in California with a bare majority, all fifty-five of its electoral votes go to that candidate, regardless of the percentage of votes the candidate received. This gives presidential candidates an incentive to focus on large states (states with lots of electoral votes) and "swing states" (states where it is unclear who will win). Winning in California with one vote gives a candidate fifty-two more votes than winning in Wyoming with one vote. In addition, winning in California with 100% of the votes gives a candidate no more electors than just barely winning the state. As a consequence, voters in the swing states and in large states have greater impact on who wins than do voters in mid-sized states where one party tends to dominate. Thus, if minorities live in large states or swing states, they will have greater impact on the outcome of presidential elections. Chapter 9 discusses the distribution of the different minority groups around the United States and concludes that the Electoral College, if anything, limits the electoral power of racial and ethnic minorities and has little effect on gender minorities.

Electoral Systems

There are many ways that elections can be conducted, and they may not be race or gender neutral. Some electoral systems result in more minorities being elected to office than others. The type of system has differing effects on women and racial and ethnic minorities. In the United States, most elections involve **single-member districts** (SMDs). In a SMD, political areas are divided into districts and each district gets one representative. SMDs are thought to be beneficial for racial and ethnic minorities since they allow for majority-minority districts.[39] However, since women and LGBT people do not tend to live in areas segregated by gender and sexual orientation, SMDs are less helpful for these groups.

SMD elections can be decided with either a plurality of votes in which whoever gets the most votes wins, even if less than 50% of the voters supported the candidate, or they can be majoritarian, requiring the winner to get a majority of the vote (50+%). These types of systems may result in run-off elections. This is an additional election between the top two vote getters. Run-off elections may be detrimental to minority voters since it may be difficult for minorities to get over 50% of the vote, even if they are the largest unified voting bloc.

Another type of electoral system involves **at-large elections.** With at-large elections, there are no districts and all citizens vote on all representatives. Prior to the 1960s, at-large systems were common, particularly for city councils. However, since it was thought that they made it difficult for racial and ethnic minorities to win elections, ward or district systems became more common. Assuming people vote based on race, if 30% of a city's residents were African American, it would be difficult for an African American to win a majority of votes. Research indicates that compared to at-large systems, SMDs result in greater representation for minorities, but only if they are highly concentrated in individual districts, such as majority-minority districts.[40] Thus, SMDs are more likely to help African Americans, American Indians, and Hispanics to win elections than to help women win. For example, McCool, Olson, and Robinson found that "In the 19 jurisdictions in our study, only six American Indians had ever been elected in the at-large system. Replacement of this system with single-member districts resulted in remarkable gains in Indian office holding. In the fifteen single-member system in our study, there are currently twenty-five native American elected officials."[41] Trounstine and Valdini also note that race and gender interact such that Hispanic and African American women candidates do not benefit from SMDs.[42]

Another type of election involves **multimember districts** (MMDs). In MMDs, multiple representatives represent a single district. Multimember districts can function like single-member districts in that there are multiple posts, and candidates choose which post to run for. For example, there could be District 1A and District 1B, both of which represent the same area, but candidates must decide if they are running for post A or B. Voters then cast one vote for a representative in District 1A and another vote in District 1B. The other type of MMD is to have one slate of candidates who run for multiple seats, and the candidates with the most votes win. If District 1 had two seats, the top two vote getters would be seated in the legislature. Women may do better in MMDs than in SMDs.[43] There are several reasons women could do better in MMDs than SMDs:[44] women are more likely to run in MMDs because they are less competitive, voters may be more likely to vote for a woman in MMDs than SMDs since they may prefer a man if they only have one representative, or political parties may be more likely to recruit women to run in MMD districts since there is less risk. Assuming voters prefer men, parties may see running a woman candidate in a winner-take-all system as a larger gamble than running a man. Research has been somewhat mixed, but generally finds that MMDs increase the representation of women.[45]

Related to MMDs is **cumulative voting.** These are MMDs where there is a slate of candidates, but voters can pack their votes. For example, if there are three positions in an election, the voters would get three votes that they can distribute as they wish. They can give three candidates one vote each or one candidate three votes, or anything in between. These elections have been used in some local races and are thought to be beneficial to minority interests since a minority group can give all their votes to one candidate, increasing that candidate's chance of winning.[46]

Proportional representation (PR) is not used in the United States but is an electoral system that tends to offer greater representation to political minorities.[47] There are many varieties of PR; a common version involves voters choosing among parties instead of individual candidates. Then the number of seats is distributed to the parties based on their vote totals. If one party receives 30% of the votes, that party would be allocated 30% of the seats. Prior to the election in these nations, parties create a rank ordered list of candidates. A party allocated five seats would select the top five people on its list to be seated in the parliament. These types of elections are widely recognized as resulting in high levels of descriptive representation for women. One reason for this is that many of these countries also have a quota system in which parties are required to put a certain percentage of women on their list of candidates. Proportional representation is not common in the United States and is unlikely to be adopted, but if it were, it would likely increase the descriptive representation of women and other minorities. Spotlight 3.2 offers a discussion of quotas.

Institutional Design

The design of political institutions can also affect the descriptive representation of minorities. One feature that could affect the representation of minorities is *term limits*. During the 1990s many U.S. states instituted limits on the number of terms legislators could serve. These limits were touted as ways to increase the diversity of legislatures, particularly as they relate to gender.[48] Since white men held most legislative positions, if they were blocked from running for reelection, then new types of people could be elected. The particulars of these laws varied from state to state. Some states limited how many terms members could serve consecutively, while others had lifetime bans. In some states the bans were based on the total number of

Spotlight 3.2

Quotas

Quotas involve reserving a certain number of elected positions for a minority group. They can involve efforts to increase the representation of either women or racial/ethnic minorities, but they are more common for women. Gender quotas are used in over seventy countries worldwide.[49] Quotas are most common in nations with proportional representation (PR) systems. In PR states, the quota requires a certain percentage of people on the party lists to be women or other minorities, depending on the law. The degree to which they work in expanding the number of women legislators depends greatly on the particular form of quota.[50]

One type of quota system is voluntary, where a party decides to have quotas. They are not binding. Another type is a legal requirement that a certain percentage of candidates on the list be women or ethnic or racial minorities, depending on the quota. These types of systems often fail to increase the diversity of legislatures because parties will place women and minorities on the bottom of the list. For example, if the quota requires 30% of the list to be women, women could fill the bottom 30%. In this situation, only parties that get more than 70% of the vote would seat any women. With another type of quota, a list placement quota, the party must place women throughout the list. Quotas with a placement requirement tend to have the greatest impact on the representation of women.[51] Some nations without PR systems have a quota where a number of seats is reserved for women or minorities. Quotas can be effective in increasing the number of women and minorities in office. Many of the nations with a large number of women in their legislatures, such as Rwanda, Sweden, South Africa, Senegal, and Nicaragua, have quotas. All of these nations have over 40% women in their legislatures.[52]

Melanie M. Hughes analyzed eighty-one countries to see how quotas affect the representation of minority women. Hughes found that 14% of these countries had both gender and minority quotas, what she called tandem quotas.[53] She found that gender quotas help majority and minority women's representation. However, minority quotas decrease the representation of majority women while they increase the representation of minority women. The real benefit for minority women, however, comes from tandem quotas. With tandem quotas, minority women's representation increases fivefold. Without quotas, the odds of a minority woman being elected compared to a majority man is one in fourteen. The ratio for majority women is one in three and it is one in two for minority men. But with tandem quotas, the majority men are only 1.5 times more likely to be elected than minority women.

years in legislative service; in other states they were based on years in one chamber. They also varied by the length of the limit from six to twelve years. Research on the mid- to long-term effects of term limits, however, suggests that minorities have not benefited from term limits.[54] Although minorities, particularly women, may have benefited initially, over time they have not had a positive effect.[55] As women reach their term limits, other women are not replacing them. To get a sense of the effects of term limits, I calculated the ratio of the percentage of a group in the population to that in the legislature.[56] For example, if 20% of a state's population is Hispanic and 10% of its legislators are Hispanic, it would have a score of .50 (10/20 = .50). These figures suggest that term limits have a modest effect on descriptive representation. In term-limited states, the ratio for African American representation was about .7, and it was about .6 in non-term-limited states. The ratios for Hispanics were about .3 and .2. For LGBT representation, the ratios were .5 and .3. However, for women there was virtually no difference. The ratio was about .5 whether or not there were term limits.

During the 1960s, many U.S. states went through a process of professionalizing their legislatures, whereby legislators were given more resources to make policy. The level of professionalism today is uneven. Legislators in some states are given full-time salaries, staff, and office budgets, and in other states, being a legislator is at best a part-time job. In some states the legislature only convenes every other year for a few months, and in others it meets year around every year. The National Conference of State Legislatures (NCSL) divides the states into three levels based on their professionalism. In states the NCSL classified as red, the most professional, legislators' average yearly salaries were $69,000, and they had 8.9 staff members. In blue states, the least professional, they average $16,000 and have 1.2 staff members.[57] Minorities are likely to be more common in less professional legislatures. Since less professional legislatures pay less and have fewer resources, there should be less competition for them, and it should be easier for disadvantaged groups to win those spots. Casellas, for example, finds that citizen, as opposed to professional, legislatures have more Hispanic representatives, all else being equal.[58] Similarly, Sanbonmatsu finds that women are more likely to be in less professional legislatures, although the effects of particular aspects of professionalism vary by party.[59]

The Fourteenth Amendment

The Fourteenth Amendment to the Constitution provides some of the strongest civil rights guarantees to minorities. Given its importance, this section will discuss the Fourteenth Amendment and its implications for minorities broadly. The first section of the amendment states:

> All persons born or naturalized in the United States and subject to the jurisdiction thereof, are citizens of the United States and of the State wherein they reside. No State shall make or enforce any law which shall abridge the privileges or immunities of citizens of the United States; nor shall any State deprive any person of life, liberty, or property, without due process of law; nor deny to any person within its jurisdiction the equal protection of the laws.

The next three sections of the amendment concern congressional apportionment of the states following the repeal of slavery, paying Civil War debts, and barring individuals who supported the Confederacy from serving in the U.S. government or state governments. The second section limits the representation of American Indians, as it indicates the number of people in a state for determining the number of House seats a state receives (apportionment) will not include "Indians not taxed." Since many treaties between the tribes prevent tribe members from paying some taxes, it has been argued they should not be able to vote to tax others. Of course, they do pay other taxes. Nevertheless, this clause has been used in the past to deny American Indians citizenship, the vote, and ability to hold office.[60]

Section 5 gives Congress the power to enforce the amendment. This section significantly expands federal power over the states in addressing issues of citizenship and civil rights. Congress is authorized to enact laws ensuring equal treatment of people. While the Fourteenth Amendment appears to apply only to actions taken by state governments, not the federal government, since it says, "No state shall make or enforce any law. . . ." the Supreme Court has ruled that the Fifth Amendment's due process clause, which prevents the federal government from denying Americans due process of law, includes or incorporates the Fourteenth Amendment. Thus, the Fourteenth Amendment limits actions on the part of the U.S. government as well as the states.

There are two clauses in the Fourteenth Amendment that are of particular interest regarding minorities and politics. The first defines U.S. citizens as people born in the United States or who have been naturalized. Prior to this, it was up to the states to determine citizenship. Citizenship as noted earlier is critical for voting rights. Its initial impact was, however, limited. It was not seen as giving citizenship to American Indians[61] even though they were born in the United States. It also did not affect naturalization policies that limited naturalization to whites.

The equal protection clause is perhaps the most important clause of the amendment. The **equal protection clause** prevents state and federal governments from denying people equal protection of the law. The courts use different standards, depending on the traits of the person involved, to determine whether the equal protection clause has been violated. For most individuals, the courts use the *rational basis standard*. With this standard, the individual claiming discrimination has to prove that he or she was discriminated against and that most people would find the discrimination unreasonable. It is more difficult to win discrimination suits with this standard than with the other standards. To date, in cases involving discrimination against LGBT Americans, the Supreme Court has reviewed claims for reasonableness. But there are signs in recent cases that the Court may use one of the more protective tests in the future.

The courts use strict scrutiny when people claim they were discriminated against based on race or ethnicity. This is because race and ethnicity are suspect classes. **Suspect classes** include minority groups based on race, religion, and national origin who have a history of being discriminated against. Under this standard, the burden of proof rests with the government, which needs to prove either that it did not discriminate against someone because of race/ethnicity or the discrimination was needed to meet a compelling governmental interest, or that it is essential for the government to meet its responsibility. Even if there is a compelling interest, the discrimination has to be the "least restrictive means" to obtain that interest. In other words, there is no other way to meet the compelling interest. For example, in the *Bakke* case (see Chapter 6), the Court ruled that some affirmative action is allowable in university enrollments since diversity in education is a compelling interest.[62] Students learn more when the student body is diverse. However, a strict quota is not narrow enough to withstand the standard. In other words, while states can try to increase diversity in education, they cannot require a certain percentage of students be of a particular group: there are other ways to increase diversity that are less likely to harm the ability of white students to attend a school. Thus, the key aspects of the **strict scrutiny** standard are that the burden of proof falls on the government, any discrimination must be based on a compelling interest, and the compelling interest cannot be met in a less restrictive way.

In cases involving sex discrimination, the courts use an intermediate standard sometimes referred to as **heightened scrutiny**. This standard is used for **quasi-suspect classes**. These classes include groups that have a history of discrimination that is less severe or more justified than the discrimination against suspect classes. The dominant suspect class is sex. Under this standard the government has to prove either that it did not discriminate or that it did so to meet an important governmental interest. An important interest is not as important as a compelling interest. If the government can prove it has an important interest with this standard, it just needs to indicate that the discrimination helps meet that interest. It does not have to be a least restrictive means to achieve the interest.

The case establishing heightened scrutiny was *Craig v. Boren* 429 U.S. 190 (1976). This case stems from a fraternity associated with Oklahoma State University that ran out of beer during a party. In Oklahoma at the time, women could buy beer at the age of eighteen, but men had to wait until twenty-one. So the fraternity brothers had to get a woman to buy the beer. Eventually they sued the state, stating the law was a violation of the equal protection clause. The state defended the law on public safety grounds: men between the ages of eighteen and twenty-one who had been drinking were more likely to cause safety problems than similar women. The court ruled the law violated the equal protection clause because the state failed to demonstrate a connection between the law and public safety.

The Fourteenth Amendment offers considerable protections to minorities against discrimination by the government, particularly minorities that fall within the suspect or quasi-suspect classes. However, there are limits to these protections. First, they only cover discrimination by governments, not private businesses. The Civil Rights Act is designed to fill that hole. Another limit is that it requires individuals who have been discriminated against to bring suit; doing so can be very costly. It is very stressful, takes time, and may involve legal expenditures.

Conclusion: Similarities, Differences, and Intersectionality in Formalistic Representation

Formalistic representation involves formal structures that give representatives the authority to act and makes them accountable to the voters. These structures can affect descriptive as well as other types of representation. This chapter can help us see the similarities and differences between the groups and how laws have affected their representation. For groups who are de facto segregated (i.e., not forced by law) but nevertheless tend to live in minority communities, majority-minority districts, made available through single-member district elections, are a significant tool for descriptive representation. However, for groups such as women and LGBT, majority-minority districts are less helpful. In fact, women—racial and ethnic minority women as well as white women—may be advantaged by multimember districts. Today, laws limiting the representation of citizens in Puerto Rico and Washington, D.C., disproportionately affect LGBT, Hispanics, and African Americans.

Voting laws also affect the ability of minorities to win elections and for minority voters to hold their representatives accountable. With the exception of LGBT, minority groups have been singled out to be disenfranchised. Women, at least white women, have been able for vote since 1920, but African Americans and to a lesser extent Hispanics were denied the franchise until the 1960s, after a series of Court cases and the passage of the Voting Rights Act. Thus, each group has its own history with relation to the vote. Today, most voting laws and systems that harm minority voting participation affect them because of their generally low levels of socioeconomic status, such as laws limiting felons' voting rights, and poor electoral infrastructures. These, too, tend to be less of an issue for women, LGBT, and Asian Americans who are less likely to be economically deprived. Thus, laws limiting voting have had and continue to have a more restrictive effect on racial and ethnic minorities than women as a category or LGBT as a category.

The Fourteenth Amendment to the Constitution has had undeniable effects, protecting racial, ethnic, and gender minorities from discrimination. The equal protection clause can be used by individuals who have been unfairly treated by the government to seek recourse. But the courts use different standards for finding discrimination unacceptable for different types of groups. For gays and lesbians, the courts use the standard affording the least amount of protection: the reasonableness test. For women, or issues of gender discrimination, the courts use a tougher standard: heightened scrutiny; and for African Americans, or issues of race, the courts use the toughest standard: strict scrutiny.

KEY TERMS

At-large elections   (p. 71)
Cumulative voting   (p. 72)
Equal protection clause   (p. 75)
Grandfather clauses   (p. 65)
Heightened scrutiny   (p. 76)
Influence districts   (p. 68)
Literacy tests   (p. 65)
Multimember districts   (p. 71)

Poll tax   (p. 64)
Proportional
   representation   (p. 72)
Quasi-suspect classes   (p. 76)
Shaw v. Reno (1993)   (p. 67)
Shelby County v. Holder
   (2013)   (p. 66)
Single-member districts   (p. 71)

Strict scrutiny   (p. 76)
Suspect classes   (p. 75)
Voter dilution   (p. 67)
Voter ID laws   (p. 69)
Voting Rights Act   (p. 65)
White primaries   (p. 65)

Chapter 4

Policy Representation and Minorities in Legislatures

On the afternoon of August 9, 2014, Michael Brown, an unarmed African American teenager, was shot several times and killed by a police officer in Ferguson, Missouri, a suburb of St. Louis. Following Mr. Brown's killing, there was a peaceful protest that turned violent, and for several nights there was rioting in the streets. The police overreacted, sending in military-equipped police, which only increased tensions. In November 2014, a grand jury decided not to indict the police officer, Darren Wilson, who shot Michael Brown. Following the decision there was another protest that turned violent.

Mr. Brown's killing was one of several killings of unarmed African American youth that have been publicized in recent years.[1] Unfortunately, there are no official statistics kept of police use of fatal force, but the FBI estimated that in 2013 there were 461.[2] There is even less information collected on the frequency of police officers killing unarmed African Americans.[3] Since some reports of the shooting indicated the Mr. Brown had his hands up when he was shot, a common symbol for concerns about the treatment of African American men by police is holding one's hands in the air.

Race played no small role in the events in Ferguson. The St. Louis area has a history of tensions between African Americans and whites dating back to the days of slavery and continues today. These issues often play out in the criminal justice system. For example, in Ferguson, a town that is two-thirds African American and one third white, only four of fifty-three police officers were African American at the time of the shooting.[4] The police department's history of treating African Americans poorly has led to a Justice Department investigation into civil rights violations. These investigations are not directly related to Mr. Brown's killing, but found a general pattern of officers who engaged in "discriminatory traffic stops, mistreated prisoners or used excessive force."[5]

Contributing to the residents' distrust was that the city of Ferguson used traffic fines and people's failure to pay them as ways to increase their revenue. Julia Ho, who works for Hands Up United, a group formed after the shooting, said "Bench warrants and traffic fines were a regressive tax on the poor and

"Hands up don't shoot" became a common protest battle cry following the killing of Michael Brown by a police officer in Ferguson, Missouri. (© *Nancy Borowick/Corbis*)

criminalization of poverty."[6] Individuals would get traffic fines, not be able to pay them, and then there would be a bench warrant for an arrest. Having a bench warrant would make it difficult for people to get jobs and housing. Then when they were stopped again by the police, they would have to pay court fees on top of their initial ticket. About 44% of the city's revenue comes from fines.[7]

The condition in Ferguson has resulted in a lack of trust between the African American community and the police. This lack of trust was not improved by the police's militancy and lack of transparency following the shooting of Michael Brown. And this lack of trust undoubtedly helped to fuel the fire of the protests following Mr. Brown's death. It has also contributed to fears and distrust of the police around the country, particularly among racial minorities, that the police are not there to protect them but may harm them. The above story indicates that the United States is not colorblind, and there are likely policies of particular importance to racial minorities. Similarly, there are several issues important to ethnic minorities, women, and LGBT. This chapter examines several key issues that are shared by many minority groups, such as criminal justice reform, economic and education equality, as well as some that are more identified with one or two groups, such as immigration, same-sex marriage, and reproductive rights. Additionally, the chapter explores conditions likely to facilitate policy or substantive representation. Policy representation occurs when policies reflect the interests of constituencies, and with minority policy representation, the key is the degree to which policymakers consider minorities' interests when they create policies. This chapter identifies and describes issues of particular importance to minorities and then explores the conditions in the states and their legislatures that affect whether governments serve minorities' interests.

Understanding what affects policy or substantive representation can be approached through different paths. Researchers can explore the degree to which the represented's interests are reflected in policy, and what affects the likelihood those policies are enacted. Or, researchers can examine the degree to which descriptive representation leads to substantive representation, that is, whether minority representatives work on issues important to minority groups. After discussing the issues important to minorities, this chapter will examine the degree to which descriptive representation advances policy representation and then examine other conditions such as public support, interest group support, and institutional traits that can affect policy representation.

The key lessons from this chapter are that two of the biggest policy concerns for minorities are economic well-being and education. Other concerns include criminal justice reform, hate crimes, immigration, voting rights, same-sex marriage, sexual assault, and immigration. The key conditions that affect minorities' levels of policy representation include descriptive representation, characteristics of the state's residents, institutional characteristics, and the use of initiatives and referenda. An additional lesson is that minority policymakers may engage in higher levels of pork barreling and constituency services than nonminorities, although these differences may be in decline.

Key Minority Policy Interests

The Economy

A set of issues that is of particular importance to minorities concerns the economy. Although most Americans are concerned about the economy, minorities are more concerned and focus that concern on employment. In a 2013 Gallup poll, 24% of whites and 29% of nonwhites identified the economy as the most important issue facing the nation; 25% of nonwhites cited unemployment as the most important issue compared to 16% of whites.[8] Women, too, were somewhat more likely to see economic hardship as a key issue (28% vs. 24% for men).[9] A 2013 Pew Research Center survey found that LGBT respondents named equal employment rights as the most important issue for their community (57%). Among LGBT respondents, lesbians were more likely to identify employment rights than gay men and bisexual respondents.

It is not surprising that economic concerns are important to minority groups since each of the minority groups suffers from discrimination in hiring and, with the exception of Asian Americans, is poorer than counterparts. African Americans, Hispanic Americans, and American Indians are significantly more likely than whites and Asian Americans to live in poverty.[10] There is some variation within nationalities of Hispanics and Asian Americans. Cubans and Salvadorans have relatively low poverty rates, 16.2% and 18.9%, respectively, with Dominicans having a higher rate of poverty (26.3%).[11] Similarly, there is some variation by nationality among Asian Americans. Filipinos (5.8%), Indians (8.2%), and Japanese (8.2%) are less likely to live in poverty, while Vietnamese (14.7%) and Koreans (15%) are more likely to live in poverty.[12] Although some Asian nationalities are more likely to live in poverty than others, each nationality is less likely to live in poverty than African Americans or Hispanics.

Additionally, women are more likely to live in poverty than men, and this is true within each racial group. According to the 2010 census, whereas 11.9% of men lived in poverty, 13.9% of women lived in poverty.[13] Among whites, 8.9% of men and 10.8% of women live in poverty. Among African Americans, the difference is 25.5% to 29.0%; among Asian Americans, the difference is 11.7% to 12.6%; and among Hispanics, the difference is 25.0% to 28.1%.

Badgett and coauthors analyzed several studies and found a consistent pattern of LGBT Americans being more likely to live in poverty than non-LGBT Americans.[14] The gap was largest for women and minority LGBT Americans. For example, they found 7.6% of lesbian couples live in poverty, compared to 5.7% for different-sex couples. One-third of lesbian couples without high school diplomas live in poverty, compared to 20.1% of gay couples. Finally, they found same-sex African American couples were twice as likely to live in poverty as different-sex African American couples.

According to a recent survey of transgender Americans, they are also more likely to live in poverty.[15] Whereas 4% of Americans have household incomes of under $10,000, 15% of transgender Americans make less than $10,000. The situation is even worse among transgender Americans of a minority race. While 14% of transgender Americans reported being unemployed, 28% of African Americans who are transgender, 24% of American Indians who are transgender, and 18% of Hispanic and multiracial individuals who are transgender reported being unemployed.[16] The unemployment rate for the general population at the time was 7%.

Being economically disadvantaged has broad implications for citizens. First, in the United States there is a strong connection between income levels and issues of representation. For example, low-income Americans are significantly less likely to vote or otherwise participate in the political process.[17] In addition, economically disadvantaged people tend to be disadvantaged in the criminal justice system. They are more likely to have to rely on public defenders or, as the story of Ferguson notes, have difficulty paying fines, which can create large legal issues. The economically disadvantaged also suffer from poor educational opportunities. Students from low-income families have dropout rates five times greater than the national average.[18]

Education

Education is another major issue for most minority groups. African Americans and Hispanics are less likely to have graduated from college than are whites and Asian Americans. However, there is not much evidence that women are less likely to have graduated from college than are men. Although Asian American women are less likely to have graduated from college than Asian American men, Asian American women are more likely to have graduated from college than any group except Asian American men. There is less information about the education levels of LGBT Americans, but according to at least one study, LGBT Americans are as likely to have a college degree as other Americans. According to a Pew Research Center survey, 32% of LGBT Americans have graduated from college, compared to only 26% of the general public.[19] Thus, African Americans and Hispanics, but not other minorities, are less likely to have a college degree.

One reason education is important to minority groups is that they have a history of being forced to go to inferior and/or segregated schools. Although the Fourteenth Amendment would appear to ensure that minority and nonminority children have equal access to schools, that has not been the case throughout U.S. history. After Reconstruction, Southern states quickly adopted Jim Crow laws that served to segregate African Americans and whites in public places, such as public transportation and schools. The Court upheld these laws in the now infamous case *Plessy v. Ferguson* (1896).[20] In the case, the Court ruled that the Fourteenth Amendment did not prevent segregation as long as there were "separate but equal" facilities.[21] Although the **separate but equal doctrine** assumed that facilities would be equal, the schools for African Americans were decidedly inferior to white schools. A 1949 Supreme Court case concerned Clarendon County, South Carolina, where white students were bused to one of two nice school buildings with a teacher-student ratio of 1:28, while the African American students had to walk to schools that were dilapidated and had a teacher student ratio of 1:48.[22] The separate but equal doctrine was overturned in the *Brown v. Board of Education of Topeka* case (1954), but schools remained largely segregated until the 1980s. Desegregation seems to have peaked in the late 1980s. According to a report by the Harvard Civil Rights Project, public schools reached the highest degree of integration in 1988, and since then schools started to become *resegregated*.[23] Part of the reason for the **resegregation** was a series of Court cases starting in the 1990s that weakened the ability of school districts to force desegregation.[24] With the resegregation there is an economic component. Where the majority of Hispanic and African American students are also economically disadvantaged, schools are segregated by income as well as race, resulting in minority students attending the lowest performing schools and having high dropout rates.[25] It is estimated that whereas only 17% Asian American and 22% of white students will fail to graduate from high school on time, the percentages are 42 for Hispanic, 43 for African American, and 46 for American Indian students. [26]

Although it is common to think of segregation in black and white terms, schools were also segregated for American Indians, Mexicans, Chinese, and Japanese. American Indian children attended a special type of segregated school—boarding schools designed to assimilate the children to the dominant culture. These were common from the late 1800s to the mid-1900s. The quality of these schools was often less of an issue than the negative psychology effects they had on children who were forced to leave their families, homes, and cultures for a foreign way of life.[27] Today, many American Indian students attend schools run by the federal government that are poorly run.[28] Some of the segregation for Mexicans, Chinese, and Japanese was due to language. Since many Chinese, Japanese, and Mexican immigrant children did not speak English at home, it was common to have separate classes or schools for these children. Education for non–native English speakers remains an issue important for Hispanics and Asian Americans with no easy solution, as learning in English is helpful for being successful, but a native language is important to maintaining cultural ties.[29]

Women, too, have had problems getting a good education. Historically, many professional and private schools and universities were male only, denying women an equal chance for an education. Today, although women and men attend college at roughly the same rate, women tend to be overrepresented in colleges of education and underrepresented in the STEM (science, technology, engineering, and math) areas.[30] That women are less likely to pursue some fields than others may partially explain why women make less money than men; however, women also make less than men within the same field upon graduation.[31]

A key problem for LGBT students is being bullied and harassed because of their gender identity and sexual orientation. A recent study of transgender Americans found that many transgender or gender nonconforming Americans who identified as such in K–12 schools, reported having been harassed (78%), physically assaulted (35%), or a victim of sexual violence (12%) at school.[32] The problems were worse for multiracial and economically poor transgender students. What further complicates the problem is that often it was a teacher or a staff member who victimized the student. Another report found that about three-quarters of LGBT students were verbally harassed because of their sexual orientation, two-thirds of LGBT students heard homophobic remarks at school, over half have felt unsafe, and 30% missed school because they felt unsafe.[33] In addition, although students were reluctant to report it, when they did schools were likely to take no action (about 60% of the time), and about half of the students heard teachers or staff make homophobic comments. One of the effects of the bullying is that a large number of LGBT students drop out of high school.[34] It is estimated that as many as one in three LGBT high school students drops out of school, triple the national average.[35]

Criminal Justice Reform

Many minority groups would benefit from criminal justice reforms, as well. Racial and ethnic minorities are more likely to be arrested than whites and to receive stiffer punishments for similar crimes. For example, the incarceration rate for African Americans is six times that of whites, for American Indians it is two times, and for Hispanics it is one and a half times the white incarceration rate.[36] The effects of a criminal record can be severe. It can make it difficult to get a job, vote, or find housing. Although one possible reason for these figures is that African Americans and Hispanics are more likely to commit crimes, such an interpretation would be misleading. For example, while it is estimated that African Americans make up about 14% of drug users in the United States, in 2006 they made up 35% of drug arrests and 53% of drug convictions.[37]

The reasons racial and ethnic minorities are more likely to be incarcerated are multiple, and include such things as low levels of income, the location of police surveillance, sentencing laws, and decisions of prosecutors.[38] For example, middle- and upper-class parents whose children exhibit antisocial behaviors can afford better treatments for their children to keep them out of trouble,[39] or poor defendants are less likely to be able to post bail, increasing their time in jail. Relatedly, if the police looked for crime in middle-class neighborhoods instead of poor neighborhoods there would be more middle-class and white people found violating the laws.[40] In addition, federal prosecutors are more likely to charge minorities than similarly situated whites with crimes that carry minimum sentences.[41]

Laws themselves have biases. Drug-free zones around schools have a larger effect in congested urban areas where minorities are more likely to live than in rural areas where whites are more likely to live since rural schools are more likely to be out in the country. Criminal justice professionals also often do not treat minorities as well as whites. As a report by the Sentencing Project finds, "From police officers' selection of whom to stop and search, judges' and administrators' bail determinations, prosecutors' charging and plea bargaining decisions, to parole board recommendations about who to release—each stage of the criminal justice system is affected by policies and discretion that often unintentionally disfavor low-income individuals and people of color."[42]

Race and ethnicity also affect the types of experiences Americans have with the criminal justice system. Whites are less likely than minorities to have had negative experiences with the police and criminal justice system. For example, police are more likely to stop minority drivers for investigatory reasons, and when they stop minorities, they are more likely to search the car than they are to stop white drivers and search their cars.[43] Compounding the problem is that whites tend to overestimate the crime rates for African American and Hispanics by about 25% to 30%.[44] That crime is raced also undermines public safety. For example, George Zimmerman overreacted to a perceived threat by an unarmed young African American man, Trayvon Martin, that resulted in Martin's death.

LGBT, too, have disproportional contact with the criminal justice system. While there are limited statistics on incarceration and arrest rates based on sexual orientation and gender identification, LGBT are believed to have higher rates.[45] For example, while 4% to 8% of youth are LGBT, it is estimated that 13% to 15% of youths in detention are LGBT.[46] In addition, once in prison, LGBT are particularly vulnerable to abuse by guards and prisoners.[47]

Women are less likely to have contact with the criminal justice system than are other minority groups. Only about 7% of the prison population are women.[48] Racial and ethnic minority women are more likely to be incarcerated than white women, but the differences are less than found among men. About half of the incarcerated women are white, 22% African American, 17% Hispanic, and 11% of another race/ethnicity.[49] Although women are less likely to be incarcerated than men, they are still affected when their fathers, sons, and mates are sent to prison. They lose income, support, and companionship.

Another issue for many minorities is protection from **hate crimes**. These are crimes that target people who belong to groups that are oppressed and less protected in society. These would include crimes such as vandalism, assault, burning crosses, or even murder against a minority group. Since hate crimes are attacks on vulnerable groups, they are seen as deserving special attention. The FBI reported 5,928 incidents of hate crimes in 2013. About 48% of these were race related, 21% sexual-orientation related, and 11% based on ethnicity or nationality, while the remaining were based on religion and on disability.[50] According to the Anti-Defamation League, all but six states have laws to protect against race-based hate crimes, thirty states protect against sexual-orientation-based hate crimes, and twenty-six against gender-identity-based hate crimes.[51]

Military Service

Another concern for some minorities is being able to serve in the military. Not only does military service provide employment opportunities, but military service has often been tied to citizenship. The citizen soldier is a common concept that indicates not only that citizens have a responsibility to serve their nation but also that having served is part of full citizenship. Additionally, although less important today, military service has at times in history been a virtual prerequisite for holding high-level offices. For example, prior to President Clinton, only twelve presidents did not have a military background,[52] and in the 1970s about three-quarters of Congress's members were veterans.[53] Even though our elected officials are less likely to be veterans today than in the past, Americans still see military service as a trait that they want in their president.[54]

Racial and ethnic minorities have been able to excel in the military in recent years, as demonstrated by the career of Colin Powell (see Chapter 7). However, women were kept out of combat positions until 2013 when the military started a process of deciding which combat positions should be opened up for women.[55] This is essential since combat experience is needed for military personnel to reach the highest ranks. Gays and lesbians were barred from the military services until 2011. During 1993, there was an effort to loosen restrictions that prevented gays and lesbians from serving with the adoption of "Don't Ask, Don't Tell" (DADT). DADT allowed gays and lesbians to serve in the military as long as they kept their sexual orientation a secret. Prior to 1993, the military asked recruits about their sexual orientation and rejected gays and lesbians. With DADT, gay and lesbian troops would be discharged if their sexual orientation was discovered, but recruits would not be asked about their sexual orientation. Transgender citizens are still barred from military service, but President Obama's administration in mid-2015 started planning to remove the ban on transgender soldiers.[56]

Individual Group Concerns

Individual minority groups also have their own sets of issue concerns. African Americans and other racial/ethnic groups are also concerned with several issues surrounding voting rights. As discussed in Chapter 3, these groups have been denied their right to vote throughout much of U.S. history, so laws affecting voting are of particular concern. Some current issues are the disenfranchisement of felons, voter ID laws, and changes to the Voting Rights Act. Hispanics are more concerned with immigration policy than the rest of America. Whereas immigration is seen as the most important issue to only about 8% of Americans, 20% of U.S. Hispanics see it as the most important issue.[57] Transgender Americans have particular issues as well, such as facing discrimination on the part of doctors and police, needing government-issued identification that reflects their genders, and unisex public bathrooms.[58] American Indians have issues concerning tribal government sovereignty and tribal relations with the federal and state governments.

LGBT Americans want legally sanctioned same-sex marriages, prevention and treatment of HIV/AIDS, and adoption rights.[59] AIDS is a disease that in the United States is often associated with gay men, since they were the first to suffer from it in large numbers. HIV (human immunodeficiency virus) refers to the condition of having been infected with the virus, and AIDS (acquired immunodeficiency syndrome) means that a person who has HIV has the disease caused by the virus. Although gay men are still the most likely to get HIV/AIDS,

African Americans and to a lesser degree Hispanics are also high-risk groups.[60] Worldwide, the disease is less concentrated among gay men. Spotlight 4.1 discusses HIV/AIDS in the world.

Spotlight 4.1

HIV/AIDS in the World

In 2013, about 1.5 million people died from AIDS worldwide, but since the epidemic started, over 39 million people have died from the disease.[61] HIV is the virus that causes AIDS. AIDS attacks blood cells, preventing the body from fighting off opportunistic illnesses. It is an often sexually transmitted disease but can be transmitted through contact with infected blood. At present there is no cure, but people can live long lives after being infected with the virus with the proper treatment. Antiretroviral drugs are the most common and can be very expensive.

Although HIV/AIDS is a worldwide problem, it is more common in some parts of the world, particularly sub-Saharan Africa. It is estimated that about 25 million people, or almost 5% of the people in this part of Africa, have the disease.[62] Sub-Saharan Africa also "accounts for almost 70% of the global total of new HIV infections."[63] The Caribbean has the next highest rate of almost 1%.[64] North America has the third highest rate (0.6%), followed by Latin America (0.4%), South and Southeast Asia (0.3%), Oceana (0.3%), North Africa and the Middle East (0.2%), Eastern Europe and Central Asia (0.2%), and Western and Central Europe (0.2%).[65] One problem with these figures is that many, perhaps half, of the people infected may not know they are infected.

As these numbers indicate, it is often the poorest parts of the world that have been hit the hardest by the disease. Since the medications are expensive,

many relief organizations and wealthy nations have offered assistance to combat the epidemic.[66] Yet even with this assistance, about two-thirds of the people infected are not receiving needed medications. This problem is even larger for children; while one-third of adults with the disease receive antiretroviral therapy (ART), only about one-fourth of children receive the medication.[67]

While much of the worldwide effort to combat the disease has focused on getting medication to people infected, prevention is another focal point. Governments and NGOs have produced numerous publications informing individuals about how to minimize the chance of becoming infected or spreading the disease. The United States has pushed an abstinence approach, while other nations have encouraged condom use and other safe-sex practices. Governments have also produced information to minimize the chance that a mother gives the disease to her newborn, and information on how to prevent transmitting the disease with needles. In addition to these approaches, there has been some advancement in the development of a vaccine. The best option now is pre-exposure prophylaxis (PrEP), which has been administered to people in high-risk groups.

Another approach to helping end the epidemic is finding a cure. Unfortunately, a cure has not been found.

There are also several issues of particular importance to women. Women are more likely to prioritize abortion policy, although they are not necessarily more pro-choice.[68] Fifty-four percent of women say abortion policy is very important, compared to 36% of men. One survey indicated women are particularly

UCSB students march between drive-by shooting crime scenes in a protest against sexual violence and hate crimes in Santa Barbara, California. (© LUCY NICHOLSON/ Reuters/Corbis)

concerned about domestic violence and sexual assault, child care, time off for family care, drug and alcohol addiction, sexual harassment, women in math, science, and technology, women in other parts of the world, and electing more women.[69] Domestic violence can involve "rape, sexual assault, robbery, and aggravated and simple assault committed by intimate partners, immediate family members, or other relatives."[70] It accounts for over 20% of all violent crime and disproportionately is against women (76%).[71]

Although the issue of sexual assault cuts across all groups of people, American Indian and immigrant women who are victims of sexual assault are often afforded less justice than other victims. Immigrant women, particularly migrant workers or those in the United States illegally, are prime targets for sexual predators, since the costs for them to report the rape may be great, even deportation. Rape of American Indian women on reservations by nontribal members often occurs in a no-man's-land where no one government may have jurisdiction over the crime, and sexual predators aware of this often go to reservations to commit sexual assaults to avoid prosecution.[72] When the federal courts can get involved, the picture is not much better; federal prosecutors only prosecute about one-third of rape cases involving American Indian women.[73] Although provisions of the 2013 reauthorization of the Violence Against Women Act were designed to help alleviate the problems, they do not fully address the issue,[74] the tribal courts' jurisdiction over nontribal members remains limited.

Does Descriptive Representation Lead to Substantive Representation?

It is often assumed that descriptive representation is important because it increases the policy representation of minorities. The exact mechanism that may cause a relationship is unknown. Miller and Stokes identified two mechanisms by which representatives can work on behalf of constituents' interests.[75] The first involves voters electing people who are similar to themselves, and as a consequence, when representatives make decisions they think are right, they are making decisions supported by voters. The other involves representatives purposely trying to make decisions that will be supported by their constituents. Constituents or groups may pressure representatives to make specific decisions. Given this ambiguity, there are several reasons why minority representatives may be likely to work on minority interests. First, as minorities, they are likely to share some of the same concerns as others of their minority status. For example, congresswomen, like most women, were socialized as girls to be primary caregivers of children, and experienced gender discrimination. Similarly, Hispanic members, like most Hispanics, are likely to have experienced discrimination, grown up in bilingual families, or lived in similar neighborhoods. And similar statements could be made of other minority members. These similarities mean that minority policymakers are likely to share the interests of others of their minority group. Minority lawmakers may bring unique insights and approaches. As an African American state legislator said, "Black women come with a different kind of attitude, it's a motherly attitude. It's a cultural thing for Black women. It's like my mama saying 'I'll eat last once everyone has found their full.' We don't come first. People just don't respect Black women."[76]

Second, minority members may also have what Jane Mansbridge called **surrogate representation**.[77] This is where representatives feel a need to work for the interests of a group of people who are not their voters, such as African American representatives feeling a need to represent African Americans regardless of where they live, Hispanic representatives representing Hispanics, and so on. Surrogate representation is strongest for representatives who share experiences with a group that is underrepresented.[78] Thus, it should be strong for minority representatives. Interviews of congresswomen find that congresswomen feel a need to work on women's issues, in part because congressmen ignored these issues. In addition, congresswomen feel as though they have a lot in common with each other because of life experiences.[79] Other minority representatives who feel a strong identity are also likely to feel a need to work on these issues, even without voter pressure. To test this, David Brockman examined whether African American politicians were more intrinsically motivated to work on African American interests, as opposed to being motivated out of electoral concerns.[80] He did so by conducting an experiment where legislators were sent letters, some from a hypothetical African American constituent from the district, and others from a hypothetical African American outside of their district.[81] He found African American legislators were more likely to respond to the nonconstituent letter from an African American than was the white legislator. Since legislators have little political incentive to respond to people outside of their district, that the African American legislator responded to a nonconstituent who was African American indicated the legislator acted out of surrogate representation, not electoral considerations. Although minorities are mostly likely to be surrogate representatives for minorities, there have been nonminorities who have been strong advocates for minority interests.

Third, policymakers may have pressure put on them from groups to work on minority issues. Numerous interest groups work to increase the number of minority officials in office, with the expectation that the officials will be advocates in office who will work on key issues. Upon retirement a lesbian state legislator said, "Because I was considered the gay politician, I had not only more work, but got more flack, more criticism, more heartache from the gay community than from the people who elected me."[82] This legislator's quote indicates the pressure she felt from the LGBT community to be its advocate. Swers, too, notes that the parties often want women members to take the lead on women's issues.[83] Having a spokeswoman on women's issues gives the party's position more credence than having a spokesman. Similar logic holds for other groups as well.

Lastly, minority representatives may be more likely to work on minority interests, not because of their minority status, but because of their party, constituents' preferences, or position in their legislature. Elected officials, regardless of race, ethnicity, or gender, want to get elected and will work to serve their voters' interests. Thus, women may work on women's issues, African Americans on African American issues, and so on, because that is what their voters want them to do. Remember, racial and ethnic minorities tend to serve majority-minority districts, and women tend to represent "women friendly" districts. Thus, it could be that, if men and whites represented districts similar to those that minorities represent, they, too, would support minority rights. Relatedly, it may be that minority policymakers support minority interests because of their political parties. The Democratic Party over the past fifty years has been the party that represents minorities.[84] As a consequence, Democrats are more likely to support minority interests, and minorities are more likely to be Democrats. Thus, when researchers compare minority legislators with white male legislators, they are largely comparing Democrats with Republicans.

A legislator's official position in office can also affect his or her work. Legislators often specialize in the issues of their committee assignment. Thus, legislators assigned to committees whose jurisdiction includes issues important to women and minorities will be more likely to serve those interests. Committees are the gatekeepers to floor debate: bills not reported out of committee are not debated. In addition, when bills are debated on the floor, it is usually committee members that take the lead. Committee leaders, too, take the lead drafting and amending bills on the topic of their committee. There is also some research indicating that women are likely to be assigned to committees such as Health, Education, Labor, and Pensions that work on traditional women's issues,[85] and likely to use committee positions to affect women's issue policies.[86] Similarly, African Americans are more likely to serve on constituent committees.[87] In addition, committee hearings with African American and Hispanic chairs are more likely to address civil rights, housing, and social issues.[88] The drawback of minority and women legislators serving on constituent committees is it may decrease the odds they serve on prestigious committees, such as Ways and Means or the Rules Committee.[89] These committees act on issues of importance to many members, so they give members the opportunity to use them to gain power in the institution.

There are also reasons minority legislators may not want to work on issues of importance to their individual minority status. If they are pigeonholed or seen as only caring about one set of issues, it may hurt their ability to work on other issues of interest to them or their constituents. This may be particularly true if the issues are not within the mainstream of their party. Also, and perhaps even most important, it could hurt their reelection chances. If they want to win reelection, they need to be seen by their constituents as someone who works for the entire district, not just a subset of the district.

Several scholars argue that if constituent preferences or the party drives minority policymakers' interest in minority concerns, then it is not really the officials' race, ethnicity, gender, and sexual orientation that affect their policy making. Instead it is their party and the district's wishes.[90] For example, Swain examined the Congress before the 1992 elections and compared the behavior of African American members to that of similar white members (specifically party and district racial makeup) and found very little difference in their behaviors.[91] As a consequence, she argued that members' race did not affect their behavior.

Although the literature on descriptive representation and policy representation is somewhat mixed, once party and district traits are controlled for, the preponderance of research suggests that minority representatives are more likely to work to advance minority interests than are nonminority representatives. The research also finds racial and ethnic minority women are the most likely to work to advance minority interests.[92] The way scholars have examined the effects of descriptive representation on policy representation is to see whether minority members are more likely to support legislation thought to be helpful to minorities. Generally, minority support is measured as voting for key pieces of legislation (roll-call votes) but has also been measured by bill sponsorship, oversight, earmarks, and speeches on the floor.[93]

An interest group's ratings can be used as an indicator of which bills are prominority. Many interest groups keep tabs on how members vote on the legislation they support or oppose and then rate members based on their support for that legislation. Another approach is for scholars to use a precise definition of minority interests to determine which bills and resolutions are pro- or anti-minority interests. Regardless of the approach, minority members are generally found to be more supportive of minority interests than nonminority members. Although in her classic noted above Swain found little difference between African American and white members, more recent work finds significant differences.[94] Canon suggests that district traits combined with members' race has a particularly strong effect.[95] African American members who represent African American districts and won election by focusing on differences between the races better represented African

American interests (as measured by Leadership Conference on Civil Rights and African American Congressional Caucus votes) than African American members who won in biracial districts and won by campaigning on commonality (issues that do not suggest race). However, both types of African American members better represented African American interests than did white members.

Compared to white members, African American and Hispanic members of Congress have also been found to be more active in congressional oversight related to minority interests.[96] Congressional oversight occurs when Congress monitors the work of the bureaucracy to make sure it is fully implementing policies. Hispanic legislators were more likely to introduce pro-Hispanic and less likely to introduce anti-Hispanic bills than were non-Hispanic members.[97] Women legislators were more likely to introduce legislation important to women, and African American state legislators were more likely to introduce legislation important to African Americans.[98] The literature on LGBT legislators paints a similar picture. LGBT legislators are significantly more likely to prioritize, introduce, and vote for pro-LGBT legislation, even after taking into consideration party and district traits.[99] Finally, research on gender differences also finds that women legislators are more likely to support compassion issues, such as education and helping the underprivileged, whether measured by bill introductions, roll-call votes, floor speeches, earmarks, or surveys of legislators.[100]

The bulk of the literature has been elitist in that it allowed either interest groups or researchers to determine minority interests, not what minorities themselves want. Little research has examined the congruence between minority voters' preferences and minority members' behavior. It tends to find that descriptive representation is less important for policy representation than the elitist approach. Tate, using the 1996 National Black Election Study (NBES) of African American voters, found that African American members of Congress were more liberal on some policies than most African Americans.[101] She also compared African American constituents' position on welfare reform with their members' vote on welfare reform, and found that on this one issue, African American voters' positions and their members' vote matched 34% of the time if their representative was an African American Democrat, 38.5% if a white Democrat, and 70% of the time if a Republican.[102] That she only looked at the issue of welfare reform certainly biased her results, and it is not likely that on most issues white Republicans are the best representatives of African Americans. For example, while 77% of African Americans favored the Affordable Care Act (Obamacare), in the 113th Congress, 100% of Republican Congress members voted for the repeal, compared to none of the African American Congress members.[103]

It may be that a critical mass is needed for descriptive representatives to contribute to policy representation. Kanter has estimated that for minorities in organizations to distinguish themselves from others, there needs to be at least 15% minorities in the group.[104] When there are few individuals of a group, they are tokens and feel a need to adopt the norms of the majority. Minority politics scholars have subsequently tested to see if minorities are more likely to work on minority issues as their numbers increase. Testing the idea that there needs to be a critical mass of a minority group in a legislature for descriptive representation to affect substantive representation has not been conclusive: some researchers have found an effect, others have not.[105]

For minority legislators to be able to affect policy, they need to be effective legislators. It is often feared that minority legislators will find it difficult to enact the legislation important to them and their constituents. Social distance theory suggests people do not want to interact with people who are different from themselves, thus minorities may find it more difficult to develop relationships with their colleagues.[106] In addition, the majority of legislators may not support the policy goals of their minority colleagues if their colleagues focus only on minority interest policies. However, most research finds that women are as effective as men in seeing the bills they introduce pass,[107] and African Americans are as effective as whites.[108] The evidence as to the effectiveness of gays and lesbians is more mixed.[109] While gay men were as effective as other legislators, lesbians had a more difficult time. Lesbians faced more discrimination, had more difficult relationships with colleagues, and were policy outliers. As a consequence they saw fewer of the bills they introduced pass.

Also, women of color may have a more difficult time in legislatures as well. African American women often feel more marginalized in legislatures and face more discrimination than African American men or white women.[110] Hawkesworth's research on the raced and gendered nature of Congress offers insight into how racial and ethnic minority women are marginalized.[111] She finds that women of color are systematically stereotyped and treated differently; they are excluded from important meetings when they should have been included, and they are silenced in ways not done to men of color or white women. Ultimately, she argues, women of color often appear to be invisible to the rest of the chamber. Brown's interviews of African American women in the Maryland state house support the idea that women of color are treated differently than other legislators.[112]

A caveat that needs to be made in reference to our understanding of whether policymakers' race, ethnicity, or gender affect policy making is that not all representatives of a minority share a political outlook. Michele Bachman and Sarah Palin have very different views about what it means to represent women than do Hillary Rodham Clinton or Nancy Pelosi. Rocha, Sanchez, and Uscinski suggest that while Hispanic representatives generally may be more liberal, other personal attributes (such as party, education, nation of birth, sex, and generation) and district traits (such as majority-minority district and region) and electoral vulnerability can also affect their roll-call voting.[113] As a consequence, they suggest that some Hispanic members are "better" representatives of Hispanics than others. Dovi offers a criterion that can be used to indicate whether or not an individual of a minority group is a good descriptive representative of that group.[114] She suggests that there need to be mutual relationships: "Mutuality requires an interactive relationship between representative and citizens. Mutual relationships require historically disadvantaged groups to recognize its descriptive representatives in a particular way as well as a descriptive representative to recognize that group in a particular way."[115] They need to recognize each other as being members of a disadvantage group and to share "a common understanding of the proper aims of a descriptive representative of the group."[116] In addition, since disadvantaged groups can be diverse, it is important that the representative has a broad understanding of who is in that group.

One way that minority legislators can advance their interests in a legislature is to create a caucus, also called a legislative service organization. These are organizations of legislators in a chamber who share an interest. Many of the minority groups we discuss have a caucus in Congress or state legislatures. The first minority caucus in Congress was the **Congressional Black Caucus** (CBC), founded in 1971. The CBC focuses on issues of importance to African Americans and is made up of African American members who choose to join. One of its better-known activities is that every year it puts out its own budget to stress the priorities important to African Americans. The CBC has a liberal reputation and tends to be dominated by Democrats. Hispanic members created the **Congressional Hispanic Caucus** in 1976. In many ways it parallels the CBC but focuses on issues of importance to Hispanics. One way it differs from the CBC is that it focuses more on foreign affairs. There is also a **Congressional Asian Pacific American Caucus**. It was founded in 1994 and focuses on issues of concern to Asian Americans and Pacific Islanders.

Women also have a caucus: **Congressional Caucus for Women's Issues.** It was founded in 1977 and tends to be more bipartisan than the other caucuses, particularly as the number of Republican women has grown. The youngest of the congressional minority caucuses is the **Congressional LGBT Equality Caucus**, founded in 2008. It is made of LGBT members and their allies. The literature on women in state legislatures tends to find that caucuses can have an important effect on the passage of women's issues.[117] However, the Congressional Caucus for Women's Issues has struggled with the increase of conservative Republican women who do not share the feminist agenda often associated with the caucus, and as Congress has become more conservative.[118] The CBC, too, has had to change as its membership has changed. In 2015, its membership took less of an outsider approach and was less urban than its original membership.[119]

What Affects Policy Representation?

Policies important to minorities can be enacted through the three different branches of government. Judges make policy when they interpret the law or the Constitution. The Constitution is known for its brevity, and with the brevity comes vague language often open to interpretation. For example, Article I section 6 of the Constitution, which gives Congress the power to regulate interstate commerce, has been used to prevent businesses engaged in interstate commerce from discriminating (e.g., Civil Rights Act). However, the Supreme Court has had to define interstate commerce to determine which businesses have to comply with the Civil Rights Act. If it is defined broadly, more businesses are involved in interstate commerce, and more businesses have to comply with the

Civil Rights Act. When judges interpret the law or the Constitution, they determine what the law means and when it is applicable. For example, when the Supreme Court used the Constitution's Fourteenth Amendment's equal protection clause to examine school desegregation in *Brown v. Board of Education of Topeka* (1954), it effectively changed policy throughout the country. After the ruling, desegregated schools was a national policy, whether or not that was the reality everywhere.

Policy can also be made in the executive branch. Perhaps this can be seen most clearly with *executive orders*. These are directives from the president to the executive branch, and in the absence of law have the same force of law. Most of the first efforts to end discrimination in the federal government came from executive orders.[120] For example, the term *affirmative action* was first used after President John Kennedy's Executive Order 10925. Executives also have veto power, which can also affect minority policies in either negative or positive ways. In the negative, Governors Arnold Schwarzenegger (R, CA) and Chris Christie (R, NJ) vetoed same-sex marriage laws that had passed their state legislatures. In the positive, in 2014 Gov. Jan Brewer (R, AZ) vetoed a bill that would have allowed businesses to not serve LGBT Americans. A key part of the executive branch is the bureaucracy. As those charged with enforcing and implementing policy do their work, they, too, can have considerable effect on the meaning of those policies. Chapter 7 examines descriptive and policy representation in the bureaucracy.

Legislatures may have the clearest role in making policy, as they pass laws. This section discusses what affects the likelihood legislators pass pro-minority legislation. Following from the previous section on descriptive representation, the proportion of minorities in a representative body can affect the likelihood that it passes pro-minority legislation. This can occur because minority legislators introduce legislation related to minority interests, helping minority interests get on the agenda. Policies to help minorities cannot be enacted until they are on the agenda. After minority interests get on the agenda, minority legislators can help steer them through the process. They can do this by persuading their colleagues to support their legislation through actions such as lobbying their colleagues, negotiating, and giving speeches on the floor. Minority legislators can affect other legislators in less overt ways as well. Contact theory suggests that as people of the majority group come in contact with minorities, they are less likely to see them as a stereotype and develop more positive views. Thus, minority members may change the views of other members of their legislatures simply by having contact with them. A lesbian state legislator from Arkansas, Rep. Kathy Webb (D), made the following observation:

> I think being there and being a gay legislator made a lot of people think about things that they have never had to think about in the past. . . . There were some people who came up and told me they were glad they met my partner and how nice she was. I think something like that helps people overcome, maybe a preconceived notion that they had.[121]

Even in the absence of persuasion, minority legislators may be in positions, such as party leadership or committee chairs, to use the rules to their advantage. Committee chairs and leaders can refuse to hold debate on legislation to ensure its failure or use procedural tools to help advance legislation. For example, although the Civil Rights Act eventually passed in 1964, it had to overcome being held up in committee by committee chairs in opposition to the bill, and sixty days of filibusters.[122] An example from a state legislature occurred in 1997, when Rep. Chuck Carpenter (R), a gay state legislator from Oregon, threatened to use a discharge procedure to bring an anti-discrimination bill to floor, which got a committee hearing for the bill.[123] A discharge procedure is a legislative tool that will bring a bill to the floor for debate without committee approval.

Legislatures with more minority members also pass legislation more favorable for minority interests. For example, Haider-Markel finds that as the number of LGBT state legislators increases, so, too, does the number of pro-LGBT pieces of legislation introduced and passed. This is true even after controlling for the ideology of the legislature and state.[124] However, he also finds **backlash effects**: as the number of LGBT legislators increases, so does the frequency that anti-LGBT legislation is introduced and passed. However, even after taking the backlash into consideration, he finds that increases in the number of LGBT legislators result in a net gain for pro-LGBT legislation. Other research, too, has found that in locations with more LGBT officeholders, policy tends to be more favorable to LGBT interests.[125]

Research on women's issues also finds that as the number of women in office increases, so does the likelihood more women's interest legislation passes. For example, Cowell-Meyers and Langbein's examination of state policy concerning women's interests in thirty-four areas from 1990 to 2000 finds that descriptive representation has a positive effect on women's policies.[126] A recent study by Bouche and Wittmer also finds that legislatures with more women are more likely to pass anti-human-trafficking legislation.[127] Bouche and Wittmer argue that part of the reason the presence of women legislators is important is because women legislators form a network that diffuses policy information. Other research also finds that the proportion of women in state legislatures affects abortion policy and child support programs.[128]

The effects of descriptive representation are not limited to women's and LGBT interests. Minto and Sinclair-Chapman argue that the presence of a larger number of minorities in the House of Representatives compared to the Senate helps explain why the House has spent more energy on civil rights and social welfare between 1951 and 2004, despite the decline of public interest in the issues.[129] Owens finds that state legislatures with more African American members spend more on health care and welfare, which are services important to African Americans.[130] However, as noted in Chapter 2, the research on majority-minority districts suggests that "too much" focus on descriptive representation may be harmful to substantive representation.[131]

The party in control of a government also affects the likelihood minority legislation passes. The Democratic Party in recent years has been more supportive of government involvement in advancing minority interests and rights than the

Republican Party. As a consequence, it makes sense that the size of the Democratic delegation would affect policy. Democratic members may support minority rights because that is their preference, their constituents' preference, or because the party leadership encourages them to support it. Similarly, liberals tend to be more supportive of minority rights, and the ideology of legislators also affects minority policies. Hero and Tolbert find that Hispanics are substantively represented because Democrats offer high levels of support for Hispanic issues.[132] Several studies also find the party in control of the government has significant effects on abortion policy, such that Republican governments enact more pro-life policy and Democrats more pro-choice.[133] Tolbert and Steuernagel also found Democratically controlled state legislatures were related to "women friendly" health care policies.[134] Although not the focus of their work, many studies find that the party or ideology of the legislative membership affects minority policy.[135]

In a democracy, it is expected that public preferences or interests will affect public policy. Although there are many debates about the relationship of preferences (what people say they want) to interests (what is really good for the people), here the focus is on preferences or wishes. Our electoral system is designed to give representatives incentives to work on constituents' preferences. Elected officials who do not represent their constituents' wishes are not likely to get reelected. Thus, it is likely public policy will reflect public attitudes toward minority rights. And indeed research suggests that policy tends to be responsive to constituent attitudes (see Chapter 8). For example, several studies on abortion policy, welfare, and immigration policy suggest public attitudes have a significant effect on these policies.[136]

Lax and Phillips conducted one of the more interesting explorations of public opinion and minority policies.[137] Although they find that policy is responsive to public opinion (e.g., places where people are more pro-choice, policy is more pro-choice), they also find what they call the **democratic deficit.** That is, there is not congruence between citizens' policy preferences and policy. For example, the majority of citizens in many states want hate crime protection for LGBT people, but a significant minority of states do not have such laws. What seems to be a significant contributor to the democratic deficit is the power of interest groups. They write: "Having a powerful interest group on the same (opposite) side as the opinion majority increases (decreases) the chance of congruence by up to 18%. A liberal (conservative) interest group increases (decreases) the likelihood of having the liberal policy, all else equal, by up to 14%."[138] They also point out that this means public opinion would have to increase nine points to make up for one powerful interest group. Also affecting the deficit is that legislators appear to be overly responsive to the dominant ideology and party. For example, if constituents are conservative, lawmakers will pass conservative laws, even if constituents are moderate on a specific issue.

As noted above, another factor that can affect minority rights is interest or advocacy groups. Pluralist theory suggests that people get representation through organized groups that can speak on behalf of their interests. Even if an individual does not vote or otherwise participate, if there is an interest group advocating for interests possessed by that individual, her interests are heard and considered by policymakers. Groups, too, have numerous ways that they can affect policy: they can lobby, work on elections, or mobilize their members. Although scholarly research suggests the ability of interest groups to influence individual policymakers may be limited, research tends to find that minority policies are in fact more favorable when there are strong minority groups and weak anti-minority groups.[139] For example, Meier and McFarlane find two of the main predictors of a state's funding for abortion were the strength of NARAL Pro-Choice America and anti-abortion religious forces.[140] The effects of interest groups on minority interests, however, are likely contextual. Haider-Markel and Meier find, consistent with the expectations of Schattschneider, the effects of interest groups on LGBT policy are affected by the scope of the conflict.[141] When issues are salient to large numbers of people, then interest groups have less influence than when the population is less aware of the issue.

The effects of large minority populations on a state's minority policies are complex. On one hand, resource mobilization theory suggests that large populations are key to affecting change.[142] If a group has a large population and this population has significant resources and identity, it is better able to advocate for itself. Certainly this makes sense. The larger their population size the larger is their vote share, and the larger their vote share, the more politicians need to listen. This is particularly true if there is general agreement on policy demands within the group. Additionally, the larger the size of a group, the better able it is to create effective organizations. And indeed some research finds the larger a group's size and resources, the better its interests are represented.[143] Sheer size is not likely to affect the representation of women since the percentage of women does not vary significantly from state to state.

On the other hand, large minority populations can cause a backlash. When a minority group grows, it can be seen as a threat to the entrenched majority group. V. O. Key coined the term **racial threat** to refer to this phenomenon.[144] With racial threat, the majority will oppose policies seen as beneficial to the minority group, and elected officials will vote to support the majority when the group is seen as a threat to the majority's way of life. Monogan, for example, found that states with the largest growth in immigrant populations enacted more policies that were detrimental to immigrants.[145] Matsubayashi and Rocha, too, found evidence that where minority populations (African American and Hispanic) were large, there was less spending on welfare.[146] However, they also found that this was less so where the economic status of African Americans was similar to that of whites. It is likely that under some conditions large minority populations will result in positive policies and in other conditions, such as perceived racial threat, it will result in negative policies.

Federalism may also affect minority rights. That is, that states as well as the federal government enact policies that affect minorities has implications for minority policies. Minority activists as well as academics debate whether the national or state governments are more likely to enact policies favorable to minorities. During the suffrage movement, the suffragettes used a state strategy for decades, believing the states were more likely to grant women the right to vote than Congress was to propose a constitutional amendment that could give women the right to vote. And while the strategy had some successes in that women living in some states were able to vote prior to the Nineteenth Amendment, ultimately the national strategy proved more successful. It is unlikely that the national strategy would have worked decades earlier, and the state by state approach resulted in at least some states allowing women to vote earlier. The civil rights movement saw its greatest successes, too, after the federal government became more active protecting African Americans' rights and liberties. It is unlikely that without federal intervention Jim Crow Laws would have ended when they did. Conversely, scholars examining the LGBT movement have argued that a state strategy is likely to be more fruitful today.[147] Several states and their legislators are supportive of LGBT rights, and the LGBT movement can, and has, seen some real successes in these states. However, the federal government is more conservative and defined by gridlock.

Relatedly, location may also affect minority interests. Southern states tend to offer few rights and protections for minorities, while Northeastern and Western states along the coast offer more. There is also a tendency for Great Lake states to offer more protections and rights than other Midwestern and Southern states. One reason for the regional variation in minority policy is what scholars refer to as **policy diffusion**.[148] *Policy diffusion* is a term that describes how policies spread from one state to another. Although there are several ways policies can spread, it is common for them to spread to neighboring states. Because neighboring states often share economic interests or communicate frequently, when one state adopts a policy and neighboring states see positive effects from the policy, they may learn from their neighbors and adopt the policy as well. Thus, one reason the first states to recognize same-sex marriage are concentrated in the northeast may be because Vermont was the first state to formally recognize same-sex relationships. It did so when it passed a law granting civil unions to same-sex couples in 2000. **Civil unions** are similar to marriage in granting certain rights. Once a state recognized same-sex relationships, then neighboring states saw it was working and followed suit. Another way location can affect policy is through political culture (political culture was discussed in Chapter 2). Traditional political cultures often have policies less favorable to minorities and are in the South.

In addition to examining specific factors that can affect minority politics, there have also been multifactor theories put forward to explain policy. For example, Mucciaroni suggests that a combination of institutional factors, public opinion, and perceived threat explain why some pro-LGBT policies have become law and others have not.[149] He suggests that when movement supporters, particularly stakeholders such as social workers or police, have greater resources, policy change is more likely than if opponents have greater resources. But also when the demands are not seen as a threat, favorable policy is more likely to occur. Finally, these all interact such that policy changes are the most likely when threat is low and supporters have greater resources. Several of these theories are designed to explain social movements and will be discussed more in Chapter 12.

Initiative and Referenda Effects on Minority Interests

A significant issue for any democracy is how to protect minorities in a majoritarian system. How can a minority group ever get its interests met if it takes a majority for a policy to be enacted? A solution taken by the founders of the United States is to not have direct democracy but to have a republic. In a republic, the people select representatives who have to deliberate and compromise in institutions that have processes that can give nonmajority members the opportunity to block legislation. At the state level, policy can change through direct democratic means with *initiatives and referenda*. Initiatives involve interested individuals outside of the government creating a petition to change a law. If enough people sign the petition, the proposed policy change will appear on a ballot, and the people can vote on whether to change the policy. With referenda, legislators want to change the law but for some reason want or need the people's approval. For example, many state constitutions require referenda to change the state's constitution. Although all states allow for referenda, only about half allow for initiatives.[150]

The existence of these processes allows researchers to test the effect of direct democracy on minority policy. The common wisdom is that minorities are harmed by these direct democratic practices. And certainly there have been numerous initiatives in the past ten years that have attacked LGBT rights, immigrants, or affirmative action. In the early twenty-first century, citizens of most states voted to ban same-sex marriage, citizens in seven states voted to limit the use of non-English languages, and citizens in four states voted to ban affirmative action.[151] However, minority rights have also been advanced through the initiative and referenda processes. In 2012, citizens in Maine, Maryland, and Washington voted to allow same-sex marriages. Additionally, women got the right to vote in Colorado (1893) and Idaho (1896) through popular vote, although similar referenda failed in California (1896) and Massachusetts (1915).

Scholarly research has produced mixed findings as to the effects of initiatives and referenda on minority rights. Some research finds evidence that antimajority ballot items are more likely to pass,[152] while other research finds that they are less likely to pass than other ballot items.[153] Lewis suggests there is a better approach to examining the effects of ballot items on minority rights: examining whether anti-minority policies are more likely to be enacted, regardless of process, in states with more direct democratic processes than in states with less direct democracy.[154] After all, ballot items can affect legislative behavior, since legislators may pass legislation to avoid an initiative from going forward. Thus, to see the effects of ballot items, scholars need to look at the larger picture. What Lewis finds is that between 1995 and 2004, states with more direct democracy passed anti-minority legislation at much higher rates (about three times greater) than other states. This clearly supports the view that direct democracy is harmful for minorities.

Demonstration

This section demonstrates the importance of several of the factors noted above that affect minority policy by looking at variation in state welfare benefits, hate crime legislation, and immigration policy. Since minorities are more likely to live in poverty, the generosity of welfare benefits is used as an indicator of minority representation. Since states vary in their wealth and cost of living, instead of just looking at welfare benefits in dollar figures, the ratio of welfare benefits to median household income is used.[155] The degree to which states offer hate crime protections is based on a four point index, where a one indicates that there are no hate crime protections and a four means that there is protection based on race, ethnicity, sexual orientation, and gender identity. The immigration scale comes from James E. Monogan and is based on laws passed in state legislatures between 2005 and 2011.[156] It ranges from −1 to +1 and takes into consideration whether a law was welcoming or hostile to immigrants as well as the scope of the law.

Figures 4.1 and 4.2 indicate the effects of direct democracy and political culture. Figure 4.1 depicts the differences in the three policy areas by whether or not a state has initiatives. It demonstrates that there is a modest tendency for states with initiatives to have less favorable welfare and hate crime policies and larger negative effects on immigration. Remembering that immigration tone's range is from −1 to +1, note that states with less direct democracy averaged .34 and those with direct democracy averaged −.15. Figure 4.2 compares states with traditional political cultures with other states. This figure demonstrates that states with traditional political cultures have less favorable minority policies. The largest effect seemed to be in the area of immigration. States with traditional political cultures averaged −.49 on the immigration tone index and nontraditional states .38.

Table 4.1 looks at how descriptive representation affects these policies. To make the analysis simple, the level of descriptive representation for each group was divided into three categories: high, medium, and low levels. Based on research on the effects of descriptive representation, we would expect that states with more minority members in a legislature would have more favorable minority policy. Generally, this is the pattern that was found, but fits least well for African American legislators. States with the highest percentage of African American legislators are not the states with the most generous welfare and hate crime policies, or most favorable immigration tone. That states with large African American populations are also southern states with conservative traditional political cultures contributes to this finding, but does not fully explain it. However, states with more women, Hispanic, and LGBT legislators had more favorable hate crime policies and immigration tone. For example, states with high levels of Hispanic legislators averaged .68 on immigration tone compared to −.58 for states with few Hispanic legislators. With women legislators, the averages ranged from .42 to −.54, and for LGBT legislators, the rates ranged from .61 to −.37. The pattern is less straightforward with regard to welfare benefits, but the states with the fewest minority legislators had the least favorable polices for minorities.

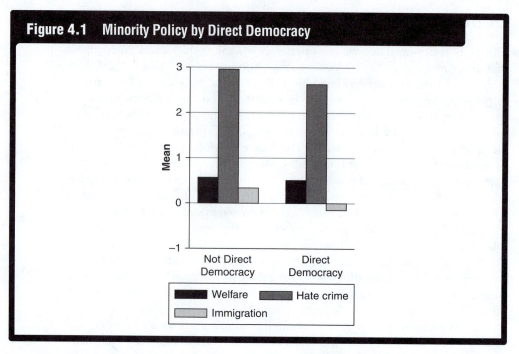

Figure 4.1 Minority Policy by Direct Democracy

Sources: Data from James E. Monogan, "The Politics of Immigrant Policy in the 50 U.S. States, 2005-2011," *Journal of Public Policy* 33, no. 1 (2013); Michael D. Tanner and Charles Hughes, "The Work versus Welfare Trade Off: 2013," August 19, 2013, http://www.cato.org/publications/white-paper/work-versus-welfare-trade; and http://www.adl.org/assets/pdf/combating-hate/state_hate_crime_laws.pdf; and http://www.ncsl.org/research/elections-and-campaigns/chart-of-the-initiative-states.aspx

Note: The difference is statistically significant at the .10 level for immigration tone.

Table 4.2 examines the effect of public opinion, party, and size of the minority population on policy. Public opinion is the percentage liberal, party is strength of the Democratic Party, and size of the minority population is the percentage of Hispanics, Asian Americans, American Indians, and African Americans, combined, in the population.[157] Each of these measures was categorized as high, medium, and low. Table 4.2 demonstrates that the liberal, Democratic, and diverse (large minority populations) states had the most hate crime protections and the most favorable immigration policies. For example, states with high levels of minority populations averaged 3.06 on the hate crimes scale, and those with low levels averaged 2.61. For the strength of the Democratic Party, the scale ranged between 3.71 and 2.25. The effects of ideology may be the strongest. The most liberal states averaged 3.91 and the least liberal states 0.94. The results were more mixed with regard to welfare benefits. The expected pattern existed for public opinion and minority population size in that the liberal states and those with large minority populations had more generous welfare benefits

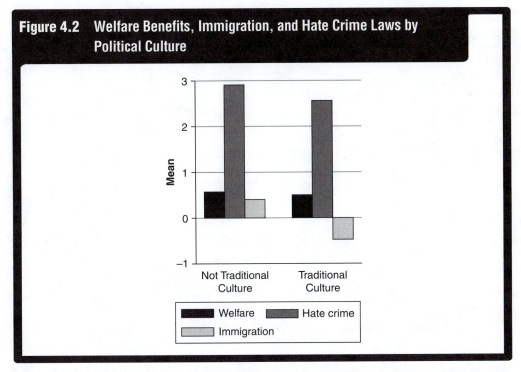

Figure 4.2 Welfare Benefits, Immigration, and Hate Crime Laws by Political Culture

Sources: Data from James E. Monogan, "The Politics of Immigrant Policy in the 50 U.S. States, 2005-2011," *Journal of Public Policy* 33, no. 1 (2013); Michael D. Tanner and Charles Hughes, "The Work versus Welfare Trade Off: 2013," August 19, 2013, http://www.cato.org/publications/white-paper/work-versus-welfare-trade; http://www.adl.org/assets/pdf/combating-hate/state_hate_crime_laws.pdf; and Daniel J. Elazar, *American Federalism: A View from the States* (New York: Thomas Y. Crowell, 1972).

Notes: 1 = traditional political culture; 0 = not traditional. The difference is statistically significant at the .05 level for immigration.

than conservative states and states with small minority populations. With party, the Democratic states had the most generous benefits, but the least Democratic did not have the least generous benefits.

A limitation of this demonstration is that it did not take into consideration that relationships could be spurious. That is, that a third condition created the appearance of relationship when none existed. However, the demonstration supports the conclusions of more sophisticated research that takes this possibility into consideration. Thus, these analyses demonstrated that descriptive representation and population characteristics (ideology, party supportive, and diversity) have greater effects than institutional traits on minority policy. In addition, direct democracy can affect policy, particularly by depressing immigration tone.

TABLE 4.1 The Effects of Descriptive Representation on Policy Representation

	Welfare Policy	Hate Crime	Immigration Tone
African American legislators high	.54	2.41	−.01
African American legislators medium	.53	3.22	.39
African American legislators low	.55	2.73	−.11
Latino legislators high	.54	3.44	.68
Latino legislators medium	.56	2.82	.26
Latino legislators low	.51	2.17	−.58
Women legislators high	.56	3.52	,42
Women legislators medium	.55	2.82	.40
Women legislators low	.51	2.00	−.54
LGBT legislators high	.55	3.5	.61
LGBT legislators medium	.58	2.86	.22
LGBT legislators low	.50	2.20	−.37

Sources: Data from NCSL.org; James E. Monogan, "The Politics of Immigrant Policy in the 50 U.S. States, 2005-2011," *Journal of Public Policy* 33, no. 1 (2013); Michael D. Tanner and Charles Hughes, "The Work versus Welfare Trade Off: 2013," August 19, 2013, http://www.cato.org/publications/white-paper/work-versus-welfare-trade; and http://www.adl.org/assets/pdf/combating-hate/state_hate_crime_laws.pdf.

Note: The levels of descriptive representation of Hispanic, women, and LGBT were statistically significant at the .05 level for immigration and hate crimes.

Table 4.2 Minority Population, Public Opinion, Party, and Policy Representation

	Welfare Policy	Hate Crime	Immigration Tone
Minority high	.57	3.06	.28
Minority medium	.53	2.73	.17
Minority low	.52	2.61	−.12
Democrat high	.61	3.71	.76
Democrat medium	.49	2.41	−.00
Democrat low	.51	2.25	−.47
Liberal high	.58	3.71	.76
Liberal medium	.53	2.71	.10
Liberal low	.51	1.94	−.58

Sources: Data from Monogan; Tanner and Hughes; http://www.adl.org/assets/pdf/combating-hate/state_hate_crime_laws.pdf; James W. Ceaser and Robert P. Saldin, "A New Measure of Party Strength," *Political Research Quarterly* 58, no. 2 (2005): 245–256. The percentage of liberals from William D. Berry, Evan J. Ringquist, Richard C. Fording, and Russell L. Hanson, "Measuring Citizen and Government Ideology in the American States 1960–1993," *American Journal of Political Science* 42, no. 1 (1998): 327–348. 2012 updated data release and figures on population percentages from Elizabeth M. Hoeffel, and Sonya Rastogi, Myong Ouk Kim, and Hasan Shahid, "The Asian Population: 2010," 2010 Census Briefs, March 2012; Sonya Rastogi, Tallese D. Johnson, Elizabeth M. Hoeffel, and Malcolm P. Drewery Jr., "The Black Population: 2010," 2010 Census Briefs, September 2011; and Sharon R. Ennis, Merarys Rios-Vargas, and Nora G. Albert, "Hispanic Population: 2010," 2010 Census Briefs, May 2011, all available from http://www.census.gov.

Note: The differences are statistically significant at the .05 levels for liberal and hate crimes and immigration tone; Democrat for all three policies.

Casework/Constituency Services and Pork Barreling by Minority Legislators

While making policy decisions is perhaps the most common way to work on behalf of a group, two other ways to represent constituents are to engage in casework/constituency services and pork barreling. **Casework/constituency** services involve legislators working as ombudsmen for their constituents: helping them with issues they may have with the government. For example, if a constituent does not receive his social security check, he might ask his member of Congress, or rather his member's staff, for some assistance in tracking it down. *Pork barreling* or earmarking involves legislators getting the government to spend money in their districts, usually on special projects, such as building new buildings or improving roads. Although these types of activities have been very common among representatives in the United States, they are less common today. Nevertheless, they can be very important for districts represented by racial and ethnic minorities. Since racial and ethnic minorities tend to represent poorer districts, their constituents are often in great need of governmental moneys or have great use of the bureaucracy. In fact, according to Tate, African Americans see the most important role for members of Congress as pork barreling, followed by constituency services; working on bills was third.[158] Early research from the 1980s also found that African American policymakers spent more time on constituency service.[159] However, more recent research does not find African American state legislators spending more time on casework or pork barreling than white legislators.[160] Early research, too, found that women policymakers were more likely to engage in constituent services since constituents expected this of women policymakers, and that women tended to prioritize these activities.[161] However, more recent work has tended to find smaller gender differences in the amount of time policymakers spend on constituency services, although women policymakers may still receive more contact from their constituents.[162] Congresswomen also still outperform their male colleagues in bringing money back to the district by about 9%.[163]

Conclusion: Similarities and Differences in Policy Representation

There are many similarities in the policy interests of minorities. Most minorities suffer from income inequality, poor educational opportunities, and injustices in the criminal justice system. These three policy areas are highly intertwined. People lacking economic resources often attend poor schools and are more likely to be arrested and less able to defend themselves. In addition, people who go to poor schools have a hard time earning money and are more likely to have trouble with the law. There is the school-to-prison pipeline where students who have problems at school are suspended, expelled, or dealt with in the criminal justice system instead of in the schools. Poor and minority students are more likely to suffer from this pipeline than others.[164] In addition, individuals with criminal records have a difficult time finding employment.

One difference in the policy issues is that white women are less likely to have contact with the criminal justice system. Other differences include: Asian Americans and Hispanics have greater interest in immigration and citizenship, gays and lesbians are more interested in marriage inequality, transgender Americans have a particular interest in health care issues, and women are more interested in domestic violence and reproductive choice.

Not only are there great similarities in the issues of interest to minorities, but also what affects their policy representation tends to be similar. First, having "one of your own" in office is helpful. Minority representatives are more likely to work for the interests of people who share their minority status. They can speak on behalf of these groups in committees, on the floor of a legislature, through legislative sponsorships, and roll-call votes. However, although minority members used to be more engaged in casework/constituency services and pork barreling, that is less so today. Similarly, the more of a minority group there is in office, the more likely that group is to have its interests reflected in policy. Other things that can affect the policy representation of minorities are the strength of interest groups supporting or opposing their cause, public opinion, party control of the government, the size of the minority population, and location (policy diffusion and political culture). Since groups, public opinion, and minority populations affect policy representation, these will all be examined in later chapters. But the next chapter examines the symbolic representation of minorities.

KEY TERMS

Backlash effects   (p. 96)

Casework/constituency   (p. 105)

Civil unions   (p. 99)

Congressional Asian Pacific American Caucus   (p. 94)

Congressional Black Caucus   (p. 94)

Congressional Caucus for Women's Issues   (p. 94)

Congressional Hispanic Caucus   (p. 94)

Congressional LGBT Equality Caucus   (p. 94)

Democratic deficit   (p. 97)

Hate crimes   (p. 85)

Plessy v. Ferguson (1896)   (p. 82)

Policy diffusion   (p. 99)

Racial threat   (p. 98)

Resegregation   (p. 83)

Separate but equal doctrine   (p. 82)

Surrogate representation   (p. 89)

Chapter 5

Minorities and Symbolic Representation

The election of Barack Obama to the presidency had great meaning to many Americans, particularly African Americans. Obama was inaugurated on the day that would have been Martin Luther King Jr.'s eightieth birthday, and to many it symbolized the promised land King spoke of in his "I Have a Dream" speech.[1] On Election Day, an eighty-year-old from Georgia said, "We marched, we sang and now it's happening."[2] Another Obama supporter said, "This is the moment black people have been waiting for, from a time when we thought none of us could ever be president. It's liberating. . . . It's not just for black people, the country can be itself."[3] To many, it symbolized hope for the future. One man attending Obama's inauguration said: "I've been a black man in America all my life, and this fills me with hope. It makes me think about my sons and their possibilities."[4] A mother said, "I used to tell my children that they can be anything and do anything that they wanted to do in their lives. . . . And with Barack Obama being the first African American president, it just means that my words did not go in vain. For my children and my grandchildren and my great grandchildren anything is possible."[5] To many African Americans, it symbolized that their vote was finally going to mean something. One first-time fifty-five-year-old voter said, "This is huge. . . . This is bigger than life itself. When I was coming up, I always thought they put in who they wanted to put in. I didn't think my vote mattered. But I don't think that anymore."[6] To some, it symbolized an improved government that will represent all of America. A woman attending the inauguration said, "Our country's going to be a better place. It's finally going to be government by the people."[7] The election of Obama demonstrates how individuals and their actions can be symbols and how those symbols can affect how people feel about the United States.

The inauguration of Barack Obama as president of the United States had great symbolic meaning to many Americans. (© *Chuck Kennedy/Pool/Corbis*)

Symbolic representation has been discussed in two different contexts. One context concerns symbols. What are the symbols that represent the government? The other concerns the degree to which constituents have positive feelings toward the government and the people who control it. This is the approach taken in this chapter. Schwindt-Bayer and Mishler describe symbolic representation thusly:

> symbolic representation refers to the extent that representatives "stand for" the represented with an emphasis on symbols or symbolization. Pitkin provides the example of a flag as a symbol representing a nation. What matters is not the symbol itself, but "the symbol's power to evoke feelings or attitudes" (Pitkin 1967, 97). Symbolic representation is concerned not with who the representatives are or what they do, but how they are perceived and evaluated by those they represent.[8]

Schwindt-Bayer and Mishler see symbolic representation as the product of the other types of representation. If individuals feel the formal rules are fair, they have high levels of descriptive and policy representation, then symbols will evoke positive feelings. In this way symbolic representation can be seen as specific support, or based on current policies. Specific support is in contrast to diffuse support. Diffuse support is a general belief that the system of government is good; individuals' levels of diffuse support are believed to come from their socialization. Having higher levels of symbolic representation may also increase peoples' willingness to contribute to the government and engage in political actions, such as voting.[9] If people's level of symbolic representation falls too low, it is often feared that it could harm the political system, but Americans' views toward the government are low, and the system is not in immediate danger of collapse.

This chapter explores minorities' feeling and attitudes toward their representatives and the government, such as their feelings when they see the flag, whether they love the country, presidential approval, levels of trust, and efficacy. Some key lessons from this chapter are that up until Barack Obama became president, African Americans and women tended to have lower levels of symbolic representation than nonminorities, but that Hispanics and Asian Americans generally have higher levels of symbolic representations because first-generation Americans tend to have higher evaluations of the government. Another key lesson is that descriptive representation affects symbolic representation. While **dyadic descriptive representation,** the congruence of constituents' minority status with that of their representatives' minority status, affects minorities' views of their individual representative; **collective descriptive representation,** the view that the government is diverse, affects minorities' views toward the government more broadly. Other things affecting symbolic representation are party, economic status, and having been discriminated against. Unfortunately, data to comparably evaluate the symbolic representation of American Indians are lacking. But given their treatment by the United States, it would not be expected to be very high.

Measuring Minorities' Attitudes

Below is a brief description of some issues concerning how to measure minority groups' attitudes. Students who are familiar with common methods of public opinion polling are familiar with random or representative samples and their value for accurately estimating public opinion. See Spotlight 5.1 for a discussion of sampling. With random sampling, everyone has an equal chance of being selected, which helps ensure that the people surveyed accurately reflect Americans. If some types of people are over-selected, then the views of these types of people will count more than they should based on population size, and the results would be biased in their direction. So if a survey over-surveyed Anglos, the survey would lead researchers to think America is more Republican than it is since Anglos are more likely to be Republicans than racial and ethnic minorities.

Most national surveys survey about 1,200 respondents. Surveys of 1,200 respondents can produce fairly accurate results: that is, they have a margin of error of about 3% or 4%.[10] However, a survey of 1,200 based on a random sample would not interview very many minorities. It would only include about 155 African Americans (African Americans make up about 13% of Americans, and 13% of 1,200 is 155), 200 Hispanics (Hispanics make up about 17% of Americans), seventy Asian Americans, and fewer than fifteen American Indians. It is risky to make generalizations based on such small numbers of respondents. One approach to deal with this problem is to have very large sample sizes. For example, during election years, Gallup has conducted tracking polls that ask the same series of questions daily of just a couple hundred respondents.[11] This enables Gallup to look at changes in voters' preferences. In 2012, this resulted in over 100,000 respondents. With such a large sample, the Gallup survey could be used to make generalizations about groups of Americans that have small populations. For example, even though LGBT respondents only make up about 3.5% of their sample, the tracking poll resulted in about 3,500 LGBT respondents. The drawback of this particular survey, however, is that the survey is limited in the number and types of questions asked. Another drawback is that it is very expensive to survey such a large number of people, and as a consequence, it is not very practical. A similar approach used by some researchers is to pool together the results of several surveys that ask identical questions.[12] The problem here is that it makes an assumption that the survey experience was identical across several different surveys.

Another approach is to over-sample minorities, or in some cases, survey only the minority group of interest. The limitation of this approach is finding a sample frame or list of minorities to draw a sample from. One way researchers have approached this problem is to sample heavily in areas where minorities live. For example, the 1990s American National Election Study (ANES) over-sampled African Americans in its Black American National Elections Study (BNES). Here, random digit dialing was done within clusters. Random digit dialing is a common sampling procedure where a sample is drawn from valid phone numbers instead

Spotlight 5.1

Brief Discussion of Sampling and Statistical Inference

It is cost-prohibitive to survey all 300 million Americans to measure their attitudes and beliefs, so researchers survey a sample, or small group. Not just any sample would do a very good job estimating everyone's views, so researchers are careful to draw samples that they think would be representative of America: that is, a sample that descriptively represents the American people. Usually, to do this they find a list that approximates a list of Americans. With telephone surveys, one of the most common survey modes, they will get a list of valid phone numbers. This assumes that everyone has a phone, they have the same number of phones, and are likely to answer it. Since there are some problems with these assumptions, credible polling firms will make some adjustments, such as selecting individuals within homes, or taking into account cell phones. Once they have all the phone numbers, they will randomly select a certain number of phone numbers to call. There are several ways to randomly draw samples, from a systematic sample where every nth number on the list is called, to using a computer to randomly select numbers.

Using a random method enables researchers to use statistical inferences to estimate the accuracy of the estimates made from the sample. Statistical inference theory assumes that results from n number of samples would be normally distributed, resembling a bell curve if placed on a graph. With a normal distribution, roughly two-thirds of the cases would fall within one standard error of the mean or average, and about 95% of the cases would fall within two standard errors. This means that researchers can be confident that in 95 out of 100 samples the true population score would fall within two standard deviations of the mean. This is how margins of error are calculated. The standard error is similar to a standard deviation and is a way to measure the dispersion of cases around the mean, based on how far each case is from the mean.

As a rule, the larger the sample the smaller the standard deviation, or the better the chances are that the scores the researcher finds are near the score that would be found if everyone had been surveyed. However, increasing the sample size beyond 1,200 to improve accuracy is not cost-effective. Researchers would have to significantly increase the sample size to have a noticeable improvement in accuracy. When researchers want to estimate scores for a subsample of their survey, for example, estimate the views of women or other minorities, they need to keep in mind that the size of the subsample is significantly smaller and adjust their confidence in their estimate.

of individual households. Clustering involves first sampling large areas and then doing further sampling within each area (cluster). The BNES used the following clusters:[13]

1. High Black Density areas (areas with black population density of 15 percent or more).

2. Medium Black Density (small communities in states with large black populations).

3. Low Black Density—all remaining telephone exchanges.

They then selected phone numbers at different rates, depending on the cluster, such that phone numbers in the high-density stratum were three times more likely to be selected than the low-density stratum and twice that of the medium stratum. The National Latino Political Survey used a similar approach in its survey of Hispanics.[14]

Another approach is not to use random sampling. Such an approach was used by a recent Pew Research Center survey of LGBT Americans.[15] Pew used an Internet polling firm that knew the sexual orientation of its research subjects and interviewed only individuals identified as LGBT. A survey of transgender Americans conducted by the National Center for Transgender Equality and the National Gay and Lesbian Task Force used a mixture of surveying members of transgender organizations and a snowball sample.[16] With snowball samples, researchers have an initial list of subjects and then ask the subjects to help recruit more subjects. While such an approach is often needed for populations of hard to identify people, its value is limited. Since it does not yield a probability sample, sample statistics based on statistical inference are inappropriate, and whether they represent the population of interest is unclear.

Levels of Symbolic Representation

To get a sense of minority individuals' emotions and attitudes toward the government, this section reports the results of several surveys that ask different questions about Americans' views and feelings toward the U.S. government. First, it examines minorities' feelings about the United States, then their levels of trust in the government, its efficacy, presidential approval, and confidence in its institutions. This section ends by examining minorities' views about whether or not the country is heading in the right direction.

Feelings toward the United States

One way to examine minorities' level of symbolic representation is to look at how they feel about the United States and how they feel about being an American. These attitudes can be estimated with the 2012 ANES Time Series data. In 2012, ANES asked respondents several questions about how they feel about the United States. One question asked how individuals feel when they see an important U.S. symbol: the flag. These results suggest minorities have lower levels of symbolic representation than nonminorities.[17] While 44.8% of Anglos said the flag made them feel extremely good, and 31.2% said very good, only 31.6% of African Americans said extremely good and 27.6% said very good. For Hispanics, the figures were between those of Anglos and African Americans; 41.2% and 32.1%. Women tended to feel somewhat better about the flag than did men; 44.2% felt extremely good and 30.2% felt very good, and for men, the scores were 40.3% and 31.0%. Within most racial groups as well, women were more likely to feel at least very good. Among Hispanics and Anglos, more women felt at least very good than did men (78.2% to 73.6% for Anglos and 75.9% to 70.7% for Hispanics). However, among African Americans, men were more likely to feel at least very good (60.2% to 58.2%). According to the same survey, LGB Americans feel less good than non-LGB Americans about the flag. While 43.0% of non-LGB Americans felt extremely good and 30% felt very good, for gays and lesbians the figures were 27.7% and 23.3%, and for bisexuals the figures were 27.9% and 25.7%.

The gap between minorities and nonminorities has changed over the past years. In 2004, the gap between the percentage of African Americans and Anglos who reported feeling extremely good was 25.8%, by 2012 it had shrunk to 13.6%.[18] Women reported high levels of symbolic representation based on the flag question in both surveys, and the gap between men and women grew from 1.4% to 3.9%. Hispanics' relative symbolic representation, however, has fallen. The gap between Hispanics and Anglos went from 0.7% in 2004 to 3.6% in 2012. While it is a hopeful sign that African Americans have views more similar to Anglos today than in the past and that women have more positive views than men, the reason for this may not be so hopeful. The reason is that minorities' feelings toward the flag declined less than nonminorities. In 2004, 31.2% of African Americans reported feeling "extremely good" when they saw the flag. In 2012, 31.2% of African Americans still felt "extremely good." For Hispanics, 56.3% reported feeling "extremely good" in 2004, and only 41.2% felt "extremely good" in 2012. The percentage of women who felt extremely good

The flag carries much meaning for Americans, as is demonstrated by its use here by illegal immigrants wanting U.S. citizenship.
(© *Atlantide Phototravel/Corbis*)

upon seeing the flag went from 52.8% to 44.2%. Among Anglos, the percentage feeling "extremely good" fell from 57.0% to 44.8%.

Minorities also tend to have generally less positive feelings about the United States. The ANES time series asked respondents whether they loved the United States. According to the survey, 68.7% of Anglos say they love the United States, compared to 58.9% of African Americans and 57.7% of Hispanics.[19] Gays and lesbians are also less likely to love the country than are non-LGB. While 65.7% of non-LGB report loving the United States, 58.8% of gays and lesbians, and 50.9% of bisexuals report loving the country. Although LGB and racial/ethnic minorities are less likely to love the United States than nonminorities, women are more likely to love the United States than are men, 66.2% to 64.3%. However, women within each racial/ethnic group are not more likely to love the United States. Although Anglo women are more likely to love the United States than Anglo men (70.1% to 67.3%), and Hispanic women more so than Hispanic men (61.9% to 53.4%), African American women are less likely to love the United States than are African American men (57.6% to 60.4%).

Similar trends were found in terms of how important minorities feel it is to be American. The ANES 2012 time series asked respondents how important it was to them to be an American. Generally women found it as important as men did, and racial and ethnic minorities found it less important than Anglos.[20] While 57.2% of women see being an American as extremely important and 26.5% as very important, 54.5% of men see it as extremely important and 28.3% see it as very important. However, other minority groups see being American as less important. Gays and lesbians see being an American as less important than non-LGB Americans. While 56.8% of non-LGB respondents say it is extremely important and 27.3% say it is very important, only 34.7% of gays and lesbians say it is extremely important and 30.4% say it is very important. For bisexuals, the figures are 38.2% and 27.5%. Compared to Anglos, African Americans and Hispanics are less likely to see being American as at least very important (83.9%, 79.7%, and 81.5%). Among Anglos and Hispanics, women were more likely to see being an American as at least very important. However, among African Americans, men were more likely to see being an American as at least very important. In fact, with almost 84% of African American men feeling that being an American was important, they were the most likely to value being an American, while African American women were the least likely to see being an American as very important (76.1%).

To summarize, except for women, minorities' responses to the flag were more negative, as were their responses to how much they love America and how important it is to be American, than nonminorities' responses. The above discussion also makes clear the risk one runs in over-generalizing about a group. Although women tend to have more positive attitudes toward the United States than men, that was not the case for African American women, and African American men often have fairly positive responses. One word of caution is needed in making these generalizations. For some groups, particularly LGB, the number of respondents in the survey was small, about 100 for lesbians and gays combined and about 100 for bisexuals. These small numbers decrease the accuracy of the results. Also these results are best thought of as measuring diffuse support, or support not based on specific policies, since they ask about general feelings toward the United States or its symbols.

Trust

Another way to gauge minorities' symbolic representation is by estimating their levels of governmental **trust,** which is a measure of symbolic representation that taps peoples' views toward the government. Trust is often measured with the following question: "How much do you trust the government in Washington to do what is right?" The options are "just about always," "most of the time," "some of the time," and "never." There are debates about whether this question taps diffuse support (long-term support based on socialization), or specific support (support for personalities and specific policies),[21] which is a weakness of this measure of trust. The strength of this measure of trust, however, is that the American National Elections Studies has been tracking it since the 1950s and surveys enough people that it can generalize about African Americans, whites, men, and women. Figures 5.1 and 5.2 depict the percentage of women, men, African Americans, whites, and Democrats who said they trusted the government just about always or most of the time from 1958 to 2012. In examining these trends, students need to keep in mind that Americans' feelings of trust have declined over the past fifty years. Students also need to keep in mind that trust is highly influenced by the congruence of party in office and individuals' party. Since African Americans are predominantly Democrats, Figure 5.2 includes information on Democrats' trust, as well as whites' trust, as means of comparison.

Figure 5.1 indicates that men and women have similar levels of trust. Men's and women's levels of trust are very close to each other throughout the years. For example, in 2012 there was virtually no difference, with 10.8% of men and 10.6% of women trusting the government at least most of the time.[22] Figure 5.1 also indicates that men's and women's trust change together, as one goes up, the other goes up with it. This indicates that similar forces may be at play affecting both men's and women's trust.

Figure 5.2 depicts the difference between African Americans, whites, and Democrats. It suggests that whites' and African Americans' levels of trust tend to trend together, as does African Americans' trust with Democrats' trust. This suggests that events have similar effects on African Americans' and whites' level of trust. However, the figure also indicates that historically, African Americans have had lower levels of trust than others. While President Bush was president, between 2000 and 2008, the gap was fairly large, about 15% points, but the gap shrank in 2008. The gap shrank not because African Americans increased their trust, but because whites' trust declined as the economic

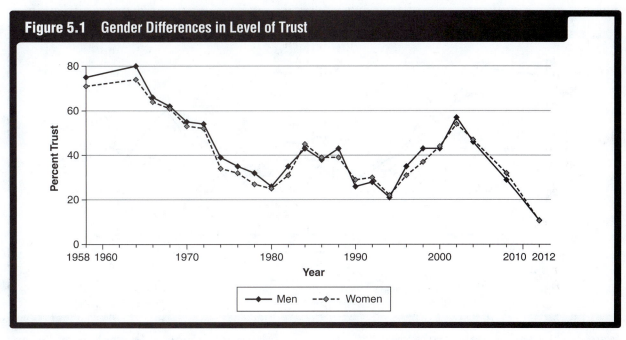

Figure 5.1   Gender Differences in Level of Trust

Source: Data from American National Election Studies (ANES, http://electionstudies.org/OurStudies/OurStudies.htm). Scores for 2012 were calculated by the author using 2012 ANES time series data (ANES 2012 Time Series Study [dataset]). Stanford University and the University of Michigan (producers).

crisis grew. Today, however, with an African American Democrat in the White House, African Americans appear to have greater trust than whites. In 2012, 15.1% of African Americans trusted the government at least most of the time compared to 9.2% of whites and 13.6% of Democrats. Other surveys have found an even larger gap.[23]

Gronke and his coauthors suggested that the above measure of trust is too broad and developed a three-prong typology of trust based on people's confidence in different institutions.[24] Their typology includes confidence in the government, confidence in institutions of opposition to the government (media, TV, unions, and education), and confidence in institutions of order (religious, military, scientific, medical, and business institutions). Their research, conducted prior to Obama's presidency, supports the findings that African Americans have low levels of symbolic representation. They find that African Americans have more confidence than whites in the opposition institutions and less confidence in government and the order institutions. Women, on the other hand, have more varied levels of confidence. Compared to men, women have more confidence in the government and less in the order institutions but do not differ in their support of opposition institutions.

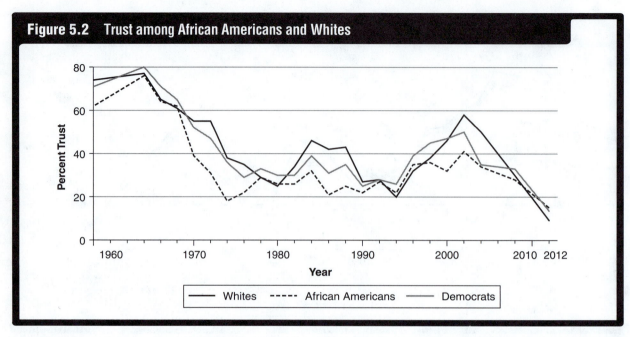

Figure 5.2   Trust among African Americans and Whites

Source: Data from American National Election Studies (ANES, http://electionstudies.org/OurStudies/OurStudies.htm). Scores for 2012 were calculated by the author using 2012 ANES time series data (ANES 2012 Time Series Study [dataset]). Stanford University and the University of Michigan (producers).

Unlike African Americans and women, who tend to have low levels of trust in the government, Hispanics tend to have high levels of trust.[25] According to the 2012 ANES, 17.4% of Hispanics trust the government most of the time. While Hispanic women have slightly lower levels of trust than do Hispanic men, there are greater differences between Hispanic nationalities than between the sexes. According to a 2013 Pew Research Center survey,[26] Cubans have the most trust, followed by Mexicans and Puerto Ricans. Abrajano and Alvarez argue that Hispanics have high levels of trust because a large percentage of Hispanics are immigrants, and immigrants tend to have more positive views of the government.[27] New Americans tend to be optimistic about their future in the United States because they compare their current lives with the lives they left behind. However, later generations and those who have assimilated may have negative views. Instead of comparing their lives to the lives of people in the country they or their ancestors left, they compare them to the lives of other Americans. Additionally, second-generation Americans are less tolerant of discrimination than are immigrants. For example, the authors find that whereas first-generation Hispanics scored 18.6 on their trust scale, fourth-generation Hispanics scored 4.6.[28] To put these figures in perspective, whites averaged 13.4. That immigrants have higher levels of trust than native citizens is true in Europe as well as in the United States (see Spotlight 5.2).

Although not much research has examined levels of trust by sexual orientation, the 2012 ANES data give us a glance. These data include only about 100 gays and lesbians and 100 bisexuals, so these are very rough estimates. However, they indicate that gays and lesbians have much lower levels of trust in the government than do bisexuals or non-LGB Americans. Only 4.1% of gays and lesbians trust the government most of the time, compared to 10.7% of non-LGB and 10.3% of bisexuals.[29]

Spotlight 5.2

Immigrants and Trust in Europe

That immigrants have more symbolic representation than native citizens is not unique to the United States. Indeed, the research looking at immigrants in Europe and Canada has found similar trends.[30] For example, Maxwell, using the European Social Survey 2002–2007, reports that on a 10-point scale first-generation Europeans scored a 5.14, second-generation a 4.51, and native Europeans scored a 4.64.[31] The scores for government satisfaction were 5.07, 4.26, and 4.33. For economic satisfaction, the scores were 5.33, 4.68, and 4.75. Thus, immigrants have more positive views of their governments than second-generation and other native-born Europeans.

Research on European immigrants' trust has attempted to explain their high levels of trust. Roder and Muhlau find that much of immigrants' high levels of trust in the government is caused by immigrants' lower expectations.[32] They look at immigrants' confidence in the government from twenty-six European countries as measured by the European Social Survey 2002–2006. They find that immigrants from the nations with the lowest quality of governments, measured by the Worldwide Governance Indicators, have the greatest confidence in their European governments. They and others also find that acculturation helps explain levels of trust. The longer immigrants have been in a nation and/or the better they speak the language of their host nation, the less trust they have in their government.[33]

Relatedly, researchers have been interested in what causes second-generation Europeans to have less trust than first-generation immigrants. One possible explanation is that experiences with discrimination help explain why trust and similar attitudes decline. Discrimination helps explain some of the decline. Discrimination can also help explain immigrants' overall levels of trust in institutions.[34] What are likely better explanations for the decline in trust over time, however, are acculturation and changes in their expectations.[35]

Since ANES interviews few Asian Americans, it is not the best survey to measure the symbolic support of Asian Americans. What is better is the 2008 National Asian American Survey. This survey asked respondents to indicate how strongly they agree or disagree that "We can trust our government in Washington to do what is right." Although these results are not fully comparable to the other surveys, they indicate Asian Americans have fairly high levels of trust.[36] Almost 20% strongly agreed that we can trust the government, 29.4% somewhat agreed,

16.5% neither agreed nor disagreed, 22.1% somewhat disagreed, and only 13.3% strongly disagreed. As with Hispanics, Asian Americans born in the United States have less trust in the government than those born elsewhere. Twenty-one percent of those born in the United States strongly disagree that the government can be trusted, compared to about 11.5% of those born abroad. Among Asian Americans, there is not much difference between men and women in their average levels of trust. However, Asian American women may be more ambivalent. They were less likely to answer the question and more likely to indicate they neither agree nor disagree.

The above discussion suggests that African Americans and gays and lesbians tend to have lower levels of trust in the government than whites, and that women's and men's levels of trust are very similar. In addition, Asian Americans and Hispanics have high levels of trust in the government because many are first-generation Americans. The trend analysis of race and gender also suggests that what affects one group's level of trust tends to affect another's level of trust, but that since President Obama has been elected president, African Americans have had somewhat higher levels of trust.

Efficacy

Related to symbolic representation may be political efficacy. **Political efficacy,** the belief that people can affect the government, is composed of both internal and external efficacy. **Internal efficacy** is an individual's belief that he or she can affect government action. **External efficacy** is the belief that the government is generally open to the influence of non-elites. External efficacy is more closely related to symbolic representation since it concerns how the government reacts to the people; whereas internal efficacy often concerns individuals' views of their own power. Again, ANES has fifty years of survey data that can be used to compare African Americans' efficacy to whites' efficacy and women's efficacy to men's efficacy. Since 1958 ANES has asked respondents whether they agree or disagree with the following statement: "People like me don't have any say about what the government does." Since 1988 respondents have also been given the option of neither agreeing nor disagreeing.[37] Given the wording, respondents who agree have low levels of external efficacy. Figure 5.3 reports the results since 1958 broken down by gender, and Figure 5.4 reports the results broken down by race and party. Figure 5.3 suggests that women have somewhat lower levels of efficacy. In 2012, which had one of the smaller gaps, 53% of women agreed that people like themselves have no say compared to 51.7% for men. The 2008 results are unique in that women had higher levels of efficacy, less likely to think the people had no say. A likely reason for this is that in 2008 Hillary Rodham Clinton made a viable run for the White House, and Sarah Palin was the Republican vice presidential candidate.

Figure 5.4 suggests that although African Americans tend to have lower levels of efficacy than whites or Democrats, something changed between 2008 and 2012. In the average year prior to 2012, 47.7% of African Americans, 42.2%

Figure 5.3   Gender Differences in Efficacy

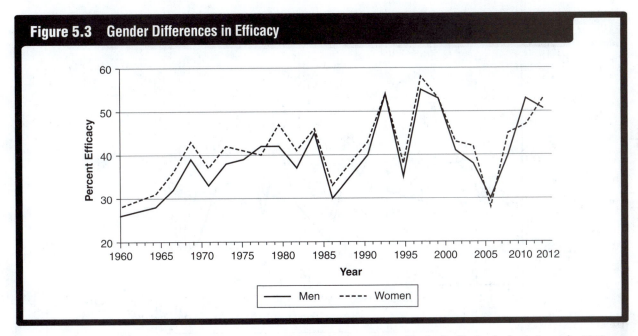

Source: Data from American National Election Studies (ANES, http://electionstudies.org/OurStudies/OurStudies.htm). Scores for 2012 were calculated by the author using 2012 ANES time series data (ANES 2012 Time Series Study [dataset]). Stanford University and the University of Michigan (producers).

Note: The figure shows the percentages of people who agree that people don't have influence and are those with low levels of efficacy.

of Democrats, and 39.2% of whites felt people like them did not have any say, that is, low efficacy. However, in 2012, African Americans had higher levels of efficacy. About 48.4% of Democrats, 53.9% of whites, and 46.3% of African Americans agreed that the people had little influence. What likely affected these trends was the election of 2008. In 2008, Barack Obama won the presidency, and African Americans have continued to outpace whites in efficacy. Note, however, that African Americans did not become markedly more efficacious, but that whites became markedly less trusting. This is consistent with some work by Claudine Gay that finds that whites are more likely to be negatively affected by minority policymakers than African Americans are positively affected.[38]

The 2012 ANES data can also be used to estimate gays' and lesbians' and Hispanics' efficacy, and the intersectionality of gender and race/ethnicity.[39] They suggest that Hispanics and gays and lesbians, but not bisexuals, have high levels of efficacy. About 44.2% of Hispanics compared to 53.8% of Anglos believe that people have no influence on what the government does. Similarly, 51.9% of non-LGB Americans, 40.4% of lesbians and gays, and 60.5% of bisexuals believe the people have no say.

The data also suggest that although women in 2012 had lower levels of efficacy, that was not true for all races. Anglo women had lower levels of efficacy

Figure 5.4   Efficacy by Race and Party

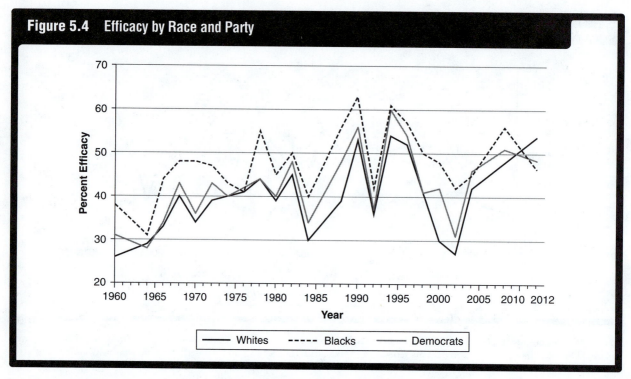

Source: Data from American National Election Studies (ANES, http://electionstudies.org/OurStudies/OurStudies.htm). Scores for 2012 were calculated by author using 2012 ANES time series data.

Note: The figures are percent who agree that people don't have influence and are those with low levels of efficacy.

(56.5% of Anglo women and 51.2% of Anglo men said people have no say), African American women had somewhat more efficacy than African American men (44.5% to 48.6%), and among Hispanics there was not a noticeable gender difference (49.5% for women and 49.2% for men).

The ANES data can also be used to estimate internal efficacy. ANES asked respondents whether or not they agreed that politics was too complicated to understand. Responses to the question suggest that gays and lesbians have high levels of internal efficacy, less likely to agree with the statement that politics is too complicated. Whereas 47.4% of gays and lesbians agreed, 60.1% of non-LGB Americans and 58.8% of bisexuals agreed.[40] African Americans and Hispanics also had higher levels of internal efficacy. Whereas 60.3% of whites agreed that politics was too complicated, only 56.6% of African Americans and 53.4% of Hispanics agreed. The one minority group that had lower levels of internal efficacy was women; only 54.1% of men agreed that politics was too complicated compared to 65.6% of women. This gender gap was similar among Anglos and Hispanics but was virtually nonexistent for African Americans. Thus, African American women have higher levels of both internal and external efficacy than other women. That African American women have higher levels of efficacy than white women may help explain why proportionally African American women are more likely to hold political offices.

Because of the small number of Asian Americans surveyed by ANES, the 2008 National Asian American Survey (NAAS) is used to describe Asian Americans' levels of efficacy. The NAAS asked respondents to what degree they agree to the following statements: "Public officials and politicians care what people like me think" and "Politics is so complicated I can't understand what is going on." These results suggest that Asian Americans believe that politicians care (high levels external efficacy) but also that politics is too complicated (low levels internal efficacy). About 33% of Asian Americans disagree and 50.8% agree that politicians care. Conversely, 23.6% disagree and 66.7% agree that politics is too complicated. Thus, Asian Americans tend to trust the government even if they do not feel as though they personally have much influence. As with trust, there are not large differences between Asian American men and women and their efficacy. The main gender differences among Asian Americans were that women were somewhat less likely to answer the question, and those who did answer were somewhat more extreme in their lack of internal efficacy.

Presidential Approval

Another way to get a sense of minority individuals' levels of symbolic representation is to look at presidential approval. People who approve of the president's job performance are likely to think the government is working well and making good decisions. Thus, it is more likely to tap specific support. Not surprisingly, racial and ethnic minorities give President Obama higher ratings than whites give him. Between 2009 and 2013, on average, 41% of whites approved of President Obama's performance in office compared to 63% of Hispanics and 89% of African Americans.[41] Women, too, give President Obama relatively high approval ratings. This gender gap ranges from about 4% to 6%.[42] Not only are women generally more likely to approve of President Obama's job performance, but so are women within each minority group. LGBT Americans also rate President Obama highly. According to the Pew Research Center 2013 survey of LGBT Americans, 76% of LGBT Americans have favorable opinions of President Obama, compared to 59% of the general public according to another 2013 Pew survey.[43]

Presidential approval ratings are highly affected by party. Thus, much of Obama's support from minorities is a function of him being a Democrat. In fact, once party is considered, there is virtually no difference between men and women.[44] In 2013, while 89% of African Americans approved of Obama's performance, 88% of liberal Democrats approved of Obama.[45] Additionally, during President George W. Bush's administration, women, African Americans, Hispanics, and Asian Americans were all less likely to approve of his performance in office than were men and Anglos, who are more likely to be Republican.[46]

Research examining the effects of Hurricane Katrina, which hit New Orleans and disproportionately harmed poor African American residents, indicates how race can affect symbolic representation.[47] Whereas non-African Americans tended to blame nature and the victims of Katrina for much of the suffering, African Americans were more likely to blame the government for the poor response to the disaster. Although some of this is related to party identification, the differences remain significant after taking party into consideration.

Unfortunately, ANES and Gallup have not asked a sufficient number of American Indians about their views of the president, so we have little information on this or other aspects of their symbolic representation. However, President Obama's administration has done much to try to improve the relationship between the federal government and American Indians. He has worked on improving Indian health care, federal collaboration with tribes, appointed more American Indians to key positions, and signed a resolution that was just shy of apologizing to American Indians for U.S. abuses.[48] Thus, it is likely that the presidency of Obama had similar effects on American Indians' symbolic representation as it did on other minorities.

Although all minority groups give President Obama higher approval ratings than their nonminority counterparts, this has more to do with the person or party who occupies the White House and less to do with their views toward the government. Thus, as a general rule, how much minorities approve of the president's job performance may tell us little about their support of the government generally or its institutions, but rather it may be an indicator of whether the current administration is likely to enact policies supported by minorities.

Direction of the Nation

Related to symbolic representation are minorities' views of how well the nation is doing. Over the years, Gallup has asked: "We'd like you to imagine a ladder with steps numbered from zero at the bottom to ten at the top. Suppose the top of the ladder represents the best possible situation for our country and the bottom represents the worst possible situation. Please tell me the number of the step on which you think the United States stands at the present time."[49] Although historically a smaller percentage of nonwhites than whites have given the United States a positive score (above 5), after 2008 the trend has reversed; in 2014, 57% of nonwhites gave a positive score compared to only 33% of whites.[50] What has puzzled researchers is that at the same time minorities appear to be more optimistic, they are doing less well economically. Spotlight 5.3 examines this puzzle. To estimate whether LGBT Americans believe the nation is heading in the right direction, Pew Research Center data can be used. According to the survey, LGBT Americans are more likely to think the United States is generally headed in the right direction than is the general public (55% to 32%). This is likely due to the advances in LGBT interests during this decade.[51]

A 2012 Pew Research Center survey, "The Rise of Asian Americans," asked 3,511 Asian Americans what they thought of the direction of the nation. It found

Spotlight 5.3

A Glass Mysteriously Half Full

Pollsters have noted that since the mid-1980s, there has been a fundamental shift in the optimism of Americans. Prior to the mid-1980s, non-Hispanic whites were more optimistic about their futures and the future of America than were African Americans and Hispanics. But there has been a reversal such that between 2008 and 2010, non-Anglos were twice as likely as Anglos to think the nation was in a good place. What puzzles researchers is that while minorities have become more optimistic, their economic circumstances have not improved. If anything, the wealth gap between Anglos and African Americans and Hispanics has increased since the recession of 2008. Researchers have not figured out the reason minorities are so optimistic despite their economic realities,

but some reasons have been circulating. One of the more common theories is the election of the first African American president, Barack Obama. Non-Anglos see his presidency more favorably than Anglos. Since race and party overlap, it is a bit unclear whether President Obama's race or party is more significant, but his election likely contributes to minority optimism. It may also be less helpful in explaining the optimism of Hispanics. While historically Hispanics' opinions tracked those of Anglos, since 2002, that has not been the case. And 2002 predates the election of President Obama. Researchers have not been able to explain what happened in 2002.

Source: This Spotlight is a summary of a report on NPR by Gene Demby, March 5, 2014.

that Asian Americans were more likely to be satisfied with the direction of the United States than other Americans (43% to 21%).[52] This survey also demonstrates that foreign-born Asian Americans have higher levels of symbolic representation than Asian Americans born in the United States. Of the native-born Asian Americans, 32% are satisfied with the direction of the United States compared to 46% of the foreign-born Asian Americans.[53] The report also demonstrates variation among different Asian groups. Fifty-six percent of Vietnamese are satisfied with the direction compared to 48% of Koreans, 47% of Indians, 41% Chinese, 36% Japanese, and 30% Filipino.[54]

The above suggests that although historically African Americans and women tended to have lower levels of symbolic representation than whites or men, the trend has changed in recent years. The trend seems to have changed with the 2008 election that sent the first African American to the White House. This not only seems to have increased minorities' views of the government but also depressed nonminorities' views. Looking at minorities' views, there is less trend data on the symbolic representation of Asian Americans and Hispanics, but evidence suggests they tend to have higher levels of symbolic representation than most Americans. The reason is that immigrants have more positive views, and a large number of Hispanics and Asian Americans are immigrants. Less is known about LGBT Americans' symbolic representation, but they appear to have low levels when measured by the love of country but higher when measured by views of the president and efficacy. For all the minority groups, having a Democratic president in office increases their symbolic representation.

What Affects the Symbolic Representation of Minorities?

As noted above, symbolic representation is influenced by party congruence; where the constituent and policymaker share party identification, symbolic representation is higher. Thus, since minorities tend to be Democrats, the symbolic representation of minorities increases when Democrats are in office. But there are several other factors that can affect symbolic representation. First, minorities may respond differently to events. Harper and Norrander's examination of President Bush's approval ratings found that the influence of some events was raced and gendered.[55] Women judged Bush more harshly because of the war with Iraq and the worsening economy, particularly after 2005. This is likely because, generally, women tend to be less supportive of use of force and tend to be more pessimistic about the economy. Compared to whites, African Americans' approval of President Bush was also more strongly and negatively influenced by the worsening economy, Katrina, and the war with Iraq. Hispanics' approval ratings of President Bush more closely mirrored Anglos' approval ratings. Yet, the levels of trust and efficacy among whites, African Americans, women, and men tend to trend together.

A couple of other factors are likely to influence symbolic representation. First, the financial situation of minorities, as well as of all Americans, affects their levels of trust.[56] People who are struggling financially or see the national economy as doing poorly have less symbolic representation. Thus, given minorities' lower levels of socioeconomic status, minorities are likely to have lower levels of symbolic representation. Research also suggests that people who have experienced discrimination are less likely to trust the government.[57]

Descriptive representation also likely affects the symbolic representation of minorities. As already noted, minorities' symbolic representation improved after President Obama was elected president. Minorities who have minority representatives, or who believe there are a large number of minorities in office, may be more likely to feel they have a voice and that policies will reflect their interests. In this discussion, symbolic representation will be loosely defined to include minorities' views about the government and its leaders as well as political engagement, such as political knowledge, interest, and participation. One of the first pieces of research to examine the relationship between descriptive and symbolic representation was Bobo and Gilliam's examination of the political engagement of African Americans in what they call **black empowerment areas**,[58] cities and towns with a black mayor. They find that African Americans living in high empowerment cities are more likely to participate in politics (vote, campaign, contact officials, and engage in community activities) because by living in an empower-ment city, African Americans' levels of knowledge, trust, and efficacy improved. Thus, there is a direct effect of descriptive representation on minorities' symbolic representation.

Since Bobo and Gilliam's work, the research on the effects of descriptive rep-resentation on minorities' symbolic representation has taken a couple of different approaches, and the approach often affects what is found. First, researchers have examined what could be called *dyadic descriptive representation,* when individu-als share race, ethnicity, or gender with their own representative. For example, Tate, using the 1996 NBES survey, found that African Americans represented by African Americans had more political knowledge about their representatives (House member and Senator) and were more interested in the 1996 elections.[59] But she also found that being represented by an African American member of Congress did not affect African Americans' approval of Congress, trust, or effi-cacy. Banducci, Donovan, and Karp confirmed that the effects of dyadic descrip-tive representation are limited to the member and do not extend to Congress or the nation.[60] They found that even after controlling for party, education, gender, age, and economy, African Americans who were descriptively represented had a .21 probability of recalling the name of their Congress members, a .12 prob-ability of having contacted their member, and a .61 probability of approving of the representative's performance; when the representative was nonminority, the probabilities were .09, .08, and .46.[61] But they also found that dyadic representa-tion had little effect on African American constituents' efficacy.

Gay also found that dyadic descriptive representation affects African Ameri-cans' relationship with their member.[62] She found African Americans had some-what more positive views of their Congress members and were more likely to contact them if an African American member of Congress represented them. For example, using a "feeling thermometer," African American Democrats gave their African American members a score of 72.9, but African Americans who were represented by white Democrats gave their member a 65.6.[63] However, she found that it was not race per se but ideological closeness that increased African Ameri-cans' feeling toward their members. The one area where dyadic descriptive rep-resentation improved symbolic representation regardless of ideology concerned contact. African Americans were twice as likely to contact their member when the member was African American than when the member was white. Brunell, Anderson, and Cremona analyzed whether individual African Americans who knew they were represented by an African American member of Congress gave that member much higher ratings than those who were represented by a non-African American member or were unaware that their representative was African American, and found that they do.[64] However, they, too, found the effects were limited and do not extend to congressional approval.

The effects of dyadic descriptive representation may be further nuanced. Reingold and Harrell tested several possible ways dyadic descriptive representation could affect women's engagement.[65] They examined whether there was a difference in the effects of dyadic representation if a woman voter matched with each of the following: a woman candidate, a woman official, or only a woman candidate of the same party as the voter and official of the same party as the voter. They found women's campaign interests, political discussions, efforts to persuade, and candidate recognition were not affected by whether they were represented by a woman or a man. However, women's engagement was affected by whether or not there was a woman on the ballot, such that women were more engaged if there was a woman on the ballot but not more engaged if a woman represented them. Additionally, they found that women's engagement was most strongly and positively influenced by the presence of a woman candidate if the woman and candidate shared party identification.

The other approach is to examine the effects of the overall levels of descriptive representation on symbolic representation: what I call *collective descriptive representation*. Collective descriptive representation concerns the proportion of minorities in office, or peoples' perceptions of the proportion of minorities in office. In examining collective descriptive representation, Tate found that African Americans who thought there were more African American members in Congress had more trust and approval of Congress than did those who perceived lower levels of descriptive representation.[66] In addition, Rocha, Tolbert, Bowen, and Clark found that African Americans and Hispanics are more likely to vote if they reside in states with large African American or Hispanic descriptive representation.[67] Brunell, Anderson, and Cremona also found that African American constituents' perceptions of the size of the African American delegation in Congress positively affected their views toward both their own member and that of Congress as a whole. Using a unique approach McCool, Olson, and Robinson asked American Indians who had been elected to city councils if they believe their elections improve American Indians' views of the government. Ten of fifteen believed they did.[68] They found that the leaders felt they were making changes in ways that made American Indians believe that their interests were being considered.[69] Finally, although Lawless found limited effects of both dyadic and collective descriptive representation, she did find that women represented by women gave higher approval ratings to women representatives.[70]

Descriptive representation can also affect symbolic representation when officeholders serve as role models for others. The beginning of this chapter indicates that many see President Obama as a role model. To some, he demonstrates that their children can grow up to be anybody. Additionally, Campbell and Wolbrecht found women politicians have a strong role model effect on adolescent girls.[71] Girls growing up where there were visible women political leaders reported more anticipated political involvement.

Thus, it appears as though having dyadic representation improves individuals' views of their own member but not necessarily their views of Congress or government as a whole, and that collective descriptive representation improves individuals' views toward the government more largely. However, there may be some variation by whether one is studying women, African Americans, candidates, officials, or political participation.

Symbolic Legislation: Representing Minorities through Symbolic Actions

Although this chapter focuses on symbolic representation as individuals' attitudes and feelings toward government, minority legislators do work that is symbolic in nature. They act in ways not directly affecting policy, but make visible minorities or symbols important to minorities. For example, most cities of any size have a governmental building or road named after Martin Luther King Jr. It is not that Martin Luther King Jr. personally had lived in the city or helped build the building or road, but that the leaders wanted to do something to reach out to the minority community by naming a public area after a civil rights icon. Tate finds that much of the legislation introduced by African American Congress members and passed is symbolic in nature.[72] For example, Cardiss Collins introduced legislation to name a Chicago post office after Charles A. Hayes, an African American who had represented part of Chicago before retiring.[73]

Another way minority policymakers can act in more symbolic ways is by discussing minorities and women when they discuss issues that do not specifically concern race and gender. For example, Gershon examined Congress members' webpages and found that not only were congresswomen more likely to discuss women's issues and African American and Hispanic members' minority issues but that they brought race, ethnicity, and gender into other discussions.[74] Canon examined the use of the frank, which is free mailing to constituents, and found that 45% of the photos in nonwhite members' mailings were of African Americans compared to 28% for white members.[75] Canon also looked at where members had their local offices and race of staff members. He found that African American members had a higher percentage of African American staff members, even after controlling for district makeup, and were more likely to have local offices in communities with large minority populations. It should be noted that Canon, too, found differences among African Americans who run on raced themes of difference or themes of commonality. Those who ran on raced themes were more likely to have African American staff members and offices in African American communities than were others.

Conclusion: Decreasing Gaps in Symbolic Representation

The election of President Barack Obama had a positive effect on the symbolic representation of minorities. Historically, African Americans had lower levels of symbolic representation than whites, but after the 2008 election, their beliefs and feelings toward the government improved. Since the election of President Obama in 2008, African Americans have had as high, if not higher, levels of symbolic representation, measured by some views of the government. Hispanics, women, Asian Americans, and African Americans, too, were more likely to approve of President Obama than of President George W. Bush, his predecessor. And LGBT gave Obama very high ratings. Although much of Obama's effect on minorities' views is likely partisan, that he is African American undoubtedly has a positive effect as well.

The symbolic representation of minorities, as well as of Americans generally, improves when they have something in common with elected officials. Two key characteristics to share are minority status and party. Minority groups tend to be Democrats, and as a consequence, tend to have higher levels of symbolic representation when Democrats are in office. In addition, minority constituents who are represented by Democrats and minority representatives, or perceive the government to have high levels of descriptive representation, have higher levels of symbolic representation. How descriptive representation affects symbolic representation depends on whether it is dyadic or collective representation. Dyadic descriptive representation improves views toward individual representatives, while collective descriptive representation improves attitudes toward the government more broadly. Unfortunately, having minority representatives tends to depress the symbolic representation of nonminority Americans.

This chapter helped to demonstrate the importance of not assuming all women or all men are similar or that all whites, African Americans, Hispanics, or Asian Americans are similar. Although white women tended to have lower levels of efficacy than men, but felt as much love for the country, among African Americans the reverse was the case. Compared to African American men, African American women tend to have higher levels of efficacy but lower levels of love for the country.

This chapter explored many ways to evaluate symbolic representation; some measure views toward the nation broadly, such as feelings toward the flag, while others were government specific, such as confidence in the branches of government and efficacy, while others such as presidential approval related more to individuals in office. The mix of support varied by minority group. Hispanics and Asian Americans had fairly high levels of all three types of views, although levels of symbolic representation vary dramatically by individuals' nativity status. While first-generation Americans have very high levels of symbolic representation, the representation of third- and fourth-generation Americans is very low. Women's symbolic representation is somewhat lower than men's symbolic representation when measured as views toward the government but not feelings toward the country. Gays and lesbians tend to feel less positively toward the country and have less trust in the government, but generally evaluate the government more positively. However, we only have recent survey results to examine. Regardless of their relative symbolic representation, minority groups still tend to feel positively toward the nation. Almost 60% of African Americans, 73% of Hispanics, 74% of women, and 51% LGBT feel at least very good when they see the flag.

KEY TERMS

Black empowerment
  areas   (p. 126)
Collective descriptive
  representation   (p. 110)

Dyadic descriptive
  representation   (p. 110)
External efficacy   (p. 120)
Internal efficacy   (p. 120)

Political efficacy   (p. 120)
Trust   (p. 116)

Chapter 6

Minority Representation and the Judicial Branch

I n 1991, Thurgood Marshall, the first African American Supreme Court justice, retired after twenty-three years on the Supreme Court of the United States (SCOTUS). During his tenure on the bench, he was a strong advocate for minority rights in such cases as *Griggs v. Duke, Mobile Alabama v. Bolden, Bowers v. Hardwick, Roe v. Wade, Regents of University of California v. Bakke, Craig v. Boren,* and *Reed v. Reed.* Upon his retirement, there was much pressure on President George H. W. Bush to appoint another African American to SCOTUS. President Bush selected Clarence Thomas, a conservative African American, to replace Marshall. Whereas Marshall's legal career focused on civil rights (see Spotlight 6.1), Thomas's focused on tax law, not civil rights. Although Thomas was appointed by President Ronald Reagan to head up the Equal Employment Opportunity Commission, as its head he made changes that were opposed by the civil rights community.[1] In 1990, he became an appellate judge for the District of Columbia. In the Supreme Court, Justice Thomas has been a consistent vote against advancing protections and rights for minorities in such cases as *Shaw v. Reno, Ledbetter v. Goodyear, Shelby County v. Holder,* and *Obergefell v. Hodges.* That President Bush felt a need to replace Thurgood Marshall with another African

American indicates the symbolic importance of descriptive representation on the courts. However, that Thomas has not been an advocate for minorities demonstrates that descriptive representation is not enough. Although there are African Americans who share Thomas's perspective, they are a numeric minority. Thus, he cannot be said to offer much substantive representation for minorities. The levels of descriptive representation in the federal and state courts, what affects it, and whether it affects policy representation are key issues of this chapter.

The judicial branch has an important role to play in minority representation. As the trial courts adjudicate justice involving minorities, they can treat minorities fairly or treat them unfairly. Much has been written about the effects of the defendant's race on sentencing, and scholars find that African American defendants

This photo depicts Thurgood Marshall when he was chief counsel for the NAACP. He later became the first African American Supreme Court justice. (© *Bettmann/Corbis*)

tend to get tougher sentences than white defendants.[2] The Supreme Court when it engages in judicial review has the ability to make policy that affects minorities. The Court can make policy that is detrimental to minorities as it did in *Bowers v. Hardwick* (1986)[3] or it can advance minority rights as it did in *Lawrence v. Texas* (2003)[4] (see below for discussion of the cases). In addition, when the courts interpret what the law means and how to apply it, it can expand or limit the rights of minorities. For example, when the Court ruled that the Civil Rights Act focuses on the effects not the intent of a law, it made it easier for minorities to win discrimination suits since it is easier to demonstrate the effect of a law than to demonstrate the intentions of legislators because there are many legislators, each with their own intention. This chapter briefly describes the federal courts, outlines the levels of descriptive representation in the courts, discusses what affects descriptive representation in the courts, and whether descriptive representation affects policy representation. The chapter ends with a brief description of several important cases involving minority rights. The key lessons of this chapter are: African Americans and women have more descriptive representation on the federal bench than they do in Congress; the diversity of state benches is affected by the selection process and state characteristics; and diversity of the federal bench is affected by time and party of president. Other key lessons are: although minority judges' decisions are similar to those of nonminority judges, panel effects are more noticeable, and while at times the Supreme Court has been a protector of minority rights, at other times it has not. Thus, any blanket statement about the Court as a protector of minorities misses the variation in the Court's decisions.

The Court Systems

The United States has a dual court system, meaning that there are state courts and federal courts. State courts solve conflicts arising from state law, and the federal courts solve conflicts arising from federal law. Regardless of the level, there are two main powers of the courts: *statutory interpretation* and *judicial review.* **Judicial review** is the power the courts have to determine if an action taken by the other branches of government violates the Constitution. This clearly gives the courts policy power, as it can block a policy with its decision. **Statutory interpretation** occurs when the courts determine what the law means. As they interpret the law, they can indicate what the policy really means. For example, in *Ledbetter v. Goodyear Tire and Rubber Company,*[5] the Court was asked to interpret the Civil Rights Act's provision that to bring a suit the discrimination had to occur within 180 days of the time of the complaint. At issue was whether the discrimination occurred with each paycheck or at the point of hire. When the Court ruled it was at the point of hire, it limited the ability of people to sue. Judicial review and statutory construction, or interpretation, are particularly noteworthy since the Constitution and many laws are vague and open to interpretation. For example, Title VII (42 U.S.C. § 2000e-2[e][1]) of the Civil Rights Act prevents discrimination unless there is a "bona fide occupational qualification reasonably necessary to the normal operation of that particular business or enterprise." What one person sees as reasonably necessary or as a bona fide occupational qualification may not be what another person sees as reasonable and bona fide. Or, as was discussed in Chapter 3, how the Court interpreted the equal protection clause of the Fourteenth Amendment determines what it means for the daily lives of Americans.

In addition to the U.S. state and federal courts, there are tribal courts. One type of tribal court is traditional courts, which can include religious courts, and make decisions based on tribal custom and are less formal than U.S. courts. There are about twenty such courts.[6] There are also about twenty Courts of Indian Offenses or Code of Federal Regulations courts.[7] They were originally created to help assimilate American Indians starting in the nineteenth century, but today mostly exist where tribes lack a tribal court. Finally, there about 150 tribal courts that deal with civil and criminal conflicts within tribes.[8]

To understand the role of the federal courts in minority politics, it is essential to understand the three main types of federal courts in the United States. First, there are the **district courts.** There are ninety-four of these trial courts, with each state having at least one. These courts examine the facts of a case and the law to determine outcomes. These can be criminal cases, where it is determined whether the defendant violated the law and what his or her sentence should be. Trial courts can also hear civil cases, where a plaintiff sues a defendant for damages the plaintiff incurred because of the defendant's actions, such as suing an employer for discrimination. In either type of case, there is one judge who oversees the trial, with either the judge or a jury determining the outcome.

The next level of court includes the **appellate courts.** There are thirteen different Circuit Courts of Appeals that examine previous decisions for mistakes of law. Twelve of the circuit courts have general jurisdiction over appeals arising from district courts in the region. The thirteenth circuit court, which is called the United States Court of Appeals for the Federal Circuit, has nationwide jurisdiction but hears only specialized cases on subjects such as international trade, patents, and veterans' benefits. Appellate courts are mostly concerned with procedure at the lower level or whether the Constitution was violated. This can include compliance with the equal protection clause or other protections for minorities. For example, in district-level discrimination cases that were decided against the plaintiff (the person bringing charges), the plaintiff may ask the appeals court to review the decision. In each circuit there is a pool of judges from which three judges are selected to hear each individual case.

The highest court is the **U.S. Supreme Court.** It is currently made up of nine justices who hear cases en banc. That is, all nine justices hear each case. The vast majority of Supreme Court cases have already been heard at the intermediate appellate level. When a case is appealed to the Supreme Court, the Court has the option of whether or not to hear the case. Only about 100 to 150 out of the 7,000 cases brought to the Court are selected for review.[9] After the Court hears a case, it announces its decision and lays out its reasoning in the majority opinion. These opinions establish precedent and indicate to the lower courts how laws and the Constitution should be interpreted. Some justices may agree with the decision but have different reasons for coming to the same conclusion. They would write what is called a concurring opinion. On rare occasions, no majority is formed for the purposes of writing the majority opinion. In these cases there is a plurality opinion, meaning it is the opinion with the most support but not a majority of support. These decisions have less ability to establish precedent. Justices who disagree with the majority decision often write a dissenting opinion that lays out why they came to a different conclusion. Although concurring and dissenting opinions do not have the precedent power of the majority opinion, occasionally they will be used by future Courts. A good example of this is Powell's concurring opinion in *Regents of the University of California v. Bakke,* 428 U.S. 265 (1978). In the *Bakke* case, the Court ruled that universities cannot use quotas as they try to increase diversity. The majority opinion did not indicate whether or not diversity was a compelling interest (remember this term from the discussion of strict scrutiny in Chapter 3) in education. In Powell's concurring opinion, he said that although he thinks quotas violate the equal protection clause, he did think diversity in education was a compelling interest. In later decisions concerning affirmative action in education, the Court has used Powell's concurring opinion.

The *U.S. v. Windsor,* 570 U.S. ___ (2013), case and its aftermath illustrate many of these points. In this case, the Court struck down the Defense of Marriage Act (DOMA), which prevented the federal government from recognizing same-sex marriages performed in states that recognize them. The Court's reasoning rested on both equal protection grounds and federalism. It reinforced that regulating marriages is a state not a federal power and interpreted the equal protection clause to mean that gays and lesbians had rights. After the decision, gay and lesbian couples living in states that did not recognize their marriages filed suit, saying the state law violated the equal protection clause. In these states, the district courts heard the cases and, relying on the *Windsor* case, ruled that the state laws violated the equal protection clause. In many of these cases, the state did not like the decision and asked the appellate courts to review the lower courts' decisions. After several appellate courts heard cases on appeal, most but not all ruled in favor of same-sex marriages. To resolve the conflict between the appellate courts, in April 2015, SCOTUS heard four cases on the issue.

The four cases were combined into the *Obergefell v. Hodges* decision. On June 26, 2015, the second anniversary of the *Windsor* case, the Court ruled that the Fourteenth Amendment's due process clause protects same-sex couples' right to marry because marriage is a fundamental right protected by the Fourteenth Amendment, and the Court found no difference between this right for same-sex and opposite-sex couples.[10] The equal protection clause was also used in the case since to deny same-sex couples the fundamental right to marry would deny them equal protection. Justice Kennedy wrote the opinion that was signed by five justices. The other four justices came to a different conclusion. Generally, they argued that the Constitution does not address the issues of same-sex marriage, and the issue should be left to the states.

Descriptive Representation: The Numbers Game

Most minorities have more proportional representation in the judicial branch than in the executive or legislative branches. This is perhaps most true with regard to African Americans. There has been at least one African American justice (11%) on the Supreme Court since 1967 when *Thurgood Marshall* became the first African American Supreme Court justice (see Spotlight 6.1). The only other African American Supreme Court justice has been Clarence Thomas. African Americans are slightly better represented on the other federal courts. Thirteen percent of district and appellate court judges are African American.[11] With 13% of Americans being African American, African Americans have fairly proportional representation in the federal courts.

Spotlight 6.1

Justice Thurgood Marshall

Whether as a lawyer, the chief legal counsel for the National Association for the Advancement of Colored People (NAACP), the Solicitor General of the United States, or a Supreme Court justice, Thurgood Marshall was a central figure in many of the most important Supreme Court cases in the twentieth century. He dedicated much of his life to ending Jim Crow laws.

At the NAACP, he helped establish the NAACP Legal Defense and Education Fund, Inc. (Inc Fund) and had thirty-six victories before the Supreme Court,[12] including some of the most important cases of his generation: *Shelley v. Kraemer, Smith v. Allwright,* and of course, *Brown v. Board of Education of Topeka*.

In 1961, President John F. Kennedy nominated Marshall to be an appellate judge for the prestigious second district. The confirmation took longer than most judgeships of the day, about eight months, due to the resistance of Southern Democrats. He had served as an appellate judge for about four years when President Lyndon B. Johnson nominated him for solicitor general. As solicitor general, he faced the Supreme Court nineteen times and won fourteen cases. Some of these were key civil rights cases, such as *Katzenbach v. Morgan* and *Harper v. Virginia Board of Elections*.

In 1967, President Johnson nominated Marshall to the Supreme Court. Although his confirmation was fairly quick, many people still opposed it. Southern Democrats opposed the nomination, claiming he was too liberal and an activist. Some criticized his nomination

on intellectual grounds. The liberal *New Republic* magazine wrote: "Mr. Marshall's performance [in the federal court and as solicitor general] was often less than brilliant."[13] Also, the Student Nonviolent Coordinating Committee (SNCC), which had become more radical and part of the black power movement, opposed the nomination. Marshall was seen as too conservative since he opposed the more militant wing of the civil rights movement and was staunchly anticommunist.

Justice Marshall had a judicial philosophy that was opposed by the growing number of conservative justices. He saw the Constitution in contextual terms, that its meaning changes with the times. He also saw what he considered racist behavior on the part of his brethren and was not afraid to point this out. He felt many of his brethren did not understand the realities of life for most Americans. As a consequence, he saw himself as an outsider.

In 1991, Justice Marshall retired from the Supreme Court and died two years later. He was an ambitious man who served the nation by working for people being denied their rights. This was dangerous work, and he faced much criticism, some involving death threats. One thing that helped him get through was his sense of humor.

Source: The information for this Spotlight comes from Howard Ball, *A Defiant Life: Thurgood Marshall and the Persistence of Racism in America* (New York: Crown, 1998).

Women, too, see greater representation in the judicial than in the executive or legislative branches. Since 1981, there has been at least one woman on the Court, and currently there are three. The first woman on the Supreme Court was *Sandra Day O'Connor*, who was appointed in 1981 by President Ronald Reagan and served until 2006. She can best be described as a moderate jurist who was often a swing vote. Today, the three women justices are Ruth Bader Ginsberg, Elena Kagan, and Sonia Sotomayor. This translates into one-third of SCOTUS being female. This is roughly the percentage of women on the district and appellate courts as well.[14] These figures are similar to the average number of justices on European supreme courts but higher than those found in Latin America. See Spotlight 6.2 for more information on women judges in Europe. Although women have greater parity in the courts than Congress, they still are noticeably underrepresented.

Spotlight 6.2

Women Judges in Europe and the Americas

Worldwide, about 27% of justices in nations' top courts are women.[15] The percentages vary dramatically by nation. In Latin America, for example, over 60% of the Eastern Caribbean Supreme Court justices are women, while none of the justices in Panama's or Uruguay's top court are women.[16] To the north of the United States, in Canada, four of the nine justices are women.[17] Generally, in the Western Hemisphere the number of women justices has grown in recent years. For example, while Brazil did not have any women in its top court in 1998, by 2010, 18% were women.[18]

Europe's rate of women judges is similar to that of the United States, 34%.[19] In 2012, Romania, Bulgaria, Luxembourg, Hungary, Latvia, Slovakia, Slovenia, and Sweden had more than 40% women judges.[20] In other nations, such as United Kingdom, Cyprus, and Portugal, the percentages of women judges on the top courts were in the single digits.[21] As in Latin America, Europe has seen a growth in the number of women judges. The yearly growth rate between 2007 and 2012 has averaged 0.7%.[22] However, only nine out of sixty-four presidents of top national courts were women in 2012.[23]

In addition to the national top courts, Europe also has two courts associated with the European Union (EU): the Court of Justice and the General Court. The Court of Justice interprets EU laws, and the general court deals with conflicts between parties. In these courts, only 20% of justices were women.[24] The Court of Justice, which is the highest of the courts, had only 15% women justices.[25]

Many nations outside of the Western Hemisphere have done well diversifying their top courts. Over 40% of the justices in Central Asia and in Central and Eastern Europe are women.[26] In developed nations the percentages are around 30, and in sub-Saharan Africa the percentage of women justices nears the world average. In the Middle East, East Asia, and the Pacific, the numbers are just below the world average. South Asia has the lowest percentage of women judges, less than 10%.[27]

One of the main impediments to women gaining top judgeships is the "good old boys' club."[28] Since most nations use executive or legislative appointments, that women lawyers tend to be less connected to power sources depresses their advancement. Where merit examinations are used to make appointments, women tend to make up a larger percentage of the judgeships.[29]

Having women judges is important. "Women's representation in the judiciary is a matter of equality and fairness, but it is also important for maintaining public confidence in the justice system. There is evidence that women judges can create more conducive environments for women in courts and can make a difference to outcomes."[30]

The representation of Hispanics in the judicial branch is fairly similar to their representation on the legislative branch, and their numbers have grown in recent years. The first and only Hispanic to serve on the Supreme Court is *Sonia Sotomayor*, who was nominated by President Obama in 2009 (see Spotlight 6.3). The other federal courts have a smaller percentage of Hispanic judges. About 10% of district judges and 8% of appellate judges are Hispanic.[31]

Spotlight 6.3

Justice Sonia Sotomayor

In 2009, when Justice David Souter announced his retirement, President Barack Obama nominated Sonia Sotomayor to replace him. In addition to her vast legal experience (prosecutor, private practice, federal district judge, and appeals judge), one of the reasons she was selected was President Obama wanted his nominee to have real-life experiences and empathy.[32] Which she has. She was born in 1954 to first-generation Puerto Ricans and grew up in the projects in the Bronx. Her father died when she was young, and she grew up with a childhood illness, diabetes. Nevertheless, she excelled at school and was able to attend Princeton as an undergraduate and then went on to Yale Law School. At both schools she was one of only a handful of women and Hispanic students. Also, at both schools she saw and fought discrimination.

During her confirmation, Sonia Sotomayor was criticized for saying "I would hope that a wise Latina woman with the richness of her experiences would more often than not reach a better conclusion than a white male who hasn't lived that life."[33] Her statement led to fears she would be an activist justice who followed her personal views instead of the law. However, the point of her comment was to inspire women of color and suggest that having judges with different life experiences is important for justice.

Eventually, she would be confirmed with the support of sixty-eight senators and become the third woman and the first Hispanic justice on the Supreme Court. As a consequence, women and Hispanic groups hoped she would give them a voice on the Court. And on the Court she has made decisions that protected affirmative action, the Voting Rights Act, and advanced LGBT rights; as an appellate judge her decisions were constrained by precedent, and she was more moderate.

To understand Justice Sotomayor's rise to power and the likely role she will play on the Court, it is important to realize the interplay of race and ethnicity. Her experiences growing up Puerto Rican in the Bronx are very different from those of Justice Elena Kagan, who grew up on the West side of Manhattan, or of Justice Ruth Bader Ginsburg, who grew up in Brooklyn, both of whom are Jewish. For example, while Justice Ginsburg's legal career distinguished her as an advocate for women's rights, Justice Sotomayor's career has been more marked by her advocacy for racial and ethnic minority rights. That Justice Sotomayor is Puerto Rican also distinguishes her from Hispanics who are Cuban, Mexican, Central American, or South American. The story of Justice Sotomayor indicates the value and limits of descriptive representation for policy representation. She is a wise Latina whose life of experience influences her decisions, yet as a judge she is also constrained by the law.

There are three exceptions to the trend of minorities having at least somewhat better or equivalent descriptive representation in the judicial than the legislative branch: American Indians, LGBT Americans, and Asian Americans.

There has never been an American Indian on the Supreme Court, and currently there is only one American Indian serving on the federal courts. In May 2014, Diane Humetewa became the first woman American Indian, and only the third American Indian to serve on the federal courts, when she was confirmed by the Senate to serve the Arizona district court.[34] LGBT Americans have slightly more proportional representation than American Indians. Although no openly LGBT has ever served on the Supreme Court, as of June 2014 nine LGBT judges have served on a district court and one on an appeals court. The first LGBT federal judge was Deborah Batts, appointed by President Bill Clinton.[35] President George W. Bush did not appoint any LGBT judges to the federal courts. In 2013, President Barack Obama appointed and the Senate confirmed Todd M. Hughes, the first LGBT judge on the court of appeals. As for Asian Americans, in May 2015 there were only four appellate Asian American judges, twenty-seven district judges, and no Supreme Court justices.[36]

Looking at the percentage of women and men of color on the bench indicates no clear pattern of women of color having more or less proportional representation than white women, although they are less likely to be on the bench than their male counterparts. On the district courts, minority women have levels of representation closer to that of their male counterparts than white women. About 22% of active district judges are white women, 6% are African American women, 1.6% are Asian American women, 3.6% are Hispanic women; and there is only one American Indian woman.[37] For men the percentages are 51%, 8%, 2%, and 7%. On the U.S. Court of Appeals, the percentage of white women is closer to the percentage of white men than the percentages of women of color to percentages of men of color. Among active judges, 29% are white women, 4% are African American women, .6% Asian women, 1.8% Hispanic women, 49% white men, 8% African American men, 1.8% Asian men, and 6% Hispanic men.[38]

In addition to judges and justices, other key judicial positions are the attorney general and the solicitor general. The attorney general heads up the Justice Department and is the chief law enforcement officer, often giving legal advice to the president and representing the government in court.[39] More will be said about the descriptive representation of the executive branch in Chapter 7, but in 2015 Loretta Lynch became the first African American woman attorney general when she replaced Eric Holder, who was also African American. Another key position is the solicitor general, who supervises and conducts cases involving the United States that are heard by SCOTUS and "is involved in approximately two-thirds of all the cases the U.S. Supreme Court decides on the merits each year."[40] The solicitors general present more oral arguments before the Supreme Court than any other person. They also decide which cases are appealed by the United States and whether the government will file amici curiae briefs. The number of Supreme Court justices who have been solicitor general evidences the importance of this role. For example, Justices John Roberts and Elena Kagan were solicitors general, as was Thurgood Marshall. Thurgood Marshall was the first African American to serve as solicitor general, from August 1965 to August 1967. Since Marshall, other African American solicitors general include Wade H. McCree Jr. (March 1977– August 1981) and Drew Days (May 1993–July 1996). Elena Kagan (March 2009–August 2010) is the only woman to have held the post.

Women and LGBT Americans appear to fare as well or slightly better in state supreme courts, while racial and ethnic groups appear to fare slightly worse. About 35% of state supreme court justices are women and 2.1% of the justices are LGBT jurists.[41] African Americans, on the other hand, hold only 7.1% of state supreme court judgeships and Hispanics 3.2%. American Indians hold 0.3% and Asian Americans 2.5% of state supreme court judgeships. As with state legislative positions, the appearance of lower levels of racial and ethnic representation on the court is due to minorities being highly concentrated in a handful of states.

Table 6.1 lists the states and the ratio of African American, Hispanic, Asian American, American Indian, LGBT, and women judges on state supreme courts. The ratios are calculated by dividing the percentage of supreme court justices who are a minority by the percentage of that minority in the population. For example, if 10% of a state's supreme court justices are women and 50% of the state's population is female, then the state would have a ratio of 0.20. This table indicates that there are a handful of states where minorities are overrepresented on the state supreme court, due in part to the small number of supreme court justices. Courts with few justices can have a high percentage of minorities with only one or two minorities on the bench. For example, although Connecticut has only one African American supreme court judge, its ratio is 1.39. It may also be that governors like to appoint minorities to the most visible positions as a way to reach out to minority voters. At lower levels of state courts there is a clearer underrepresentation of minorities throughout the states.[42]

What Affects Descriptive Representation in the Judicial Branch?

To understand what affects the level of descriptive representation in the judicial branch one needs to understand how judges are selected. In the federal judiciary, judges are nominated by the president and then confirmed by the Senate. Thus, a significant influence on the appointment of minority judges is the president. As a rule, Democratic presidents are more likely to nominate minorities than are Republicans. Table 6.2 indicates the nominations of minority judges since President Jimmy Carter. Carter was the first president to try to diversify the courts, so his presidency is a good starting point. The table lists the number of appointments the president made to the appeals and district courts, as well as the number of minority judge appointments made to each type of court. As the table makes clear, Democratic presidents—Carter, Clinton, and Obama—are more likely to appoint gender, race, and ethnic minorities. For example, while Presidents Carter, Clinton,

TABLE 6.1 Ratio of Percentage of Minorities on State Supreme Courts to Percentage of Minorities in the Population

	African Americans	Hispanics	Women	LGBT	American Indian	Asian American
Alabama	0.00 (0)	0.00 (0)	0.64 (33)	0.00 (0)	0.00 (0)	0.00 (0)
Alaska	0.00 (0)	0.00 (0)	0.83 (40)	0.00 (0)	0.00 (0)	0.00 (0)
Arizona	0.00 (0)	0.00 (0)	0.40 (20)	0.00 (0)	0.00 (0)	0.00 (0)
Arkansas	0.00 (0)	0.00 (0)	0.57 (29)	0.00 (0)	0.00 (0)	0.00 (0)
California	0.00 (0)	0.00 (0)	1.13 (57)	0.00 (0)	0.00 (0)	1.95 (29)
Colorado	0.00 (0)	0.68 (14)	0.83 (43)	4.38 (14)	0.00 (0)	0.00 (0)
Connecticut	1.39 (14)	1.04 (14)	0.29 (14)	4.12 (14)	0.00 (0)	0.00 (0)
Delaware	0.00 (0)	0.00 (0)	0.39 (20)	0.00 (0)	0.00 (0)	0.00 (0)
Florida	1.81 (29)	0.62 (14)	0.57 (29)	0.00 (0)	0.00 (0)	0.00 (0)
Georgia	0.95 (29)	0.00 (0)	0.27 (14)	0.00 (0)	0.00 (0)	0.00 (0)
Hawaii	0.00 (0)	0.00 (0)	0.80 (40)	3.92 (20)	0.00 (0)	1.05 (60)
Idaho	0.00 (0)	0.00 (0)	0.00 (0)	0.00 (0)	0.00 (0)	0.00 (0)
Illinois	0.97 (14)	0.00 (0)	0.84 (43)	0.00 (0)	0.00 (0)	0.00 (0)
Indiana	2.20 (20)	0.00 (0)	0.00 (0)	0.00 (0)	0.00 (0)	0.00 (0)
Iowa	0.00 (0)	0.00 (0)	0.00 (0)	0.00 (0)	0.00 (0)	0.00 (0)
Kansas	0.00 (0)	0.00 (0)	0.84 (43)	0.00 (0)	0.00 (0)	0.00 (0)
Kentucky	0.00 (0)	0.00 (0)	0.57 (29)	0.00 (0)	0.00 (0)	0.00 (0)
Louisiana	0.44 (14)	0.00 (0)	0.84 (43)	0.00 (0)	0.00 (0)	0.00 (0)
Maine	0.00 (0)	0.00 (0)	0.57 (29)	0.00 (0)	0.00 (0)	0.00 (0)
Maryland	0.99 (29)	0.00 (0)	0.83 (43)	0.00 (0)	0.00 (0)	0.00 (0)
Massachusetts	2.12 (14)	0.00 (0)	0.83 (43)	3.18 (14)	0.00 (0)	2.33 (14)
Michigan	0.99 (14)	0.00 (0)	0.84 (43)	0.00 (0)	0.00 (0)	0.00 (0)
Minnesota	5.58 (29)	0.00 (0)	0.57 (29)	0.00 (0)	0.00 (0)	0.00 (0)
Mississippi	0.30 (11)	0.00 (0)	0.21 (11)	0.00 (0)	0.00 (0)	0.00 (0)
Missouri	1.21 (14)	0.00 (0)	0.84 (43)	0.00 (0)	0.00 (0)	0.00 (0)
Montana	0.00 (0)	0.00 (0)	0.58 (29)	0.00 (0)	0.00 (0)	0.00 (0)
Nebraska	0.00 (0)	0.00 (0)	0.27 (14)	0.00 (0)	0.00 (0)	0.00 (0)
Nevada	1.73 (14)	0.00 (0)	0.59 (29)	0.00 (0)	0.00 (0)	0.00 (0)

	African Americans	Hispanics	Women	LGBT	American Indian	Asian American
New Hampshire	0.00 (0)	0.00 (0)	0.79 (40)	0.00 (0)	0.00 (0)	0.00 (0)
New Jersey	0.00 (0)	0.80 (14)	0.84 (43)	0.00 (0)	0.00 (0)	0.00 (0)
New Mexico	0.00 (0)	1.30 (60)	0.40 (20)	0.00 (0)	0.00 (0)	0.00 (0)
New York	0.88 (14)	0.80 (14)	0.83 (43)	0.00 (0)	0.00 (0)	0.00 (0)
North Carolina	0.65 (14)	0.00 (0)	1.11 (57)	0.00 (0)	0.00 (0)	0.00 (0)
North Dakota	0.00 (0)	0.00 (0)	0.81 (40)	0.00 (0)	0.00 (0)	0.00 (0)
Ohio	0.00 (0)	0.00 (0)	1.11 (57)	0.00 (0)	0.00 (0)	0.00 (0)
Oklahoma*	1.49 (11)	0.00 (0)	0.44 (22)	0.00 (0)	1.22 (11)	0.00 (0)
Oregon	0.00 (0)	0.00 (0)	0.57 (29)	0.00 (0)	0.00 (0)	0.00 (0)
Pennsylvania	0.00 (0)	0.00 (0)	0.57 (29)	0.00 (0)	0.00 (0)	0.00 (0)
Rhode Island	0.00 (0)	0.00 (0)	0.39 (20)	0.00 (0)	0.00 (0)	0.00 (0)
South Carolina	0.72 (20)	0.00 (0)	0.78 (40)	0.00 (0)	0.00 (0)	0.00 (0)
South Dakota	0.00 (0)	0.00 (0)	0.40 (20)	0.00 (0)	0.00 (0)	0.00 (0)
Tennessee	0.00 (0)	0.00 (0)	1.17 (60)	0.00 (0)	0.00 (0)	0.00 (0)
Texas*	0.00 (0)	0.29 (11)	0.44 (22)	0.00 (0)	0.00 (0)	0.00 (0)
Utah	0.00 (0)	0.00 (0)	0.80 (40)	0.00 (0)	0.00 (0)	0.00 (0)
Vermont	0.00 (0)	0.00 (0)	0.79 (40)	5.10 (25)	0.00 (0)	0.00 (0)
Virginia	1.49 (29)	1.39 (11)	0.29 (14)	0.00 (0)	0.00 (0)	0.00 (0)
Washington	0.00 (0)	0.00 (0)	0.88 (44)	0.00 (0)	0.00 (0)	0.00 (0)
West Virginia	0.00 (0)	0.00 (0)	0.79 (40)	0.00 (0)	0.00 (0)	0.00 (0)
Wisconsin	0.00 (0)	0.00 (0)	1.13 (57)	0.00 (0)	0.00 (0)	0.00 (0)
Wyoming	0.00 (0)	0.00 (0)	0.41 (20)	0.00 (0)	0.00 (0)	0.00 (0)
Average	0.52 (7)	0.12 (3)	0.63 (32)	0.33 (2)	0.22 (.02)	0.11 (2)

Sources: http://ialgbtj.org/; http://www.judicialselection.us/judicial_selection/bench_diversity/index.cfm?state=; Elizabeth M. Hoeffel, and Sonya Rastogi, Myong Ouk Kim, and Hasan Shahid, "The Asian Population: 2010," 2010 Census Briefs, March 2012; Sonya Rastogi, Tallese D. Johnson, Elizabeth M. Hoeffel, and Malcolm P. Drewery, Jr., "The Black Population: 2010," 2010 Census Briefs, September 2011; and Sharon R. Ennis, Merarys Rios-Vergas, and Nora G. Albert, "Hispanic Population: Census Brief 2010," May 2011 (available from http://www.census.gov/). U.S. Census data as found at http://www.indexmundi.com/facts/united-states/quick-facts/all-states/female-population-percentage#table. Gary Gates and Frank Newport, "LGBT Percentage Highest in D.C., Lowest in North Dakota," February 15, 2013, http://www.gallup.com/poll/160517/lgbt-percentage-highest-lowest-north-dakota.aspx.

*Oklahoma and Texas have two state supreme courts; these figures do not include their Court of Criminal Appeals. Numbers in parenthesis are the percentage of minorities on the bench.

TABLE 6.2   Presidential Appointment of Minorities to the Appeals and District Courts

	Carter	Reagan	GHW Bush	Clinton	GW Bush	Obama*
Appeals						
Total	56	83	42	66	62	53
African Americans	9	1	2	9	6	9
Hispanics	2	1	2	7	3	4
Asian Americans	1	2	0	1	0	4
Women	11	6	7	20	17	23
District						
Total	203	290	148	305	261	233
African Americans	28	6	10	53	18	46
Hispanics	14	13	6	18	27	27
Asian Americans	2	2	0	4	4	16
American Indians	1	0	0	1	0	1
Women	29	24	29	88	54	99

Source: Calculated by author from Federal Judiciary Center data, http://www.uscourts.gov/JudgesAndJudgeships/BiographicalDirectory OfJudges.aspx.

*As of November 30, 2014. Figures are raw numbers.

and Obama each appointed nine African Americans to the court of appeals, this is the same number as appointed by both Bush presidents and Reagan combined. The table also indicates that as time passes more and more minorities are nominated to the federal courts. For example, on the Democratic side, Carter appointed twenty-nine women to district courts, Clinton eighty-eight, and Obama ninety-nine. On the Republican side, Reagan appointed twenty-four, George H. W. Bush twenty-nine, and George W. Bush fifty-four.

Making generalizations about the selection of minority judges to state courts is more complex since states differ in how they select judges. Some states select judges much the way the federal government selects judges; with the chief executive, in this case the governor, making a nomination and the legislature confirming it. Some states use a merit system, also called the Missouri plan. With a merit system, a commission makes a short list of candidates, then the governor selects someone from the list. Since this system lacks a legislative confirmation process, these judges will face the electorate in a retention election every few years. In retention elections, voters just vote whether or not they want the judge to remain on the bench. If a judge is voted out, the governor will appoint another judge.

Some states have nonpartisan elections of judges; some partisan elections and some states use some combination of these systems. In addition, two states have legislative selection where the legislature selects judges.

The research examining whether one system or another is more likely to select minority judges has been inconclusive. A reason there is not one system that is best is because the effects of selection processes are contextual. Williams's research suggests that the effects of the selection process depend on the level of court.[43] She finds that states with nonpartisan elections see more women on the trial courts, and those with merit plans see fewer women on the appellate courts. Bratton and Spill find that the governor's party and the makeup of the court affect which selection method is best. They find women are more likely to be seated to an open state judgeship through the appointment process, but this is contingent on there being a Democratic governor and the court being all male.[44] Frederick and Strebs find that at the appellate level in the early 2000s, women judicial candidates are as likely, if not slightly more likely, to win than men judicial candidates.[45]

Opportunity may also affect the seating of minorities on the courts. A larger number of positions on a court may depress the prestige of the court, and minorities may be more likely to be selected for less prestigious judgeships. Also, just by odds, a bench with twenty judges is more likely to have a minority member than a bench with ten judges. Research confirms that minority judges are more likely to be appointed or elected to larger benches. The number of judgeships affects the percentage of women on the courts—the more district and appellate seats, the higher the percentage of women who fill those seats,[46] and the more seats a state has on its supreme court, the sooner it was to seat a woman or a racial/ethnic minority on its supreme court.[47]

The legal experiences of minorities, too, affect their representation on the courts. First, the ability of minorities to become lawyers is critical. The proportion of minority lawyers in a state affects the number of minority judges.[48] Although in recent years the number of minority lawyers has increased, currently only about 10% of lawyers are racial or ethnic minorities, and only about one-third of lawyers are female. These small percentages limit the ability of minorities to be appointed to judgeships.[49] What affects the likelihood that minority lawyers become judges is whether minority lawyers get prestigious legal jobs. Historically, white males have dominated top legal jobs. For example, women lawyers make only about 75% as much money as men lawyers.

Minority lawyers are also likely to become judges only if they have the ambition to do so. Jensen and Martinek find women and African American trial judges in New York have as much if not more ambition to be on the appellate court.[50] However, Williams finds lawyers and judges in Texas believe there are more barriers to women becoming judges.[51] Such beliefs can discourage women from seeking judicial positions.

Conditions within a state can also affect the descriptive representation of the judicial branch. The culture of a state can affect the proportion of minorities on the state courts. Williams, for example, finds that liberal states have more women judges on the district, but not the appellate courts.[52] Goelzhauser finds state ideology interacts with selection systems to affect when minority judges are seated on state supreme courts.[53] He finds that liberal states that use an appointment process seated their first African American and female judge sooner than more conservative states that use an appointment process. Liberal states that use partisan elections seated their first African American, but not female, supreme court judge sooner than conservative states. But ideology had no effect on the seating of minority judges where there are nonpartisan elections. Hurwitz and Lanier find that states with liberal elites have more African American judges (except on the supreme court), and that state ideology interacts with the selection system such that liberal states with the merit system have more African American judges than conservative states with merit systems.[54] Gruski, Zuk, and Barrows as well as Goelzhauser find that the more African American voters there are in a state, the more African American federal district court judges serve that state.[55] Further, Goelzhauser finds that states with strong economies have more Hispanic judges. Thus, more minorities are on the bench in states that use executive appointments and nonpartisan elections, and states with strong economies and a liberal populous may have more minority judges.

Descriptive and Substantive Representation in the Courts

Does the presence of minority judges result in decisions more favorable to minority interests? The behavior of the current U.S. Supreme Court justices would not offer a clear answer to the question. Although many of the white men justices, such as Antonin Scalia, Samuel Alito, Stephen Breyer, and John Roberts, tend to vote against minority interests, they have been joined by Justice Clarence Thomas. Conversely, while the women justices are a dependable vote for minority interests, they are often joined by Justice Anthony Kennedy. In addition, historically some white men justices have been defenders of minority rights, such as Chief Justice Earl Warren. In addition, Justice Sandra Day O'Connor was a swing vote on the Court and sometimes advanced minority rights, and sometimes did not. Part of the reason it is difficult to generalize about justices' behavior based on race, ethnicity, or gender is that presidents will select judges who match their ideology. O'Connor and Thomas were nominated by Republicans, while Marshall, Ginsburg, Sotomayor, and Kagan were nominated by Democrats.

There are two ways minority judges can affect policy representation. Keep in mind that the Constitution and laws are vague, and how they are interpreted affects their implications for society. The first is by making decisions that differ from their counterparts. Much like minority legislators have an interest in helping protect minorities, minority judges may as well. However, unlike legislators, their decisions are constrained by the law and the precedents in interpreting the law. The other way, often called **panel effects**, concerns how in a panel of judges the

The current justices are (seated) Clarence Thomas, Antonin Scalia, John Roberts, Anthony Kennedy, and Ruth Bader Ginsburg; and (standing) Sonia Sotomayor, Stephen Breyer, Samuel Alito, and Elena Kagan. (*Courtesy of Steve Petteway, Collection of the Supreme Court of the United States*)

presence of a minority judge will affect other judges' decisions. There are three mechanisms that can contribute to a panel effect:[56] deliberation (minorities offer unique information), votes (that a judge votes in one direction can encourage others to vote likewise), and presence (the presence of a minority judge may affect other judges' votes). For example, having a minority judge on the bench may affect how nonminority judges see the case or understand its effects.

The evidence on whether minority judges make decisions beneficial to minority policy interests is very much mixed. The research on women trial judges at the local level finds that women judges are less patriarchal and tend to be tougher on women defendants, sending women to prison for longer terms.[57] At the appellate level, Boyd, Epstein, and Martin examined thirteen different policy areas, and the only area where they found men and women judges to differ is in the area of sex discrimination, with women judges being more likely to find that sex discrimination occurred.[58] Similarly, Songer, Davis, and Haire find women appellate judges vote in a more liberal direction on employment discrimination but do not differ from men on obscenity and search and seizure cases.[59] Segal, too, finds little effect of gender on judicial behavior.[60] She examines federal district judges who were appointed by Clinton and finds women judges LESS supportive of women's issues and personal liberty, more supportive of African American issues, and not differing from men in other minority issues, criminal rights, and federal economic regulation. For example, while 26.5% of women judges supported women's issues, 50% of men judges did, for African American issues the difference was 37.1% to 17.5%, and for personal liberties it was 49.3% to 35.6%.[61] Songer and Crews-Meyer examine women state supreme court justices and find women vote in a more liberal direction on civil liberty and death penalty cases; and Farhang and Wawro find that women appellate judges' decisions, compared to men's, are more liberal on employment discrimination cases.[62]

The research concerning African American judges has also been mixed. Segal's examination of Clinton's appointees finds that African American judges are not significantly more supportive of African American issues, women's issues, other minority issues, criminal rights, or federal economic regulations than white judges. For example, 31.8% of African American judges and 29.5% of white judges voted in favor of African American issues.[63] The largest difference she found was that African American judges were more likely to oppose, not support, civil liberty claims, 28.4% to 45.6%.[64] Farhang and Wawro find African American federal appellate judges do not differ from white judges in their decisions on discrimination cases.[65] But, Kastellec finds African American appellate judges to be more supportive of affirmative action than non-African American judges.[66] Cox and Miles find African American judges more likely to make liberal decisions concerning the Voting Rights Act, and Scherer finds African American judges to be more liberal on search and seizure cases.[67]

Some research examines sentencing and conviction rates of judges and finds African American judges are more equitable in their treatment of defendants,[68] and others find no difference at all.[69] There is less research on whether minority women judges are unique in their decisions, but there is some evidence that minority women judges are more likely to support criminal defendants.[70] Bonneau and Rice suggest that part of the reason for the mixed findings is that the research examines different times and places, and that race differences are most likely to occur where the court has greater control over its docket.[71] They examine whether appellate judges vote to overturn convictions, or sentences of defendants convicted of a criminal offense, and find that the race of the judge matters more in states lacking an intermediate appellate court.

There have been more consistent findings concerning panel effects. White judges on appellate panels are more likely to support affirmative action[72] and the Voting Rights Act[73] if they serve with an African American judge. Similarly, Boyd and coauthors find that men judges serving on panels with women are more likely to make liberal decisions on sex discrimination cases than those on men-only panels.[74] Farhang and Wawro find panel effects of women judges but not African American judges in employment discrimination cases.[75]

A reasonable conclusion from this summary of the literature is that minority judges can affect the outcome of cases, but that the effects are limited. This makes sense since all judges, regardless of race, ethnicity, and gender, receive similar legal training and need to follow the law and deal with the facts of the case at hand. Also, it has been argued that ambitious judges will guard against any appearance of being unique for fear it would prevent them from gaining more prestigious positions in the future. Even if minority judges have limited effects on the outcome of cases, they can still be important role models, make the court appear more impartial, help correct for past and current discrimination against minorities, or affect the behavior of other judges.

Key Court Cases

A debate among judicial scholars concerns the degree to which the courts serve to protect minorities against abuse by the masses. Some argue that the courts are less constrained by popular will since, once appointed, it is difficult to remove a judge. There is also no lobbying or other way for the public to influence judicial decisions. This independence allows judges to protect minorities, even if the other policymakers and the public are reluctant to do so. However, others note that there are significant limitations to court action since courts cannot control their agenda or enforce their decisions. Also, since judges are dependent on the other more democratic branches to enforce their decisions, judges' actions are constrained. And indeed some empirical examinations suggest that the courts tend to serve the majority.[76] A quick review of some of the more significant Supreme Court cases demonstrates the reason for the debate; at some points in history, the Court was reluctant to protect minorities, but at other times, particularly during the **Warren Court,** the Court seemed to protect rights. The Warren Court refers to the time in which Earl Warren was chief justice of the Supreme Court (1953–1969).

Several key Court cases are described below, divided into those concerning race/ethnicity, gender, and sexual orientation. This should help demonstrate the varied history of the Court with regard to minorities as well as introduce students to the most significant cases. In addition to these cases, elsewhere in the book the following cases are discussed: *Plessy v. Ferguson* (1896), *Brown v. Board of Education of Topeka* (1954), *Loving v. Virginia* (1967), *Craig v. Boren* (1976), *Shaw v. Reno* (1993), *Shelby County v. Holder* (2013), *Regents of the University of California v. Bakke* (1978), *United States v. Windsor* (2013), *Griggs v. Duke Power Company* (1971), *U.S. Steelworkers v. Weber* (1979), *Ledbetter v. Goodyear* (2006), *Schuette v. Coalition to Defend Affirmative Action* (2014), and *Obergefell v. Hodges* (2015).

Gender Cases

Muller v. Oregon **(208 U.S. 412, 1908).** This case upheld a state law that prevented employers from having women work for more than ten hours, while no such limit existed for men. Muller argued that these laws prevented women from being free to engage in contracts. The Court, however, upheld the law, reasoning that women were not physically able to work such long hours, indicating that women were less capable than men and could be treated differently by the state.

Griswold v. Connecticut **(381 U.S. 479, 1965).** Up until this case, many states had laws that prevented doctors from distributing or discussing contraception with their patients. This case is important for two reasons. First, it indicated these laws were unconstitutional, which enabled women to receive contraception to help prevent unwanted pregnancies. Second, the Court ruled that the Constitution implied that Americans had a right to privacy. This right has been important in advancing abortion rights and LGBT rights.

Reed v. Reed (404 U.S. 71, 1971). This case comes out of a controversy between an estranged couple in the administration of their child's estate (the child had died). Idaho law stipulated "males must be preferred to females" in establishing administrators of estates, yet both Sally and Cecil Reed wanted to be administrators. The Court ruled that such sex-based laws violate the Constitution's equal protection clause because there was no rational basis for it. Thus, the Court here used the rational basis test of the equal protection clause.

Roe v. Wade (410 U.S. 113, 1973). At the time of this case, many states outlawed abortion. This case is important because the Court recognized that through the right of privacy, women had rights regarding their bodies and the decision to terminate a pregnancy. The right is not absolute and must be weighed against the rights of the fetus. Thus, the Court ruled that the right to abortion was strongest in the first trimester when the fetus could not survive outside the womb. Since this case, there have been several other cases where the Court has limited some aspects of abortion rights and allowed states to regulate them. However, the case has not been overturned.

Meritor Savings Bank v. Vinson (477 U.S. 57, 1986). After losing her job, Mechelle Vinson sued her former employer, saying that she had been discriminated against because her employer had sexually harassed her, and that the harassment created a hostile work environment. In the case, the Court ruled that discrimination does not have to be tangible and that a hostile work environment violates the Civil Rights Act.

LGBT Cases

Bowers v. Hardwick (478 U.S. 186, 1986). In 1986, many states had laws that criminalized oral and anal sex when engaged in by gay men, but not by heterosexuals. This case comes out of such a law in Georgia. Although these laws were later found to violate the Fourteenth Amendment's due process clause in *Lawrence v. Texas*, in this case, these laws were upheld.

Romer v. Evans (517 U.S. 620, 1996). In 1992, the voters of Colorado voted to amend the state's constitution in such a way that it would prevent gays, lesbians, and bisexuals from seeking minority status or protection from the state. The Supreme Court ruled that, since the law singled out LGB people to prevent them from seeking laws to protect their rights and there was no rational basis to do so, the law violated the equal protection clause.

Lawrence v. Texas (539 U.S. 558, 2003). This case concerned a law similar to the one in *Bowers v. Hardwick*. However, here the Court found the law to be unconstitutional because it singled out same-sex couples and intruded into private acts. This case served to invalidate laws in thirteen states. It is also important because it indicated that LGBT Americans had the same rights as non-LGBT to privacy in intimate relationships.

Race and Ethnicity Cases

***Dred Scott v. Sanford* (60 U.S. 393, 1856).** Dred Scott was a slave living on free land when his owner died. He sued to gain his freedom since he lived in a free state. The Court ruled that as a slave, he was not a citizen and did not have the right to bring a case. This case is often cited as one of the Court's worst decisions; it was overturned with the ratification of the Fourteenth Amendment.

***The Civil Rights Cases* (109 U.S. 3, 1882).** These cases invalidated the Civil Rights Act of 1875 that sought to bar discrimination in privately owned but public places, such as theaters, transportation, and hotels. The Court ruled that since the Fourteenth Amendment pertains only to government action, the federal government had no authority to regulate private business.

***Elk v. Wilkins* (112 U.S. 94, 1884).** Elk was born on a reservation but moved off of the reservation and wanted to claim U.S. citizenship and vote. Although the Fourteenth Amendment gives citizenship to people born in the United States, the Court ruled he was not a U.S. citizen and could not vote. He was not born in the United States because he was born on tribal lands.[77] This case meant that Congress would have to act to give American Indians the right to vote.

***United States v. Wong Kim Ark* (169 U.S. 649, 1898).** Wong Kim Ark was born in the United States to Chinese parents. At issue in the case was whether he was a U.S. citizen under the citizenship clause of the Fourteenth Amendment. The Court gave a broad interpretation of the clause and sided with Mr. Ark, indicating anyone born on U.S. territory is a U.S. citizen.

***Korematsu v. United States* (323 U.S. 214, 1944).** During World War II, people of Japanese descent were prevented from being in parts of the west coast and were relocated into internment camps. Korematsu refused to leave and was arrested. The Court upheld the law and conviction of Korematsu, even though the only reason he was arrested was due to his ancestry. This was the first case where the Court used strict scrutiny, although it was originally presented in Footnote 4 in *U.S. v. Carolene Products, Co.* (1938).

***Shelley v. Kraemer* (334 U.S. 1, 1948).** At the time of this case many home buyers' contracts had **restrictive covenants**. These were clauses that prevented people from selling their homes to African Americans. In this case the Court ruled that states could not enforce restrictive covenants without violating the equal protection clause.

***Smith v. Allwright* (321 U.S. 649, 1944).** After Texas gave the Democratic party the authority to set up primary elections, the Democratic party denied African Americans the right to vote in primaries. Since the state was solidly Democratic, whoever won the primary effectively won the office. They argued that the Fifteenth Amendment's voting rights clause involved only state action, not party action. The Court in this case, however, ruled that these "white primaries" did violate the Fifteenth Amendment because the state had jurisdiction over elections.

***Harper v. Virginia Board of Elections* (383 U.S. 663, 1966).** In this case the Court was asked to rule on whether the Virginia poll taxes that required voters to pay a tax violated the equal protection clause. It ruled that it did because the ability to pay the tax had no bearing on one's ability to vote. The Court also ruled that the interpretation of the equal protection clause can change with time. The case affected only local elections; the Twenty-Fourth Amendment outlawed poll taxes for elections for federal offices.

***Katzenbach v. Morgan* (384 U.S. 641, 1966).** Earlier, the Court had upheld the constitutionality of literacy tests, and the Voting Rights Act sought to make them illegal. The case centered on whether Congress had the power to do so because section 5 of the Fourteenth Amendment gave Congress the power to enforce the equal protection clause. In the case, the Court upheld Congress's power to regulate elections in order to ensure the Fourteenth Amendment was followed.

***Lau v. Nichols* (414 U.S. 563, 1974).** This was a class action lawsuit on behalf of Chinese students in the San Francisco area. Although many of the students did not speak English, the schools did not offer English-language instruction to all. Although the students claimed they were denied equal protection as provided by the Fourteenth Amendment because they were denied an equal opportunity for education, the Court ruled that failure to provide Chinese students with English classes effectively denied them an education, in violation of the Civil Rights Act. Thus, the Court required English instruction but did not base the decision on the Fourteenth Amendment.

Conclusion: Improving Descriptive Representation but Mixed Record of Courts' Protection of Minorities

The minority groups discussed in this chapter have much in common when it comes to descriptive representation in the courts in that they are underrepresented and that at the federal level, time and the party of the president have much effect on their representation. However, while women and African Americans have comparatively high levels of descriptive representation on the federal courts, other minorities do not. In addition, each group shares being underrepresented at the state level, with their levels of underrepresentation varying across the states. However, women and LGBT tend to have greater representation at the state than the federal level, while other minorities tend to do as well or better at the federal level. There is no clear pattern of women of color having more or less proportional representation on the federal bench than white women, although they have less than men of color.

The research across minority groups is mixed as to whether descriptive representation in the courts results in policy representation. On one hand, there is no clear evidence that minority judges offer minorities policy representation; some research finds that minority judges substantively represent minority interests, while some finds they do not. One exception to this generalization is that women of color who are on the bench may be more sympathetic to defendants. On the other hand, the research finds panel effects fairly consistently. That is, nonminority judges on panels with minority judges alter their behavior.

Also shared by the groups is a mixed record as to whether the courts are protectors of minority rights. At some times, such as during the Warren Court, the Supreme Court has helped advance the interests of minorities, while at other times the Court has been less willing to protect minorities against tyranny by the masses.

Overall, then, there is much similarity in the representation of minorities in the judicial system. Although the degree to which each minority group lacks descriptive representation varies, they all are underrepresented, and at least at the federal level have improved as time has gone by, especially under Democratic presidents. Research also suggests that the effects of descriptive representation on the courts have ambiguous effects on policy representation. The courts generally also have a mixed record as to whether they protect minorities against discrimination or collude with others to harm minorities.

KEY TERMS

Appellate courts   (p. 135)
District courts   (p. 135)
Judicial review   (p. 134)
Panel effects   (p. 146)

Regents of the University of California v. Bakke (1978)   (p. 136)
Restrictive covenants   (p. 151)

Statutory interpretation   (p. 134)
U.S. Supreme Court   (p. 135)
Warren Court (1953–1969)   (p. 149)

Chapter 7

Representative Bureaucracy

Dennis Mallon was born male in 1940. As a young child, however, Dennis knew that she was really a girl.[1] She tried to "man-up" playing football, getting married, and joining the army, yet at the same time knew that acting as a man was not really who she was.[2] By the time she was forty, Dennis, now Denee, was living as a woman. Ever since she was eleven years old, she wanted sex reassignment surgery. In 2012, when she was in her seventies, she finally decided to have the surgery. However, Medicare, the health care insurance for seniors, had a rule against paying for such surgery. The rule started in the 1980s when there was less known about gender dysphoria, the depression and stress many transgender people feel and how surgery can help with the condition. Today, sex reassignment surgery is an accepted treatment, and she challenged the rule. A Health and Human Services board reviewed the request and allowed Medicare to pay for her surgery. When it did this, it changed a policy that has the potential to drastically improve the lives of transgender seniors needing the surgery. However, this policy change did not come about by an act of Congress, an executive order, or even a court decision, but because a board within the bureaucracy had the power to change the policy and allow seniors with gender dysphoria the possibility of an effective treatment.

As the above example demonstrates, the bureaucracy has considerable power to affect policy. In this case in a positive way for a minority group, but it can also make policy that is more detrimental. However, there are very few democratic controls to make bureaucrats accountable to the people. This can make minorities particularly vulnerable to the discretion of bureaucrats. For example, police departments have been known to engage in **racial profiling,** which involves the police targeting individuals because of their personal traits, such as race or ethnicity, to be investigated for possible criminal activity. Because bureaucrats can affect policy and are not accountable to the people, it is most important that the United States has a **representative bureaucracy,** or a diverse bureaucracy with individuals who reflect a variety of views.[3] A diverse bureaucracy can help ensure that more voices or perspectives are heard and considered as policies are implemented. Those who advocate for a representative bureaucracy tend to make certain assumptions about the way the bureaucracy works: that government decisions affect most aspects of society, bureaucrats can affect those decisions, bureaucrats

Denee Mallon, shown here, was able to change policy regarding Medicare benefits through bureaucratic action. The policy change enabled her to get sexual reassignment surgery. *(AP Photo/Craig Fritz)*

use their own values to make decisions, and that their values are related to socio-demographic traits due to socialization and experiences.[4] These assumptions are generally accepted but are not absolute; bureaucrats do not use their personal values to make all decisions all the time, as they are also influenced by rules, procedures, and institutional values.[5] In addition, the ability of bureaucrats' values to affect their work depends on the amount of discretion they have in their jobs.

Scholars who study representative bureaucracy often use different terminology for descriptive and substantive representation: passive and active. **Passive representation** is similar to descriptive representation, and **active representation** is similar to substantive/policy representation. Mosher defines active representation as when "An individual (or administrator) is expected to press for the interests and desires of those whom he is presumed to represent, whether they be the whole people or some segment of the people;" and defines passive representation as concerning "the source or origin of individuals and the degree to which, collectively, they mirror the total of society."[6] This chapter will discuss the kinds of influence bureaucrats can have over policy, then it discusses the levels of passive representation, what affects levels of passive representation, and concludes with a discussion of the effects of passive representation on active representation. It suggests that passive representation is increasing but remains imperfect, as there is job segregation, minorities tend to have lower level positions, and levels of passive representation vary from state to state. It also suggests that affirmative action and other government policies can be helpful for increasing passive representation and that passive representation does increase active representation.

The Influence of Bureaucrats on Policy

Although the term *bureaucracy* has several meanings, for the purposes of this chapter it refers to the part of a government housed in the executive branch that implements policies. In the federal government, this usually includes the fifteen departments: The Departments of Agriculture, Commerce, Defense, Education, Energy, Health and Human Services (HHS), Homeland Security, Housing and Urban Development (HUD), Interior, Justice, Labor, State, Transportation, Treasury, and Veterans Affairs. But it also includes independent agencies, such as the National Aeronautic and Space Administration (NASA); government corporations, such as AMTRAK and the postal service; as well as independent regulatory agencies, such as the Securities and Exchange Commission. States, counties, and cities, too, have bureaucracies broken down into departments and agencies within their executive branches to execute state and local policies.

The types of work bureaucrats do differ greatly. Presidents, governors, or mayors/city managers appoint some of the most powerful positions. At the state level, several states also elect some of the key administrators, such as attorney general and secretary of state. High ranking bureaucrats advise chief executives (i.e., president, governor, or mayor) about policy needs and outcomes, as well as supervise personnel and oversee vast operations. For example, Sec. Julián Castro, who heads up HUD, oversees several programs involving community development block grants, public housing, housing loans, discrimination in housing, and community development; and each state has a secretary of state who oversees elections, the administration of professional and drivers' licenses, as well as maintaining state records. Many departments are multibillion dollar operations with thousands of employees.

At the federal level, departmental secretaries and a handful of other positions make up the president's cabinet. Although the role of the cabinet has waned under recent presidents,[7] the cabinet members are key policymakers (see Spotlight 7.1 for a list of cabinet members in the Obama administration). As the overseers of key parts of the government, they are in a good position to make recommendations to Congress and the president as to what policies work and which need adjustments, or even to recommend new policies. As such, they meet with the president and Congress on a regular basis. In addition, they create policies for their departments or agencies that can affect the outcomes of policies.

In addition to these political positions, there are also civil service positions. In the federal government, grade levels are used to distinguish between higher and lower level positions. The top positions are senior executive service (SES) positions, and the others are graded from General Service 15 at the top to General Service 1 at the bottom. It is difficult to generalize about types of jobs within the different grades because they vary dramatically from department to department, and from the people who deliver the mail, to FBI agents, scientists, to clerical workers, and park rangers. At the state level, bureaucrats include school teachers, police officers, social workers, as well as people doing clerical work, and countless other jobs, including managers and supervisors.

Governmental or public, as well as private, bureaucracies are known for having a fairly rigid hierarchy with clear rules and procedures to help ensure fairness and efficiency. The rules and procedures can help ensure fairness such that individuals, regardless of race, ethnicity, or gender, who apply for the same government service, are to follow the same procedures, and the criteria of who gets the service are established by rules. These rules and procedures can minimize the discretion that bureaucrats have to use their own values to make decisions. Also, bureaucrats are often socialized into the culture of their agencies, which, too, can minimize individual discretion.

Even though there are limits to bureaucrats' actions, they do have considerable policymaking power. One avenue for their power is administrative discretion. The term *administrative discretion* is used to describe the leeway bureaucrats have in interpreting and carrying out policies. For example, police officers can decide whether or not to stop a car that is speeding, and teachers can decide whether or not to send a student to the principal's office. The race, gender, or ethnicity of clients can affect how a bureaucrat treats individuals. In addition to discretion, many agencies have rulemaking or regulatory powers. Often when Congress passes a law, it gives power to agencies to create the rules to implement the policy.

Spotlight 7.1

President Obama's Cabinet

Vice President of the United States Joseph R. Biden (white man)

Department of State Secretary John Kerry (white man)

Department of the Treasury Secretary Jack Lew (white man)

Department of Defense Secretary Ashton Carter (white man)

Department of Justice Attorney General Loretta Lynch (African American woman)

Department of the Interior Secretary Sally Jewell (white woman)

Department of Agriculture Secretary Thomas J. Vilsack (white man)

Department of Commerce Secretary Penny Pritzker (white woman)

Department of Labor Secretary Thomas E. Perez (Hispanic man)

Department of Health & Human Services Secretary Sylvia Mathews Burwell (white woman)

Department of Housing & Urban Development Secretary Julián Castro (Hispanic man)

Department of Transportation Secretary Anthony Foxx (African American man)

Department of Energy Secretary Ernest Moniz (white man)

Department of Education Secretary Arne Duncan (white man)

Department of Veterans Affairs Secretary Robert McDonald (white man)

Department of Homeland Security Secretary Jeh Johnson (African American man)

The following positions have the status of Cabinet-rank:

White House Chief of Staff Denis McDonough (white man)

Environmental Protection Agency Administrator Gina McCarthy (white woman)

Office of Management & Budget Director Shaun L. S. Donovan (white man)

United States Trade Representative Ambassador Michael Froman (white man)

United States Mission to the United Nations Ambassador Samantha Power (African American woman)

Council of Economic Advisers Chairman Jason Furman (white man)

Small Business Administration Administrator Maria Contreras-Sweet (Hispanic woman)

Source: From http://www.whitehouse.gov/administration/cabinet, accessed September 26, 2014, updated.

These rules can determine the extent of the policy: who is affected and how they are affected. The Civil Rights Act created the *Equal Employment Opportunity Commission* (EEOC) to investigate and resolve complaints of discrimination. It is up to the EEOC to decide the procedures and criteria to use to evaluate complaints. These procedures and criteria can determine who is protected and how hard or easy it is to prosecute discrimination cases. For example, the EEOC ruled that protections against sex discrimination include gender identity. This interpretation has expanded the protections that transgender Americans receive.

Level of Passive Representation

Understanding the levels of passive representation is complicated. There are three levels of government. Thus, we can talk about passive representation at the federal, state, and local levels. Within each of these levels there is a fair amount of *gender segregation*. The term *gender segregation* comes from gender studies and refers to the tendency for women to hold some types of jobs and men others. For example, women city employees are more likely to work for school districts than for fire departments or police forces. The idea of **job segregation** can be used more broadly to describe how racial and ethnic minorities are more likely to hold some types of jobs than nonminority workers. Additionally, compared to white men, women and racial/ethnic minorities are more likely to have civil service instead of political or policy jobs, and within civil service jobs minorities tend to hold jobs found in the lower pay grades. One can speak of passive representation at several types of jobs within each level of government and across several different pay grades. To deal with this complexity, this section will focus on the federal government and briefly summarize state and local passive representation.

Passive Representation at the Federal Level

Cabinet-level positions are considered the most powerful positions within the federal bureaucracy, and there were few minorities in cabinet-level positions until the last few presidents. Cabinet-level officials are nominated by the president and confirmed by the Senate. Table 7.1 lists recent presidents and the numbers of women and other minorities they appointed to cabinet positions. The pattern is similar to that of minority judicial appointments: Democratic presidents nominate more women and minorities than Republican presidents, and throughout time the number of minority appointments has increased. For example, President Obama (D) appointed nine racial/ethnic minorities in his first term, which is the same number President George W. Bush (R) appointed in both of his terms, and President Clinton (D) appointed fifteen in his two terms. Keep in mind as you look at the table that the size of the president's cabinet has varied with the man in office and that presidents have varied in the number of years they served. Those who serve longer have more opportunities to appoint minorities to their cabinet.

The first woman cabinet member was Frances Perkins, who was nominated by President Franklin D. Roosevelt in 1933 to head up the Department of Labor. After Perkins, it would be another twenty years before the next woman cabinet member would be appointed, Oveta Culp Hobby (secretary of health, education and welfare, 1953–1955). As of May 2015, forty-six women (including Perkins) have held cabinet-level positions. Carter was the first president to nominate more than one woman to the cabinet. There has been a fair amount of job segregation with regard to cabinet positions. As of May 2015, seven women have been secretary of labor, and four secretary of health and human services and of the Environmental Protection Agency, but no woman has been secretary of defense, secretary of treasury, or secretary of veterans affairs.[8]

TABLE 7.1   Minority Appointment to the Cabinet by President

Presidents and years in office	African American	Hispanic	Asian American	Women	Number of cabinet positions
Obama 2009–2012	4	2	3	8	23
GW Bush 2001–2009	3	4	2	8	21
Clinton 1993–2001	8	5	1	14	22
GHW Bush 1989–1993	1	1	0	4	17
Reagan 1981–1989	1	1	0	4	17
Carter 1977–1981	1	0	0	4	17
Ford 1974–1977	1	0	0	1	18
Nixon 1969–1974	0	0	0	1	22
Johnson 1963–1969	1	0	0	0	13
Kennedy 1961–1963	0	0	0	0	11
Eisenhower 1953–1961	0	0	0	1	11

Sources: "Women Appointed to Presidential Cabinets," 2013, http://www.cawp.rutgers.edu/sites/default/files/resources/prescabinet.pdf; McClain and Stewart, *Can We All Get Along*, 146–158; John A. Garcia, *Latino Politics in America: Community, Culture, and Interests* (Boulder, CO: Rowman & Littlefield, 2003), 135.

The first African American cabinet member was Robert C. Weaver, who was appointed by President Lyndon B. Johnson as secretary of housing and urban development. After Secretary Weaver's appointment, every president except President Nixon has appointed at least one African American to his cabinet. The first real growth in the number of African American cabinet members, however, occurred during President Bill Clinton's administration: he appointed eight African Americans. The first Hispanic cabinet member, Lauro Cavazos, was appointed as secretary of education by President Ronald Reagan. Since his appointment, every president has had at least one Hispanic cabinet member. And just as President Clinton was the first president to have multiple African American cabinet members, Reagan was the first to have multiple Hispanic members. Although President Clinton did not have multiple Asian American cabinet members, he was the first president to appoint an Asian American to the cabinet. The first Asian American to serve was Norman Mineta, as secretary of commerce.

In addition, there have been a handful of racial and ethnic minority women who have served in presidential cabinets.[9] As of May 2015, there have been six African American women in the cabinet (Secretary of Housing and Urban

Development Patricia Roberts Harris, 1977; Secretary of Labor Alexis M. Herman, 1997; Administrator of the Environmental Protection Agency Lisa P. Jackson, 2009; Secretary of State Condoleezza Rice, 2005; Rice also served as national security advisor, 2001; Ambassador to the United Nations Susan Rice, 2009; and Attorney General Loretta Lynch, 2015). There have been three Hispanic women in the cabinet: Administrator of the Small Business Administration Aida Alvarez, 1997; Administrator of the Small Business Administration Maria Contreras-Sweet, 2014; and Secretary of Labor Hilda Solis, 2009. Finally, there has been only one woman Asian American in the cabinet; Secretary of Labor Elaine Chao, 2001.

Hispanics and African Americans, like women, have seen a fair amount of job segregation within presidential cabinets. As of May 2015, two Hispanics have been secretary of the interior, secretary of energy, and secretary of HUD, and one has been secretary of labor and one secretary of education. The other cabinet-level positions have not had a Hispanic head. Although African Americans have had more varied cabinet positions, they have been concentrated in HUD, HHS, transportation, veterans affairs, and state. Additionally, like women and Hispanics, several African Americans have been secretary of education, secretary of labor, attorney general, and secretary of energy. One post that historically was seen as one of the most important positions was secretary of state. The secretary serves as a representative of the United States in negotiating with other countries and is often the face of the United States abroad. In 1997, President Clinton appointed the first woman as secretary of state: Madeleine Albright. She was followed by Colin Powell in 2001, the first African American secretary of state. After Powell, Condoleezza Rice became the first African American woman secretary of state in 2005. Hillary Clinton was secretary of state from 2009 to 2013. Spotlights 7.2 and 7.3 give brief biographies of Colin Powell and Madeleine Albright.

While cabinet-level positions are important policy making positions, street-level bureaucrats affect what policies mean to clients. Table 7.2 depicts the rates of minority employment in the 2012 federal government, the civilian labor force, and senior executive service of the federal government. One way to gauge the degree of passive representation is to compare the federal workforce with that of the civilian workforce. These data do not suggest that the federal government is more or less likely to employ minorities than private business. It hires slightly fewer Anglos (65.4% to 68.5%), but this is largely because it is significantly more likely to hire African Americans (17.9% to 10.1%), and it is slightly more likely to hire Asian Americans (5.8% to 4.9%) and American Indians (1.7% to 0.9%). One reason for the high levels of African American employment is that Washington, D.C., has a large African American population. A likely reason American Indians are more likely to work for the government is several governmental agencies, such as the Bureau of Indian Affairs, focus on American Indian affairs and are expected to hire American Indians. However, the federal government is noticeably less likely to hire Hispanic workers (8.2% to 14.2%).

Spotlight 7.2

Secretary Colin Powell

Colin Powell was the son of Jamaican immigrants. This made his experience different from many other African Americans of his era. His parents did not grow up in the segregated United States, instead, they had an immigrant experience. As a consequence, Powell grew up in a neighborhood that was ethnically diverse.

Although he never excelled at school, he joined and found a home in ROTC. In 1958, he became a second lieutenant in the U.S. Army. Eventually, he was deployed to Vietnam, where he was wounded during a patrol and received a Purple Heart. Powell is not ashamed of his service in Vietnam. In a speech by the Vietnam Memorial in Washington, D.C., he said "the parades and celebrations are not needed to restore our honor as Vietnam veterans, because we never lost our honor."[10]

After Vietnam, Powell earned a Master of Business Administration, then served as a White House Fellow for the Office of Management and Budget, where he made numerous important contacts. He also attended the prestigious National War College. Although he was recruited to work in the White House to fill several posts, he was reluctant to accept them, but eventually did. Some of the important positions he held include: being an aide to Deputy Defense Secretary Frank Carlucci , deputy national security adviser, and his most significant positions were national security adviser to President Reagan, chairman of the Joint Chiefs of Staff during George H. W. Bush's and Clinton's administrations, and secretary of state for George W. Bush.

While he was chairman of the Joint Chiefs of Staff, President Bill Clinton proposed allowing gays and lesbians to serve openly in the military. Powell played an instrumental role in blocking the change and the resulting "Don't Ask Don't Tell" policy, indicating that minorities of different groups do not always support each other.

As secretary of state, Powell's tenure was dominated by the war in Iraq. When he entered office, he was known for the Powell Doctrine, which held that military missions should be well defined, use significant force, and have a clear exit strategy.[11] Yet, the war he is associated with did not meet those criteria. He was skeptical of the war but was a "loyal soldier" and publicly defended it, most notably at a United Nations' Security Council meeting in February 2003. Today, these statements are seen as false. His defenders focus on his skepticism of the war, and his detractors believe he should have stood up for his beliefs, resigned, or been more persuasive in the White House.[12]

Sources: Information on Colin Powell's early life is from David Roth, *Sacred Honor: A Biography of Colin Powell* (San Francisco, CA: HarperSanFrancisco, 1993); Richard Steins, *Colin Powell: A Biography* (Westport, CT: Greenwood Press, 2003).

In addition, the federal government is less likely to hire women (43.5% to 46.3%). Not only is the federal government no more or less diverse than the civil workforce, but minority employees are concentrated at the lower grades. Whereas 56.5% of the total workforce is male, men hold 66.5% of SES positions. Additionally, whereas 65.4% of the workforce is white, white employees hold 80.6% of SES positions. The limited levels of passive representation for minorities at higher levels hold true across all minority groups depicted in Table 7.3.

Table 7.2 fails to take into consideration the intersectionality of race/ethnicity and gender, but there are some interesting interactions. First, Anglo women and

Spotlight 7.3

Secretary Madeleine Albright

Madeleine Albright was born in Prague, Czecho-slovakia, in 1937. After World War II, her father was appointed United Nations (UN) ambassador and while in New York, they decided to seek political asylum. Eventually, her family moved to Denver. After graduating from high school, she attended Wellesley College and eventually earned a doctorate from Columbia University. In 1976, she became chief legislative assistant to Sen. Ed Muskie. After a few years, she was hired by the National Security Council to work on congressional relations where she met Zbigniew Brzezinski, who was national security adviser and became her mentor. In the 1980s, she worked on Walter Mondale's presidential campaign, as foreign policy advisor for Geraldine Ferraro, and as Gov. Michael Dukakis's foreign policy adviser in his failed presidential bid. Also during the 1980s she became president of the Center for National Policy, a think tank.

In 1993, Madeleine Albright was appointed UN ambassador. It was an interesting time to be at the UN. The cold war had recently ended. Some of the key conflicts during her tenure at the UN included those in Somalia, Rwanda, Haiti, and Bosnia. During her time at the UN, gender played a role. She referred to the Security Council as fourteen suits and one skirt, referring to the gender makeup of the council. She was able to chair the U.S. delegation to the Fourth World Conference on Women, in Beijing, China.

Albright's time at the UN would end with Clinton's first term, at which point he appointed her as secretary of state. Gender played a role in her appointment.

I was disturbed, however, by the extent to which women seemed to be for me and—with rare exceptions—the men for someone else. Many of my supporters were convinced that the opposition from males was a kind of discrimination, but I did not want to use that word.[13]

As secretary of state, there were numerous conflicts around the world Albright had to contend with, such as Saddam Hussein, Iran, the Kosovo-Serbia conflict, the Middle East, Libya, and Cuba. She also worked on NATO expansion, human rights issues, and nuclear weapons reduction. In addition, she wanted the State Department to take women's issues more seriously.[14]

Source: Madeleine Albright, Madam Secretary (New York: Miramax Books, 2003).

Hispanic women are less likely to be in the federal government workforce than in the civilian labor force (25.5% to 31.5% for Anglo women and 3.4% to 6% for Hispanic women). Conversely, African American women and American Indian women are more likely to be in the federal workforce (10.6% to 5.4% for African American women and 1% to 0.4% for Native American women). The difference for Asian American women is negligible (2.6% to 2.3%). This suggests that minority women are more similar to minority men than to white women.

Just as with cabinet-level positions, data regarding the distribution of minorities by executive departments suggest a fair amount of job segregation. Minorities are often concentrated in departments that deal with issues related to minority interests. Not surprisingly, African Americans are concentrated in the Department of Education and the Department of Housing and Urban Development (HUD)

TABLE 7.2   Breakdown of Federal and Civilian Employment by Race, Ethnicity, and Gender

	Federal Workforce (%)	Civilian Labor (%)	SES (%)	State and Local Government (%)
Men	56.5	53.7	66.6	54.1
Women	43.5	46.3	33.5	45.9
Hispanic	8.2	14.2	4.1	10.6
White	65.4	68.5	80.6	65.9
African American	17.9	10.1	10.5	18.8
Asian/Pacific Islander	5.8	4.9	3.3	4.0
American Indian	1.7	0.9	1.4	0.7
Non-Hispanic/multiracial	1.0	1.4	0.6	no data

Sources: Data for federal, civilian, and SES are for 2012 and are from http://www.opm.gov/policy-data-oversight/pay-leave/salaries-wages/#url=2012. Data on state government employment are for 2011 and come from http://www.eeoc.gov/eeoc/statistics/employment/jobpat-eeo4/2011/table1/table1.html.

TABLE 7.3   Occupational Category by Group, 2012

	African American (%)	Hispanic (%)	Asian American (%)	American Indian (%)	Women (%)
Professional	10.7	5.2	9.2	1.2	46.1
Administrative	18.4	8.1	4.6	1.2	43.1
Technical	24.2	9.1	4.5	2.8	57.8
Clerical	27.4	11.2	4.9	2.7	66.4
Other	14.5	21.1	2.8	1.6	13.1
White collar	17.8	8.3	5.8	1.7	47
Blue collar	18.4	7.6	5.6	2.2	9.8
Total	17.9	8.2	5.8	1.7	43.5

Source: Data from the U.S. Office of Personnel Management, 2012, http://www.opm.gov/policy-data-oversight/pay-leave/salaries-wages/#url=2012, 12, 21, 30, 39, 48.

and have low rates of employment in the Department of Agriculture, Department of the Interior, and Department of Energy. Hispanics are concentrated in the Department of Homeland Security and have small numbers in the Department of Health and Human Services (HHS) and Department of Commerce. American Indians are concentrated in the HHS and Department of the Interior. This makes sense since the Indian Health Services is in HHS and the Bureau of Indian Affairs is in the Department of the Interior. Women are concentrated in the departments of Education, HHS, HUD, and Treasury and less likely to be employed by the Air Force, Transportation, and Navy. Asian American bureaucrats are less concentrated in a couple of departments; however, they are more likely to be employed by the Department of Commerce and Department of the Navy and least likely to be employed by the Department of the Interior.

The data in Tables 7.1 and 7.2 do not discuss the employment of LGBT workers. In large part that is because less data are collected on these workers. However, to date no LGBT Americans have held cabinet-level positions, and according to the 2000 census, gays and lesbians are somewhat less likely to be employed by the federal government than non-LGBT workers. That the federal government is less likely to hire LGBT employees is not too surprising given its history of discriminating against LGBT workers. For example, one of the founders of the LGBT movement was Frank Kameny, who became an activist when he lost his government job in the 1950s for being gay.[15] Lewis and Pitts found some differences by sex, however.[16] Gay men are less likely to work in the federal bureaucracy than non-gay men, but lesbians are no more or less likely to work in the government than non-lesbian women. About 4% of men with male partners worked for the federal government compared to 5% of men with female partners, 3.9% of women with male partners work for the government compared to 4.0% of women with female partners.

Passive Representation at the State and Local Levels

State and local governments tend to have higher levels of passive representation for African Americans, Hispanics, and women, but not for American Indians, than the federal government. In 2011, 18.8% of state and local government employees were African American, 10.6% Hispanic, 4% Asian, 0.7% American Indian, and 45.9% women.[17] The percentages in the federal government were 17.9, 8.2, 5.8, 1.7, and 43.5. As with all other employers, states employ minorities, with the exception of Asian Americans, at lower pay grades. While the average Anglo state and local government employee was paid about $49,000, the average African American was paid $42,000, average Asian American was paid $61,000, the average Hispanic $47,000, and the average American Indian $43,000. Men were paid $52,000 on average and women $43,000.[18] In addition, women did less well than men within each racial/ethnic grouping. However, some women did better than some men. For example, Asian American women were paid on average $57,000 compared to $64,000 for Asian American men, but this is more than any other gender/race group. Anglo men were paid on average $53,000, Hispanic men $52,000, American Indian men $49,000, African American men $44,000, Anglo women $44,000, Hispanic women $42,000, African American women $40,000 and American Indian women averaged the lowest incomes at $38,000.

Although the above suggests states have fairly high passive representation, even if it is at lower pay grades, there is much variation by state. Table 7.4 lists each state and the percentage of African Americans, Hispanics, Asian Americans,

TABLE 7.4 Passive Representation in the States by Race and Gender: Ratio of Civil Servants to Population

	African Americans	Hispanics	Asian Americans	American Indian	Women
Alabama	1.24 (33.2)	0.15 (0.6)	0.57 (0.8)	0.43 (.3)	0.97 (50.0)
Alaska	0.70 (3.3)	0.53 (2.9)	0.94 (6.7)	0.53 (7.8)	0.97 (46.6)
Arkansas	1.55 (25)	0.14 (0.9)	0.33 (0.5)	0.44 (0.4)	0.90 (45.7)
Arizona	1.08 (5.4)	88 (26.1)	0.67 (2.5)	0.45 (2.4)	0.90 (45.1)
California	1.69 (12.2)	0.70 (26.3)	0.99 (14.7)	0.47 (0.8)	0.96 (48.3)
Colorado	0.94 (4.7)	0.79 (16.4)	0.46 (1.7)	0.56 (0.9)	0.91 (45.2)
Connecticut	0.84 (9.5)	0.47 (6.3)	0.20 (0.9)	0.20 (0.1)	0.54 (27.6)
Delaware	1.32 (25.7)	0.35 (2.9)	0.39 (1.5)	0.57 (0.4)	0.92 (47.7)
Florida	1.1 (22.5)	0.59 (13.2)	0.7 (2.1)	0.8 (0.4)	0.91 (46.5)
Georgia	1.21 (38.1)	0.28 (2.5)	0.34 (1.3)	0.40 (0.2)	0.94 (48.1)
Idaho	0.5 (.5)	0.38 (4.2)	0.47 (0.9)	0.35 (0.6)	0.95 (47.2)
Illinois	1.31 (20.1)	0.49 (7.7)	0.56 (2.9)	0.50 (0.3)	0.86 (44.1)
Indiana	1.01 (10.2)	0.33 (2.0)	0.40 (0.8)	0.50 (0.2)	0.90 (45.6)
Iowa	0.70 (2.6)	0.30 (1.5)	0.52 (1.1)	0.60 (0.3)	0.89 (45.0)
Kansas	1.06 (7.5)	0.44 (4.6)	0.41 (1.2)	0.67 (0.8)	0.91 (45.8)
Kentucky	1.11 (9.7)	0.19 (0.6)	0.36 (0.5)	0.67 (0.2)	0.88 (44.7)
Louisiana	1.22 (39.9)	0.23 (1.0)	0.47 (0.9)	0.43 (0.3)	1.05 (53.6)
Maine	0.56 (0.9)	0.38 (0.5)	0.43 (0.6)	0.57 (0.4)	0.82 (41.9)
Maryland	1.25 (38.6)	0.22 (1.8)	0.28 (1.8)	0.60 (0.3)	0.89 (46.1)
Massachusetts	1.46 (11.4)	0.49 (4.7)	0.37 (2.2)	0.40 (0.2)	0.71 (36.6)
Michigan	1.38 (20.9)	0.57 (2.5)	0.34 (1.0)	1.43 (1.0)	0.91 (46.2)
Minnesota	0.77 (4.8)	0.36 (1.7)	0.55 (2.6)	0.69 (0.9)	0.96 (48.5)
Mississippi	1.11 (41.8)	0.19 (.5)	0.45 (0.5)	0.30 (0.2)	1.05 (54.0)
Missouri	1.18 (14.7)	0.29 (1.0)	0.38 (0.8)	0.80 (0.4)	0.95 (48.4)
Montana	0.25 (0.2)	0.34 (1.0)	0.45 (0.5)	0.29 (1.9)	0.94 (47.0)
Nebraska	0.85 (4.6)	0.36 (2.9)	0.41 (0.9)	0.31 (0.4)	0.86 (43.2)

	African Americans	Hispanics	Asian Americans	American Indian	Women
Nevada	1.01 (9.5)	0.37 (9.9)	0.61 (5.5)	0.75 (1.2)	0.95 (46.8)
New Hampshire	0.47 (0.8)	0.32 (0.9)	0.27 (0.7)	1.66 (0.5)	0.90 (45.7)
New Jersey	1.66 (24.5)	0.55 (9.8)	0.31 (2.8)	0.38 (2.3)	0.89 (45.8)
New Mexico	0.75 (2.1)	1.19 (55.0)	0.50 (1.0)	0.39 (4.0)	0.82 (41.5)
New York	1.51 (26.0)	0.63 (11.1)	0.68 (5.6)	0.30 (0.3)	0.80 (41.2)
North Carolina	1.14 (25.8)	0.24 (2.0)	0.50 (1.3)	0.79 (1.1)	1.01 (51.6)
North Dakota	0.25 (0.4)	0.25 (.7)	0.29 (0.4)	0.20 (1.1)	0.98 (48.7)
Ohio	1.19 (15.9)	0.39 (1.2)	0.43 (0.9)	1.00 (0.3)	0.91 (46.8)
Oregon	0.96 (2.5)	0.49 (5.6)	0.69 (3.4)	0.72 (1.3)	0.95 (47.9)
Oklahoma	1.09 (9.5)	0.34 (3.0)	0.73 (1.6)	0.73 (6.6)	0.92 (46.9)
Pennsylvania	1.51 (18.0)	0.46 (2.6)	0.25 (0.8)	0.34 (0.1)	0.82 (42.3)
Rhode Island	0.85 (6.3)	0.28 (3.5)	0.29 (1.0)	0.44 (0.4)	0.76 (39.2)
South Carolina	1.18 (34.0)	0.24 (1.2)	0.44 (0.7)	0.60 (0.3)	0.91 (46.6)
South Dakota	0.34 (0.6)	0.30 (0.8)	0.23 (0.3)	0.15 (1.3)	0.88 (43.9)
Tennessee	1.30 (22.7)	0.17 (0.8)	0.34 (0.6)	0.50 (0.2)	0.87 (44.4)
Texas	1.45 (18.3)	0.75 (28.2)	0.61 (2.7)	0.50 (0.5)	0.92 (46.2)
Utah	0.56 (0.9)	0.42 (5.4)	0.93 (2.6)	0.60 (0.9)	0.79 (39.2)
Vermont	0.47 (0.7)	0.47 (0.7)	0.35 (0.6)	1.25 (0.5)	0.91 (46.2)
Virginia	1.34 (27.8)	0.32 (2.5)	0.34 (2.2)	0.60 (0.3)	0.90 (45.8)
Washington	1.23 (5.9)	0.31 (3.5)	0.79 (7.1)	0.83 (1.5)	0.89 (44.7)
West Virginia	0.81 (3.4)	0.17 (0.2)	0.44 (0.4)	0.50 (0.1)	0.88 (44.6)
Wisconsin	0.92 (6.5)	0.41 (2.4)	0.48 (1.3)	0.55 (0.6)	0.92 (46.5)
Wyoming	0.69 (0.9)	0.51 (4.5)	0.67 (0.8)	0.08 (0.2)	0.94 (46.0)
Average	*100.1 (13.4)*	*40.0 (5.8)*	*45.2 (1.9)*	*54.2 (1.1)*	*87.9 (44.5)*

Sources: http://www.eeoc.gov/eeoc/statistics/employment/jobpat-eeo4/2011/; Elizabeth M. Hoeffel, and Sonya Rastogi, Myong Ouk Kim, and Hasan Shahid, "The Asian Population: 2010," 2010 Census Briefs, March 2012, http://www.census.gov/prod/cen2010/briefs/c2010br-11.pdf; Sonya Rastogi, Tallese D. Johnson, Elizabeth M. Hoeffel, and Malcolm P. Drewery Jr., "The Black Population: 2010," 2010 Census Briefs, September 2011, http://www.census.gov/prod/cen2010/briefs/c2010br-06.pdf; and Sharon R. Ennis, Merarys Rios-Vergas, and Nora G. Albert, "Hispanic Population: 2010," Census Briefs 2010, May 2011, http://www.census.gov/prod/cen2010/briefs/c2010br-04.pdf.

Note: Numbers in parenthesis are the percentages of a minority group in the states' civil service. Information on Hawaii's is missing.

American Indians, and women in its bureaucracies and the ratio of each minority group's passive representation with population. Looking at women first, the average ratio was 0.88 but the ratios ranged between 0.54 and 1.05. The New England states of Connecticut, Massachusetts, and Rhode Island as well as Utah have low levels of representation, while the southern states of Alabama, Louisiana, Mississippi, and North Carolina have high levels. This is the opposite of the trends in women's representation is state legislatures. New England states tended to have high levels of women's legislative representation, and southern states had low levels. A likely reason for this difference is that the strength of women in the workforce is related to levels of descriptive representation.[19]

There is considerable variation between the states when looking at African Americans' passive representation as well, but the average state has a ratio of 1.00, or proportional passive representation. Several states have ratios of population percentage to employment percentages of over 1.5 (Arkansas, California, New Jersey, and Pennsylvania), indicating high levels of passive representation. Southern states also tend to have ratios over 1.00. States with small African American populations tend to have low ratios of 0.50 or less (Idaho, Montana, New Hampshire, North Dakota, South Dakota, and Vermont).

The ratios for Hispanic, Asian American, and American Indian passive representation indicate that these groups have low levels of passive representation. The average ratio for Hispanic passive representation is only 0.40, and New Mexico is the only state with a ratio over 1.00. Some states, mostly southern, have ratios of less than 0.20 (Alabama, Kentucky, Mississippi, and West Virginia). Although no state has a ratio over 1.0 for Asian American passive representation, California's ratio is 0.99 and Alaska's is 0.94. The average ratio for Asian Americans is higher than that for Hispanics, 0.45. Although several states have passive representation ratios over 1.0 for American Indians (Michigan, New Hampshire, Ohio, and Vermont), the average is 0.54. In addition, some states, such as Wyoming (0.08), have very low ratios.

The above figures do not include those for LGBT bureaucrats, but Lewis and Pitts' examination of the 2000 census can give us some idea of LGBT employment in state and local governments.[20] They find that women partnered with women are more likely to be employed by both state and local governments than women partnered with men (8.3% to 6.4% at the state level, and 8.9% to 8.0% at the local level), and gay men are more likely to be employed by states than non-gay men (5.0% to 4.4%) but less likely at the local level (5.2% to 6.8%).[21]

To summarize, although the federal government hires minorities at similar rates as private employers, states and localities tend to hire minorities at higher rates. To put this another way, state and local governments have higher levels of passive representation than the federal government. Governments at all levels tend to hire minorities at lower pay grades and also tend to segregate them into traditional fields. For example, women are likely to be found in departments dealing with compassion issues, such as HHS, and minorities generally see higher rates of employment in HUD. Finally, it should be noted that while minorities generally see higher rates of employment in state and local government than in the federal government, there is a fair amount of variation across states.

What Affects Passive Representation?

Several things can affect levels of passive representation, such as the diversity and skills of the workforce, antidiscrimination laws, criteria used in hiring decisions, and descriptive representation. While these will be discussed later, the next few paragraphs will discuss affirmative action and the controversies surrounding it.

Affirmative Action

One of the most discussed ways to increase passive representation is affirmative action. **Affirmative action** involves any positive action taken to help minorities improve their status, usually in employment and education.[22] The United States is not the only nation to have used affirmative action to diversify the government or workplace; Spotlight 7.4 discusses affirmation action programs outside the United States, with a focus on South Africa. Although affirmative action can be used to diversify employment in private as well as governmental employment, this section focuses on government employment and contract authority. **Contract authority** involves the government hiring businesses to conduct work. Affirmative action with regard to contract authority involves the government ensuring that the contracts it makes with private businesses to do work go to minority-owned businesses or businesses that employee minorities. To be legal, affirmative action plans for private employers must comply with the **Civil Rights Act** (CRA). The CRA does several things, but most notably for passive representation, it prohibits

Abigail Fisher was the plaintiff in the 2013 case *Fisher v. University of Texas*. In this case the Court issued a narrow decision that allowed limited use of affirmative action in college admission decisions. The Court reheard the case in December 2015, and as of the book going to press, it had not decided the case. (*AP Photo/ Susan Walsh*)

Spotlight 7.4

Affirmative Action in South Africa

Throughout the world, nations vary in their use of affirmative action. Some nations, such as Great Britain, do not have affirmative action programs, while others, such as South Africa, rely heavily on them. South Africa has a troubling past with regard to race issues. Between World War II and 1994, South Africa had an oppressive policy of apartheid: the nation was divided into areas for blacks (native Africans) and whites (mostly Dutch settlers). All the good jobs and schools were reserved for the whites, while blacks had poor housing, jobs, schools, and limited mobility. After a strong movement on the part of the Africans, such as Desmond Tutu and Nelson Mandela, and much pressure from the world community, the minority white government agreed to end apartheid and to have elections with universal suffrage. In 1994, elections were held and Nelson Mandela became president, and his party, the African National Congress (ANC), had the majority of votes in the parliament.

The Employment Equity Act, 55 of 1998, is designed to achieve equity in the workplace by "promoting equal opportunity and fair treatment in employment through the elimination of unfair discrimination; and implementing affirmative action measures to redress the disadvantages in employment experienced by designated groups, to ensure their equitable representation in all occupational categories and levels in the workforce."[23] It barred discrimination based on several criteria, such as race, gender, sexual orientation, age, disability (including HIV and pregnancy), marital status, and religion. The law required businesses to have a person responsible for overseeing affirmative action programs and mandated "identification and elimination of barriers with an adverse impact on designated groups; measures which promote diversity; making reasonable accommodation for people from designated groups; retention, development and training of designated groups (including skills development); and preferential treatment and numerical goals to ensure equitable representation. This excludes quotas."[24]

In addition to the Employment Equity Act, which concerns employment in public as well as private sectors, South Africa also had the Black Economic Empowerment policy, a more broad-based policy designed to improve blacks' economic status. Yet despite these policies, the wealth of black South Africans has not improved much since 1993.[25] Regardless, affirmative action is popular in South Africa with close to 70% of respondents to a recent poll approving of it for blacks and women,[26] with black South Africans more supportive than whites. While 76% of blacks and women support it, 22% of whites and 42% of men support it.

race- and sex-based discrimination in education and employment. In employment it prevents private businesses involved in interstate commerce or that receive government funds from discriminating against job applicants because of race/ethnicity or sex. Yet giving preferences to women or racial/ethnic minorities appears to do just that. Nevertheless, the court ruled in *U.S. Steelworkers v. Weber* (1979)[27] that affirmative action is consistent with the intent of the CRA and is permissible if it addresses a manifest imbalance, it does not trammel others' rights, and it is temporary until minorities are hired at proportional rates. Thus, to be allowed, affirmative action programs have to address imbalances that are detectable, it cannot treat nonminorities unfairly, and it has to end when the imbalances have been addressed. Affirmative action by governments must be consistent with the CRA and also meet the strict scrutiny standard of the equal protection clause (see Chapter 3). Nevertheless, many plans have been approved.

Presidents since Franklin Roosevelt have taken steps to reduce discrimination in federal employment, but the early steps involved **antidiscrimination policies.**[28] These first efforts to reduce discrimination established rules designed to prevent minority applicants from being discriminated against and relied on victims of discrimination to bring complaints against the government. For example, in 1941 President Roosevelt issued **Executive Order 8802.** It created the President's Committee on Fair Employment Practices (FEPC), which would serve as a model for future presidents' efforts to combat discrimination in the government. The FEPC took and investigated complaints that the federal government and its contractors had discriminated against workers and applicants, and publicized the discrimination. However, it had no enforcement power. Although the order seems weak by today's standards, it was attacked by conservatives in Congress and eventually lost funding. As a rule, the antidiscrimination policies were ineffective since many victims were reluctant or unable to file complaints or prove their cases, and those doing the hiring had little incentive to comply since the penalties for discrimination were mild if they existed at all.[29]

Because antidiscrimination policies were generally ineffective, presidents developed new ways to improve these policies, eventually leading to affirmative action. The term *affirmative action* comes from President John Kennedy's **Executive Order 10925.** It required government contractors to take "Affirmative action to ensure that applicants are employed and that employees are treated during employment without regard to their race, creed, color or national origin." It also required contractors to file compliance reports, and required similar steps to be taken by U.S. departments and agencies. Although the term *affirmative action* comes from President Kennedy, the first requirement of federal government to take a positive step came in 1953 when President Dwight D. Eisenhower issued **Executive Order 10479.**[30] Along with other things, this order required government contractors to post antidiscrimination policies. This can be seen as affirmative action since it went further than responding to victim complaints; it required contractors to take an action.[31] Affirmative action can take a variety of forms, including tracking information on minority employment, recruitment efforts, informing minorities of their rights, considering race in employment decisions, or even establishing hiring quotas.[32] Other executive orders have further expanded affirmative action at the federal level. **Executive Order 11246,** signed by President Lyndon Johnson in 1967, requires government contractors to have affirmative action plans to ensure that racial and ethnic minorities are hired and not discriminated against.[33] **Executive Order 11375,** signed by President Johnson in 1967, prohibits discrimination and requires affirmative action based on sex. Starting with the passage of the **Equal Employment Opportunity Act of 1972,** local governments that want to receive federal dollars are prohibited from discriminating against minority applicants and employees and must have affirmative action plans. Recently, President Obama has tried to end discrimination against LGBT applicants by federal contractors by using executive orders to amend previous Executive Orders 11478 and 11246. As with most of the discrimination-oriented executive orders, this was signed when Congress failed to pass needed legislation.

Three major concerns with affirmative action are: its legality, its effectiveness, and its costs. The Supreme Court's willingness to permit affirmative action has evolved through several cases, but to be allowed, a governmental affirmative action program must meet the strict scrutiny standards. That is, the government must prove that the affirmative action program meets a compelling government interest, and that the interest cannot be met in a less restrictive way. This makes it difficult, but not impossible, for affirmative action programs that discriminate in hiring to meet Constitutional muster.

Evaluating the effectiveness of affirmative action is difficult. At about the same time the government started affirmative action programs, the civil rights movement strengthened, public opinion started to change, and the education of women and racial and ethnic minorities improved.[34] That several things happened at once that could affect minority employment means it is difficult to isolate the effects of affirmative action. In addition, affirmative action programs have changed over the years with changes in Court rulings and political support.[35] Added to this is the diversity of affirmative action programs. They can include such things as quotas, making sure minorities know their rights, targeted recruitment, or taking minority status into consideration when making decisions. Thus, it is difficult to parcel out the effects of affirmative action on federal employment. Nevertheless, there is support for the idea that affirmative action increases the diversity of public employment. Holzer and Neumark reviewed numerous articles on the effectiveness of affirmative action and concluded that there is no question that affirmative action increases minority hires, but that questions remain as to how much it increases minority hires and which groups are most likely to benefit.[36]

Using hiring in police departments helps demonstrate some of these issues. The research on passive representation of police officers and affirmative action suggests affirmative action is a valuable tool. Examining the hiring of women police officers, Sass and Troyer found that affirmative action suits had one of the most significant effects on whether women were hired.[37] Although Miller and Segel found less effect of affirmative action on the employment of women, they found that it had a fairly strong effect on African Americans; 4.5% increase for lower level positions and 6.2% increase for professional positions.[38] McCray also confirms that affirmative action increases minority employment in police forces, finding affirmative action resulted in 14% more African Americans in new hires.[39]

Affirmative action has not been applied to gays and lesbians, but the federal government and several states offer antidiscrimination protections. These policies appear to have some success. Lewis and Pitts found that states with either antidiscrimination laws or executive orders protecting gays and lesbians had more gays and lesbians employed in their state and local governments.[40]

Regardless of the effectiveness of affirmative action, affirmative action is unpopular (see Chapter 8). Although affirmative action may increase diversity, some fear that there may be costs associated with it, such as people with lower credentials being hired, **reverse discrimination,** or that it may harm people who have benefited from it; that their coworkers will see them as less qualified.[41] Whether or not these concerns are well founded, many states have acted to remove affirmative action programs. For example, in 1996 California's voters supported **Proposition 209,** which outlawed the strongest forms of affirmative action. Prop. 209 stated: "Neither the State of California nor any of its political subdivisions or agents shall use race, sex, color, ethnicity, or national origin as a criterion for either discrimination against, or granting preferential treatment to, any individual or group in the operation of the State's public employment, public education, or public contracting." Since Californians passed Prop. 209, several other states have followed suit: Washington, Nebraska, Oklahoma, New Hampshire, Florida, Arizona, Michigan, and Texas.[42] In 2014, the Court ruled in *Schuette v. Coalition to Defend Affirmative Action*[43] that such bans are Constitutional.

As affirmative action lost its support, a new approach has become more popular: diversity management.[44] **Diversity management** can take any number of forms including: affirmative action, diversity training, mentoring for minorities, evaluating managers based on diversity, or networking for minorities. Although they examined private employment, not public employment, Kalev, Kelly, and Dobbin examined the employment of women and African American managers and concluded: "The most effective practices are those that establish organizational responsibility: affirmative action plans, diversity staff, and diversity taskforces. Attempts to reduce social isolation among women and African Americans through networking and mentoring programs were less promising. Least effective are programs for taming managerial bias through education and feedback."[45] The analysis by Kalev and associates indicates that although white women and African American men benefit from affirmative action, white and African American women and African American men benefit more from diversity staff and committees (employees or taskforces dedicated to diversifying the workforce). But the other programs, diversity training, diversity evaluations, networking, and mentoring programs, had mixed effects on minority hires.

What some people may see as a form of affirmative action is the preference given to American Indian applicants to the Bureau of Indian Affairs and other agencies directly responsible for Indian policies. However, it is not the same as affirmative action. In 1934, Congress passed the Indian Reorganization Act to allow the Department of the Interior, which oversaw the Bureau of Indian Affairs, to allow Indians to be hired "without regard" to civil service laws and to be given preference in hiring. This law was upheld by the Court even after the 1972 Equal Employment Opportunity Act, which prevents racial discrimination in hiring, in *Morton v. Mancari*, 417 U.S. 535 (1973). Jerry Stubben summarizes the court ruling thusly: "'that the purpose of these preferences, as variously expressed in the legislative history, has been to give Indians a greater participation in their own self-government;' to further the Government's trust obligation toward Indian Tribes; and 'reduce the negative effect of having non-Indians administer matters that affect Indian tribal life.'"[46] In essence, race is not the driving factor in these preferences but, rather, they help ensure greater self-governance and sovereignty for political entities: tribes.[47]

Other Influences on Passive Representation

Although affirmative action and management diversity are the most discussed ways to increase passive representation, the minority status of political leaders (or descriptive representation in city councils, state legislatures, mayors, or governors) may affect it as well.[48] However, the research examining the effects of descriptive representation has been mixed, suggesting the effects may vary by minority group. For example, Kerr Miller, Schreckhise, and Reid found that cities with African American mayors have more African Americans in administrative positions, but that the number of African Americans on city councils has a limited effect on African American employment.[49] However, they also found that Hispanic employment in administrative positions was affected by Hispanic representation on city councils, but that Hispanic mayors have limited effect on Hispanic employment.[50] In addition, the presence of gays and lesbians on the school board affects the frequency of gay and lesbian school administrators and teachers,[51] and the presence of racial minorities on school boards increases the presence of minorities in administrative positions but not the presence of teachers.[52] The effects of women elected officials may have little effect on women's employment. Sass and Troyer found that women city councilors and mayors did not affect the number of women recruited for police forces.[53]

To demonstrate the relationship of political representation to passive representation, Figures 7.1 to 7.3 plot the relationship between the ratio of bureaucrats to population size with the ratio of legislators to population size in the states. Figure 7.1 depicts the relationship for African Americans. The general upward trend of the plots demonstrates that states with a larger ratio of legislators to population size also have a larger ratio of bureaucrat to citizen. Figure 7.2 depicts the relationship for Hispanics. Compared to Figure 7.1, the upward trend is clearer and steeper, indicating an even stronger relationship. Compare these figures to Figure 7.3, which depicts the relationship for women. Notice the trend is fairly flat, indicating that the percentage of women in the legislature has little to no relationship with the percentage of women in the bureaucracy. These figures demonstrate the effects of political representation on passive representation.

Figure 7.1 Scatterplot of African American Bureaucrats and Legislators

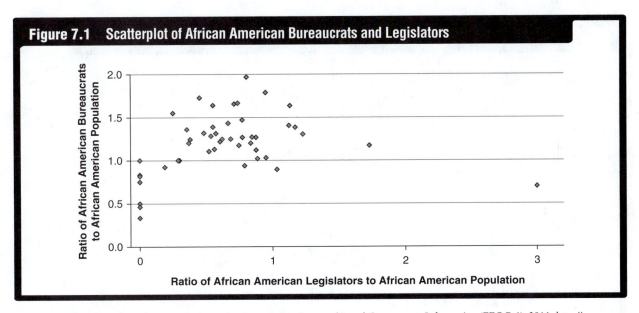

Source: Data from Equal Employment Opportunity Commission State and Local Government Information (EEOC-4), 2011, http://www.eeoc .gov/eeoc/statistics/employment/jobpat-eeo4/2011/table1/table1.html and Table 2.1.

The criteria used to make hiring decisions can also affect passive representation. For example, Sass and Troyer found that male-dominated police forces that used fitness tests recruited fewer women to police academies.[54] Because criteria can make some applicants appear unqualified for a position, to be compliant with federal antidiscrimination laws, employers cannot construct unnecessary tests that could prevent minorities from being hired. This relates to the concept of **disparate impact**. Disparate impact is an interpretation of the Civil Rights Act that suggests that criteria used in hiring that disproportionately harm minorities, regardless of intent, constitute a form of discrimination that violates the Civil Rights Act, unless the criteria can be demonstrated to be related to job performance. The disparate impact standard comes from *Griggs v. Duke Power Company* (1971)[55] and was codified into the CRA in 1991. In the *Griggs* case, Duke Power Company had a history of overt discrimination against African Americans. After the CRA was passed, they changed their criteria for promotion to higher paid jobs to include a test that African Americans tended to perform poorly on. The test, however, had no bearing on how workers performed and therefore violated the CRA.[56]

Several other factors may affect passive representation. Several studies found that areas with large minority populations have more minority employees than those with small minority populations.[57] States with larger minority populations have more minority bureaucrats. Stewart and his colleagues also found that region of country affects the percentage of minority teachers.[58] Differences in

Figure 7.2   Scatterplot of Hispanic Bureaucrats and Legislators

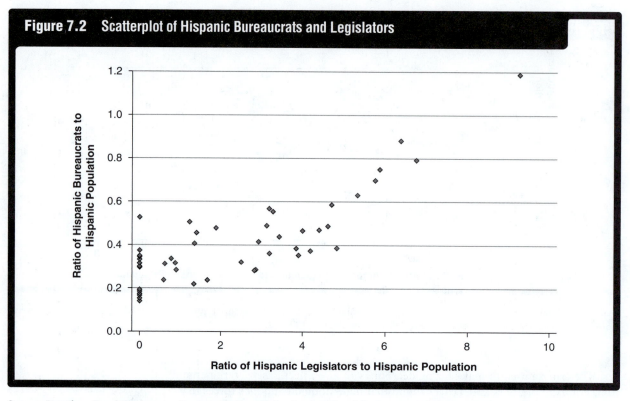

Sources: Data from Equal Employment Opportunity Commission State and Local Government Information (EEOC-4), 2011, http://www.eeoc
.gov/eeoc/statistics/employment/jobpat-eeo4/2011/table1/table1.html and Table 2.1.

education, too, can account for job segregation or minority employees being concentrated in lower pay grades.[59] Women's limited employment in higher positions may also be affected by family responsibilities.[60] It has also been suggested that newer or expanding agencies find it easier to diversify, but the findings have been mixed as to whether that is the case.[61] Economically well-off cities may also find it easier to diversify their workforce.[62] Focusing on variation in federal agencies, Kellough found greater racial and gender integration in smaller agencies, greater racial but not gender integration in agencies with more blue-collar and clerical workers.[63] However, he did not find that greater opportunities to hire new employees or labor union strength affected integration. Similar results have been found elsewhere.[64]

This section suggests that affirmative action is effective in increasing passive representation, but remains unpopular and can violate antidiscrimination and equality laws. Other things that can affect passive representation are the size of minority populations in a state, the political representation of a group, and the criteria used to make hiring decisions.

Figure 7.3   Scatterplot of Women Bureaucrats and Legislators

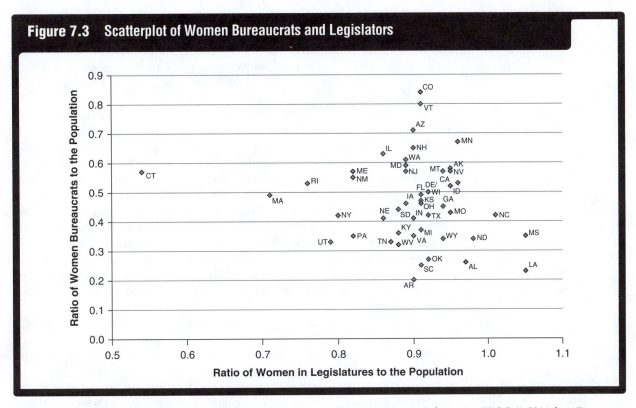

Sources: Data from Equal Employment Opportunity Commission State and Local Government Information (EEOC-4), 2011, http://www.eeoc .gov/eeoc/statistics/employment/jobpat-eeo4/2011/table1/table1.html and Table 2.1.

The Effects of Passive Representation on Active Representation

There are several ways that minority bureaucrats could be beneficial for the active representation of minorities. First, minority representatives may have a better understanding of the needs of minority clients. For example, Bradbury and Kellough found that African American citizens and local bureaucrats in Georgia had similar perspectives on issues important to their communities.[65] Second, minority bureaucrats may serve as role models, providing inspiration to minority clientele.[66] Third, minority bureaucrats may want to be advocates for minorities.[67] Sowa and Selden, for example, found that minority bureaucrats in the Farmers Home Administration (FmHA) were more likely to see representing minorities as one of their roles.[68] Also, minority bureaucrats may be better able to communicate with minority clients,[69] and clients tend to prefer agencies with street and administrative bureaucrats who look like them.[70] In addition, passive representation may have indirect effects such that nonminority bureaucrats change their behaviors because of the presence of minorities, or that the clientele change their behavior because of passive representation.

However, organizational theory suggests that the characteristics of the organization minimize the effects of bureaucrats' traits and values on their behaviors. One such limitation is that employees are socialized into the organization's norms. Wilkins and Williams find evidence that African American and Hispanic police officers engage in more, not less, racial profiling due to socialization,[71] and Dolan finds that the top-level bureaucrats' spending priorities are affected as much by their department as their gender.[72] An additional limit is that bureaucrats vary in the amount of discretion they have to affect minority interests. Only bureaucrats with discretion, particularly discretion in a policy with racial/ethnic/gender importance, and with less socialization in the organization are likely to offer active representation. Because of this, it is important to make a distinction between administrators (high-level SES) and **street-level bureaucrats**, or bureaucrats who work directly with clientele. Minority street-level bureaucrats tend to offer more active representation for minorities since they have greater discretion and less organizational socialization. The effects of passive representation on active representation are also likely affected by other contexts, such as region and socioeconomic status.[73]

Much of the research on passive/active representation has focused on education and policing, so this section will focus on this research. However, areas outside of police departments and school districts also offer evidence of the value of passive representation. Individuals receiving treatment for HIV-AIDS prefer to have someone help them who shares their race/ethnicity, gender, and sexual orientation and to a lesser extent prefer agencies with directors who share these social demographic traits.[74] Child-support collection is improved if there is a woman supervisor.[75] Women top-level executives have somewhat different spending priorities.[76] The allocation of resources by the Farmers Home Administration (FmHA) was affected by the supervisors' view of their representative role.[77] More federal contract dollars go to minority-owned firms from agencies with greater passive representation.[78] Finally, within the EEOC there are more complaints filed where there are more minority bureaucrats.[79] Selden's examination of the effects of passive representation on resource allocation at the FmHA was unique in that it examined several minority groups: Hispanics, African Americans, Asian Americans, and American Indians.[80] She found passive representation leading to active representation for each group except American Indians.

In education there is a fair amount of research indicating that minority students perform better in school districts with minority teachers. For example, Meier and Stewart examined the effects of minority teachers and principals (administrators) on the experiences of minority students in Florida schools.[81] They found that African American students in school districts with more African American teachers were less likely to be placed in classes for students with mental retardation, more likely to be placed in gifted programs, less likely to be punished, and performed better on standardized tests than were African American students in districts with fewer minority teachers. Other studies have tended to confirm the value of minority teachers for minority students. For example, Dee found minority students taught by minority teachers performed better in reading and math,[82] Fraga, Meier, and England found Hispanic students in districts with a large number of Hispanic teachers were more likely to complete high school and go to college,[83] Aaron and Powell found African American teachers gave less negative feedback to African American students than did white teachers,[84] and several studies find minority students in districts with a large number of minority teachers are more likely to pass exams[85] and less likely to drop out.[86] Research also suggests minority teachers have more positive perceptions of minority students, are less likely to give them negative labels, and more likely to put them in gifted programs.[87] The research has also found positive effects of women math teachers on female students' math scores.[88] Not only does having teachers that look like students improve their textbook learning, but it may have advantages outside the classroom. One study found African American female teens were less likely to become pregnant if at least 20% of their teachers were African American.[89]

If students perform better when they have teachers who look like them, then there is the possibility that white students may perform less well with minority teachers. The research has been mixed on this point. While Pitts' research found evidence that nonminority students did less well with minority teachers,[90] Meier and colleagues found nonminority students can benefit from minority teachers.[91] In addition, Rocha and Hawes found that African American students benefit from Hispanic teachers and vice versa.[92]

While minority teachers help minority students succeed, minority principals and administrators have less effect on students' experience.[93] For example, Pitts found that districts with more minority managers did not see higher passage or lower dropout rates of minority students.[94] It is likely that the socialization of top level administrators and principals to the norms of the institution is greater than that of street-level bureaucrats, teachers in this case, which limits the effects of their earlier socialization and experiences. However, research also suggests that the race/gender of the principal may affect minority teachers. Stewart, England, and Meier found there were more minority teachers where there were more minority administrators.[95] In addition, Grissom and Keiser found that minority teachers reported higher levels of job satisfaction and were less likely to quit if they had a minority principal.[96] They also found that African American teachers were paid more if they had an African American principal than if they had a white principal. In addition, passive representation may provide a training ground for minorities who can work their way to top leadership positions. Meier and Smith examined school districts and found that districts that had more minority teachers had more minority administrators and board members.[97]

The research on policing also tends to confirm that passive representation leads to active representation.[98] Minority drivers are less likely to be ticketed or have their cars searched if stopped by minority officers than by white officers.[99] Meier and Nicholson-Crotty's examination of sixty cities over eight years found women were more likely to bring sexual assault charges in cities with more women police officers, and that cities with more women officers had higher arrest rates for sexual assault cases.[100] Brown and Frank found that African American officers were more likely to arrest African American suspects[101] and that this may reflect a desire to limit crime in minority neighborhoods.[102] Supporting this idea is that African American officers are likely to perform community support activities in minority neighborhoods.[103] Finally, citizens are more likely to see a police action as legitimate if a police officer of their race is present.[104]

However, not all research suggests positive effects of diversifying police forces. Hur's 2013 study of 464 municipalities with populations over 50,000 found there may be some costs associated with a diverse police force.[105] He found that cities with more racially diverse police forces had higher rates of employee turnover (dismissal, resignation, and total) and lower clearance rates for violent, property, and total crimes. And as noted earlier, Wilkins and Williams found that socialization in police forces may trump minority status in some cases: police divisions that had more Hispanic and African American officers also made more traffic stops involving Hispanics (racial profiling).[106]

One debate about representative bureaucracy is whether the size of passive representation affects the degree to which passive representation leads to active representation. This is similar to the issues of critical mass discussed in Chapter 4. For example, does the first minority employed in an agency feel as free to make decisions based on her values as a minority employee in an agency with several minority employees? Meier has argued that the effects are not linear, but that a critical mass must be met before passive representation results in active representation.[107] Specifically, he found that the relationship between the presence of minority principals improved the performance of Hispanic students only after about 16% of a school district's principals were Hispanic. Hindera and Young's examination of the EEOC's discrimination complaint filings found that the relationship was nonlinear as well.[108] They found that when a critical mass was met, the more African Americans in district offices, the more of the agencies' resources were allocated to helping African Americans. When African Americans made up a plurality (less than 50% but the most common minority group) in an office, the number of white employees also increased resources for African American interests. However, once African American employees made up a majority, the relationship of passive to active representation was similar to that of a critical mass.

Conclusion: Similarities and Differences in Minority Representation in the Bureaucracy

Minority groups differ in their levels of passive representation. African Americans and women are unique in their relatively high levels of passive representation at both the federal and state levels, while Hispanics have the lowest levels of passive representation. In some cases, the differences in levels are significant. For example, the average state has a ratio between the percentage of African

American civil servants and African Americans in the population of about 1.00 for African Americans, while the ratio of Hispanic civil servants to the Hispanic population is only 0.40.

However, minority groups share being concentrated at lower grades and in certain occupations. While this is bad from the perspective of individuals wanting high paying government work, it may lead to greater active representation: passive representation by street-level bureaucrats results in greater active representation than passive representation by bureaucrats at higher levels. Job segregation results in higher levels of passive representation in some departments than others. For example, most minorities have high levels of federal employees in HHS.

Other characteristics shared by most minority groups are the causes and consequences of passive representation. Passive representation increases active representation. Minority students, for example, perform better in school where there are minority teachers, and minority teachers have greater job satisfaction where there are minority administrators. And, levels of passive representation are affected by affirmative action, time, the size of a minority population, and the criteria used in hiring. There tends to be greater passive representation where there are programs designed to increase diversity, as the number of minorities increase, and where there are not unnecessary tests or requirements. In addition, passive representation at the highest levels has increased in recent years. However, the effects of political representation, that is, descriptive representation in elected positions, are less clear or uniform across groups. Another significant difference is that, although giving preferences to American Indians in hiring may seem like race-based affirmative action, it is more accurately seen as a way to help ensure tribal self-governance.

KEY TERMS

Active representation   (p. 156)

Affirmative action   (p. 169)

Antidiscrimination policies   (p. 171)

Civil Rights Act (CRA)   (p. 169)

Contract authority   (p. 169)

Disparate Impact   (p. 175)

Diversity management   (p. 173)

Equal Employment Opportunity Act of 1972   (p. 171)

Executive Order 8802   (p. 171)

Executive Order 10479   (p. 171)

Executive Order 10925   (p. 171)

Executive Order 11246   (p. 171)

Executive Order 11375   (p. 171)

Job segregation   (p. 159)

Passive representation   (p. 156)

Proposition 209   (p. 173)

Racial profiling   (p. 155)

Representative bureaucracy   (p. 155)

Reverse discrimination   (p. 173)

Street-level bureaucrats   (p. 178)

Chapter 8

Public Opinion and Minority Interests

President Obama's position on same-sex marriage has "evolved." When he ran for president in 2008, he stated he opposed same-sex marriage, but by the time he ran for reelection in 2012, he supported it. Publically, he indicated that he came to support it after much soul-searching. According to a White House webpage:

> It's no secret the President has gone through some soul-searching on this issue. He's talked to the First Lady about it, like so many couples do. He's heard from folks—gay and lesbian friends, staff members in long-term, loving relationships, as well as brave young servicemen and women he got to know through the fight to end Don't, Ask Don't Tell.
>
> He's sat around his kitchen table with Sasha and Malia, who have friends whose parents are same-sex couples. As the President said during the interview, "it wouldn't dawn on them that somehow their friends' parents would be treated differently. It doesn't make sense to them. And frankly, that's the kind of thing that prompts a change of perspective—not wanting to somehow explain to your child why somebody should be treated differently when it comes to eyes of the law."
>
> In the end, the President said, he believes it's important to "treat others the way you would want to be treated." We need to recognize that people are going to have differing views on marriage and those views, even if we disagree strongly, should be respected."[1]

While the above quote is the official position, many believe that personally he supported same-sex marriage long before 2012 but for political reasons left that position in the closet until 2012. As early as 1996, when he was a state legislator, he indicated he supported it, but that his public support disappeared for political reasons as he ran for higher office.[2] What happened is that by 2012 the public had changed its collective opinion enough that supporting marriage equality was no longer a political liability.

Each interpretation of Obama's evolution reinforces some lessons about public opinion and minority rights. Assuming the first interpretation is correct, Obama is not the only American to have changed his position on this issue between 2008 and 2012, as there has been much change in American attitudes toward LGBT issues in recent years. The reasons he gives for changing his position is also illustrative of what likely happened around many kitchen tables. People who have contact with minorities are likely to change their views and as same-sex marriage became framed as a civil rights issue or an issue of fairness it

Same-sex marriage divides not only America but also people around the world. This photo is of a protest in Belfast, Ireland. In 2015, 61% of the Irish voted for a marriage equality referendum. (*Liam McBurney/PA Wire via AP Images*)

received more support. Assuming the second interpretation is correct, it demonstrates the importance of public opinion in affecting public policy: policy makers follow public opinion.

Since the United States is a democracy, public policy is expected to reflect public opinion. The primary pathways by which public opinion impacts policies are related to elections. One pathway is that voters elect officials who share their policy views, and these officials make decisions based on shared views. Another pathway is based on officials acting in ways to win reelection. Officials who want to win reelection are fearful that they will be voted out of office if they fail to serve their constituents, and as a consequence, make decisions consistent with their interpretation of constituents' preferences. These pathways appear to lead to officials acting in ways consistent with public opinion. In their much-cited examination of opinion-policy congruence in the aggregate at the national level, Page and Shapiro found the two moved together about two-thirds of the time.[3] That is, as opinion toward a policy area became more liberal/conservative, policy became more liberal/conservative about two-thirds of the time. They also found that when the opinion change was large, policy change was even more likely to occur. Focusing on several issues related to minorities at the state level, Lax and Philips, too, found that states were responsive to citizens such that states whose voters were more liberal had more liberal policies.[4] Since public opinion tends to affect policy, this chapter examines public opinion toward minorities and minority interests and what affects it. The first sections of this chapter will examine Americans' attitudes toward minority groups. They will be followed by examinations of Americans' attitudes toward policies and what affects those attitudes.

There are four key lessons to be learned from this chapter. First, Americans' attitudes toward minority groups have changed dramatically since the middle of the twentieth century, such that there are fewer negative stereotypes and overt prejudice is less common, although less-overt prejudice persists. Second, although Americans express more positive attitudes toward minorities than in the past, their support for some policies beneficial for minorities has seen more modest change. That is, there is more support for equality in principle than in practice. Third, the results of surveys designed to measure Americans' opinions about minorities and their interests are influenced by the way questions are phrased. Therefore, citizens need to be careful in interpreting survey results. Finally, Americans' demographic traits, party identification, ideology, contact with minorities, perceptive threat from minorities, and events affect their attitudes toward minorities and their interests. This chapter relies heavily on public opinion research. Spotlight 8.1 describes four polling organizations whose polls are extensively used in this and other chapters.

Attitudes toward Racial and Ethnic Minorities

As noted above Americans have more positive views toward minorities today than in the past. This is particularly evident when looking at **attitudes** toward African Americans. Since pollsters have been asking Americans about their views toward

Spotlight 8.1

Reputable Polling Organizations

One way students can help ensure that the polling data they use are accurate is to rely on surveys from reputable polling organizations. This Spotlight describes four polling organizations that tend to produce high quality surveys and often make their data available through their webpage.

The Pew Research Center conducts most of its surveys by phone, but also utilizes other forms of surveys. One of its subdivisions is the Pew Research Hispanic Trends Project, which collects information regarding Hispanics. The Pew Research Center has also conducted research on LGBT and Asian Americans. The margin of error for its studies vary from about ±2 to ±4.

The American National Election Studies, at the University of Michigan, is another reputable polling organization. ANES is best known for its time series studies conducted during election years. ANES does most of its surveys in person. Additionally, it conducts pilot studies between election years to test changes to these surveys. Some of its studies are panel studies, where the same people are surveyed more than once. This allows researchers to see how individuals change during the election. One of the benefits of ANES data is that ANES has been conducting surveys since the 1940s and can be used to identify long-term trends. Given the complexity of its sampling design, the margin of error is not easily calculated, but its 2012 time series survey is estimated to have a margin of error of less than ±1.5.

A third reputable polling organization is the General Social Survey (GSS), conducted by the National Opinion Research Center (NORC) located at the University of Chicago. GSS has a more comprehensive set of questions on Americans' attitudes toward minorities and their interests than ANES does, but has been asking them for a shorter time period. It conducts its surveys in person. The GSS does not calculate a margin of error for its studies given the complexity of its sampling.

A fourth polling organization is Gallup, Inc., founded by George Gallup, a pioneer in survey research in the 1930s. Gallup is a for-profit business. The Gallup Poll division conducts most of its political polling in the United States. It conducts numerous surveys every year, and the margin of error for each survey varies from as low as 1% to as high as about 5%. It is less likely to make its raw data available than the other organizations discussed here.

There are many other reputable firms: for example, Harris Poll and many major news outlets conduct good polls. Even when using results from a respected polling firm, students still need to pay attention to the particular polling data they wish to use and make sure they address their specific needs.

African Americans for several decades, there is considerable trend data that demonstrate the change. For example, since the mid-1970s the General Social Survey (GSS) has asked respondents what they believe is the cause of African Americans' low socioeconomic status (SES) with the following questions:[5]

The question asked:
"On average (Negroes, Blacks, African-Americans) have worse jobs, income and housing than white people. Do you think this is because"

Possible responses:
"Most (Negroes, Blacks, African-Americans) don't have the chance for education that it takes to rise out of poverty."

"Most (Negroes, Blacks, African-Americans) have less inborn ability to learn."

"Mainly due to discrimination."

Respondents could answer yes or no to each option. The results from these questions are depicted in Figure 8.1, which demonstrates that there has been a dramatic decline in the percentage of Americans who believe that African Americans have lower SES because of innate inabilities. Whereas about a quarter of Americans thought African Americans' low SES was due to inborn disabilities in 1977, by the 2000s, less than 10% attributed their low SES to inborn disabilities. This belief that African Americans have less innate ability than whites has been referred to as **old fashioned racism**.

Although old fashioned racism has declined dramatically, it is unlikely that racism has died. Rather, it is more likely that it has taken a different form. The term **symbolic racism** describes a type of racism that is more common today. Symbolic racism includes four beliefs: "(1) racial discrimination is no longer a serious obstacle to blacks' prospects for a good life, so that (2) blacks'

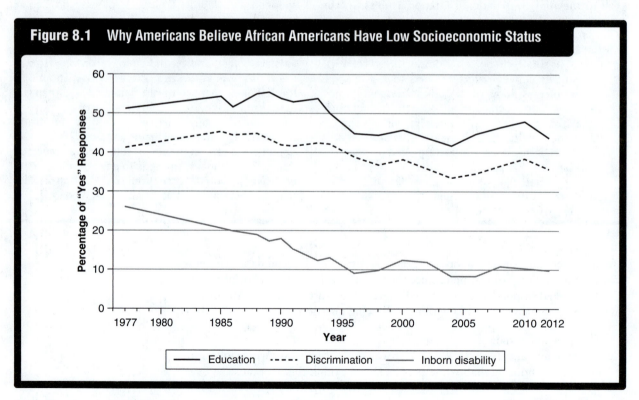

Figure 8.1 Why Americans Believe African Americans Have Low Socioeconomic Status

Source: Data from https://gssdataexplorer.norc.org.

continuing disadvantages are largely due to their unwillingness to work hard enough. As a result, both their (3) continuing demands and (4) increased advantages are unwarranted."[6] Tarman and Sears note that in a 2000 ANES survey, 59% percent agreed with the statement, "It's really a matter of some people not trying hard enough; if blacks would only try harder, they could be as well off as whites."[7] Figure 8.1 also demonstrates that a growing number of Americans believe that discrimination is NOT a cause of African Americans' low SES. In 1977, when GSS first asked the question, 41% indicated that discrimination was a main cause of African Americans' low SES compared to 35% in 2012. Figure 8.4, which will be discussed later, also demonstrates the low levels of support for affirmative action, which would be consistent with the new symbolic racism.

Further, Figure 8.1 shows that almost half of Americans believe education plays a role in African Americans' low levels of SES. In fact, this is the most common response. However, note that even here there has been a decline. A smaller percentage of Americans today (44%) think education contributes to African Americans' low SES than did in 1977 (51%).

Not only have attitudes toward racial and ethnic minorities improved over the years, but so, too, has Americans' belief that segregation is unacceptable. For example, according to an ANES survey, while in 1962 almost a quarter of Americans supported segregation, by 1978 only about 5% supported segregation.[8] Similarly, the General Social Survey has found that during the 1970s about 40% of Americans believed whites had a right to segregated neighborhoods but by the 1990s, only about 10% believed whites had such a right.[9] Although these examples demonstrate an improved environment for minorities, they also demonstrate the importance of question wording. In the 1970s the vast majority of Americans did not support segregation but still believed whites had a right to segregated neighborhoods. There are a couple of ways students can interpret opinions when question wording significantly affects the conclusions drawn from surveys. It could mean that respondents do not have clear or strong positions and the results may be measuring "nonattitudes." Or, it could mean that they have sophisticated understanding of the issue such that subtle changes in context affect their responses. Often students must rely on their own judgment to decipher the meaning of these polls.

Attitudes toward Women

Much like attitudes toward African Americans have improved over the last fifty years, so have attitudes toward women. GSS data are used to make Figure 8.2, which demonstrates changes in opinions about women. GSS has asked four questions over the years to measure Americans' views toward sex roles.

The specific questions are:

Now I'm going to read several more statements. As I read each one, please tell me whether you strongly agree, agree, disagree, or strongly disagree with it. For example, here is the statement:

A. A working mother can establish just as warm and secure a relationship with her children as a mother who does not work.

B. It is more important for a wife to help her husband's career than to have one herself.

C. A preschool child is likely to suffer if his or her mother works.

D. It is much better for everyone involved if the man is the achiever outside the home and the woman takes care of the home and family.[10]

Figure 8.2 illustrates the fundamental change in Americans' views toward sex roles that occurred during the 1970s and 1980s. Although there have been ups and downs since the 1980s, by the 2000s, a significant majority of Americans are less supportive of traditional sex roles. For example, in 1977, 77% of the respondents agreed that it is better for society if men are the achievers outside of the home, and 68.2% believed preschool children were hurt when their mothers work outside the home, but in 2012, only 32.1% and 34.6%, respectively, agreed. Similar changes occurred with regard to believing children are hurt when their mothers' work and believing a wife should prioritize her husbands' career over her own. Although support for traditional sex roles has fallen dramatically, still a significant minority, about a third of Americans, supports traditional roles.

Much like old fashioned racism has been replaced by symbolic racism, Swim, Aikin, Hall, and Hunter have noted that **old fashioned sexism,** the idea that women are less competent than men in some areas, should be treated different, and support for traditional gender roles, has been replaced by **modern sexism.**[11] People harboring modern sexism "believe that discrimination against women is a thing of the past, feel antagonistic toward women who are making political and economic demands, and feel resentment about special favors for women."[12] The behavior of people who harbor modern sexism is consistent with these beliefs, for example, being less likely to vote for women candidates.[13]

Attitudes toward LGBT Persons

Americans' attitudes toward LGBT, too, have changed dramatically over the past fifty years. Figure 8.3 depicts Americans' responses to two questions asked several times by Gallup. One question is: "Do you feel that homosexuality should be considered an acceptable alternative lifestyle or not?"[14] The other question asks: "In your view, is being gay or lesbian [ROTATED: something a person is born with, (or) due to factors, such as upbringing and environment?]"[15] Figure 8.3 demonstrates that whereas in the mid-1980s about a third of Americans saw

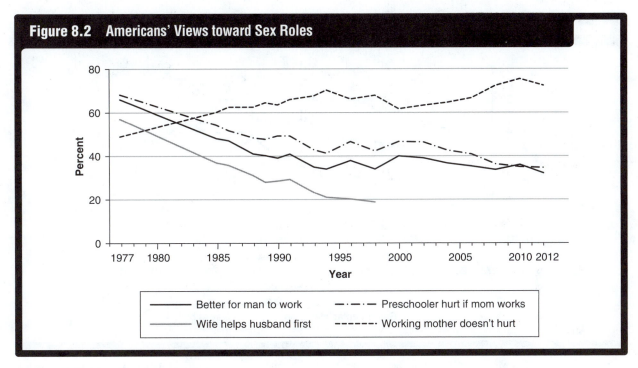

Figure 8.2 Americans' Views toward Sex Roles

Source: Data from https://gssdataexplorer.norc.org.

being gay or lesbian as an acceptable "lifestyle," by the 2000s, the figure was over 50%. Although this is a dramatic change, there is still a sizable minority of Americans who do see being gay as unacceptable.

Attribution theory suggests people who believe that sexual orientation is innate will not blame gays and lesbians, and will be more tolerant toward LGBT and supportive of their rights.[16] Some research, however, suggests it is just as likely that the causal order goes the other way, that is, people who do not see same-sex relations as immoral are more likely to see sexual orientation as innate.[17] Regardless of interpretation, Figure 8.3 demonstrates the dramatic change in Americans' attitudes toward the causes of sexual orientation. In 1978, 13% of Americans thought gays and lesbians were born gay and lesbian, and 56% thought upbringing/environment caused homosexuality, and by 2013 the figures were 47% and 33%.

Americans tend to have more negative views toward transgender Americans than gays and lesbians. Using a feeling thermometer, where respondents indicate how warmly they feel toward transgender people, the average was a freezing 32 degrees.[18] The warmest average temperature was among women, the college educated, young people, egalitarians, people who do not believe in gender binary, and the less religious.

Figure 8.3   Americans' Attitudes toward LGBT Persons

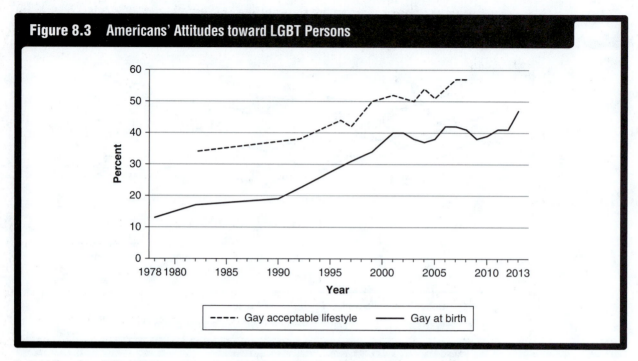

Sources: Data from Jeffrey M. Jones, "More Americans See Gay, Lesbian Orientation as Birth Factor by 47% to 33%, Americans Say It Is Inherent Rather Than Product of Environment," May 16, 2013, http://www.gallup.com/poll/162569/americans-gay-lesbian-orientation-birth-factor.aspx; Gallup, "Gay and Lesbian Rights," October 14, 2014, http://www.gallup.com/poll/1651/Gay-Lesbian-Rights.aspx.

To summarize, Americans' attitudes toward minorities changed dramatically in the last fifty years. We have less old fashioned prejudice when it comes to women and African Americans. Unfortunately, old fashioned racism and sexism have been replaced with modern racism and sexism. The modern versions do not hold that minorities are less capable but rather that there is little discrimination, so programs designed to ensure equality are likely to give special benefits to minorities at the expense of others. There has also been a dramatic change in Americans' views toward gays and lesbians. As a rule, Americans are less likely to see being gay or lesbians as a negative trait. Even with the dramatic change, many Americans still see homosexuality as undesirable, and the view toward transgender Americans is even worse.

Attitudes toward Affirmative Action

Although Americans' attitudes toward minority groups have improved over the years, changes in their support for many policies beneficial to minorities have not kept up. This is clear when examining Americans' support for affirmative action (see Chapter 7 for a discussion of affirmative action), or whether the government should be involved in helping ensure minority rights. The American National Elections Studies (ANES) has asked respondents about their views toward affirmative action since the 1960s, and the GSS since the 1970s. Figure 8.4 depicts the results of four questions concerning affirmative action. Three questions are general questions about whether the government should help blacks/minorities:

Some people feel that the government in Washington should make every effort to improve the social and economic position of blacks . . . Others feel that the government should not make any special effort to help blacks because they should help themselves . . . Where would you place yourself on this scale, or haven't you thought much about it?[19]

Some people feel that if black people are not getting fair treatment in jobs, the government in Washington ought to see to it that they do. Others feel that this is not the federal government's business. Have you had enough interest in this question to favor one side over the other?" If yes, "How do you feel? Should the government in Washington see to it that black people get fair treatment in jobs?"[20]

Some people think that (Blacks/Negroes/African-Americans) have been discriminated against for so long that the government has a special obligation to help improve their living standards. Others believe that the government should not be giving special treatment to (Blacks/Negroes/African-Americans). Where would you place yourself on this scale, or haven't you made up your mind on this?[21]

One question asks whether or not women should be given preferences in hiring.

Some people say that because of past discrimination, women should be given preference in hiring and promotion. Others say that such preference in hiring and promotion of women is wrong because it discriminates against men. What about your opinion—are you for or against preferential hiring and promotion of women? . . . Do you favor/oppose preference in hiring and promotion strongly or not strongly?[22]

Figure 8.4 suggests that support for government assistance for African Americans has declined over the years. During the 1960s and 1970s, about 40% of Americans agreed that the government should see to it that African Americans are treated fairly, but by the 2000s only about 30% agreed. Although this indicates a decline in support for affirmative action, the pattern is not linear. In the late 1980s, less than 20% supported affirmative action, and around the turn of the century (2000), closer to 35% supported it. The other questions concerning affirmative action also indicate low support in the 1980s followed by a rise and then decline.

There are several reasons why Americans' support for affirmative action declined while their levels of old fashioned prejudice fell. One is the insurgence

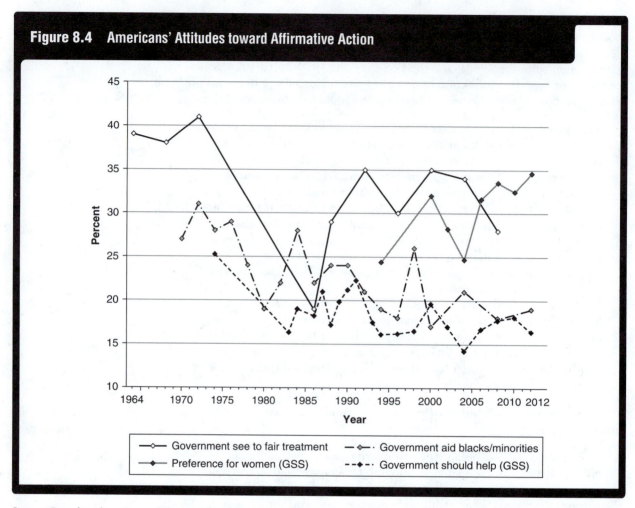

Figure 8.4   Americans' Attitudes toward Affirmative Action

Sources: Data from http://www.electionstudies.org/nesguide/toptable/tab4b_4.htm, http://www.electionstudies.org/nesguide/toptable/tab4b_8 .htm, and http://www3.norc.org/GSS+Website/.

of symbolic racism. If African Americans are less successful because they do not work hard enough, many people might argue that governmental assistance will not be helpful to eradicate inequalities. Also, many Americans do not believe the affirmative steps taken have benefited society. Much polling data find that Americans feel men and whites have been disadvantaged by affirmative action. According to a 2006 GSS survey, about two-thirds of Americans believe that it is somewhat likely that affirmative action results in less qualified African Americans getting jobs at the expense of whites.[23] Another reason is that the United States is more conservative today than in the past, in that there is less faith that government action can fix problems. Later in this chapter, there will be greater discussion on what affects Americans' attitudes toward minority policy.

Figure 8.4 depicts the results of a question asking about preferential hiring of women. This question was first asked in the 1990s, and since then there has been a general increase in support from 24.4% in 1994 to 34.6% in 2012. Nevertheless, most Americans still oppose affirmative action for women.

Figure 8.4 also can be used to compare support for affirmative action for women with support for racial minorities. This comparison suggests that preferential hiring for women has grown while support of affirmative action for racial minorities has declined. However, the wording of these questions is not identical, and responses to questions on affirmative action can change based on question wording. There is evidence of this in Figure 8.4. With the exception of the mid-1980s, Americans report higher levels of support for the statement that "The government in Washington should ensure fair treatment," than support the statement that the "government in Washington should make every possible effort to improve the social and economic position of blacks (minorities)" or to the statement "Some people think that (Blacks/Negroes/African-Americans) have been discriminated against for so long that the government has a special obligation to help improve their living standards." Luckily GSS used the same question wording to tap respondents' attitudes toward preferential treatment for women and for African Americans in 2012. These results suggest that Americans are more supportive of affirmative action for women than for African Americans: 34.6% supported preferences for women, and only 18.9% supported preferences for African Americans.[24]

This section demonstrates that Americans oppose affirmative action for African Americans, and that opposition continues to climb. Although Americans also oppose affirmative action for women, opposition has fallen, and more Americans support affirmative action for women than for African Americans.

Attitudes toward LGBT Issues

Although Americans' attitudes toward affirmative action have not kept pace with their views toward minorities generally, Americans' attitudes toward LGBT policies have seen more positive changes. This can be seen by responses to two questions asked in a series of Gallup surveys:

> Do you think marriages between same-sex couples should or should not be recognized by the law as valid, with the same rights as traditional marriages?
>
> As you may know, there has been considerable discussion in the news regarding the rights of homosexual men and women. In general, do you think homosexuals should or should not have equal rights in terms of job opportunities?[25]

Figure 8.5 depicts responses to these questions over the past thirty years. It indicates a dramatic increase in Americans' support for policies protecting gays and lesbians against discrimination in employment. According to Figure 8.5, whereas in 1982 only 59% of Americans supported employment protection for gays and lesbians, by 2008 almost 90% did. Although there has been a large increase in support for employment protection policies, perhaps the most dramatic change is in support for same-sex marriage. Also in Figure 8.5, whereas in 1996 only 27% of Americans, believed same-sex couples should be legally recognized the same as traditional marriages, by 2013 just over 50% of Americans believed they should be legally recognized. In addition to these trend data, recent studies show Americans in strong support of adoption rights (61%), the right of LGBT to serve in the military (70%), and inheritance rights for same-sex couples (78%).[26] Although Americans may not have positive views toward transgender people, they are generally supportive of their rights. A survey by the Public Religion Research Institute found that 89% of Americans believe transgender Americans should have the same rights as others, and three-quarters believe Congress should pass hate crime language to include gender identity.[27]

Figure 8.5   Americans' Attitudes toward LGBT Rights

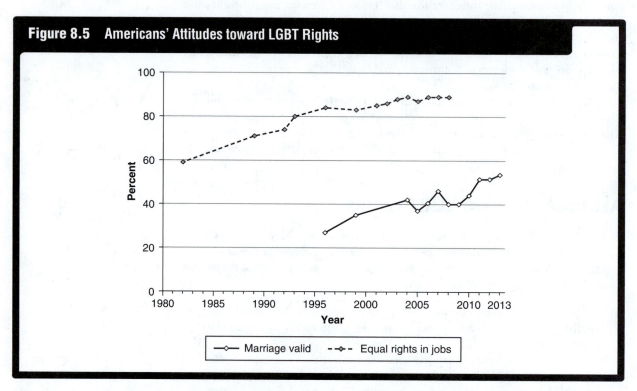

Source: Data from Gallup, "Gay and Lesbian Rights," October 14, 2014, http://www.gallup.com/poll/1651/Gay-Lesbian-Rights.aspx.

Attitudes toward Abortion

One of the key issues for women's groups is abortion rights. Without control over reproductive choice, it is difficult for women to finish school, succeed in the workplace, or have control over their lives. Since *Roe v. Wade*, there have been countless dollars spent and actions taken to try to affect public policy and opinion on this issue. Figure 8.6 depicts trends in Americans' views toward abortion rights since 1995 based on two series of questions used by Gallup. One series asks respondents: "Do you think abortions should be legal under any circumstances, legal only under certain circumstances or illegal in all circumstances?" Respondents who said only under certain circumstances were asked a follow-up question: "Do you think abortion should be legal in most circumstances or only in a few circumstances?" The other question asked respondents, "With respect to the abortion issue, would you consider yourself to be pro-choice or pro-life?"

One of the fascinating things demonstrated by Figure 8.6 is the general stability of Americans' views toward abortion. Note the scale on the figure is truncated, going from 10 to 60, not 0 to 100, yet the movement of the lines is fairly slight. This lack of movement is despite considerable effort to change opinions. To the degree there is a change, there tends to be slight movement toward the pro-life position. This is particularly surprising given that both LGBT rights and abortion rights are often considered morality issues. Morality issues deal less with facts and more with individuals' views of what is right and wrong. Thus, voters often feel confident to make decisions.[28] In this case, on issues related to sexual freedoms. One significant difference between LGBT and abortion rights likely to explain some of the difference in public opinion is that LGBT rights have been framed as civil rights issues.

Figure 8.6 also demonstrates the importance of understanding the question being asked and the potential biases of question wording. If one took the question asking respondents whether they are pro-choice or pro-life, one could conclude that America is highly polarized on the issue since about half of Americans are pro-life and the other half pro-choice. Additionally, one could incorrectly see that about half of Americans are pro-life and assume these people want no abortion rights. This would be a misinterpretation of the survey results. Most Americans are in the middle, relatively few want a ban on all abortions or no limits on abortion rights.

Attitudes toward Immigration

An issue important to Hispanic and Asian Americans is immigration. Survey firms have not consistently asked questions about immigration policy over several decades. However, Gallup has surveyed Americans about their views toward immigration for about fifteen years.[29] One question Gallup has asked concerns

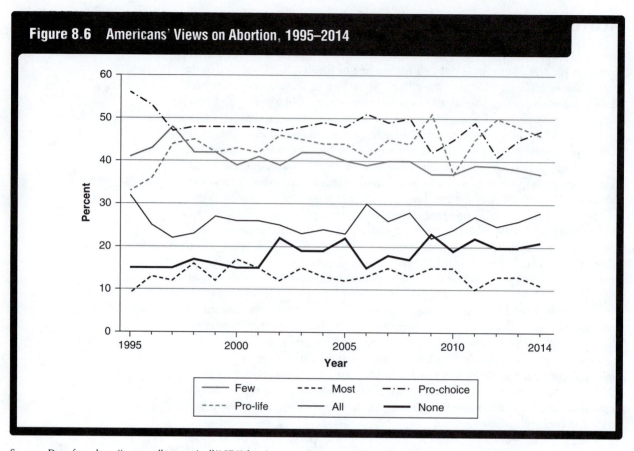

Figure 8.6   Americans' Views on Abortion, 1995–2014

Sources: Data from http://www.gallup.com/poll/1576/abortion.aspx. For years with multiple surveys, the spring surveys were used.

whether immigration should increase or decrease, and another question asked whether immigration is a good thing or a bad thing. The questions read:[30]

> Thinking now about immigrants—that is, people who come from other countries to live here in the United States—in your view, should immigration be kept at its present level, increased or decreased?
>
> On the whole do you think immigration is a good thing or a bad thing for this country today?

The results from these questions are depicted in Figure 8.7, which shows the percentages of Americans who believe the number of immigrants should increase or decrease. They indicate a growth in the percentage of people who want immigration to increase. In 1999, only about 10% of respondents felt immigration should increase, but by 2013 the percentage had more than doubled.

Immigration is a controversial issue dividing America. Here is a protest in support of immigration reform. (*Saul Loeb/ AFP/Getty Image*)

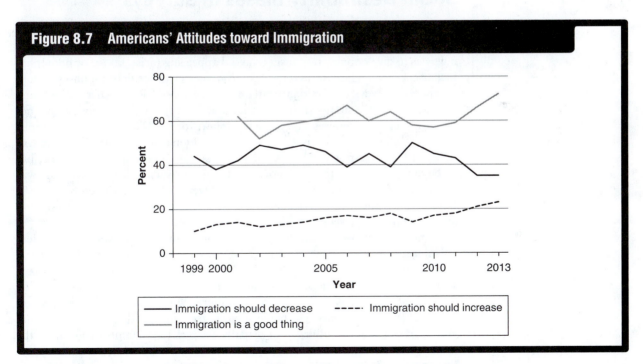

Figure 8.7   Americans' Attitudes toward Immigration

Source: Data from Lydia Saad, "Americans More Pro-Immigration Than in Past," July 11, 2013, http://www.gallup.com/poll/163457/americans-pro-immigration-past.aspx.

The percentage who felt it should decrease fell less sharply, from 41% to 35%; the remaining respondents felt it should stay the same. However, these results still indicate that most Americans do not want more immigration. Figure 8.7 also demonstrates an increase in the percentage of Americans who believe immigration is a good thing. In 1999, 62% of Americans felt immigration was good, and that number jumped to 72% in 2013.

Recent surveys also indicate that most Americans want undocumented immigrants to be able to stay in the United States. According to a 2015 Pew Research Center survey, 72% of Americans believe "undocumented immigrants currently in the U.S. who meet certain requirements" should be able to stay.[31] The Pew survey also found that while most Americans want undocumented immigrants to be able to stay, only about 42% support allowing these immigrants to apply for citizenship.[32] Overall, Americans express some ambivalence toward immigration policy. They generally think immigration is good, but do not want immigration to increase, and while they want undocumented immigrants to be able to stay in the United States, that's conditional, and they do not want undocumented immigrants to become citizens.

Social Desirability Biases in Surveys

Students must be concerned about the social desirability biases of public opinion surveys concerning minority rights. That is, people may answer questions in such a way as to give popular responses to avoid appearing racist, sexist, or homophobic, rather than an honest response. There is some evidence that responses to public opinion surveys on gay rights inflate public support. Researchers have found that when using a survey technique that allows people to give anonymous, not just confidential responses, there is less support for LGBT policies. For example, one study found that when asked with a traditional format offering confidentiality, 14% of respondents opposed antidiscrimination policies for LGBT, but when the responses were anonymous, 25% opposed such policies. This study was designed to examine survey bias, not actual levels of support, therefore the 25% figure should not be seen as indicating the percentage of Americans who oppose antidiscrimination policies.[33]

Another approach to dealing with this problem is a list experiment.[34] Here all subjects are given a list of identical statements, usually in the neighborhood of three or four; half of the subjects are given an additional statement about a socially sensitive issue such as views about minorities. Each subject is then asked how many statements make him or her angry. Researchers can then compare the number of statements that made subjects feel angry within the experimental groups to estimate overall levels of negative feelings to the minority group. If the group given the extra statement indicates more statements made them angry, this can be attributed to the extra statement and that there are high levels of negative feelings toward the minority group. This method does not allow for measuring an individual's attitude, as it is not possible to tell which statements make people feel angry; however, it can give an idea as to how many in a group or subgroup have more negative views. This method has been used to indicate that Southerners may still harbor greater prejudice against African Americans than other Americans, many white Americans are uncomfortable with African American or women presidents, and that Americans want more restrictive immigration policies.[35] Other approaches to deal with social desirability biases, such as affect misattribution procedure and experiments, are discussed in Chapter 2.

To summarize this section, although Americans' support for policies to advance other minorities' interests has not increased with the decline of old fashioned racism and sexism, support of policies advancing LGBT interests have seen dramatic improvement. This may be because many of the policy changes to advance LGBT address policies that are overt in their discrimination, whereas policies to advance African Americans' and women's interests address economic inequalities that appear to come at a greater cost to the dominant groups.

Influences on Americans' Attitudes toward Minority Interests

Several factors are related to Americans' attitudes toward minority issues: socio-demographic traits, political party, ideology, contact with minorities, and perceptions of threat. Many of these same factors affect Europeans' attitudes toward minorities as well (see Spotlight 8.2). This section will explore these influences on attitudes toward minority interests. First, socio-demographic traits, such as age, race, religion, gender, and socioeconomic status affect Americans' attitudes toward minority issues. These traits affect their experiences and interests that in turn affect their values, beliefs, and attitudes. **Values** are the long-term standards people use to make evaluations.[36] For example, some people value equality, and some people value liberty. People who value equality tend to offer more support for minority rights because they want all people to be treated the same. Conversely, people who value liberty may be less supportive of minority policies if they infringe on a person's right to control his or her property. **Beliefs** are views about how the world works or information we have about how the world works.[37] For example, does nature or nurture better explain gender differences, or sexual orientation? Are people poor because of economic systems or their own limitations? Attitudes are peoples' relatively enduring predispositions to respond favorably or unfavorably toward someone or something, such as whether they support same-sex marriage, hate crime legislation, immigration reform, or affirmative action.[38] Individuals' interests are also influenced by their traits. For example, minority individuals may support affirmative action because they are more likely to benefit from it.

Traits, values, beliefs, and interests all interact to affect attitudes. This can be demonstrated by examining why age is related to people's attitudes. Although there are several ways age can affect people's political attitudes, two are particularly relevant: life cycle effects and generational effects. **Life cycle effects** predict that as people go through different stages of their lives, different things are important to them, and this can affect their attitudes or opinions. For example, people in their fifties or older may be more supportive of social security and Medicare than people in their twenties out of pure self-interest. To seniors, these programs can strongly affect their well-being, but younger people are more

Spotlight 8.2

Attitudes toward Minorities in Europe

In 2012, the Eurobarometer asked several questions about Europeans' attitudes toward minorities.[39] These data indicate that about 56% of Europeans believe that discrimination against ethnic minorities is widespread,[40] followed by 46% for sexual orientation, and 45% for gender identity.[41] Only 36% believed gender discrimination was widespread.[42]

Europeans' attitudes toward minorities are not evenly distributed across all nations. In fact, there is considerable variation from nation to nation. Also indicating European attitudes toward minorities is their comfort level with having minority political leaders. Although not absolute, many of the countries that were comfortable with one minority were comfortable with other minority leaders. Residents of Denmark and Sweden were either the most comfortable or the second most comfortable with each minority.[43] Ireland, Luxemburg, and the United Kingdom, too, were often near the top, while residents of Southern and Eastern Europe tended to feel less comfortable.

Besides nationality, there were several factors that affect individuals' comfort levels. The strongest of these was the diversity of individuals' social circles. Individuals with diverse social circles had the greatest levels of comfort. Individuals who were well educated and politically left of center were also consistently more likely to feel comfortable with a minority leader, although the strength of the effect was smaller than the effect of individuals' social circles. Women tended to feel more comfortable with women, transgender, and LGB leaders and ethnic minority leaders. People

under the age of fifty-five were more comfortable with every type of leader except women. And sexual minorities were more comfortable with transgender and LGB leaders. Europeans who had experienced discrimination were also more comfortable with LGBT and ethnic minority leaders.

Europeans were generally supportive of their governments doing more to help end discrimination in the workplace. About 79% of respondents supported diversity training, 76% monitoring of recruitment, and 69% monitoring the composition of the work force.[44] Four conditions increased Europeans' support for these measures: being young, perceiving discrimination as high, having a diverse social circle, and being well educated. However, Europeans by and large do not think the current programs have been effective.[45] Again, there was variation by nation. On a 10-point scale, with an average of 5.1, Ireland and Malta scored 5.8, while Hungary scored 3.9.[46] Not surprisingly, respondents who had experienced discrimination or were ethnic minorities felt it was widespread and were more likely to see government programs as ineffective.

Differences in question wording mean we cannot compare Americans' perceptions of discrimination and what needs to be done about it with Europeans' perceptions of the same things. However, what is uncanny is the similarity of factors related to views toward minorities: having contact, high levels of education, being a minority, experiencing discrimination, and being young.

focused on starting their careers than on retirement. Generational effect can also result in people of different ages having different attitudes. **Generational effect** refers to how key historical events in the lives of a cohort affect their values and beliefs. The historical events that occurred during the lives of individuals as they enter adulthood are thought to be of particular importance. For example, people who came of age during the civil rights era are likely to have different perceptions of race relations than those who came of age before or after the civil rights era. Thus, individuals within an age cohort are likely to share many beliefs, values, and opinions. While this paragraph focused on the effects of age, other socio-demographic traits affect individuals' experiences that can affect their beliefs, values, interests, and attitudes.

One socio-demographic trait that affects Americans' views toward minority interests, as the above suggests, is age. Younger Americans are more support-ive of minority rights than are older Americans. According to a Pew Research Center survey, whereas 66% of millennials (those born after 1981) support mar-riage equality for same-sex couples, only 35% of the silent generation (those born between 1928 and 1945) support same-sex marriage.[47] Younger Americans are also more supportive of allowing undocumented immigrants to stay in the coun-try. According to another Pew Research Center survey, 78% of those between nineteen and twenty-nine support allowing undocumented immigrants to stay in the United States, compared to 69% of those over sixty-five.[48] Younger people were also less supportive of traditional sex roles. Younger people (those born in or after 1977) were less likely to agree that it would be good for women to return to traditional roles than were older people (born before 1946), by 63% to 38%.[49] Americans in their middle years were the least supportive of affirmative action. About 16% of those in their middle years supported affirmative action, compared to 23% of Americans under twenty-seven, and 22% of those over fifty-six years old.[50] Supporters of minority rights might find the support of young Americans encouraging because of generational replacement. **Generational replacement** occurs when one generation dies off and is replaced by a new generation. Since each generation becomes more and more supportive of minority interests, over time generational replacement should result in Americans becoming more and more supportive of minority interests.

Not surprisingly, racial and ethnic minorities are often more supportive of minority interests than are nonminorities. According to the 2008 ANES survey on affirmative action, 44% of African Americans said the government should help African Americans compared to only 12% of whites.[51] Although African Americans are clearly more supportive, it is instructive to point out that most people of either race do not support affirmative action. In the area of immigra-tion, again we see some differences in attitudes based on race. Hispanics (80%) and African Americans (82%) are more supportive of allowing undocumented immigrants to stay in the United States legally than are whites (67%).[52] How-ever, there is no clear trend of racial minorities being more or less supportive than whites of same-sex marriage.

According to the Pew survey used earlier, African Americans are less supportive of same-sex marriages. Whereas 50% of whites support same-sex marriage, only 38% of African Americans support it. A common reason given for African Americans' lack of support for marriage equality is that they tend to be more religious, and religiosity is highly related to opposition to LGBT rights. While religiosity helps explain some of African Americans' views toward LGBT issues, it does not fully explain their low levels of support.[53] Religiosity of African Americans may also interact with class such that the gap between whites and African Americans is larger for the middle class than for the higher and lower classes, and the middle class tends to be church leaders.[54] However, on issues less related to religion, such as gays and lesbians in the military or employment nondiscrimination, most research suggests that African Americans are as supportive of LGBT rights as whites.[55] There is also evidence that Hispanics have similar levels of support for same-sex marriage (52%) as whites.[56] Thus, the growing diversity is likely to increase support for most, but not all, minority interests.

Religion has one of the strongest effects on attitudes toward LGBT and women's interests.[57] According to a Pew survey, 64% of Catholics and 60% of people without a religion disagreed with the statement that women should return to their traditional roles in society, but only 42% of white evangelical Protestants and 51% of white mainline protestants disagreed.[58] When given the opportunity to indicate why respondents opposed same-sex marriage, religion was a common theme. Below are some of the respondents' statements.[59]

> "It's Biblical. God didn't make anybody that way." —an eighty-six-year-old woman

> "It's my Christian views on what God says. It's wrong." —a fifty-eight-year old woman

> "It's against scripture and God's order." —a seventy-year-old man

> "That is not the way it is supposed to be. This is a religious belief." —a seventy-five-year-old man

> "It's just Biblical. That's an undesirable lifestyle." —a sixty-one-year-old man

> "According to God's book, he didn't make gay people. He made Adam and Eve." —a sixty-four-year-old man

> "I'm a Christian and the Bible says it's a sin and there's no two ways around it." —a twenty-eight-year-old man

> "Because I believe in the Bible and I love the Lord." —a seventy-year-old woman

Given that the Christian right has been one of the strongest opponents to LGBT rights and some women's issues, such as abortion rights, and that there are biblical interpretations supporting notions of traditional families, the role of religion is not surprising.

Religion also affects Americans' attitudes toward immigration. Whereas 62% of white evangelical and 65% of white mainline Protestants support allowing undocumented immigrants to stay in the United States, 84% of African American Protestants, 73% of Catholics, and 74% of the unaffiliated support it.[60] Religion's effect on attitudes toward immigration are less likely biblical and more likely cultural. McDaniel, Nooruddin, and Shortle argue that "the cultural opposition to immigrants appears to be rooted in a particular understanding of America's origins as a Christian nation. This belief, which we label Christian nationalism, finds its adherents most strongly among Evangelical Protestants, making them least likely to be favorable toward immigrants."[61]

Although race, age, and religion have the strongest relationships to Americans' attitudes toward minority interests, education and gender are also related to Americans' attitudes. Women are more supportive of minority rights than are men. For example, whereas 56% of women support marriage rights for same-sex couples and 20% support affirmative action, only 46% of men support same-sex marriage, and 18.8% of men support affirmative action.[62] In addition, the more education Americans have, the more supportive they are of minority rights. Americans with college degrees are more supportive of allowing undocumented immigrants to stay in the United States (84%) than those without a high school diploma (62%),[63] and more supportive of same-sex marriage (62% to 46%). The pattern is less clear when examining affirmative action. While 17.4% of respondents to a GSS survey who had a high school diploma supported affirmative action, 28.2% of those without a high school diploma and 20.9% of those with at least a college degree support it.[64]

The above evidence given to support the idea that race, age, religion, education, and gender affect Americans' attitudes toward minority issues has been *bivariate* to keep the analysis easy for students. That is, relationships between each socio-demographic trait and each policy were examined one pair at a time. However, it is possible that these relationships could be spurious since there tend to be strong relationships between several of these socio-demographic traits. For example, age, race, and gender are related to education and religion. Spurious relationships are associations that appear to exist because of a third factor. So, hypothetically, it is possible that educated Americans appear to be more supportive of minority rights, but that it is only because they are younger and that it is age, not education, that drives attitudes toward minority rights. However, as outlined earlier, researchers who have tested for possible spurious relationships still find socio-demographic traits related to views toward minority rights.

Americans' attitudes toward minority interests also vary by **party identification**. Party identification has a couple of different definitions. One definition focuses on individuals' psychological attachment to a party that comes from one's socialization or upbringing.[65] Americans, whether intentionally or not, may be raised to be Democrats or Republicans, and their party becomes part of their identity. Thus, people who identify as Democrats will take cues from other Democrats, and those who identify as Republicans will take cues from other Republicans. Thus, since the Democratic party and its leaders are seen as more supportive of minority interests than Republicans, Democrats are likely to adopt that view and be supportive. The other view of party identification is that of a running tally.[66] With this view, although Americans come to adulthood predisposed to support one party or the other, they evaluate the parties and change their party identification in response to the positions parties take on the issues they care about. Therefore, people who support minority interests would be more likely to be Democrats because the party shares their attitude.

Although with the psychological attachment model, party affects issue positions, with the running tally model, issue positions affect party; in either event, Democrats are expected to be more supportive of minority issues. And for the past forty years that has tended to be the case. According to the ANES 2008 survey, Democrats are more supportive of affirmative action than Republicans (28% to 7%).[67] There are also partisan differences in views toward same-sex marriages. According to a 2013 Pew survey, 59% of Democrats and 29% of Republicans support same-sex marriage (independents are at 57%).[68] Democrats are also more likely to disagree with the statement that women should return to traditional roles than are Republicans (60% to 41%).[69] Similarly, Democrats are more supportive of allowing undocumented immigrants to stay in the United States than are Republicans (76% to 64%).[70]

Americans' views toward minority policies also vary by ideology. An **ideology** can be thought of as a set of attitudes that are held together by some larger understanding of the proper role of government, such that the set of attitudes people have should follow a logical pattern. Although the underlying understandings of liberals and conservatives are less clear today than in the past, liberals are thought to be more supportive of civil and minority rights. And indeed, surveys indicate people who identify as liberals are more supportive of minority interests. Again, according to the ANES 2008 survey, liberals were more supportive of affirmative action than were conservatives (35% to 10%).[71] Also, according to a 2013 Pew survey, 73% of liberals and 30% of conservatives support same-sex marriage.[72]

One of the strongest theoretical explanations for variation in people's attitudes toward minorities and their interests is **contact theory**.[73] According to contact theory, people not in a minority group have negative attitudes about that group due to ignorance. Thus, the more contact they have with minorities, the less likely they are to harbor negative stereotypes and be prejudiced. To demonstrate contact theory, a few responses to a Pew survey that allowed respondents to indicate, in their own words, why they supported or opposed same-sex marriages are given below.[74]

"My best friend's mom is gay and I have a gay friend." —a nineteen-year-old woman

"I work with people who are gay. I believe they are born that way." —a thirty-nine-year-old man

"Over time knowing more gay people." —a seventy-year-old woman

"My sister is a lesbian and I love my sister incredibly!" —a fifty-one-year-old man

"I lived close to a gay community. It helped me relate to what they are dealing with." —a forty-two-year-old man

"I have two lesbians living beside me and they seem like all right people." —a fifty-year-old man

"Knowing quite a few people involved in this. They are good and honest people." —an eighty-one-year-old woman

Table 8.1 also demonstrates the effects of contact theory by looking at the results of a 2006 GSS survey. In 2006, GSS asked a series of questions about how many acquaintances respondents have who are gay/lesbian, Hispanic, and African American. The specific questions were:

I'm going to ask you some questions about all the people that you are acquainted with, meaning that you know their name and would stop and talk at least for a moment if you ran into the person on the street or in a shopping mall. Some of these questions may seem unusual but they are an important way to help us understand more about social networks in America. Please answer the question as best you can.

Respondents were then asked how many gay men or lesbians, Hispanics, and African Americans they were acquainted with. These questions can be used to measure how much contact they had with these groups.

TABLE 8.1 Effects of Contact with Minorities on Support for Minority Policy

Number of Acquaintances	Same-sex Marriage	Affirmative Action	Immigration
0	3.87 (193)	3.52 (106)	3.91 (148)
1	3.53 (45)	3.24 (33)	3.85 (48)
2–5	3.12 (126)	3.49 (123)	3.67 (124)
6–10	2.91 (23)	3.38 (47)	3.63 (46)
More than 10	2.41 (22)	3.42 (67)	3.54 (57)
N	409	376	423

Source: Calculated by the author using 2006 GSS data, http://www3.norc.org/GSS+Website/Download/SPSS+Format/.

Notes: For same-sex marriage the numbers are means of a scale where 1 = strongly favor and 5 = strongly oppose. For affirmative action the numbers are means for a scale where 1 = strongly favor and 4 = strongly oppose. For immigration the numbers are means for a scale where 1 = increase immigration a lot and 5 = decrease immigration a lot. Numbers in parenthesis are number of cases.

GSS also asked a question about respondents' support for same-sex marriage, whether immigration should increase, stay the same or decrease, and about whether they support affirmative action. The same-sex marriage and immigration questions have already been described. The affirmative action question was: "Some people say that because of past discrimination, blacks should be given preference in hiring and promotion. Others say that such preference in hiring and promotion of blacks is wrong because it discriminates against whites. What about your opinion—are you for or against preferential hiring and promotion of blacks?" Respondents were then asked how strongly they favor or oppose preferential hiring. For affirmative action the scores range from 1 to 4 and for the other questions they range from 1 to 5. In each case, higher numbers indicate less support than lower numbers. If contact with a minority group is related to support for that group's interest, we would expect people who have more contact would be more supportive of these policies or have lower scores.[75] And that is what Table 8.1 shows. For LGBT, the relationship is clearest. Those who know at least ten gays or lesbians score more than 1 point lower on the 5-point scale than those who are not acquainted with any gays or lesbians, and there is a nice linear pattern in which for each gay or lesbian a respondent knows, he or she becomes more supportive.

A similar but less dramatic pattern exists for immigration policy and knowing Hispanic Americans. Respondents who are acquainted with at least ten Hispanic Americans scored almost one-half point lower on a 5-point scale. The pattern is weakest for African Americans. The pattern is not linear, but there is a small decline in opposition to affirmative action between those who are not acquainted with any African Americans and those who are acquainted with at least one African American.

Although there is more consistent support of contact theory when examining attitudes toward LGBT than racial minorities, there is fairly strong support in both areas. One reason for some variation in the findings is that the context of the contact may affect its influence on people's attitudes. For example, contact between people of majority and minority status may be more successful if the interaction is among equals who work cooperatively as opposed to people of unequal status who compete against each other. Another reason may be that since sexual orientation is not visible, gays and lesbians only come out to people who are supportive of gay and lesbian interests.

In a study of race relations in Detroit, Welch, Sigelman, Bledsoe, and Combs examined the effects of residential patterns on contact between whites and African Americans and racial attitudes.[76] They find that African Americans living in interracial neighborhoods have more contact with whites and feel less group solidarity with African Americans. Similarly, whites living in interracial neighborhoods have more contact with African Americans and hold fewer negative stereotypes and have less prejudice against African Americans. In addition to levels of contact, Welch and coauthors also expect that where people live affects people's perceptions by affecting the quality of their schools, opportunities, crime rates, and social pathologies. Thus, they also compare suburbanites with urban dwellers. They found that after taking into account the racial mix of neighborhoods, white urban dwellers, compared to suburbanites, held more negative stereotypes toward African Americans but were more likely to support interracial marriage. Urban dwellers in general also had more negative views of public services.

The contact individuals have with minorities can be virtual as well as in person. That is, individuals can have virtual contact with minorities by seeing them on TV, in movies, or other media. Some research suggests that the increased presence of gay and lesbian characters on TV, in shows such as *Ellen* and *Will and Grace*, has had a positive effect on Americans' attitudes toward gays and lesbians.[77] Of course, if the images reinforce negative views, such as the disproportional number of racial minority criminals in TV shows, the virtual contact would not improve views of minorities.

Another explanation for variation in support for minorities and their interests may conflict with contact theory, the **racial threat hypothesis.** The racial threat hypothesis suggests that members of a majority group who live in an area where there is a large number of minorities may come to fear that a minority group will threaten their way of life.[78] These fears may intensify if the minority group appears to be gaining in power with such successes as the election of minorities to office. The threat will increase individuals' willingness to support policies that limit minority economic and political growth. It is therefore expected that people in the majority who live near minorities will be less supportive of minority interests. And indeed research has found some support, particularly when looking at attitudes toward racial minorities.[79] For example, Tolbert and Grummel found that white Californians who lived in more diverse areas (large Latino, Asian American, and African American populations) were more likely to support Proposition 209, which was designed to end affirmative action.[80] There is some evidence, however, that the racial threat hypothesis may explain less about Americans' attitudes today than in the pre–civil rights era, whether applied to racial and ethnic minorities or LGBT.[81] For example, neither Voss nor Giles and Buckner found much evidence that the racial makeup of areas where whites lived affected their vote for Ku Klux Klan leader David Duke for governor and senator in Louisiana.[82] The validity of the racial threat hypothesis may also vary based on context or individual traits. For example, Key's original thesis was designed to explain Southern white views, and Giles and Hertz found it was most valid for people with low socioeconomic status.[83]

It may be possible to reconcile the racial threat hypothesis with the contact hypothesis. Although it may be that the strong effects of contact theory are due to self-selection, that is, people who are less prejudiced are more likely to seek contact with minorities, Oliver and Wong find self-selection is unlikely the case.[84] In addition, Rocha and Espino find that the distribution of minorities in a geographical area affects findings related to support for English-only and immigration policies.[85] The racial threat Anglos feel from Hispanics, particularly those who do not speak English, most likely occurs in communities where there is a large number of Hispanics, but only when Hispanics and Anglos are segregated. Thus, Anglos may feel a threat or competition from Hispanics for jobs, social status, and political power but do not have much contact with Hispanics.

Another way to think of threat is not based on the minority group but on the specific policy. In an investigation of why some pro-gay policies are more likely to be enacted than others Mucciaroni examines variation in the perceived threat posed by different policies.[86] He finds that legislation that had a more difficult time being accepted, like same-sex marriage, is perceived as more threatening than hate crime protections, which are perceived as less threatening.

Public opinion may also be affected by the positions of political elites, such as elected officials and interest groups. Rational choice models suggest that for most Americans there is little value in becoming well informed on all issues. As a consequence, they find easy cues for figuring out their positions. One such cue is to see what the elites are saying. For example, in 1993 when President Bill Clinton announced he planned to allow gays and lesbians to serve openly in the military, the opinions of his strongest supporters followed suit.[87] Zaller argues that elites can affect individuals' opinions through their use of the media.[88] The media will report and reflect their statements. Thus, elites will have the greatest influence on those who are attentive to the news. However, people who are attentive also tend to have firmer positions and are more likely to reject ideas that are in conflict with their own. Thus, they will be more receptive to elite positions of those they tend to agree with and more likely to reject those of elites with whom they disagree. Brewer's examination of Americans' attitudes about civil unions and same-sex marriage supported Zaller's theory.[89] Elites may also affect public opinion since the way they discuss, or frame, issues may affect the way people think about them. So, for example, is same-sex marriage an issue of civil rights or one of traditional family values? More will be said about frames in Chapter 12.

A final factor that can affect Americans' attitudes toward minorities and their interests concerns events. Figures 8.1 to 8.6 show fluctuations in Americans' opinions. Some of these ups and downs can be explained by knowing about key events. For example, Figure 8.5 shows a drop in the percentage of Americans who saw immigration as a good thing after the 9/11 attacks in 2001. In 2002, only 52% of Americans said immigration was a good thing. Court cases or policy adoption can also cause change in Americans' attitudes. Same-sex marriages became law in Iowa because of a court case, *Varnium v. Brien,* in 2009. Kreitzer, Hamilton, and Tolbert use the decision to examine the effects of the case.[90] They found almost immediately after the case many people changed their opinion to become more supportive. The people who became more supportive tended to be those with characteristics suggesting a predisposition to be supportive who did not support marriage rights before the case. Although this case improved public opinion, not all cases have a positive effect.

Conclusion: Varied but Increasing Acceptance of Minorities and Their Issues

There are many similarities between the different minority groups in public support for them. Each group has seen increased acceptance in Americans' views toward the group, although not necessarily increased support for policies designed to serve minority interest. For many but not all groups there is widespread tolerance; the exception is LGBT. However, although opinions have improved, there are still problems. The old fashioned racism and sexism that argued African Americans and women were inherently different from whites and men may have all but disappeared, but there is a new kind of racism/sexism suggesting that policies are not needed to ensure these groups are treated fairly.

Perhaps because of new forms of racism and sexism, as well as differences in the nature of the policies, the decline of old fashioned forms of prejudice have not resulted in uniform increases in the public's support for policies believed to be in their interests. Americans are less supportive of segregation, less willing to limit women to traditional roles, more supportive of LGBT rights, immigration, and allowing undocumented workers to stay in the United States, but at the same time are less supportive of affirmative action and abortion rights. This means that while improved attitudes toward groups and declines in prejudice are good, they do not necessarily translate into policy achievements.

There are, however, many similarities in the types of people who support minorities and their policy interests. The types of people who tend to be supportive are the young, well educated, less religious, liberals, and Democrats, as well as people who have contact with minorities. One possible exception is that although African Americans tend to support most minority issues, they may be less supportive of same-sex marriage.

There is another lesson to be learned from this chapter. People need to be very careful in interpreting survey data. Question wording and social desirability can easily get in the way of finding the truth about Americans' attitudes toward minorities and their rights. And, while this chapter has relied heavily on survey results, they may overestimate Americans' support for minorities and their rights.

KEY TERMS

Attitudes (p. 184)

Attribution theory   (p. 189)

Beliefs (p. 199)

Contact theory (p. 204)

Generational effect   (p. 201)

Generational
    replacement   (p. 201)

Ideology   (p. 204)

Life cycle effects   (p. 200)

Modern sexism   (p. 188)

Old fashioned racism   (p. 186)

Old fashioned sexism   (p. 188)

Party identification   (p. 203)

Racial threat hypothesis   (p. 207)

Symbolic racism   (p. 186)

Values   (p. 199)

Chapter 9

Minority Groups and Political Resources

When the Reagan administration deleted almost one-third of the Bureau of Indian Affairs' budget, Native Nations were encouraged to start or expand gaming operations.[1] Since then their revenues from casinos, bingo halls, and similar businesses have grown dramatically. By 2008, 233 tribes ran 411 "gaming operations" that created 636,000 jobs and produced $26.7 billion in gaming revenues and about $3 billion in revenues from hotels, restaurants, and entertainment associated with gaming.[2] As a point of reference, the revenues in 1999 were $9.8 billion.[3] During the economic downturn in 2008, gaming revenues remained fairly constant as did the economic gains for their communities, but the number of tribes involved in gaming has continued to increase.[4] In 2013, the gaming revenues were about $28 billion.[5] For the tribes that have gaming operations, this has resulted in an economic boom, but readers should realize that not all the tribes have gaming businesses, and the remaining are economically poor. For example, during the 1990s, the unemployment rate in gaming tribes dropped 5% compared to a 2.5% drop for nongaming tribes.[6] The gaming revenues in some, but not all, states have improved tribal relations with states that have gained tax revenue because of the gaming boom. Another effect of the gaming boom has been an increased political presence of American Indians at the federal, state, and local levels. In the 2014 elections, Indian gaming contributed $12.4 million to candidates, up from $193,100 in 1994.[7] The Chickasaw nation alone contributed close to $800.000.[8] In 2003, two tribes contributed over $2 million each. In addition, gaming money has allowed tribes to engage in high stakes lobbying. In 2009, more than thirty tribes and related groups lobbied federal agencies; the Indian gaming industry spent $17.8 million in lobbying at the national level.[9] In 2014, the Gila River Indian Community alone spent over $3.5 million. The National Congress of American Indians has engaged in voter registration drives, is building office space in Washington, D.C., to have a greater presence there, and is partnering with the National Conference of State Legislatures to improve policy making on Indian issues at the state level.[10] The increased revenues have also contributed to an increased interest and participation in U.S. federal, state, and local elections by individual American Indians.[11]

The effects of Indian gaming's resources on the political behavior of American Indians and their tribes demonstrates the importance of financial resources for the political incorporation of minority groups. Although financial resources are

Casinos like this one, the Sho Ka Wah Pomo Casino in California, have provided many Indian tribes with resources that have increased their political sway. (© Marilyn Angel Wynn/Nativestock Pictures/Corbis)

important, there are also other resources that increase a group's political power. This chapter explores the levels of key resources held by individuals within each minority group and that are needed to effectively lobby for the group's interests. These include population size and distribution, the eligibility of the group members to vote, socioeconomic status, and **civic engagement**. Civic engagement has many meanings but here it refers to individuals being active in their community, such as attending church and volunteering with community groups. Civic engagement is important since it helps individuals learn civic skills, gain political knowledge, and it increases the likelihood individuals are recruited and mobilized.[12] Another characteristic of minority groups that is critical for political success is that their members share an identity and interests. The more a group of people share interests and the more they identify with their minority status, the more time, money, and energy they will donate to advancing their group's interest. Shared identity and interests will be explored in Chapter 10.

Some of the key points of this chapter are that the groups vary in their resource strengths. For example, while Hispanics have a large population, they tend to have less wealth and education. Asian Americans, on the other hand, are few in number but have higher levels of wealth and education. Both of these groups' political power, however, is further weakened because many Asian Americans and Hispanics are young, and many others are not U.S. citizens. This means relatively high percentages of Asian Americans and Hispanics are not eligible to vote. African Americans make up a sizeable population, most of whom are citizens, and they have high levels of civic engagement; however, they tend to be economically poor. American Indians, too, are poor economically, are less likely to complete college, but are more likely to complete high school. And although we lack equivalent data as to their civic engagement, their political engagement in tribal issues is likely to help American Indians develop civic skills. LGBT Americans make up a small, youthful group with modest resources, while women make up a large well-educated group that is civically engaged.

Size and Distribution of Minority Populations

The chapters that examined levels of representation noted that descriptive and policy representation are influenced by the population size of each minority group. The larger a group, the more likely it is to see its members holding office and its interests reflected in policy. Population size is important because it gives a group a power base with individuals who can be recruited for grassroots actions, voting, and whose financial resources and talents can be tapped. There are several ways that one can think about the size of the minority group. The national population size could be important for lobbying Washington or collecting funds for national issue campaigns, and to some extent presidential elections. However, the national electorate selects no politician, not even the president. Remember, the president is selected by the Electoral College whose delegates are selected by the states, usually with a winner-take-all system. Thus, the national size may be less important than the distribution of minorities.

The debates over immigration reform offer a nice illustration of this point. Many political observers believe that one reason Mitt Romney lost the 2012 presidential election was because Hispanic voters were significantly more likely to support presidential candidate Barack Obama and believe that if the Republican party wants to win the White House, it needs to do more to reach Hispanic voters. A good way for the Republican party to attract Hispanic voters may be to take the lead on immigration reform. However, the number of Republican House members and senators who need Hispanic voters to win reelection is quite small. Thus, even though Hispanics are a quickly growing voting bloc, few Republican Congress members have enough Hispanics in their districts for them to have a political interest in supporting immigration reform.

Figuring out all the nuances of where it is best for minority populations to be concentrated to maximize their political powers is likely futile since the specifics change with issues and over time. Instead, this section will present national population figures and discuss where the different minority groups are concentrated. Finally, it will explore the minority makeup of **swing states** and large states. Swing states are states whose voters are divided in their support for the Democratic and Republican candidates. Presidential candidates focus their campaigns on these states, and the candidate who wins in the swing states tends to win elections. As a consequence, swing states have the greatest effect on presidential elections. The key swing states of the 2012 presidential race were Colorado, Florida, Iowa, New Hampshire, Ohio, Virginia, and Wisconsin.[13] Additionally, given that state population size also affects electoral votes as well as number of House seats, this section will discuss the minority makeup of the five largest states: California, Texas, New York, Florida, and Illinois.

Racial and Ethnic Minorities

According to the U.S. Census, in 2013 African Americans made up about 13.2% of the U.S. population[14] indicating they have some potential to be a significant political force. This national population figure, however, may underreport their potential to be a significant political force since their populations are concentrated. Map 9.1 depicts the distribution of African Americans across the United States by county. In some localities, particularly in the southeast, African Americans make up a majority of the population, indicating they have the ability to dominate local politics. In many other areas, they may lack a majority but have large enough populations (30% or so) to be significantly influential. However, the distribution of African Americans may also limit their ability to influence very many Congress members or presidential elections. In the vast majority of counties, African Americans make up less than 10% of the population.

Table 9.1 suggests a mixed picture of whether or not African Americans live in powerful states. African Americans are not concentrated in swing

Map 9.1   African American Population, Percent by County

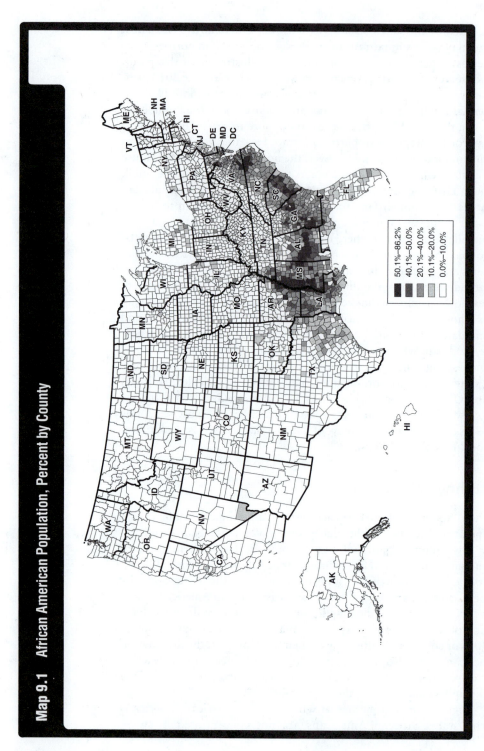

50.1%–86.2%
40.1%–50.0%
20.1%–40.0%
10.1%–20.0%
0.0%–10.0%

Source: U.S. Census Bureau, 2013 American Community Survey 5-Year Estimates, Table B03002, http://factfinder.census.gov/.

TABLE 9.1 Minority Populations in Swing States and Large States

	African American	Hispanic	Asian American	American Indian	Women	LGBT
CO	4.3	21.0	3.0	1.6	49.8	3.2
FL	16.6	23.2	2.7	0.5	51.1	3.5
IA	3.2	5.3	2.0	0.5	50.4	2.8
NH	1.4	3.0	2.4	0.3	50.6	3.7
OH	12.5	3.3	1.8	0.3	51.1	3.6
VA	19.7	8.4	6.0	0.5	50.9	2.9
WI	6.5	6.2	2.5	1.1	50.4	2.8
CA	6.6	38.2	13.9	1.7	50.3	4.0
TX	12.3	38.2	4.2	1.0	50.3	3.3
NY	17.5	18.2	8.0	1.0	51.6	3.8
IL	14.5	16.3	5.0	0.6	51.0	3.8

Sources: Data from http://quickfacts.census.gov/qfd/index.html; Gates and Newport, "LGBT Percentage Highest in D.C."; Lindsay M. Howden and Julie A. Meyer, "Age and Sex Composition: 2010," 2010 Census Briefs, May 2011, http://www.census.gov/prod/cen2010/briefs/c2010br-03.pdf.

states. They make up less than 10% of residents in five of the six swing states. However, they make up more than 10% in all of the large states, and in all but one of the large states, the African American population is higher than the national average. In addition, one of the large states is also the swing state of Florida.

The size and distribution of Hispanics indicates that they are a larger political force than African Americans. First, according to the U.S. Census, Hispanics made up 17.1% of the U.S. population in 2013.[15] Map 9.2 indicates that they are heavily concentrated in certain locations, indicating they have the potential to be large voting blocs locally. This is particularly true in the Southwestern states. In looking at powerful states, again the picture is mixed. On one hand, Hispanics make up over one-third of the population in the large states of California and Texas, and over 20% in Florida. In addition, in the other large states the Hispanic population is as large or larger than the national average. On the other hand, with the exception of Colorado and Florida, they are not concentrated in swing states.

Asian Americans and American Indians are not likely to be significant forces in national politics. According to the U.S. Census, Asian Americans made up about 5.3%[16] of the U.S. population in 2013, and American Indians only about 1.2% of the U.S. population.[17] However, both groups are large enough in a handful of

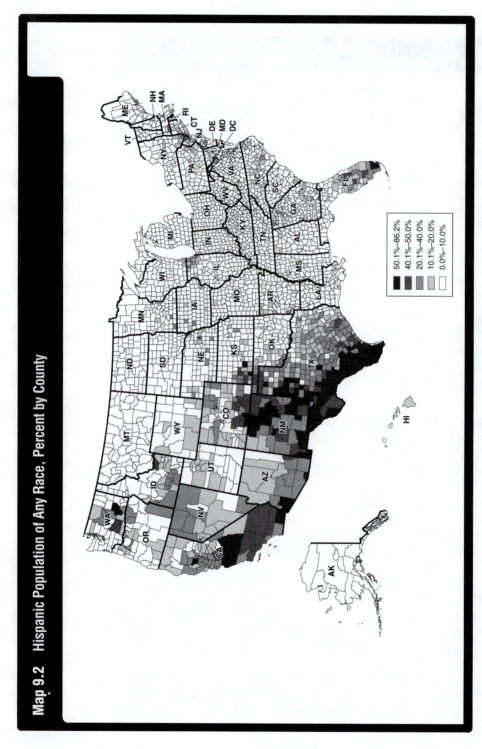

Map 9.2   Hispanic Population of Any Race, Percent by County

Source: U.S. Census Bureau, 2013 American Community Survey 5-Year Estimates, Table B03002, http://factfinder.census.gov/.

states to play a role in local and state politics. American Indians are about 14% of the population of Alaska, 10% of New Mexico, and 9% of Oklahoma and South Dakota. In Hawaii, 38% of the population is Asian and 10% native Hawaiian.[18] Unfortunately, these states are neither swing states nor large states. There is, however, one large state that does have a sizable Asian American population. About 14% of Californians are Asian Americans (see Table 9.1).

The information above just describes the current percentages of the minority groups. However, what might be equally important are their trends, or whether they are becoming a smaller or larger percentage of America's population. Politicians will be particularly interested in reaching minority groups that are growing in numbers, as they will become a larger share of future voters. Figure 9.1 depicts the percentage of the different minority groups from the 1960 census to the 2010 census. It demonstrates that each minority group has become a larger share of the American people over the years. For the groups that see the smallest amount of immigration, American Indians and African Americans, growth has been less dramatic. In 1960, 10.5% of Americans were African American, and in 2010, 13.6% of Americans were African American. The percentage of American Indians has risen from 0.3% to 1.7%. Part of the reason for this apparent growth is that recent censuses have allowed individuals to list more than one race, and only 0.9% in 2010 said they were American Indian alone and 12.6% African American alone.

Although both American Indians and African Americans have experienced gains, Asian Americans and Hispanics have seen even larger gains. In the ten years between 2000 and 2010, the population growth of both groups was over 40%.[19] The percentage of Asian Americans was only 0.5% in 1960 and today is eleven times larger at 5.6%. The first census to ask about Hispanic status was in 1980, and in that year, 6.4% of Americans were Hispanic. In 2010, the number was 16.3%. Since the economic recession of 2008 the number of immigrants has declined and with it the growth rate of Hispanic and Asian Americans. The Hispanic population grew about 2.1% between 2010 and 2013, and the Asian American Population grew about 2.9%.[20] The increase in Asian Americans is still largely the result of immigration, but the Hispanic increase is also the result of a high birth rate.[21] Overall, though, minority populations are growing, indicating the increasing power of minority groups.

Women

Unlike racial and ethnic minorities, women make up a large percentage of the population and are fairly evenly distributed across the states. More than half of America is female (50.8%),[22] and in the vast majority of counties and states women and men are fairly evenly balanced. Thus, based on population size women have the potential to be a significant political force in most every governmental unit.

Within most of the racial/ethnic groups, women outnumber men. In 2012, 51.3% of whites, 53.0% of Asian Americans, and 54.9% of African Americans

Figure 9.1   Percentage of Minority Populations over the Years

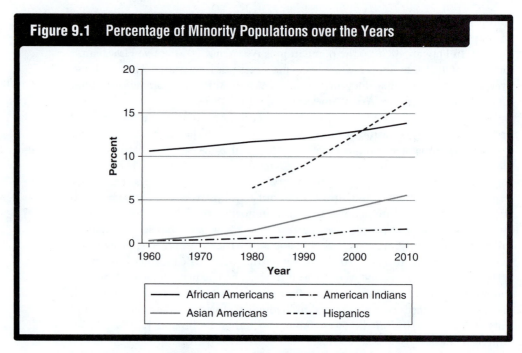

Sources: http://www.census.gov/population/www/documentation/twps0056/tab01.pdf; Elizabeth M. Hoeffel, and Sonya Rastogi, Myong Ouk Kim, and Hasan Shahid, "The Asian Population: 2010," 2010 Census Briefs, March 2012, http://www.census.gov/prod/cen2010/briefs/c2010br-11.pdf; Karen R. Humes, Nicholas A. Jones, and Roberto R. Ramirez, "Overview of Race and Hispanic Origin: 2010," 2010 Census Briefs, March 2011, http://www.census .gov/prod/cen2010/briefs/c2010br-02.pdf; Sharon R. Ennis, Merarys Rios-Vergas, and Nora G. Albert, "Hispanic Population: 2010," Census Brief 2010, May 2011, http://www.census.gov/prod/cen2010/briefs/c2010br-04.pdf.

were women. African American women outnumber African American men by the highest percentage. A likely reason for this is the African American women out-live African American men. In 2012, the average life span of an African American man was 70.8 years compared to 77.5 for an African American woman. For whites, the difference was smaller (76.2 to 81.2).[23] The minority group where men outnumber women is Hispanics: 50.1% of Hispanics are men. It is likely Hispanic men somewhat outnumber Hispanic women because men are more likely to have immigrated. According to the 2010 census, among Hispanics over the age of 18, women outnumber men in the number of native-born Hispanics, but men outnumber women among the foreign-born Hispanics.[24]

Unlike racial and ethnic minorities, women make up a large percentage of the population. About 51% of Americans are women.[25] Also unlike other minor-ity groups, women are fairly evenly distributed across the United States. Alaska has the smallest percentage of women (47.9%) and Rhode Island the largest (51.7%).[26] Thus, based on population size, women have the potential to be a significant political force throughout the nation.

LGBT Persons

Based on population size, LGBT comprise a weak lobby. Most estimates suggest that the gay, lesbian, and bisexual population is less than 5% of the U.S. population,[27] and the percentage of transgender Americans is less than 1% (about 0.3%).[28] Using the 2012 Gallup tracking polls, Gates and Newport estimate about 3.5% of Americans are LGBT.[29] However, this figure likely underestimates the size of the LGBT population since many LGBT are closeted. Morin cites unpublished work by Katherine B. Coffman, Lucas C. Coffman, and Keith M. Marzilli Ericson that offered respondents to a survey anonymity, not just confidentiality, and found much higher levels of people indicating they were LGBT.[30] Confidentiality means the researcher knows the respondent's response but will not tell anyone else, and anonymity means the researcher does not know the respondent's response. With this study, the researchers found that while 11% of respondents said they were not heterosexual and 17% had had a same-sex sexual experience in the confidential version of the survey, in the anonymous version of the survey, 19% said they were not heterosexual and 27% had had a same-sex sexual experience.[31] Because the study did not rely on a random sample, these figures do not indicate the percentage of Americans who are LGBT, but just that the traditional surveys undercount LGBT Americans.

Further evidence of the political weakness of LGBT is that they are not concentrated enough to be a majority of voters, or even a minority of influence in any state or city. According to Gates and Newport, the state with the highest LGBT population was Hawaii at 5.1%.[32] Other states where the LGBT population neared 5% were Vermont, Oregon, Maine, and Rhode Island. North Dakota had the smallest LGBT population (only 1.7%) followed by Montana, Mississippi, Tennessee, Utah, Idaho, Nebraska, Pennsylvania, Iowa, and Wisconsin. Not only are none of the states with large LGBT populations swing states, but two of the states with small LGBT populations are swing states: Iowa and Wisconsin. Gates and Newport also estimate that about 10% of the residents in Washington, D.C., are LGBT.[33] Although this may mean LGBT are a significant voting bloc, residents of Washington, D.C., have limited influence nationally. D.C. has only three electoral votes and is solidly Democratic (so not a swing state). In addition, its only congressional member is a shadow member of Congress. **Shadow members** lack voting authority but otherwise participate in congressional activities. Of course, it is impossible to know whether these states actually vary in LGBT population size or whether LGBT people are just more likely to answer the question in some states than others.

With the exception of women, each of the minority groups has limited power based on size and distribution. Although the racial and ethnic minorities can have power in certain locations and their numbers have increased, they are not concentrated in swing states. Similarly, LGBT make up a small percentage of the U.S. population and are not concentrated enough in any state to make a constant and strong political force. This means their power is limited. Women comprise about half of the U.S. population, which gives them the potential to be politically powerful. That they are evenly distributed means their power is isolated to just a few locations.

The Voting Eligibility of American Minorities

Not only is population size important to the political power of a group, but perhaps even more important is the population size of those who are eligible to vote. Although the eligibility of felons to vote can affect the eligibility of minorities to vote (see Chapter 3), the two main eligibility requirements that tend to affect individuals' eligibility to vote are age and citizenship.

Citizenship

LGBT, women, and American Indians are likely to have high levels of citizenship since they are not disproportionately immigrants. First, since 1924 American Indians have had the right of citizenship, so virtually all American Indians are U.S. citizens. Second, women are not less likely to be citizens than men.[34] Thus, women are no more or less likely to be eligible to become citizens. In looking at LGBT Americans, it is clear that they are less likely to be immigrants than non-LGBT Americans. Whereas about 3.5% of Americans are LGBT, only about 2.7% of undocumented immigrants and 2.4% of documented immigrants are LGBT.[35] Within the LGBT community, women are less likely to be immigrants than men. Thus, LGBT living in the United States are highly likely to be U.S. citizens.

However, African Americans, Hispanics, and Asian Americans are less likely than Anglos to be citizens. Although African Americans are less likely to be citizens than Anglos, the difference is quite small. According to the U.S. Census in 2012, about 95% of African Americans are citizens,[36] compared to 99% of Anglos.[37] Thus, citizenship is not likely to limit the ability of many African Americans to participate.

Not only are Asian Americans a small percentage of the population, but 74% are immigrants,[38] meaning they would need to apply to become naturalized citizens. The days of denying citizenship to foreign-born Asians have gone, and non-native-born Asian Americans are becoming naturalized citizens at high rates. Just under 60% of non-native-born Asian Americans are citizens, compared to 45% of non-native-born in the United States for all groups.[39] Nevertheless, 69.6% of Asians living in the United States are citizens.[40] This means that although 5.6% of Americans are Asian, only about 4% of U.S. citizens are Asian American. The rates of citizenship vary by nationality. Vietnamese are the most likely to become citizens (76%), followed by Filipino (67%), Chinese (59%), Korean (58%), Indian (50%), and Japanese (33%).[41]

Hispanics fare better than Asian Americans when it comes to citizenship. Most Hispanics (64.5%) are citizens by birth, having been born in the United States.[42] However, of the 35.5% foreign-born Hispanics, only about one-third have become citizens.[43] This means just over 75% of all Hispanics are citizens. Thus, although about 17% of U.S. residents are Hispanic, only about 12% of U.S. citizens are Hispanic. As with Asian Americans, there is much variation among different Hispanic nationalities and their rates of citizenship. Since Puerto Rico is a U.S. territory, Puerto Ricans are citizens by birth, and virtually all of Puerto Ricans are citizens. Among foreign-born Hispanics, Mexicans are less likely to become naturalized citizens. Only 36% of Mexicans living in the United States who were born outside of the United States are citizens, compared to 61% of other foreign-born Hispanics, and to 68% for all immigrants.[44]

While citizenship is a stumbling block for immigrants throughout the world, what it takes to be a citizen and vote varies throughout the world. Spotlight 9.1 depicts some of these difference.

Spotlight 9.1

Citizenship Requirements around the World

As a general rule, nations can be divided by whether they grant citizenship by jus soli or jus sanguinis. With jus sanguinis, citizenship is conferred based on citizenship of parents, and with jus soli, citizenship is conferred based on place of birth, having been born in a nation or territory. The Americas are most likely to use jus soli, while most other nations rely more heavily on jus sanguinis. Nations also vary in terms of such things as whether one or two parents need to be a citizen, if it has to be a custodial parent, or even if grandparents allow for jus sanguinis. A particular case is Israel, which confers citizenship on all Jews. Most Europeans have two citizenships, one to their nation and one to the European Union (E.U.). Citizenship in the E.U. is comparatively easy to get and gives an individual a right to vote in E.U. elections, but not in national elections.

Based on parentage or place of birth, some people can have dual citizenship. For example, a child who has parents of different nationalities, or one born in a jus soli nation of parents who are citizens of jus sanguinis nations, could be born a citizen of two nations. Nations differ in how they treat such persons. Some nations allow their citizens to be citizens of more than one nation (dual citizenship), while others require citizens to renounce all other citizenships. The particulars of these laws vary dramatically. In some nations individuals lose citizenship immediately upon gaining another citizenship. In some nations, minors can have dual citizenship, but at some point, often age 18 or 21, they have to choose one nation.

It is also possible in virtually all nations for noncitizens to become naturalized citizens, that is, choose to become a citizen of a nation they live in instead of the one they were born into. Nations vary in what is required but here are some common requirements: applicants must be adults; have lived in a nation for a period of time; not have a criminal record; speak the native language; demonstrate knowledge of the government or history of the nation; and be able to support themselves. Several nations also require applicants to be of good character and/or follow the Constitution. A handful of nations, such as Egypt, have different requirements for men and women. Many nations will alter these requirements if the applicant is married to or, in some cases, in a civil partnership with a national or is a descendent.

Age

Age can be another barrier to full participation. If a large share of a minority group is under the age of 18, then a large share is not eligible to vote. Additionally, since middle aged Americans are more likely to vote than younger Americans, if a minority group is older, its political power is likely to be greater. Although groups with a high percentage of young people may have fewer voters today, keep in mind that in the future these young people will be potential voters. So having a large number of young people today may bode well for the future political power of the minority groups, even though they have fewer voters today.

Most racial and ethnic minorities are younger that Anglos. While 20.1% of whites are nineteen or younger, 30.9% of African Americans,[45] 22.8% of Asians,[46] and 33.8% of Hispanics are under nineteen.[47] Looking at median ages tells a similar story. The median is similar to the average (or mean) in that it tells us what is typical; it is determined by listing all the scores, in this case ages, and picking the middle value. The median is preferred when looking at age since there are often outliers or extreme cases that can make the average less likely to indicate a typical value. The median age for Anglos is 37.7, 30.2 for African Americans, 28.0 for American Indians, 32.7 for Asian Americans, and 25.8 for Hispanics.[48] That minorities tend to be younger may also help explain their growing population sizes. They have more people of childbearing age than Anglo Americans.

Whereas the current political power of racial and ethnic groups may be diminished by their youthfulness, the potential power of women is likely enhanced by their age. Women tend to live longer than men and the average age of women is 38.5, compared to 35.8 for men.[49] Unlike women, LGBT tend to be younger than their counterparts. According to the Pew Research Center survey, whereas 22% of Americans are between the age of eighteen and twenty-nine, 30% of LGBT are in this age group.[50] Seventeen percent of Americans are in the over-sixty-five category, compared to 9% of LGBT. The seeming youth of LGBT Americans is likely caused by older Americans being less likely to indicate they are gay or lesbian in a survey. It is likely that younger Americans are more likely to self-identify as LGBT since older Americans would have found greater discrimination in their youth had they come out. Also, some people do not realize their sexual orientation until later in life.[51]

When looking at the intersection of race and gender with regard to eligibility, some differences emerge. Within Hispanic populations, there are not large differences between men and women in terms of age. The average Hispanic woman is twenty-eight years old and the average Hispanic man twenty-seven.[52] There is a greater difference in the median age of African Americans. The median age for African American women is thirty-four; it is thirty-one for African American men.[53] The median age of Anglo women and Asian-American women is two years greater than their male counterparts. The medians for Anglos are forty-three and forty-one, and for Asians they are thirty-seven and thirty-five.[54] In terms of citizenship, women are somewhat more likely to be citizens than their male counterparts. For African Americans, 94.2% of women are citizens compared to 93.1%

of men. For Hispanics the percentages are 68.1% and 64.4% and for Anglos they are 93.2% and 92.2%. Asian American men are slightly more likely to be citizens 67.7% and 67.8%.[55]

In terms of eligibility, Asian Americans' and Hispanics' ability to participate is limited by their youth and lack of citizenship. African Americans, too, tend to be young and less likely to be citizens than Anglos, but the differences between African Americans and whites are small. There is little evidence that political power of American Indians, women, and LGBT will be harmed by their ability to meet eligibility requirements, as women and LGBT Americans are likely to be citizens, and women are likely to be older.

The Socioeconomic Status of Minorities

The socioeconomic status of individuals making up a minority group can also affect its power and influence. The term **socioeconomic status** (SES) is used instead of class in the United States; it refers to individuals' levels of education and wealth. The more resources individuals belonging to a minority group have, the more resources they can give to the movement. Individuals' SES can also affect their political behavior. It has long been recognized that socioeconomic status affects Americans' voting behavior as well as their work on other types of political activities.[56] Individuals who are of a higher socioeconomic status (SES) may find it more cost-effective to participate. The **rational choice model** has been used extensively to explain political participation. It assumes that individuals will engage in activities if they personally benefit more by the engagement than it costs them to participate.

Individuals' costs and benefits may be affected by their socioeconomic status. People with a higher socioeconomic status may incur fewer costs since it may be easier to understand the process, and they have more resources that can help them get to the voting location. For example, people with more education may find it easier to read and process information about elections, including where to vote and the candidates' positions on issues. People with higher SES may also see greater benefits to participation since they tend to have higher levels of civic attitudes,[57] such as civic duty and efficacy. Civic duty is the belief that Americans have a responsibility to participate in society, and efficacy is the belief that individuals' participation matters. People with high levels of socioeconomic status may also receive more encouragement to participate. In essence, SES affects political participation by affecting individuals' engagement and resources, including civic skills and recruitment.[58]

Table 9.2 gives information on the SES of racial and ethnic minorities. It clearly demonstrates that African Americans and Hispanics average a lower SES than Asian Americans and Anglos. While over 50% of Asian Americans and 30% of Anglos have college degrees, only 20% of African Americans and 14% of Hispanics have college degrees. Also, while the median income is $62,500 for Anglos and $75,000 for Asian Americans, the median income of African Americans is only $38,400 and $39,700 for Hispanics. Although not depicted in Table 9.2,

TABLE 9.2   Income and Education by Race and Ethnicity

	% College Graduate*	Median Income**
Anglos	30.3	62,545
African Americans	19.8	38,409
Hispanics	13.9	39,730
Asian Americans	52.4	75,027

Sources: College graduation data from "Table 229: Educational Attainment by Race and Hispanic Origin 2010," http://www.census.gov/compendia/statab/2012/tables/12s0229.pdf; income data from "Table 697: Money Income of Families—Median Income by Race and Hispanic Origin in Current and Constant (2009) Dollars: 1990–2009," http://www.census.gov/compendia/statab/2012/tables/12s0697.pdf.

Note: Income figures presented are for 2009.

racial and ethnic minorities experience job segregation as well. Asian American workers are disproportionately found in management and professional positions and less likely to be found in service jobs.[59] Conversely Hispanic and African American workers are less likely to be found in management and professional positions and more likely to be found in sales and service jobs.[60] Thus, African Americans and Hispanics are less likely to graduate from college, make less money, and have lower status jobs than Anglos, while the Asian Americans tend to do somewhat better.

Women, too, encounter job segregation and tend to have smaller incomes. Women workers are concentrated in the low paying sales and service jobs but are close to parity in managerial and professional jobs.[61] Within these categories as well there is job segregation. For example, among managers, women are concentrated in the areas of social and community service, but are lacking among chief executives.[62] In addition, women who work outside of the home make less money than men who work. In 2012, the median income for men was $33,900, and it was $21,500 for women.[63] Although women may choose careers that pay less, there may be gender biases in why jobs traditionally held by women, such as nursing and teaching, are paid less. Regardless of the reason, women earn less money than men.

To get a sense on whether minorities' SES is likely to improve in the future, Figure 9.2 depicts changes in income levels for the different minority groups. The data come from the U.S. Census and are based on per capita income standardized in 2012 dollars. Table 9.2 shows that during the 1980s and 1990s all groups' economic situation was improving. Then, starting around 2000, the growth stalled and then fell during the recession. Not only did income growth stall, but income gaps between the wealthier groups (Asian Americans and whites) and the poorer groups (African Americans and Hispanics) have grown. In 1982, African Americans' per capita income was $12,400 and whites' was $21,800; a gap of $9,400. For Hispanics the gap was somewhat larger: $9,600. In 2012, the per

Figure 9.2 Trends in Per Capita Income by Race

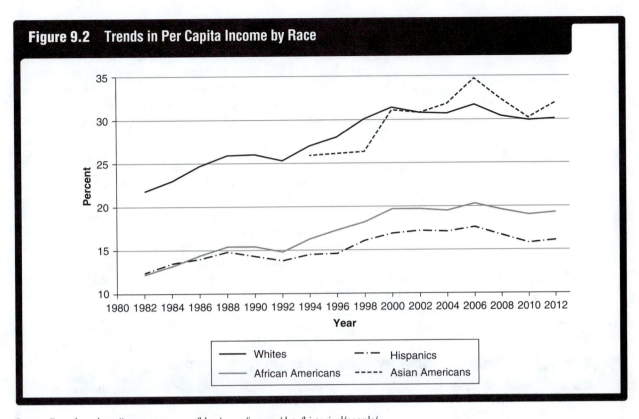

Source: Data from http://www.census.gov/hhes/www/income/data/historical/people/.

Notes: The data are median incomes standardized for 2013 dollars and include people identifying with a single race. With Asians after 2000 the data include Pacific Islanders, with Whites the data include Hispanics.

capita income for whites was $30,100 and for African Americans $19,300; a $10,800 gap. The gap for Hispanics grew to $13,200. Something to note about these data is that the white category included Hispanics, so the gaps would have been larger had African Americans and Hispanics been compared to Anglos.

The above figures do not include information on American Indians, but work by Akee and Taylor offers some insights on the SES of American Indians living on reservations. First, American Indians tend to be economically poor. The median per capita income for American Indians between 2006 and 2010 was about $12,500, for the rest of America it was $26,900.[64] Although using a different population, census data similarly find American Indians generally earn less than other Americans, although the difference is smaller.[65] However, Akee and Taylor also find that American Indians' real per capita income has grown at faster rates than other Americans' and that if current trends continue, they would have higher than average incomes by the year 2054.[66] Summarizing the education levels of American Indians is not straightforward. Although they have higher than average levels of high school completion (or the equivalent), they are significantly less likely to have completed college.[67]

Figure 9.3 replicates Figure 9.2 but includes information on gender. It, too, shows that incomes were on the rise until about 2000. For men the income growth lasted a little longer than it did for women. Unlike racial and ethnic minorities, however, the gap between men's and women's incomes has shrunk. In 1982, the per capita income for women was $13,400 and for men it was $31,900; a $18,500 gap. In 2012, the income for women was $21,500 and for men it was $33,900; a $12,400 gap. Although the gap for women has shrunk while the gap for racial and ethnic minorities grew, the gender gap today is larger than the gap between whites and African Americans, but smaller than the gap between Hispanics and whites. Overall, the trends indicate that women's and American Indians' relative SES status is likely to improve, but Hispanics' and African Americans' is not.

Table 9.3 takes into consideration the possibility that race and gender intersect such that women may have higher or lower SES than men, depending on their race or ethnicity. For groups with higher SES, women tend to do less well than men. Anglo women make about $22,900 annually, and Anglo men make $38,800. For Asian Americans the annual incomes are $23,300 to $40,200. For American Indians the incomes are $30,993 and $35,912. For African American

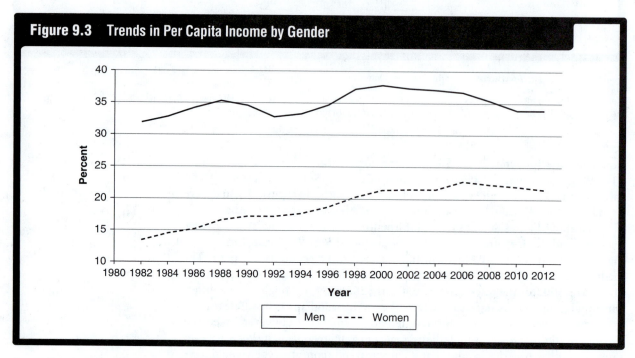

Figure 9.3   Trends in Per Capita Income by Gender

Source: Data from http://www.census.gov/hhes/www/income/data/historical/people/.

Note: Data are median incomes standardized for 2013 dollars.

TABLE 9.3   Income and Education by Race and Ethnicity Broken Down by Gender

	Men		Women	
	% College Graduate	Median Income	% College Graduate	Median Income
Anglos	30.8	38,751	29.9	22,902
African Americans	17.7	24,923	21.5	20,021
Hispanics	12.9	24,592	14.9	16,725
Asian Americans	55.6	40,227	49.5	23,335
American Indians	12.1	35,912	14.4	30,993

Sources: Graduation data from "Table 230: Educational Attainment by Race, Hispanic Origin, and Sex: 1970–2010." http://www.census .gov/compendia/statab/2012/tables/12s0230.pdf (2010 data); income data from http://www.census.gov/hhes/www/income/data/historical/ people/index.html (2012 data); all data on American Indians from http://factfinder.census.gov/faces/tableservices/jsf/pages/productview .xhtml?src=bkmk.

and Hispanics, although women make less than their male counterparts, the differences are smaller. For African Americans the difference is about $4,900 ($20,000 to $24,900) and for Hispanics the difference is $7,900 ($16,700 to $24,600). Although Asian American and Anglo women make substantially less than Asian American and Anglo men, they do, however, have higher incomes than African American and Hispanic women but not men.

Table 9.3 also indicates that although women make less money than men in each racial or ethnic group, African American, Hispanic, and American Indian women are more likely to have a college degree than are their men counterparts. On the other hand, Anglo and Asian American women are less likely to have a college degree than are their men counterparts, although the difference for Anglos is quite small. Similar to income, Asian American and Anglo women are more likely to have college degrees than are African American and Hispanic women. These findings, therefore, paint a mixed picture of women's SES compared to men's. While women in all racial/ethnic categories earn less money, they tend to be as educated.

The SES of LGBT Americans is similarly mixed. Although they tend to be poorer than most Americans,[68] they also tend to be better educated.[69] According to a Pew Research Center study, 43% of Americans have less than a high school education, but only 33% of LGBT Americans have not graduated from high school.[70] Also, while 26% of Americans have a college degree, 32% of LGBT Americans have at least a college degree. According to Gallup data, "about 16% of LGBT-identified individuals have incomes above $90,000 per year, compared with 21% of the overall adult population."[71] On a related note, LGBT Americans are less likely to be Anglo than of a racial or ethnic minority group.[72] According to Gallup data, 3.2% of non-Hispanic whites identify as LGBT, 4.6% African American, 4.0% Hispanic, and 4.3% Asian Americans identify as LGBT.

Sexual orientation and race/ethnicity interact to affect individuals' SES. Badgett, Durso, and Schneebaum report poverty rates for gay male couples, lesbian couples, and different sex couples by race.[73] They find that white gay men couples are less likely to be poor (3.1%) than married different-sex couples (4.8%) and lesbian couples (5.8%). The trend is similar for Hispanics and American Indians. For Hispanics, the percentages of couples living in poverty are 8.5, 15.3, and 12.4, respectively, and for American Indians the percentages are 8.1, 12.6, and 18.4. However, gay African American male couples are much more likely to be poor than different-sex African American couples. About 18.8% of African American gay men couples live in poverty, compared to 8.0% for different-sex African American couples and 17.9% of lesbian couples. Although African American lesbian couples are somewhat less poor than their male counterparts, by and large lesbians are the most likely to be poor within each racial/ethnic group. There is

Spotlight 9.2

Gender and Foreign-Born Economic Disparities in Europe

Much like American women, European women make less than European men. According to a recent European Union report, women make on average about 16.4% less than European men, but there is much variation by nation.[74] In Slovenia the gap was only 2.5%, but in Estonia it was 30.0%.[75] There was also variation by employment sector. In most nations the gender gap was smaller in the public sector than in the private sector, the exceptions being Sweden, Bulgaria, Latvia, and Hungary.[76] The gap was the largest in the financial sector.[77] Although women tend to work in lower paying segments of the economy, across all segments women make less than men. Women did make more than men in construction in several but not most nations. A promising sign is that the wage gap is smaller for younger workers than for older workers.

Immigrants living in Europe also fare poorly economically.[78] While the average unemployment rate among twenty-five- to fifty-four-year-olds in Europe is 8%, for those with non-EU state citizenship (third country nationals), the rate is 18%. While the unemployment rate for third country nationals in some nations is smaller, less than 10% in the Czech Republic, Greece, Cyprus, the Netherlands, and the United Kingdom, it is over 29% in Belgium and 28% in Spain.[79] And in every nation it is higher. Women third country nationals do somewhat better. They average 17% unemployment, compared to 19% for men third country nationals.[80]

Another way to look at the economic well-being of third country nationals is to look at their median incomes. How well they do depends greatly on where they live. In Belgium, their proportion of median equivalized disposable income is only 55, but it is 136 in Bulgaria and 110 in Malta. The proportion of income earned by men who are third country nationals to men who are EU nationals is not always larger or smaller than the proportion of income earned by women third country nationals. In some nations, such as the United Kingdom and Denmark, women do comparatively better; in other nations, such as Latvia and Estonia, men do comparatively better, and in some nations, such as Belgium and Spain, men and women third country nationals do similarly compared to their counterparts. Most likely the particulars of a nation's economy, labor needs, and gender roles interact to affect the relative success of men and women third country nationals.

one major exception to this trend, however. Asian American lesbian couples are the least likely to be poor (2%).

The previous paragraphs suggest that with the exception of Asian Americans, ethnic and racial minorities have lower levels of socioeconomic status. This suggests that they will have less time, money, civic skills, and political engagement than others. Additionally, it suggests they may be less likely to be mobilized or recruited for political actions. Women and LGBT Americans present a more mixed picture, and although they tend to be poor (although this varies some by racial groupings), they tend to have equivalent levels of education. That minorities tend to have lower standards of living than majorities is found throughout the world. See Spotlight 9.2 for a discussion of the incomes of minorities in Europe.

The Civic Engagement of Minorities

Along with socioeconomic status, the degree to which minorities associate with others and join various groups may affect their political influence and power. Earlier, it was noted that SES affects political participation by affecting individuals' engagement and their resources, including civic skills and recruitment, but civic engagement, being active in organizations such as churches and social services groups, can also affect individuals' civic skills and likelihood to be recruited for political participation.[81] As a consequence, this section examines variation in volunteerism and association with religious institutions among the minority groups. The more active minorities are in nonpolitical activities, the more likely they are to become active in political activities. In examining the political participation of Asian Americans, for example, Wong, Ramakrishnan, Lee, and Junn found that Asian Americans who were active in secular and religious organizations were more likely to vote, give money to candidates, contact officials, protest, and engage in community activism.[82]

Volunteerism

Volunteering is a great way to make contacts and develop skills helpful for political activism. Thus, this section compares the volunteer rates of several groups. According to the 2014 Current Population Survey, African Americans are less likely to volunteer than are whites. Although the survey indicates that whites are somewhat more likely to volunteer than African Americans (26.7% to 19.7%),[83] African Americans who volunteer put in the same number of hours as whites (fifty-two to fifty-two hours annually).[84] Although African Americans and whites may have similar overall levels of volunteerism, Asian Americans and Hispanics are less likely to volunteer: 18.2% of Asian Americans and 15.5% of Hispanics reported having volunteered. Additionally, Asian Americans, but not Hispanics, report

Becoming a naturalized citizen is an important step to enable immigrants to fully participate in U.S. politics. (*John Moore/Getty Images*)

putting in fewer volunteer hours (thirty-six for Asian Americans and fifty-one for Hispanics).[85] This suggests that Asian Americans and Hispanics may be less likely to be mobilized to be active in politics or develop civic skills.

There are also gender differences in volunteer rates, with women volunteering more than men. According to the 2014 Current Population Survey, 28.3% of women report volunteering compared to 22.0% of men.[86] According to the same survey, women volunteer slightly fewer hours a year (fifty to fifty-two hours). Again, it may be that there is variation by race and gender. According to results of a 2012 GSS survey mentioned above, when broken down by race and gender, gender differences in volunteer rates vary dramatically by race.[87] Women are more likely to volunteer than their men counterparts for whites and African Americans but not Hispanics, and the difference is most pronounced for African American women. Almost 45% of African American women reported having volunteered in the past month, compared to 34% of African American men. White women, on the other hand, volunteer at only slightly higher rates than men. About 35% of white women reported volunteering, compared with about 32% of white men. Among Hispanics, only 23% reported volunteering in the past month, and Hispanic women were less likely to participate than Hispanic men. Only 21% of Hispanic women reported volunteering, compared with 25% of Hispanic men.

Religiosity

Examining religious activities also suggests that women and African Americans may be civically engaged enough to develop civic skills and to be recruited for political activities. According to 2012 GSS data, African Americans are the most likely to attend church on a regularly basis.[88] Whereas only 11.3% of African Americans report never attending church, 27.6% of whites and 22.5% of other races report never attending church. At the other end of the scale, 11.4% of African Americans report attending church more than once a week, compared to only 5.5% of whites and 4.8% of other races. For weekly attendance the percentages are 18.4% for African Americans, 18.0% for whites, and 27.6% for other races. Thus, African Americans are highly likely to gain civic skills and networks through their religious activities.

Looking at the Asian Americans' and Hispanics' attendance at religious services gives a mixed picture: Asian Americans are somewhat less likely to attend church than other Americans, and Hispanics are more likely to attend services. According to a Pew Research Center study, whereas 32% of Asian Americans attend church at least weekly, 36% of the general public does;[89] and according to a 2014 survey from the Pew Research Center, 40% of Hispanics attend church at least weekly, compared to 37% of the general public.[90] These differences are likely caused by differences in religion in Asia and Latin America. Asian Americans who are less acculturated and live in areas with more Asian immigrants are less likely to be active in their religious community,[91] while Hispanics who were foreign-born attend religious services frequently.[92]

As with volunteerism, the data on church attendance also suggest women are more active. GSS asks respondents how often they attend religious services and these data indicate that whereas 27.6% of men never attend church, only 21.8% of women never attend church.[93] Conversely, 19.5% of women attend church weekly, and 7.6% attend church more than once weekly. For men the percentages are 19.0% and 4.7%. Women within each racial/ethnic group also attend church more regularly. For example, 8.6% of African American women never attend church, compared to 17.6% of African American men. In addition, 15.5% of African American women attend church more than weekly compared to 6.5% of African American men. The gaps are smaller for whites and other races, but within each category women are more likely to attend church more than weekly and less likely to never attend.

LGBT Americans are less religious than others. According to the Pew Research Center survey of LGBT Americans, they are twice as likely as non-LGBT Americans not to be affiliated with any church.[94] It also reports that whereas 65% of LGBT Americans seldom or never attend church, only 29% of non-LGBT Americans seldom or never attend church.[95] Although LGBT Americans may be less likely to attend church, they may be more likely than non-LGBT Americans to develop civic skills and gain recruitment through other activities. About 80% of LGBT Americans use social networking, and about half have engaged in some form of LGBT rights activity, such as joining a group or attending a pride event.[96] But how these activities compare to religious activities in building networks and civic skills is unknown.

Based on their high levels of volunteerism, women, and to a lesser extent African Americans, are likely to have higher levels of civic skills, engagement, and recruitment than Asian Americans and Hispanics. There is less information on LGBT civic engagement, but they appear to have low levels based on religious affiliation. Although the above surveys did not survey enough American Indians to offer comparable information about their volunteer activities and religious attendance, American Indians have additional ways to gain civic skills. American Indians are not only citizens of the United States but are also citizens of sovereign tribes, and many living on reservations need to navigate U.S. national, state, and local political institutions as well as American Indian institutions. American Indians tend to be more active in tribal politics than U.S. politics.[97]

Conclusion: Variation among Groups in Their Resources

A review of the resources of the different minority groups suggests that while all groups can be said to be resource poor, the different minority groups have different resources to bring to the table. Asian Americans have high levels of SES, but are small in number (although large in some localities) and are less civically engaged than individuals in other groups (volunteer and attend church less). Not only are Asian Americans small in number, but there is also a significant percentage of Asian Americans who are not citizens and/or under the age of eighteen. Hispanics comprise a large group of Americans; however, they are otherwise resource poor. They are younger, less likely to be citizens, have low levels of SES, and have less civic engagement. African Americans are a fairly large percentage of Americans, tend to be citizens, and civically engaged. However, African Americans tend to have low levels of SES. American Indians are small in numbers and have low SES, but are likely to be eligible to vote. Women make up a large percentage of the U.S. population, tend to be as well educated, are older, and are more civically engaged than men. LGBT make up a small percentage of Americans, they tend to be less well off (except for non–African American gay men in relationships) but better educated.

This chapter also demonstrates the importance of not assuming all women are alike or all members of a minority group are alike. For example, although women tend to outnumber men, there are more Hispanic men than Hispanic women in the United States. Also, while for most minority groups women are more likely to be citizens, that is not the case among Asian Americans. Also, while Asian American and Anglo women tend to make less money than their men counterparts, they still average higher median incomes than Hispanic and African Americans of either sex. Similarly, while Anglo and Asian American women are less likely to have college degrees than their men counterparts, they are more likely to have a college degree than Hispanics or African Americans of either sex. In addition, African American, Hispanic, and American Indian women are more likely to have college degrees than their men counterparts. There were intersectional differences in volunteerism. Although women tended to be more active volunteering, among Hispanics that was not the case.

To be politically powerful, groups not only need members who have important resources but also need those individuals to expand their resources in the groups' interests. Organizations have to be able to mobilize the resources. One thing that is helpful for mobilization is that there is some cohesion and consciousness among the individuals of the group. This is the topic of the next chapter.

KEY TERMS

Civic engagement   (p. 212)   Shadow members   (p. 219)   Swing states   (p. 213)
Rational choice models   (p. 223)   Socioeconomic status   (p. 223)

Chapter 10

Acculturation, Group Consciousness, and Cohesion among Individuals with Shared Minority Status

In 1977 Sonia Johnson was a forty-two-year-old college-educated Mormon housewife when she received a call from her old friend Hazel.[1] It had been fifteen years since Sonia had really spoken with Hazel, and in that time Hazel had become a feminist. Hazel inspired Sonia to start reading about feminism. To describe how she was transformed into a feminist, Sonia writes, in her book *From Housewife to Heretic*,

> Women have a unique file entitled "what it means to be female in a male world," and from the moment we are born female and a voice says, "It's

a girl," we begin dropping pieces of data into it. For some women, this file is readily accessible; they can look into it whenever they wish, and it often offers its contents to them spontaneously. For still others, this file opens only infrequently and is so threatening that it is quickly closed, though the owner knows and remembers what she has glimpsed there. There are all degrees of awareness and willingness to cope with this file until at the other end of the continuum are women like the woman I was, traditional women, deeply male-oriented and patriarchal in our view of the world and ourselves. . . . . We, more than other women, fear the knowledge that file contains, so much so that even when we are forced

Many women, such as Sonia Johnson (pictured here), had to have their consciousness raised in order to become active in the women's movement. (© *Bettmann/Corbis*)

to look, we deny what we have seen, we distort the data to make it fit the myth patriarchy teaches women to live, and we thrust the file deeper, down into the bottom corridor and underneath stacks of files we never open. . . . Data about being female under male rule still drops at an alarming rate into that file, and the file grows fuller and fuller—there is so much data!—until the seams begin to crack. We reinforce them frantically (perhaps by fighting the ERA). Finally, however, no matter how strong that file—and patriarchal women have almost bionic files—there comes along the one piece of data that breaks it wide open.[2]

For Sonia the file broke open in the winter of 1978 when she went to hear a church official speak about why the church opposed the Equal Rights Amendment. The speaker had not prepared for the speech and only read a simplistic article on the amendment just prior to the meeting. That the speaker had not prepared and used simplistic terms indicated to Sonia that he lacked both an interest in the issue and a respect for women. The summer after her file broke, she marched in Washington, D.C., behind a banner that read "Mormons for the ERA," and testified before a Senate subcommittee on the proposed amendment.[3] A few months later she founded an interest group, "Mormons for the ERA." The conversion of Sonia Johnson to feminism indicates the importance of individuals' group consciousness in activating them to work on issues important to their group.

In that vein, this chapter focuses on three characteristics of minorities to explore the likelihood individuals of a group will become active working on a common purpose: acculturation, group consciousness, and group solidarity/cohesion. When members of a group share values, attitudes, and goals, it is easier for political elites to mobilize them for a common collective goal. If individuals within a group share political views, a greater proportion of their resources can be tapped to foster that goal. Group solidarity or cohesion is related to group consciousness, which can also increase the willingness of individuals in a group to work to advance their interests. African Americans who identify as African American, Hispanics as Hispanics, Asian Americans as Asian Americans, and so on, and see that identification as politically relevant are likely to participate to advance their interests. In addition, individuals who are acculturated are likely to be politically active, which should increase their political power. However, individuals with high levels of acculturation also tend to have low levels of group consciousness and cohesion, which could depress the political power of minority groups. This chapter examines the degree to which individuals in each minority group have group cohesion (shared religion, ideology, party identification, and vote choice), have a group consciousness (identify with a group and see that group as facing discrimination), and acculturation (whether individuals feel like typical Americans, were born in the United States, and speak English).

Some takeaways from this chapter are that LGBT Americans and African Americans have high levels of acculturation, group cohesion, and group consciousness. Asian Americans and Hispanics have modest levels of acculturation, group cohesion, and group consciousness. Women have high levels of acculturation and modest levels of group cohesion and group consciousness. Women, including women within each minority group, tend to have higher levels of cohesion and consciousness than men. In addition, it shows that minorities by and large are more liberal and Democratic than their counterparts. Finally, the end of the chapter looks at whether acculturation and group consciousness are related to whether minorities voted for President Barack Obama.

Acculturation: The Extent to Which Minorities Are Part of the Dominant Culture

Acculturation refers to how well individuals can function in the dominant U.S. culture and economy.[4] It tends to be measured by how long individuals have lived in the United States and their ability to speak English. Levels of individuals' acculturation are politically important. Given the term's focus on language and length of time in the United States, acculturation is most likely to affect minorities that have large numbers of immigrants. Generally, individuals with low levels of acculturation have a greater sense of ethnic identity and are more liberal on issues. For example, Branton examined Hispanics' attitudes on several policies and found that those with lower levels of acculturation tended to have more positive attitudes toward immigration, government spending and services, affirmative action, and education reform.[5] Also, individuals with lower levels of acculturation were more likely to see descriptive representation as important and to vote for candidates of their own race or ethnicity.[6]

These findings suggest that minority groups with low levels of acculturation may be able to work collectively to advance their interests. However, high levels of acculturation may be helpful in increasing political behavior since individuals who have lived in the United States longer may have a better understanding of the process and find it easier to participate. Although not the topic of his research, Sanchez found that the longer Hispanics had lived in the United States the more likely they were to register to vote, vote, and participate in Hispanic-specific activities such as attending a demonstration concerning a Hispanic issue or working on the candidacy of a Hispanic candidate.[7] Given the effects of acculturation on political attitudes and participation, this chapter explores minority individuals' levels of English proficiency, length of residence in the United States, and feeling as though one is a typical American where available.

Women and LGBT have high levels of acculturation. Women and men are similar in the likelihood that they are first-generation Americans. In 2012, about 12.9% of women were first generation, 11.1% second and 75.8% third or higher. For men the figures are 13.0%, 11.8%, and 75.2%.[8] There is not much difference in the likelihood men and women speak English at home. About 79.3% of women speak English at home compared to 79.0% of men.[9] Less is known about LGBT Americans' acculturation, but estimates tend to have well over 90% of

LGBT Americans being born in the United States.[10] Thus, most LGBT Americans can be assumed to be acculturated.

In looking at racial and ethnic minorities, the most acculturated group is African Americans. Of the racial and ethnic groups, African Americans are the most unified in speaking English. Only 8.3% of African Americans speak a language other than English at home; this compares to 5.8% of white Americans.[11] In addition, about 92% of African Americans were born in the United States.[12]

On the other side of the coin, the group that is least acculturated is Asian Americans. According to the Pew Research Center's 2012 Survey of Asian Americans, only 42.5% of Asian Americans said they thought of themselves as typical Americans, and 57.5% said they felt very different.[13] In addition, about 75% of Asian Americans are first-generation Americans, 18% are second-generation, and only 6% are third-generation or higher.[14] Also according to the Pew survey, 36.5% of Asian Americans speak English less than very well.[15] The main factor affecting Asian Americans' language proficiency is place of birth. Asian Americans born in the United States are more likely to speak English proficiently than those born abroad.

There are modest gender differences among Asian Americans' acculturation, with women having somewhat lower levels. According to the Pew survey noted above, 43.7% of Asian American men feel they are typical Americans compare to 41.1% of Asian American women.[16] The survey also found that whereas 42.8% of Asian American women said they could carry on a conversation in English, 54.3% of Asian American men said they could carry on a conversation in English. However, the survey also found a tendency for Asian American men to be somewhat more likely to be first generation (76.6% to 74.1%). That Asian American men are more likely to be first generation but feel more like typical Americans and more likely to be proficient in English suggests that nativity status does not account for the gender gap in acculturation.

While African Americans have high levels of acculturation and Asian Americans low levels, Hispanics are somewhere in between but more similar to Asian Americans in their low rates of acculturation. According to the 2012 National Survey of Latinos, 49.7% of Hispanics feel like typical Americans,[17] and about half were born on U.S. territory, including Puerto Rico. Because of this, 39.3% report speaking English less than very well.[18] Thus, about 60% of Hispanics speak English very well. The main factor affecting Hispanics' language is place of birth. Of Hispanics born in the United States, 39.7% speak only English at home, compared to only 4.4% of non-native U.S. Hispanics.[19]

As with Asian Americans, Hispanic women may be somewhat less acculturated than Hispanic men. According to the 2012 National Survey of Latinos, 24.9% of Hispanic women and 27.3% of Hispanic men have high levels of proficiency in the English language.[20] Finally, 51.2% of Hispanic men and 49.9% of Hispanic women feel like typical Americans.

The acculturation of American Indians is not straightforward. On one hand, the vast majority of American Indians are native-born Americans and speak English. The U.S. Census, for example, estimates that among American Indians living in American Indian or Alaskan Native Areas, 87% speak only English.[21] On the other hand, in many ways they have two countries, the United States and their tribe, which can divide their loyalties. Wilkins and Stark discuss unpublished work by Diane Duffy that discusses different types of patriotism held by American Indians. Below is a listing:

Indigenous patriotism: primary allegiance to their tribe and they speak their native language.

Measured-separatism patriotism: some support for the United States but primary allegiance is to the tribe.

Anti-American patriotism: considerable hostility toward the United States, although not necessarily supportive of tribe.

Environmental patriotism: similar to indigenous patriotism but extends to all creation not just human.

Assimilative patriotism: the United States is supreme and tribes are secondary.

Co-optive or colonized patriotism: lacks a tribal political consciousness or allegiance.

Apatriotic: has no patriotism.[22]

Based on this review of acculturation, Asian Americans and Hispanics have low levels of acculturation, which is likely the result of their high levels of immigration. On the other hand, women, LGBT Americans, and African Americans have high levels of acculturation. In addition, Asian American and Hispanic women are likely to be less acculturated than white women or men sharing their race/ethnicity. American Indians have high levels of acculturation based on usual measures but nonetheless have a unique relationship to the United States.

Group Consciousness: The Extent to Which Minorities See Group Status as Politically Important

A key concept in understanding minorities' attitudes and behaviors is group consciousness. **Group consciousness** is the idea that an individual identifies with a group and sees that identity as politically important. Specifically, researchers have suggested that group consciousness is comprised of some mix of the following:[23]

1. Individuals identifying with or seeing themselves as part of group.

2. A belief that the group faces discrimination or that failure of individuals to succeed is caused by systemic or institutional racism.

3. Dissatisfaction with the group's status compared to other groups and desire for collective action.

4. Individuals prefer to be with people of their group, or feel close to their group.

5. A commitment to the group and/or that the group has a linked fate. **Linked fate** refers to the belief that individuals of a group are distinguished by society such that the fate of one person in the group is linked to the fate of all in the group.

Much of the research on group consciousness comes from studying African Americans, and suggests that group consciousness is the result of a group having had a history of being treated differently in profound ways because of their group status such that an individual's life is greatly affected by being part of that group. Because of this, individuals socialize with and rely heavily upon people of this group's status.[24] Although this theory is based on studying African Americans, it has been extended to other groups. Generally, individuals' levels of group consciousness increase with their socioeconomic status since SES effects individuals' awareness of a group's history, the length of a group's history in the United States, nativity status, mobilization, and awareness of discrimination.[25] Wright Austin, Middleton, and Yon have found similar traits affect the group consciousness of African Americans and Black ethnics.[26] For Hispanics, as well, experiencing discrimination increases their panethnic identity.[27] The term **panethnic identity** refers to individuals feeling part of a group that has many nationalities or ethnicities,[28] such as Mexican Americans identifying as Hispanic instead of Mexican, or Chinese Americans identifying as Asian American instead of Chinese.

The political implications of group consciousness have been examined by estimating the effects of group consciousness generally, as well as individual aspects of group consciousness, such as the effects of discrimination. Therefore, in summarizing these implications, I will refer to general effects unless an aspect has unique effects. Group consciousness can affect individuals' attitudes and vote choice such that individuals with higher levels of group consciousness have less trust in the government, prefer the Democratic Party and Democratic candidates, prefer **co-ethnic candidates** or candidates who share their race or ethnicity,[29] and the concept of descriptive representation.[30] Generally, group consciousness is thought to increase participation in political activities, such as voting, attending rallies, contacting officials, donating funds, meeting officials, signing petitions, picketing/boycotting, and volunteer activities.[31]

The research is somewhat mixed as to the effects of group consciousness on voting but tends to find stronger effects on minority-specific activities, such as working on a co-ethnic candidate's campaign.[32] One caveat about the general view that group consciousness affects political attitudes and behaviors is that its effects are conditional. They tend to be the strongest when group interests or identity are in play or have been primed.[33] **Priming** occurs when a factor affects the standards someone uses to evaluate something else.[34] For example, Hispanics are expected to be more likely to vote for Hispanic candidates when there are anti-immigration items on the ballot because the ballot item increases the chances that voters use a candidates' ethnicity to evaluate the candidate.

The effects of discrimination on individuals' political attitudes and behaviors are complex. Researchers have found that individuals who believe that their group faces much discrimination may have less trust in the government,[35] a decreased likelihood of voting,[36] or have little effect on political attitudes and behaviors.[37] The reason for the varied findings is that having experienced discrimination and perceiving the likelihood a group is discriminated against are different, and the effects differ based on levels of group identity or consciousness. For example, Schildkraut found that although individuals who have experienced discrimination are less likely to vote, individuals who have experienced discrimination and have high levels of group consciousness are more likely to vote.[38] She also found that whether individuals perceive their group to suffer from discrimination, as opposed to a personal experience, has little effect on voting. Valdez also found an interaction between group identification and discrimination. She found among Hispanics that although generally people with a panethnic identity are less likely to vote, those with a panethnic identity who perceive high levels of discrimination against Hispanics are more likely to vote.[39]

While the term *group consciousness* is often used to describe a sense that one's ethnicity or race has important political implications, the term **gender consciousness** has been used to describe the belief that one's gender has important political implications. Tolleson-Rinehart has defined gender consciousness as "one's recognition that one's relationship to the political world is at least partly but nonetheless particularly shaped by being female or male. This recognition is followed by identification with others in the "group" of one's sex, positive affect toward the group, and a feeling of interdependence with the group's fortunes.[40] Relatedly, the term **feminist consciousness** is often seen as a particular type of gender consciousness with an emphasis on equality between the sexes.[41] This is what Sonia Johnson describes at the beginning of the chapter. A gender or feminist consciousness is related to people's political attitudes and voting behavior such that women with high levels of gender consciousness are more liberal and supportive of women candidates and active in women's issues.[42] Whereas group consciousness stems from a group's shared history of being treated poorly by society, gender consciousness is thought to come from personal experiences, such as gender consciousness raising activities, having been sexually harassed, and personality traits, such as low levels of traditional moralism.[43]

Although gender and group consciousness have a different focus, group consciousness focuses on group experiences and gender consciousness on individual experiences; they both suggest that if people of a group are treated poorly, they are more likely to develop a specific consciousness. Generally, women are thought to have less of a gender consciousness than individuals of racial and ethnic minority groups have a group consciousness.[44] This may be caused by heterosexual married women's and men's economic well-being being collective in nature, that men and women interact on a regular basis, that the gender inequalities may not be as strong as racial inequalities, and that women tend to have greater equality in the United States than in many parts of the world.[45] Most of the work on feminists and gender consciousness has focused on the United States, though there is growing interest in feminist consciousness elsewhere. Spotlight 10.1 discusses feminist consciousness in Russia.

Black feminist consciousness is a particular type of consciousness felt by African American women who recognize that African American women have a unique set of experiences. There has been considerable debate on the effects of multiple minority identities on individuals' attitudes and behaviors. Do different group consciousnesses compete with each other such that either race or gender trumps the other? Or, do they reinforce each other such that minority women

Spotlight 10.1

Feminist Consciousness in Russia

An individual's group consciousness is dependent on her environment. Thus, the frequency and effects of feminist consciousness on Russians is likely different than that of Americans. Henderson-King and Zhermer's research suggests that the gender environments of the nations are very different.[46] During the Soviet days, there was an official position of gender equality and the communal good was valued over an individual's good, while at the same time they still valued traditional gender roles at home. Thus, the issue of women having to work full-time both in and out of the home (the so-called second shift) may be particularly severe. Abortion is not a political issue in Russia; abortions have been legal since the Soviet days. Thus, Henderson-King and Zhermer expect that a feminist consciousness will be weaker in Russia than in the United States and that the effect of feminist consciousness on abortion and the second shift problem will differ in the two nations.

To measure feminist consciousness, Henderson-King and Zhermer conducted surveys among college students in the United States and Russia. Their measure of feminist consciousness has many aspects: feminist identity, positive feelings about feminists, feminist beliefs, social instability (the possibility that the society can change to yield greater gender equality), and sensitivity to sexism. The results of their study suggest that few men or women of either nation identify as

feminists even though many have high levels of the other indicators of a feminist identity. According to most indicators, Americans had greater femininist consciousness than Russians, and women had greater femininist consciousness than men.[47]

Henderson-King and Zhermer also looked at Russians' and Americans' views on abortion and whether they think the second shift problem would be better solved by women getting more time off from work or men doing more housework. Russians were more supportive of abortion, and Americans were less supportive of abortion rights. Russian men were outliers in their opposition to men sharing housework.

The authors were also interested in the relationship between feminist consciousness and positions on the two issues. Feminist consciousness did not have much effect on American women's issue positions. For Russian women, sensitivity to sexism affected views toward women having more time off work and feelings toward feminists affected their views toward shared work. For Russian men, sensitivity to sexism was related to views toward abortion, and perceptions of social instability were related to whether women should have more time off. For American men, feelings about feminists and social instability were related to views on whether men and women should share housework. Social instability also affected their views toward women having more time off from work.

with both a race and gender consciousness are particularly aware of the political importance of both identities? The research on black feminist consciousness suggests the two consciousnesses are reinforcing: African American women with a strong gender consciousness also have a strong race consciousness.[48] Additionally, there is evidence that people with a black feminist consciousness have unique political attitudes where race and gender merge[49] and are more likely to vote.[50]

Less is known about the group consciousness of LGBT individuals. But an LGBT identity has some unique traits. Egan suggests that for most groups, individuals are part of the group from the day they are born, and in the case of racial and ethnic minorities, individuals are part of a family that shares the group membership.[51] Thus, they may share a political socialization. In addition, individuals in the group are thought to share political attitudes and behaviors because of life experiences and mobilization by organizations and politicians who use that identity to gain their support. But Egan suggests individuals chose whether or not to identify as LGB. Although sexual orientation is innate, many people who have same-sex relations do not identify as gay, lesbian, or bisexual. What determines whether individuals identify as LGB is their background. For example, younger people with liberal, educated families living in urban areas are more likely to identify as LGB. And that it is this background, as much as mobilization, that accounts for the cohesion among LGBs' attitudes.

Discrimination among Minorities

Given the importance of individuals' experiences with and perceptions of discrimination for political identity and political participation, this section examines individuals' experiences and perceptions of discrimination. First, the Pew Research Center's Survey of LGBT Americans suggests that most LGBT individuals experience some type of discrimination. About 58% of LGBT people have been the subject of a slur or joke, 39% have been rejected by friends or family, 30% physically threatened, upwards of 20% have also been poorly treated in a place of worship or other public place or been treated unfairly at work.[52] Although there is not much difference between African American and white LGBT Americans in their experiences of discrimination based on their LGBT status, gay men (84%) are more likely to have experienced discrimination than lesbians (73%) or bisexuals (49%). LGBT individuals also feel they face lots of discrimination and are not widely accepted in the United States. Over 50% of LGBT individuals believe LGBT face a lot of discrimination and an additional 39% percent believe they face at least some discrimination.[53]

A recent study of transgender Americans indicates the extent of discrimination they experience.[54] It indicated that 90% have been harassed at the workplace, 26% have been fired, 22% have been harassed by the police, 19% have been refused medical treatment by health care professionals, and 19% have been denied housing. Discrimination is even greater among racial minorities who are also transgender.[55] While 26% of transgender Americans have lost a job because of their gender identity, the figures are 36% for American Indians and multiracial individuals, 32% for African Americans, and 30% for Hispanics.[56] Racial and ethnic transgender Americans also experience greater levels of most types of discrimination and assault. Male-to-female (MTF) transgender Americans also tend to experience greater discrimination in the workforce than female-to-male (FTM) transgender Americans.

Women, too, feel discrimination. According to the 2010 General Social Survey (GSS), 5% of Americans believe they have been discriminated against because of gender. Not surprisingly, women are more likely to feel they were discriminated against because of sex than were men (7.2% to 1.8%).[57] African American women and white women reported similar levels of discrimination. According to another study, about 40% of women said they experienced gender discrimination.[58]

Asian Americans are the least concerned about discrimination of the racial and ethnic minority groups. In 2012, only 13% of Asian American felt that discrimination was a major problem for them as a group, 48% said it was a minor problem, and 35% said it was not a problem at all.[59] However, about 20% say they have experienced discrimination in the past year, and half that many say they have been called a racial slur during the past year.[60] There does not seem to be a significant difference in these experiences by sex.[61]

Compared to Asian Americans, Hispanics are more likely to be aware of discrimination. In a 2010 survey, 61% of Hispanics said that discrimination was a major problem, and an additional 24% said it was a minor problem.[62] According to a 2013 Pew survey, Hispanics see discrimination as a greater problem today than ten years ago.[63] Not only do Hispanics believe they are discriminated against, but about one-third have experienced discrimination or have had a family member face discrimination in the past five years.[64] Hispanic women are somewhat more likely to have experienced discrimination. According to the 2012 GSS, while 11.9% of Hispanics reported having been discriminated against at work, 13.4% of Hispanic women and 11.0% of Hispanic men reported having experienced discrimination because of their ethnicity.[65]

Another group that has unifying experiences or beliefs about discrimination is African Americans. In a 2013 Pew Research Center survey, 46% of African Americans said there was a lot of discrimination against African Americans, and 42% of African Americans said there was some discrimination.[66] As far as having personally experienced discrimination, 35% of African Americans reported having been discriminated against in the last year; this is higher than the 10% of whites.[67] There are gender differences in African Americans' experiences with discrimination, with African American women being more likely to have reported experiencing race discrimination at work (19.6% to African American men 10.1%).

The above suggests that minorities, with the exception of Asian Americans, have considerable experience with discrimination and believe that their group faces much discrimination. Individuals with the double minority status of being female and of a racial/ethnic minority often have the greatest awareness of both gender and race discrimination. As noted earlier, whether this discrimination motivates minorities to participate is likely dependent on their levels of group identity.

The Group Identity of American Minorities

Since group identity can affect Americans' political attitudes and behavior, this section explores feelings of group identity among individuals who are a minority. First, although LGBT people are heterogeneous in race, class, and gender, they tend to have high levels of LGBT identity. According to a 2013 Pew Research Center survey of gay, lesbian, bisexual, and transgender Americans, 37% of LGBT Americans said that being LGBT was a very or extremely important part of their identity and an additional 26% said it was somewhat important.[68] However, among LGBT, bisexuals are less likely to see it as an important part of their identity. Only 20% of bisexuals said the identity was very or extremely important and 25% said it was somewhat important. There were not enough transgender respondents to the survey to report their feelings of identity.

The above question just asked about identity within the specific groups—whether lesbians identify with lesbians and gay men as gay men, it does not

Transgender Americans and other gender nonconforming individuals are likely to face discrimination than most other minorities. Greater protection for these Americans is likely to become a significant issue in the culture wars. (© Marcel Steger/Corbis)

suggest whether, for example, gay men and lesbians feel as though they have much in common with each other. The Pew study also asked the respondents if they have much in common with each other. And the results suggest that many feel they have much in common (see Table 10.1), and there is a gender dimension to their feelings of commonality. Three-quarters of lesbians feel they share at least some concerns with gay men, and 70% of gay men feel they share at least some concerns with lesbians. About 60% of gay men and lesbians feel they share at least some concerns with bisexuals. There is a noticeable decline in their shared concerns with transgender people. Only about half of gays and lesbians feel they share the same concerns as transgender people. The table also demonstrates that among bisexuals there are fairly strong levels of perceived common concerns with gay men and lesbians, but more so for people of their own sex.

To get a sense of the degree to which women have a gender consciousness, an American National Elections Studies (ANES) question about linked fate can be used. The ANES asked women if they felt their life was affected by what happens to women and how much their life was affected by being a woman. Generally, women have high levels of linked fate, with 66% saying their life was affected.[69] This was somewhat stronger for Anglos (67.4%) than African Americans (64.3%) or Hispanic women (60.3%), but it was strong for all women. Although Hispanic women were less likely to feel their lives were linked to other women, among those who did, they felt the effect more strongly. Whereas 42.4% of Hispanic women said their lives were affected "a lot" by being a woman, 37.0% of African Americans and 32.7% of Anglo women said "a lot." Anglo women and Hispanic women were the most likely to say their life was not affected very much (10.0% for Anglos, 15.9% for Hispanic women, and 5.3% for African American women).

The ANES data can also be used to estimate the degree to which women have a feminist consciousness. It asked respondents to use a feeling thermometer to

TABLE 10.1   How Much LGBT People Have in Common with Each Other (Percentage of a Group Who Say They Have a Lot in Common with Another Group)

	Lesbians (%)	Gay men (%)	Bisexuals (%)	Transgender (%)
Lesbians		75	60	47
Gay men	70		65	52
Bisexual men	37	66		24
Bisexual women	75	55		38

Source: Pew Research Center for People and the Press, "A Survey of LGBT Americans: Attitudes, Experiences and Values in Changing Times," June 13, 2013, http://www.pewsocialtrends.org/files/2013/06/SDT_LGBT-Americans_06-2013.pdf, 84.

Note: Numbers are percentages of a group who say they share a lot or some common concerns with each groups. The rows are respondents and the columns are the targets. For example, 70% of gay men believe they have a lot or some in common with lesbians.

indicate their feelings toward feminists. The average temperature given by women was a temperate 53.9 degrees, somewhat higher than the 46.5 degrees men gave feminists.[70] Among women, Anglos felt the least warmly toward feminists, giving them only 51.8 degrees, while African American women gave feminists 57.2 degrees and Hispanic women gave feminists 56.8 degrees. In fact, the score feminists received from Anglo women was lower than that received by African American men (55.4).

Much like Asian Americans lack a sense of discrimination, they also lack a panethnic identity. The Pew Research Center survey of Asian Americans asked respondents: "People sometimes use different terms to describe themselves. In general, which one of the following terms do you use to describe yourself most often."[71] About 64.6% of Asian Americans said their nationality, 19.4% said Asian, and 14.2% said American. Also indicating the strength of their national identity is that they tend to associate with people who share their nationality. To the question, "How many of your friends in the U.S. are from the same Asian background as you?" about 42.6% said most or all of their friends were of their nationality, and another 42.3% said some of their friends shared their nationality, leaving only 15.9% saying hardly any or none of their friends shared their nationality. With both of these questions there were small gender differences, with women having more ties to their home country. For example, 63.9% of men and 65.7% of women said they identify with their nationality. For the friends question: 41.5% of men said most or all of their friends were of their nationality, compared to 41.6% of women who said most of their friends shared their nationality.

Hispanics, too, have a moderate sense of panethnic identity. Only 20% of Hispanics interviewed in a recent survey said they identify as Hispanic/Latino, 54% identify as their nationality, and 23% identify as American, the remaining either said it depends, they did not know, or refused to answer the question.[72] In addition, Hispanics were asked, "How much do you think (people of country of origin) living in the U.S. and Latinos/Hispanics from different countries living in the U.S. today share values in common? Would you say . . . a lot in common, some in common, only a little in common, or almost nothing in common?" To this question 39% said a lot, 39% some, and 19% said only a little or almost none.[73] In another Pew Survey, Hispanic respondents were asked: "Please listen to the following statements and tell me which comes closer to your view. Hispanics/Latinos in the U.S. share a common culture, Hispanics/Latinos in the U.S. have many different cultures." Almost 70% of respondents said Hispanics are made up of many different cultures. Looking at gender differences in Hispanics' identity suggests that women have higher levels of group identity than men. In 2011, 27.7% of women and 23.3% of men identified as Hispanic/Latino and 31.7% of women and 27.8% of men believe Hispanics/Latinos share a common culture.[74]

Hispanics have modest levels of linked fate. According to the 2012 ANES, only 24.7% of Hispanics believe that their lives are affected "a lot" by what happens to Hispanics, and 59.5% believe it is only somewhat affected.[75]

Hispanic women are less likely to believe their lives are linked to other Hispanics. Only 48.1% believe their lives are affected by what happens to other Hispanics, and only 23.8% believe it is affected a lot. The figures for men were 53.1% and 25.6%.

African Americans are often thought to have the highest levels of group consciousness. According to a 2008 ABCNews/USA Today/Columbia University survey, about two-thirds of African Americans believed they have a common fate with other African Americans.[76] In addition, 63.7%, according to an ANES survey, believed their lives were affected by what happens to African Americans, and 35.5% believe their lives are affected "a lot," and only 8% believe they are not affected very much.[77] African Americans also feel close to other African Americans. According to a 2012 GSS survey, whereas less than 1% of African Americans said they did not feel at all close to African Americans on a 9-point scale, 59.9% said they felt very close (scored a 9).[78] As a point of comparison, 30% of whites said they felt very close to whites. Within both groups there was a tendency for men to say they felt closer to their race than for women to do so. Among African Americans, 60.7% of men said they felt very close to African Americans, compared to 56.6% for African American women. As with Hispanics, African American women had lower levels of linked fate than did men. Only 59.8% of women compared to 68.3% of men believed their lives were affected by what happens to African Americans, while 40.2% of men believe their lives are affected a lot, only 31.0% of women believe their lives are affected a lot.[79]

To conclude: LGBT and African Americans have high levels of group identity and Asian Americans and women low levels, with Hispanics falling somewhere in between. Among African Americans and Asian Americans, women tend to have somewhat lower levels of racial identity whereas among Hispanic women tend to have somewhat higher levels of Hispanic identity. Anglo women have lower levels of feminist consciousness than other women.

Group Cohesion: Level of Shared Beliefs, Values, and Attitudes among Individual Minorities

Groups that share beliefs, values, and attitudes are more likely to be able to coalesce their resources behind a single candidate or cause and to be more effective than groups whose members are at cross-purposes. Individuals who share a minority status are likely to share many values and attitudes because they share interests, political socialization, and experiences. First, they share many interests that could affect their political attitudes. For example minorities are more likely to directly benefit from affirmative action than nonminorities and so may be more likely to support it. Second, they are likely to have similar **political socialization.** Political socialization is the process by which individuals learn about politics, its actors and issues. Minorities are likely taught unique lessons by parents, teachers, or others as to how the government works to either aid or harm their interests. Following incidents like the one in Ferguson, Missouri, in 2012, families talk to their African American sons and daughters about how they have to be careful around the police.[80] Similarly, girls are likely to be socialized to be caregivers and boys breadwinners. Third, minorities are likely to have unique experiences because of their minority status, such as having experienced discrimination. In addition, some feminist theorists argue that the experiences of giving birth and bonding with young children have unique effects on women's view of the world. Although biological explanations for differences between racial and ethnic groups are both offensive and inaccurate, there has been some recent research suggesting biological differences between men and women may contribute some to gender differences in political attitudes and behaviors.[81]

To get a sense of the unity of purpose shared by individuals within the groups, I look at the religious, ideological, partisan preferences, and vote choice of individuals of the different minority groups. In addition, within the Hispanic and Asian American populations, I examine levels of acculturation, consciousness, and cohesion among different nationalities. Differences between nationalities will depress the cohesion of these groups.

Religion

If individuals within a minority group share a religious faith, then they are likely to share other political views that could facilitate greater cooperation. Individuals' religious faith has a strong influence on their views toward many key political issues, from gay rights and abortion to immigration (see Chapter 8). In addition, among African Americans the church has reinforced perceptions of racial groups and contributes to group consciousness.[82] Table 10.2 lists the religious preferences of Hispanics, Asian Americans, whites, African Americans, men, and women.[83] These data suggest African Americans are highly unified by religious preference with 68.3% of African American respondents to a GSS survey indicating they are Protestants. In addition, with 6% of African Americans identifying as Catholic and 8.3% as simply Christian, over 80% of African Americans are Christians, suggesting strong religious agreement. Further supporting the cohesiveness of African Americans' religious preferences is that among Protestant African Americans there is a fair amount of agreement in denomination, with 60% indicating they are Baptists.[84]

Hispanics, too, are predominantly Christian. According to a Pew 2012 survey of Latinos, 85.4% of Hispanics are Christian, divided between Catholic (55%) and Protestant (22%).[85] In addition, there is evidence that Hispanics are increasing their affiliation with Protestant denominations. A recent study found that the percentage of Hispanics who are Catholic is declining and that nearly one-quarter of Hispanics are former Catholics.[86] Thus, religion may become less unifying for Hispanics.

TABLE 10.2 Religion by Race, Ethnicity, and Gender (Percentage of Each Group That Shares a Faith)

	Catholic (%)	Protestant (%)	Christian (%)	None (%)	Other (%)	N
Asian Americans	18.7	14.1	8.4	25.8	33.0	3,489
Hispanic	47.4	20.9	11.8	15.6	4.3	1,683
African Americans	6.6	66.4	6.8	16.8	3,4	300
Whites	25.0	44.3	5.4	20.7	4.6	1,472
Men	24.9	39.5	4.9	23.7	7.0	882
Women	23.7	48.6	6.9	16.4	4.4	1,085
Asian American women	19.7	14.7	9.9	26.3	29.4	1,745
Asian American men	17.7	13.7	10.6	25.6	32.4	1,743
Hispanic men	45.5	20.6	10.6	21.2	6.4	836
Hispanic women	49.4	21.2	13.0	13.5	9.3	847
White women	24.9	47.7	7.3	17.1	3.0	801
White men	25.2	40.3	3.5	25.0	6.0	671
African American men	3.9	58.8	5.5	25.5	6.3	114
African American women	8.4	71.5	7.7	11.0	1.4	186

Source: These figures were calculated by the author. For whites and blacks, 2012 GSS data (http://www3.norc.org/GSS+Website/Download/SPSS+Format/) were used; for Hispanics, the Pew Research Center 2012 National Survey of Latinos was used; for Asian Americans, the Pew Research Center 2012 survey "Rise of Asian Americans" was used.

Asian Americans are the least unified in their religious beliefs. The most common religion is Christian. However, according to the Pew survey of Asian Americans, less than one-half of Asian Americans are Christian and they differ in denomination. Only about 18.7% of Asian Americans identify as Catholic, 14.1%, Protestant, and 8.4% as just Christian. In addition to Christianity, there are sizeable Buddhist (14.2%) and Hindu (10.6%) populations among Asian Americans.[87]

Many of the large national surveys do not include enough American Indians to indicate their religious preferences. However, according to a survey out of City University of New York, American Indians' religious views are similar to those of Anglos. About 20% of American Indians identify as Baptist, 17% Catholic, 17% no religious preference, and only 3% said Indian or tribal.[88] Thus, there is not a unifying religion for American Indians.

Women tend to be highly unified in their religious faith. As with other minority groups, the most common faith is Christianity, with about 79% of women listing some type of Christianity as their religious preference, compared to 69% of men who are Christian.[89] Table 10.2 presents information on the intersectionality of race/ethnicity and gender as they relate to religion. These data demonstrate that across racial and ethnic groups, women are more unified in their religious affiliation than are men. For example, almost 90% of African American women are Christian, including 72% who are Protestants, while about 68% of African American men are Christian and 59% Protestant. Among Hispanics, as well, more women are Christians than are men. About 87% of Hispanic women and 84% of Hispanic men are Christians. Asian American women are also more Christian than their male counterparts, and Asian American men are more likely to be affiliated with the "other religions."

LGBT Americans are less religious than others. A Pew Research Center survey found that whereas 73% of the general public is affiliated with Christianity, only 42% of LGBT respondents identify as Christian.[90] The most common response LGBT respondents gave to the religious affiliation question was "unaffiliated" (48%). There are not significant differences between lesbians, gay men, and bisexuals in their lack of affiliation.

To summarize, African Americans are the most unified in their religious beliefs with 80% identifying as Christian and about 70% as Protestant. Hispanics, too, are fairly unified in religion with over 80% identifying as Christian, just over half of those as Catholics. There is less detailed information about American Indians' religious faith, but they do not appear to be highly unified. LGBT Americans and Asian Americans are the least unified in religion with less than half in each group identifying as Christian, the most common faith among LGBT. With Asian Americans, a sizeable percentage identify as Hindu and Buddhist as well as not religious. Within the LGBT population, almost half do not identify with any religion. Women in general, as well as within each group, tend to be more unified in their religion than their male counterparts.

Political Ideology

Political ideology adds structure to individuals' political attitudes. It is based on their understanding of how the world works or their views about how it should work. Americans are thought to align their ideology on a single dimension, from liberal on one end to conservative on the other. Although there are questions about whether the single continuum accurately reflects Americans' ideologies, it is common to treat it as a single continuum, and for simplicity the following discussion does so as well. Liberals tend to want larger government involvement, particularly in the economy and to ensure equality. Conservatives, on the other hand, want less government intervention in the economy and tend to value freedom over equality. One reason these descriptions may not fall on a single dimension is that many people who identify as conservatives want government intervention in issues like abortion and to limit LGBT rights, and those who identify as liberal want less government intrusion in these areas.[91]

There is stronger unity among LGBT Americans than among women. The 2012 Gallup tracking poll found that LGBT respondents were solidly liberal, or at least not conservative. About 45% of LGBT respondents self-identified as liberal and 20% conservative. This compares to 23% and 39% for non-LGBT respondents.[92] Using the 2012 GSS data, it is clear that women, too, are more liberal than men. About 23.6% of men self-identify as at least slightly liberal, 36.4% identify as moderate, and 44.1% as at least slightly conservative. About 27% of women identify as at least slightly liberal, 36.5% identify as moderate, and 30.7% identify as at least slightly conservative. Although these data indicate women are more liberal than men, they do not indicate that women are as solidly liberal or united in a political ideology as LGBT Americans.

Turning our attention now to race: Although African Americans are stereotyped as liberals, they are fairly diverse in their ideology. The 2012 GSS indicated that 27.7% of African Americans identify as at least slightly liberal, 44.3% as moderate, and 22.7% as at least slightly conservative. As a point of comparison, among whites the percentages are 31.1%, 34.9%, and 35.0%. Thus, African Americans are less conservative than whites, but not more liberal. Part of the reason African Americans are not more unified in a liberal ideology is that many are conservative on some key social policies, such as same-sex marriage.

Table 10.3 breaks these data down by race and gender and finds some interesting interactions. The most unified liberal group is African American women: 31% of African American women are liberal, 46.3% are moderate, and only 16.7% are conservative. African American men are more conservative with only 22.8% identifying as liberals, 41.2% moderates, and 29.8% conservative. White women and white men are more solidly conservative than African Americans generally or than women of other races. One of the lessons of this table is that although women tend to be more liberal than their male counterparts, this is less true for white women.

Asian Americans are also more liberal than conservative. Whereas 25.8% of Asian Americans are conservative, 33.5% are liberal and 40.8% are moderates.[93] Table 10.3 also demonstrates that among Asian Americans, women are somewhat more liberal than their male counterparts. However, note that Asian American women are also slightly more conservative than Asian American men. The reason is that Asian American women are less likely to be moderates than are Asian American men. Nevertheless, 8.7% more Asian American women are liberal than conservative, and only 6.3% more Asian American men are liberal than conservative. Thus, Asian American women can be said to be at least somewhat more liberal than Asian American men.

Hispanics, too, are ideologically diverse. Only 28.5% of Hispanics are liberal, 40.3% are moderates, and 31.2% conservative.[94] Similar to other minority groups, according to Table 10.3 Hispanic women are more liberal than Hispanic

TABLE 10.3   Gender and Race Differences on Ideology (Percentage of Each Group That Is Liberal, Moderate, or Conservative)

	Liberal	Moderate	Conservative	N
White women	25.9	34.4	34.0	766
White men	24.0	35.5	36.2	645
African American women	31.0	46.3	16.7	172
African American men	22.8	41.2	29.8	108
Hispanic women	26.0	33.7	29.0	127
Hispanic men	24.2	40.5	28.2	126
Asian American women	35.5	38.2	26.2	1,593
Asian American men	31.5	43.2	25.2	1,634

Source: These figures were calculated by the author. For whites and blacks, 2012 GSS data (http://www3.norc.org/GSS+Website/Download/SPSS+Format/) were used; for Hispanics, the Pew Research Center 2012 National Survey of Latinos was used; for Asian Americans, the Pew Research Center 2012 survey "Rise of Asian Americans" was used.

men and like Asian Americans, Hispanic women are also more conservative than Hispanic men because they are less likely to be moderates.

Unlike other minorities, there is some evidence that American Indians are more conservative than liberal. McClain and Stewart combined eighteen years of ANES data to give estimates on American Indian ideology.[95] They find that 2.5% are extremely liberal, 12.0% liberal, 11.6% slightly liberal, 33.1% moderate, 16.6% slightly conservative, 18.0% conservative, and 6.3% extremely conservative.

To summarize, with the exception of Hispanics and American Indians, minorities tend to be more liberal than nonminorities. This is particularly true for LGBT Americans and African Americans, who are fairly unified in their ideology. Also, women within each racial and ethnic minority group tend to be more liberal than men, indicating they have the greatest cohesiveness. Asian American and Hispanic men also tend to be more moderate than women.

Party Identification

Besides sharing a political ideology, another way to examine whether minorities share political interests and values is to look at party identification, which is one of the key ways to organize political preferences, along the lines of party identification (see Chapter 8 for a definition of party identification). Generally in the United States, people who are supportive of larger government, minority interests, and helping the poor and working classes through the government identify with the Democratic Party, and people who are less supportive of large government intervention in the economy and in minority interests, but support government regulation of social policies, are more likely to be Republican. Although most liberals identify as Democrats, and conservatives identify as Republicans, ideology and party identification are not the same. At times, such as prior to the 1990s, a large number of conservatives had strong allegiances to the Democratic Party, and numerous Republicans were moderate or even liberal.[96] Parties are groups that try to control the government by running candidates and having people in office. And party identification is an attachment to one of the parties. Ideology, on the other hand, is a set of beliefs.

Women and LGBT are solidly Democratic. Women are more supportive of the Democratic Party than the Republican Party, but they are less unified than other minority groups. According to the 2012 GSS, 36.6% of women are Democrats or are independents who lean toward the Democratic Party, 21.6% are true independents, and 29.5% are Republicans or independents who lean toward the Republican Party. For men the percentages are 34.8%, 17.5%, and 34.9%.[97] LGBT Americans are more solidly Democratic than women. According to the 2012 Gallup tracking poll, 65% of LGBT respondents were Democrats or leaned toward the Democratic Party. This figure is similar to that found by the Pew survey.[98] It found 8% LGBT respondents identified as Republican, 56% as Democrats, and 30% as independents, with some variation among lesbians, gay men, and bisexuals. Only about 8% of gay men were Republican, compared to 67% who were Democrats (the remaining were independents). Among lesbians, only 4% were Republicans compared to 64% Democrats. For bisexuals the percentages were 7% and 44%.[99] The strong support for the Democratic Party is understandable given the policy positions of the two parties in recent years.

Although LGBT Americans are solidly Democratic, the most unified partisans are African Americans. According to GSS data, 80.6% of African Americans identify with the Democratic Party (this includes those independents who lean toward the Democratic Party), 13.4% identify as independents, leaving only 6% of African Americans identifying with the Republican Party.[100] For whites the percentages are 38.8%, 18.7%, and 27.6%.[101] Hispanics, too, are highly Democratic. According to the 2012 Pew Survey of Hispanics, 68.8% are Democrats, 21.3% Republicans, with the others being either independents or identifying with another party.[102] Although Asian Americans are less Democratic than African Americans or Hispanics, they are still highly Democratic. According to the Pew Research Center survey of Asian Americans, about 58% of Asian Americans identify with the Democratic Party compared to 32.7% for Republicans; the remaining are independents.[103] The immigration experience of Asian Americans and Hispanics undoubtedly affects their party identification. Wong and associates find that among Asian Americans, those who are less acculturated (in the United States for a shorter period of time and do not speak English) are less likely to have a party identification, while acculturated Asian Americans are clearly more likely to be Democrats.[104]

Although American Indians differed from other minorities by being conservative, they share a Democratic preference. McClain and Stewart's examination of ANES data from 1990 to 2008 found that among American Indians, 14.2% identified as strong Democrats, 16.4% as weak Democrats, 16.2% as Democratic-leaning independents, 13.2% as independents, 14.8% as Republican-leaning independents, 13.9% as weak Republicans, and 11.2% as strong Republicans. A potential reason that American Indians are more likely to be Democratic than Republican is that Democratic officials are more likely to support tribal self-determination and spending to improve social conditions,[105] and American Indians support candidates who support native causes.[106]

Table 10.4 depicts the interaction of race and gender in terms of party identification. It demonstrates that while white women, Asian Americans, and Hispanic women are more Democratic than their male counterparts, that is not the case for African Americans. Among African Americans, men are slightly more likely to identify with the Democratic Party than are women.

The above discussion demonstrates that among minorities there is a high level of support for the Democratic Party. Well over half of LGBT Americans, African Americans, Asian Americans, and Hispanics identify with the Democratic Party, and for LGBT Americans and African Americans very few, less than 10%, identify with the Republican Party. Even American Indians, who tend to be conservative, are solidly Democratic. Although women are more Democratic than men in general as well as within most of the minority groups, African American women are not as solidly Democratic as African American men.

TABLE 10.4   Party Identification by Race/Ethnicity and Gender (Percentage of Each Group Identifying with the Parties)

	Democrats	Independents	Republicans	N
White women	39.3	20.4	37.6	779
White men	38.1	17.7	40.1	669
African American women	79.8	14.5	4.8	185
African American men	81.9	11.9	2.8	115
Hispanic women	43.6	37.1	18.6	819
Hispanic men	45.6	25.7	12.3	839
Asian Women	61.3	7.9	30.9	1,448
Asian men	55.1	10.5	34.4	1,532

Source: These figures were calculated by the author. For whites and blacks, 2012 GSS data (http://www3.norc.org/GSS+Website/Download/SPSS+Format/) were used; for Hispanics, the Pew Research Center 2012 National Survey of Latinos was used; for Asian Americans, the Pew Research Center 2012 survey "Rise of Asian Americans" was used.

Note: For Asians, "no preference" and "something else" were eliminated.

Vote Choice

Not only are minorities unified in their party identification but they are unified in their voting behavior. To demonstrate this point, this section looks at the 2012 presidential election. Women are the least unified of the minority groups, but in the 2012 presidential race between President Barack Obama and Mitt Romney, 55% of women voted for Obama, compared with 45% of men.[107] LGBT voters were even more unified in their support for Obama, with 76% casting a vote for him over Mitt Romney.[108] The other minorities were similarly unified in their support for President Obama. In 2012, 93% of African Americans voted for Obama, as did 71% of Hispanics and 73% of Asian Americans.[109] Women who are racial and ethnic minorities tend to be particularly unified in their support of President Obama. About 96% of African American women voted for Obama in 2012, compared with 76% of Hispanic women.

Although these data do not include American Indians, American Indians, too, were strong supporters of Obama in 2008. In 2008, about 90% voted for Obama over Sen. John McCain.[110] Gender differences in voting among American Indians differed from whites. American Indian men were slightly more likely to vote for Obama in 2008 than were American Indian women.

Variation by Nationality

As noted earlier, most Asian Americans feel they make up several different cultures and most Hispanics feel that they make up several different cultures. Yet, individuals of a group need to feel as though they share a common interest for them to come together to effect change. If most Mexican Americans, for example, do not feel as though they have much in common with Cuban Americans, it will be difficult for Cubans and Mexicans to come together and build a Hispanic movement. In that case, the 17% percent of Hispanics would not be a voting bloc; they would not pool their resources behind groups and lobbying efforts. Important here is the degree to which individuals of different nationalities have a shared identity and feel as though they have similar issue positions. So far this chapter has treated everyone within a gender, racial, or ethnic group the same regardless of nationality. This section examines the indicators of acculturation, cohesion, and group consciousness broken down by nationality for Asian Americans and Hispanics.

Table 10.5 presents different aspects of acculturation, cohesion, and consciousness for Asian Americans, broken down by nationality. The table demonstrates a fair amount of variation. First, Filipinos and Japanese are more likely to feel like typical Americans than other Asian Americans. In addition, Filipinos, Indians, and Japanese are the most likely to speak English.[111] Part of the reason Filipinos and Indians have greater English proficiency than other nationalities may be because English is frequently spoken in the Philippines and India. Perhaps because of their greater acculturation, Filipinos, Indians, and Japanese also report less concern with discrimination. Less than 11% of these groups see

TABLE 10.5 Acculturation, Consciousness, and Cohesion among Different Asian Nationalities

	Chinese	Filipino	Indian	Japanese	Korean	Vietnamese	Other
Discrimination major problem	16.7	7.7	10.7	8.5	24.7	12.9	15.3
Experience discrimination	21.8	18.7	18.1	9.4	19.9	14.5	28.4
Identify as Asian	27.3	10.0	20.3	16.0	14.0	16.8	31.1
Typical American	40.9	52.2	34.6	53.6	31.4	36.6	41.1
Speak English	52	78	76	82	54	41	52
Christian	31.0	85.6	16.9	37.3	71.2	37.8	21.4
Democrat	52.0	45.5	67.9	55.9	52.3	39.3	55.9
Liberal	34.0	21.2	39.3	30.7	32.7	39.3	38.1

Source: Data from the Pew Research Center 2012 survey "Rise of Asian Americans." All but language were calculated by the author.

discrimination as a major problem. Compare this to the nearly 25% of Koreans who see it as a major problem. Japanese also report being least likely to experience discrimination. Three nationalities stand out with regard to their Asian identity: Chinese, other Asians, and Indians. In terms of religion, again there is much variation, with over 85% of Filipinos identifying as Christian, compared to only 21% of the "other Asians" category. Filipinos also differ from other Asian nationalities in their political ideology and party identification. Only 21% of Filipinos describe themselves as liberals and 46% as Democrats. This compares to 39% of Indians who are liberal and 67% who are Democrats. Although these figures suggest that Filipinos are unique among the Asian nationalities, they do not present a clear picture of what might cause stronger levels of identity or cohesion.

Similar to Asian Americans, Hispanics' acculturation, cohesion, and consciousness vary by nationality (see Table 10.6). First, Puerto Ricans and Cubans are the most likely to feel like typical Americans, and South Americans, other Central Americans, and Salvadorans are the least likely to.[112] That Puerto Ricans are born U.S. citizens and that Cubans have been welcomed in the United States may help explain their acculturation. Puerto Ricans also stand out in their English proficiency with Mexicans also having high levels of English proficiency. However, that does not seem to affect their group consciousness. Although most Hispanics of each nationality see discrimination as a major problem, Salvadorans have the greatest issue with discrimination and Cubans the least. Similarly, with regard to having had friends or family members experience discrimination, Salvadorans report higher levels than do Cubans. Although Salvadorans have the greatest issue with discrimination, they are the least likely to identify as Hispanic. Cubans and Dominicans are the most likely to identify as Hispanic. This may be in part because Salvadorans have come to the United States more recently than Cubans. Additionally, Salvadorans are the least likely to see Hispanics as having

TABLE 10.6   Acculturation, Consciousness, and Cohesion among Different Hispanic Nationalities (by Percentage)

	Salvadoran	Dominican	Other Central American	Cuban	Mexican	South American	Puerto Rican
Discrimination major problem	75.4	63.4	66.1	56.3	62.8	62.0	70.1
Experienced discrimination	38.3	28.6	33.9	18.8	34.4	30.0	33.3
Identity Hispanic	49	66	54	63	57	60	55
Shared values	51	44	43	40	38	38	36
Typical American	40.4	45.7	42.4	50.0	48.7	42.4	66.6
English proficiency	8.1	7.1	8.3	8.7	21.1	9.9	35.1
Christian	44.1	59.4	45.0	32.7	51.0	58.3	36.2
Democrat	68.7	82.9	72.2	54.3	67.1	75.0	75.4
Liberal	33.3	27.0	36.5	21.3	30.4	33.8	26.9

Sources: The measures for identity and shared values come from Mark Lopez, "Three-fourths of Hispanics Say Their Community Needs a Leader," October 22, 2013, http://www.pewhispanic.org/files/2013/10/National_Latino_Leader_10-2013_FINAL.pdf. The measures for Christianity and party were calculated by the author using the Pew Research Center 2012 National Survey of Latinos. Ideology was calculated by the author using the Pew Research Center 2011 National Survey of Latinos. The rest were calculated by the author using the Pew Research Center 2010 National Survey of Latinos.

shared values. Cubans also stand out in their values and beliefs. They are least likely to be Christian, Democrats, or liberal.

The above suggests that the national diversity of Asian Americans and Hispanics may make it more difficult for there to be a panethnic movement on the part of Asian American or Hispanics. Some nationalities have considerable similarities but others do not. While this creates some difficulties, they are not the only issues. Research also suggests that racial differences among Hispanics can also affect vote choice.[113]

Effects of Acculturation and Group Consciousness on Voting Cohesion

To help demonstrate the effects of acculturation and group consciousness on voting cohesion, this section takes a closer look at vote choice. It looks at whether Asian Americans and Hispanics who were more concerned with discrimination, who identified more with their panethnic identity, and who were more acculturated were more likely to vote for Barack Obama for president. The Pew Research Center's 2012 Survey of Asian Americans asked respondents whether they thought discrimination was a major problem, a minor problem, or not a problem at all, if they had been discriminated against, if they saw themselves as typical Americans, and if they described themselves by their nationality, Asian American, or American. It also asked respondents if they voted for Barack Obama or John McCain in the 2008 election. These data indicate Asian Americans who saw discrimination as a greater problem were more likely to vote for Obama. About 77.8% of those who said it was a major problem voted for Obama, compared to 73.6% of those who said it was a minor problem, and 64.2% who said it was not a problem at all. Similarly, 75.8% of those who had experienced discrimination in the past year voted for Obama, compared to 69.1% of those who had not. Individuals who identify as Asian American were also more likely to have voted for Obama. About 77.2% of those who had a pan-ethnic identity voted for Obama, compared to 67.8% who had a national identity and 68.6% who identify as American. While Asian Americans who had high levels of group consciousness were more likely to have voted for Obama, those who were acculturated were less likely to have voted for President Obama. About 68.7% of Asian Americans who said they were typical Americans voted for Obama, compared to 71.4% who said they felt very different and 78.5% who said it depends.

Turning our attention to Hispanics, the Pew Research Center's 2012 National Survey of Latinos asked respondents who they would vote for, Barack Obama or Mitt Romney. To measure acculturation it asked respondents whether they were born in the United States, and it created an English proficiency scale. To measure discrimination it asked whether being Hispanic/Latino helps, hurts, or does not make a difference in getting a job. These results suggest that the less acculturated Hispanics were more likely to support President Obama's reelection effort. About 71% of those who spoke English supported Obama, compared to 76.1% of those who were bilingual and 83.2% of those who spoke primarily Spanish. Voting based on location of birth were more muted; 74.8% of those who were born in the United States supported Obama, compared to 84.3% of those born in Puerto Rico and 75.6% of those born elsewhere. Looking at discrimination, 82.4% who think being Hispanic hurts getting a job supported Obama, compared to 74.1% who think it helps, and 75.1% who said it doesn't make a difference. The Pew Center's 2012 survey did not have a question about panethnic identity.

Although the next chapter examines the degree to which minorities participate in politics, this section will demonstrate the relationship between group consciousness and acculturation and the likelihood that individuals vote. The Asian American survey used above also asked respondents whether or not they voted in the 2012 election. Responses to this question suggest that Asian Americans who feel like typical Americans were more likely to have voted than others (75.6% to 68.4%), and those who identify as Asian American were somewhat more likely to vote (73.8% to 71.1%). However, those who see discrimination as a major problem were less likely to vote than those who saw it a minor problem or not at all a problem. The percentages were 68.6% to 72.3% to 74.1%. Asian Americans who identify as Asian American and who perceive discrimination as a major problem were even less likely to vote. Whether or not someone had experienced discrimination made virtually no difference on the likelihood of voting.

Acculturation and group consciousness also are related to the likelihood that Hispanics vote. The 2012 National Survey of Latinos asked respondents how likely they were to vote in the 2012 election. Hispanics who were only proficient in Spanish were less likely to vote than those who were proficient in English or who were bilingual. The percentages of those who said they were absolutely sure they were going to vote were 57.8%, 70.2%, and 72.0%, respectively. Hispanics born in the United States were only modestly more likely to vote than those born in Puerto Rico or another country. The percentages of those who were absolutely sure they were going to vote were born in the United States: 69.7%, born in Puerto Rico: 65.7%, and born in another country: 68.4%. The results also suggest that those who see discrimination as a problem were less likely to vote. About 66.1% of those who said being Hispanic hurts the ability of people to get a job were absolutely sure they were going to vote, compared to 68.1% of those who said it helps and 74.0% of those who say it does not matter.

ANES data can be used to examine the relationships of acculturation and linked fate with African Americans' voting behavior.[114] African Americans who were born abroad were somewhat more likely to vote for Barack Obama in 2012 than were those born in the United States. Of those born in the United States (not including Puerto Rico), 95.4% voted to reelect President Obama compared to 98.0% of those born outside of the United States or in Puerto Rico. Whether African Americans were born in the United States also had a modest effect on whether they voted. While 83% of those born in the United States reported voting, 81% of those born abroad reported voting. African Americans who had a sense of a linked fate were more likely to vote and more likely to vote for Obama. About 85.2% African Americans who felt their lives were affected by what happens to African Americans voted, and 97.1% of them voted for Obama; of those who did not believe their lives were affected, 76.4% voted and 93.0% of them voted for Obama.

These results present a bit of a conundrum for organizers of minority interest groups. While low levels of acculturation and high levels of group consciousness tend to increase the unity of the Asian American, African American, and Hispanic vote, they also tend to depress the likelihood that individuals will vote. Thus it is unclear if encouraging a group consciousness or acculturation would be beneficial or not. A possible solution may be to frame elections in a way to mobilize individuals with low levels of acculturation but high levels of group consciousness. This could be done by discussing how issues important to the minority group can be affected by the election or by using important minority symbols to mobilize voters.

Conclusion: Similarities, Differences, and Intersectionality among Minority Individuals

As with the other chapters, this chapter suggests that while the different minority groups have much in common, they also differ in significant ways. As a rule Hispanics and Asian Americans have low levels of acculturation, group consciousness, and cohesion, while African Americans and LGBT Americans have high levels of all three. American Indians are unique in their acculturation and consciousness since they were born in the United States and speak English, but many remain active citizens of their tribe. They also lack strong levels of cohesion. Women tend to have high levels of acculturation and lower levels of group consciousness and cohesion.

Many of the differences between the groups can be explained. One thing that helps explain some of the differences is how recently there has been a large immigration of a group. Asian Americans and Hispanics tend to stand out in the lower levels of acculturation, group consciousness, and cohesion because they are comprised of many nationalities that have recently immigrated to the United States. Thus, they do not share a U.S. history or socialization. Members of these groups who do have high levels of panethnic identity do tend to vote in the same direction, as do those with low levels of acculturation, but these individuals are also less likely to vote. While American Indians are not immigrants, they share a common experience with Asian Americans and Hispanics of having come from many different nations with each having its own culture. In addition, American Indians who grew up on reservations have, in some ways, lived outside of the Eurocentric-dominant U.S. culture.

The chapter also demonstrated the importance of looking at intersectionality. Asian American and Hispanic women are less acculturated than their men counterparts or other women. Individuals who have a double minority status, such as women and LGBT who are racial or ethnic minorities, experience more discrimination. While African American and Asian American women have higher levels of racial identity, Hispanic women tend to have lower levels than their men counterparts. Interesting, too, while women are more liberal than men, this is less true for Anglo women than women of color. In party identification there are also differences. While white, Asian American, and Hispanic women are more Democratic than their men counterparts, among African Americans, men are more Democratic than women.

Although there are differences in the levels of acculturation, consciousness, and cohesion across the groups, the effects of each of these factors affect their representation. Individuals of a group who have low levels of acculturation are less likely to participate in politics, though they are more unified in their political ideology and party identification. Individuals who have high levels of consciousness and cohesion are more likely to vote for similar candidates.

KEY TERMS

Acculturation   (p. 237)

Co-ethnic candidates   (p. 240)

Feminist consciousness   (p. 241)

Gender consciousness   (p. 241)

Group consciousness   (p. 239)

Linked fate   (p. 240)

Panethnic identity   (p. 240)

Political socialization   (p. 248)

Priming   (p. 240)

Chapter 11

Minorities and Political Participation

When President Barack Obama campaigned in 2012, he used a Spanish-language TV personality, Cristina Saralegui, in several ads.[1] He also ran several ads that were in Spanish. One can be translated as "In the young people known as the DREAMers, I see the same qualities that Michelle and I try to instill in our daughters. They respect their parents, they study for a better life, and they want to give back to the only country they know and love. As a father, they inspire me. And as a President, their courage has reminded me that no obstacle is too great. No road too long."[2] Mitt Romney, his opponent, also ran ads in Spanish. In one ad, his son said, "I'm Craig Romney. I want to tell you what my father, Mitt Romney, thinks. He values very much that we are a nation of immigrants. My grandfather George was born in Mexico. . . . For my family, the magnificent thing about the United States is how we all respect and help each other, no matter where we came from. As president, my father will work toward a permanent solution to our immigration system—".[3] The keynote speaker at the Democratic convention was San Antonio mayor Julian Castro, and Cuban-born Sen. Marco Rubio introduced Mitt Romney at the Republican convention.[4] What the above indicate is that both parties in the last presidential race made significant efforts to reach Hispanic voters. In fact, both parties focused more on the Hispanic vote in that election than in another election. The reason Hispanic voters were targeted was because Hispanics are a large and growing demographic that make up a noticeable share of the vote. This story indicates the power minority voters can have when they participate and their votes are needed to win.

Minority representation is enhanced when large numbers of minorities participate in the political process. A key way for minority groups to get their preferred candidates elected and policies enacted is for individuals from that group to participate in politics. This chapter explores political participation rates among minorities. **Political participation** has many definitions but generally involves activities on the part of citizens to affect government decisions and decision makers. In a representative democracy, such as the United States, a key way to participate is by voting in elections to choose policymakers. But in addition to voting, individuals can work on campaigns, discuss politics and try to affect others' votes, contact representatives, and participate in unconventional political activities. **Unconventional political participation** involves using noninstitutionalized means

Candidates, such as Mitt Romney, have engaged in greater outreach to Hispanic voters by using Spanish language ads. (*AP Photo/ Charles Dharapak, File*)

to influence the government, and includes actions such as boycotts, demonstrations, and **civil disobedience.** Civil disobedience is breaking the law to convey a political message. Unconventional participation is in contrast to **conventional political participation,** which involves using processes within the government to effect change, such as those related to elections and contacting representatives. This chapter will focus more on conventional types of participation.

There are several takeaways from the chapter. First, participation rates of minorities have increased in the past fifty years. African Americans and LGBT Americans tend to participate, including but not limited to voting, at fairly high rates, while Asian Americans and Hispanics participate at lower levels. Women tend to have high levels of voting, but lower levels of other forms of participation. African American women, however, have high levels of participation beyond voting. Although minorities tend to have lower levels of socioeconomic status (SES), which should depress their turnout, they may see greater benefits to voting because of their elevated sense of civic duty, relational goods, and group consciousness. Asian Americans and Hispanics are less likely to vote because a significant proportion of these Americans are immigrants who are not eligible to vote. American Indians also have low levels of political participation in U.S. politics, but their participation rates are increasing. Another takeaway is that because of the diversity of America; minorities can have a significant effect on the outcome of national and some state and local races.

The Vote

As noted in Chapters 1 and 3, many minority groups were denied the right to vote until the middle of the twentieth century. Although the Fifteenth Amendment (1870) to the Constitution would appear to give all men the right to vote regardless of race, African Americans living in the South were effectively denied that right until the 1960s. Figure 11.1 gives voting trends for African Americans and whites according to American National Election Studies (ANES) surveys in presidential elections from 1952 to 2012. The figure shows that in the 1950s whites were significantly more likely to vote than were African Americans, but the gap in voter turnout closed during the last half of the twentieth century. In 1952, only 33% of African Americans reported voting, compared to 78% of whites, a 45-point gap. By 1964, the gap had fallen to 15 points (65% to 80% reported voting). From the 1970s into the 1990s, the gap fluctuated from 6 to 12 points. Although African Americans voted at lower levels, Verba and Nie's research suggests that the low voting rates of African Americans had less to do with race than with socioeconomic status.[5]

When comparing the voting rates of African Americans with that of whites within the same levels of SES, African Americans voted at similar rates as whites. Although low levels of socioeconomic status lowered voting rates of African Americans in the twentieth century, by 2008 African Americans voted at similar rates as whites even without taking SES into consideration. In addition, during the 2012

Figure 11.1 Turnout for African Americans and Whites, 1952–2012

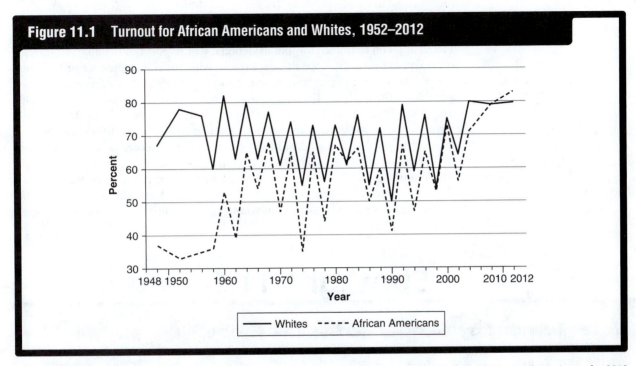

Sources: Data from American National Election Studies (ANES, http://electionstudies.org/nesguide/2ndtable/t6a_2_2.htm). Scores for 2012 were calculated by the author using 2012 ANES time series data (ANES 2012 Time Series Study [dataset]). Stanford University and the University of Michigan (producers).

presidential election African Americans outpaced whites. Many believe that the prospect of an African American president inspired a record number of African Americans to vote in 2008 and 2012. Research indicates that African Americans are more likely to vote in elections where there are minority representatives. For example, African Americans are more likely to vote in cities with African American mayors,[6] particularly where there have not been African American mayors in the past.[7] African Americans also vote at high levels where there are African American members of Congress.[8] However, it should be noted that some research has found more muted effects of descriptive representation on voter turnout of African Americans.[9]

Although many estimates indicate that African Americans voted at higher rates than whites in 2008 and 2012, some question these results. The information we have about voting rates by demographic traits is based on self-reports of voting or intentions to vote. The problem with these data is the tendency for people to over-report their voting. That is, they are more likely to say they voted than they actually voted or say that they will vote when in fact they will not. There is some evidence that African Americans may over report more than whites. One study estimated that once overreporting was taken into consideration, the voting gaps in 1992 and 1994 were about 20 points each election.[10] The raw data in Figure 11.1 suggest about a 12-point gap. There are also reasons to expect that African Americans may have had greater social pressures to overestimate the likelihood that they voted in the historic 2008 election. Since self-reporting results in overreporting, McKee, Hood, and Hill examined turnout in Georgia, which reports individual information on registered voters.[11] Since the state tracks who voted and the race of the voter, these data are not dependent on self-reports. They find that African Americans were not more likely than whites to overreport their votes, and that between 2004 and 2008 there was an 8.1% increase in the African American vote. This increase virtually wiped away the gap in voting rates of whites and African Americans.[12] Thus, it appears as though African Americans voted at record numbers during the 2008 election and likely surpassed whites in their turnout.

Women got the right to vote in 1920, but tended to vote in lower numbers than men until the 1980s. Since polling was in its infancy during the 1920s and 1930s, there is limited research on women's voting in the early years. However,

Spotlight 11.1

Voter Turnout by Gender across the Globe[13]

Women have the right to vote in virtually all nations, though this has been granted only recently. However, women have only recently been afforded that right in many Middle Eastern and African nations. Yet, this right to vote gives women political influence only if they choose to use it. In most nations, such as the United States, women voted at low rates up until the mid- to late twentieth century, and in most developed nations women vote at rates as high as or higher than men.

Pippa Norris examined data from eight nations that keep official turnout data by sex, and found that during the last half of the twentieth century women went from voting at significantly lower levels to voting at somewhat higher levels.[14] However, the nations for which these data were available were not very representative of all nations, thus she also examined survey data. Using data from a survey from the 1990s from nineteen different nations, she found that women were less likely to vote than men. She indicated 15.5% of women reported not voting compared to 13.7% of men. These nations included former communist nations, some in Latin America, Europe (northern and southern), and Asia. She observed great variation by nation. In Norway, women were 3.5 points more likely to vote than men, in most nations there were not significant differences but in Romania, Hungary, Poland, the Netherlands, and Australia, women voted at lower levels than men.

Norris was also interested in trying to explain variation in voting by gender. She found that much of the gap was generational. Among young voters, men and women voted at similar levels (27.5% of men reported not voting, and 27.1% of women reported not voting), but among older cohorts women voted at a markedly lower level (13.1% of men and 16.8% of women reported not voting). She also found that variation in education explained much of the difference. Among those who did not complete a primary education, 22.9% of men and 29.1% of women reported not voting. However, among those with a graduate degree, 14.1% of men and 15.8% of women reported not voting. There also tended to be a smaller gender voting gap in suburbs than in either rural or urban areas. Finally, she noted that women living in established democracies voted at more equitable rates (12.5% of men not voting and 13.1% of women not voting) than those living in newer democracies (32.4% of men compared to 34.0% of women).

Corder and Wolbrecht estimate that the gender gap in voting rates during the 1920s was around 20%.[15] Likely reasons women voted in smaller numbers were that that social norms implied women should not vote, and they had not yet developed the habit of voting. Figure 11.2 examines the voting rates of men and women in presidential races between 1952 and 2012. At the beginning of this time period there was a sizeable gap between the sexes, with men voting at higher rates, but over time the gap vanished and then reversed. The gender gap in voting rates tends to be smaller than the race gap. In 1952, 69% of women reported voting compared to 80% of men, for an 11-point gap. The gap declines significantly with the 1964 election between Barry Goldwater and Lyndon B. Johnson. By the 1980s, the gap had become very small and reversed by the 2000s. Some plausible explanations for the decrease in the gap are that the women's movement of the 1970s increased women's awareness and interest in politics, generational replacement as women who were socialized prior to the Nineteenth Amendment die off

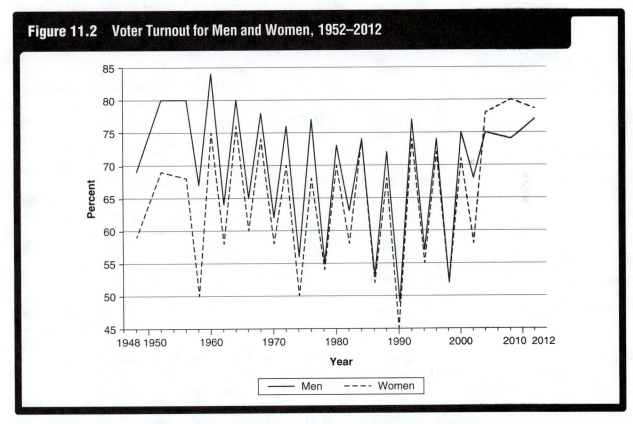

Figure 11.2   Voter Turnout for Men and Women, 1952–2012

Source: Data from American National Election Studies (ANES, http://electionstudies.org/nesguide/2ndtable/t6a_2_2.htm and http://election-studies.org/OurStudies/OurStudies.htm). Scores for 2012 were calculated by the author using 2012 ANES time series data (ANES 2012 Time Series Study [dataset]). Stanford University and the University of Michigan (producers).

and are replaced by later generations, and the campaign of Barry Goldwater. However, note that the gap is caused as much by men voting at lower rates as women voting at higher rates. Some of these trends are similar to those found around the world; see Spotlight 11.1 for a discussion.

Since the voting rates of other minority groups have only recently drawn much attention there are less trend data available. However, with the exception of LGBT, the other minority groups vote at very low levels. Depending on the survey and the question, LGBT may participate at similar or slightly lower levels than other Americans. According to the Pew Research Center study, LGBT Americans and non-LGBT Americans vote at similar levels. It found 77% of LGBT respondents said they were registered to vote, compared to 74% of the general population, and 50% of the general public said they almost always vote, compared to 49% of LGBT Americans.[16] The 2012 Gallup poll indicated LGBT Americans were slightly less politically active than others. About 74% of LGBT respondents said they were registered or planned to register to vote in 2012 compared to 80% of non-LGBT respondents. In addition, 75% of LGBT respondents said they would definitely vote compared to 81% of the non-LGBT.[17] Although the Gallup poll suggests somewhat lower levels of participation, exit polls suggest otherwise. Exit polls from 2012 suggest that 5% of voters were LGBT,[18] but most estimates suggest about 3.5% of America is LGBT.

Understanding the voting rates of Hispanics and Asian Americans is a bit complicated. Hispanic and Asian Americans tend to be younger than other Americans, meaning a significant share is less than eighteen years old and not yet eligible to vote. In fact, whereas about 17% of America is Hispanic, only 15.0% of those over eighteen are Hispanic, and whereas 5.6% of Americans are Asian American, only 5.3% of those over the age of eighteen are Asian American.[19] In addition, since most Hispanics and Asian Americans are not born on U.S. territory, they have to become naturalized citizens to be able to vote (see Chapter 9 for more details on naturalization rates). Since many have not done so, a significant percentage of Asian Americans and Hispanics are not eligible to vote. Only 67.8% of Asian Americans over eighteen years old (including Asian Americans who are mixed race) are citizens, and only 66.3% of age-eligible Hispanics are citizens.[20] Based on U.S. Census Population reports, if Asian American voting rates are calculated without regard to citizenship, only 32.5% of Asian Americans reported voting in 2012, but once noncitizens are removed from the equation, 47.9% reported voting.[21] With Hispanics, voting rates go from 31.8% when including noncitizens to 48.0% when excluding noncitizens.[22] Although taking into consideration citizenship has a strong effect on Asian American and Hispanic voting rates, both groups still vote at low levels. Based on the same survey, the voting rate of U.S. citizens regardless of race and ethnicity is 61.8%.[23] Although the voting rates for Asian American and Hispanic citizens are low, they have grown in recent elections. In 2000, 45.1% of Hispanic citizens and 43.4% of Asian American citizens reported voting; the figures went up to 47.2% and 44.2% in 2004 and 49.9% and 47.2% in 2008.[24]

A key reason for their low voting rates concerns their immigration experience. Asian American and Hispanic citizens who are born in the United States and speak English well are significantly more likely to vote than are other Asian Americans and Hispanics.[25]

Looking at the intersectionality of race/ethnicity and gender suggests some variation in the size of the gender gap by race and ethnicity. Much like women generally are more likely to vote, women within each racial ethnic group are more likely to vote. African American women were the most likely to vote. About 69.3% of African American women reported voting compared to 61.3% of African American men (an 8-point gap).[26] The gender gap is smaller for the other races. In 2012, 60.4% of Anglo men and 63.7% of Anglo women voted, for a 3.3% gap. Among Hispanics, 46.0% of men and 48.9% of women reported voting (a 2.9% gap), and among Asian Americans 46.4% of men and 49.1% of women reported voting (2.7% gap). While women tend to outvote men in most elections, this has only recently been the case for Asian Americans. Although in 2008, Asian American women outvoted Asian American men by about 2.5%, in 2004 it was about even, and in 2000 Asian American men outvoted Asian American women by about 2%.

Little is known about American Indian voters, but Stubben found that during the 1990s they registered and voted at lower rates than African Americans and whites but at higher rates than Hispanic and Asian Americans.[27] Stubben also found that American Indians voted at higher rates in tribal elections than in U.S. elections. McDonald also notes that there has been a dramatic increase in the political participation of American Indians since the 1990s.[28] He argues the increase is caused by increased wealth from gaming and other business development, greater need to interact with nontribal governments, Indian Health care, education improvements, as well as water and mining concerns.

To conclude this section, African Americans, women, and LGBT Americans vote at high levels. The rates for African Americans and women have grown since the 1950s and may even surpass those of whites and men. However, Asian Americans and Hispanics tend to vote at lower levels, this is even true after taking into consideration citizenship and age. Within each racial/ethnic group, women are more likely to vote than men. Although less is known about the electoral behavior of American Indians, it is generally thought that they are less active than whites.

Other Forms of Political Participation

Although voting is the most common way for Americans to participate in politics, it is not the only way to participate. They can work on campaigns, join groups, attend rallies, and talk to others. It may be that some of the constraints on minorities' voting may be less strong in other forms of participation. For example, if Asian Americans and Hispanics tend to vote at lower levels because of voting ineligibility, we may find that the gap is smaller when it comes to other forms of participation. In addition, minorities may be more likely to engage in nonvoting actions due to their heightened levels of group consciousness. Research consistently finds that group consciousness has stronger effects on nonvoting activities.[29] Nevertheless, in Verba, Schlozman, and Brady's 1995 classic where they asked respondents whether they had engaged in eight different activities, they found Hispanics participated at low levels.[30] The average Anglo participated in 2.2 activities, African American in 1.9, and Hispanic 1.2 (1.4 if a citizen).[31] Thus, Hispanics appear to participate in fewer political activities than Anglos or African Americans. Additionally, looking at specific types of actions they found African Americans and Hispanics less likely to contact an official, engage in informal community activity, and be affiliated with a political organization. In addition, Hispanics were less likely to work on or donate money to a campaign. African Americans were more likely than Anglos to protest, work on a campaign, or engage in informal community activity. Interestingly, Verba and his coauthors also found that once African Americans were engaged, they tended to work more hours on a campaign and made more contacts. Nonetheless, African Americans did give less money to campaigns. Verba and colleagues also found modest differences between men and women, with the average man engaged in 2.3 political activities and the average woman engaged in 2.0.[32] Additionally, women were somewhat less likely to contribute money, engage in informal community activities, and be affiliated with a political organization.

It has been twenty years since Verba, Scholzman, and Brady's research was conducted and they did not examine Asian Americans, LGBT Americans, or the intersection of race/ethnicity and gender. Table 11.1 updates the findings by listing the 2012 ANES results with regard to several types of activities for Anglos, African Americans, Hispanics, men, women, LGBT Americans, and non-LGBT Americans. It demonstrates that African Americans have increased their levels of participation and now are the most active in attending school/community meetings, showing support with buttons, yard signs, and bumper stickers, attending political events, working on campaigns, and contributing money to candidates and political parties. African Americans are about twice as likely to engage in some of these activities as either Anglos or Hispanics. Hispanics, on the other hand, remain noticeably less active in many activities, such as contacting an official, talking about candidates, and contributing money. There is one activity that Hispanics are more likely to participate in: protests. Whereas about 7.8% of Hispanics attended a protest or march in the past four years, only 6.4% of African Americans and 4.8% of Anglos participated in a protest. In the other activities, while Hispanics may be less likely to engage in them, they are not too dissimilar from Anglos.

The gender differences in participation rates tend to be muted compared to the race differences, but women tend to be less active than men. The largest differences are in the area of giving money to candidates, political parties, and groups, talking about candidates, and contacting officials. The smallest difference was in attending a school or community meeting, which supports the research indicating women are more interested in and knowledgeable about local issues. The results concerning sexual orientation are interesting but should be interpreted cautiously

TABLE 11.1 2012 Participation Rates According to the ANES (Percentages)

	Whites	African Americans	Hispanics	Women	Men	Gay	Bisexual	Heterosexual
Contacted official	27.1	23.6	16.4	18.9	22.3	38.0	19.1	20.4
Attend school/community meeting	23.6	29.8	22.1	24.3	24.9	28.5	14.0	24.9
Attend political meeting/rally/speech	5.2	9.4	4.1	5.3	6.1	6.3	11.3	5.5
Button, yard sign, bumper sticker	12.8	28.9	12.5	14.4	15.3	21.4	13.5	14.7
Talk about candidate	40.8	40.6	34.8	37.8	42.1	45.6	31.9	40.3
Work on campaign	3.0	5.6	3.1	2.9	4.1	7.0	7.5	3.3
Contribute to party	7.3	11.5	5.0	6.8	8.4	13.5	6.4	7.6
Contribute to candidate	11.0	13.5	7.4	9.9	12.3	19.9	6.9	11.1
Contribute to a group	4.7	2.1	1.8	2.5	5.8	8.0	3.3	4.0
Protest	4.8	6.4	7.8	4.4	6.8	15.1	5.4	10.2

Source: Figures calculated by the author using the American National Election Studies (ANES) 2012 Time Series Study [dataset], http://www.electionstudies.org. Stanford University and the University of Michigan (producers).

since very few of the respondents were gay, lesbian, or bisexual (only about 124 gays and lesbians and 116 bisexuals). These results demonstrate that by and large gays and lesbians are more active than bisexuals or non-LGB Americans. They were the most likely to contact an official; attend a community or school meeting; display a button, yard sign, or bumper sticker; talk about candidates; contribute money to a political party, candidate, or group; and protest. Bisexuals tended to be less active but engaged in high levels of attending political events and working on campaigns.

To summarize, Table 11.1 demonstrates that minorities, with the exception of Hispanics, engage in high levels of political participation, including giving money. Although women are less likely to engage in political actions than men, the differences tend to be fairly small. However, the gender differences are large with regard to giving money to groups, talking about candidates, contacting officials, and working on campaigns. In addition, although Hispanics tend to participate the least, they are the most likely to engage in protests or marches, and in many activities they do not differ much from Anglos.

Table 11.2 uses the 2012 ANES data to look at the intersectionality of race, ethnicity, and gender. It demonstrates that although women tend to be less politically active than men, this is mostly the case for Anglos. Hispanic women are more likely to attend school/community meetings, display their support, give

TABLE 11.2   2012 Participation Rates by Race and Gender (Percentages)

	White Women	White Men	African American Women	African American Men	Hispanic Women	Hispanic Men
Contacted official	19.6	23.1	18.6	30.1	13.5	22.5
Attended school/community meeting	23.1	24.0	29.7	30.0	22.5	21.6
Attended political meeting/rally/speech	4.6	5.9	8.7	10.3	5.0	3.2
Button, yard sign, bumper sticker	11.9	13.7	30.2	27.3	12.8	12.1
Talked about candidate	38.3	43.5	42.1	30.7	32.8	36.8
Contributed to party	6.6	8.1	9.7	13.5	4.9	5.0
Contributed to candidate	9.9	12.1	11.2	16.3	7.5	7.2
Contributed to a group	2.9	6.5	2.0	2.2	0.5	3.2
Protested	3.7	6.0	5.1	8.0	7.0	8.6

Source: Figures calculated by the author using the American National Election Studies (ANES) 2008 Time Series Study [dataset], http://www.electionstudies.org. Stanford University and the University of Michigan (producers).

money to a candidate, and attend a political event than their male counterparts. Although African American women are only more likely than African American men to participate in two activities (displaying their support with buttons, yard signs, and bumper stickers, and talking about candidates), African American women are more active than Anglo or Hispanic men in attending community/school meetings, displaying their support with buttons, yard signs, and bumper stickers, attending a political meeting/rally/ speech, and contributing money to a political party. This demonstrates the importance of looking at gender differences within racial groupings. Without doing so we would conclude that women are less active than men, but this is only true for Anglo women.

To estimate the nonvoting participation of Asian Americans, I used the 2008 National Asian American Survey. Although these data are not completely comparable to the ANES data since they ask different questions, they suggest that like Hispanics, Asian Americans remain less active than Anglos and African Americans. Only about 3.9% of Asian Americans worked on a campaign, 10.5% contacted their representative or government official, and 4.8% participated in a protest.[33] They were more active when it came to giving money to candidates, parties or other political organizations (13.5%) or discussing politics with family and friends (69.8%). The data also suggest that Asian American women are less active than Asian American men. Whereas 72.5% of Asian American men discuss politics with friends and family, only 63.8% of Asian American women discuss politics.[34] Asian American men were also more likely to contribute money to a candidate/party/political organization (13.5% to 11.7%), contact a government official (11.4% to 7.2%), and attend a protest or rally (4.9% to 3.7%). There was very little gender difference in working for a candidate/party or political organization (3.1% men and 3.8% women), but Asian American women were more likely to work for candidates/parties/groups.

Wong and coauthors find that the immigration experience has significant effects on Asian Americans' political behavior.[35] The longer Asian Americans have been in the United States, are not first or second generation, and the more proficient they are in English, the more likely they are to contribute money, contact officials, and work collectively to solve community problems, as well as vote. In addition, Wong et al. find that the length of time Asian Americans have been in the United States, their generational status, and English proficiency have less of an effect on protest actions. They also find that Asian Americans are more likely to be "super participants" if they are well off (highly educated and own their home), are Democrats, have been recruited, are active in civic and religious organizations, have experienced discrimination or hate crimes, and believe Asian Americans share common interests. In addition, Asian Americans who live in places with direct democracy and have nonpartisan ballots are more likely to participate.

The Pew Research survey of LGBT Americans also suggests that LGBT Americans are very active in issues related to their interests. About 52% have attended a pride event, 51% have boycotted a product, 40% have attended a LGBT rally or march, 39% have joined an LGBT organization, and 32% have given money to a pro-LGBT candidate.[36] About 70% of LGBT Americans have engaged in at least one of these activities, and 46% have done so in the past year.[37] Indicating the importance of identity to high levels of participation, LGBT who say their sexual orientation is very important are more likely to be active in LGBT events; the gaps tend to be around 20%.[38]

There are some differences among LGBT Americans in their political behavior. Gay men tend to be the most active, and bisexual Americans, particularly bisexual men, the least active. Gays and lesbians are more likely to have ever joined an LGBT organization than bisexuals (48%, 49%, and 28%) and to have done so in the past year (16%, 23%, and 9%).[39] Gay men (58%) are more likely to have ever boycotted services or products because of a company's position on LGBT issues than are lesbians (44%) or bisexuals (34%), and more likely to have done so in the past year (45%, 35%, and 20%).[40] Gay men are also more likely to have attended an LGBT rally or march (58%, 44%, and 25%), but the difference is smaller in looking at the past year's actions (13%, 13%, and 6%).[41] Gay men are also more likely to have given money to candidates and parties because of their stands on LGBT issues (44%, 39%, and 21%).[42] The differences are muted when looking at donations in the past year (21%, 20%, and 8%).[43] It should be noted that although lesbians tend to be less active than gay men, women who are bisexual are often more active than men who are bisexual. They are more likely to have boycotted a product (36% to 26%), been a member of an LGBT organization (34% to 12%), donated money to candidates and organizations (23% to 12%), and attended an LGBT march or rally (26% to 23%).[44]

The above indicates that African Americans have increased their levels of participation significantly and today participate at levels similar to whites. Hispanics and Asian Americans, on the other hand, are the least active in politics, with the exception of joining protests. White women participate at lower levels than white men, but minority women participate at higher levels than their men counterparts. In fact, African American women are among the most active. LGBT are also active in LGBT-specific activities, although bisexuals participate at lower levels than lesbians and gays.

Explaining Political Participation

There are several theories designed to explain why some individuals are more likely than others to participate in politics, but this section focuses on the rational choice model. It does so since other theories can be discussed within this framework. The rational choice model suggests that individuals evaluate the costs and benefits and will participate if the benefits they receive from participation outweigh the costs. So the key to understanding whether minorities are more or less likely to participate is to understand how their minority status affects the costs and benefits of their participation.

The socioeconomic model of participation[45] argues that individuals with lower levels of socioeconomic status are more likely to participate than others, and socioeconomic status can affect individuals' costs and benefits. For example, low-income individuals may find it more costly to participate because they have greater limitations with transportation, may find it more difficult to get off from work, and individuals with less education may find it more difficult to read accounts of issues and candidates. In addition, poorer communities tend to have long voting lines and antiquated voting machines (see Chapter 3). Individuals with higher levels of socioeconomic status, white-collar jobs, and high levels of education may also have greater civic skills,[46] which could lower the costs and increase the benefits. People with high levels of socioeconomic status are more likely to be recruited by others to participate, in part because of their civic skills and networks. Thus, they may not have to expend resources to become informed about political happenings. Since low socioeconomic status is related to low levels of participation and minority status, it is likely that minorities are less likely to participate. Yet as noted above, that is not necessarily the case. Nevertheless, much research suggests that the costs of voting are greater for people with low levels of socioeconomic status (SES), and this is true for minorities as well as nonminorities.[47] Additionally, as noted earlier, Verba and Nie found that even in the late 1960s, African Americans voted at higher levels than whites once socioeconomic status was taken into account;[48] therefore, the appearance of a race gap was really caused by African Americans being more likely to be poor.

Other models of political participation note that individuals who are contacted to participate are more likely to participate.[49] Potential voters who are encouraged to vote by parties, groups, candidates, or social contacts are likely to know where to vote and how to register to vote without incurring any costs. They may also instill in would-be voters the importance of voting or the importance of voting for a particular candidate. Similarly, individuals contacted by groups about events or grassroots actions are more likely to be relatively well informed about them and participate.

Unfortunately for increased minority participation, minorities are less likely to be recruited than nonminorities. The ANES asks respondents: "Did anyone from one of the political parties call you up or come around and talk to you about the campaign?" According to these data, in 2012, 41% of African Americans and 44.8% of whites reported being contacted by a party about voting. In 2008, 37% of African Americans and 45% of whites reported being contacted by a major party. In 2004, the figures were 28% and 50%.[50] Hispanics, too, are less likely to be contacted by a political party. In 2012, only 32.6% of Hispanics were contacted. Also according to the ANES data, gays and lesbians were less likely to be contacted by the parties than were non-LGB and bisexuals (37.5%, 42.5%, and 45.1%, respectively).

Unlike other minorities, women, in 2012, were more likely to report being contacted than men (43.5% to 40.8%). In 2008 there was no gender gap (42% to 42%), and in 2004 women were more likely to be contacted (46% to 40%). The race or ethnicity of women and men affected the likelihood they were contacted. In 2012, white and Hispanic women were more likely to be contacted than their men counterparts (46.8% to 42.6% for whites and 35.3% to 29.8% for Hispanics), but African American women were slightly less likely to be contacted than African American men (41.1% to 42.1%). Although the ANES does not allow for examining levels of contact for Asian Americans, the 2008 National Asian American Survey (NAAS) does. It suggests Asian Americans were not likely to be contacted by candidates or parties. Only about 26% of Asian Americans reported having been contacted.[51] The lack of contact is greater for Asian American women than men. Whereas 28% of men said they had been contacted, only 24% of women indicated they had been contacted. This may depress voter turnout, as Wong and coauthors also found that Asian Americans who were contacted were more likely to vote.[52]

Related to being recruited is civic engagement (see Chapter 9). Individuals who are part of social networks at work, church, or volunteer activities may make contacts that will recruit them to participate.[53] People with high levels of civic engagement may also find it easier to participate. Civic engagement helps people build civic skills and can educate individuals about politics and mobilize them to action. As noted in Chapter 9, Asian Americans and Hispanics are less likely to volunteer in their community and less likely to attend religious services. However, African Americans are more likely to be active in civic and religious organizations.

Most models designed to explain political behavior tend to downplay the likelihood that people participate to affect the outcomes of elections or policy debates. Using a rational choice model, Downs noted that although the costs of voting are small, the benefits of voting solely to affect who wins are virtually zero.[54] This is because the chance of a voter's single vote determining the winner is virtually zero. In looking at collective action, Olson suggests the free rider problem makes participating to affect policy irrational in most situations.[55] The **free rider problem** occurs because most policies are umbrella policies. These are policies that cannot be denied to an individual. Thus, if the policy is enacted, an individual benefits even if she did not work to enact the policy. For example, if same-sex couples are afforded the right to marry, the right is given to all same-sex couples, not just those who worked to gain that right. As such, any costs the individual incurred are wasted from an individual's perspective—she would get the benefit without any costs. As a consequence, some theories focus on the psychological benefits people get from participating.

Two key psychological benefits that can increase participation are psychological engagement (interest in politics) and feeling good about voting because of high levels of civic duty.[56] Table 11.3 lists responses from the 2008 Pew Research Center's Value study to the question asking respondents the degree to which they agreed with the following statement: "I'm interested in keeping up with national affairs."[57] The options were "completely agree," "mostly agree," "mostly disagree," or "completely disagree." Table 11.3 indicates that there is little difference between the races in their interest in national affairs. Although the differences are not large, more whites expressed interest in national affairs (than African Americans and Hispanics). There is a somewhat larger gender difference, with men expressing greater interest than women. These gender differences become more

TABLE 11.3   Interest in National Affairs by Race, Ethnicity, and Gender (Percentages)

	Anglos	African Americans	Hispanics	Other	Men	Women
Completely agree	47.1	46.2	47.0	46.3	49.9	44.2
Mostly agree	43.5	42.0	40.1	42.5	41.6	44.1
Mostly disagree	7.1	7.7	9.3	7.8	6.2	8.7
Completely disagree	2.3	4.1	3.6	3.4	2.3	3.0
	4,480	685	662	321	3,005	3,210

	Women	Anglo men	African American women	African American men	Hispanic women	Hispanic men
Completely agree	41.4	49.2	43.2	53.2	41.4	52.3
Mostly agree	32.4	42.6	45.3	37.4	40.7	39.5
Mostly disagree	15.8	6.2	9.4	5.4	13.2	5.6
Completely disagree	10.4	2.2	4.2	3.9	4.6	2.6
	2,310	4,480	398	287	325	337

Source: Calculated by author using 2002–2009 Pew Research Center's "Trends in Political Values and Core Beliefs," http://www.people-press.org/2007/03/22/2007-values-update.

pronounced when we examine gender differences among whites and Hispanics but not African Americans. About 92% of white men express an interest compared to only 73% of white women. Among Hispanics the difference is 93% to 82%. For African Americans the difference is only 91% to 89%. In fact, of all women, African American women have the greatest interest in national affairs.

The 2008 NAAS can be used to assess the political interest of Asian Americans. It suggests Asian Americans have fairly low levels of interest in politics. About 21% said they were not at all interested, 37% somewhat interested, 25% interested, and only 16% very interested.[58] Among Asian Americans, women tend to be less interested in politics than men. For example, while about 20% of Asian American men said they were very interested in politics, only about 13% of Asian American women said they were very interested.

Based on the Pew Research Center's survey of LGBT Americans, they may be less interested in politics as well. Whereas 51% of the general public closely follows the government most of the time, only 31% of LGBT Americans closely follow the government.[59] In addition, 71% of LGBT respondents closely follow the government at least some of the time compared to 77% of the general public. There is some variation among LGBT respondents in how closely they follow politics. About 42% of gay men follow politics most of the time; only 28% of lesbians and 25% of bisexuals follow politics most of the time. About 37% of gay men, 40% of lesbians, and 41% of bisexuals follow politics some of the time.[60]

Another key psychological benefit related to political participation concerns **civic duty**. Civic duty is the belief that citizens have a responsibility to vote or participate. People who have high levels of civic duty are thought to endure negative emotions (feel bad) if they do not vote and positive emotions if they vote. Thus, for people with high levels of civic duty there is the benefit of feeling good. To examine differences in the levels of minority individuals' civic duty, again the Pew Research Center's Value Study is used. The question asked respondents to what degree they agree with the following statement "I feel it's my duty as a citizen to always vote." The options were completely agree, mostly agree, mostly disagree or completely disagree.

Table 11.4 reports these findings. Table 11.4 demonstrates that African Americans have high levels of civic duty and Hispanics low levels. About 92% of African Americans, 81% of whites, and 82% of Hispanics expressed high levels of civic duty. Not only do racial and ethnic minorities have high levels of civic duty but so too do women. Although men and women both tend to agree, the difference is in the strength of agreement. Almost 68% of women completely agreed with the statement compared to 62% of men. Also, within each racial or ethnic pairing of men and women, women were more likely to completely agree than were their male counterparts. This was most pronounced for African Americans where 73% of women completely agreed compared to 66% of African American men. Efficacy may also affect voting behavior.[61] People with high levels of efficacy are also more likely to participate and as was discussed in Chapter 5, minorities tend to have lower levels of efficacy.

The psychological benefits individuals feel when they participate may be affected by whether they are on the winning or losing side of a political campaign.

TABLE 11.4 Citizens Feel a Duty to Vote by Race, Ethnicity, and Gender

	Completely agree (%)	Mostly agree (%)	Disagree (%)	Completely disagree (%)	Total number of responses
Anglo	65.5	26.1	5.7	2.8	4,477
African American	70.1	22.0	4.8	3.1	688
Hispanic	57.2	32.9	7.2	2.7	661
Men	62.1	28.2	6.5	3.2	2,996
Women	67.7	24.8	4.9	2.6	3,212
Anglo women	68.0	24.9	4.6	2.4	2,315
Anglo men	62.8	27.3	6.8	3.1	2,162
African American women	73.1	18.9	4.3	3.7	401
African American men	66.0	26.1	5.6	2.4	287
Hispanic women	58.2	31.0	8.8	2.0	320
Hispanic men	56.2	34.6	5.8	3.4	341

Source: Calculated by author using 2002–2009 Pew Research Center's "Trends in Political Values and Core Beliefs," http://www.people-press .org/2007/03/22/2007-values-update.

Unfortunately for African American voters, they are less likely to see their preferred candidates win than are individuals in other major demographic groups.[62] Between 1994 and 2006, 59% of African Americans voted for the losing presidential candidate, 55% voted for the losing Senate candidate, and 53% the losing gubernatorial candidate. Hispanics, too, were likely to vote for the losing candidate. Whites were most likely to vote for the winning candidate, followed by Asian Americans.[63] The one office where African Americans and Hispanics were likely to vote for the winner was for a member of the U.S. House of Representatives. These are elections where majority-minority districts are likely to exist. There is little in the way of gender differences in whether voters' preferred candidates won.[64]

Although the above suggests majority-minority districts would increase voter turnout, there are some debates. One train of thought is that majority-minority districts should result in higher voter turnout because minority voters will feel empowered since their candidate will have a good chance of winning. The other thought is that majority-minority districts will depress turnout because they tend to be less competitive. Noncompetitive races tend to be less interesting and decrease the chance that one vote will affect the outcome. In comparing these two ideas, Barreto, Segura, and Woods find that Asian Americans and Hispanics who live in majority-minority districts are more likely to vote.[65] Other research also supports the belief that majority-minority districts increase voter turnout. Wong and coauthors find Asian Americans living in areas with Asian American representatives are more likely to vote.[66] In addition, Haye and Mckee find that when African Americans are redistricted into districts with African American representatives, the likelihood they vote increases but when they are redistricted out of a district with an African American representative into a white district, they are less likely to vote.[67] Also supporting the idea that majority-minority districts increase minority turnout is that Barreto finds voting levels of Hispanics increase when there is a Hispanic on the ballot.[68]

In traditional models of rational choice, the calculations are at the individual level: comparing the benefits individuals personally receive with their personal costs. However, with minorities "relational goods" may affect the calculation. **Relational goods** are "incentives enjoyed by individuals as members of groups."[69] As such, minorities may see a benefit of voting in helping advance the interests of people with their minority status. Minorities can often be mobilized to vote to benefit the group. Thus, the benefits for minorities can either be individual or collective. Jang finds that because the potential for group benefits are higher where there is a large number of minorities, Asian Americans and Hispanics are more likely to vote where their numbers are greater.[70]

Relatedly, as noted in Chapter 10, minorities' voting rates can also be affected by their group consciousness. Individuals with high levels of group consciousness are likely to participate and be easily recruited to vote when issues important to the group are campaign issues. For example, based on a series of experiments, Merolla, Pantoja, Cargile, and Mora found that Hispanics, but not other groups, vote at higher levels when the media frame immigration negatively.[71] As noted in Chapter 10, research also finds among Asian Americans and Hispanics those who have experienced discrimination and see that either Asian Americans share interests or that Hispanics share interest are more likely to vote than other Asian Americans and Hispanics.[72]

There are also some specific models designed to explain the voting rates of specific minority groups. With regard to Asian Americans and Hispanics, it is likely that immigration experiences affect their participatory rates. Asian Americans and Hispanics, as noted in Chapter 9, are less likely to be proficient in English. This lack of proficiency may increase the costs for Asian Americans and Hispanics as well as other naturalized citizens. Even though ballots must be printed in languages spoken by a large number of citizens in an area, non-English speakers are likely to find getting information about the election's procedures and candidates more costly. Wong and coauthors found that Asian Americans are more likely to vote if they live where there is language assistance with ballots.[73] And much research finds that English-language proficiency of Asian Americans and Hispanics increases their political participation.[74]

Given the low participation rates but growing population rates of Hispanics there is much interest in understanding why Hispanics vote at low levels. Cassel looks at several possible reasons for their low voting rates: low SES, being young, cultural issues such as language, immigration rates, and attachment to the homeland, and that candidates and parties are less likely to recruit or mobilize Hispanic citizens.[75] She found that once SES and being contacted to vote are taken into consideration, Hispanic citizens vote at rates similar to African Americans and Anglos for presidential races and that the cultural explanations are not needed. In looking at midterm elections, she finds that even after taking into consideration SES and recruitment, Hispanics still vote at lower levels. She speculates that new immigrant groups may need extra contact in midterm elections to understand the importance of these races.

The voting rates of Asian Americans present a bit of a conundrum. SES is thought to be one of the largest factors affecting voting behavior, yet Asian Americans vote at low levels despite having high levels of SES. Part of the reason is that SES does not have the same effect on Asian Americans' voting as it does on other Americans.[76] Instead, assimilation has a strong effect, whether measured by having been born in the United States or living in communities where Asian Americans interact with other racial groups.[77] Diaz also found that Asian Americans who lived in areas with panethnic organization were more likely to participate.[78] Also affecting Asian Americans' political participation is whether they have experienced a hate crime or similar action, and have high levels of civic and religious engagement; those who have are more likely to be politically active.[79] And as noted elsewhere in this text, Asian Americans have lower levels of civic engagement and high levels of immigration. Thus, the conditions needed for high levels of Asian American participation are not plentiful.

Although national surveys do not give much information on what affects the voting behavior of LGBT Americans, some research examines what affects voter turnout of LGBT Americans. Although these studies have not had consistent findings as to the effects of SES, contact, group consciousness, and the like, on LGBT Americans' voting behavior, a recent study found that the more educated gays and lesbians, those with a public gay or lesbian identity, those who have experienced a hate crime, have collective efficacy, and belong to an LGB organization are more politically active (vote, sign a petition, and wrote a letter about an LGB issue to a representative).[80]

One final yet simple way to get a sense of why individuals in minority groups do not vote is to ask them. The 2012 Census Current Population Survey asks nonvoters why they did not vote.[81] The survey indicates African Americans are more likely to miss the vote due to issues related to low incomes. Transportation is a bigger problem for African Americans than other groups. African Americans and Hispanics are more likely to have registration problems preventing them from voting. African Americans are also the most likely to find the location inconvenient. African Americans and women are significantly more likely not to vote because of illness or disability. Asian Americans and men are more likely to miss voting because they were out of town. Some other differences include: African Americans and Hispanics are more likely to forget, but Anglos and men are most likely to lack interest. Women and whites are less likely to be too busy. Anglos are more likely not to vote because they didn't like the candidates.

To summarize, this discussion offers some understanding of the voting rates of minorities. African Americans are likely to vote at high levels because they have high levels of civic engagement and psychological benefits, such as interest and civic duty. Additionally, that an African American is currently president likely increases their relational goods, particularly since they have high levels of group consciousness. This is despite having low levels of socioeconomic status and recruitment. Hispanics' and Asian Americans' low levels of participation are partially explained by their high levels of immigration status that likely increase their cost of voting. Additionally, they tend to have low levels of civic engagement and civic duty. Relational goods and group consciousness, too, may contribute to their participation rates. Hispanics, but not Asian Americans, too, have low levels of SES. Their high levels of civic duty and recruitment likely contribute to women's high levels of participation. The participation rates of LGBT Americans are likely influenced by their levels of group consciousness, and despite having low levels of income, being less likely to be recruited by the parties, and having below average levels of political interest, they participate at rates similar to non LGBT Americans.

The Impact of the Minority Vote

There are two ways to estimate the impact of minority voters on elections: their share of the vote and the likelihood that their votes determine who wins. Both ways demonstrate the importance of the minority vote. First, minorities make up a growing and significant share of the vote. In 1996, for example, 82.5% of people who cast votes were Anglo and by 2012 the figure was down to 73.7%.[82] The group with the largest increase was Hispanics, which went from 4.7% in 1996 to 8.4% in 2012. African Americans also saw a sizeable gain. African Americans' vote share went from 10.8% to 13.4% in the same time period.[83] Asian Americans' vote share went from 1.7% to 2.9%. And women have comprised the majority of voters for at least thirty years. With presidential elections being decided by just a few points, candidates need minority votes in order to win elections.

Not only does the sheer volume of minority voters indicate their political power, but what also makes their vote significant is that voters of each minority status tend to share political interests and vote for the same candidate. In addition, the candidate supported by minorities is often not supported by nonminority voters. As a consequence, winning candidates' victories are often dependent on a given minority or coalition of minorities. This can be demonstrated by looking at the 2012 presidential election. In 2012, since the majority of Anglo voters voted for Mitt Romney for president, President Obama would have lost reelection without racial and ethnic minorities. In addition, a majority of men supported Romney, while a majority of women supported Obama. Thus, Obama could not have won without the women's vote. Finally, there are estimates that Obama could not have won without the LGBT vote. Gates demonstrates that Obama would have lost the popular vote nationally and in the swing states of Ohio, Florida, and Virginia had 51% of LGBT voters supported Romney.[84]

The above paragraphs have focused on the national vote, but the impact of minority voters is also substantial in many state and local races. Women are a majority of voters in most states. However, because of the residency patterns of racial and ethnic minorities, their voting impact is uneven. In most southern states, African Americans make up over 20% of the voters, and in most southwestern states, Hispanics make up more than 20% of the voters.[85] However, in many rural Midwestern and New England states, African American, Hispanic, and Asian American voters comprise a small minority of voters. For example, less than 1% of the electorate in South Dakota and Maine are African American and less than 3% of voters in South Dakota and 1% in Maine is Hispanic.[86] In some of these states minorities may have influence in individual districts due to the creation of majority-minority districts and districts of influence. However, as a rule, minorities have little impact in these states.

Although American Indians are unlikely to have a significant effect on national elections given their small numbers, at the local level they can have an important effect. In 2000, American Indian voters helped Maria Cantwell defeat incumbent Slade Gorton for the Washington's U.S. Senate seat since Sen. Gorton was seen as anti-Indian.[87] Jerry Stubben noted that in 2002, Tim Johnson, who won his U.S. Senate seat by 528 votes, owes his victory to American Indians.[88] Johnson campaigned on reservations, which supported his candidacy and saw a 20% increase in the Indian vote. In 2004, American Indian voters likely helped Stephanie Herseth win a U.S. House seat in South Dakota.[89]

Efforts to Reach Minority Voters

Since the majority of minorities tend to vote for Democratic candidates and the United States is diversifying, the victory of many Democrats is dependent on minority voters. Thus, Democrats have an incentive to register and mobilize these voters while Republicans have an incentive to draw as many away from the Democratic Party as they can. Parties and candidates are well aware of this and engage in numerous activities to win minority voters. This was evident in the 2012 presidential election, as noted in the introduction to this chapter.

Minority voters have become a significant share of all voters. Having ballots and instructions in languages other than English encourages minorities to vote. *(Moment Mobile EDI/Allison Achauer/Getty Images)*

There are numerous examples of how the parties and candidates courted the Hispanic vote in 2012. By October 2012, over $11 million had been spent on Spanish-language ads in Colorado, Nevada, and Florida, half of this in Miami, Orlando, and Tampa alone.[90] Although this is a small share of the money spent, it is eight times the amount spent in 2008.[91] Both campaigns used Spanish-language ads, with Obama significantly outspending Romney. Although Obama significantly outspent Romney on Spanish-language ads, both campaigns used Spanish-language ads. Candidates also appeared on Spanish-language TV, spoke in Spanish, and addressed Latino interests in speeches and other campaign materials.

Hispanics were not the only minority group to receive targeted appeals. A Romney campaign consultant noted Romney's desire to reach African American voters:

> The governor is committed to competing in the black community. The odds are high, it's challenging, but every percentage point that we chip away from President Obama counts. . . . There are shared values with this community around faith, family, free enterprise and education. He will highlight his record in terms of addressing health, wealth and disparity gaps and show clear distinctions between him and Obama.[92]

In that regard, Mitt Romney spoke at the NAACP annual conference, hired a senior consultant for outreach to the African American community, and visited a charter school with predominantly African American students.[93] Obama, too, made efforts to attract African American voters with several actions, such as creating a webpage and video for African Americans,[94] voter turnout and registration drives targeting African American communities, and making appeals in speeches. Although still not a primary focus of candidates, Asian Americans received more attention in 2012 than in previous elections. The increase in attention is the result of their increased population, and that they are less clearly aligned to the Democratic Party than other minorities.[95]

Women, particularly single women, were also a key demographic in the candidates' strategies. The Democratic Party tried to appeal to women voters by stating that Republicans were in a war against women through their efforts to challenge Medicare, collective bargaining, and reproductive rights. At the same time, the Republican Party reached out to women voters by discussing how women were negatively affected by the economy.[96]

Examining the parties' national conventions reveals the significance of minority voters to the parties. Parties' national conventions have become significant public relations campaigns in recent elections, giving parties the opportunity to sell themselves to the voters. As a consequence, who speaks during prime time indicates what kind of image a party wants to send to the American people. The Republican Party had at least ten Hispanic-themed events and included Governor Susana Martinez (NM) in its prime-time lineup, while the Democratic Party included San Antonio mayor Julian Castro as its keynote speaker.[97] Although the Republican Party received negative attention for racism on the part of its virtually homogeneously white delegates, the Republican Party featured several African Americans at its convention: Artur Davis, Condoleezza Rice, and Mia Love.[98] Other minority Republican politicians were also well represented at the convention. A *Huffington Post* article noted:

> If you're a female GOP governor, there's a 75 percent chance you're speaking at the Republican convention. Including Puerto Rico, the GOP has five governors who are of either Latin or Indian descent. All five were offered prime speaking gigs. Of the two black male House GOP freshmen, one, Tim Scott of South Carolina, has already spoken.
>
> The Huffington Post compared the GOP convention speakers list to the roster of available politicians and found that if you're a white male House member, there's less than a 3 percent chance you're getting on the stage. A white governor's shot at the prized podium is only one in six. For white male senators, the chance is closer to one in 10.

The more diverse Democratic Party not only saw racially and ethnically diverse speakers, but many spoke of advances in LGBT rights during Obama's first term[99] and Obama's endorsement of gay marriage.

In 2004 there was a major push to increase the number or American Indian voters.[100] The National Congress of American Indians and several local Indian groups made concerted efforts to increase American Indian voters. Realizing that the election was going to be close and that American Indians could vote for either party, the Republican Party as well as the Democratic Party worked to gain their vote. This was particularly true in swing states with a large number of Indian voters, such as Arizona and New Mexico, where they ran get-out-the-vote drives and made promises to improve relationship with tribes. In 2008, the Indian vote again was seen as important, as illustrated by candidates Hillary Clinton and Barack Obama visiting reservations.[101]

Conclusion: Increased Participation and Power but Differences Remain among Groups

Minorities share having seen a rise in their levels of political participation and voting power over the past several elections cycles such that the parties and many of their candidates know they need to reach minority voters in order to win. Much of the change has to do with changing laws and procedures that make it easier and more meaningful for minorities to vote. Some of it too has to do with the presidency of Barack Obama and the growing diversification of the United States. For example, fifty years ago African Americans voted and participated at much lower levels than white Americans. Today, they not only vote at higher levels but are more likely to participate in other activities such as contributing money, contacting officials, attending meetings and rallies, and wearing buttons, putting up yard signs and bumper stickers. Women, too, have seen great increases in their voting level. Until the 1980s, they voted at lower levels than men, but today they vote at somewhat higher levels than men.

Although minorities are voting at higher levels than in the past, there is great variation among minorities in their relative levels of voting. As noted in the previous paragraph, women and African Americans vote at rates as high or higher than their counterparts. LGBT too are thought to vote at levels similar to non-LGBT. However, unlike African Americans, LGBT, and women, American Indians, Asian Americans, and Hispanics participate at low levels. Much of this has to do with the immigrant experience. Hispanics' low levels of SES also contribute to their low level of participation. Since native-born Asian Americans and Hispanics vote at higher levels than non–native-born Americans, it is likely that as there are more second- and third-generation Asian Americans and Hispanics, their voting rates will increase. For American Indians, it has little to do with immigration but, instead, their torn allegiance between their tribe and the United States, or hostility toward the United States.

This chapter also demonstrates the importance of examining intersectionality. Although women of all races tend to vote at higher rates than men, African American women are uniquely active in political participation. African American women vote at higher rates than any other group. In addition, while non–African American women remain less likely to participate in nonvoting actions than their men counterparts, African American women are more likely to engage in these actions. One reason why women and African Americans may vote and participate at high levels despite high levels of poverty is that they tend to have high levels of civic duty and group consciousness.

As minorities have increased in numbers and solidarity their voting impact has increased as well. As this has happened candidates and parties have developed strategies to gain their votes. Whether or not this will impact policy it is too soon to tell. This chapter focused on the political behavior of individuals who are minorities, and while this is important for minority representation, minority representation can also be enhanced by the work of groups and movements. As a consequence, Chapter 12 examines minority-focused social movements and interest groups.

KEY TERMS

Civic duty   (p. 277)

Civil disobedience   (p. 264)

Conventional political
   participation   (p. 264)

Free rider problem   (p. 276)

Political
   participation   (p. 263)

Relational goods   (p. 279)

Unconventional political
   participation   (p. 263)

Chapter 12

Minority Movements and Interest Groups

"On strike! Shut it down!" From November 1968 to March 1969, those words rang out daily on the campus of San Francisco State College. Like clockwork, between noon and 3 P.M. striking students would gather at the Speaker's Platform on campus for a rally, then turn in mass and march on the Administration Building, intent upon confrontation with President Smith or Hayakawa.[1]

After the college paper printed an editorial in November 1967 asking the school to stop funding organizations such as the Black Student Union (BSU), a black consciousness-raising group, six students attacked the editor.[2] The students were arrested. Upon their arrest there was picketing at the school. In December protesting students broke into the administration building and the president closed the campus. In February, another action occurred when 300 minority high school and junior college students come to the campus demanding to be admitted for the fall semester. In March, the Third World Liberation Front (TWLF) occupied the campus YMCA. TWLF was a coalition of African American, Mexican American, and Asian American groups that wanted to make parallels between the colonialization of the third world with the treatment of minorities in the United States. In May, students took over the administration building to protest the ROTC's presence on campus (remember this was during the Vietnam War), the firing of a Hispanic faculty member, and the desire to have more minority faculty members. The police were called and twenty-six students were arrested. However, the main action does not occur until November 6, 1968, when BSU and TWLF started a university-wide strike following the reassignment of George Murray, a teaching assistant, who was active in the Black Panthers. The groups' demands included Murray back in the classroom, more minority faculty and students, and ethnic studies programs. When the students marched on the administration building, the president called the police, and on November 13 the campus was closed. Although efforts were made to reopen the campus, the strike continued with the support of a faculty union until March 21 when most of the students' demands were met. A similar strike started in January 1969 at University of California, Berkeley. During this strike, the police and National Guard were called, students were injured, and hundreds were arrested. It, too, resulted in the creation of an ethnic studies program.

These student-led protests were just the tip of the iceberg when it came to actions that occurred from the 1950s through the 1970s designed to improve the

Minority students who protested to improve their college experience and start minority studies programs often faced resistance. (© *Bettmann/Corbis*)

lives of minorities and society's appreciation of their contributions to the United States. This chapter briefly describes six social movements to advance minority interests of the last half of the twentieth century, a time of great change: the civil rights movement, the Chicano movement, the American Indian movement, the Asian American movement, the women's rights movement, and the LGBT movement. In addition, this chapter discusses some of the key interest groups acting to advance or halt their interests today. Although people often use the terms *political movement* and *social movement* interchangeably, scholars see them as very different. Social movements tend to be much broader in scope and based on an ideology, while political movements tend to be more issue focused. Social movements tend to be mass-based movements of individuals often socially located on the margins of society because of a minority status who share a group consciousness.[3] They also tend to be decentralized, with numerous organizations and leaders working alone or in concert to achieve change. Political movements, on the other hand, tend to have a single leader and be made up of the haves as opposed to the have-nots.

One of the tensions found in most social movements concerns whether the strategies and goals should be assimilationist or liberationist.[4] Assimilationists "embrace a rights-based perspective, works within the broader framework of pluralist democracy—one situated within classical liberalism—and fights for a seat at the table."[5] Liberationists want the political, economic and social structures to undergo fundamental changes such that the minority perspective is incorporated. Liberationists often work outside of the current political structures. As is apparent in the brief descriptions of various minority movements listed below, many movements are successful by incorporating both strategies.

The Civil Rights Movement

The **civil rights movement** is a term used to describe a period of time starting in the mid-twentieth century during which there was much activity and advancement in the rights of African Americans. Although the civil rights movement is thought to start in the 1950s, its origins predate the 1950s. Between the 1930s and 1950s, there were several events that helped lead the way; there were key court cases, creation of organizations, World War II (WWII), and the presidencies of Franklin D. Roosevelt and Harry S. Truman.[6] The NAACP, which was established in 1909, used a legal strategy that eventually led to a series of court cases that struck at the heart of Jim Crow laws (see Chapter 1) and ended white primaries. Perhaps the most significant case was the 1954 *Brown v. Board of Education* case that overturned the separate but equal doctrine and required schools to desegregate. This case not only inspired many African Americans, but also the South's resistance to the case would lead to events that would affect the movement. World War II had its effects as well. Soldiers, particularly African American soldiers who had fought for equality and freedom in Europe, returned home with a desire to fight for equality and freedom at home. But others as well drew parallels between the treatment of Jews under the Nazis with the treatment of the African Americans at home. The war also increased the mobility of African Americans, many of whom moved north in search of wartime jobs. Under FDR's presidency, there was a sense that leaders cared about the plight of African Americans. In addition, President Truman desegregated the armed forces and pushed for civil rights legislation. In 1955, the race-based brutal murder of Emmitt Till, an African American man, and the acquittal of his white attackers was covered throughout the nation, incensing many northern whites as well as African Americans. Some of the events gave individuals hope that action could lead to change, and some were galvanized to work for change.

One of the first major actions of the civil rights movement was the *Montgomery Bus Boycott* in 1955–1956. The catalyst for the boycott was Rosa Parks being arrested for sitting in the front of the bus. At the time, African Americans had to give up their seats in the front of the bus and move to the back or stand if a white person wanted the seat. When the leader of the local NAACP heard that Ms. Parks,[7] who had been active in the organization, had been arrested, he decided to use her as a figurehead/catalyst for a planned bus boycott. To get the word out and to have space to organize the boycott, he solicited the help of a new young minister in Montgomery, Martin Luther King Jr. (MLK). Although initially the boycott was to last one day, the organizers decided to keep it going until the busses were no longer segregated.

The boycott was hard on African Americans, many of whom had no other transportation and often had to walk miles to work or other activities. To keep the boycott organized, the *Montgomery Improvement Association* (MIA) was created, with MLK as its leader. The MIA held rallies to keep up the boycotters' spirit, provide resources, negotiate, and work with the courts. During the nearly yearlong boycott, the MIA received aid from outside of Montgomery to do such things as help find transportation for African Americans. Eventually, segregated busses were ruled unconstitutional, and the boycott ended. The boycott not only succeeded in desegregating the busses, it also helped to start the broader movement by deepening the commitment of activists, developing leaders, and taking the movement from the courts to direct action.[8] MLK and the other leaders from the movement formed what eventually became the Southern Christian Leadership Conference (SCLC). Ella Baker, who was hired by SCLC, helped to bring students into the movement. And these students created the Student Nonviolent Coordinating Committee (SNCC), which was more radical in orientation than the SCLC. Although SCLC remained active, it was not until 1963 that it had its next major success. In the meantime, the movement saw successes from other sources.

One of these successes was in Greensboro, North Carolina, in 1960.[9] Here four men, who were inspired by MLK, started a sit-in at the Woolworth department store. They sat down at the white-only lunch counter and said they would wait until they were served. When the store closed, they left but returned the next day. Over the next week, they returned and as word got out, more and more people joined the sit-in and by the end of the week, leaders of Greensboro agree to negotiate. When these negotiations failed, the sit-in continued, and after several protesters were arrested, many African Americans started to boycott businesses. About six months after the initial sit-in, Greensboro was desegregated. This inspired many other sit-ins, which became a staple of the movement.

Another success occurred with the *Freedom Rides* (May to September 1961). Although the Supreme Court had ruled that segregation in interstate travel violated the Constitution, many of the facilities in bus terminals remained segregated. The Freedom Rides, which were organized by the Congress of Racial Equality, CORE (see below), involved sending groups of African Americans and whites into the Deep South to challenge segregation. African Americans and whites sat on the bus together and then went into terminals together, sat in waiting rooms and restaurants together. The brutal attacks of the initial busses that occurred with police complacency received national and international news coverage, which resulted in more people volunteering to be part of the action. The attacks also increased involvement from MLK, SNCC, and the federal government. Not only did the freedom riders face physical threats, but many were also arrested for violating local segregation laws. Eventually, and reluctantly, the Kennedy administration and the federal government got involved to help protect the freedom riders. The most obvious success of the Freedom Rides was that the Interstate Commerce Commission, which regulates interstate travel, issued rules to enforce desegregation, and ensured desegregated travel. The rides also made CORE a player in the civil rights movement, demonstrated that with the aid of the federal government change could occur in the Deep South, and demonstrated to much of the nation and world the brutality of white segregationists in the South.[10]

With the encouragement of the Kennedy administration[11] student leaders in SNCC and CORE turned their attention to voter registration. They held schools to teach African Americans how to register to vote (many states required literacy tests to register to vote). However, many graduates of the school were turned away by registration agents, and many were physically attacked. Not only did individuals who tried to register to vote face violence, but so, too, did those who tried to help them. In 1963, the voter registration efforts got a boost when white students from the north came to help. This is referred to as *Freedom Summer*. At the time, in Mississippi alone about sixty-three African Americans had been killed for registration related activities, and registration had increased only 1.4%.[12] However, the summer of 1963 saw the violence continue, and when two white workers disappeared and local authorities did nothing, President Johnson sent in the FBI. The FBI found the bodies and made arrests. Yet, even in the presence of the FBI, the violence continued.

SCLC was instrumental in two significant events in 1963. By late 1962, MLK had realized that it would take federal action to change the South and that it took large actions to get the federal government involved.[13] With that in mind, SCLC planned a campaign in Birmingham, Alabama, since Birmingham was one of the more segregated and violent cities. The action was designed to provoke a response from the notoriously racist police commissioner, Bull Conner. In early April, the campaign started with a rally and boycotts. On Good Friday, MLK and others marched to city hall, at which point Connor released the police dogs on the marchers and arrested them. It was while in jail that MLK wrote his "Letter from the Birmingham Jail." The letter was in response to criticism the movement had received from religious leaders as to the tactics and timing of the actions. In the letter he defended the actions and was critical of those not active in the movement of nonviolent resistance to racial prejudice.

> I must make two honest confessions to you, my Christian and Jewish brothers. First, I must confess that over the past few years I have been gravely disappointed with the white moderate. I have almost reached the regrettable conclusion that the Negro's great stumbling block in his stride toward freedom is not the White Citizen's Counciler or the Ku Klux Klanner, but the white moderate, who is more devoted to "order" than to justice; who prefers a negative peace which is the absence of tension to a positive peace which is the presence of justice; who constantly says: "I agree with you in the goal you seek, but I cannot agree with your methods of direct action"; who paternalistically believes he can set the timetable for another man's freedom; who lives by a mythical concept of time and who constantly advises the Negro to wait for a "more convenient season." Shallow understanding from people of good will is more frustrating than absolute misunderstanding from people of ill will. Lukewarm acceptance is much more bewildering than outright rejection.[14]

In May, the **Children's Crusade** started when children marching out of church singing and praying were arrested in front of national media. Over the next few days as children continued to march, the police started to use dogs and fire hose on the children. Again, the media were there, and the nation was horrified. As the violence continued into the next week, city officials agreed to desegregate Birmingham.

The events of early 1963 led to a greater commitment by the Kennedy administration. In June, President Kennedy gave a televised speech on the need for action on civil rights. The speech was followed by the introduction of significant civil rights legislation. In support of the legislation MLK and others, particularly the Urban League, held a march on Washington. The *1963 March on Washington* was one of the best known actions of the civil rights movement and culminated with MLK's "I Have a Dream" speech. Although there were fears that the march of 250,000 would be violent, it was a peaceful event. Although Kennedy was assassinated in November of that year, President Lyndon Johnson pledged to work on the slain president's agenda and helped pass the 1964 Civil Rights Act (see Chapter 7).

By the end of 1964, the relationship between the movement and President Johnson had become strained. Frustration over the inability of African Americans to participate in Southern elections resulted in the creation of the **Mississippi Freedom Democratic Party** (MFDP). It sought to have its delegation recognized at the Democratic convention. When MFDP failed in its efforts, leaders felt betrayed by white liberals. On the other side, President Johnson was irritated that they caused trouble at his convention. When Johnson was elected, further expansion of civil rights through voting protection was not part of his agenda. Frustrated by this, in 1965 MLK and the SCLC organized a campaign in Selma, Alabama. Selma was a majority African American community that was controlled by its white citizens and had a violent history when it came to race. The campaign involved a series of marches, many of which resulted in marchers being beaten and arrested.

Spotlight 12.1

Brief Biographies of Some Key Leaders of the Civil Rights Movement

Ella Baker (1903–1986) After graduating from college, in 1927 Ella Baker moved to New York and started working on many social causes, such as the Young Negros Cooperative League. Between 1940 and 1946, she worked for the NAACP. In 1955, she started an organization named "Friendship" to help end Jim Crow laws in the south. Two years later she moved to Atlanta to help organize SCLC. Three years later she helped organize the SNCC and was active with the freedom rides and freedom summer.[15]

John Lewis (1940–present) As a student at Fisk University in the 1960s, John Lewis became active in the civil rights movement, including becoming a freedom rider. He helped to form SNCC and was its chair between 1963 and 1966. At twenty-three years old, he was one of the youngest organizers of the March on Washington and keynote speakers. While engaged in direct action protest, he was physically attacked and injured numerous times, including having his skull fractured in Selma, Alabama. In addition, he was arrested over forty times. In 1986, he was elected to Congress. In and out of Congress, Rep. Lewis continues to work on many social justice policies. As the only living keynote speaker from the 1963 march, he has been called an icon of the civil rights movement and a moral voice in the divided Congress.[16]

Malcolm X (1925–1965) Malcolm X's father was a Baptist minister active in Marcus Garvey's Universal Negro Improvement Association. After his father was killed, Malcolm went into foster care and ended up in prison. In prison, he was transformed by the teaching of Black Muslims. In 1952, when he left prison he became the spokesperson for a Black Muslim group.

He was critical of the civil rights movement's assimilationist and nonviolent strategy. He argued for separatism, believing African Americans were best off taking care of themselves. After a pilgrimage to Mecca in 1964, he came to believe in the humanity of all people, regardless of race. A year later he was murdered.[17]

A. Philip Randolph (1889–1979) A. Philip Randolph was a socialist labor activist throughout the twentieth century. During WWI, he helped found *The Messenger*, a socialist magazine for African Americans that opposed the war.[18] He also organized the first African American trade union in 1925, the Brotherhood of Sleeping Car Porters. During Franklin Roosevelt's administration, he threatened to have a march on Washington of African American workers. To stop the march, Roosevelt issued Executive Order 8802 (see Chapter 7). These plans were instrumental in the 1963 March on Washington.[19]

Bayard Rustin (1912–1987) A. Philip Randolph and Mahatma Gandhi were significant influences on Bayard Rustin's philosophy on social change. Rustin was also a gay man who refused to live in the closet. Throughout his life he would be arrested for his pacifism (not registering for the draft), civil rights work (civil disobedience defying Jim Crow laws), and homosexuality. He was an early adviser to Martin Luther King, and helped develop his strategies of nonviolent civil resistance. He is best known as chief architect of the March on Washington and strategist during the Montgomery bus boycott. His sexual orientation denied him the opportunity to take more visible leadership roles in the movement.[20]

The best known involves an MLK-led march from Selma to Montgomery in which considerable violence was unleashed against the marchers by state troopers and other officials. This all occurred in front of TV cameras, and again it increased the nation's support for the civil rights cause. Eventually, the president pushed for and Congress passed the 1965 Voting Rights Act (see Chapter 3).

This brief description of the civil rights movement focused on the nonviolent, more assimilationist groups and actions. These groups wanted African Americans incorporated into the established political and economic systems. However, there were also those, such as Stokely Carmichael, who led SNCC from 1966 to 1967 and was associated with the Black Panthers, and Malcolm X who were more liberationist; they advocated for **black nationalism** and considered violence a reasonable tactic. Black Nationalism and black power movements believed in self-determination of people of African descent, taking pride in that heritage, and separating from the white culture. They also tended to be associated with a militant form of masculinity. The Black Panthers Party was a militant Black Nationalist group that started to protect African Americans from police brutality. It took up arms but also offered social services to African Americans. There were also numerous divisions and conflicts within the nonviolent groups as to strategies and feelings about MLK. Many felt MLK was weak and unwilling to sacrifice enough for the cause. Although MLK is the best known of the civil rights leaders, Spotlight 12.1 briefly describes several other significant leaders.

The 1965 VRA was the last significant national success for the civil rights movement, but many activists continue to fight for the rights of African Americans and other racial/ethnic minorities. Although the movement saw significant policy changes throughout the nation, its effects extend beyond that. First, it helped inspire other movements that took off in the 1960s and 1970s (see below). Much of the inspiration was fueled by the significant policy changes that occurred. It also helped inspire a women's movement by its mistreatment of women in the movement. Ella Baker, for example, complained of the "condescending attitude" leaders had toward women.[21] Second, it helped educate white Americans as to the conditions faced by African Americans, particularly those living in the South, and resulted in a fundamental change in public opinion (see Chapter 8). Finally, it expanded the repertoire of actions available to peoples' movements. It helped Americanize nonviolent civil disobedience, making sit-ins, demonstrations, boycotts, and similar actions mainstays of many groups that followed.

The Chicano Movement

Munoz defined the **Chicano movement** of the 1960s "as a quest for a new identity and for political power. The movement represented a new and radical departure from the politics of past generations of Mexican American activists. It called for new political institutions to make possible Chicano self-determination."[22] Although organizations, such as LULAC (see below) and Mexican-American Movement (MAM) started during the interwar years, these organizations had a much different approach and agenda than the Chicano movement. These organizations were assimilations in that their goals tended to focus more on helping Mexican Americans/Chicanos achieve the American dream and less on Mexican nationalism or taking pride in a Mexican ancestry and identity. Immediately after World War II, many of the Mexican American organizations were middle class, focusing on the concerns of Mexican Americans in various professions. Instead of seeing Mexican Americans as a minority group facing discrimination, they tended to see Mexican Americans as needing to change by, among other things, gaining access to better education. Remember that Mexican Americans are not a racial group but an ethnicity, and many activists identified as white and distinguished themselves from the concerns of African Americans.

During the 1960s, Mexican Americans/Chicanos, particularly Chicano students, became more radical and disillusioned by the American political process. Several things helped contribute to the greater radicalism in the 1960s. First, the student movements associated with the anti-war and civil rights movement offered new ways for students to think about society and ways to try to react to social ills. Relatedly, although Munoz does not put Caesar Chávez's farm workers movement as part of the Chicano movement since its concerns focused on farm workers not Mexican Americans, it did inspire many middle-class Mexican Americans to take action.[23] The disillusionment associated with the Kennedy and Johnson administrations also helped lead to the Chicano movement. During the 1960 election, the Kennedy campaign reached out to Mexican Americans and created **"Viva Kennedy Clubs"** of Mexican American supporters of JFK. However, after Kennedy was elected, he did very little to help advance Mexicans' concerns or appoint Mexicans to key positions. When the Johnson administration did little more than JFK's administration, many Chicano activists came to distrust conventional political processes. Third, there was the publication of the poem "I Am Joaquín," which described a Chicano struggling to find his identity in the United States. The poem starts:

Yo soy Joaquín, perdido en un mundo de confusión:

I am Joaquín, lost in a world of confusion,

caught up in the whirl of a gringo society,

confused by the rules, scorned by attitudes,

suppressed by manipulation, and destroyed by modern society.

My fathers have lost the economic battle

and won the struggle of cultural survival.

And now! I must choose between the paradox of

victory of the spirit, despite physical hunger,

or to exist in the grasp of American social neurosis,

sterilization of the soul and a full stomach.[24]

Another event leading to the movement was the takeover of the Crystal City, Texas, city council in 1963. This largely Mexican American town had had an all-white city council prior to 1963, but in the 1963 election, the city council became all Mexican American. The success of this election inspired many Mexican Americans, particularly the youth, to become more active.

One of the first actions associated with the Chicano movement occurred in March 1968, when Chicano students at Abraham Lincoln High School in Los Angeles, California, walked out in protest of "racist teachers and school policies, the lack of freedom of speech, the lack of teachers of Mexican descent, and the absence of classes on Mexican and Mexican American culture and history."[25] Students from other high schools followed suit and in the end, 10,000 Chicano students in Los Angeles had walked out of school. The "blow out," as it was often called, received national attention. When the organizers of the action were arrested for disturbing the peace, activists from other southwestern states were inspired to organize other walk-outs. And by the end of the year, Chicano high school and college students were organizing not only to have "progress through education," the call of earlier generations, but also to alter the education system to better recognize the history and culture of Mexicans.

After the success of the blow outs, Chicano student organizers held meetings and conferences, such as the Crusade for Justice and the Santa Barbara Conference to develop strategies and goals for the growing movement. The Crusade for Justice, a weeklong conference, resulted in the "El Plan Espiritual de Aztlan" (The Spiritual Plan of Aztlan); its manifesto stated:

> In the spirit of a new people that is conscious not only of its proud historical heritage, but also of the brutal "Gringo" invasion of our territories, we, the Chicano inhabitants and civilizers of the northern land of Aztlan, from whence came our forefathers, reclaiming the land of their birth and consecrating the determination of our people of the sun, declare that the call of our blood is our power, our responsibility and our inevitable destiny. . . . Brotherhood unites us, and love for our brothers makes us a people whose time has come and who struggle against the foreigner "Gabacho" who exploits our riches and destroys our culture . . . we are Bronze People with a Bronze Culture. . . . We are Aztlan.[26]

This conference was followed by one in Santa Barbara that laid out strategies to effect change. In an effort to organize the various campus organizations, leaders encouraged all groups to take the name Movimiento Estudiantil Chicano de Aztlan.[27] Its acronym was **MEChA**, which means matchstick. One of the goals of MEChA was to be active on college campuses to make them more amenable for Mexican American students, including the creation of Chicano Studies programs. MEChA continues today as a college student organization active in educational issues important to Mexican Americans, such as bilingual education, and was active opposing Proposition 209.

In Texas, one of the dominant groups was Mexican American Youth Organization (MAYO). Founded in 1967 with the aid of José Ángel Gutiérrez, it had a strong nationalist militant approach. MAYO had numerous chapters throughout Texas, particularly on college campuses, and engaged in numerous confrontational actions. Yet, it is also known for helping establish a political party: **La Raza Unida**. Many Mexican Americans felt that neither the Democratic nor Republican Party represented their interests. These feelings were particularly strong among the left-leaning activists. In this vein, La Raza Unida (the united race or people), was created. While the party was active in Texas, Colorado, and California, it was most active and successful in Texas, where it was able to elect several members to local offices. Although the party still exists, it has not been successful in electing candidates since the 1970s.

A more radical and liberationist part of the Chicano movement was the Brown Berets. In addition to advocating for better education for Mexican

Spotlight 12.2

Brief Biographies of Leaders of the Chicano Movements

Caesar Chavez (1927–1993) When he was a boy, Caesar Chavez's family became migrant workers. In eighth grade he had to quit school and work full-time as a migrant worker. He left this work during WWII to serve in the western Pacific. In 1952, he became a community organizer working on Hispanic voter registration drives and an end to police brutality. In 1962, he started focusing on the issues of migrant workers. Along with Dolores Huerta, he helped organize the National Farm Workers Association (NFWA), which held protests, boycotts, pickets, marches, and hunger strikes. Associated with the NFWA was El Teatro Campensino, a theatrical group that performed short skits on pickup flatbeds depicting the lives of migrant workers. One of the best known actions of the NFWA was the grape boycott. His work also helped increase Americans' awareness of the effects of pesticides on the health of farmer workers and other people.[28]

Rodolfo "Corky" Gonzales (1928–present) Corky Gonzales's father instilled in him a pride and love of Mexico. He is best known as author of the poem "Yo Soy Joaquín" and founder of the Crusade for Justice. He, along with the Crusade, organized the first

Chicano Youth Liberation Front and the La Raza Unida Party in Colorado. The Crusade also "included a school teaching 'liberation classes,' a nursery, gym, Mayan ballroom dancing, art gallery, shops, library, dining room, community center, legal aid service, skill bank, a barrio policy board, health and housing, social workers, athletic leagues, newspaper (*El Gailo*), bail bond service, and revolution theater."[29] Until he became disillusioned with party politics, Gonzales was active in the Democratic Party, coordinating a "viva Kennedy" campaign, and worked on Johnson's war on poverty.[30]

Dolores Huerta (1930–present) Dolores Huerta was a teacher who noticed that the children of farm workers lacked basic necessities. She helped start a Community Services Organization to help the lives of farm workers. Among the things it worked on were segregation, police brutality, and voter registration. In 1960, she helped create the Agricultural Workers Association to help migrant workers get pensions and Spanish-language ballots. In 1962, she and Chavez cofounded the NFWA. In their work together, Chavez is the charismatic face and she the skilled negotiator and organizer.[31]

Americans, it also fought police brutality and for the return of the southwestern United States to Mexico. During the height of the Chicano movement, the **Brown Berets** helped organize one of the largest events, the **Chicano Moratorium,** which was an anti–Vietnam War march protesting the disproportionately large number of Chicanos who were dying on the front lines of the war. An estimated 20,000 people showed up for the event in Los Angeles. Unfortunately, the police fired on the protesters, killing three.

The Chicano movement was fairly short lived and lacks the legislative successes of the civil rights movement; nevertheless, it was successful in inspiring Mexican Americans to embrace their heritage, improve their educational opportunities, and increase the number of Chicano studies programs on college campuses. Many people were active in the Chicano movement. Spotlight 12.2 describes three leaders in the movement. The movement suffered from FBI infiltration, internal conflicts, and poor timing. It started to take off as the nation was tiring of protest and becoming more conservative. As with the civil rights movement, the Chicano movement was plagued by sexism.

The American Indian Movement

The 1960s to 1970s also saw an increase in the activism of American Indians. Although Indian tribes had been active since the founding of the United States as organizations trying to influence the federal government, the 1960s brought in a new era of greater pan-Indian organization and collective action and media use.[32] Similar to the other movements, there were organizations, such as the National Congress of American Indians (NCAI), that had been active prior to the 1960s that helped the initial stages of the movement. Also similar to the civil rights movement, many of the activists were concerned with discrimination and poor economic conditions, and similar to the Chicano movement and the black power movement, many of the actions concerned a greater recognition and appreciation for a minority culture. However, a unique feature of the American Indian movement (AIM) was the goal of greater recognition and enhancement of tribal sovereignty. As Wilkins and Stark write,

> For much of this nation's history, the general thrust of most racial and ethnic groups and their members has been to seek inclusion (to become constitutionally incorporated) into the American social contract; by contrast, the general thrust of most indigenous nations and their citizens (notwithstanding their American citizenship) has been to retain their political and cultural exclusion from absorption or incorporation in the American polity.[33]

Thus, most American Indian actions and groups tended to be more liberationist than assimilationist, although some groups, such as the NCAI, were more willing to support and work with the Bureau of Indian Affairs (BIA) and other governmental agencies.

Among the first actions in the movement were the 1964 "fish-ins" in Washington state. The state had passed several laws that limited the right of local indigenous people to fish as guaranteed in treaties. In response to the enforcement of the law, Survival of the American Indian Society (SAIS) was formed to defend treaty rights, and to fight cultural assimilation through radical tactics.[34] SAIS received aid from other organizations and before long, the fish-in was able to get celebrities such as Marlon Brando to participate. With the arrest of Brando and others, the media covered the story. The protest, which originally planned to have American Indians fishing off of the reservation using nets, the traditional way of fishing, for five days, lasted until the 1970s when they were afforded half the fish.[35]

While the fish-ins were a departure from most previous Indian efforts to affect policy by using a protest-style action with significant media presence, the takeover of Alcatraz prison in 1969 has also been seen as the start of the Indian movement. It was not tribal based, and individual American Indians from all over the nation came to protest the general mistreatment of American Indians by the federal government, including efforts to dismantle their cultures. Based on treaties, American Indians of All Tribes, Inc., a pan-Indian protest organization, argued that the island of Alcatraz should be returned to the indigenous people. To draw attention to this as well as general concerns over termination and assimilation policies, they took over the island from June 1969 to November 1971. The protest brought national attention to the growing Indian movement; following Alcatraz, there were seventy-four other militant actions.[36]

One of the actions following Alcatraz was the weeklong takeover of the Bureau of Indian Affairs in 1972. The action followed the Trail of Broken Treaties, also called the Caravan, a cross-country walk on the part of American Indians from across the country to bring attention to the failed government policies. After the Caravan, protesters had planned an action in front of the BIA building in Washington, D.C. During the action, several AIM members broke into the BIA and occupied the building, threatening to burn it down. Although the action received much press, the action was less successful than Alcatraz in giving a favorable view of their cause to non-Indians.[37]

Another significant action was the seventy-one-day occupation of the town of Wounded Knee on the Pine Ridge Reservation in South Dakota in 1973. It left two dead. The situation leading up to the occupation of Wounded Knee concerned the corruption of the tribal chief, who was supported by the BIA and mix-raced Indians, and opposed by the traditionalist Indians and tribal leaders. Christine K. Gary writes, "Native Americans might understand how and why that internal battle was shaped in part by the history of exploitation, the ongoing economic pressures, the injustices, and the factionalism that BIA paternalism prompted. It is fair to say, however, that the public at large could understand none of those things."[38] The overall effects of the action for American Indian policy are difficult to determine.

The overall policy effects of the actions were mixed.[39] On one hand, there were negative effects such as those to discredit groups like AIM and the introduction of bills to limit the gains of American Indian interests. On the other hand, some lands were returned to tribes, and legislation to improve tribal self-determination and recognize indigenous religions was passed. Spotlight 12.3 briefly discusses two leaders of AIM.

Spotlight 12.3

Biographies of Two American Indian Leaders

Dennis Banks (1937–present) Dennis Banks is Chippewa and was born on a reservation in Northern Minnesota in 1937. As a child he was forced to attend an assimilation boarding school. At age 19, he joined the army. When he returned, he found racism and alienation from his culture. He was co-founder of AIM and helped lead the actions at Alcatraz, the Bureau of Indian Affairs, and at Wounded Knee. In 1975, he was convicted of action taken during a riot in 1973 and sentenced to prison. Fearing for his life in prison, he fled and lived as a fugitive for nine years before turning himself in and serving his time. He remains active, and in 2011 he helped organize a walk across America to bring awareness to the epidemic of diabetes among American Indians. Banks has also played in movies such as *War Party*, *The Last of the Mohicans*, and *Thunderheart*.[40]

Russell Means (1939–2012) Russell Means was Oglala Sioux and born on the Pine Ridge reservation in South Dakota. His family moved to the San Francisco area when he was three. For much of his early adulthood, he lacked direction and suffered from alcoholism and drug abuse. In 1969, he was hired by the Rosebud Sioux tribal council in South Dakota, and later took a job helping Indians adapt to urban life in Cleveland. He met Dennis Banks and became active in AIM, and worked for AIM until 1988. He played a significant role in the major actions taken by AIM. Both he and Banks were put on trial for their actions at Wounded Knee, but the case was thrown out for prosecutorial misconduct. He had other problems with the law and served one year in a South Dakota prison, where he was stabbed by an inmate. He has also been shot three different times. "He styled himself a throwback to ancestors who resisted the westward expansion of the American frontier. With theatrical protests that brought national attention to poverty and discrimination suffered by his people, he became arguably the nation's best-known Indian since Sitting Bull and Crazy Horse." He had many critics, including some in the Indian movement who saw him as a self-promoter. He ran for president, for governor of New Mexico, and acted in a dozen movies.[41]

The Asian American Movement

Just as the other racial ethnic minority groups had social movements during the last half of the twentieth century, Asian Americans had a social movement. This movement came out of the anti-war movement as well as the civil rights movement. Many Asian Americans had been active in the anti-war movement and from it learned protest techniques and a need for inter-Asian coalitions to fight racism against Asians, and from the black power movement took the desire for cultural nationalism.[42] The Vietnam War also resulted in Asian Americans, regardless of nationality, being lumped together by the American public. The movement

> has been essentially a middle-class reform movement for racial equality, social justice, and political empowerment in a culturally pluralistic America. It has functioned as an inter-Asian coalition that embraces the entire spectrum of Asian ethnic groups, acknowledging their common experience in American society and calling for a higher level of solidarity among the groups.[43]

Some of its more specific demands included ethnic studies programs at colleges, reparations to Japanese harmed by the internment camps during WWII, less stereotypical representation of Asians in the media, and ending discrimination against Asian Americans.

The Asian American movement is the least well known of the movements.[44] It lacked a strong charismatic leader, a unifying ideology or plan, and lacked a large population of Americans. Nevertheless, there were groups and actions across the country during the last half of the twentieth century designed to unify Asian Americans and improve their lives in the United States while maintaining their identity. The actions at San Francisco State College and Berkeley, mentioned at the beginning of the chapter, are two of those most identified with the Asian American movement.

Women's Movements

The women's movement is often broken into three waves. The **first wave women's or feminist movement** was the suffrage movement. It started at the Seneca Falls Convention in 1848 and culminated with the ratification of the Nineteenth Amendment in 1920. Following this success, the women's movement faltered until the 1960s. During the 1960s, there was a rebirth of a women's movement that is often referred to as the **second wave women's or feminist movement**. This movement was divided between those who wanted legal assurances of equality (assimilationist) and those who felt the legal protections were not enough, but that society needed to change for women to reach their full potential (liberationists).[45] Many have also argued that a third wave woman's or feminist movement started near the end of the twentieth century.[46] This movement is less political and embraces women's power and autonomy as well as diversity among women, including the expression of a variety of genders. Although this section will focus on the second wave, a brief description of the first wave is needed for an understanding of the women's movement.

In 1848, Elizabeth Cady Stanton helped organize a meeting in Seneca Falls, New York, to address the lack of rights afforded women. At the meeting, she presented the Declaration of Sentiments. It was based on the Declaration of Independence and laid out several grievances that women had against the government and society. One of the more radical ideas coming out of the convention was women's suffrage. Many of the early suffragettes were also abolitionists who saw parallels between the lack of rights possessed by slaves and the lack of rights possessed by women. When the Fifteenth Amendment was proposed, it gave voting rights to African American males, but expressly excluded women. As such, it created a schism between the suffragettes who supported the Fifteenth Amendment and those who opposed it. Throughout the next few decades there were two different national women's groups; one that was more radical and wanted large social change led by Elizabeth Cady Stanton and Susan B. Anthony, and a more moderate group led by Lucy Stone and others. There were two possible strategies to gaining the right to vote for women. One approach focused on getting each state to allow suffrage, and the other was to try to amend the U.S. Constitution. Initially, the suffrage movement focused on the state approach. After a handful of successes, such as in Wyoming and Utah, the momentum stalled, and by the early 1900s there was a greater focus on amending the Constitution. Although the early suffragettes were abolitionists, by the twentieth century the movement became more conservative, and race and the enfranchisement of minority women

Although most women activists in the women's movement were white, women of many racial and ethnic groups were active as well. In this photo, female activists from fifteen countries, led by American feminist Gloria Steinem, march near the military demarcation line on the Korean Peninsula on May 24, 2015. (*Kyodo via AP Images*)

became a dividing issue. Eventually, different factions within the movement came together to gain the right to vote, and in 1920 the Nineteenth Amendment was ratified, giving women the right to vote.

Following the success of the Nineteenth Amendment, the women's movement faltered and there was not a viable movement between the 1920s and 1960s, though there were still activists and organizations interested in expanding women's rights and gender equality. Many of these groups, such as the National Women's Party and the Business and Professional Women's Club, led activities supporting the candidacy of John Kennedy, believing he would support women's rights. When he appointed very few women to top governmental positions, they were upset. To appease them, President Kennedy created the Commission on the Status of Women (CSW) in 1961. The CSW was important since it documented the inequalities women faced in the economy and also brought together successful women who were advocates of women's rights. These women eventually formed the National Organization for Women (NOW), a leading organization for women's rights (see below).

These events led to one of the earliest successes of the second wave movement, the passage of the Equal Pay Act in 1963. The act required that men and women receive the same pay for doing the same job. Organizations, such as NOW, are liberal assimilationist organizations trying to enact political and economic change by using established means within the existing institutions. The types of political activities include lobbying elected officials and litigation. For example, when it was clear the Equal Employment Opportunity Commission was not enforcing the Equal Pay Act or Title VII of the Civil Rights Act, NOW pressured the EEOC to do more, lobbied to increase the EEOC's power, picketed EEOC centers and businesses in violation of the law, and brought a lawsuit against the EEOC for not enforcing Title VII.[47]

In addition to the liberal assimilationist efforts to enact political change, there were more radical liberationist efforts to change society. Many of these efforts start with consciousness raising groups. Consciousness raising groups were local in nature, were made up of small groups of women, and were designed to increase their awareness of the many ways in which the patriarchy limits women's potential. Patriarchy refers to the pervasiveness of men's domination of women in most every walk of life, from family to work to entertainment to religious institutions. Some of the activists in these radical efforts advocated for women-only spaces where women could be free from the patriarchy. Many of these activists had roots in communism, the anti-war movement, and the civil rights movement. They also used more radical techniques often designed to get attention, such as throwing underwear, cosmetics, and false eyelashes into a trash can at the 1968 Miss America contest.[48]

Although there were many political efforts and accomplishments during the second wave, one of the main efforts was trying to enact the **Equal Rights Amendment** (ERA) to the Constitution. With the exception of enforcement language, the amendment had less than twenty-five words: "Equality of rights under the law shall not be denied or abridged by the United States or by any State on account of sex." To amend the Constitution, two-thirds of both houses of Congress must ratify a proposal. The proposal is then sent to the states to be ratified. Three-fourths of the states must support the amendment. Although an equal rights amendment was first introduced in Congress in 1923, it was not until 1972 that two-thirds of both houses voted for the amendment, and it was officially proposed. The passage of the ERA proposal in 1972 had its origins in 1970.

In 1970, a local chapter of NOW pressured Senator Birch Bayh to promise to hold hearings, and Congresswomen Martha Griffiths and Edith Green used a discharge petition to force debate on the amendment.[49] The discharge petition, which is a rare legislative maneuver to force debate on a bill that is stuck in committee, was successful, and the bill passed in the House. The Senate made changes to the resolution that proposed the ERA and effectively killed the bill. This led the way to changing the resolution such that it would easily pass both chambers with bipartisan support. Since the ERA sailed through Congress in 1972, those in the women's movement expected it to be quickly ratified. It needed thirty-eight states for ratification, and within a year thirty states had ratified the ERA. However, ratification stalled and only thirty-five states had ratified it by the 1978 deadline. Although an extension was made giving the ERA until 1982 to get the additional three states needed, no more states ratified the amendment, and it died.

Although the two different branches of the second wave did not agree on the needed scope of change, they both tended to support the ERA. However, when NOW signed on to the ERA, it lost support from women who wanted laws offering additional protection for women, such as shorter workdays. One of the criticisms of the pro-ERA strategy was that it focused on a national approach, which, although helpful in Congress, did not lend itself to what was a state level ratification process. The types of actions orchestrated by the pro-ERA groups included supporting pro-ERA candidates, conducting research, economic boycotts of states that had not ratified the amendment, letter writing campaigns, and demonstrations in state capitals.[50]

One reason the ERA ultimately failed was the strong groups opposing it, such as the Eagle Forum and the Concerned Women for America (see below for a discussion of these groups). These groups effectively organized at the state level where ratification took place. Their arguments in opposition tended to focus on the loss of the traditional family, the potential for women to be drafted, unisex bathrooms, and advocating homosexuality. Ford lays out several other reasons why scholars have suggested the ERA failed: a backlash against court cases, such as *Roe v. Wade* (1973), the politicization of the religious right, emergence of ultra conservative leadership in the Republican Party, gender imbalance in state legislatures, decline of progressive reforms, supporters failing to convince enough Americans of the need, people identify-ing the amendment with the conflict around the amendment, and issues involv-ing the draft and abortion.[51]

Much like the civil rights and Chicano movements were plagued with sexism, the second wave women's movement was plagued with racism and heteronorma-tivity. The leaders of the movement were largely middle-class to well-off white women who identified as heterosexual. Although many lesbians were active in

Spotlight 12.4

Brief Biographies of Key Leaders of the Women's Right Movement

Gloria Steinem (1934–present) Gloria Steinem was a freelance author when she wrote a piece about being a Playboy Bunny. This and her reporting on an abor-tion conference raised her feminist consciousness. In 1971, she co-founded the National Woman's Political Caucus. She also helped found *Ms Magazine.* She may be best known as a spokesperson for the women's movement. Traister, author of *Big Girls Don't Cry*, said, "She was a figurehead chosen by the media for complicated reasons. She was young and white, and pretty, and she looked great on magazine covers." Another reason she become a spokesperson was her wit. After Geraldine Ferraro's vice presidential can-didacy ran into problems because of her husband's taxes, Steinem said, "What has the women's move-ment learned from Geraldine Ferraro's candidacy for vice president? Never get married."[52]

Billie Jean King (1943–present) Although Billie Jean King is best known as a tennis player, she was also an advocate and spokesperson for women's rights. Realizing that women tennis players were paid sub-stantially less than men, she spearheaded a move-ment for equal pay that resulted in the creation of the Women's Tennis Association. She also started *Wom-enSports* magazine and the Women's Sports Founda-tion. She is also well known for winning the "battle of the sexes" tennis match against "male chauvinist pig" Bobby Riggs in 1974 before fifty million viewers.[53]

Betty Friedan (1921–2006) Betty Friedan graduated from Smith College in 1942 with a degree in psychol-ogy. In 1947, she married and stayed home to be a housewife and take care of their children. But she was unhappy and decided to survey other Smith gradu-ates to see if they were happy as stay-at-home moth-ers. This resulted in her book the *Feminine Mystique* (1963), which helped start the second wave feminist movement. Friedan is also known for helping start NOW, NARAL-Pro-Choice America, and the National Women's Political Caucus. She is also known for warn-ing feminists of the "lavender menace."[54]

Susan B. Anthony (1820–1906) Susan B. Anthony was a Quaker socialized to believe women were equal to men. As a young woman, she was active in the abolitionist and temperance movements. In 1851, she met Elizabeth Cady Stanton and dedicated the rest of her life to suffrage. While Stanton was a writer and theorist, Anthony was a visible spokesperson and movement strategist. She traveled around the country advocating for suffrage. In 1872, she was arrested and fined for voting. As a woman she could not speak dur-ing the trial, and the jury was all male. Anthony was well known in her time; she met with presidents, and the lady with the alligator purse in "Miss Lucy Had a Baby" may have been her.[55]

the movement, there were concerns that visible lesbians in the movement would be harmful. In addition, there were few racial or ethnic minorities active in the largely white national organizations, and these organizations did little to speak to the concerns of women of color. As a consequence, there were organizations and movements designed specifically for minority women. For example, Wei notes that there was an Asian American women's movement that paralleled the largely white women's movement. Asian American women, as a group, felt the women's movement was too polarizing and minimized individuals' responsibilities to others.[56] Many Asian American women who were activists in the Asian American or anti-war movements had been treated in overtly sexist ways. They started having Asian American women "Rap sessions" that eventually became service and political groups.

The women's movement, like the civil rights movement, is not as visible today as it was in the twentieth century, but there remain several organizations working to advance women's interests. Many of these are discussed below. Spotlight 12.4 gives brief biographies of some of the key leaders of the women's movement.

The LGBT Movement

The United States, like many nations, has seen a growing LGBT movement that started at the end of the twentieth century (see Spotlight 12.5 for a discussion of the LGBT movement in Namibia). A common starting point to discuss the LGBT movement is the **Stonewall Riot**. Stonewall was a gay bar in New York City that was frequently raided by the police. In June 1969, during such a raid, the gay patrons of the bar refused to cooperate with the police and fought back. Following the riot, which lasted several days, LGBT organizers decided to use the momentum to try to energize a LGBT movement. Although Stonewall was a pivotal event, World War II was critical in laying some groundwork.[57] Because of the war there was a fair amount of sex segregation as the young men were in the military and women stayed home. This segregation allowed individuals to develop a gay or lesbian awareness. Also facilitating a gay community was that many soldiers who were discharged because they were gay were sent to San Francisco or other port cities where gay communities developed. By the 1950s, gay organizations started to form. Key among these was the **Mattachine Society** created by Harry Hay, a leftist organizer, and the **Daughters of Bilitis** (DOB) in 1955. The Mattachine Society tended to cater to men and DOB to women. These and similar organizations were accommodationist, focusing on educating the general population and on tolerance instead of pushing for their rights. By the late 1960s, but before Stonewall, there were signs of change as there were a handful of protests, LGBT candidates started to run for office, and the ACLU had endorsed some LGBT protections.

Spotlight 12.5

LGBT Movement in Namibia

Most nations have an LGBT movement. This is a brief description of the movement in Namibia. In 1989, South West Africa People's Organization (SWAPO), which led a fight to end apartheid, became the ruling government. The new South Africa constitution guaranteed equality based on race and gender, and 1992 antidiscrimination laws included sexual orientation. This allowed for greater visibility of LGB individuals, and during the 1990s the Social Committee of Gays and Lesbians (SCOG) was active. The SCOG also created a political arm, the Gay and Lesbian Organization of Namibia (GLON). GLON was short-lived because it was ambivalent about being visible, and many blacks did not feel welcome in the organization. Today the main LGBT groups are Out-Right Namibia (ONR) and LGBT Network Namibia. Out-Right Namibia is still in its infancy. LGBT Network Namibia is a largely upper-class white organization.

In 1995, SWAPO leaders made several homophobic comments, such as "Most ardent supporters of this [sic] perverts are European who imagine themselves to be the bulwark of civilisation and enlightenment. They are not only appropriating foreign ideas in our society but also destroying the local culture by hiding behind a facade of the very democracy and human rights we created."[58] Many nations and organizations around the world condemned this type of comment. And the comments gave LGBT activists a collective identity and motivated them to become more active.

In 1997, the LGBT movement held its first public event, a panel discussion to dispel negative views of LGBT. The movement was aided by its close ties with activists in South Africa, but the conditions seemed to deteriorate. In 1998, a government official threatened to increase penalties for homosexual behavior and another said gays and lesbians should be eliminated. Many believed that these attacks were designed to divert attention away from economic problems and corruption within the government. The LGBT movement in and out of Namibia demanded that these comments be recanted. But they continued, and non-gender-conforming men became victims of special field forces assaults.

In 2005, a new president was sworn in, Hifikepunye Pohamba. The hate speech seems to have stopped, but gay men still fear imprisonment. There are few public meeting places for LGBT. In Windhoek there is a gay bar frequented by black LGBT Namibians, and a nice restaurant frequented by white LGBT Namibians. ORN (Out-RightNamibia) also has an office where LGBT people can drop in. For LGBT Namibians living in rural areas, which are very poor and underdeveloped, there are very few resources; there is not much Internet presence so even Internet information is not available. The ORN has established some outposts to try to reach some of these people.

Sources: http://www.globalgayz.com/gay-life-in-namibia-2011/398/, accessed October 6, 2014; Ashley Currier, *Out in Africa: LGBT Organizing in Namibia and South Africa* (Minneapolis, MN: University of Minnesota Press, 2012).

Following Stonewall, however, there was a new enthusiasm. Prior to Stonewall, there were about fifty LGBT organizations nationwide, but by 1973 there were over 800.[59] In addition there was a move away from assimilationism to militancy. There were sit-ins, protests, and occupation of buildings. In addition, there were calls to come out of the closet and be visible and proud. By the end of the 1970s, gays and lesbians had seen about half of the states repeal their sodomy laws, three dozen cities had anti-gay ordinances, and homosexuality was no longer classified as an illness by the American Psychiatric Association.[60] By the 1980s, however, there was a growing division within the gay community as lesbians and racial minorities experienced racism and sexism from the large organizations dominated by white gay men. Also by the 1980s, there was a growing conservatism in the United States and an anti-gay movement often identified with Anita Bryant's Save the Children Campaign. Save the Children Campaign argued that LGB individuals recruited children and threatened children's ability to have a decent childhood.

As the movement appeared in disarray and challenged by strong political opponents, HIV/AIDS hit the gay community. HIV/AIDS, a sexually transmitted virus that was usually terminal at the time, first appeared in the United States among gay men in the early 1980s. It quickly spread throughout the United States as it killed thousands of gay men. Other groups highly affected by the disease are IV drug users and African Americans. The Centers for Disease Control and Prevention estimates that in 1981, 318 Americans died of AIDS and by 1992, over 75,000 Americans died yearly from the disease.[61] The Reagan administration was slow to react to the epidemic because the people harmed by the illness had few sympathizers in the administration. In addition, Reagan had campaigned on less federal action and a smaller government.

When the government did act, it seemed to do so in ways that were not seen as helpful by LGBT activities. There were calls for quarantining people with the disease and abstinence to prevent it from spreading. Because the government was slow to act and ineffective when it did, activists were outraged and the movement was reinvigorated. It gave the movement a unified purpose, forced men with the disease out of the closet, and increased many Americans' awareness of discrimination against LGBT. It also spawned new organizations such as ACT UP, as well as numerous local groups created to help AIDS victims. **ACT UP (AIDS Coalition to Unleash Power)** combined an insider-with-an-outsider approach to change.[62] On one hand, it conducted street protests and grassroots actions to increase Americans' awareness of AIDS and put pressure on officials. ACT UP and other LGBT organizations engaged in zaps. Zaps were quick public actions designed to bring attention to the cause with disrupting or shocking actions. For example, when Anita Bryant, a former Miss America and anti-LGBT activist, was on camera, an AIDS activist threw a pie in her face. Another action involved several people lying down, playing dead, to disrupt Mass at St. Patrick's cathedral in New York. The Church had done little to help with the epidemic. One zap even involved disrupting the CBS evening news. Not only did ACT UP engage in zaps and similar actions, it also engaged in more traditional lobbying of officials to get help for HIV/AIDS victims.

In recent years, the movement has tended to focus on marriage equality. Most of the national organizations identify this as a major issue. There is also Freedom to Marry, an organization founded in 2003 to win marriage rights in the courts.[63] It works through coalitions of several, often local, organizations. Its strategy involves winning marriage rights in enough states that most Americans will live in states with marriage equality, that 60% of Americans support marriage equality and then ultimately have the Supreme Court rule in favor of same-sex marriage. In 2015, the Supreme Court said gays and lesbians have a right to marry. Although most marriage equality victories have come through court decisions, ten state legislatures voted to allow same-sex marriages and two states have used the initiative process.[64] The focus on marriage equality is not without its critics in the LGBT movement.[65] There are concerns that it takes the focus off of other important issues, such as transgender rights, youth suicides, HIV/AIDS, and employment discrimination. There are also individuals who see marriage as an oppressive institution and heteronormative.

The LGBT movement has largely been assimilationist in its strategies, focusing more on political gains than social reforms.[66] Most organizations focus on lobbying, litigation, and electing LGBT officials (see the description of LGBT groups listed below). Within the assimilationist model, there are debates over how hard and fast to push for rights. It is feared that quick dramatic change might lead to a backlash that would result in less overall progress. Some fear, too, that using the courts could backfire.[67] When the Court ruled in *Bowers v. Hardwick* (1986; see Chapter 6) against the LGBT community, it set a precedent that would take twenty years to change. While most national groups focus on assimilation, groups also encourage individuals, famous and otherwise, to come out, or encourage Hollywood to feature positive nonstereotypical LGBT characters who can transform Americans' view of LGBT and acceptance of diversity.

Looking at the activities of recent presidents presents a mixed picture of the utility of the assimilationist approach.[68] When Democratic president Bill Clinton was elected in 1992 the LGBT activists were hopeful that he would be a supporter. During his campaign he had reached out to the LGBT community and had made promises to spend more on HIV/AIDS and end the ban on gays in the military. Although he appointed an AIDS czar, the position turned out to be symbolic, and the czar did little to end the epidemic. Additionally, he signed the Defense of Marriage Act and created the policy of Don't Ask Don't Tell (DADT). Following President Clinton, Republican president George W. Bush was not expected to be an advocate for LGBT policies since he had not been a supporter in the past and relied heavily on the Christian right during his campaign, and he met those expectations. With the election of President Barack Obama there was a renewed hope that the president would advocate for more LGBT-friendly policies. And during his administration, DADT ended, the government did not defend DOMA in the courts, and when the Court ruled it unconstitutional, the Obama administration has been quick to recognize same-sex marriages. He also signed an executive order to prevent discrimination based on sexual orientation and gender identity in the federal workplace and among federal contractors. In addition, President Obama has appointed more openly LGBT officials/judges to the bureaucracy and courts than any other president.

Although LGBT groups focus on an assimilation strategy, LGBT Americans are divided as to the correct approach. In a recent Pew survey, 49% of LGBT respondents believe the best way to achieve equality is to become part of mainstream institutions and culture, while 49% believe it is important to maintain a distinct way of life.[69] Lesbians tend to take the assimilationist approach

(55% to 42%), while gay men the liberation approach (53% to 47%). Just as there were significant leaders of the other movements, there have been many leaders of the LGBT movement. Spotlight 12.6 briefly describes several.

Spotlight 12.6

Brief Biographies of LGBT Leaders

Larry Kramer (1935–present)   Larry Kramer attempted suicide while attending Yale because of the aloneness he felt as a gay man. After graduating from Yale, he had some success as a playwright and author, earning an Academy Award nomination for *Women in Love*. It was not until the AIDS epidemic that he became an activist. In 1982, he became active in New York City's Gay Men's Health Crisis. When he decided GMHC and the government were moving too slowly, he helped form ACT UP.[70] *New York Magazine* author Jesse Green wrote of Kramer: "Temperamentally unsuited to ceding the pulpit, he has never accepted the national gay organizations as competent advocates for gay people, and, in the wake of New York's failure to pass a same-sex-marriage law, can only repeat his contention that state-by-state incrementalism on such matters is "a waste of time."[71] He has used his writing skills to advance Americans' awareness of AIDS. Most notably he wrote and produced the play *Normal Heart*.

Barbara Gittings (1932–2007)   Barbara Gittings was attending Northwestern University, but became so interested in learning more about homosexuality that she dropped out of school to focus on these studies. She started a Daughters of Bilitis chapter in New York in 1958 and became editor of the national organization's magazine, *The Ladder*, from 1958 to 1966. Her passion was to try to find and print positive images of gays and lesbians. She was also involved in several homophilia organizations in the pre-Stonewall era, and in the gay rights movement after Stonewall. She also has been active in the American Library Association's gay and lesbian caucus, and helped lead the effort to remove homosexuality from the American Psychological Association's list of mental illnesses.[72]

Harvey Milk (1930–1978)   When Harvey Milk followed his partner to San Francisco, he opened a camera shop on Castro Street that became a hangout for people wanting to discuss politics. His nickname became the "Mayor of Castro Street," and in 1973 he ran for the Board of Supervisors. Although he lost in 1973, he ran again two years later and won. This is the highest ranking elected office held by a gay man up until this date. Three years later, he and the mayor of San Francisco, George Moscone, were assassinated by Dan White. White was convicted of manslaughter instead of murder because of what has been referred to as the "Twinkie defense." White argued that he was mentally disturbed because he had eaten too much junk food the day of the killings.

Social Movement Theories

Not all social movements get off the ground; some stay small and are relatively unsuccessful, while others develop into large movements with many followers and see notable successes. Several social movement theories offer potential explanations for the rise and fall of movements. I will briefly describe four social movement theories and how they can be applied to the movements discussed above:

rational choice/collective action theory, resource mobilization, political opportunity, and framing.

Collective action or rational choice models can help explain why some movements are more successful.[73] It predicts that people will engage in social movements or join organizations if the benefits they personally gain from the engagement exceed the costs. As a general rule, for large social movements the costs exceed the benefits if the only benefit is social or policy change. That is because individuals will receive the benefits of the policy change even if they are not active. For example, if same-sex marriage is afforded gay couples, marriage cannot be denied to a specific gay couple because they did not help the cause. As a consequence, any costs individuals expend are unnecessary.

This free rider problem can be overcome if individuals receive something else for their participation. Individuals could receive material goods, such as T-shirts, magazine subscriptions, or the prospect of a job. They can receive psychological benefit, such as feeling good by filling a need to be civically engaged or doing the right thing, or being part of history. They can also receive social goods, such as friendship. Benefits can also be expressive or participatory. Expressive benefits refer to how people have a need to express their views. Thus, participants in the civil rights movement may be afforded the ability to express their outrage over how they have been treated. People often have a need to go on record to support a movement. With participatory benefits there is value to the participation itself. It could be a rite of passage, or make someone a more interesting person. Although civil rights activists who were physically threatened or jailed incurred much cost, that they were jailed or threatened could increase their credentials for people in their community. Chong argues that the benefits are greater if there is assurance that the movement will be successful.[74] The expression or participatory benefits participants receive will be strongest if the movement has numerous participants or receives considerable attention. Thus, for movements to be successful they need to be able to assure potential participants that they will not be alone. With that in mind, the impact of the Montgomery bus boycotts or Greensboro sit-ins becomes apparent. Both of these started relatively small, and once they appeared to be successful in getting attention, they grew. They also demonstrated to other communities the value and potential success of similar actions.

Chong also notes that the free rider problem can be overcome if a single individual can make the difference between a group being successful or not.[75] He notes that the civil rights movement's participants could maintain their nonviolent stance amid much violence against them because the strategy would fail if one person became violent.

A second theory designed to explain why some movements are more successful is the resource mobilization theory. **Resource mobilization theory**[76] focuses on organizations' resources. Organizations with more resources are more successful. Some of the key resources for groups are a large group of people with a shared identity that can be mobilized, wealth, organizational capacity, and leadership.[77] Andersen identifies eight resources helpful for LGBT movements to be successful in the courts: legal expertise, internal organization, skill in forming coalitions with others, extra legal publicity, funding, "control over the initiation and progress of litigation," time, and support from the Department of Justice.[78] Many of these resources are already discussed in earlier chapters, such as group size and shared identity. Organizational strength of groups for and opposed to minority rights affects the likelihood minorities get elected and that their policies get enacted. In addition, the brief discussions of the movements above all demonstrate the importance of having leaders, such as MLK, who can organize, mobilize supporters, and develop strategies. In an examination of pro-choice groups, Staggenberg found that groups with professional leadership had more formalized organizations and that formalized organizations were good for maintenance, affected the tactics used, and helped build coalitions.[79] Many of the studies using resource mobilization suggest that many movements are resource poor and need to rely on allies or wait for the costs to decline.[80]

A third theory is **political opportunity structure**.[81] It focuses on how political and cultural institutions can affect the ability of movements to be successful. Although there are many aspects of institutions that can affect social movements, there are three dimensions that are widely recognized: "access to the formal institutional structure, availability of allies and the configuration of power with respect to relevant issues/challengers."[82] For example, the civil rights movement was aided by its white allies who participated in the freedom summers and as freedom riders. Often minority groups use the courts to effect change because the judicial interpretations can be more amenable to equal rights claims than political institutions. The political climate of Washington, D.C., too, may affect whether movements focus on using the federal government or the states to enact change. For example, the configuration of Washington when George W. Bush was president and the Republicans controlled the Congress gave few opportunities for gender, ethnic, or racial minorities to advance their interests in Washington; thus, some activists turned to states to try to change state policy. Another dimension is the underlying political culture.[83] In a conservative political culture, minority-based movements are less likely to be successful. For example, that the Chicano movement started to take off at the same time as the Reagan revolution likely helped it falter.

A final theory is based on framing. "Successful framing occurs when a speaker's discussion of a subject leads the receiver of the discussion to alter the criteria on which she judges the subject."[84] In other words, a frame is how we make sense of something or how we interpret it. According to Costain, Braustein, and Berggren, "framing take place as dissatisfaction and anger among individuals get reinterpreted as a public rather than a private problem."[85] Was the dissatisfaction of women in the 1950s and 1960s the fault of women or their families, or was it a societal problem that prevented women from achieving their full potential? Movements often struggle to find the best frame for their cause, particularly early in the movement before frames have had time to be tested.[86] The best frame can also change depending on the specific issue. Brewer notes that the morality frame, that homosexuality is immoral and should not be tolerated, used by antigay groups was less successful against employment nondiscrimination acts as Americans began to see sexual orientation as an inherited trait, but remains effective in banning marriage equality where religious and moral views are more relevant.[87] Frames can also vary by group. Prior to the 1960s, the Republican Party was more favorable to women's rights than the Democratic Party, and that is because the issue was framed as individual equality.[88]

Frames can greatly affect Americans' perceptions of movements and their causes and ultimately the success of the movement. For example, a common frame by opponents to minority rights it is that minorities are asking for special rights: that a group is asking for a unique benefit denied to others. Such a frame makes the request seem undemocratic and unfair. But framing it as a civil right changes Americans' perception of the legitimacy of the claim. We all are guaranteed civil rights. For another example, women's rights activists will try to frame the abortion issue as one of women controlling their bodies, preventing government from intervening in personal issues, and the need for women's safety. Opponents, on the other hand, may try to frame the issue as one of morality, anti-family, and killing an unborn child. There can be many sources of frames, but a recent study of media stories on gay rights issues found that interest groups were the main source of frames, followed by the courts.[89] There are two ways that exposure to a frame can affect people's opinions. Exposure to a particular frame can make it more accessible, easier to remember, or it can affect which values are used to evaluate a policy. In either event, exposure to frames, under some circumstances, can affect Americans' views toward a policy. Some of these circumstances include the credibility of the source and the availability of competing frames.

Andersen uses a combination of political opportunity structure and framing to understand variation in LGBT success in the courts.[90] In terms of access to the courts, it is easier for some problems to give plaintiffs standing to sue than others. To have standing, plaintiffs must have suffered some direct harm that they can get restitution for. For example, an anti-sodomy law that is not enforced has not caused clear harm. So using the courts to remove these laws was difficult until someone was arrested and charged. Similarly, gay rights advocates could not sue for employment discrimination where it was legal to discriminate against gays and lesbians.

The importance of the configuration of political elites can be demonstrated by the importance of the makeup of the Supreme Court to the outcome of cases. Andersen argues that changes to the Supreme Court as well as societal changes in the understanding of homosexuality help account for the different decisions in the *Bowers* and the *Lawrence* cases (see Chapter 6). The ability of LGBT groups to be successful in the courts also varies by their allies as well as opponents. Amicus curiae, which are briefs filed by groups or individuals not directly involved in the case, written by LGBT allies indicated to the courts the legitimacy of LGBT plaintiffs' claims. The legal and cultural frames used also affected legal success. Cultural frames concern how society frames issues and legal frames concern legal argument to frame an issue in court. These are distinct but interrelated. Andersen notes that legal criteria can be used by groups to frame issues. To successfully frame same-sex marriage as a right required society and judges to see it as such. Once the Hawaiian court in *Baehr v. Lewin* viewed same-sex marriage as a right, it was easier to frame it as right in other cases.

As Andersen's research suggests, the different social movement theories are not mutually exclusive but can be seen as complementary. Each focuses on a different aspect of what makes a social movement succeed, and it is likely that the most successful movements are those that have resources, frame issues well, and have a political system that is willing to hear what they have to say.

Interest Groups

Pluralist theory argues that for individuals' interests to be heard by the government, organizations are needed to advocate for their interests. As noted in Chapter 4, interest groups or advocacy groups can have a strong influence on public policy, and as noted above, organizations were critical to the different minority movements. There are many tactics available to aid interest groups in their efforts. They can be active in elections in numerous ways. Many will either endorse candidates to let group members know which candidate is "best" on the issues or conduct surveys to provide voters with information on the candidates' positions without a formal endorsement. Sometime endorsements can come with other benefits, such as the recruitment of campaign volunteers or financial donations to candidates' campaigns. Campaign finance law is very complicated, but some organizations can give money directly to candidates, and others can create and finance their own campaign materials to aid candidates. Aiding candidates' campaigns can affect policy either by helping ensure candidates who support their cause are elected, or by building relationships between a cause and officials that may increase access to the official and make it easier to lobby the official.

Direct lobbying is another way interest groups can affect policy. Lobbying generally involves representatives of an organization meeting directly with officials or their staff to persuade them as to the merits or limitations of a policy. When lobbying occurs outside of a formal work setting, it is often referred to as social lobbying. Such direct lobbying efforts can be expensive, so many minority groups rely heavily on grassroots efforts. Grassroots efforts involve citizens contacting government officials either directly or indirectly to affect officials' decisions. These efforts can involve demonstrations in the streets, petition-signing drives, or telephone/email/letter-writing campaigns.

Many groups also engage in education or efforts to affect public opinion. Think tanks are a type of group that engages in research to gain information about the substantive or political effects of a policy. This information can be used either in lobbying efforts or as a means to try to affect public opinion. Because of the complexity of tax and campaign finance laws, larger organizations will often have spin-off organizations that focus on a type of action. Organizations that give money directly to candidates are called political action committees (PACS), and those that focus on education are called foundations. Because of the importance of interest groups, I offer a brief description of some of the key interest groups that focus on minorities. Since most groups focus on advancing the interests of a single minority group, the list is organized by minority group.

African American Interest Groups

National Association for the Advancement of Colored People. The NAACP is one of the largest and oldest civil rights groups in the United States. It was founded in 1909 by whites and African Americans concerned by the growing violence against African Americans, including lynchings and a riot in Springfield, Illinois. Among the founders was W. E. B. Du Bois, a leading African American scholar and activist in the early 1900s. During the twentieth century, the NAACP focused on using the courts as a means to improve the status of African Americans by ending legal discrimination and segregation, ensuring voting rights, and other issues related to racial equality. Thurgood Marshall, who later became a Supreme Court justice (see Chapter 6), was one of its leaders during this time. Its legal defense fund played a major role in some of the landmark cases, such as *Brown v. Board of Education.* Today, it has 500,000 members, and some of its key issues include equal education and job opportunities, reforming the criminal justice system, and ensuring housing and health care.[91]

National Urban League. The National Urban League was founded in New York in 1920, but has origins dating back to 1910. It is less hierarchical and more community based than the NAACP. It played a critical role in the 1963 March on Washington. It is also more service based than the NAACP; its mission is to "enable African Americans to secure economic self-reliance, parity, power and civil rights." Whitney M. Young Jr. was its director during the 1960s and helped the organization to prosper during the civil rights era. In 2015, it had almost 100 chapters in thirty-five states.[92]

Southern Christian Leadership Conference. The SCLC was founded in 1957 by Martin Luther King Jr. and traces its origins to the Montgomery bus boycott. Its early goals included equality, desegregation, equal education, and voter registration. It has espoused nonviolent tactics such as boycotts and demonstrations. During the civil rights movement, the SLCL was considered more radical than the NAACP, which relied on lobbying and legal actions, but less radical than CORE, which relied more on civil disobedience. Today its interests are not limited to the southern United States, but are national and international. It lists its current objectives as:

> To promote spiritual principles within our membership and local communities.
>
> To educate youth and adults in the areas of personal responsibility, leadership potential, and community service.
>
> To ensure economic justice and civil rights in the areas of discrimination and affirmative action.
>
> To eradicate environmental classism and racism wherever it exists.[93]

Congress of Racial Equality. The founders of CORE, which was founded in Chicago in 1942, were influenced by Mahatma Gandhi. The organization they created was dedicated to achieving racial equality through nonviolent resistance.

CORE was active during the civil rights era, engaging in boycotts, sit-ins, and demonstrations but is best known for its work on the Freedom Rides and Freedom Summer. Although there are numerous CORE affiliates across the globe, it is less strong today than it was in the 1960s.[94]

Black Lives Matter. Black Lives Matter is a new movement that started after the killing of Trayvon Martin in 2013 by George Zimmerman. It started as a hashtag and as it became used, it has turned into a movement made up of several local organizations. It focuses on the poor treatment of African Americans in the criminal justice system and has affected the 2016 presidential election by pressuring candidates to address their concerns.[95]

Hispanic Interest Groups

League of United Latin American Citizens. LULAC was founded in 1929 in Texas when three Mexican American organizations merged. It is the oldest and one of the best-known Hispanic organizations. Its mission is to "advance the economic condition, educational attainment, political influence, housing, health and civil rights of the Hispanic population of the United States."[96] In that regard it supports affirmative action, immigration reform, and reforming the criminal justice system. It also conducts voter registration drives. It is less radical than some other organizations and has a decentralized mass membership structure.

National Council of La Raza. NCLR was founded in 1968 and has its origins in the Chicano movement. It is the largest Hispanic organization and has a decentralized structure with over 300 community-based organizations in forty-one states and the District of Columbia. The national organization conducts research and focuses on advocacy. Key issues include "assets/investments, civil rights/immigration, education, employment and economic status, and health."[97] La Raza has a close tie with Hispanic businesses. Although originally focused on Mexican Americans in the southwest, today it addresses issues of concern to all Hispanic nationalities.

United Farm Workers. UFW was founded in 1962 by Caesar Chavez in California to help the deplorable conditions of migrant workers, who were largely Mexican. It is often associated with a grape boycott in the 1960s and 1970s that resulted in negotiations between farm workers (Filipino as well as Hispanic) and table grape farm owners. Today, it is active in ten states.[98]

U.S. Hispanic Chamber of Commerce. USHCC was founded in 1979 to help Hispanic business owners. Its mission is "to foster Hispanic economic development and to create sustainable prosperity for the benefit of American society."[99] It has over 200 local chapters.

Southwest Voter Registration and Education Project. SVREP was founded in 1974 to ensure Mexican Americans are afforded their voting rights. Today, its primary focus is increasing the voter turnout of all Hispanics through voter registration drives and education. It has also worked on immigration policy, community organizing, training community leaders, and foreign policy such as the North American Free Trade Agreement (NAFTA).[100]

Asian American Interest Groups

National Association for Asian and Pacific American Education. NAAPAE was founded in 1977 to work on issues related to Asian American education issues, from bilingual education to promoting the inclusion of Asian American history in school curriculum.[101] NAAPAE has been less active the last few years.

Leadership Education for Asian Pacifics. LEAP was founded in 1982 with the goal of "growing leaders" in Asian American Pacific Islander communities. LEAP focuses on developing leader development programs for students, government agencies, and businesses.[102] It created the Asian Pacific American Public Policy Institute to study issues related to Asian Pacific Americans, including their representation in corporate America.

Asian Pacific American Labor Alliance. APALA was founded in 1992 and is affiliated with the AFL-CIO. It has eighteen chapters and 660,000 members.

> The stated goals of APALA were to create an organization, which would educate APA workers; promote political education and voter registration programs among APAs; and promote training, empowerment, and leadership of APAs within the labor movement and APA community. APALA further set out to defend and advocate for the civil and human rights of APAs, immigrants and people of color and to develop ties within international labor organizations, especially in the Asia-Pacific Rim.[103]

In recent years, it has opposed the Trans-Pacific Partnership and supported the Dream Act.[104] In addition, it rates members of Congress as to their support of its policy positions.

American Indian Interest Groups

National Congress of American Indians[105] was founded in 1944 to fight assimilation and termination policies. Termination policies were efforts to end U.S. recognition of tribes and the U.S. relationship with them. Its current goals of enhancing tribal sovereignty, culture, and improving the lives of Indians reflect its origins. It is the largest and oldest intertribal interest group.[106] Intertribal interest groups have members of different tribes "acting on the basis of tribal affiliation in pursuit of common political or economic goals."[107] One of its programs is Native Vote, designed to increase American Indians' political participation, and another concerns reviewing the federal budget for its effect on American Indian interests.

American Indian Movement (AIM) was founded in Minneapolis in 1968 in response to police brutality and a desire for protecting Indian rights. It also had a desire to renew native culture. It states its mission as: "Pledged to fight White Man's injustice to Indians, his oppression, persecution, discrimination and malfeasance in the handling of Indian Affairs. No area in North America is too remote when trouble impends for Indians. AIM shall be there to help the Native People regain human rights and achieve restitutions and restorations."[108] It is known most for its radical, even violent actions in the 1970s, such as the takeover of the Bureau of Indian Affairs (1972) and Wounded Knee, South Dakota (1973). AIM has struggled, and in the 1990s there were two splinter groups: National American Indian Movement and International Confederation of Autonomous AIM.[109] AIM is a liberationist organization.

Native American Rights Fund (NARF) was founded in 1970. It is a nonprofit legal firm that focuses on cases dealing with the "the preservation of tribal existence; the protection of tribal natural resources; the promotion of Native American human rights; the accountability of governments to Native Americans; and the development of Indian law and educating the public about Indian rights, laws, and issues."[110] It is careful in the cases it selects and has had some success in about 200 cases.[111] In 2014, NARF filed and won a court case concerning the availability of voting information in native languages in Alaska.[112] Although NARF has been successful, it has been criticized for being elitist since it accepts money from the government and the Ford Foundation, as well as for the control that a small group of lawyers has over its agenda.[113]

Women's Interest Groups

National Organization for Women (NOW) was founded in 1966 with Betty Friedan, author of *The Feminine Mystique*, as its first president. *The Feminine Mystique* describes the discontent of women, particularly housewives, in the 1950s. NOW is a large organization that addresses many issues of concern to women, including reproductive rights, violence against women, economic equality, women's health issues, LGBT issues, and racism. It is the largest women's group, with hundreds of thousands of members and 500 chapters. It uses the full spectrum of activist methods but identifies as a grassroots group. It has both a PAC and foundation.[114]

The Feminist Majority was founded in 1987 and is a broad-based organization working on many of the same issues as NOW. Its foundation works on research and policy development, grassroots organizing, and leadership training. The Feminist Majority does strictly political work.[115]

EMILY's List is a PAC founded in 1985 to help pro-choice women candidates get campaign funds. The name is an acronym for Early Money Is Like Yeast and symbolizes the importance to candidates of having seed money so that they can raise more money. EMILY's List also was one of the first PACs to engage in bundling. Bundling allows PACs to help candidates beyond their campaign funding limits. Its membership is roughly three million.[116] In 2014, it gave $4.7 million to candidates and spent about $8.2 million on independent expenditures.[117]

Concerned Women for America (CWA) was founded in 1978 by Beverly LaHaye as a women's group in opposition to feminism and the ERA. CWA is a conservative Christian organization with a mission to "protect and promote Biblical values among all citizens—first through prayer, then education, and finally by influencing our society—thereby reversing the decline in moral values in our nation."[118] Its key issues are sanctity of life, defense of family, education, religious liberty, national sovereignty, sexual exploitation, and support for Israel. It is a large national organization with 500 local chapters that are called prayer/action chapters and about 600,000 members.[119] CWA is affiliated with the Beverly LaHaye Institute, which is a think tank that conducts research.

The Eagle Forum was founded in 1972 by Phyllis Schlafly. It was founded in part to oppose the Equal Rights Amendment, which it saw as radical feminism. Its work extends beyond women's issues. Its mission "Is to enable conservative and pro-family men and women to participate in the process of self-government and public policy making so that America will continue to be a land of individual liberty, respect for family integrity, public and private virtue, and private enterprise."[120] In this regard it supports American sovereignty, American identity, the Constitution, exposing radical feminists, and supports traditional education. It has roughly 80,000 members,[121] a PAC, and a foundation. In 2014, according to opensecrets.org, it contributed $180,950 to candidates, spent $40,000 on lobbying, and $10,000 on outside spending.[122]

WISH List was founded in 1992 and stands for Women in the House and Senate. It is a PAC designed to help pro-choice Republican women win election to all levels of office. In addition to giving money to candidates, it helps identify and train Republican women candidates. It has given about $3.5 million to candidates it has endorsed.[123]

Susan B. Anthony List (SBA) is a pro-life organization that uses suffragettes' opposition to abortion as an important symbol. It was founded in 1993 and has an affiliated PAC. It has a six point mission that includes: Elect pro-life candidates, educate voters about pro-life issues and legislation, train pro-life activists, promote "positive response to media," advocate for passage of pro-life legislation, and connect "legislative and electoral consequences."[124] According to opensecrets.org, Susan B. Anthony and affiliated groups contributed about $2 million to candidates' campaigns, spent $380,000 on lobbying, and $943,362 in outside spending in 2014.[125]

LGBT Interest Groups

Human Rights Campaign (HRC) was founded in 1980. It is the largest LGBT group in the United States with 1.5 million supporters. It has a broad agenda. Its mission statement is:

The Human Rights Campaign is America's largest civil rights organization working to achieve lesbian, gay, bisexual and transgender equality. By inspiring and engaging all Americans, HRC strives to end discrimination against LGBT citizens and realize a nation that achieves fundamental fairness and equality for all.[126]

Although it tends to be a national organization, it does advocacy work at the state and local level as well. Some of its key issues are marriage equality, workplace discrimination, parenting rights, hate crimes, HIV, education, and several issues faced by transgender individuals such as discrimination, health care, and identification documentation. It is a well-funded organization. In 2013 it raised and spent over $32 million dollars.[127] In 2014, HRC spent $1.2 million on lobbying,[128] about $79,000 in outside spending,[129] and gave about $39,000 directly to candidates.[130]

The National LGBTQ Task Force was founded in 1973 in New York. Although the Task Force has a think tank, it is more community based than HRC. Until 2014, the Task Force was named the National Gay and Lesbian Task Force. However, it changed its name to be more inclusive. According to its webpage:

We're building a future where everyone is free to be themselves in every aspect of their lives. Today, despite all the progress we've made to end discrimination, millions of LGBTQ people fact barriers in every aspect of their lives: in housing, employment, healthcare, retirement, and basic human rights. These barriers must go. That's why the Task Force is training and mobilizing millions of activists across our nation to deliver a world where you can be you.[131]

The Gay and Lesbian Victory Fund was created in 1991 to mirror EMILY's List. An offshoot of the Victory Fund is the Victory Institute, and together they train, endorse, and offer campaign funding to LGBT candidates. In addition to its general electoral work, it has programs specific to Hispanic and women LGBT candidates.[132] In 2013, the Victory Fund and Victory Institute had a combined income of roughly $4.5 million.[133]

National Center for Transgender Equality (NCTE) was created in 2003 to afford an effective lobby designed to advance the interests of transgender people. It also is designed to keep its members informed as to the policies affecting these interests. In 2011, its budget was roughly $700,000. Its issues concern discrimination, documentation, economic opportunity, health, homelessness, education, military and veterans, seniors, immigration, prison reform, family recognition, hate crimes, and travel. Its mission is:

The National Center for Transgender Equality is a national social justice organization devoted to ending discrimination and violence against transgender people through education and advocacy on national issues of importance to transgender people.

By empowering transgender people and our allies to educate and influence policymakers and others, NCTE facilitates a strong and clear voice for transgender equality in our nation's capital and around the country."[134]

Focus on the Family is a Christian ministry focused on the traditional family and is opposed to LGBT rights. It was founded in 1977 by Dr. James Dobson and is known for its radio programming as well as other uses of the media to advocate and educate based on its beliefs.[135] Although it spent over $2 million in the 2012 election, it only spent about $750,000 in the 2014 elections.[136]

Log Cabin Republicans was founded in California during the 1970s. It is made up of Republicans who want to advocate for LGBT within the Republican Party.[137] There is also a Democratic LGBT group called Stonewall Democrats.

Summary

African American groups are among the oldest, but all minority groups saw a growth in the number of advocacy groups the last half of the twentieth century during the civil rights era. Although the above list only includes Hispanic and Asian American groups that are panethnic, there are numerous groups that focus on just one nationality, such as Cuban Committee for Democracy, Cambio Cubano, Puerto Rican Legal Defense and Education Fund, the Mexican American Legal Defense and Education Fund, Japanese American Citizens League, Chinese American Citizens' Alliance, Organization of Chinese Americans, and the National Organization of Korean Americans. In addition, many American Indian tribes serve as interest groups working on their own behalf. There are also many "legal defense funds" that focus on promoting rights by bringing suit through the courts. Within the women's groups there are those such as NOW and the Feminist Majority that want to advance women's opportunities, as well as those such as the Eagle Forum that support a more traditional role for women. In addition, there are organizations working on both sides of the abortion debate, such as NARAL and the National Right to Life Committee.

Conclusion: Much Change since the 1950s

The different minority groups shared a period of great activity in the forty years following World War II. There was the civil rights movement associated with Martin Luther King Jr., Selma, the March on Washington, as well as a more militant Black Power movement. This movement saw numerous successes in voting rights and desegregation. There was the Chicano movement that increased Americans' awareness and appreciation of the contribution and culture of Mexican Americans. The Asian American movement increased pan-Asian identity. The American Indian movement protected tribal sovereignty. The women's rights movement saw advancements in women's liberty to choose their own futures, and the LGBT movement saw the end of the ban on LGB in the military, a decriminalization of homosexual behavior, and marriage equality. The movements also affected universities, making them less limited to teaching only about the dominant Eurocentric and male history and culture.

The minority groups also share similarities in the reasons for the rise of their movements: greater resources including a faith that change will come, effective leaders, a political system with greater willingness to incorporate their interests, and effective frames. There were of course differences. The Chicano movement and the Asian American movements were noticeably smaller and less successful than the others. The LGBT movement came later in time and has seen its greatest success in the twenty-first century. The American Indian movement was more militant and less focused on political incorporation into the United States and more interested in tribal sovereignty. Parts of the women's movement did not fully incorporate minority women, who started their own groups and actions.

With the exception of the LGBT movement, which is still very strong, the movements are less active today. Nevertheless, there are still numerous organizations, many working within the system, to try to continue, and in some cases maintain, the advances they made in the twentieth century.

KEY TERMS

ACT UP (AIDS Coalition to Unleash Power)   (p. 307)
Black nationalism   (p. 293)
Brown Berets   (p. 297)
Chicano Moratorium   (p. 297)
Chicano movement   (p. 293)
Children's Crusade   (p. 291)
Civil rights movement   (p. 288)
Collective action or rational choice models   (p. 310)

Daughters of Bilitis   (p. 305)
Equal Rights Amendment   (p. 302)
First wave women's or feminist movement   (p. 300)
La Raza Unida   (p. 296)
Mattachine Society   (p. 305)
MEChA   (p. 295)
Mississippi Freedom Democratic Party   (p. 291)

Political opportunity structure   (p. 311)
Resource mobilization theory   (p. 310)
Second wave movement or feminist movement   (p. 300)
Stonewall Riot   (p. 305)
Viva Kennedy Clubs   (p. 294)

Chapter 13

Multiminority Coalitions and the Future of Minority Representation

In 1996, California voters passed Proposition 209 and banned affirmative action in the state, including its use in college admissions. In 2014, the California Senate passed a bill that could overturn the proposition by allowing voters to vote to allow affirmative action in public schools. After the state senate voted, the bill stalled because of "unexpected pushback from families of Asian descent who mobilized through Chinese-language media, staged rallies and organized letter-writing campaigns."[1] They also used emails and social media and encouraged Asian Americans to register as Republicans to prevent the Democratic Party from taking their votes for granted.[2] While African American and Hispanic students often receive poorer K–12 education, making it harder to be admitted in the top colleges and universities, Asian Americans tend to get into top schools in high numbers. Thus, some Asian Americans fear that although African Americans and Hispanics would benefit from affirmative action, Asian Americans would not, and they might even suffer.

As an Asian American running for the California senate, and who opposes the bill, said, "I can't go and tell my kids, Hey, Because you're Asian you can't get into the school you want."[3]

Some Asian American groups targeted Asian American lawmakers who supported the bill and three Democratic Asian American senators withdrew their support of the bill, apparently because of the pressure. The 80–20 PAC, which wants to use the ballot box to help ensure equal opportunity and justice for Asian Americans, said in their newsletter:

> The 3 senators have a role in causing the "NOT to proceed." But they are NOT forgiven until the final defeat of SCA 5 is done. After that, 80–20's California leaders will seek a chance to talk to the three senators and report the result of their discussions to you. After that, you may decide if they are worthy of your continued support.[4]

In retaliation for their withdrawal of support, some African American and Hispanic members have withdrawn support from an Asian American senator's reelection bid and another legislator's bill.[5]

It is not that all Asian Americans oppose affirmative action, and Asian Americans in support of affirmative action have started their own campaign, with organizations such as Chinese for Affirmative Action and Asian Americans Advancing Justice taking the lead. Asian Americans have also sent out tweets, such as #notyouraffirmativeaction or #noliesnohate.[6]

Although it is common for the person on the street to think that minorities should be able to work together to improve their representation, the above story indicates that it is not so easy since their interests do not always align. One of the goals of this chapter is to explore the odds of multiminority coalitions. The conclusions from this section are that while multiminority coalitions are possible, there remains a fair amount of distance between the minorities

Recently there have been efforts to repeal Proposition 209. Prop. 209 was a California initiative that banned the state from considering race, ethnicity and gender in education, contracts, and employment, even to increase diversity. (*AP Photo/Paul Sakuma*)

of the different groups that make it difficult for coalitions to form within the electorate or legislatures.

Racial, ethnic, and gender minorities have been underrepresented historically and remain so today. But that does not mean the same groups will forever be underrepresented. Historically, different groups, such as Italians and Irish, were underrepresented but today are fairly represented and face little discrimination. While it is unlikely that the groups discussed in this book will have equal representation anytime soon, their levels of representation may improve in the medium to short run. Thus, another goal of this chapter is to explore the likelihood of such improvement. A good sign for improved representation of minorities is that current trends have been positive. Each group has seen remarkable improvements in recent decades in its representation. Also seeing remarkable improvement is Americans' attitudes toward minority groups. In addition, many conditions exist that bode well for the future of representation for each minority group, although these conditions very for each group. While Asian Americans and Hispanics have growing populations that will increase their voting power, African Americans and LGBT Americans have high levels of group consciousness and cohesion as well as political eligibility and participation, while women have high levels of voting eligibility, engagement, and participation. On a more negative note, however, each group remains severely underrepresented and just as there are conditions that bode well for their futures, there are conditions that may stifle improvements in representation. Asian Americans and Hispanics have low rates of civic engagement and participation related to immigration; women have low levels of a group consciousness; African Americans have low SES; and LGBT Americans have small numbers. Racial/ethnic and gender minorities are not the only underrepresented groups in the United States. Thus, this chapter will also briefly explore the representation of three other groups that are likely to receive more attention in the future: Muslims, atheists, and the economically poor.

Multiminority Coalitions

So far the book has discussed each individual minority group and what affects its levels of representation without discussing the possibility of coalitions forming between different minority groups. Yet, it is possible that different minority groups could work together to affect the interests they share. I use the term *multiminority coalitions* to refer to coalitions of two or more minority groups. Most of the research examining these types of coalitions has used the term **biracial coalitions,** which refers to the coalition of two different racial groups designed to affect policy and win elections. Most such research focuses on the relationship of African Americans and Hispanics or the relationship of Anglos with either Hispanics or African Americans. However, since it is possible that coalitions could involve more than two groups and the groups could be based on gender or religion as well as race, the term *multiminority coalitions* is used.

A 2013 Gallup survey offers some mixed evidence as to the strength of the relationship between Hispanics and African Americans.[7] About 60% of Americans believe the relationship between Hispanics and African Americans is at least very good and the number has been on the rise since 2006. In addition, more African Americans believe the relationship between African Americans and Hispanics is at least somewhat good (76%) than think the relationship between African Americans and whites is at least somewhat good (66%). While these are good signs, there are also some less positive signs. More Americans think that the relationship between Anglos and Hispanics is at least very good (70%) and Anglos and African Americans is at least very good (70%). In addition, more Hispanics believe the relationship between Hispanics and Anglos is at least somewhat good (71%) than believe the relationship between Hispanics and African Americans is at least somewhat good (64%).

The above figures demonstrate several conclusions drawn by research looking at the relationship of Hispanics and African Americans. First, the research is very mixed as to what Hispanics and African Americans think of each other. Second, the relationship between Anglos and Hispanics or Anglos and African Americans is often better than the relationship between Hispanics and African Americans. Third, African Americans often feel closer to Hispanics than Hispanics feel to African Americans.

Several theories have been offered to help predict the likelihood of multiminority coalitions. First, there are several varieties of theories that predict multiminority coalitions should be likely since minorities tend to have much in common: the **rainbow coalition theory**, the **cooperative theory**, and the **shared interest theory**. Some of the traits minorities have in common include: minorities tend to be liberal and share many interests, such as wanting more equitable education, employment, voting rights, and protections against hate crimes. Thus, if they would work together and combine their voting power, they could accomplish many goals.

Other theories predict that coalitions are unlikely to form. The **competition theory** predicts that instead of minorities having much in common, they are in competition for jobs, housing, or a limited number of electoral positions. Many interests are zero-sum, meaning if one group gains, another must lose. For example, in single-member districts, if an African American wins an election, it means there cannot be an Asian American, American Indian, or Hispanic representative. How much competition really exists between minority groups is debatable. On one hand, Hispanics tend to do less well socioeconomically and politically as the number of African Americans in a community grows or becomes a plurality,[8] and that as the number of Hispanic elected officials increases the number of African American officials decreases.[9] However, there is also evidence that many of these effects are conditional, and as one group improves economically the other does as well.[10]

Another theory that predicts coalitions are difficult is the **power hypothesis**. The power hypothesis suggests that coalitions are unlikely to form where there is social distance between groups and that social distance is affected by how similar groups are to each other. Its earliest formation suggests that there is greater social distance between African Americans and Anglos than Anglos and Hispanics, and as a consequence coalitions between Anglos and Hispanics will be more common than those between Hispanics and African Americans. Later versions of the theory have argued there is greater social distance between Anglos and Hispanics, particularly where there are large immigrant populations of Hispanics.[11] Relatedly, the racial threat hypothesis has also been used to suggest that coalitions are unlikely to form (see Chapter 8 for more on the racial threat hypothesis).

The **empowerment theory**, which focuses the formation of electoral coalitions, also predicts that coalitions are unlikely. It states that minorities receive psychological benefits when one of their own is elected, and that these benefits are unlikely to extend to other minorities.[12] For example, Hispanic voters are not likely to feel empowered when an African American is elected, and vice versa. While most of the theories focus on whether there is cooperation or conflict, Hero and Preuhs suggest that there are other options: negotiation (ideological difference but shared issue salience) or tacit noncooperation (have different issues but share ideology).[13] They find that minority groups often work on different issues but share an ideology. Thus, they would not be in conflict, but also not likely to work on the same issues.

Views of the Masses

To appraise the prospects of multiminority coalitions and test some of the theories mentioned above, researchers have examined minorities' perceptions of each other. It is often assumed that for sustainable coalitions to form, individuals with different minority status need to see each other positively and feel they have something in common. And indeed research suggests people who believe they have something in common with a different minority group are more likely to support coalitions.[14] Researchers have examined feelings of commonality with two different types of questions. One approach is to examine feelings of social distance. This measures how comfortable individuals are with other types of individuals: the less comfortable, the greater the social distance. The other measure asks respondents how much they feel they have in common with other groups. For simplicity, I will summarize these literatures collectively.

Commonality

The evidence has been somewhat mixed as to the levels of feelings of commonality or social distance held by minorities. African Americans have a greater sense of commonality with Hispanics than Hispanics have a sense of commonality with African Americans.[15] For example, Kaufman finds that while 75% of African Americans feel they have at least a fair amount in common with Hispanics, only 33% of Hispanics feel they have at least a fair amount in common with African Americans.[16] Feelings of commonality are also likely contextual. Jackson, Gerber, and Cain find that while African Americans living in Los Angeles have a strong sense of commonality with Hispanics and Asian Americans (although less for Asian Americans), this was less true nationally.[17] What is discouraging for those wanting multiminority coalitions between Hispanics and African Americans is that individuals in each group generally believe they have more in common with Anglos than with each other.[18] That minorities tend to feel they have more in common with Anglos than other minorities could have several roots: such as seeing other minorities as competition for jobs, housing, or power; people's tendency to want to identify with the people with power, or frustration-aggression.[19] Frustration-aggression argues that people who are oppressed displace their frustration onto groups that are weaker.[20] In addition, African Americans, Asian Americans, and Hispanics may have had less contact with each other because Asian Americans and Hispanics have recently immigrated to the United States in large numbers.[21] This means that African Americans and Anglos have had more contact with each other. This is compounded because Asian and Hispanic immigrants have had little contact with African Americans in their home countries.

Several factors affect individuals' sense of commonality with other minorities. First, among Hispanics those who have a panethnic group consciousness are more likely to have high levels of commonality with other minority groups.[22] Also, people born in the United States or who have higher levels of acculturation have higher perceived commonality with other minorities.[23] These two points may help explain why African Americans feel they have more in common with Hispanics, than vice versa. Feelings of commonality are also affected by attitudes, such as having low levels of efficacy[24] or not holding stereotypical views of a group.[25] Exposure to elite cues may also affect views of commonality. Wallsten and Nteta recently found evidence that Democratic Hispanics exposed to positive messages about the commonality between Hispanics and African Americans by Hispanic Democratic leaders saw greater political, but not economic, commonality.[26] Republican Hispanics were not affected by elite messages regardless of which party the source belonged to. Finally, while several studies have examined the effects of socio-demographic traits, such as age, education, and income, they do not show consistent findings as to their effects.[27]

One point of contention in the literature is the effect of perceiving much discrimination or having experienced discrimination on feelings of commonality. That is, for example, do African Americans who believe that African Americans face much discrimination feel greater commonality with other minority groups who suffer discrimination? One view is the **common in-group identity model**.[28] According to this model what often leads to one group discriminating against another is not prejudice against the out-group but a preference for the in-group. What helps individuals from different groups get along is for them to see each other as being part of the same group. In this regard, discrimination could be a unifying experience that brings individuals together. Minorities who believe that their group suffers from discrimination will see others who have been discriminated against as having something in common with themselves, discrimination, and feel closer to that group. Another theory, **social identity threats theory**,[29] argues quite the opposite. Social identity threats theory holds that when people feel threatened, they build their own self-esteem by seeing out-groups in a negative light. Thus, those who believe their group suffers from discrimination will see others negatively. The empirical tests of the effects of discrimination on feelings of commonality have been mixed: some find discrimination has no effect;[30] some find it increases feelings of commonality;[31] while other research supports social identity threat theory.[32] Further research is needed to sort out the effects of discrimination on the prospects for multiminority coalitions.

Prejudice and Stereotypes

Related to research on feelings of commonality is research that looks at levels of prejudice, stereotypes, or hostile feeling between members of different minority groups. The literature examining African Americans' views toward Hispanics has tended to be disheartening for those wanting multiminority coalitions.[33] There is also evidence that African Americans hold fewer negative stereotypes of Hispanics than Hispanics hold of African Americans.[34] Efforts to explain the levels of hostility minorities hold toward each other have tested some of the theories noted above.

Oliver and Wong test the racial threat hypothesis by comparing it with contact theory (see Chapter 8).[35] Remember contact theory predicts people who have contact with individuals from a minority groups will have more positive views of the group, and racial threat suggests that as a minority group grows in size others feel their own well-being may be threatened. Oliver and Wong find little support for the racial threat hypothesis. Hispanics and African Americans have less prejudice against other minorities when there are more minorities in their neighborhood, and that this was strongest in racially diverse cities. Ha also finds that African Americans living in neighborhoods with large Hispanic populations have more positive views toward immigrants and immigration policy, although African Americans living among Asian Americans have less favorable view toward immigration and immigration policy.[36] Oliver and Wong also find that Asian Americans tend to be unique, and attribute the uniqueness to the language and culture.

Whether competition between minority groups breeds hostility between groups has also been tested. A key expectation is, if competition increases hostility, then minorities who are poor are more likely to have hostile views toward other minorities. This research has been inconclusive, most likely because the relationship is complicated. For example, Gay finds that what triggers negative views by African Americans toward Hispanics is an interaction between the size of the Hispanic population and relative economic well-being.[37] African Americans who live in areas where there is a large number of Hispanics and the Hispanics are better off than African Americans; African Americans have more negative views of Hispanics than other African Americans have of Hispanics. However, overall levels of well-being are not as important as the relative well-being of African Americans compared to Hispanics.

Perceptions of Competition

While the above concern feelings of commonality and prejudice, they do not directly look at whether minorities feel they are in competition with other minorities. Bobo and Hutchings find moderate levels of competitive threat and offer four theories as to what increases minorities' belief that other minority groups are a competitive threat: self-interest theory, classical prejudice, stratification beliefs model, and group position model.[38] **Self-interest theory** holds that individuals may fear that other minorities make it harder for them personally to find jobs, housing, or otherwise decrease the quality of their own lives. **Classic prejudice theory** holds that racial conflict is the result of individuals' "socially learned feelings of dislike and aversion, as well as the stereotypes"[39] The **stratification beliefs** model predicts that individuals who have high levels of individualism, believing people's fate depends on their own abilities, see less conflict than those who believe that individuals' fates are affected by their race, class, or gender. The **group position model** predicts that individuals who have high levels of racial alienation will see other groups in a more competitive light. Racial alienation occurs when individuals see their group as having a history of subordination that persists. Bobo and Hutchings find some support for all four theories but that the group position model is strongest.

Behavior

The above discussion looked at attitudes and not behaviors, yet it is possible that individuals may have positive attitudes and still not vote for candidates of a different minority status or support coalitions with their time and resources. The evidence of the prospects for multiminority electoral coalitions is mixed. Much of the research on city governments has had difficulty finding long-lasting electoral coalitions between different racial groups.[40] Although the research can find voters of one minority group willing to vote for candidates of another minority group, these coalitions can easily fall apart based on the behavior of elected officials or the emergence of new candidates. Looking at state House races, Casellas's work finds that majority African American districts elect African Americans and Hispanic districts elect Hispanics.[41] On the other hand, Casellas also finds that for U.S. House races African American candidates benefit from Hispanic votes. In addition, President Obama would not be president without multiminority voting coalitions. That is, Obama would not have won the presidency in either 2008 or 2012 without garnering the minority vote.

In both elections, women, LGBT voters, Hispanics, Asian Americans, and African Americans were all significantly more likely to vote for him than either of his Republican opponents. Table 13.1 indicates the percentage of African Americans, Hispanics, Asian Americans, Anglos, lesbians and gays, bisexuals, non-LGBT voters, women, and men who voted for Obama. This table offers strong evidence that minorities were more likely to support Obama's candidacy. Minorities are also

TABLE 13.1   Minorities' Vote for President in 2012 (Percentages)

	Obama	Romney	Other	N
African Americans	95.5	5.1	1.5	542
Hispanics	71.3	26.5	2.2	402
Anglos	41.6	55.0	3.4	3,081
Gays and lesbians	92.2	3.2	4.6	86
Bisexuals	65.7	27.1	7.3	67
Non-LGBT	50.8	46.1	3.1	4,035
Women	55.1	42.9	2.0	2,212
Men	48.8	46.9	4.3	2,035

Source: Figures calculated by the author using the American National Election Studies (ANES) 2012 Time Series Study [dataset], www.electionstudies.org. Stanford University and the University of Michigan (producers).

more likely to vote for women. Table 13.2 indicates the percentage that responded of each minority and whether they think it would good for a woman to be president. It demonstrates that each minority group is more likely to think it would be good for there to be a woman president than the matching nonminority groups.

Research on ballot items, too, provides evidence of minorities supporting each other. Morris examined the voting behavior of African Americans in California for Proposition 187, a ballot item that would block undocumented immigrants from getting services from the state, finding that most African Americans did not vote for Proposition 187 and were less likely to support it than were whites, 46.8% to 62.6%.[42] However, African Americans and Hispanics voted to ban gays' and lesbians' rights to marry in California. In the 2008 Proposition 8 vote, it is estimated that 70% of African Americans and 53% of Hispanics voted for the ban on same-sex marriages.[43] What is likely is that the prospects of multiminority electoral coalitions are conditional. Rocha suggests multiracial electoral coalitions are likely where there are partisan elections that allow minorities to coalesce around the Democratic candidate, since minorities tend to be Democrats.[44] In addition, he finds that they are more common where no one minority group is a majority.

The empowerment theory, mentioned earlier, suggests that voters may not receive the same psychological benefits from voting for people of a minority status other than their own. Kaufmann tests this and finds that although African American voters are more likely than whites to vote for Hispanics, and vice versa, voters are still more likely to vote for candidates of their own race/ethnicity.[45] She also examined African American and Hispanic voters' evaluation of their city by race of mayor and found some support for the shared interest hypothesis but

TABLE 13.2   How Good Would It Be for There to Be a Woman President?

	Extremely good	Moderately good	A little good	Neither good nor bad	A little bad	Moderately bad	Extremely bad
African American	29.5	19.2	1.4	41.4	2.3	1.4	4.8
Hispanic	24.6	20.0	2.4	48.9	0.3	1.4	2.4
Anglos	17.3	17.4	1.6	58.6	0.7	2.3	2.0
Gays and Lesbians	43.0	18.6	0.7	35.5	0	2.1	0.1
Bisexuals	27.2	13.2	4.6	51.1	1.3	0.2	2.5
Non-LGBT	18.8	18.1	1.7	55.7	0.9	2.2	2.5
Women	23.6	19.9	1.8	49.5	1.0	2.3	2.0
Men	15.3	16.0	1.9	60.6	0.8	2.3	3.1

Source: Figures calculated by the author using the American National Election Studies (ANES) 2012 Time Series Study [dataset], www.election studies.org. Stanford University and the University of Michigan (producers).

more for the empowerment hypothesis. Her findings generally suggest that while shared interests can bring groups together, voters' empowerment is limited to voters who share the minority status of the winning candidate.

Coalitions among Elites

So far the discussion of the prospects for multiminority coalitions has focused on the masses. However, elites, such as policymakers, may work together and form coalitions even without most minorities supporting such coalitions. One type of elite includes interest groups or advocacy groups. Although there is little research examining coalitions of groups, Hero and Preuhs examined the prospect of conflict or cooperation between Hispanics' and African Americans' advocacy work in Congress and the courts.[46] They find no evidence of minority advocacy groups in direct conflict with each other, that is, taking different positions on the same issue, and much evidence that they share a liberal ideology. However, they also find that minority advocacy groups work on different issues and conclude that although minority advocacy groups are not in direct competition with each other, they are unlikely to form coalitions either.

History presents a mixed picture as to the likelihood of coalitions forming that are made up of gender and racial groups. The first suffragettes were abolitionists, suggesting the potential for coalitions. But many became suffragettes because their ability to work in the abolitionist movement was limited due to sexism. Some suffragettes supported the Fifteenth Amendment, which gave African American men the right to vote, others refused to support it because the amendment explicitly excluded women. And when African American men got the right to vote before women, there was a schism in the movement. By the twentieth century, too, there was much racism among many of the newer activists in the suffrage movement. A similar story played out during the civil rights movement. The sexism in the civil rights movement spurred many women to become active in the women's movement. And the women's movement, although not hostile to civil rights, rights for racial and ethnic minorities were not its focus. There have been tensions too between LGBT group, women's groups, and racial/ethnic groups. For example, Betty Friedan, first president of NOW, coined the term the *lavender menace* to refer to the danger lesbians posed to the women's movement. Also, gay men discriminated against many women active in the early LGBT groups. In addition, racial minorities often feel unwelcome in the main LGBT groups and form their own. Rimmerman quotes an early activist in the LGBT movement:

> Despite the push toward a gynandrous center, the sexism of some of the men was—for me, at least—the biggest obstacle toward immediately and completely immersing myself in GLF [Gay Liberation Front]. A number of men were more oppressive to women than any heterosexual guy I had known. A few of the men looked at me with such unveiled contempt that I started to give credence to the old adage that some men were gay because they hated or feared women. I'm sure that these guys would have preferred for the women to leave so that the GLF would become an all-men's group, sort of like a political bathhouse. . . . If we were going to be there, however, a few men thought we might as well make ourselves useful by baking some cookies and making coffee. Some of the other women and I were constantly correcting men who called us "girls."[47]

Within the LGBT community, transgender individuals and their concerns are often marginalized. Some LGBT groups were willing to support an antidiscrimination bill that excluded gender identity to increase the odds that the bill passed. The bill ultimately failed. Today, however, many groups are more likely to realize the commonalities of their causes.

A more common way to look at elites is to look at legislators. At this level, coalitions may be likely. Minority legislators tend to share a Democratic Party identification (see Chapter 2), a liberal ideology,[48] and liberal constituents (see Chapter 2). In addition, policy making or legislating tends not to be a zero-sum game. That is, if one legislator gets what she wants in a piece of legislation, it does not necessarily mean another legislator does not get what he wants. Rather, they can work together to advance each others' goals. Additionally, legislators are a relatively small group, so there is some accountability: members who do not follow through with their promises will find it difficult to make deals in the future. Research that looks at the legislative behavior of elites tends to find that minority legislators support each others' interests; for example, African American legislators support bills of importance to Hispanics, women and LGBT Americans, and women legislators tend to support legislation of importance to Hispanics, African Americans, and LGBT Americans, and so on.[49]

TABLE 13.3   Multiracial Coalitions in Congress: Support of Different Groups for Different Causes

	NAACP	HRC	AAUW	Immigration
African Americans	93.4	86.6	83.8	92.4
Hispanics	74.8	72.3	66.8	75.1
Anglos	41.9	33.8	34.5	36.6
Women	69.2	69.1	64.2	73.2
Men	44.7	35.3	36.5	37.7
LGBT	98.0	99.0	98.0	93.6
Non-LGBT	48.1	40.2	40.4	43.1
Democrats				
African Americans	97.4	91.1	88.1	92.4
Hispanics	94.4	91.2	86.8	91.1
Anglos	91.8	87.2	87.1	89.8
Women	94.3	96.3	91.5	92.4
Men	92.8	85.6	88.9	89.0
LGBT	98.0	99.0	98.0	93.6
Non-LGBT	93.1	88.1	87.0	90.3
Women				
African Americans	98.5	94.5	92.9	93.6
Hispanics	95.0	97.0	89.0	92.0
Anglos	92.3	97.0	91.3	94.3
Men				
African Americans	96.9	89.4	85.7	91.9
Hispanics	94.2	88.8	86.0	90.6
Anglos	91.6	84.3	85.9	88.1

Sources: Data from Human Rights Campaign, "Congressional Scorecard: Measuring Support for Equality 112th Congress," http://towardequality.org/HRC-112th_CongressionalScorecard_Updated.pdf, http://www.naacp.org/pages/report-cards; AAUP Action Fund, "Congressional Voting Record: 112th Congress 2011–2012," http://www.aauwaction.org/wp-content/uploads/2012/09/CVR2012.pdf; 2014 National Immigration Scorecard, http://www.immigrationscores.com/.

To demonstrate this, Table 13.3 compares African American, Anglo, Hispanic, women, men, LGB legislators, and non-LGB legislators in their support for the legislative positions of several different minority advocacy groups:

NAACP, Human Rights Campaign, Association of American University Women (AAUW), and a consortium of Asian American and Hispanic groups' rating on immigration.[50] According to Table 13.3, minorities are significantly more likely to support other minority groups' positions than are nonminority groups. Anglo members of Congress averaged less than 45% on the NAACP, HRC, AAUW, and the 2014 national immigration scorecards, while Hispanics and African Americans averaged between about 94% and 66%. Similarly, while women scores averaged in the 60th and 70th percentiles, men averaged in the 30th and 40th, and while LGBT legislators' scores averaged in the 90th percentiles, non-LGBT legislators' scores averaged in the 40s. Some political scientists might say that these comparisons are really tapping party differences since minorities are predominantly Democrats. Another view is that people may be Democrats because of their support for a variety of minority rights. Thus, the comparison is fair. Nevertheless, the middle of Table 13.3 limits the comparisons to just Democrats. Although the differences are less dramatic, Anglos, men, and non-LGBT legislators averaged lower scores than minorities.

Since some legislators have double minority status, such as being a woman and a racial/ethnic minority, Table 13.3 also looks at the scores for minorities broken down by gender. These findings offer general but incomplete evidence that people with a double minority status offer the most support for minority issues, even those not directly related to their own minority status. Or stated differently, minority women are the most likely to support policy that helps other minority groups. African American women have the highest average on the NAACP scorecard, followed by African American men, Hispanic women, Hispanic men, Anglo women, and Anglo men. This suggests a nice pattern where having a double minority status increases support.

That double minority status increases support for most minority policies is supported by members' scores on other groups' scorecards, as well. Although Anglo and Hispanic women's averages are the same for AAUW ratings, they are highest, followed by African American women, African American men, Hispanic men and Anglo men. And African American women average the highest AAUP scores, with Anglo women, Hispanic women, and men being fairly similar. Although Anglo men offer the least support for LGBT interests, Anglo women offer the most, followed by African American women, Hispanic women, African American men, and Hispanic men. That minority women may be more likely to engage in coalitions is supported by research by Frago, Lopez, Martinez-Ebers, and Ravirez.[51] They find that Hispanic women are more likely than Hispanic men to prioritize working on African American and Asian American interests. In addition, they found Hispanic women are more likely to want to smooth out conflicts and effect compromise with other policymakers.

For multiminority coalitions to form, minorities at both the elite and general public levels need to feel they have similar interests and can trust each other. While our understanding of minorities' shared feeling of commonality, hostility, and competition are not overly discouraging; they do not depict a picture of people with a strong sense of commonality. The most encouraging evidence is that minority voters may support candidates of other minority groups, unless in direct competition with someone of their own group, and minority legislators tend to support similar pieces of legislation.

The Future: Trends in Representation

One way to gauge the future levels of minority representation is to look at recent trends in levels of representation (substantive representation, formalistic representation, descriptive representation, symbolic representation), and the factors that can affect representation (levels of participation, resources, cohesion, acculturation, and public opinion). The trends indicate that there are many hopeful signs about the future of minority representation. First, in terms of policy, many of the worst laws are history. The Jim Crow laws are gone, the Civil Rights Act and its parallels at the state and local level outlawed discrimination based on race, ethnicity, and gender (including gender identity) at work, school, and other public areas. The federal and a growing number of state governments offer hate crime protection for LGBT populations, and although there is no federal protection against workplace discrimination based on sexual orientation and gender identity, the number of states offering LGBT workers such protections is growing. In addition, same-sex marriages are allowed in every state. The United States has abandoned its assimilationist policies in favor of greater tribal sovereignty. In the area of formalistic representation, the laws have certainly improved for racial and ethnic minorities since the days before the Voting Rights Act, or the Twenty-Fourth Amendment. Gone are literacy tests, poll taxes, and white primaries.

In terms of symbolic representation, if we look at the relationship between minorities and nonminorities in their levels of symbolic representation, African Americans and women have as positive views as do whites and men. Hispanics and Asian Americans may have even more positive views of the United States. Each minority group has seen improvement in its descriptive representation as well. The number of minority policymakers has increased. For example, while in the 108th Congress there were sixty women, thirty-nine African Americans, twenty-four Hispanics, two American Indians, four Asian Americans, and three openly LGB House members, ten years later in the 113th Congress there were seventy-nine women, forty-three African Americans, twenty-eight Hispanics, ten Asian Americans, two American Indians, and seven openly LGB members in the House. The 114th Congress saw some increases as well, eighty-four women, forty-five African Americans, twenty-nine Hispanics, and eight Asian Americans.[52] In addition, President Obama has appointed more minorities to the courts and to high ranking executive branch posts than any other president.

If we look at conditions that are favorable for representation, again there are several positive signs. Public opinion toward all the minority groups has improved dramatically since the mid-twentieth century. Few Americans today hold old-fashioned racist or sexists views, and people are much more accepting of LGBT Americans. For example, virtually all Americans report that they would vote for an African American, women, or Hispanic candidate for president, and about 60% would vote for an LGBT candidate. In addition, few people want to go back to the days when laws denied women and other minorities equal education or job opportunities. In addition, a majority of Americans support marriage equality, as well as antidiscrimination policies for LGBT workers.

There are numerous interest groups at the national, state, and local levels advocating on behalf of minorities, and African Americans, women, and LGBT Americans vote at high levels. For example, prior to the 1980s African Americans and women voted at lower rates than whites and men, however in the most recent elections they have voted at as high or higher rates. There is little trend data on voting behavior of LGBT Americans, but in 2012 they voted at similar levels as non-LGBT Americans. LGBT Americans and African Americans also have many traits that bode well for their continued participation, such as high levels of voter eligibility, civic engagement, acculturation, group consciousness, cohesion, and civic duty. And while women have low levels of group consciousness, they have high levels of eligibility, civic duty, acculturation, and civic engagement. Although Asian Americans and Hispanics vote at low levels, the percentages of voters who are Asian American or Hispanic is rapidly growing. Since the main reasons individuals from these groups vote at low levels are related to their high levels of immigration, including lacking voter eligibility and acculturation, future generations should see significantly higher rates of voting. Among minorities in America, African American women stand out in terms of their high voting rates, consciousness, civic engagement, civic duty, and political interest.

While there is much to be hopeful about, there are also several points of concern. If policies are evaluated by outcomes, then there is great reason to be concerned about the future. The wealth gaps between men and women, and Anglos and racial and ethnic minority groups, with the exception of Asian Americans, remain large. With education, as well, there are signs of resegregation, and racial and ethnic minority students remain concentrated in poorer performing schools, many of which are pipelines to prison. For LGBT students, bullying is a significant problem that can prevent them from attending school. When looking at specific policies there are some points of concern as well. Although the Supreme Court has upheld some types of affirmative action in education, programs designed to help minorities gain education and employment have been under attack as several states have passed laws to prevent affirmative action. Many women's groups are concerned about what they see as an attack on their reproductive rights, as many states are passing laws making abortions more difficult.

With regard to formalistic representation, there are grave concerns about the effects of the Court's 2013 case, *Shelby v. Holder*, which nullified a key provision of the Voting Rights Act. Within a year of the case, six of the nine states affected by the *Shelby* case had passed stricter voter ID laws and some are working on limiting early voting and same-day registration.[53] Although the research has been inconclusive as to the effects of voter ID laws, many activists fear that minorities will find it more difficult to obtain identification and so be disenfranchised. It is also unlikely that many new laws will pass to increase minority participation. Legislation that would give a pathway to citizenship for illegal immigrants is unlikely to pass in Congress. Also not likely to pass are major changes to the electoral system, such as altering the Electoral College or going to proportional representation that could increase participation or equalize the value of a vote.

In terms of symbolic representation, there are also negative signs. Although minorities tend to be similar to nonminorities in their views toward the government, levels of symbolic representation are in decline. For example, in 2004, 56.4% of Hispanics reported feeling "extremely good" when they saw the flag, but in 2012 the figure fell to 41.2%. The percentage of women who felt extremely good upon seeing the flag went from 52.8% to 44.2%. With regard to descriptive representation, even though the government is more diverse today than in the past, all groups remain significantly underrepresented. In addition, the increase for African Americans members (from 38 to 43 in the ten years from the 108th to the 113th Congress) is small. In addition, while Hispanic population grew over 40%, the number of Hispanic House members increased by less than 20% (from 24 to 28). The 114th Congress saw just one more Hispanic member take a seat in the House. At the state and local levels, the increases in descriptive representation have been uneven. For example, while over 40% of legislators in Colorado are women, less than 13% of legislators in South Carolina are women. Minorities in the executive branch tend to be concentrated in certain types of departments and at lower pay grades.

There are also several points of concern when it comes to factors likely to increase representation. First, although Americans have less overt prejudice against minorities, a new form of racism and sexism based on stereotypes remains, and there is little support for some key policies, such as affirmative action. In addition, each minority group comprises a diverse group of individuals and this diversity is unlikely to decline. Thus it may be difficult for minorities to develop greater cohesion or group consciousness. After all, what do African American urban lesbians, Sudanese immigrants, poor rural African American farm workers, and middle-class professional African American men have in common? Or what do fairly well off Cubans who fled communist Cuba and were welcomed in the United States have in common with poor Central Americans fleeing violence and poverty who are arriving here illegally today? In terms of participation, most Hispanics and Asian Americans, even those who are citizens, do not vote in a given election, and there is little reason to expect that to change soon. They have low levels of civic engagement, acculturation, cohesion, and consciousness. And although Asian Americans have high levels of SES, one of the main factors associated with voting, other minorities have low levels of SES. Also, while African Americans voted at high levels in 2008 and 2012, it is likely that the candidacy of Barack Obama contributed to those levels and whether they will continue to participate at high levels after he leaves office is an unknown, but their low levels of turnout in the 2014 midterm elections are discouraging. How much minorities vote in the future will likely depend on whether they have developed the habit of voting, and the minority status of future candidates.

Although there are significant points of concern, I remain optimistic about the future for representation of minorities. As the nation continues to diversify, candidates and parties need to be inclusive in order to win elections. In addition, although minorities, with the exception of women, are less likely to be contacted by candidates and parties than heterosexual Anglos, recent elections have seen an uptick in the mobilization of minority voters. However, with this diversity will also come some challenges for minority activists. Chief among these may be how to gain or maintain cohesion within a group. For example, how well will they be able to get Asian Indians, Japanese, Chinese, Koreans, and Southeast Asians living in America to see their similarities and unite to effect positive change for Asian Americans?

Minorities of the Future (Past and Present)

Although racial/ethnic and gendered minorities have received most of the attention by scholars examining minorities in American politics, they are not the only groups who are underrepresented. This section will briefly explore the representation of two religious minorities, Muslims and atheists, and one economic minority, the poor. The attention scholars and political pundits pay to these groups is increasing and is likely to continue to do so.

Muslims

September 11, 2001, and its aftermath increased Americans' awareness of Muslim Americans. The greater presence of Muslims in Western nations is not limited to the United States; Spotlight 13.1 discusses the growth of Muslims in Europe. Since the U.S. Census does not collect information on religion, there is not reliable historical information on Muslims in the United States. However, estimates indicate roughly 0.5% of Americans are Muslim.[54] To get a sense of who these Americans are and their political power, Pew conducted a survey in 2011.[55] This section will highlight the results of this survey. Almost two-thirds of Muslims are foreign born, about 40% of whom come from Northern Africa or the Middle East. Most of the foreign born (70%) have become citizens, and 80% of Muslims living in the United States are U.S. citizens.[56] Muslim Americans are racially diverse; 30% are white, 23% black, 21% Asian, 6% Hispanic, and 19% are other or mixed race.[57] Their incomes and levels of education are similar to those of other Americans. Although Muslim Americans attend religious services more often than other Americans, they are not extremists. They also reject terrorism. For example, 80% say suicide bombings are never justified, and 70% have a very unfavorable view of al Qaeda.[58] Most believe that Muslims coming to the United States today want to assimilate (56%).[59] However, most also see that being Muslim is more important to them than being an American (49% to 26%).[60]

They are more optimistic about their personal economic situation and the direction of the country than other Americans. However, most believe that 9/11 made it harder to be an American Muslim (55%) and have suffered discrimination and prejudice. For example, 28% of respondents report having been "treated or viewed with suspicion" in the past year, 22% have been "called an offensive name," 21% of respondents have been "singled out by airport security," 13% report having been "singled out by police," and 6% have been "physically threatened or attacked."[61] Almost half (43%) of the respondents have experienced one of these forms of discrimination happen to them in the past year.

Spotlight 13.1

Muslims in Western Europe

Muslims make up the largest religious minority in Europe.[62] France has the highest percentage of Muslims in Western Europe (8%–9.6%),[63] and Albania (70%) the most in Eastern Europe.[64] The large number of Muslims has created policy conflict in Europe.[65] One of the more visible conflicts occurred in France and revolved around the wearing of hijab, or burka. In 2011, France started enforcing a law that makes the wearing of or forcing women to wear face coverings illegal.[66] This law is seen by many as an attack on Muslim women.

According to a Pew survey, attitudes toward Muslims vary across Europe. In Italy, 63% of respondents reported negative views toward Muslims, compared to 53% of respondents in Greece, 50% in Poland, 46% in Spain, 33% in Germany, 27% in France, and 26% in the U.K.[67] Older and conservative Europeans tend to have more negative views.

European Muslims are aware of the hostility. A Pew survey found 51% of German, 42% of British, 39% of French, and 31% of Spanish Muslims said Europe was hostile to them.[68] However, Muslims tended to have greater concern about unemployment.[69]

Scholars using resource mobilization theory suggest that Muslims in different nations have different resources and that where Muslims have greater resources, they do better.[70] Those examining political opportunity structures note that the centralization of power in France may limit Muslims' ability to affect change, while the relative ease with which they can become a British citizen may increase their power there. In addition, the variation in Muslims' experiences may have to do with how much nations want immigrants to assimilate, their views of nationalism, the relationship between church and state, and economic conditions.

Muslims affected the outcome of France's 2012 presidential race. It is estimated that Hollande, the socialist candidate, would not have won without their support.[71] However, Muslims have not done well gaining descriptive representation.[72] It is estimated that there are only eleven Muslims out of 785 members of the European Parliament. In addition, only six of the twenty-seven nations in the European Parliament have a Muslim representative.[73] Muslims do slightly better at the national and local level, but there is considerable variation from nation to nation.

Politically, Muslims share much with other minorities. Muslims are solidly Democratic (70% Democratic, 11% Republican, and 19% independent).[74] They are more liberal than the general population, but more identify as moderates than either liberal or conservative (27% liberal, 38% moderate, and 25% conservative, compared to 22%, 36%, and 38% for the general public).[75] They are also more likely than other Americans to approve of President Obama's performance in office and less likely to have approved of President G. W. Bush's performance in office. Generally, too, they see President Obama and the Democratic Party as friendly to Muslims. As with other groups with large immigration growth, such as Asian Americans and Hispanics, Muslims vote at lower rates and are less politically engaged than other Americans. Whereas 64% of Muslims reported voting in 2008, 76% of the general public reported voting.[76] Similarly, while 37% of Muslims reported following what's going on in the government most of the time, 50% of the general public reported following what's going on most of the time. The Pew survey also asked about the role of women and acceptance of LGBT Americans. It found that as with other Americans, Muslim Americans have become more accepting of LGBT Americans in recent years, but they still lag other Americans in their levels of acceptance. They are also more likely to see men as better leaders than women. Whereas 27% of Muslims prefer a man and 4% prefer a woman, the percentages for the rest of America are 13% and 12%.[77] They also are more likely to see immigrants as strengthening America (71% to 45%).[78] In foreign policy, they are less likely to support actions in the war on terrorism than other Americans. For example, while 57% of Americans think using force in Afghanistan was the right thing to do, only 38% of Muslims think it was the right thing to do.[79]

While the Pew survey provides much information about Muslim Americans, it does not indicate what Americans think about Muslims. To estimate Americans' views toward Muslims, the Arab American Institute conducted a poll in the summer of 2014.[80] It indicates that only 27% of Americans view Muslims favorably and that the percentage had fallen since 2010 (35%). Additionally, it showed that a plurality of Americans (42%) support racial profiling of Muslims, and 42% believe if a Muslim American gained a "an important position of influence in the government" that his or her religion would influence their decision making compared to 32% who are confident the person could do the job. The survey also supports contact theory. Whereas 36% Americans who know someone who is Muslim have a favorable view of Muslims, only 23% of Americans who do not know someone Muslim have a favorable view.

Muslims, too, lack descriptive representation. Keith Ellison (D, MN) became the first Muslim elected to Congress when he won his seat in 2006. In 2008 there were only two members of Congress, nine state legislators, and ten local officials who were Muslim.[81] Even though Muslims are a small percentage of Americans at about 0.5%, with 435 members of Congress, 7,300 state legislators, and countless local officials, they are grossly underrepresented. The number of Muslim officials is unlikely to see dramatic increases. According to Gallup, only 58% of Americans report they would vote for a Muslim of their party who was well qualified for president.[82] All this would suggest that Muslims need greater representation in places of power.

Atheists

Atheists could also be among the most underrepresented groups in American politics.[83] According to a *Huffington Post* article, in the 113th Congress there were no sitting, self-identifying, atheist Congress members.[84] There is one member, Rep. Kyrsten Sinema (D, AZ) who has claimed to be a nonbeliever in the past but now says she has a "secular approach." In the 112th Congress, there was one member who identified as atheist, Rep. Pete Stark (D, CA), and one member who, after he left office, announced he was a nonbeliever, Rep. Barney Frank (D, MA). The article also noted that there is only one self-claimed atheist among the 7,300 state legislators, Sen. Ernie Chambers (D, NE), and that several states still require elected officials to believe in god.

While there may only be one or two atheist elected officials in state and federal roles, the number of atheists in the general public is 2.4%,[85] larger than Native Americans or Muslims. The 2.4% figure is based on a Pew survey where people specified that they were atheists. In addition, another 3.3% identify as agnostic, and an additional 13.9% have no religion in particular. This would mean that about 20% are not religious. Atheists tend to be male, young, and highly educated.

To get a sense of the political attitudes and behaviors of atheists, I use the 2012 ANES time series survey to calculate statistics. Although atheists were not identified as such on the survey, nonreligious people were, thus I will use the terms *nonreligious* and *religious*. Nonreligious are similar to the general public in levels of trust, interest, and voting. About 2% of nonreligious feel they can always trust the government to do what is right, and 8% feel they can trust it most of the time. This is similar to religious people's levels of trust (1% and 10%, respectively). Nonreligious people report similar, but slightly lower, levels of interest in politics. Almost 16% of nonreligious people say they always pay attention to politics compared to 17.3% of religious people. About 32% of nonreligious people pay attention most of the time compared to 36% of the religious. Although they are less likely to register to vote, among those registered, they are as likely to vote. About 76% of nonreligious people were registered to vote compared to 84% of the religious. About 84% of religious people and nonreligious who are registered to vote reported voting in the November 2012 elections.

Where nonreligious people stand out is in their liberal views and support for the Democratic Party and its candidates. Also, a higher percentage of nonreligious people are independents and moderates. And of those who voted, they overwhelmingly supported President Obama. Almost 71% of nonreligious people reported voting to reelect President Obama, compared to about 51% of the religious. A likely reason they voted for President Obama at high levels is that they are overwhelmingly Democrats. About 22% of nonreligious people reported being strong Democrats, 33% at least lean, but not strongly, toward the Democratic Party, 21% are independents, 18% at least lean, but not strongly, toward the Republican Party, and an additional 6% are strong Republicans. Among religious people, 47% at least lean toward the Democratic party, only 14% are independents, and 39% Republicans. Nonreligious people also tend to be liberals. Among nonreligious people, 35% are at least weak liberals, 41% are moderates, and 22% are conservative. For religious people the percentages are 33%, 35%, and 41%.

A likely reason that there are few atheists in office is that many Americans would not vote for them. According to a Gallup survey, only 54% of Americans say they would vote for a qualified atheist candidate of their party for president.[86] Americans also tend to have negative views toward atheists. The 2012 ANES asked respondents to place atheists on a feeling thermometer scale. Feeling thermometer scores range from 0 for feeling cold or unfavorable toward a group to 100 for feeling warm or favorable toward a group. Atheists scored a cool 35 degrees. To put it in perspective, Americans gave LGBT Americans 46 degrees, Muslims 38 degrees, big business 47 degrees, feminists 49 degrees, Christian fundamentalists 41 degrees, welfare recipients 44 degrees, Catholics 52 degrees. One of the few groups to score as low as Atheists was Congress. It also scored 35 degrees.

Mansbridge (1999) argues descriptive representation is needed for a group when it does not trust that others can represent its interests and policies do not reflect its interests. Whether atheists meet that criterion is hard to say since there are few advocates espousing unique atheist interests. However, that might be changing. Atheists are starting to get organized. In 2013, Freethought Equality Fund PAC became the first atheist political action committee.[87] FEF PAC's goal is to increase the number of humanist, atheists, agnostics, and their allies in office.[88] In 2014, FEF PAC contributed about $41,000 to congressional candidates.[89]

The Economically Poor

During the fall of 2011 it seemed as though a new movement concerned with economic inequality was starting. In September of that year, protesters in the **Occupy Wall Street** movement took over Zuccotti Park in New York City to protest the growing disparity between the wealthy 1% and the remaining 99%. Similar actions sprang up throughout the nation and in the next few months 8,000 protesters were arrested.[90] After a few months the movement died down and was no longer making headlines. Their goals, which included politicians less focused on the wealthy, a Robin Hood tax, and relief for large student loans, have not been met.[91] In fact, the larger issue of income inequality continues to grow. Although there are several ways to measure income inequality, they tend to indicate that prior to the 1970s income tended to grow at similar rates across the

In 2011, the Occupy Wall Street activists took over Zuccotti Park in New York City to protest growing economic disparity in the United States. (© Bo Zaunders/Corbis)

economic spectrum, but since then the top income brackets have done significantly better.[92] According to estimates from the Congressional Budget Office, while incomes of the bottom 60th percentile grew 49% between 1979 and 2012, the incomes of the top 1% grew 201%.[93] Net worth is also concentrated in the top percentile. The top 1% has 35% of the wealth in the United States and the bottom 90% owns only 27%.[94]

Income disparity is found in American politics as well, with poor Americans being grossly underrepresented. In 2012, about 15% of Americans lived below the poverty line,[95] while the average House member had a net worth estimated at just under $850,000 and the average Senator at $2.7 million.[96] While a handful of members are in debt, they earn $174,000 annually and have a good benefits package. There are also several members who have been middle class and some who have been on welfare and/or grew up poor. However, that they were able to move up the economic ladder makes them unique and less representative of the poor. Given the role of money in elections, it is not too surprising that our representatives tend to be wealthy. Voters may also want successful people to represent them. Nevertheless, there are concerns that the interests of the poor are ignored and that politicians' wealth prevents them from understanding the lives of their constituents.

Politicians often make comments that reinforce these concerns. For example, President George H. W. Bush was unaware of scanners in grocery stores.[97] In addition, Republican presidential nominee Mitt Romney said:

> There are 47 percent of the people who will vote for the president no matter what. All right, there are 47 percent who are with him, who are dependent upon government, who believe that they are victims, who believe the government has a responsibility to care for them, who believe that they are entitled to health care, to food, to housing, to you-name-it—that that's an entitlement. And the government should give it to them. And they will vote for this president no matter what. . . . These are people who pay no income tax. . . . [M]y job is not to worry about these people. I'll never convince them they should take personal responsibility and care for their lives.[98]

In 2014, Hillary Rodham Clinton, a socially liberal woman Democrat, made the insensitivity of the haves apparent in an interview with Diane Sawyer. She complained that she and President Bill Clinton left the White House "dead broke" and in debt in 2000. This is despite having earned over $400,000 in 1999 and receiving an $8 million advance on a book.[99] She and President Clinton also earned $109 million in the next seven years.

What is troubling to many supporters of democracy is that poor Americans tend to be less engaged in politics and to vote at low levels. According to ANES data, in 2008, 26% of the poorest 16% of Americans were not registered to vote compared to 11% for the top 5%.[100] Additionally, in 2008, 64% of the poorest group voted, while 89% of the wealthiest group voted. Not only are poor people less active politically, they are solidly Democratic. In 2008, 68% of the poorest voters voted for the Democrat (Obama) for president compared to 27% of the wealthiest group.[101] For congressional elections the numbers were 75% to 33%.[102] That poor Americans are supporters of the Democratic Party has been the case for as long as ANES has been surveying the electorate.

Perhaps part of the reason that poor Americans participate at lower levels is that they have more negative views of the government. They are somewhat less trusting of the government than the middle classes but somewhat more trusting than the wealthiest group.[103] They have less efficacy; are more likely to think the government doesn't care what people think (63% to 43%).[104] And more likely to think politics is too complicated (72% to 40%).[105]

It is important to point out that the poor may have more negative views about American politics because the government is less responsive to their needs. For example, poor Americans are less likely to be contacted by the parties or candidates during elections. In 2012, whereas 37% of the poorest groups were contacted, 52% of the wealthiest groups were contacted.[106] There is likely a bit of a catch-22: one reason they are not contacted is they are less likely to vote, but one reason they are less likely to vote is that they are less likely to be contacted. It has been argued that if poor people participated at higher levels, it would transform the political system. The issues discussed by politicians wanting to get elected would change. Of course, it is impossible to know.

Final Thoughts: Should Minorities Be Lumped Together or Split into Different Groups?

In 1857, Charles Darwin wrote to friend and botanist Joseph Dalton Hooker, "It is good to have hair-splitters & lumpers."[107] Lumpers are taxonomists known for "submerging many minor varieties under a single name, whereas a splitter does the opposite, naming the varieties as subspecies or even full species."[108] Lumpers would likely feel comfortable classifying minorities as a single group, while splitters would feel a need to split minorities into many different groups.

Lumpers would note that each of the minority groups lacks proportional descriptive representation in the government. This is true in all branches and at all levels (local, state, and federal). Lumpers would also note that the reasons for their underrepresentation are similar: (1) some voters harbor prejudice and harmful stereotypes; (2) minorities may not have the backgrounds, such as law degrees, associated with office holders; (3) minorities may be less likely to run for office; (4) the media may cover their elections differently; and (5) some laws disadvantage minority candidates. In addition, the minority groups share being resource poor, which may depress their political participation and ability to mobilize. The value of proportional representation, too, may be similar. It is likely that dyadic descriptive representation has nominal effects on their symbolic representation, but that collective descriptive representation has more effect on views toward the government.

In addition, the groups share many similarities in reference to policy or substantive representation. They share many policy goals such as equal employment and education opportunities and criminal justice reform. Minorities share histories of facing discrimination and having experienced significant social movements during the last half of the twentieth century. Many of the conditions that are conducive to minority policy representation are similar across groups as well, such as descriptive representation, Democratic government, large minority populations, favorable public opinion, and strong interest groups that support their interests. In addition it is likely that direct democracy is harmful to interests of each minority group. The ability of minorities to get their policies enacted are also affected by mass opinion, and there is less prejudice toward the minority groups today than fifty years ago, at least in the old-fashioned sense. Some of the factors that affect public opinion toward the groups are also fairly consistent. For example, having contact with a minority group improves support for that group's interests. In addition, the same types of people, other minorities, Democrats, well-educated, and young, tend to be supportive of minorities' interests.

While lumpers would be happy classifying minorities as a single group, splitters would be displeased. Although all groups may lack proportional representation, some groups such as women and Hispanics have less proportional representation than do African Americans or Asian Americans. What can help them gain representation varies some by group. For example, since racial and ethnic minorities tend to live in segregated areas, the demographic makeup of districts has a greater effect on their levels of descriptive representation than district makeup has on women's and LGBT's representation. Another notable difference is that since many Asian Americans and Hispanics are not U.S. citizens, they lack the voting power to elect one of their own. That these groups are made up of large numbers of immigrants affects their levels of participation and symbolic representation. Also, there are some issues of greater interest to some groups than others, such as marriage equality, immigration, tribal sovereignty, and reproductive rights.

Another difference between the groups is that each of the groups has a unique set of resources. For example, although Hispanics are a large minority group, they have low levels of SES and are less civically engaged than other groups. Asian Americans have a small population and tend to be wealthier and better educated. The groups vary in their levels of acculturation, cohesion, and group consciousness. Hispanics and Asian Americans tend to have low levels of acculturation, group consciousness, and cohesion, while African Americans and LGBT Americans tend to have high levels of acculturation, cohesion, and group consciousness, and women tend to have low levels of group consciousness and cohesion but high levels of acculturation.

Finally, the groups differ in their levels of participation. In recent elections, African Americans, LGBT Americans, and women tended to vote at fairly high levels, while Asian Americans and Hispanics tended to participation at low levels. The key reason for this is that a large percentage from each group is not native born.

Splitters, too, would want to divide groups even further since there is an intersection of race and gender. This book supports the idea that race and gender intersect in such a way that the representation individual Americans receive depends on their mix of race, ethnicity, and gender. Minority women tend to outpace white women in descriptive representation. African American women, in particular, tend to have high levels of group consciousness, cohesion, and participation rates. Women minorities in office also have unique experiences working on a unique set of issues.

As Darwin wrote to his friend, lumpers and splitters are both good. By lumping minorities together, we can see the big picture of what is helpful for underprivileged groups to gain representation. By splitting hairs, we can see that the political experiences and realities of each group are unique. It can be dangerous to assume that what will help white women become incorporated into the political system will help minority women. Not all groups even see the same value of incorporation; the American Indian movement wanted greater tribal sovereignty, and the Chicano and Asian American movements wanted incorporation, but also greater appreciation of their cultures.

KEY TERMS

Biracial coalitions   (p. 324)

Classic prejudice theory   (p. 329)

Common in-group identity
   model   (p. 327)

Competition theory   (p. 325)

Cooperative theory   (p. 325)

Empowerment theory   (p. 326)

Group position model   (p. 329)

Occupy Wall Street   (p. 342)

Power hypothesis   (p. 325)

Rainbow coalition theory   (p. 325)

Self-interest theory   (p. 329)

Shared interest theory   (p. 325)

Social identity threats theory   (p. 327)

Stratification beliefs   (p. 329)

Glossary

Acculturation refers to how well individuals can function in the United States and how long their families have lived in the United States

ACT UP (AIDS Coalition to Unleash Power) is a group created to help AIDS victims and improve policy responses to AIDS. It combined an insider with an outsider approach.

Active representation is similar to **substantive or policy representation** but usually refers to the bureaucracy.

Affect misattribution procedure is a way to measure implicit prejudice. Subjects in an experiment are shown Chinese characters (writing) and asked to evaluate them. Just before each character, subjects are shown a photo of either an African American man or a white man so quickly they are barely aware that they saw it. Those giving negative evaluations of Chinese characters following photos of African Americans are thought to have higher levels of implicit prejudice than those giving positive evaluations following a photo of an African American.

Affirmative action involves any positive action taken to help minorities improve their status, usually in employment and education.

Antidiscrimination policies were the first efforts to reduce discrimination. They allowed people who were victims of discrimination to bring complaints against government or businesses if they had discriminatory practices.

Appellate courts hear cases that arise from district court trials and are mostly concerned with the procedure at the lower level. There are twelve appellate circuits and one federal appellate circuit. In each circuit, there is a pool of judges from which three judges are selected to hear individual cases.

At-large elections occur where there are no districts and all citizens vote for representatives for every position. These types of elections are thought to harm the descriptive representation of racial and ethnic minorities.

Attitudes are peoples' relatively enduring predispositions to respond favorably or unfavorably toward someone or something.

Attribution theory predicts that when Americans think sexual orientation is innate, they are more tolerant toward LGBT and supportive of their rights.

Backlash effects occur when minority causes see a setback after some success.

Beliefs are views about how the world works or information we have about how the world works.

Biracial coalitions refer to efforts where people of two or more races, often minority races, work together to help mutual interests, including affecting policy and winning elections.

Black empowerment areas are areas where African Americans have significant levels of descriptive representation. Bobo and Gilliam define these as cities with black mayors.

Black nationalism and black power involve the belief in the self-determination of people of African descent, taking pride in that heritage and separating from the white culture.

Blood quantum is an approach to determining a person's race based on percentage of a person's ancestry that was of a minority race.

Bradley Effect refers to a problem often faced by minority candidates: they tend to poll better in surveys than on Election Day.

Brown Berets is an organization of Mexican Americans who advocate for returning land to Mexico. It helped organize one of the largest events of the Chicano movement, the **Chicano Moratorium**.

Brown v. Board of Education of Topeka (1954) is a Supreme Court case that ruled segregated schools violated the equal protection clause.

Casework/constituency services involve legislators working as ombudsmen for their constituents, helping them with issues they may have with the government.

Chicano Moratorium was an anti–Vietnam War march protesting the disproportionately large number of Mexican Americans who were dying on the front lines of the war.

Chicano movement was a 1960–1970s movement advocating for greater power of Mexican Americans. It is often associated with an increase in pride and identity of Mexicans.

Children's Crusade was part of the Birmingham campaign. It involved children being attacked by police as they marched out of churches singing and praying. The media covered the campaign, increasing Americans' awareness of conditions in the South.

Civic duty is the belief held by individuals that they have a responsibility to participate in society.

Civic engagement has many meanings, but here it refers to individuals being active in their community.

Civil disobedience is breaking the law to convey a political message.

Civil Rights Act (CRA) does several things, but most notably it prevents race- and sex-based discrimination in education and employment.

Civil rights movement is a term used to describe a series of actions occuring in the mid-twentieth century where there was much activity and advancement in the rights of African Americans.

Civil unions are similar to marriages in granting rights to same-sex couples, but are only governmental actions. Vermont was the first state to formally recognize same-sex relationships when it created civil unions in 2000.

Clarence Thomas Hearings are the confirmation hearing of Justice Thomas. He was plagued by allegations of sexual harassment, but no women served on the Senate Judiciary Committee, which held the hearings. The hearings are thought to contribute to 1992 being the year of the woman.

Classic prejudice theory holds that individuals are socialized to dislike or have stereotypes of minorities and that these feelings contribute to racial conflict.

Co-ethnic candidates are candidates who share a voter's race or ethnicity.

Collective action or rational choice models can help explain why some movements are more successful. They predict that people will engage in social movements or join organizations if the benefits they personally gain from doing so exceed the costs.

Collective descriptive representation is when individuals believe the government has high levels of descriptive representation. Minorities who believe there are high levels of descriptive representation tend to see the government in a better light than those with lower levels.

Common in-group identity model holds that discrimination is a unifying experience that brings individuals together.

Competition theory predicts that since minorities are often in competition for jobs, housing, or a limited number of electoral positions that muliminority coalitions are unlikely to form.

Congressional Asian Pacific American Caucus (founded in 1994) is an organization of members of Congress that focuses on issues of concern to Asian Americans and Pacific Islanders. Most members are of Asian or Pacific Island descent.

Congressional Black Caucus (founded in 1971) is an organization of members of Congress that focuses on issues of importance to African Americans.

Congressional Caucus for Women's Issues (founded in 1977) is an organization of members of Congress that focuses on issues of concern to women. Its membership includes congresswomen from both parties.

Congressional Hispanic Caucus (founded 1976) is an organization of members of Congress that focuses on issues of importance to Hispanics. It is made up of Hispanic members of Congress

Congressional LGBT Equality Caucus (founded in 2008) is an organization of members of Congress that focuses on issues important to the LGBT community. Its membership includes LGBT members of Congress and their allies.

Contact theory assumes nonminority individuals have negative attitudes about a minority group due to ignorance. Thus, the more contact they have with minorities, the less likely they are to harbor negative stereotypes and be prejudiced.

Contract authority involves the government hiring businesses to conduct work.

Conventional political participation involves using regular governmental processes to effect change, such as those related to elections and contacting representatives.

Cooperative theory (also see **rainbow coalition** and **shared interest**) predicts that since minorities have much in common, multiminority coalitions are likely.

Cumulative voting occurs in MMDs where there is a slate of candidates, but voters can distribute their votes to one or multiple candidates. Elections with cumulative voting are thought to be helpful for minority descriptive representation.

Daughters of Bilitis was an early lesbian rights organization started in 1955.

Democratic deficit refers to the lack of congruence between policy and public opinion. That is, policy preferences are not the same as policy.

Deracialization refers to the strategy of minority candidates to avoid discussing issues related to their minority status. The strategy is thought to help minority candidates reach nonminority voters.

Descriptive representation concerns whether representative bodies resemble the people they are to represent in that their membership corresponds to the demographic makeup of the people.

Disparate impact is an interpretation of the Civil Rights Act that suggests that criteria used in hiring that disproportionately harm minorities, regardless of intention, constitute a form of discrimination that violates the Civil Rights Act, unless the criteria can be demonstrated to be needed.

District courts are trial courts that examine the facts of a case and the law to determine outcomes. There is one judge who oversees the trial, but either the judge or a jury determines the outcome.

Diversity management can take any number of forms, including affirmative action, diversity training, mentoring for minorities, evaluating managers based on diversity, or networking for minorities.

Dyadic descriptive representation is when individuals share race, ethnicity, or gender with their own representative. Minorities with dyadic descriptive representation see their representative in a better light than those without dyadic representation; however, dyadic descriptive representation has little effect on views toward the government more generally.

Eligibility pool refers to the people who are likely to hold elective office because they have the traits associated with politicians, such as being successful businesspeople or lawyers or having military experience or previous electoral experience. Minorities are less likely to be in the eligibility pool.

Empowerment theory is primarily interested in the formation of electoral coalitions and predicts that minorities receive psychological benefits when one of their own is elected, but that this is unlikely to extend to other minorities.

Equal protection clause of the Fourteenth Amendment prevents state and federal governments from denying people equal protection of the law. It has been interpreted to prevent the government from unfairly discriminating against people.

Equal Rights Amendment was a proposed amendment to the Constitution that was the focus of much of the **second wave** feminist movement. It stated, "Equality of rights under the law shall not be denied or abridged by the United States or by any State on account of sex."

Ethnicity concerns categories of people based on shared cultural traits, such as language or religion.

Executive Order 8802 was issued by President Franklin Roosevelt and created the President's Committee on Fair Employment Practices (FEPC), which has served as a model for future presidents' efforts to combat discrimination in the government.

Executive Order 10479 was signed by President Eisenhower, and along with other things, it required government contractors to post antidiscrimination policies.

Executive Order 10925 was issued by President Kennedy in 1965 to help eliminate discrimination against African Americans and was the first to use the term *affirmative action*. It required the government and government contractors to take "affirmative action," or positive steps to increase employment of African Americans.

Executive Order 11246 was signed by President Lyndon Johnson in 1967 and requires government contractors to have affirmative action plans to ensure that racial and ethnic minorities are hired and not discriminated against.

Executive Order 11375 prohibits discrimination and requires affirmative action on account of sex. President Johnson signed it in 1967.

External efficacy is the belief that the government is generally open to the influence of non-elites. Although historically African Americans and women had low levels of external efficacy, that has changed in recent years.

Feminist consciousness is a particular type of **gender consciousness** with an emphasis on equality between the sexes.

First wave women's or feminist movement was the suffrage movement, which started at the Seneca Falls Convention in 1848 and culminated with the ratification of the Nineteenth Amendment in 1920.

Formalistic representation refers to how the formal rules or laws affect how individuals are selected as representatives.

Free rider problem suggests that since people will receive the benefits associated with umbrella policies, it is not rational to participate.

Gender is a social construct referring to differences between men and women due to societal pressures or socialization. When referring to gender, the norm is to use the terms *men* and *women*.

Gender consciousness has been used to describe the belief that one's gender has important political implications.

Gender identity refers to the sex individuals identify with and perform in society. Political issues related to gender identity tend to affect people who are transgender.

Gender nonconformity refers to not identifying or presenting oneself as any one gender or sex.

Gendered institutions are institutions whose processes, norms, rules, and structures have a gender in that they were made with gender biases, and people's gender affects the way they are treated in the institution. Many political institutions are thought to be masculine.

Generational effect refers to the manner in which key historical events in the lives of an age cohort affect its members' values and beliefs.

Generational replacement refers to younger generations replacing older generations as older ones die off. Generational replacement is likely to result in more support for minority interests.

Grandfather clauses were clauses attached to laws, such as poll taxes, that essentially indicated if your grandfather could not vote, then you would have to pay the tax. The Supreme Court ruled these unconstitutional in 1915.

Group consciousness generally is the idea that an individual is aware of her identity with a group and sees that identity as politically important.

Group position model holds that individuals who have high levels of racial alienation will see other groups in a more competitive light.

Hate crimes are crimes that target people who belong to groups that are oppressed and less protected in society.

Heightened scrutiny is a standard used in sex discrimination cases. With this standard, the government has to prove either that it did not discriminate or that it did so to meet an important governmental interest. An important interest is not as important as a compelling interest. If the government can prove it has an important interest with this test, it just needs to indicate that the discrimination helps meet that interest.

Ideology is a set of attitudes that are held together by some larger understanding of the proper role of government such that the set of attitudes people have should follow a logical sequence. Minorities are more likely to be liberal than conservative.

Implicit prejudice is less visible than explicit prejudice.

Individualistic culture is a type of political culture found in U.S. states. It is associated with more government corruption and the idea that the government is there to foster private interests.

Influence districts are legislative districts where minorities do not make up a majority but are a large enough voting bloc that they have influence over who wins.

Internal efficacy is an individual's belief that he or she can affect government action. Minorities tend to have relatively high levels of internal efficacy.

Intersectionality suggests that there is variation among people based on the combination of race, gender, and class: what it means to be an African American man is different from being a white man, or an African American woman is different from what it means to be a white, Asian, or American Indian woman, or an African American lesbian is different than a straight African American woman.

Jim Crow laws were predominantly found in Southern states in the mid-1900s that segregated African Americans and whites in public places, such as public transportation and schools.

Job segregation is a term from gender studies that refers to the tendency for women to hold some types of jobs and men others. The term can also be applied to employment variation with regard to race and ethnicity.

Judicial review is the power the courts have to determine if an action taken by the other branches of government violates the Constitution. It gives the courts policymaking power.

La Raza Unida is a political party of Mexican Americans. It elected local candidates in Texas during the 1960s and 1970s.

Life cycle effects suggest that as people go through different stages of their lives, different things are important to them, and that this can affect their attitudes or opinions.

Linked fate refers to the belief that individuals of a group are distinguished by society such that the fate of one person in the group is linked to the fate of all in the group.

Literacy tests required would-be voters to pass a test before they could register to vote. The Voting Rights Act prohibits literacy tests.

Loving v. Virginia (1967) is a case that declared antimiscegenation laws unconstitutional because they violate the equal protection class.

Majority-minority districts are electoral districts that have a majority of racial or ethnic minority voters. They were created to increase the number of minority members of Congress.

Mattachine Society was an early gay rights organization started in 1951.

MEChA means "matchstick" and stands for Movimiento Estudiantil Chicano de Aztlan. MEChA is active on college campuses and encourages universities to be more open to Mexican American students, including the creation of Chicano studies programs.

Minorities are defined as groups of people who are underrepresented in and by the government.

Mississippi Freedom Democratic Party was a party created by African Americans in Mississippi. It sought to have its delegate recognized at the 1964 Democratic convention.

Modern sexism is the belief held by some people that women are no longer discriminated against, and they therefore do not support programs to increase gender equality.

Moralistic culture is a type of political culture found in U.S. states. It is associated with the view of government as a social good and is associated with high levels of participation by the masses.

Multimember districts occur where there are multiple representatives for a single district. They are thought to increase the representation of women but not racial and ethnic minorities.

Occupy Wall Street movement was a short-lived movement that started in 2011 in Zuccotti Park in New York City to protest the growing disparity between the wealthy 1% and the remaining 99%.

Old fashioned racism is the belief that African Americans have less innate ability than whites.

Old fashioned sexism is the belief that women are less competent, and that traditional gender roles are preferred.

Panel effects are the effect that the presence of a minority judge has on other judges' decisions.

Panethnic identity involves individuals feeling part of a group that has many nationalities or ethnicities, such as Mexican Americans identifying as Hispanic instead of Mexican, or Chinese Americans identifying as Asian American instead of Chinese.

Party identification has two definitions. One is that of a psychological attachment to a party that comes from one's socialization or upbringing. The other view of party identification is that of a running tally. People who identify with the Democratic Party tend to more strongly support policies supported by minorities or to advance minority rights, than those who identify with the Republican Party.

Passive representation is similar to **descriptive representation**.

Plessy v. Ferguson (1896) is a court case that established the "separate but equal" doctrine, which permitted Jim Crow laws and weakened the impact of the Fourteenth Amendment's equal protection clause.

Policy diffusion describes how policies spread from one state to another. Although there are several ways policies can spread, it is common for them to spread to neighboring states.

Political efficacy is the belief that people can affect the government. Minorities have relatively low levels of efficacy.

Political opportunity structure focuses on how political and cultural institutions can affect the ability of movements to be successful.

Political participation has many definitions but generally involves activities on the part of citizens to affect government decisions and decision makers.

Political socialization is the process by which individuals learn about politics, its actors, and issues.

Poll tax is a fee or tax people had to pay before they could vote. These were used to disenfranchise African Americans and were prohibited by the **Twenty-Fourth Amendment** (1964) and the Voting Rights Act.

Power hypothesis suggests that coalitions are unlikely to form where there is social distance between groups and that social distance is affected by how similar groups are to each other.

Priming occurs when a stimulus affects what individuals are thinking about or how they perceive something.

Proportional representation occurs when the number of legislative seats is distributed to the parties based on their vote totals. These electoral systems allow for quotas and are thought to be beneficial for minorities.

Proposition 209 outlawed the strongest forms of affirmative action; it was passed by California's voters in 1996.

Quasi-suspect classes are minority groups that have a history of being discriminated against, but the discrimination is not as severe or may be more justifiable than with suspect classes. Sex is the main quasi-suspect class. When individuals in a quasi-suspect class bring a discrimination suit, the court will use the heightened or intermediate scrutiny standard.

Race is a way to categorize individuals by a physical trait (often color of skin) caused by a shared ancestry. Race is best thought of as a social construct.

Raced institutions are institutions whose processes, norms, rules, and structures have biases based on the experiences of white people. Most U.S. political institutions are thought to be raced.

Racial profiling involves the police targeting individuals to investigate for possible criminal activity because of personal traits, such as race or ethnicity.

Racial threat initially referred to a phenomenon that whites had more negative views toward African Americans in areas with larger African American populations. The idea has been expanded to include a general phenomenon where people in a dominant group feel threatened when a minority group gains power.

Racial threat hypothesis suggests that members of a majority group who live in an area where there is a large number of minorities may come to fear that a minority group will threaten their way of life.

Rainbow coalition theory (also see **cooperative theory** and **shared interest theory**) predicts that since minorities have much in common, multiminority coalitions are likely.

Rational choice models predict that people will engage in activities if they benefit more by the engagement than it costs them. It has been used extensively to explain political participation.

Reconstruction refers to a period following the Civil War when the federal government oversaw the treatment of the African Americans in the South.

Regents of the University of California v. Bakke (1978) is a case in which the Court ruled that universities cannot use quotas as they try to increase diversity. It is also known for Powell's opinion that indicated diversity in education is a compelling interest.

Relational goods are benefits individuals may receive by being members of group.

Representative bureaucracy refers to the importance of having a diverse bureaucracy for the fair implementation of policies. It assumes government decisions affect most aspects of society, bureaucrats affect those decisions, bureaucrats use their own values to make decisions, and their values are related to socio-demographic traits because of socialization and experiences.

Resegregation refers to schools becoming segregated after they had become more desegregated in the 1980s.

Resource mobilization theory focuses on organizations' resources and how they affect a movements' success.

Restrictive covenants were clauses in contracts that prevented people from selling their home to African Americans. They violate the equal protection clause.

Reverse discrimination is a term used to describe a program that has the effect of discriminating against nonminorities.

Second wave women's movement or feminist movement started in the 1960s. It is most strongly associated with the battle for the **Equal Rights Amendment.**

Self-interest theory holds that individuals may fear that other minorities may make it harder for them personally to find jobs, housing, or may otherwise decrease the quality of their lives.

Separate but equal doctrine was established in *Plessy v. Ferguson* (1896), which indicated that the Fourteenth Amendment did not prevent segregation as long as there were "separate but equal" facilities.

Sex refers to the biological differences between males and females, such that females tend to have two X chromosomes and can give birth, whereas males tend to have one X and one Y chromosome and produce sperm. Generally the terms *male* and *female* are used in reference to sex differences.

Sexual orientation refers to whether individuals are romantically attracted to people of their own sex or people of the other sex, either sex, or neither sex.

Shadow members of Congress are members who lack voting authority but otherwise can participate in Congressional action.

Shared interest theory (also see **cooperation** and **rainbow coalition theory**) predicts that since minorities have much in common, coalitions are likely.

Shaw v. Reno (1993) is a case in which the Court ruled in a 5–4 decision that drawing district boundaries based on race was unconstitutional. The ruling limits the ability of states to create majority-minority districts.

Shelby County v. Holder (2013) is a Supreme Court case that invalidated section 4 of the Voting Rights Act. This section concerned the requirements for preclearance and had the effect of negating sections 4 and 5.

Single-member districts are political areas divided into districts with each district getting one representative; they are associated with higher racial and ethnic descriptive representation since they allow for majority-minority districts.

Social constructs are categories that have meaning because society treats those in that category uniquely, but the category may not have an intrinsic meaning.

Social identity threats theory holds that when people feel threatened, they build their own self-esteem by seeing other minorities in a negative light. It predicts that discrimination will make multiminority coalitions more difficult.

Socioeconomic status (SES) is a term used instead of class in the United States. It refers to individuals' levels of education and wealth. Minorities tend to have lower levels of income but not necessarily education than nonminorities.

Statutory interpretation occurs when the courts determine what the law means. As courts interpret the law, they can indicate what the policy really means, giving courts policymaking power.

Stonewall Riot was a riot that broke out when police raided a New York City gay bar in 1969. It is often seen as the start of the modern LGBT movement.

Stratification beliefs model suggests that individuals who have high levels of individualism, believing people's fate depends on their own abilities, see less conflict between minority groups than those who believe that individuals' fate is affected by their race, class, or gender.

Street-level bureaucrats are bureaucrats who work directly with clientele. Minority street-level bureaucrats tend to offer more active representation for minorities than administrators.

Strict scrutiny is a standard used to interpret the equal protection clause in discrimination cases involving race. With this standard, the government needs to prove either that it did not discriminate against someone because of race or doing so met a compelling governmental interest. Even if there is a compelling interest, discrimination has to be the "least restrictive means" to obtain that interest.

Substantive representation, also called **policy representation**, concerns whether representatives or the government act in a manner that affects the represented's interests.

Surrogate representation occurs when representatives feel a need to work on the interests of a group of people who are not their voters, such as African American representatives feeling a need to represent African Americans regardless of where they live.

Suspect classes are minority groups who have a history of being discriminated against. Race, religion, and national origin are the primary suspect classes. When individuals in a suspect class bring a discrimination suit, the court will use the strict scrutiny standard.

Swing states are those that have the greatest effect on presidential elections since they can swing toward either party. They get the most focus in presidential elections. Minorities were not as likely as nonminorities to live in swing states during the 2012 presidential election, depressing their electoral power.

Symbolic racism describes a common form of racism today. It involves people believing that African Americans' lack of success is due to their not working hard enough as opposed to discrimination or innate abilities. Thus, programs like affirmative action are not needed.

Symbolic representation focuses on how people, places, and things can "stand for" or be a symbol of something else, such as a rainbow has come to represent LGBT rights. Since it concerns how people feel about or react to the government, this book examines symbolic representation by examining minorities' attitudes toward the government and policymakers.

Traditionalistic culture is a type of political culture found in U.S. states. It is concentrated in the South and is associated with a belief that the government is there to maintain order. It also tends to have a group of people who govern with the masses being less active. States with a traditional culture tend to have lower levels of descriptive representation.

Trust is a measure of symbolic representations that taps peoples' views toward the government. It is often measured by the following question: "How much do you trust the government in Washington to do what is right?" Women and African Americans tend to have relatively low levels of trust, but Hispanics and Asian Americans tend to have relatively high levels.

Unconventional political participation is using non-institutionalized means to influence the government, and involves actions such as boycotts, demonstrations, and civil disobedience.

U.S. Equal Employment Opportunity Act of 1972 requires local governments that want to receive federal dollars to not discriminate and to have affirmative action plans.

U.S. Supreme Court is the highest court in the United States. Most of the cases are heard on appeal after the cases have been heard at the appellate level.

Values are the long-term standards people use to make evaluations.

Viva Kennedy Clubs were groups of Mexican Americans who supported John F. Kennedy's 1960 presidential campaign. Many members were disappointed by Kennedy's lack of interest in their issues after he was elected.

Voter dilution involves efforts to minimize the impact of minority votes. It includes such things as cracking the minority vote into many districts.

Voter ID laws require voters to show some form of identification before casting their votes. These laws vary from requiring a government-issued photo ID before submitting a ballot, to presenting almost any type of identification.

Voting cues are shorthand cues, such as race, ethnicity, and gender, that voters use to guess candidates' traits and issue positions.

Voting Rights Act is a key piece of legislation passed in 1965 that prohibits state and local governments from enacting laws that have voting requirements that deny or limit voting on account of race, regardless of the intention of the law.

Warren Court (1953–1969) refers to the time during which Earl Warren was chief justice of the Supreme Court. It is known for having made numerous decisions advancing minority rights.

White primaries prevented African Americans from voting in Southern primaries. The Supreme Court ruled in 1944 that white primaries violated the Fifteenth Amendment.

Widow effect describes the phenomenon of women following their husbands into Congress upon their husbands' death.

Women friendly districts are districts that are likely to have women candidates and officials. They tend to be in Northern and Western states, urban areas, have residents who have high levels of SES, and tend to have a large percentage of women in the workforce.

Year of the woman (1992) was known for a large number of women who ran for and won seats in Congress.

Notes

Preface

1. Hope Yen, "Census: White Majority in U.S. Gone by 2043," *USNews* and *NBC News*, June 13, 2013, http://usnews.nbcnews.com/_news/2013/06/13/18934111-census-white-majority-in-us-gone-by-2043?lite
2. Judith Lorber, *Gender Inequality: Feminist Theories and Politics*, 3rd ed. (Los Angeles, CA: Roxbury, 2005), 200.
3. Hanna Fenichel Pitkin, *The Concept of Representation* (Berkeley: University of California Press, 1967).
4. Jim Endersby, "Lumpers and Splitters: Darwin, Hooker and the Search for Order." *Science* 362 no. 5959 (2009) 1496–1499. http://www.sciencemag.org/content/326/5959/1496.full#ref-14.

Chapter 1

1. Paula D. McClain and Joseph Stewart Jr., *Can We All Get Along? Racial and Ethnic Minorities in American Politics* (Boulder, CO: Westview, 2014), 153–155.
2. McClain and Stewart, *Can We All Get Along?* 154.
3. Charles W. Carery Jr., *A to Z of African Americans: African-American Political Leaders* (New York: Facts on File, 2004).
4. Shirley Chisholm, *Unbought and UnBossed* (Boston, MA: Houghton Mifflin, 1970), 53.
5. LaVerne McCain Gill, *African American Women in Congress: Forming and Transforming History* (New Brunswick, NJ: Rutgers University Press, 1997).
6. Amy Alexander, *Fifty Black Women Who Changed America* (New York: Kensington Publishing, 2003).
7. Gill, *African American Women,* 28.
8. Judith Lorber, *Gender Inequality: Feminist Theories and Politics*, 3rd ed. (Los Angeles, CA: Roxbury, 2005), 200.
9. Kimberle Crenshaw. "Mapping the Margins: Intersectionality, Identity Politics, and Violence against Women of Color," *Stanford Law Review* 43, no. 6 (1991): 1241–1299.
10. Jessica Trounstine and Melody E. Valdini, "The Context Matters: The Effects of Single-Member versus At-Large Districts on City Council Diversity," *American Journal of Political Science* 52, no. 3 (2008): 554–569.
11. Hope Yen, "Census: White Majority in U.S. Gone by 2043," *USNews and NBC News*, June 13, 2013, http://usnews.nbcnews.com/_news/2013/06/13/18934111-census-white-majority-in-us-gone-by-2043?lite.
12. Will Oremus, "Here Are All the Different Genders You Can Be on Facebook," *Slate*, February 13, 2014, http://www.slate.com/blogs/future_tense/2014/02/13/facebook_custom_gender_options_here_are_all_56_custom_options.html.
13. Oremus, "Here Are All the Different."
14. See Michael LeMay, *The Perennial Struggle: Race, Ethnicity, and Minority Group Relations in the United States,* 3rd ed. (Upper Saddle River, NJ: Prentice Hall, 2009), 4–12, for a discussion.
15. See the following link for information on indigenous Latin Americans: http://www.iwgia.org/regions/latin-america/indigenous-peoples-in-latin-america.
16. Sibylla Brodzinsky, "African Heritage in Latin America," *Christian Science Monitor*, February 12, 2013, http://www.csmonitor.com/World/Americas/2013/0212/African-heritage-in-Latin-America.
17. For a discussion of the tensions between ethnic minorities and the Chinese government, see Chinafile, "Are Ethnic Tensions on the Rise in China," *The World Post*, March 3, 2014, http://www.huffingtonpost.com/2014/03/03/china-ethnic-tensions_n_4892675.html.
18. Ian Traynor, "The Language Divide at the Heart of a Split That Is Tearing Belgium Apart," *The Guardian*, May 9, 2010, http://www.theguardian.com/world/2010/may/09/belgium-flanders-wallonia-french-dutch.
19. Traynor, "The Language Divide."
20. Raphael Minder, "Catalonia Overwhelmingly for Independence from Spain in Straw Poll," *New York Times*, November 9, 2015, http://www.nytimes.com/2014/11/10/world/europe/catalans-vote-in-straw-poll-on-independence-from-spain.html?_r=0.
21. Calculated from information from http://www.dailymail.co.uk/news/article-2758795/Europe-divided-Map-shows-continent-look-separatist-movement-got-wish.html.
22. http://www.oecd.org/els/mig/imo2013.htm.
23. Patrick Ireland, *Becoming Europe: Immigration, Integration and the Welfare State* (Pittsburgh, PA: University of Pittsburgh Press, 2004).
24. Cecile Alduy, "The Devil's Daughter," *The Atlantic*, October 2013, http://www.theatlantic.com/magazine/archive/2013/10/the-devils-daughter/309467/.

25. Bruce Stokes and Russ Oates, "A Fragile Rebound for EU Image on Eve of European Parliament Elections: EU Favorability Rises, but Majorities Say Their Voice Is Not Heard in Brussels," May 12, 2014, http://www.pewglobal.org/2014/05/12/chapter-4-views-of-roma-muslims-jews/.

26. McClain and Stewart, *Can We All Get Along?* 58–63.

27. McClain and Stewart, *Can We All Get Along?* 9; Noelani Goodyear-Kaopua, Ikaika Hussey, and Erin Kahunawaikaala Wright, eds., *A Nation Rising: Hawaiian Movements for Life, Land, and Sovereignty* (Durham, NC: Duke University Press, 2014).

28. In Middle Eastern areas of Africa, Egyptians and other Middle Easterners are white.

29. The question asked: "Some people say the term "African-American" should be used instead of the word "black." Which term do you prefer—"African-American" or "black,"—does it not matter to you either way?" Frank Newport, "Black or African-American? African American slightly preferred among those who have a preference," September 28, 2007, http://www.gallup.com/poll/28816/Black-African-American.aspx.

30. https://www.cia.gov/library/publications/the-world-factbook/wfbExt/region_cam.html, accessed April 6, 2015.

31. Sonya Rastogi, Tallese D. Johnson, Elizabeth M. Hoeffel, and Malcolm P. Drewery, Jr., "The Black Population: 2010: 2010 Census Briefs," September 11, http://www.census.gov/prod/cen2010/briefs/c2010br-06.pdf.

32. Ira Berlin, "The Changing Definition of African-American: How the Great Influx of People from Africa and the Caribbean since 1965 Is Challenging What It Means to Be African-American," *Smithsonian*, February 2010, http://www.smithsonianmag.com/departments/presence-of-mind/The-Changing-Definition-of-African-American.html?c=y&page=2.

33. Elizabeth M. Grieco, "Race and Hispanic Origin of the Foreign-Born Population in the United States: 2007," January 2010, http://www.census.gov/prod/2010pubs/acs-11.pdf, Table 1.

34. Jesse McKinnon, "Black Population: 2000," August 2001, http://www.census.gov/prod/2001pubs/c2kbr01-5.pdf.

35. According to the census, 12.6% identified only as African American, and 13.6% identified as African American or as African American, and at least one other race. Karen R. Humes, Nicholas A. Jones, and Roberto R. Ramirez, "Overview of Race and Hispanic Origin: 2010," March 2011, http://www.census.gov/prod/cen2010/briefs/c2010br-02.pdf.

36. 4.8% identified as only Asian, and an additional 0.9% identified as Asian along with another race (Elizabeth M. Hoeffel, Sonya Rastogi, Myong Ouk Kim, and Hasan Shahid, "The Asian Population: 2010: 2010 Census Briefs," March 2012, http://www.census.gov/prod/cen2010/briefs/c2010br-11.pdf, 4). These figures do not include Native Hawaiians or other Pacific Islanders. Collectively, this group is only about 0.5% of the population.

37. Hoeffel, Rastogi, Kim, and Shahid, "The Asian Population," 4.

38. For a quick summary of discrimination faced by Chinese, see Kenneth J. Guest, "Chinese Exclusion Act of 1882," in *Encyclopedia of Racism in the United States: Vol. 1: A–H*, ed. Pyong Gap Min (Westport, CT: Greenwood Press, 2005), 117–121.

39. Daisuke Akiba, "Japanese American Internment," in *Encyclopedia of Racism in the United States: Vol. 2: I–R*, ed. Pyong Gap Min (Westport, CT: Greenwood Press, 2005), 318–326.

40. Sookhee Oh, "South Asians, Ambiguity in Racial Identity Among," in *Encyclopedia of Racism in the United States: Vol. 3, S–Z*, ed. Pyong Gap Min (Westport, CT: Greenwood Press, 2005), 592–594.

41. Elizabeth M. Hoeffel, Sonya Rastogi, Myong Ouk Kim, and Hasan Shahid, "The Asian Population: 2010." Note, however, that some groups increase at a higher rate, but their numbers were very small in 2000. For example, the number of Bhutanese went from 192 to almost 19,000, an increase of over 9600%.

42. Clyde Tucker, Brian Kojetin, and Roderick Harrison, "A Statistical Analysis of the CPS Supplement on Race and Ethnic Origin," 1995, http://www.census.gov/prod/2/gen/96arc/ivatuck.pdf, Table 4.

43. About 0.9% only identified as American Indian, and an additional 0.7% identified as American Indian and at least one other race.

44. Stephen L. Pevar, *The Rights of Indians and Tribes*, 4th ed. (New York: Oxford University Press, 2012), chap. 3.

45. David E. Wilkins and Heidi K. Stark, *American Indian Politics and the American Political System*, 3rd ed. (Lanham, MD: Rowman & Littlefield, 2011), chap. 10.

46. Wilkins and Stark, *American Indian Politics*, chap. 2.

47. Wilkins and Stark, *American Indian Politics*, chap. 2.

48. Wilkins and Stark, *American Indian Politics*, 45.

49. Daniel McCool, Susan M. Olson, and Jennifer L. Robinson, *Native Vote: American Indians, the Voting Rights Act, and the Right to Vote* (New York: Cambridge University Press 2007), 9.

50. Goodyear-Kaopua, Hussey, and Wright, *A Nation Rising.*

51. For more on the Freedmen, see http://www.okhistory.org/publications/enc/entry.php?entry=FR016.

52. Sean Murphy, "Cherokee Freedmen Controversy: Court Lets Slaves' Descendants Sue Cherokee Chief," December 14, 2012, http://www.huffingtonpost.com/2012/12/14/cherokee-freedmen-court-slaves-descendants-sue-chief_n_2302124.html; Will Chavez, "Update: Freedman Descendants Have Citizenship Restored and May Vote Sept. 24," *Cherokee Phoenix*, September 21, 2011.

53. Wilkins and Stark, *American Indian Politics.*

54. Lemay, *Perennial Struggle*, chap. 4.

55. The categorization of people by use of the Spanish language was instigated by the census in 1970.

56. D'Vera Cohn, "Hispanic? Latino? Or...?" April 4, 2012. http://www.pewsocialtrends.org/2012/04/04/hispanic-latino-or/.

57. Sharon R. Ennis, Merarys Rios-Vergas, and Nora G. Albert, "Hispanic Population: Census Brief: 2010," May 2011, http://www.census.gov/prod/cen2010/briefs/c2010br-04.pdf.

58. Ennis, Rios-Vergas, and Albert, "Hispanic Population."

59. http://quickfacts.census.gov/qfd/states/00000.html.

60. McClain and Stewart, *Can We All Get Along?* 18.

61. http://www.usimmigrationsupport.org/wetfoot-dryfoot.html.

62. Mark Lopez, "Three-fourths of Hispanics Say Their Community Needs a Leader," October 22, 2013, http://www.pewhispanic.org/files/2013/10/National_Latino_Leader_10-2013_FINAL.pdf.

63. Lemay, *Perennial Struggle*, chap. 4.

64. Lemay, *Perennial Struggle,* 124.

65. Lemay, *Perennial Struggle*, 124–126.

66. http://www.isna.org/ or http://aiclegal.org/.

67. Judith Lorber, *Gender Inequality: Feminist Theories and Politics*, 3rd ed. (Los Angeles, CA: Roxbury, 2005), 29.

68. Judith Lorber, *Gender Inequality,* chap. 11.

69. Lindsay M. Howden and Julie A. Meyer, "Age and Sex Composition: 2010: 2010 Census Briefs," May 2011, http://www.census.gov/prod/cen2010/briefs/c2010br-03.pdf.

70. Edith Barrett, "The Policy Priorities of African American Women in State Legislatures," *Legislative Studies Quarterly* 20, no. 2 (1995): 223–247.

71. Luis Ricardo Fraga, Linda Lopez, Valerie Martinez-Ebers, and Ricardo Ramirez, "Gender and Ethnicity: Patterns of Electoral Success and Legislative Advocacy among Latina and Latino State Officials in Four States," *Journal of Women, Politics & Policy* 28, no. 3–4 (2006): 121–145.

72. Gary J. Gates, "How Many People Are Lesbian, Gay, Bisexual and Transgender?" The Williams Institute at UCLA School of Law, April 2011, http://williamsinstitute.law.ucla.edu/research/census-lgbt-demographics-studies/how-many-people-are-lesbian-gay-bisexual-and-transgender/.

73. Lorber, *Gender Inequality,* 9.

74. There are several limitations to relying on behavior as a measure of sexual orientation. Some people are celibate but still may be attracted to individuals of one sex or the other. Additionally, some gays and lesbians may have partners of the opposite sex but do so to hide their sexual orientation. Or people may have same-sex partners but do not identify as gay or lesbian.

75. Jaime M. Grant, Lisa A. Motter, and Justin Tanis, "Injustice at Every Turn: A Report of the National Transgender Discrimination Survey," 2011, http://www.thetaskforce.org/downloads/reports/reports/ntds_full.pdf.

76. Michelle A. Gibson, Jonathan Alexander, and Deborah Meem, *Finding Out: An Introduction to LGBT Studies* (Thousand Oaks, CA: Sage, 2014), chap. 5.

77. Gary Gates and Frank Newport, "LGBT Percentage Highest in D.C., Lowest in North Dakota," February 15, 2013, http://www.gallup.com/poll/160517/lgbt-percentage-highest-lowest-north-dakota.aspx.

78. Gates, "How Many People Are Lesbian."

79. The question asked, "Do you, personally, identify as gay, lesbian, bisexual or transgender?"

80. Rich Morin, "Study: Polls May Underestimate Anti-gay Sentiment and Size of Gay, Lesbian Population," October 9, 2013, http://www.pewresearch.org/fact-tank/2013/10/09/study-polls-may-underestimate-anti-gay-sentiment-and-size-of-gay-lesbian-population/.

81. Hanna Fenichel Pitkin, *The Concept of Representation* (Berkeley: University of California Press, 1967).

82. Although Pitkin (1967) classifies symbolic and descriptive representation both as part of "stand for" representation, for the purposes of this book it helps to discuss them separately.

83. Quoted in Pitkin, *The Concept of Representation*, 60.

84. Jane Mansbridge, "Should Blacks Represent Blacks and Women Represent Women? A Contingent Yes," *Journal of Politics* 61, no. 3 (1999): 628–657.

85. Suzanne Dovi, "Preferable Descriptive Representatives: Will Just Any Woman, Black or Hispanic Do?" *American Political Science Review* 96, no. 4 (2002): 729–743.

86. Katherine Tate, *Black Faces in the Mirror: African Americans and Their Representatives in the U.S. Congress* (Princeton, NJ: Princeton University Press, 2003); Donald D. Haider-Markel, *Out and Running: Gay and Lesbian Candidates, Election, and Policy Representation* (Washington, DC: George Washington University Press, 2010); Kimberly Cowell-Meyers and Laura Langbein, "Linking Women's Descriptive and Substantive Representation in the United States," *Politics & Gender* 5, no. 4 (2009): 491–518; Michael B. Berkman and Robert O'Connor, "Do Women Legislators Matter?" *American Politics Quarterly* 2, no. 1 (1993): 102–124; Chris T. Owens, "Black Substantive Representation in State Legislatures from 1971–1994," *Social Science Quarterly* 86, no. 4 (2005): 780–791.

87. Dovi, "Preferable Descriptive Representatives," 730, summarizes Anne Phillips, "Democracy and Representation: Or, Why Should It Matter Who Our Representatives Are?" *Feminism and Politics* (Oxford: Oxford University Press, 1998), 224–240.

88. Haider-Markel, *Out and Running*; Tate, *Black Faces*; Jason P. Casellas, "Coalitions in the House? The Election of Minorities to State Legislatures and Congress," *Political Research Quarterly* 62, no. 1 (2009a):120–131; Jason P. Casellas, "The Institutional and Demographic Determinants of Latino Representation," *Legislative Studies Quarterly* 34, no. 3 (2009): 399–426; Robert E. Hogan, "The Influence of State and District Conditions on the Representation of Women in the U.S. State Legislatures," *American*

Politics Research 29, no. 4 (2001): 4–24; Heather L. Ondercin and Susan Welch, "Comparing Predictors of Women's Congressional Election Success: Candidates, Primaries, and the General Election," *American Politics Research* 37, no. 4 (2009): 593–613; Heather L. Ondercin and Susan Welch, "Women Candidates for Congress," in *Women and Elective Office: Past, Present, and Future*, ed. Susan Thomas and Clyde Wilcox (New York: Oxford University Press, 2005), 60–80; Barbara Palmer and Dennis Simon, *Breaking the Political Glass Ceiling: Women and Congressional Elections* (New York: Routledge, 2006), chap. 6.

89. B. Keith Payne, Jon A. Krosnick, Josh Pasek, Yphtach Lelkes, Omair Akhtar, and Trevor Thompson, "Implicit and Explicit Prejudice in the 2008 American Presidential Election," *Journal of Experimental Social Psychology* 46, no. 2 (2010): 367–374; Cindy D. Kam, "Implicit Attitudes, Explicit Choices: When Subliminal Priming Predicts Candidate Preference," *Political Behavior* 29, no. 3 (2007): 343–367; Mark S. Leeper, "The Impact of Prejudice on Female Candidates: An Experimental Look at Voter Inference," *American Politics Quarterly* 19, no. 2 (1991): 248–261;Virginia Sapiro, "If U.S. Senator Baker Were a Woman: An Experimental Study of Candidate Images," *Political Psychology* 3, no. 1 (1981–1982): 61–83; Rebekah Herrick and Sue Thomas, "Gays and Lesbians in Local Races: A Study of Electoral Viability," *Journal of Homosexuality* 42, no. 1 (2001): 103–126.

90. Richard L. Fox and Jennifer L. Lawless, "Entering the Arena? Gender and the Decision to Run for Office," *American Journal of Political Science* 48, no. 2 (2004): 264–280; Gbemende Johnson, Bruce I. Oppenheimer, and Jennifer L. Selin, "The House as a Stepping Stone to the Senate: Why Do So Few African American House Members Run?" *American Journal of Political Science* 56, no. 2 (2012): 387–399.

91. Pitkin, *Concept of Representation*; Leslie A. Schwindt-Bayer and William Mishler, "An Integrated Model of Women's Representation," *Journal of Politics* 67, no. 2 (2005): 407–428.

92. William H. Flanigan, Nancy H. Zingale, Elizabeth A. Theiss-Morse, and Michael W. Wagner, *Political Behavior of the American Electorate*, 13th ed. (Washington, DC: Sage/CQ Press, 2015), 83–84.

93. Operationalized is a fancy way to talk about how a researcher measures important concepts.

94. Rodney E. Hero and Caroline Tolbert, "Latinos and Substantive Representation in the U.S. House of Representatives: Direct, Indirect, or Nonexistent?" *American Journal of Political Science* 39, no. 3 (1995): 640–652.

95. Michelle L. Swers, *The Difference Women Make: The Policy Impact of Women in Congress* (Chicago: University of Chicago Press, 2002), 10.

96. Tate, *Black Faces in the Mirror*, chap. 4.

97. Schwindt-Bayer and Mishler, "An Integrated Model"; Pitkin, *Concept of Representation*.

98. Pitkin, *The Concept of Representation*, 97.

99. Schwindt-Bayer and Mishler, "An Integrated Model," 408.

100. Schwindt-Bayer and Mishler, "An Integrated Model."

101. Crenshaw, "Mapping the Margins."

102. Mary Hawkesworth, "Congressional Enactments of Race-Gender: Toward a Theory of Raced-Gendered Institutions," *American Political Science Review* 97, no. 4 (2003): 529–550.

103. Hawkesworth, "Race-Gender," 546.

Chapter 2

1. Michael Doyle, "Momentum for Revising Military Assault Law Shifts: 2 Democratic Senators Are Sparring over the Best Way to Proceed," *Charlotte Observer*, March 17, 2013, 9A.

2. The following sources were used in this description of the role women senators played in passage of the military assault law: Halimah Abdullah, "Political Fight over Military Sex Assaults Divides Women Senators," *CNN Wire*, March 7, 2014, http://www.cnn.com/2014/03/07/politics/military-sexual-assaults/; Jay Newton-Small, "Senate Women Tackle Sexual Assault in the Military," *Time*, November 19, 2013, http://swampland.time.com/2013/11/19/senate-women-tackle-sexual-assault-in-the-military/; Targeted, News Service, "Mikulski, Collins Lead Bipartisan Group of Senate Women Speaking on Senate Floor against Sexual Assault in the Military," November 20, 2013.

3. Newton-Small, "Senate Women Tackle"; Targeted News Service, "Mikulski, Collins Lead Bipartisan Group."

4. Abdullah, "Political Fight over Military Sex Assaults"; Newton-Small, "Senate Women Tackle."

5. Newton-Small, "Senate Women Tackle."

5. Newton-Small, "Senate Women Tackle"; Targeted News Service, "Mikulski, Collins Lead Bipartisan Group."

6. Newton-Small, "Senate Women Tackle"; Targeted News Service, "Mikulski, Collins Lead Bipartisan Group."

7. Julie Dolan, Melissa Deckman, and Michele L. Swers, *Women and Politics: Paths to Power and Political Influence* (Upper Saddle River, NJ: Pearson/Prentice Hall, 2007), 36.

8. http://www.cawp.rutgers.edu/fast_facts/levels_of_office/congress.php. Alma Adams (D) won in a special election in November 2014 and took office immediately. Thus, during the last two months of the 113th Congress, there were 80 women in the House and 100 in Congress.

9. http://history.house.gov/People/Listing/C/CARAWAY,-Hattie-Wyatt-(C000138)/, accessed April 17, 2015.

10. http://www.cawp.rutgers.edu/fast_facts/levels_of_office/documents/widows.pdf, accessed April 17, 2015.

11. http://www.senate.gov/artandhistory/history/common/briefing/minority_senators.htm.

12. Josephson, *Jeannette Rankin*.

13. Smith, *Jeannette Rankin*, 102.

14. Quoted by Josephson, *Jeannette Rankin*, 97–98.

15. Josephson, *Jeannette Rankin*, 80.

16. There were only 243 House members in the 1870s.

17. These figures were taken from *Vital Statistics of Congress*, http://www.brookings.edu/~/media/Research/Files/Reports/2013/07/vital-statistics-congress-mann-ornstein/Vital-Statistics-Chapter-1-Demographics-of-Members-of-Congress_UPDATE.pdf?la=en.

18. http://history.house.gov/People/Listing/R/REVELS,-Hiram-Rhodes-(R000166)/.

19. The first Hispanic to serve in Congress was Delegate Joseph Marion Hernández, who represented the Florida Territory in the 17th Congress from 1821 to 1823 and lost as a candidate for the 18th Congress. He had no party affiliation, though he later unsuccessfully ran for the Senate as a Whig. He was of Cuban descent.

20. http://history.house.gov/HistoricalHighlight/Detail/35356; http://history.house.gov/People/Listing/P/PACHECO,-Romualdo-(P000003)/; http://bioguide.congress.gov/scripts/biodisplay.pl?index=P000003.

21. http://history.house.gov/People/Listing/P/PACHECO,-Romualdo-(P000003)/.

22. These numbers were calculated from https://www.senate.gov/artandhistory/history/common/briefing/minority_senators.htm.

23. Lorraine H. Tong, "CRS Report for Congress: Asian Pacific Americans in the United States Congress," *FAS* June 12, 2013, http://fas.org/sgp/crs/misc/97-398.pdf.

24. Dalip Singh Saund, http://www.encyclopedia.com/doc/1G2-2506300146.html.

25. Paula D. McClain and Joseph Stewart Jr., *Can We All Get Along? Racial and Ethnic Minorities in American Politics* (Boulder, CO: Westview, 2014), 161.

26. McClain and Stewart, *Can We All Get Along?* 164.

27. https://www.kshs.org/kansapedia/charles-curtis/12029 (accessed April 17, 2015).

28. http://www.senate.gov/artandhistory/history/common/generic/American_Indian_Heritage_Month.htm; McClain and Stewart, *Can We All Get Along?* 164.

29. Interview with Claudia Dreifus in September and October 1995, published in *Times Magazine*, February 4, 1996.

30. Michael Berenbaum and Fred Skolnik, *Encyclopaedia Judaica*, 2nd ed. (Detroit, MI: Macmillan Reference USA, 2007), 179–180.

31. "Rep. Frank Says He Is a Homosexual," *CQ Weekly Reports*, June 6, 1987, 1186.

32. "Rep. Frank Says He Is a Homosexual," 1186.

33. http://naacp.3cdn.net/cb0f6053dfa585f0ff_dom6vrdc6.pdf.

34. http://hrc-assets.s3-website-us-east-1.amazonaws.com//files/assets/resources/112thCongressionalScorecard_2012.pdf#__utma=149406063.212690201.1355933003.1410808303.1410808598.45&__utmb=149406063.1.10.1410808598&__utmc=149406063&__utmx=-&__utmz=149406063.1410808598.45.6.utmcsr=yahoolutmccn=(organic)lutmcmd=organiclutmctr=HRC%20scorecard&__utmv=-&__utmk=164084415.

35. http://www.aauwaction.org/wp-content/uploads/2012/09/CVR2012.pdf.

36. http://lulac.org/assets/pdfs/108thcongress-1-2.pdf. This figure is for the 108th Congress, the most recent scorecard available.

37. Shawn Zeller, "Frank Fights Old Allies after Axing Transgender Provision," *CQ Weekly Reports,* October 15, 2007, 2978.

38. "Frank Response," *CQ Weekly Reports*, May 22, 1993, 1303.

39. Janet Hook, "House Reprimands Frank, Refuses to Censure Him," *CQ Weekly Reports*, July 28, 1990, 2379.

40. Hook, "House Reprimands Frank," 2379.

41. Calculated by the author using data from CAWP, http://www.cawp.rutgers.edu/fast_facts/levels_of_office/documents/color.pdf.

42. Michael S. Rocha, Gabriel R. Sanchez, and Jason L. Morin, "The Institutional Mobility of Minority Members of Congress," *Political Research Quarterly* 54, no. 4 (2011): 897–909.

43. http://www.cawp.rutgers.edu/fast_facts/levels_of_office/documents/conglead.pdf.

44. Al Kamen and Colby Itkowitz, "Where Are the Women at Capitol Hill Hearings," *Washington Post*, September 11, 2014, http://www.washingtonpost.com/politics/where-are-the-women-at-capitol-hill-hearings/2014/09/11/ae08739a-39f3-11e4-bdfb-de4104544a37_story.html?wpisrc=nl_politics&wpmm=1.

45. The percentage of African Americans in Mississippi came from http://factfinder.census.gov/faces/nav/jsf/pages/index.xhtml, accessed April 16, 2015.

46. The percentage of African Americans in Vermont came from http://factfinder.census.gov/faces/nav/jsf/pages/index.xhtml, accessed April 16, 2015.

47. Becki Scola, "Women of Color in State Legislatures: Gender, Race, Ethnicity and Legislative Office Holding," *Journal of Women, Politics & Policy* 28, no. 3/4 (2006): 45.

48. http://history.house.gov/Exhibitions-and-Publications/BAIC/Historical-Data/Black-American-Representatives-and-Senators-by-Congress/; Norman J. Ornstein, Thomas E. Mann, Michael J. Malbin, Andrew Rugg, and Raffaela Wakeman, *Vital Statistics of Congress*, July 2013, brookings.edu/vitalstats; http://www.cawp.rutgers.edu.

49. Karen Grigsby Bates, "Why Did Black Voters Flee the Republican Party in the 1960s?" *NPR*, July 14, 2014, http://www.npr.org/blogs/codeswitch/2014/07/14/331298996/why-did-black-voters-flee-the-republican-party-in-the-1960s.

50. Melanie M. Hughes, "The Intersection of Gender and Minority Status in National Legislatures: The Minority Women Legislative Index," *Legislative Studies Quarterly* 38, no. 4 (2013): 489–516.

51. Hughes, "The Intersection of Gender," 506.

52. Tom Rea, "The Ambition of Nellie Tayloe Ross," http://www.wyohistory.org/essays/ambition-nellie-tayloe-ross, accessed April 14, 2015.

53. Her husband did not die but was impeached and could no longer hold office.

54. Governors James E. and Miriam "Ma" Ferguson Collection #3795, http://www.baylor.edu/content/services/document.php/155338.pdf, accessed April 14, 2015.

55. http://www.cawp.rutgers.edu/fast_facts/index.php.

56. Dolan, Deckman, and Swers, *Women and Politics,* 189.

57. http://www.cawp.rutgers.edu/fast_facts/index.php.

58. Laura van Assendelft, "Entry-Level Politics? Women as Candidates and Elected Officials at the Local Level," in *Women and Elective Office: Past, Present, and Future,* 3rd ed., ed. Sue Thomas and Clyde Wilcox (New York: Oxford University Press, 2014).

59. These were calculated by Anthony Gonzales in October of 2013 using the gay and lesbian victory fund information. It may slightly undercount mayors, as it only tracks those it endorses.

60. There was an African American lieutenant governor who was an acting governor for a brief period during Reconstruction.

61. Dwayne Yancey, "L. Douglas Wilder (1931-)," *Encyclopedia Virginia,* http://www.encyclopediavirginia.org/Wilder_Lawrence_Douglas_1931-#start_entry (accessed April 17, 2015).

62. McClain and Stewart, *Can We All Get Along?*

63. According to http://African Americandemographics.com/culture/African American-politics/African American-mayors/, there were forty-nine African American mayors, and according to the 2012 IMCA municipal yearbook 2012, there are roughly 680 cities with populations over 50,000.

64. Gov. Bill Richardson of New Mexico ran unsuccessfully for the Democratic Party nomination in 2008.

65. There have also been a handful of Hispanic governors of U.S. territories.

66. McClain and Stewart, *Can We All Get Along?* 171.

67. These were calculated by author from NALEO's directory.

68. In 2011 the question asked "Between now and the 2012 political conventions, there will be discussion about the qualification of presidential candidates—their education, age, religion, race and so on. If your party nominated a generally well-qualified person for president who happened to be a _____, would you vote for that person?"

69. Richard Matland and David King, "Women as Candidates in Congressional Elections," in *Women Transforming Congress*, ed. Cindy Simon Rosenthal (Norman: University of Oklahoma Press, 2002), 119–145; Jeffrey M. Jones, "Atheists, Muslims See Most Bias as Presidential Candidates: Two-Thirds Would Vote for Gay or Lesbian," June 21, 2012, http://www.gallup.com/poll/155285/atheists-muslims-bias-presidential-candidates.aspx.

70. Herbert Asher, *Polling and the Public*, 8th ed. (Washington, DC: CQ Press, 2014).

71. Dwayne Yancey, "L. Douglas Wilder (1931-)," *Encyclopedia Virginia,* http://www.encyclopediavirginia.org/Wilder_Lawrence_Douglas_1931-#start_entry, accessed April 17, 2015.

72. Daniel J. Hopkins, "No More Wilder Effect, Never a Whitman Effect: When and Why Polls Mislead about Black and Female Candidates," *Journal of Politics* 71, no. 3 (2009): 769–781.

73. Kate Zernike and Dalia Sussman, "For Pollsters the Racial Effect That Wasn't," *New York Times,* November 5, 2008, http://www.nytimes.com/2008/11/06/us/politics/06poll.html?_r=0 (accessed April 14, 2015).

74. Hopkins, "No More Wilder Effect."

75. Mark S. Leeper, "The Impact of Prejudice on Female Candidates: An Experimental Look at Voter Inference," *American Politics Quarterly* 19, no. 2 (1991): 248–261; Virginia Sapiro, "If U.S. Senator Baker Were a Woman: An Experimental Study of Candidate Images," *Political Psychology* 2, no. 1 (1981–1982): 61–83.

76. Rebekah Herrick and Sue Thomas, "Gays and Lesbians in Local Races: A Study of Electoral Viability," *Journal of Homosexuality* 42, no. 1 (2001): 103–126; Rebekah Herrick and Sue Thomas, "The Effects of Sexual Orientation on Citizen Perceptions of Candidate Viability," in *Gays and Lesbians in the Democratic Process: Public Policy, Public Opinion, and Political Representation*, ed. Ellen D. B. Riggle and Barry L. Tadlock (New York: Columbia University Press, 1999), 170–191.

77. Ewa A. Golebiowska, "Group Stereotypes and Political Evaluation," *American Politics Research* 29, no. 6 (2001): 535–565.

78. Herrick and Thomas, "Gays and Lesbians in Local Races."

79. Benjamin Highton, "White Voters and African American Candidates for Congress," *Political Behavior* 26, no. 1 (2004): 1–25.

80. B. Keith Payne, Jon A. Krosnick, Josh Pasek, Yphtach Lelkes, Omair Akhtar, Trevor Thompson, "Implicit and Explicit Prejudice in the 2008 American Presidential Election," *Journal of Experimental Social Psychology* 46, no. 2 (2010): 367–674.

81. Cindy D. Kam, "Implicit Attitudes, Explicit Choices: When Subliminal Priming Predicts Candidate Preference," *Political Behavior* 29, no. 3 (2007): 343–367.

82. Leeper "The Impact of Prejudice on Female"; Sapiro, "If U.S. Senator Baker"; Deborah Alexander and Kristi

Andersen, "Gender as a Factor in the Attribution of Leadership Traits," *Political Research Quarterly* 46, no. 3 (1993): 527–545; Leonie Huddy and Nayda Terkildsen, "Gender Stereotypes and the Perception of Male and Female Candidates," *American Journal of Political Science* 27, no. 1 (1993): 119–147; Kim Fridkin Kahn, "Does Gender Make a Difference? An Experimental Examination of Sex Stereotypes and Press Patterns in Statewide Campaigns," *American Journal of Political Science* 38, no. 1 (1994): 162–195; Kira Sanbonmatsu and Kathleen Dolan, "Do Gender Stereotypes Transcend Party?" *Political Research Quarterly* 62, no. 3 (2009): 485–494; Kim L. Fridkin and Patrick J. Kenney, "The Role of Gender Stereotypes in U.S. Senate Campaigns," *Politics and Gender* 5, no. 3 (2009): 301–324.

83. Herrick and Thomas, "The Effects of Sexual Orientation."

84. Monica Schneider and Angela L. Bos, "An Exploration of the Context of Stereotypes of Black Politicians," *Political Psychology* 32, no. 2 (2011): 205–232.

85. Monica L. McDermott, "Race and Gender Cues in Low Information Races," *Political Research Quarterly* 51, no. 4 (1998): 895–918.

86. Barbara Palmer and Dennis Simon, *Breaking the Political Glass Ceiling: Women and Congressional Elections* (New York: Routledge, 2006), chap. 6.

87. Robert E. Hogan, "The Influence of State and District Conditions on the Representation of Women in the U.S. State Legislatures," *American Politics Research* 29, no. 4 (2001): 4–24; Heather L. Ondercin and Susan Welch, "Comparing Predictors of Women's Congressional Election Success: Candidates, Primaries, and the General Election," *American Politics Research* 37, no. 4 (2009): 593–613; Heather L. Ondercin and Susan Welch, "Women Candidates for Congress," in *Women and Elective Office: Past, Present, and Future*, ed. Susan Thomas and Clyde Wilcox (New York: Oxford University Press, 2005): 60–80; Barbara Palmer and Dennis Simon, *Breaking the Political Glass Ceiling*, chap. 6.

88. Donald D. Haider-Markel, *Out and Running: Gay and Lesbian Candidates, Election, and Policy Representation* (Washington, DC: George Washington University Press, 2010), chap. 2–3.

89. Daniel J. Elazar, *American Federalism: A View from the States* (New York: Thomas Y. Crowell, 1972).

90. Rodney Hero, *Faces of Inequality: Social Diversity in American Politics* (New York: Oxford University Press, 1998).

91. Katherine Tate, *Black Faces in the Mirror: African Americans and Their Representatives in the U.S. Congress* (Princeton, NJ: Princeton University Press, 2003); Jason P. Casellas, "Coalitions in the House? The Election of Minorities to State Legislatures and Congress," *Political Research Quarterly* 62, no. 1 (2009): 120–131; Jason P. Casellas, "The Institutional and Demographic Determinants of Latino Representation," *Legislative Studies Quarterly* 34, no. 3 (2009): 399–426.

92. Casellas, "Coalitions in the House?"; Casellas, "The Institutional and Demographic."

93. Casellas, "Coalitions in the House?"; Casellas, "The Institutional and Demographic."

94. Haider-Markel, *Out and Running*.

95. For simplicity, I include Senate and House members in these figures. Had I only examined House members, the size of the minority populations in district would have been much larger. I used 2010 census data.

96. Adrienne R. Smith, Beth Reingold, and Michael Leo Owens, "The Political Determinants of Women's Descriptive Representation in Cities," *Political Research Quarterly* 65, no. 2 (2012): 315–329.

97. Tate, *Black Faces in the Mirror*; Gbemende Johnson, Bruce I. Oppenheimer, and Jennifer L. Selin, "The House as a Stepping Stone to the Senate: Why Do So Few African American House Members Run?" *American Journal of Political Science* 56, no. 2 (2012): 387–399.

98. These figures were calculated by author using census data for members serving in the 113th Congress.

99. Amanda Noss, "Household Income 2013: American Community Survey Brief," September 2014, https://www.census.gov/content/dam/Census/library/publications/2014/acs/acsbr13-02.pdf, Table 1, accessed April 14, 2015.

100. Linda L. Fowler and Jennifer L. Lawless, "Looking for Sex in All the Wrong Places: Press Coverage and the Electoral Fortunes of Gubernatorial Candidates," *Perspectives on Politics* 7, no. 3 (2009): 519–536; Kim Fridkin Kahn, "Does Gender Make a Difference?"; Kahn, "Does Being Male Help?"; Sarah Allen Gershon, "Media Coverage of Minority Congresswomen and Voter Evaluations: Evidence from an Online Experimental Study," *Political Research Quarterly* 66, no. 3 (2013): 702–714; Dianne G. Bystrom, Terry A. Robertson, and Mary Christine Banwart, "Framing the Fight—An Analysis of Media Coverage of Female and Male Candidates in Primary Races for Governor and U.S. Senate in 2000," *American Behavioral Scientist* 44, no. 12 (2001): 1999–2013; Lindsey Meeks, "Is She 'Man Enough'? Women Candidates, Executive Political Offices, and News Coverage," *Journal of Communication* 62, no. 1 (2012): 175–193; Stephen M. Caliendo and Charlton D. McIlwain, "Minority Candidates, Media Framing: Racial Cues in the 2004 Election," *Harvard International Journal of Press/Politics* 11, no. 4 (2006): 45–69; David T. Canon, *Race, Redistricting, and Representation: The Unintended Consequences of Black Majority Districts* (Chicago: University of Chicago Press, 1999), chap. 5; Brian Schaffner and Mark Gadson, "Reinforcing Stereotypes? Race and Local Television News Coverage of Congress," *Social Science Quarterly* 85, no. 3 (2004): 604–623; Nayda Terkildsen and David F. Damore, "The Dynamics of Racialized Media Coverage in Congressional Elections," *Journal of Politics* 61, no. 3 (1999): 680–699.

101. Caliendo and McIlwain, "Minority Candidates, Media Framing."
102. Caliendo and McIlwain, "Minority Candidates, Media Framing."
103. Kevin B. Smith, "When All's Fair: Signs of Parity in Media Coverage of Female Candidates," *Political Communication* 14, no. 1 (1997): 71–82.
104. Sarah Allen Gershon, "Media Coverage of Minority Congresswomen."
105. Kathleen Dolan, "Do Women Candidates Play to Gender Stereotypes? Do Men Candidates Play to Women? Candidate Sex and Issue Priorities on Campaign Websites," *Political Research Quarterly* 58, no. 1 (2005): 31–44; Kahn, "Does Gender Make a Difference?"; Virginia Sapiro, Katherine Cramer Walsh, Patricia Strach, and Valerie Hennings, "Gender, Context, and Television Advertising: A Comprehensive Analysis of 2000 and 2002 House Races," *Political Research Quarterly* 54, no. 1 (2011): 107–119.
106. Martha Kropf and John Boiney, "The Electoral Glass Ceiling? Gender, Viability, and the News in U.S. Senate Campaigns," *Women & Politics* 23, no. 1/2 (2001): 79–83; Kahn, "Does Being Male Help?"; Gershon, "Media Coverage of Minority Congresswomen."
107. Gershon, "Media Coverage of Minority Congresswomen."
108. Rebekah Herrick and Jeanette Morehouse Mendez, "Women and Campaigns," in *Women and Elective Office: Past, Present, and Future*, 3rd ed., ed. Sue Thomas and Clyde Wilcox, (New York: Oxford University Press, 2014), 97–110.
109. These figures were calculated by author.
110. Ondercin and Welch, "Women Candidates for Congress."
111. Haider-Markel, *Out and Running*, chap. 3.
112. Paru Shah, "It Takes a Black Candidate: A Supply-Side Theory of Minority Representation," *Political Research Quarterly* 67, no. 2 (2014): 266–279; Regina Branton, "The Importance of Race and Ethnicity in Congressional Primary Elections," *Political Research Quarterly* 62, no. 3 (2009): 459–473.
113. Calculated by dividing the number of women candidates by the number of potential candidates assuming a two-way race. Data on the number of women candidates come from http://www.cawp.rutgers.edu/fast_facts/elections/documents/can_histsum.pdf.
114. Robert Darcy, Susan Welch, and Janet Clark, *Women, Elections and Representation* (Lincoln: University of Nebraska Press, 1994).
115. The American Bar Association's Commission on Women in the Profession, "A Current Glance at Women in the Law," July 2014, http://www.americanbar.org/content/dam/aba/marketing/women/current_glance_statistics_july2014.authcheckdam.pdf, accessed April 21, 2015; Caroline Fairchild, "Women CEOs in Fortune's 1000: By the Numbers," July 8, 2014, http://fortune.com/2014/07/08/women-ceos-fortune-500-1000/ (accessed April 21, 2015).
116. Richard L. Fox and Jennifer L. Lawless, "Entering the Arena? Gender and the Decision to Run for Office," *American Journal of Political Science* 48, no. 2 (2004): 264–280.
117. Fox and Lawless, "Entering the Arena?"
118. There were thirty-three seats open and three special elections, resulting in thirty-six races.
119. Johnson, Oppenheimer, and Selin, "The House as a Stepping Stone."
120. Johnson, Oppenheimer, and Selin, "The House as a Stepping Stone."
121. Herrick and Mendez, "Women and Campaigns," 101.
122. Calculated by author using Federal Election Commission campaign finance data reports.
123. Nadia E. Brown, "Black Women's Pathways to the Statehouse: The Impact of Race/Gender Identities," in *Black Women in Politics*, ed. Michael Mitchell and David Covin (New Brunswick, NJ: Transaction Publishers, 2014).
124. Canon, *Race, Redistricting, and Representation*; Baodong Lui, "DeRacialization and Urban Racial Contexts," *Urban Affairs Review* 38, no. 4 (2003): 572–591.
125. Ravi K. Perry, "Kindred Political Rhetoric: Black Mayors, President Obama, and the Universalizing of Black Interests," *Journal of Urban Affairs* 33, no. 5 (2011): 567–589.
126. Perry, "Kindred Political Rhetoric"; Ravi K. Perry, *Volume 18: 21st Century Urban Race Politics: Representing Minorities as Universal Interests* (Bingley, UK: Emerald Group Publishing, 2013).
127. Dolan, "Do Women Candidates Play"; Kahn, "Does Gender Make a Difference?"
128. Rebekah Herrick, "Sex Differences in Constituent Engagement," *Social Science Quarterly* 91, no. 4 (2010): 947–963.
129. David T. Canon, *Race, Redistricting, and Representation: The Unintended Consequences of Black Majority Districts* (Chicago: University of Chicago Press, 1999).
130. Luis Ricardo Fraga, Linda Lopez, Valerie Martinez-Ebers, and Ricardo Ramirez, "Gender and Ethnicity: Patterns of Electoral Success and Legislative Advocacy among Latina and Latino State Officials in Four States," *Journal of Women, Politics & Policy* 28, no. 3–4 (2006): 121–145; Carol Hardy-Fanta, Pei-te Lien, Dianne M. Pinderjughers, and Christine Marie Sierra, "Gender, Race, and Descriptive Representation in the United States: Findings from the Gender and Multicultural Leadership Project," *Journal of Women, Politics & Policy* 28, no. 3/4 (2006): 7–41.
131. R. Darcy, Charles D. Hadley, and Jason F. Kirksey, "Election Systems and the Representation of Black Women in American State Legislatures," *Women & Politics* 13, no. 2 (1993): 73–89.
132. Brown, "Black Women's Pathways," 85–86.
133. Brown, "Black Women's Pathways."

134. Tasha S. Philpot and Hanes Walton, Jr., "One of Our Own: Black Female Candidates and the Voters Who Support Them," *American Journal of Political Science* 51, no. 1 (2007): 59.

135. Becki Scola, "Predicting Presence at the Intersections"; Becki Scola, "Women of Color in State Legislatures: Gender, Race, Ethnicity and Legislative Office Holding," *Journal of Women, Politics & Policy* 28, no. 3/4 (2006): 43–69.

136. These tendencies are supported with data presented in Chapters 10 and 11.

137. See, for example, Georgia Duerst-Lahti, "Governing Institutions, Ideologies, and Gender: Toward the Possibility of Equal Political Representation," *Sex Roles* 47, no. 7/8 (2002): 371–386; Joan Acker, "Gendered Institutions: From Sex Roles to Gendered Institutions," *Contemporary Sociology* 21, no. 5 (1992): 565–569; Mary Hawkesworth, "Congressional Enactments of Race-Gender: Toward a Theory of Raced-Gendered Institutions," *American Political Science Review* 97, no. 4 (2003): 529–550; Sally Kenney, "New Research on Gendered Political Institutions," *Political Research Quarterly* 49, no. 3 (1996): 445–466.

138. Acker, "Gendered Institutions," 567.

139. Sally Kenney, "New Research on Gendered Political Institutions," *Political Research Quarterly* 49, no. 3 (1996): 445–466.

140. Kenny, "New Research on Gendered Political Institutions," 456.

141. Duerst-Lahti, "Governing Institutions."

142. Dotty Lynch, "Big Girls Don't Cry," *CBS News* August 6, 2002, http://www.cbsnews.com/news/big-girls-dont-cry/, accessed April 14, 2015.

143. For example, see Carol Gilligan, *In a Different Voice* (Cambridge, MA: Harvard University Press, 1982).

144. Mary Hawkesworth, "Congressional Enactments of Race-Gender."

145. Maya Rhodan, "Senator Says Male Colleague Told Her 'You're Even Pretty When You're Fat,'" *Time*, August 27, 2014, http://time.com/3197103/kirsten-gillibrand-senate-sexism/.

146. http://thedianerehmshow.org/shows/2014-09-10/sen-kirsten-gillibrand-sidelines.

147. http://www.huffingtonpost.com/news/obama-tax-returns/.

148. Jennifer E. Manning, "Membership of the 113th Congress: A Profile," August 26, 2014, http://www.senate.gov/CRSReports/crs-publish.cfm?pid=%260BL%2BR%5CC%3F%0A.

149. Alec MacGillis, "Obama Assembles an Ivy-tinged League," *Washington Post*, December 7, 2008, http://www.washingtonpost.com/wp-dyn/content/story/2008/12/06/ST2008120602443.html.

150. NAACP, *NAACP Legislative Report Card of the 104th Congress*, http://naacp.3cdn.net/cf6cd26c1fc7f106fc_v3m6bpg2z.pdf.

151. Michael S. Rocha, Gabriel Sanchez, and Joseph Uscinski, "Personal Attributes and Latino Voting Behavior in Congress," *Social Science Quarterly* 89, no. 2 (2008): 392–405.

152. https://www.aauwaction.org/wp-content/uploads/2014/09/CVR-2013-14.pdf, accessed April 21, 2015.

153. David T. Canon, *Race, Redistricting, and Representation: The Unintended Consequences of Black Majority Districts* (Chicago: University of Chicago Press, 1999).

154. Stefanie Chambers and William E. Nelson Jr., "Black Mayoral Leadership in New Orleans: Minority Incorporation Revisited" in *Black Women in Politics*, ed. Michael Mitchell and David Covin (New Brunswick: Transaction Publishers, 2014), 117–134.

155. Suzanne Dovi, "Preferable Descriptive Representatives: Will Just Any Woman, Black or Hispanic Do?," *American Political Science Review* 96, no. 4 (2002): 729–743.

156. Dovi, "Preferable Descriptive Representatives," 735.

Chapter 3

1. John Herbers, "Selma Negroes Tell of Attack: 3 in One Family Recovering after Clash with Police," *New York Times*, February 22, 1965, 12.

2. Herbers, "Selma Negroes Tell of Attack."

3. Herbers, "Selma Negroes Tell of Attack."

4. John Herbers, "Dr. King and 770 Others Seized in Alabama Protest," *New York Times,* February 2, 1965, 1.

5. Hanna Fenichel Pitkin, *The Concept of Representation* (Berkeley: University of California Press, 1967), chaps. 2, 3.

6. *Ginn v. U.S.*, 238 U.S. 347, 355 (1915).

7. *Smith v. Allwright,* 321 U.S. 649 (1944).

8. Francois Pierre-Louis, "Literacy Test," *Encyclopedia of Racism in the United States, Vol. 2: I-9,* ed. Pyong Gap Min (Westport, CT: Greenwood Press, 2005), 364–365.

9. F. Chris Garcia and Gabriel R. Sanchez, *Hispanics and the U.S. Political System: Moving into the Mainstream* (Upper Saddle River, NJ: Pearson Prentice Hall, 2008), chap. 6.

10. Garcia and Sanchez, *Hispanics and the U.S. Political System,* 121.

11. Daniel McCool, Susan M. Olson, and Jennifer L. Robinson, *Native Vote: American Indians, the Voting Rights Act, and the Right to Vote* (New York: Cambridge University Press, 2007), chap. 1.

12. "Alaska Must Translate Election Material into 2 Indigenous Languages," *National Public Radio*, October 10, 2014, http://www.npr.org/blogs/codeswitch/2014/10/07/354230888/alaska-must-translate-election-material-into-2-indigenous-languages.

13. 570 U.S. ____ (2013).

14. The American National Election Studies is a highly respected survey of national elections housed at the University of Michigan. See Spotlight 8.1 in Chapter 8 for more information on ANES.

15. http://electionstudies.org/nesguide/2ndtable/t6a_2_2.htm.

16. McCool, Olson, and Robinson, *Native Vote*, chap. 7.

17. McClain and Stewart, *Can We All Get Along?* 66–70; Wilkins and Stark, "American Indian Politics," chap. 7; McCool, Olson, and Robinson, *Native Vote*, 81–85.

18. Wilkins and Stark, "American Indian Politics" chap. 7; McCool, Olson and Robinson, *Native Vote*, 81–85.

19. 509 U.S. 630 (1993).

20. See, for example, Charles Cameron, David Epstein, and Sharyn O'Halloran, "Do Majority-Minority Districts Maximize Substantive Black Representation in Congress?" *American Political Science Review* 90, no. 4 (1996): 794–812.

21. Richard Engstrom, "Redistricting: Influence Districts—a Note of Caution and Better Measure," Research Brief for The Chief Justice Earl Warren Institute on Law and Social Policy, May 2011, http://www.law.berkeley.edu/files/Influence_Districts.pdf, accessed April 18, 2015.

22. http://www.ncsl.org/legislatures-elections/elections/felon-voting-rights.aspx.

23. Christopher Uggen, Sarah Shannon, and Jeff Manza, "State-Level Estimates of Felon Disenfranchisement in the United States, 2010," July 2012, http://www.sentencingproject.org/doc/publications/fd_State_Level_Estimates_of_Felon_Disen_2010.pdf.

24. Melanie Bowers and Robert R. Preuhs, "Collateral Consequences of a Collateral Penalty," *Social Science Quarterly* 90, no. 3 (2009): 722–743.

25. The Sentencing Project, "Black Lives Matter: Eliminating Racial Injustice in the Criminal Justice System," 2015, 15, http://sentencingproject.org/doc/publications/rd_Black_Lives_Matter.pdf, accessed April 18, 2015.

26. The Sentencing Project, "Black Lives Matter."

27. The Sentencing Project, "Black Lives Matter."

28. The percentage of citizens varies by nationality; nearly all Puerto Ricans are citizens but less than half of Hondurans. Pew Hispanic Center, "The 10 Largest Hispanic Origin Groups: Characteristics, Rankings, Top Counties," June 27, 2013, http://www.pewhispanic.org/files/2012/06/The-10-Largest-Hispanic-Origin-Groups.pdf.

29. Paru Shah, "Racing Toward Representation: A Hurdle Model of Latino Incorporation," *American Politics Research* 38, no. 1 (2010): 84–109.

30. Jeffrey S. Passel, D'Vera Cohn, and Ana Gonzalez-Barrera, "Population Decline of Unauthorized Immigrants Stalls, May Have Reversed New Estimate: 11.7 Million in 2012," September 23, 2013, http://www.pewhispanic.org/2013/09/23/population-decline-of-unauthorized-immigrants-stalls-may-have-reversed/.

31. The Twenty-Third Amendment to the Constitution grants Washington, D.C., three electoral votes.

32. http://factfinder2.census.gov/faces/tableservices/jsf/pages/productview.xhtml?pid=DEC_10_DP_DPDP1.

33. Ben Pershing, "Eleanor Holmes Norton Again Offers Bill to Make DC the 51st State," *Washington Post,* January 15, 2015, http://www.washingtonpost.com/blogs/dc-wire/post/eleanor-holmes-norton-again-offers-bill-to-make-dc-the-51st-state/2013/01/15/524f88a0-5f4c-11e2-a389-ee565c81c565_blog.html.

34. http://www.ncsl.org/legislatures-elections/elections/voter-id.aspx.

35. M. V. Hood III and Charles S. Bullock III, "Much Ado about Nothing? An Empirical Assessment of the Georgia Voter Identification Statute," *State Policy and Politics Quarterly* 12, no. 4 (2012): 394–414.

36. David Graham, "Here's Why Black People Have to Wait Twice as Long to Vote as Whites," *The Atlantic*, April 8, 2013, http://www.theatlantic.com/politics/archive/2013/04/heres-why-black-people-have-to-wait-twice-as-long-to-vote-as-whites/274791/.

37. Michael C. Herron and Jasjeet S. Sekhon, "Black Candidates and Black Voters: Assessing the Impact of Candidate Race on Uncounted Vote Rates," *Journal of Politics* 67, no. 1 (2005): 154–177.

38. Since each state gets two votes for the Senate, small states have a disproportionately large number of electors. In Wyoming there are about 19,000 residents per electoral vote, and in California there are 677,345 residents per electoral vote (calculated by author using census data from Factfinder2.gov).

39. Wilma Rule and Joseph F. Zimmerman, *United States Electoral Systems: The Impact on Women and Minorities* (New York: Greenwood Press, 1992).

40. See, for example, Shah, "Racing Toward Representation"; Jessica Trounstine and Melody E. Valdini, "The Context Matters: The Effects of Single-Member versus At-Large Districts on City Council Diversity," *American Journal of Political Science* 52, no. 3 (2008): 554–569; Melissa J. Marschall, Anirudh V. S. Ruhil, and Paru Shah, "The Racial Calculus: Electoral Institutions and Black Representation in Local Legislatures," *American Journal of Political Science* 54, no. 1 (2010): 107–124.

41. McCool, Olson, and Robinson, *Native Vote,* 175.

42. Trounstine and Valdini, "The Context Matters."

43. Rule and Zimmerman, *United States Electoral Systems.*

44. Susan Welch and Donley T. Studlar, "Multimember Districts and the Representation of Women: Evidence from Britain and the United States," *Journal of Politics* 52, no. 2 (1990): 391–412.

45. Kira Sanbonmatsu, "Political Parties and the Recruitment of Women to State Legislatures," *Journal of Politics* 64, no. 3 (2002): 791–809.

46. Shaun Bowler, Todd Donovan, and David Brockington, *Electoral Reform and Minority Representation: Local Experiments with Alternative Elections* (Columbus: Ohio University Press, 2003).

47. Rule and Zimmerman, *United States Electoral Systems.*
48. Robert Darcy, Susan Welch, and Janet Clark, *Women, Elections, and Representation,* 2nd ed. (Lincoln: University of Nebraska Press, 1994).
49. http://www.idea.int/gender/quotas.cfm.
50. Mark Jones, "Quota Legislation and the Election of Women: Learning from the Costa Rican Experience," *Journal of Politics* 66, no. 4 (2004): 1203–1223.
51. Jones, "Quota Legislation and the Election of Women."
52. http://www.quotaproject.org/country.cfm.
53. Melanie M. Hughes, "The Intersection of Gender and Minority Status in National Legislatures: The Minority Women Legislative Index," *Legislative Studies Quarterly* 38, no. 4 (2013): 489–516.
54. Jason P. Casellas, "The Institutional and Demographic Determinants of Latino Representation," *Legislative*

Studies Quarterly 34, no. 3 (2009): 399–426; Susan J. Carroll and Krista E. Jenkins, "Unrealized Opportunity? Term Limits and the Representation of Women in State Legislatures," *Women & Politics* 23, no. 4 (2001): 1–30.
55. Carroll and Jenkins, "Unrealized Opportunity."
56. The equation used was percentage of minority legislator divided by percentage of minority in the population.
57. http://www.ncsl.org/legislatures-elections/legislatures/full-and-part-time-legislatures.aspx#average.
58. Casellas, "The Institutional and Demographic."
59. Sanbonmatsu, "Political Parties and the Recruitment of Women."
60. McCool, Olson, and Robinson, *Native Vote,* chap. 1.
61. *Elk v. Wilkins,* 112 U.S. 94 (1884).
62. *Regents of the University of California v. Bakke,* 438 U.S. 265 (1977).

Chapter 4

1. David Von Drehle, "Fatal Encounter: A Police Shooting in Missouri Puts the Spot Light on Race," *Time,* August 25, 2014, 15–16.
2. Eugene Robinson, "What the Police Don't Want Us to Know," *Chicago Tribune,* December 3, 2014, http://www.chicagotribune.com/news/opinion/commentary/ct-police-shootings-ferguson-brown-perspec-1204-jm-20141203-story.html.
3. Von Drehle, "Fatal Encounter."
4. Matt Apuzzo, "Federal Inquiry of Ferguson Police Will Include Apparent Racial Profiling," *New York Times,* September 5, 2014, 16.
5. Apuzzo, "Federal Inquiry of Ferguson."
6. Frances Robles, "Ferguson Set Broad Change for City Courts," *New York Times,* September 8, 2014.
7. Robles, "Ferguson Set Broad Change."
8. Joy Wilke, "In U.S. More Nonwhites Than Whites Say Jobs Is Top Issue," 2013, http://www.gallup.com/poll/164000/nonwhites-whites-say-jobs-top-issue.aspx.
9. Lydia Saad, "US Subgroups Say Economy and Jobs Most Important Problem," 2011, http://www.gallup.com/poll/148001/subgroups-say-economy-jobs-important-problem.aspx#1.
10. Suzanne Macartney, Alemayehu Bishaw, and Kayla Fontenot, "Poverty Rates for Selected Detailed Race and Hispanic Groups by State and Place: 2007-2011," February 2013, http://www.census.gov/hhes/www/poverty/publications/acsbr11-17.html.
11. Macartney, Bishaw, and Fontenot, "Poverty Rates for Selected Detailed Race"; Mexicans', Puerto Ricans' and Guatemalans' poverty rates were similar to that of the Hispanic average.
12. Macartney, Bishaw, and Fontenot, "Poverty Rates for Selected Detailed Race."
13. http://www.census.gov/hhes/www/cpstables/032011/pov/POV01_100.htm.
14. W. V. Lee Badgett, Laura E. Durso, and Alyssa Schneebaum, "New Patterns of Poverty in the Lesbian, Gay, and Bisexual Community," June 2013, http://williamsinstitute.law.ucla.edu/wp-content/uploads/LGB-Poverty-Update-Jun-2013.pdf.
15. Jaime M. Grant, Lisa A. Mottet, and Justin Tanis, "Injustice at Every Turn: A Report of the National Transgender Discrimination Survey," 2011, http://www.thetaskforce.org/downloads/reports/reports/ntds_full.pdf.
16. Grant, Mottet, and Tanis, "Injustice at Every Turn."
17. Sidney Verba and Norman H. Nie, *Participation in America: Political Democracy and Social Equality* (Chicago: University of Chicago Press, 1972); Sidney Verba, Kay Lehman Schlozman, and Henry E. Brady, *Voice and Equality: Civic Voluntarism in American Politics* (Cambridge, MA: Harvard University Press, 1995).
18. http://www.apa.org/pi/families/resources/school-dropout-prevention.aspx.
19. Here is brief description of the survey: "The analysis of the experiences and attitudes of the LGBT population in this report is based on a survey conducted April 11–29, 2013, among a sample of 1,197 self-identified LGBT adults, 18 years of age or older. The survey was conducted by the GfK Group using KnowledgePanel, its nationally representative online research panel. KnowledgePanel members are recruited through probability sampling methods and include both those with Internet access and those without (KnowledgePanel provides internet access for those who do not have it and, if needed, a device to access the Internet when they join the panel). A combination of random digit dialing (RDD) and address-based sampling (ABS) methodologies were used to recruit panel members (in 2009 KnowledgePanel switched its sampling methodology for recruiting panel members from RDD to ABS). The panel

comprises households with landlines and cellular phones, including those only with cell phones, and those without a phone. Both the RDD and ABS samples were provided by Marketing Systems Group (MSG). KnowledgePanel continually recruits new panel members throughout the year to offset panel attrition as people leave the panel. The survey was conducted in English." Pew Research Center for People and the Press, "A Survey of LGBT Americans: Attitudes, Experiences and Values in Changing Times," June 13, 2013, http://www.pewsocialtrends.org/files/2013/06/SDT_LGBT-Americans_06-2013.pdf, 23.

20. 156 U.S. 537 (1896).

21. This case concerned transportation, not education, but the ruling had implications for education and other public accommodations.

22. Howard Ball, *A Defiant Life: Thurgood Marshall and the Persistence of Racism in America* (New York: Crown, 1998), 114–115.

23. Kevin Drew, "Law Center: Today's Battle in the Classrooms: Resegregation," *CNN,* May 18, 2004, http://www.cnn.com/2004/LAW/05/15/schools.desegregation/index.html?_s=PM:LAW; Gary Orfield, John Kucsera, and Genevieve Siegel-Hawley, *E Pluribus ... Separation: Deepening Double Segregation for More Students* (Los Angeles, CA: UCLA, 2012), *The Civil Rights Project/Proyecto Derechos Civiles,* September 2012, http://civilrightsproject.ucla.edu/research/k-12-education/integration-and-diversity/mlk-national/e-pluribus...separation-deepening-double-segregation-for-more-students/orfield_epluribus_revised_omplete_2012.pdf.

24. Orfield, Kucsera, and Siegel-Hawley, *E Pluribus ... Separation.*

25. http://www.apa.org/pi/families/resources/school-dropout-prevention.aspx; Orfield, Kucsera, and Siegel-Hawley, *E Pluribus ... Separation.*

26. Alliance for Excellent Education, "The High Cost of High School Dropouts: What the Nation Pays for Inadequate High Schools," November 2011, http://all4ed.org/reports-factsheets/the-high-cost-of-high-school-dropouts-what-the-nation-pays-for-inadequate-high-schools/, accessed April 22, 2015.

27. PBS American Experience, "We Shall Remain: Episode 5, Wounded Knee." May 11, 2009; Carla Bear, "American Indian Boarding School Haunts Many," *NPR,* May 12, 2008, http://www.npr.org/templates/story/story.php?storyId=16516865, accessed April 25, 2015.

28. Josh Hicks, "Federally-Run Indian Schools Are in Rough Shape Because of a Broken Bureaucracy" *Washington Post,* April 24, 2015, http://www.washingtonpost.com/blogs/federal-eye/wp/2015/04/24/federally-run-indian-schools-are-in-rough-shape-because-of-a-broken-bureaucracy/.

29. F. Chris Garcia and Gabriel R. Sanchez, *Hispanics and the U.S. Political System: Moving into the Mainstream* (Upper Saddle River, NJ: Pearson Prentice Hall, 2008), chap. 12.

30. http://trends.collegeboard.org/education-pays/figures-tables/students-stem-fields-gender-and-race-ethnicity,

accessed April 23, 2015; http://www.census.gov/compendia/statab/2012/tables/12s0302.pdf, accessed April 23, 2015; http://www.esa.doc.gov/sites/default/files/womenin-stemagaptoinnovation8311.pdf.

31. Natalie Kitroeff and Jonathan Rodkin, "Women's Career Choices Don't Explain Gender Pay Gap," *Bloomberg Business,* November 14, 2014, http://www.bloomberg.com/bw/articles/2014-11-14/women-make-less-than-men-even-when-they-are-equally-qualified-mbas, accessed April 21, 2015.

32. Grant, Mottet, and Tanis, "Injustice at Every Turn."

33. Joseph G. Kosciw, Emily A. Greytak, Neal A. Palmer, and Madelyn J. Boesen, "The 2013 Nation School Climate Survey: The Experiences of Our Lesbian, Gay, Bisexual, and Transgender Youth in Our Nation's Schools," *GLSEN,* 2014, http://www.glsen.org/sites/default/files/2013%20National%20School%20Climate%20Survey%20Full%20Report_0.pdf, accessed April 23, 2015.

34. http://www.apa.org/pi/families/resources/school-dropout-prevention.aspx.

35. http://www.apa.org/pi/families/resources/school-dropout-prevention.aspx.

36. Christopher Hartney and Linh Vuong, "Created Equal: Racial and Ethnic Disparities in the US Criminal Justice System," National Council on Crime and Delinquency, March 2009, http://www.nccdglobal.org/sites/default/files/publication_pdf/created-equal.pdf, accessed April 23, 2015.

37. "Reducing Racial Disparity in the Criminal Justice System: A Manual for Practitioners and Policymakers," *The Sentencing Project,* 2008, http://www.sentencingproject.org/doc/publications/rd_reducingracialdisparity.pdf, accessed April 23, 2015.

38. Hartney and Vuong, "Created Equal."

39. "Reducing Racial Disparity in the Criminal Justice System."

40. Hartney and Vuong, "Created Equal."

41. The Sentencing Project, "Race and Punishment," 25.

42. The Sentencing Project, "Race and Punishment," 25.

43. The Sentencing Project, "Race and Punishment."

44. The Sentencing Project, "Race and Punishment," 14.

45. Jody Marksamer and Harper Jean Tobin, "Standing with LGBT Prisoners: An Advocate's Guide to Ending Abuse and Combating Imprisonment." National Center on Transgender Equality, April 2014, http://transequality.org/sites/default/files/docs/resources/JailPrisons_Resource_FINAL.pdf, accessed April 23, 2015.

46. Marksamer and Tobin, "Standing with LGBT Prisoners," 2.

47. Marksamer and Tobin, "Standing with LGBT Prisoners."

48. Calculated by author from data provided by E. Ann Carson, "Prisoners in 2013," Bureau of Justice Statistics, September 30, 2014, Table 7, http://www.bjs.gov/content/pub/pdf/p13.pdf, accessed April 26, 2015.

49. Calculated by author from data provided by Carson, "Prisoners in 2013," Table 7.

50. Calculated by author from data available at https://www.fbi.gov/about-us/cjis/ucr/hate-crime/2013/

tables/1tabledatadecpdf/table_1_incidents_offenses_victims_and_known_offenders_by_bias_motivation_2013.xls.

51. http://www.adl.org/assets/pdf/combating-hate/state_hate_crime_laws.pdf.

52. Herbert Mitgang, "Hail to Chiefs without Military Pasts," *New York Times*, January 3, 1993, http://www.nytimes.com/1993/01/03/us/hail-to-chiefs-without-military-pasts.html, accessed April 21, 2015.

53. Rachel Wellford, "By the Numbers: Veterans in Congress," *PBSNewshour*, November 11, 2014, http://www.pbs.org/newshour/rundown/by-the-numbers-veterans-in-congress/ accessed April 21, 2015.

54. Pew Research Center, "For 2016 Hopefuls, Washington Experience Could Do More Harm Than Good: Military Service Top Positive, Atheism Top Negative for Potential Candidates," May 19, 2014, http://www.people-press.org/2014/05/19/for-2016-hopefuls-washington-experience-could-do-more-harm-than-good/, accessed April 21, 2015.

55. Tom Vanden Brook, "Women Moving Closer to Combat Front Lines" *USAToday*, November 20, 2014, http://www.usatoday.com/story/news/nation/2014/11/20/pentagon-women-combat/70010930/, accessed April 15. 2015.

56. Sandhya Somashekhar and Craig Whitlock, "Military to Allow Transgender Members to Serve Openly," *Washington Post*, July 13, 2015, http://www.washingtonpost.com/politics/pentagon-to-allow-transgender-members-to-serve-openly/2015/07/13/fe9b054a-298d-11e5-a5ea-cf74396e59ec_story.html.

57. Saad, "Hispanics Put Other Issues."

58. Grant, Mottet, and Tanis, "Injustice at Every Turn."

59. Pew Research Center for People and the Press, "A Survey of LGBT."

60. http://www.cdc.gov/hiv/statistics/basics/ataglance.html.

61. http://www.who.int/mediacentre/factsheets/fs360/en/.

62. http://www.avert.org/worldwide-hiv-aids-statistics.htm.

63. http://www.who.int/mediacentre/factsheets/fs360/en/.

64. http://www.avert.org/worldwide-hiv-aids-statistics.htm.

65. http://www.avert.org/worldwide-hiv-aids-statistics.htm.

66. http://www.who.int/mediacentre/factsheets/fs360/en/.

67. http://www.who.int/mediacentre/factsheets/fs360/en/.

68. Pew Research Center, "For Voters It's Still the Economy."

69. "Progress and Perils: New Agenda for Women," Center for the Advancement of Women. As presented in Nancy E. McGlen, Karen O'Connor, Laura van Assendelft, and Wendy Gunther-Canada, *Women, Politics, and American Society* (New York: Longman, 2011).

70. Jennifer L. Truman and Rachel E. Morgan, "Special Report: Nonfatal Domestic Violence, 2003-2012," *BJS*, April 2014, http://www.bjs.gov/content/pub/pdf/ndv0312.pdf.

71. Truman and Morgan, "Special Report: Nonfatal Domestic Violence."

72. Louise Erdrich, "Rape on the Reservation," *New York Times*, February 26, 2013. The recent Violence Against Women Act improves the situation somewhat by allowing tribes limited authority in domestic violence cases involving nontribal citizens.

73. Erdrich, "Rape on the Reservation."

74. Kavitha Chukuru, "Violence Against Women Act Includes New Protections for Native American Women," *Huffington Post*, March 10, 2013, http://www.huffingtonpost.com/2013/03/10/violence-against-women-act-native-americans_n_2849931.html.

75. Warren E. Miller and Donald E. Stokes, "Constituency Influence in Congress" *American Political Science Review* 57, no. 1 (1963): 45–56.

76. Nadia E. Brown, "Black Women's Pathways to the Statehouse: The Impact of Race/Gender Identities," in *Black Women in Politics*, ed. Michael Mitchell and David Covin (New Brunswick, NJ: Transaction, 2014), 87.

77. Jane Mansbridge, 1999. "Should Blacks Represent Blacks and Women Represent Women? A Contingent Yes," *Journal of Politics* 61, no. 3 (1999): 628–657; Jane Mansbridge, "Rethinking Representation," *American Political Science Review* 97, no. 4 (2003): 515–528.

78. Mansbridge, "Should Blacks Represent Blacks"; Mansbridge, "Rethinking Representation."

79. Susan J. Carroll, "Representing Women: Congresswomen's Perceptions of Their Representative Roles," in *Women Transforming Congress*, ed. Cindy Simon Rosenthal (Norman: University of Oklahoma Press, 2002), 50–68.

80. David E. Brookman, "Black Politicians Are More Intrinsically Motivated to Advance Blacks' Interests: A Field Experiment Manipulating Political Incentives," *American Journal of Political Science* 57, no. 3 (2013): 521–536.

81. David E. Brookman, "Black Politicians Are More Intrinsically Motivated."

82. Quoted in David Rayside, *On the Fringe: Gays and Lesbians in Politics* (Ithaca, NY: Cornell University Press, 1998), 270.

83. Michelle L. Swers, *The Difference Women Make: The Policy Impact of Women in Congress* (Chicago: University of Chicago Press, 2002).

84. Karen Grisbey Bates, "Why Did Black Voters Flee the Democratic Party in the 1960s?" *NPR*, July 14, 2014, http://www.npr.org/blogs/codeswitch/2014/07/14/331298996/why-did-black-voters-flee-the-republican-party-in-the-1960s.

85. Laura W. Arnold and Barbara M. King, "Women, Committees, and Institutional Change in the Senate," in *Women Transforming Congress*, ed. Cindy Simon Rosenthal (Norman: University of Oklahoma Press), 284–316.

86. Noelle H. Norton, "Transforming Policy from the Inside: Participation in Committee," in *Women Transforming Congress*, ed. Cindy Simon Rosenthal (Norman: University of Oklahoma Press), 316–340.

87. Katherine Tate, *Black Faces in the Mirror: African Americans and Their Representatives in the U.S. Congress* (Princeton, NJ: Princeton University Press, 2003).

88. William Curtis Ellis and Walter Clark Wilson, "Minority Chairs and Congressional Attention to Minority Issues: The Effect of Descriptive Representation in Positions of Institutional Power," *Social Science Quarterly* 94, no. 5 (2013): 1207–1221.

89. Tate, *Black Faces in the Mirror*; Arnold and King, "Women, Committees, and Institutional Change in the Senate."

90. For example, Carol M. Swain, *Black Faces, Black Interests: The Representation of African Americans in Congress* (Cambridge, MA: Harvard University Press, 1993); Rodney E. Hero and Caroline Tolbert, "Latinos and Substantive Representation in the U.S. House of Representatives: Direct, Indirect, or Nonexistent?" *American Journal of Political Science* 39, no. 3 (1995): 640–652.

91. Swain, *Black Faces, Black Interests.*

92. Luis Ricardo Fraga, Linda Lopez, Valerie Martinez-Ebers, and Ricardo Ramirez, "Gender and Ethnicity: Patterns of Electoral Success and Legislative Advocacy among Latina and Latino State Officials in Four States," *Journal of Women, Politics & Policy* 28, no. 3–4 (2006): 121–145; Edith Barrett, "The Policy Priorities of African American Women in State Legislatures," *Legislative Studies Quarterly* 20, no. 2 (1995): 223–247; Byron D. Orey, Wendy Smooth, Kimberly S. Adams, and Kisha Harris-Clark, "Race and Gender Matter: Refining Models of Legislative Policy Making in State Legislatures," *Journal of Women, Politics & Policy* 28, no. 3/4 (2006): 97–119.

93. Brinck Kerr and W. Miller, "Latino Representation, It's Direct and Indirect," *American Journal of Political Science* 41, no. 3 (1997): 1066–1071; Tate, *Black Faces in the Mirror*; David T. Canon, *Race, Redistricting, and Representation: The Unintended Consequences of Black Majority Districts* (Chicago: University of Chicago Press, 1999); Kerry L. Haynie, *African American Legislators in the American States* (New York: Columbia University Press, 2001); Michael D. Minto and Valeria Sinclair-Chapman, "Diversity in Political Institutions and Congressional Responsiveness to Minority Interests," *Political Research Quarterly* 66, no. 1 (2013): 127–140; Michelle. L. Swers, "Are Women More Likely to Vote for Women's Issue Bills Than Their Male Colleagues?" *Legislative Studies Quarterly* 23, no. 3 (1998): 435–448; Sue Thomas and Susan Welch, "The Impact of Gender on Activities and Priorities of State Legislators," *Western Political Quarterly* 44, no. 2 (1991): 445–456; Sue Thomas, *How Women Legislate* (New York: Oxford University Press, 1994); Sue Thomas, "The Impact of Women on State Legislative Policies," *Journal of Politics* 53, no. 4 (1991): 958–976; Sarah Poggione, "Exploring Gender Differences in State Legislators' Policy Preferences," *Political Research Quarterly* 58, no. 2 (2005): 305–314; Kathryn Pearson and Logan Dancey, "Speaking for the Underrepresented in the House of Representatives: Voicing Women's Interests in a Partisan Era," *Politics and Gender* 7, no. 4 (2011): 493–519; Rebekah Herrick, "The Effects of Sexual Orientation on State Legislators' Behavior and Priorities," *Journal of Homosexuality* 56, no. 8 (2009): 1117–1133; Fraga, Lopez, Martinez-Ebers, and Ramirez, "Gender and Ethnicity."

94. Tate, *Black Faces in the Mirror*; Canon, *Race, Redistricting, and Representation*; Haynie, *African American Legislator*.

95. Canon, *Race, Redistricting, and Representation.*

96. Michael D. Minto, "Legislative Oversight and the Substantive Representation of Black and Latino Interests in Congress," *Legislative Studies Quarterly* 34, no. 2 (2009): 193–218.

97. Walter Clark Wilson, "Descriptive Representation and Latino Interest Bill Sponsorship in Congress," *Social Science Quarterly* 91, no. 4 (2010): 1043–1062.

98. Kathleen A. Bratton and Kerry L. Haynie, "Agenda Setting and Legislative Success in State Legislatures: The Effects of Gender and Race," *Journal of Politics* 61, no. 3 (1999): 658–679.

99. Herrick, "The Effects of Sexual Orientation."

100. Swers, "Are Women More Likely"; Swers, *The Difference Women Make*; Thomas, *How Women Legislate*; Thomas and Welch, "The Impact of Gender"; Poggione, "Exploring Gender Differences"; Barrett, "The Policy Priorities of African American Women"; Pearson and Dancey, "Speaking for the Underrepresented."

101. Tate, *Black Faces in the Mirror.*

102. Tate, *Black Faces in the Mirror*, 94.

103. The survey was a Pew Research Center survey, and the roll-call vote was the thirty-ninth vote in the House to repeal the act: two African American members did not vote (Clyburn and John Lewis), though they have supported the act throughout the years.

104. Rosabeth Moss Kanter, *Men and Women of the Corporation* (New York: Basic Books, 1977).

105. Kathleen A. Bratton, "Critical Mass Theory Revisited: The Behavior and Success of Token Women in State Legislatures," *Politics and Gender* 1, no. 2 (2005): 97–125; Lyn Kathlene, "Power and Influence in State Legislative Policymaking: The Interaction of Gender and Position in Committee Hearing Debates," *American Political Science Review* 88, no. 3 (1994): 560–576; Thomas, "The Impact of Women"; Thomas, *How Women Legislate*.

106. Bratton and Haynie, "Agenda Setting and Legislative Success."

107. Bratton, "Critical Mass Theory Revisited"; Bratton and Haynie, "Agenda Setting and Legislative Success"; Alana Jeydel and Andrew J. Taylor, "Are Women Legislators Less Effective? Evidence for the U.S. House in the 103rd–105th Congress," *Political Research Quarterly* 56, no. 1 (2003):19–27; Thomas and Welch, "The Impact of Gender."

108. Canon, *Race, Redistricting, and Representation*; Tate, *Black Faces in the Mirror*; but see Bratton and Haynie, "Agenda Setting and Legislative Success."

109. Rebekah Herrick, "The Legislative Effectiveness of Gay and Lesbian Legislators," *Journal of Women, Politics & Policy* 31, no. 3 (2010): 243–259.

110. David Hedge, James Button, and Mary Spear, "Accounting for the Quality of Black Legislative Life: The View from the States," *American Journal of Political Science* 40, no. 1 (1996): 82–98.

111. Mary Hawkesworth, "Congressional Enactments of Race-Gender: Toward a Theory of Raced-Gendered Institutions," *American Political Science Review* 97, no. 4 (2003): 529–550.

112. Nadia E. Brown, "Black Women's Pathways to the State-house: The Impact of Race/Gender Identities," in *Black Women in Politics*, ed. Michael Mitchell and David Covin (New Brunswick, NJ: Transaction, 2014), 85–86.

113. Michael S. Rocha, Gabriel Sanchez, and Joseph Uscinski, "Personal Attributes and Latino Voting Behavior in Congress," *Social Science Quarterly* 89, no. 2 (2008): 392–405.

114. Suzanne Dovi, "Preferable Descriptive Representatives: Will Just Any Woman, Black or Hispanic Do?" *American Political Science Review* 96, no. 4 (2002): 729–743.

115. Dovi, "Preferable Descriptive Representatives," 735.

116. Dovi, "Preferable Descriptive Representatives," 736.

117. Sue Thomas, "The Impact of Women on State Legislative Policies," *Journal of Politics* 53, no. 4 (1991): 958–976.

118. Irwin N. Gertzog, *Women & Power on Capitol Hill: Reconstructing the Congressional Women's Caucus.* (Boulder, CO: Lynne Rienner, 2004).

119. Tate, *Black Faces in the Mirror*, chap. 5.

120. J. Edward Kellough, *Understanding Affirmative Action* (Washington, D.C.: Georgetown University Press, 2007).

121. Quoted in Donald D. Haider-Markel, *Out and Running: Gay and Lesbian Candidates, Election, and Policy Representation* (Washington, DC: George Washington University Press, 2010), 84.

122. A filibuster is a legislative tool that individuals in opposition to a bill can use to prevent a vote. It involves a senator taking the floor to speak and not relinquishing the floor.

123. Haider-Markel, *Out and Running*, 105.

124. Haider-Markel, *Out and Running*.

125. Donald D. Haider-Markel, Mark R. Joslyn, and Chad J. Kniss, "Minority Group Interests and Political Representation: Gay Elected Officials in the Policy Process," *Journal of Politics* 62, no. 2 (2000): 568–577.

126. Kimberly Cowell-Meyers and Laura Langbein, "Linking Women's Descriptive and Substantive Representation in the United States," *Politics & Gender* 5, no. 4 (2009): 491–518.

127. Vanessa Bouche and Dana E. Wittmer, "Gendered Diffusion on Gendered Issues: The Case of Human Trafficking," *Journal of Public Policy* 35, no. 1 (2015): 1–33.

128. Michael B. Berkman and Robert O'Connor, "Do Women Legislators Matter?" *American Politics Quarterly* 21, no. 1 (1993): 102–124; Jocelyn Crowley, "When Tokens Matter," *Legislative Studies Quarterly* 29, no. 1 (2004): 109–134.

129. Minto and Sinclair-Chapman, "Diversity in Political Institutions."

130. Chris T. Owens, "Black Substantive Representation in State Legislatures from 1971–1994," *Social Science Quarterly* 86, no. 4 (2005): 780–791.

131. For example, see Charles Cameron, David Epstein, and Sharyn O'Halloran, "Do Majority Minority Districts Maximize Substantive Black Representation in Congress?" *American Political Science Review* 90, no. 4 (1996): 794–812.

132. Hero and Tolbert, "Latinos and Substantive Representation."

133. Marshall H. Medoff, Christopher Dennis, and Kerry Stephens, "The Impact of Party Control on the Diffusion of Parental Involvement Laws in the U.S. States," *State Politics & Policy Quarterly* 11, no. 3 (2011): 325–347; Marshall H. Medoff, "State Abortion Politics and TRAP Abortion Laws," *Journal of Women, Politics & Policy* 33, no. 3 (2012): 239–262; John F. Camobreco and Michelle A. Barnello, "Democratic Responsiveness and Policy Shock: The Case of State Abortion Policy," *State Politics & Policy Quarterly* 8, no. 1 (2008): 48–65.

134. Caroline J. Tolbert and Gertrude A. Steuernagel, "Women Lawmakers, State Mandates and Women's Health," *Women & Politics* 22, no. 2 (2001): 1–39.

135. Owens, "Black Substantive Representation"; Haider-Markel, *Out and Running*; but see Cowell-Meyers and Langbein, "When Tokens Matter."

136. Medoff et al., "The Impact of Party"; Medoff, "State Abortion"; Barbara Norrander and Clyde Wilcox, "Public Opinion and Policymaking in the States: The Case of Post-*Roe* Abortion Policy," *Policy Studies Journal* 27, no. 4 (1999): 707–722; Kenneth J. Meier and Deborah R. McFarlane, "The Politics of Funding Abortion—State Responses to the Political Environment," *American Politics Quarterly* 21, no. 1 (1993): 81–101; Owens, "Black Substantive Representation"; James E. Monogan, "The Politics of Immigrant Policy in the 50 U.S. States, 2005–2011," *Journal of Public Policy* 33, no. 1 (2013): 35–64.

137. In one piece, Lax and Phillips examine LGBT policies (Jeffrey Lax and Justin H. Phillips, "Gay Rights in the States: Public Opinion and Policy Responsiveness," *American Political Science Review* 103, no. 3 (2009): 367–386), and in the other (Jeffrey R. Lax and Justin H. Phillips, "The Democratic Deficit in the States," *American Journal of Political Science* 56, no. 1 (2012): 148–166), they examine thirty-nine specific policies in eight larger policy areas, many of which directly concern a minority interest (abortion, immigration, or gay rights), and almost all are of interest to minorities (such as health care and education).

138. Lax and Phillips, "The Democratic Deficit," 163.

139. Lax and Phillips, "The Democratic Deficit"; Norrander and Wilcox, "Public Opinion and Policymaking"; Meier

and McFarlane, "The Politics of Funding Abortion"; but see Cowell-Meyers and Langbein, "Linking Women's Descriptive."

140. Meier and McFarlane, "The Politics of Funding Abortion."

141. Donald D. Haider-Markel and Kenneth J. Meier, "The Politics of Gay and Lesbian Rights: Expanding the Scope of the Conflict," *Journal of Politics* 58, no. 2 (1996): 332–349; E. E. Schattschneider, *The Semisovereign People: A Realistic View of Democracy in America* (Hinsdale, IL: Dryden Press, 1975).

142. For example, see Kenneth D. Wald, James W. Button, and Barbara A. Rienzo, "The Politics of Gay Rights in American Communities: Explaining Antidiscrimination Ordinances and Policies," *American Journal of Political Science* 40, no. 4 (1996): 1152–1178; James W. Button, Barbara A. Rienzo, and Kenneth D. Wald, "The Politics of Gay Rights at the Local and State Level," in *The Politics of Gay Rights*, ed. Craig A. Rimmerman, Kenneth D. Wald, and Clyde Wilcox (Chicago: University of Chicago Press, 2000).

143. Wald et al., "The Politics of Gay Rights in American Communities"; Button et al., "The Politics of Gay Rights"; Haider-Markel, *Out and Running*.

144. V. O. Key Jr., *Southern Politics in the State and Nation* (Knoxville: University of Tennessee Press, 1949).

145. Monogan, "The Politics of Immigrant Policy."

146. Tetsuya Matsubayashi and Rene R. Rocha, "Racial Diversity and Public Policy in the States," *Political Research Quarterly* 65, no. 3 (2012): 600–614.

147. Gary Mucciaroni, *Same Sex, Different Politics: Success and Failure in the Struggles over Gay Rights* (Chicago: University of Chicago Press, 2008).

148. Frances Stokes Berry and William D. Berry, "State Lottery Adoptions as Policy Innovations: An Event History Analysis," *American Political Science Review* 84, no. 2 (1990): 395–415; David M. Glick and Zoe Friedland, "How Often Do States Study Each Other? Evidence of Policy Knowledge Diffusion," *American Politics Research* 42, no. 6 (2014): 956–985; Christopher Z. Mooney, "Modeling Regional Effects on State Policy Diffusion," *Political Research Quarterly* 54, no. 1 (2001): 103–124.

149. Gary Mucciaroni, *Same Sex, Different Politics*.

150. http://NCSL.org.

151. Calculated by author from data available at NCSL.org.

152. For example, see Barbara S. Gamble, "Putting Civil Rights to a Popular Vote," *American Journal of Political Science* 41, no. 2 (1997): 245–269.

153. For example, see Todd Donovan and Shaun Bowler, "Direct Democracy and Minority Rights: An Extension," *American Journal of Political science* 42, no. 3 (1998): 1020–1024.

154. Daniel C. Lewis, "Bypassing the Representational Filter? Minority Rights Policies under Direct Democracy Institutions in the U.S. States," *State Politics and Policy* 11, no. 2 (2011): 198–222.

155. Welfare benefit figures were for 2013 (http://www.census.gov/hhes/www/income/data/incpovhlth/2012/statemhi2_12.xls) and were calculated by the CATO institute (Michael D. Tanner and Charles Hughes, "The Work versus Welfare Trade Off: 2013," August 19, 2013, http://www.cato.org/publications/white-paper/work-versus-welfare-trade), a conservative think tank, and median income was based on census figures that average 2011–2012 figures.

156. Monogan, "The Politics of Immigrant Policy."

157. The percentage of liberals comes from William D. Berry, Evan J. Ringquist, Richard C. Fording, and Russell L. Hanson, "Measuring Citizen and Government Ideology in the American States 1960–1993," *American Journal of Political Science* 42, no. 1 (1998): 327–348, 2012 Updated Data Release. The percentage of minorities comes from NCSL.org. Democratic strength comes from James W. Ceaser and Robert P. Saldin, "A New Measure of Party Strength," *Political Research Quarterly* 58, no. 2 (2005): 245–256.

158. Tate, *Black Faces in the Mirror*, 127–128.

159. Sue Thomas, "The Effects of Race and Gender on Constituency Service," *Western Political Quarterly* 45, no. 1 (1992): 169–180.

160. Mark C. Ellickson and Donald E. Whistler, "Explaining State Legislators' Casework and Public Resource Allocations," *Political Research Quarterly* 54, no. 3 (2001): 553–569.

161. Thomas, "The Effects of Race and Gender."

162. Ellickson and Whistler, "Explaining State Legislators' Casework"; Rebekah Herrick, "Sex Differences in Constituent Engagement," *Social Science Quarterly* 91, no. 4 (2010): 947–963.

163. Sarah F. Anzio and Christopher R. Berry, "The Jackie (and Jill) Robinson Effect Why Do Congresswomen Outperform Congressmen?" *American Journal of Political Science* 55, no. 3 (2011): 478–493.

164. Carla Amuroa, "Fact Sheet: How Bad Is the School-to-Prison Pipeline," *PBS*, http://www.pbs.org/wnet/tavissmiley/tsr/education-under-arrest/school-to-prison-pipeline-fact-sheet/, accessed April 25, 2015.

Chapter 5

1. Kevin Sack, "After Decades, a Time to Reap," *New York Times*, November 5, 2008, A1; Clyde Haberman, "In Honoring Dr. King, Rote Finds Relevance in Obama: NYC," *New York Times*, January 20, 2009, A29; Sheryle Gay Stoleberg, "'From Slavery to History: Americans Witness a Day of Clarity," *New York Times*, January 21, 2009, 4; Susan Saulny, "On Bus to Washington, Old Friends and Organizers from Chicago Will Reminisce," *New York Times*, January 19, 2009, A15.

2. Sack, "After Decades, a Time to Reap."

3. Jim Dwyer, "A Proud Day for Black America, and for the Rest of the Nation, Too," *New York Times*, January 21, 2009, A29.

4. Marc Fisher, "From a Landscape of Faces, a Singular Feeling," *Washington Post*, January 21 2009, A43.

5. Michael E. Ruane, Nikita Stewart, and David Nakamura, "A Vast, Diverse Sea of Humanity Celebrates the Dawn of an Era: From Across the Country, a Jubilant Crowd Converges," *Washington Post*, January 21, 2009, A13.

6. Susan Saulny, "Obama-Inspired Black Voters Find Politics Is for Them, Too," *New York Times*, November 2, 2008, 1.

7. Fisher, "From a Landscape of Faces."

8. Leslie A. Schwindt-Bayer and William Mishler, "An Integrated Model of Women's Representation," *Journal of Politics* 67, no. 2 (2005): 407–428.

9. Marisa A. Abrajano and R. Michael Alvarez, "Assessing the Causes and Effects of Political Trust among U.S. Latinos," *American Politics Research* 38, no. 1 (2010): 110–141.

10. Margin of error reflects the likely range of scores that would have been found if all of a population and not just a sample had been interviewed. For example, if 45% of a sample said X with a margin of error of plus or minus 3, the actual percentage of Americans who would say X would likely be somewhere between 42% and 48%. It is based on statistical inference theory.

11. http://www.gallup.com/services/170948/u.s.%20daily-tracking.aspx; Gary Gates and Frank Newport, "LGBT Percentage Highest in D.C., Lowest in North Dakota," February 15, 2013, http://www.gallup.com/poll/160517/lgbt-percentage-highest-lowest-north-dakota.aspx.

12. See, for example, Ryan L. Claassen, "Political Opinion and Distinctiveness: The Case of Hispanic Ethnicity," *Political Research Quarterly* 57, no. 4 (2004): 609–620.

13. Katherine Tate, "National Black Election Study," 1996. ICPSR version. Columbus: Ohio State University [producer], 1997. Ann Arbor, MI: Inter-university Consortium for Political and Social Research [distributor], 2004. http://doi.org/10.3886/ICPSR02029.v1.

14. Rodolfo de la Garza, Angelo Falcon, F. Chris Garcia, and John A. Garcia, "Latino National Political Survey, 1989–1990," ICPSR06841-v3. Ann Arbor, MI: Inter-university Consortium for Political and Social Research [distributor], 1998. http://doi.org/10.3886/ICPSR06841.v3.

15. Pew Research Center for People and the Press, "A Survey of LGBT Americans: Attitudes, Experiences and Values in Changing Times," June 13, 2013, http://www.pewsocialtrends.org/files/2013/06/SDT_LGBT-Americans_06-2013.pdf.

16. Jaime M. Grant, Lisa A. Motter, and Justin Tanis, "Injustice at Every Turn: A Report of the National Transgender Discrimination Survey," 2011, http://www.thetaskforce.org/downloads/reports/reports/ntds_full.pdf.

17. These figures were calculated by the author using the American National Election Studies (ANES) 2012 Time Series Study [dataset], http://www.electionstudies.org.

18. Calculated by the author using the American National Election Studies (ANES) 2004 Time Series Study [dataset], http://www.electionstudies.org). Stanford University and the University of Michigan (producers). In 2004, 57.0% of Anglos and 51.4% of men reported feeling "Extremely good." In 2012, the figures were 44.8% and 40.3%.

19. These figures were calculated by the author using 2012 ANES Time Series Study.

20. These figures were calculated by the author using 2012 ANES Time Series Study.

21. For discussion, see Paul Gronke, James Hicks, and Timothy E. Cook, "Trust but Verify: Three Lenses on Americans' Trust in Government," in *Understanding Public Opinion*, 3rd ed., ed. Barbara Norrander and Clyde Wilcox (Washington, DC: CQ Press, 2010), 197–214.

22. Calculated by the author using the American National Election Studies (ANES) 2012 Time Series Study [dataset], http://www.electionstudies.org. Stanford University and the University of Michigan (producers).

23. http://www.people-press.org/files/legacy-pdf/01-31-13%20Views%20of%20Government.pdf.

24. Gronke et al., "Trust but Verify."

25. Abrajano and Alvarez, "Assessing the Causes."

26. The Pew Research Center for People and the Press, "Views of Congress: The Problem Lies with Members Not the System," January 31, 2013, http://www.people-press.org/files/legacy-pdf/01-31-13%20Views%20of%20Government.pdf.

27. Abrajano and Alvarez, "Assessing the Causes."

28. Abrajano and Alvarez, "Assessing the Causes," 124.

29. These figures were calculated by the author using 2012 ANES data.

30. Antje Roder and Peter Muhlau, "Low Expectations or Different Evaluations: What Explains Immigrants' High Levels of Trust in Host Country Institutions," *Journal of Ethnic and Migration Studies* 38, no. 5 (2012): 777–792.

31. Rahsaan Maxwell, "Evaluating Migrant Integration: Political Attitudes across Generations in Europe," *International Migration Review* 44, no. 1 (2010): 25–52.

32. Roder and Muhlau, "Low Expectations or Different Evaluations."

33. Peter T. Dinesen and Marc Hooghe, "When in Rome, Do as the Romans Do: The Acculturation of Generalized Trust among Immigrants in Western Europe," *International Migration Review* 44, no. 3 (2010): 697–727.

34. Antje Roder and Peter Muhlau, "What Determines the Trust of Immigrants in Criminal Justice Institutions in Europe?" *European Journal of Criminology* 9, no. 4 (2012): 370–387.

35. Antje Roder and Peter Muhlau, "Discrimination, Exclusion and Immigrants' Confidence in Public Institutions in Europe," *European Societies* 13, no. 4 (2011): 535–557.

36. Calculated by the author using National American Asian Survey 2008. Karthick Ramakrishnan, Jane Junn, Taeku Lee, and Janelle Wong, National Asian American Survey, 2008 [Computer file]. ICPSR31481-v2. Ann Arbor, MI: Inter-university Consortium for Political and Social Research [distributor], 2012-07-19. doi:10.3886/ICPSR31481.v2. See more at http://www.naasurvey.com/data.html#sthash.3s62isqO.dpuf.

37. http://electionstudies.org/nesguide/toptable/tab5b_2.htm.

38. Claudine Gay, "The Effect of Black Congressional Representation on Political Participation," *American Political Science Review* 95, no. 3 (2001): 589–602.

39. These were calculated by the author using 2012 ANES time series data.

40. These were calculated by the author using 2012 ANES time series data.

41. Frank Newport and Jan Sonnenschein, "Obama Approval Fluid among Hispanics, GOP Moderates," August 27, 2013, http://www.gallup.com/poll/164150/obama-approval-fluid-among-hispanics-moderate-gop.aspx.

42. Steve Crabtree, "Gender Gap in Obama Approval Constant since Term Began," May 9, 2013, http://www.gallup.com/poll/154562/Gender-Gap-Obama-Approval-Constant-Term-Began.aspx.

43. Pew Research Center for People and the Press, "A Survey of LGBT Americans: Attitudes, Experiences and Values in Changing Times," June 13, 2013, http://www.pewsocialtrends.org/files/2013/06/SDT_LGBT-Americans_06-2013.pdf.

44. Crabtree, "Gender Gap in Obama Approval."

45. Newport and Sonnenschein, "Obama Approval Fluid among Hispanics."

46. Jeffrey M. Jones, "Conservative Republicans Still Widely Support President Bush," December 11, 2008, http://www.gallup.com/poll/113083/Conservative-Republicans-Still-Widely-Support-Bush.aspx; Joseph Carroll, "Congressional Approval Ratings at 20%; Bush's Approval at 32%," November 7, 2007, http://www.gallup.com/poll/102829/Congress-Approval-Rating-20-Bushs-Approval-32.aspx#2.

47. Lonna Rae Atkenson and Cherie D. Maestas, "Race and the Formation of Attitudes: Responses to Hurricane Katrina," in *Understanding Public Opinion,* 3rd ed., ed. Barbara Norrander and Clyde Wilcox (Washington, DC: CQ Press, 2010), 105–122.

48. Wilkins and Stark, *American Indian Politics,* chap. 4.

49. Justin McCarthy, "Stark Differences in Views on U.S. Status," January 28, 2014, http://www.gallup.com/poll/167072/stark-racial-differences-views-status.aspx.

50. Justin McCarthy, "Stark Differences in Views."

51. Pew Research Center for People and the Press, "A Survey of LGBT Americans," 11.

52. Pew Research Center for People and the Press, "Rise of Asian Americans," April 4, 2013, http://www.pewsocialtrends.org/files/2013/04/Asian-Americans-new-full-report-04-2013.pdf, 154.

53. Pew Research Center for People and the Press, "Rise of Asian Americans," 154.

54. Pew Research Center for People and the Press, "Rise of Asian Americans," 154.

55. Tiffany Harper and Barbara Norrander, "The Rise and Fall of George W. Bush: Popular Support for the President," in *Understanding Public Opinion,* 3rd ed., ed. Barbara Norrander and Clyde Wilcox (Washington, DC: CQ Press, 2010), 215–238.

56. Abrajano and Alvarez, "Assessing the Causes and Effects."

57. Abrajano and Alvarez, "Assessing the Causes and Effects."

58. Lawrence Bobo and Franklin Gilliam, "Race, Sociopolitical Participation and Black Empowerment," *American Political Science Review* 84, no. 2 (1990): 377–393.

59. Katherine Tate, *Black Faces in the Mirror: African Americans and Their Representatives in the U.S. Congress* (Princeton, NJ: Princeton University Press, 2003).

60. Susan A. Banducci, Todd Donovan, and Jeffrey A. Karp, "Minority Representation, Empowerment, and Participation," *Journal of Politics* 66, no. 2 (2004): 534–556.

61. Banducci, Donovan, and Karp, "Minority Representation," 550.

62. Claudine Gay, "Spirals of Trust? The Effect of Descriptive Representation on the Relationship between Citizens and Their Government," *American Journal of Political Science* 46, no. 4 (2002): 717–732.

63. Gay, "Spirals of Trust?" 722.

64. Thomas L. Brunell, Christopher J. Anderson, and Rachel K. Cremona, "Descriptive Representation, District Demography, and Attitudes toward Congress among African Americans," *Legislative Studies Quarterly* 33, no. 2 (2008): 223–244.

65. Beth Reingold and Jessica Harrell, "The Impact of Descriptive Representation on Women's Political Engagement: Does Party Matter?" *Political Research Quarterly* 63, no. 2 (2010): 280–294.

66. Tate, *Black Faces in the Mirror.*

67. Rene R. Rocha, Caroline Tolbert, Daniel C. Bowen, and Christopher Clark, "Race and Turnout: Does Descriptive Representation in State Legislatures Increase Minority Voting?" *Political Research Quarterly* 63, no. 4 (2010): 890–907.

68. Daniel McCool, Susan M. Olson, and Jennifer L. Robinson, *Native Vote: American Indians, the Voting Rights Act, and the Right to Vote* (New York: Cambridge University Press, 2007), chap. 7.

69. Brunell et al., "Descriptive Representation."

70. Jennifer Lawless, "Politics of Presence: Women in the House and Symbolic Representation," *Political Research Quarterly* 53, no. 1 (2004): 81–99.

71. David E. Campbell and Christina Wolbrecht, "See Jane Run: Women Politicians as Role Models for Adolescents," *Journal of Politics* 68, no. 2 (2006): 233–247.

72. Tate, *Black Faces in the Mirror*.

73. Tate, *Black Faces in the Mirror*, 81.

74. Sarah Allen Gershon, "Communicating Female and Minority Interests Online: A Study of Web Site Issue Discussion among Female, Latino, and African American Members of Congress," *Harvard International Journal of Press/Politics* 13, no. 12 (2008): 120–140.

75. David T. Canon, *Race, Redistricting, and Representation: The Unintended Consequences of Black Majority Districts* (Chicago: University of Chicago Press, 1999).

Chapter 6

1. http://www.oyez.org/justices/clarence_thomas, accessed April 30, 2015.

2. David B. Mustard, "Racial, Ethnic, and Gender Disparities in Sentencing: Evidence from the U.S. Federal Courts," *Journal of Law & Economics* 44, no. 1 (2001): 285–314.

3. 478 U.S. 186 (1986).

4. 539 U.S. 558 (2003).

5. 550 U.S. 618 (2007).

6. David E. Wilkins and Heidi K. Stark, *American Indian Politics and the American Political System*, 3rd. ed. (Lanham, MD: Rowman & Littlefield, 2011), 74–75.

7. Wilkins and Stark, *American Indian Politics*, 75.

8. Wilkins and Stark, *American Indian Politics*, 76–78.

9. http://www.uscourts.gov/about-federal-courts/educational-resources/about-educational-outreach/activity-resources/supreme-1.

10. http://www.oyez.org/cases/2010-2019/2014/2014_14_556.

11. Calculated by author from http://www.uscourts.gov/JudgesAndJudgeships/BiographicalDirectoryOfJudges.aspx.

12. Howard Ball, *A Defiant Life: Thurgood Marshall and the Persistence of Racism in America* (New York: Crown, 1998), 174.

13. Quoted in Ball, *A Defiant Life*, 194.

14. Calculated by the author from http://www.uscourts.gov/JudgesAndJudgeships/BiographicalDirectoryOfJudges.aspx.

15. Sital Kalantry, "Judges, Gender, Justice," Summer 2012, http://www.americasquarterly.org/women-in-robes.

16. Kalantry, "Judges, Gender, Justice."

17. Kalantry, "Judges, Gender, Justice."

18. Kalantry, "Judges, Gender, Justice."

19. "Women and Men in Leadership Positions in the European Union 2013: A Review of the Situation and Recent Progress," October 2013, http://ec.europa.eu/justice/gender-equality/files/gender_balance_decision_making/131011_women_men_leadership_en.pdf.

20. "Women and Men in Leadership."

21. "Women and Men in Leadership."

22. "Women and Men in Leadership."

23. "Women and Men in Leadership."

24. "Women and Men in Leadership."

25. "Women and Men in Leadership."

26. UN Women, "Progress of the World's Women 2011–2012: In pursuit of Justice," 2011, http://progress.unwomen.org/pdfs/EN-Report-Progress.pdf.

27. UN Women, "Progress of the World's Women."

28. Kalantry, "Judges, Gender, Justice."

29. Kalantry, "Judges, Gender, Justice."

30. UN Women, "Progress of the World's Women," 61.

31. Calculated by author from http://www.uscourts.gov/JudgesAndJudgeships/BiographicalDirectoryOfJudges.aspx.

32. Antonia Felix, *Sonia Sotomayor: The True American Dream* (New York: Berkley Books, 2010).

33. Felix, *Sonia Sotomayor*, 223.

34. Jennifer Bendery, "Senate Confirms First-Ever Native American Woman as Federal Judge," *Huffington Post*, May 15, 2014, http://www.huffingtonpost.com/2014/05/15/native-american-judge_n_5330273.html, accessed April 28, 2015.

35. Mark Joseph Stern, "Obama's Most Enduring Gay Rights Achievement," *Slate*, June 17, 2014, http://www.slate.com/blogs/outward/2014/06/17/openly_gay_federal_judges_are_obama_s_most_enduring_gay_rights_achievement.html.

36. Calculated by the author from http://www.fjc.gov/servlet/nFsearch, accessed April 7, 2014.

37. Calculated by the author from http://www.uscourts.gov/JudgesAndJudgeships/BiographicalDirectoryOfJudges.aspx, accessed May 2, 2015.

38. Calculated by the author from http://www.uscourts.gov/JudgesAndJudgeships/BiographicalDirectoryOfJudges.aspx, accessed May 2, 2015.

39. http://www.justice.gov/ag/about-office-0.

40. http://www.justice.gov/osg/about-osg.html, updated August 2011.

41. Anthony Gonzalez calculated these figures.

42. Author calculated percentages based on data from American Juricature Society's "Diversity of the Bench" listing found at http://www.judicialselection.us/judicial_selection/bench_diversity/index.cfm?state=.

43. Margaret Williams, "Women's Representation on State Trial and Appellate Courts," *Social Science Quarterly* 88, no. 5 (2007): 1192–1204.

44. Kathleen A. Bratton and Rorie Spill, "Existing Diversity and Judicial Selection: The Role of Appointment Method in Establishing Gender Diversity in State Supreme Courts," *Social Science Quarterly* 83, no 2 (2002): 504–518.

45. Brian Frederick and Matthew J. Strebs, "Women Running for Judge: The impact of Sex on Candidate Success in State Intermediate Appellate Court Elections," *Social Science Quarterly* 89, no. 4 (2008): 937–954.

46. Williams, "Women's Representation on State Trial."

47. Greg Goelzhauser, "Diversifying State Supreme Courts," *Law & Society Review* 45, no. 3 (2011): 761–781; Mark S. Hurwitz and Drew Nable Lanier, "Explaining Judicial Diversity: The Differential Ability of Women and Minorities to Attain Seats on State Supreme and Appellate Courts," *State Politics & Policy Quarterly* 3, no. 4 (2003): 329–352.

48. Williams, "Women's Representation on State Trial"; Goelzhauser, "Diversifying State Supreme Courts"; Hurwitz and Lanier, "Explaining Judicial Diversity."

49. Nancy E. McGlen, Karen O'Connor, Laura van Assendelft, and Wendy Gunther, *Canada, Women, Politics, and American Society* (New York: Longman, 2011), 225.

50. Jennifer M. Jensen and Wendy L. Martinek, "The Effects of Race and Gender on the Judicial Ambitions of State Trial Court Judges," *Political Research Quarterly* 62, no. 2 (2009): 379–392.

51. Margaret Williams, "In a Different Path: The Process of Becoming a Judge for Women and Men," *Judicature* 90, no. 3 (2006): 104–113.

52. Williams, "Women's Representation on State Trial."

53. Goelzhauser, "Diversifying State Supreme Courts."

54. Hurwitz and Lanier, "Explaining Judicial Diversity."

55. Gerald S. Gryski, Gary Zuk, and Deborah J. Barrows, "A Bench That Looks Like America? Representation of African Americans and Latinos on the Federal Courts," *Journal of Politics* 56, no. 4 (1994): 1076–1086; Goelzhauser, "Diversifying State Supreme Courts."

56. Jonathan Kastellec, "Racial Diversity and Judicial Influence on Appellate Courts," *American Journal of Political Science* 57, no. 1 (2013): 167–183.

57. John Gruhl, Cassua Spohn, and Susan Welch, "Women as Policymakers: The Case of Trial Judges," *American Journal of Political Science* 25, no. 2 (1981): 308–322.

58. Christina Boyd, Lee Epstein, and Andrew D. Martin, "Untangling the Causal Effects of Sex on Judging," *American Journal of Political Science* 54, no. 2 (2010): 389–411.

59. Donald R. Songer, Sue Davis, and Susan Haire, "A Reappraisal of Diversification in the Federal Courts: Gender Effects in the Courts of Appeals," *Journal of Politics* 56, no. 2 (1994): 425–439.

60. Jennifer Segal, "Representative Decision Making on the Federal Bench: Clinton's District Court Appointees," *Political Research Quarterly* 53, no. 1 (2000): 137–150.

61. Segal, "Representative Decision Making," 144.

62. Donald R. Songer and Kelley A. Crews-Meyer, "Does Judge Gender Matter? Decision Making in State Supreme Courts," *Social Science Quarterly* 81, no. 3 (2000): 750–762; Sean Farhang and Gregory Wawro, "Institutional Dynamics on the U.S. Court of Appeals: Minority Representation under Panel Decision Making," *Journal of Law, Economics, & Organization* 20, no. 2 (2004): 299–330.

63. Segal," Representative Decision Making," 145.

64. Segal," Representative Decision Making," 145.

65. Farhang and Wawro, "Institutional Dynamics."

66. Kastellec, "Racial Diversity."

67. Adam B. Cox and Thomas J. Miles, "Judicial Ideology and the Transformation of Voting Rights Jurisprudence," *University of Chicago Law Review* 73, no. 4 (2008): 1493–1539; Nancy Scherer, "Blacks on the Bench," *Political Science Quarterly* 119, no. 4 (2004/5): 655–675.

68. For example, see Susan Welch, Michael Combs, and John Gruhl, "Do Black Judges Make a Difference?" *American Journal of Political Science* 32, no. 1 (1988): 126–136.

69. For example, see Cassia Spohn, "The Sentencing Decisions of Black and White Judges: Expected and Unexpected Similarities," *Law and Society* 24, no. 5 (1990): 1197–1216.

70. Todd Collins and Laura Moyer, "Race, Gender and Intersectionality on the Federal Appellate Bench" *Political Research Quarterly* 61, no. 2 (2008): 219–227.

71. Chris Bonneau and Heather Marie Rice, "Impartial Judges? Race, Institutional Context, and U.S. State Supreme Courts," *State Politics and Policy Quarterly* 9, no. 4 (2009): 381–403.

72. Kastellec, "Racial Diversity."

73. Cox and Miles, "Judicial Ideology."

74. Boyd, Epstein, and Martin, "Untangling the Causal Effects."

75. Farhang and Wawro, "Institutional Dynamics."

76. See, for example, Robert A. Dahl, "Decision Making in a Democracy: The Supreme Court as a National Policymaker," *Journal of Public Law* 6 (1957): 279–295.

77. Daniel McCool, Susan M. Olson, and Jennifer L. Robinson, *Native Vote: American Indians, the Voting Rights Act, and the Right to Vote* (New York: Cambridge University Press 2007), 6.

Chapter 7

1. Miranda Leitsinger, "Sex Reassignment Surgery at 74: Medicare Win Opens Door for Transgender Seniors," *NBC*, January 3, 2015, http://www.nbcnews.com/news/us-news/sex-reassignment-surgery-74-medicare-win-opens-door-transgender-seniors-n276986; GLAD, "How 75-Year-Old Army Veteran Denee Mallon Took on Medicare—and won," February 2, 2015, http://www.glad.org/current/post/how-75-year-old-army-veteran-denee-mallon-took-on-medicare-and-won.

2. Leitsinger, "Sex Reassignment Surgery at 74."

3. Frederick C. Mosher, *Democracy and the Public Service* (New York: Oxford University Press, 1968); Mark D. Bradbury and Edward Kellough, "Representative Bureaucracy: Exploring the Potential for Representation in Local Government," *Journal of Public Administration Research and Theory* 18, no. 4 (2008): 697–714.

4. Mosher, "Democracy and the Public Service"; Kenneth J. Meier, Robert D. Wrinkle, and J. L. Polinard, "Representative Bureaucracy and Distributional Equity: Addressing the Hard Question," *Journal of Politics* 61, no. 4 (1999): 1025–1039.

5. Gregory B. Lewis and David W. Pitts, "Representation of Lesbians and Gay Men in Federal, State and Local Bureaucracies," *Journal of Public Administration Research and Theory* 21, no. 1 (2011): 159–180.

6. Mosher, "Democracy and the Public Service," 12.

7. George C. Edwards III and Stephen J. Wayne, *Presidential Leadership: Politics and Policy Making*, 7th ed. (Belmont, CA: Thomson Wadsworth, 2006), chap. 6.

8. Center for American Women and Politics, "Women Appointed to Presidential Cabinets," 2014, http://www.cawp.rutgers.edu/fast_facts/levels_of_office/documents/prescabinet.pdf.

9. http://www.cawp.rutgers.edu/fast_facts/levels_of_office/documents/prescabinet.pdf, accessed September 26, 2014.

10. Quoted in David Roth, *Sacred Honor: A Biography of Colin Powell* (San Francisco, CA: HarperSanFrancisco, 1993).

11. Walter Isaacson, "Colin Powell's Redeeming Failures," *New York Times*, November 16, 2004, accessed September 28, 2014.

12. Walter Isaacson and Editorial Desk, "Good Soldier Powell," *New York Times*, November 16, 2014, accessed September 28, 2014.

13. Madeleine Albright, *Madam Secretary* (New York: Miramax Books, 2003), 219.

14. Albright, *Madam Secretary*, 341.

15. Martin Weil and Emily Langer, "Frank Kameny Dies; Was Leading Gay Rights Activist," *Washington Post*, October 11, 2011, http://www.washingtonpost.com/local/frank-kameny-dies-wasleading-gay-rights-leader/2011/10/11/gIQAIsUwdL_story.html.

16. Lewis and Pitts, "Representation of Lesbians and Gay Men."

17. "Equal Employment Opportunity Commission State and Local Government Information (EEOC-4)," 2011, http://www.eeoc.gov/eeoc/statistics/employment/jobpateeo4/2011/table1/table1.html.

18. "Equal Employment Opportunity Commission State and Local Government Information (EEOC-4)."

19. Barbara Palmer and Dennis Simon, *Breaking the Political Glass Ceiling: Women and Congressional Elections* (New York: Routledge, 2006).

20. Lewis and Pitts, "Representation of Lesbians and Gay Men."

21. Lewis and Pitts, "Representation of Lesbians and Gay Men," 167.

22. J. Edward Kellough, *Understanding Affirmative Action* (Washington, D.C.: Georgetown University Press, 2007).

23. "Summary of the Employment Equity Act," 55 of 1998, issued in terms of Section 25(1) from http://www.labour.gov.za/DOL/legislation/acts/employment-equity/employment-equity-act-and-amendments, accessed September 26, 2014.

24. "Summary of the Employment Equity Act," 55 of 1998.

25. Justice Malala, "Does Race Matter in South Africa?" *BBC News*, August 29, 2012, http://www.bbc.com/news/world-africa-19402353, accessed September 26, 2014.

26. Ben Roberts, Gina Weir-Smith, and Vasu Reddy, "South African Social Attitudes Survey: Affirmative Action," http://www.hsrc.ac.za/uploads/pageContent/1607/Affirmative%20Action.pdf, accessed September 26, 2014.

27. 443 U.S. 193 (1979).

28. J. Edward Kellough, *Understanding Affirmative Action* (Washington, DC: Georgetown University Press, 2007).

29. Kellough, *Understanding Affirmative Action.*

30. Kellough, *Understanding Affirmative Action.*

31. Kellough, *Understanding Affirmative Action.*

32. Kellough, *Understanding Affirmative Action.*

33. http://www.dol.gov/ofccp/regs/compliance/aa.htm.

34. Kellough, *Understanding Affirmative Action.*

35. L. A. Harris, "Revisiting Affirmative Action in Leveling the Playing Field: Who Have Been the True Beneficiaries Anyway?" *Review of Public Personnel Administration* 29, no. 1 (2009): 354–372.

36. Harry J. Holzer and David Neumark, "Affirmative Action: What Do We Know?" *Journal of Policy Analysis and Management* 25, no. 2 (2006): 471.

37. Tim R. Sass and Jennifer L. Troyer, "Affirmative Action, Political Representation, Unions, and Female Police Employment," *Journal of Labor Research* 20, no. 4 (1999): 571–587.

38. Amalia R. Miller and Carmit Segal, "Does Temporary Affirmative Action Produce Persistent Effects? A Study of Black and Female Employment in Law Enforcement," *Review of Economics and Statistics* 94, no. 4 (2012): 1124.

39. Justin McCrary, "The Effect of Court-Ordered Hiring Quotas on the Composition and Quality of Police," *American Economic Review* 97, no. 1 (2007): 318.

40. Lewis and Pitts, "Representation of Lesbians and Gay Men."

41. Kellough, *Understanding Affirmative Action*, chap. 4.

42. http://www.ncsl.org/research/education/affirmative-action-state-action.aspx.

43. 527 U.S. ____ (2014).

44. Kellough, *Understanding Affirmative Action*, chap. 4.

45. Alexandra Kalev, Erin Kelly, and Frank Dobbin, "Best Practices or Best Guesses? Assessing the Efficacy of Corporate Affirmative Action and Diversity Policies," *American Sociological Review* 71, no. 4 (2006): 589–617.

46. Jerry D. Stubben, "Indian Preferences: Racial Discrimination or a Political Right?" in *American Indian Policy: Self-Governance and Economic Development*, ed. Lyman

H. Legters and Fremont J. Lyden (Westport, CT: Greenwood Press, 1994), 109.

47. Stubben, "Indian Preferences," 103–117.

48. Joseph Stewart Jr., Robert E. England, and Kenneth J. Meier, "Black Representation in Urban School Districts: From School Board to Office to Classroom," *Western Political Quarterly* 42, no. 2 (1989): 287–305; Brinck Kerr, Will Miller, William Schreckhise, and Margaret Reid, "When Does Politics Matter? A Reexamination of Determinants of African-American and Latino Municipal Employment Patterns," *Urban Affairs Review* 49, no. 6 (2013): 888–912; Kenneth D. Wald, Barbara A. Rienzo, and James W. Button, "Sexual Orientation and Education Politics: Gay and Lesbian Representation in American Schools," *Journal of Homosexuality* 42, no. 4 (2002): 145–168; Brinck Kerr and Kenneth R. Mladenka, "Does Politics Matter? A Time-Series Analysis of Minority Employment Patterns," *American Journal of Political Science* 38, no. 4 (1994): 918–943; Lana Stein, "Representative Local Government: Minorities in the Municipal Work Force," *Journal of Politics* 48: no. 3 (1986): 694–713; Kenneth R. Mladenka, "Barriers to Hispanic Employment Success in 1200 Cities," *Social Science Quarterly* 70, no. 2 (1989): 391–407.

49. Kerr et al., "When Does Politics Matter?"; Also: Peter K. Eisinger, "Black Employment in Municipal Jobs: The Impact of Black Political Power," *The American Political Science Review* 76, no.2 (1982): 380–392, also found that African American mayors had a large effect on municipal employment of African Americans. But others did not find mayors having an effect at lower positions. (Kerr and Mladenka, "Does Politics Matter?"; Mladenka, "Blacks and Hispanics in Urban Politics."

50. This is also supported by Kerr and Mladenka, and by Mladenka's examination of lower level positions. Earlier work, however, found little effect of political representation on the employment of Hispanics (Susan Welch, Albert K. Karnig, and Richard Eribes, "Changes in Hispanic Local Public Employment in the Southwest," *Western Political Quarterly* 36, no. 4 (1983): 660–673.

51. Wald, Rienzo, and Button, "Sexual Orientation and Education Politics."

52. Stewart, England, and Meier, "Black Representation in Urban School Districts."

53. Sass, and Troyer, "Affirmative Action."

54. Sass, and Troyer, "Affirmative Action."

55. 401 U.S. 424 (1971).

56. Kellough, *Understanding Affirmative Action*.

57. Stewart, England, and Meier "Black Representation in Urban School Districts"; Peter K. Eisinger, "Black Employment in Municipal Jobs": Welch, Karnig, and Eribes, "Changes in Hispanic"; Stein, "Representative Local Government"; Mladenka, "Barriers to Hispanic Employment."

58. Stewart, England, and Meier "Black Representation in Urban School Districts."

59. Zhou Chen, Kakoli Roy, and Carol A. Gotway Crawford, "Examining the Role of Gender in Career Advancement at the Centers of Disease Control and Prevention," *American Journal of Public Health* 100, no. 3 (2010): 426–434; Cynthia Bowling, Christine Kelleher, Jennifer Jones, and Deil Wright, "Cracked Ceilings, Firmer Floors, and Weakening Walls: Trends and Patterns in Gender Representation among Executives Leading American State Agencies, 1970–2000," *Public Administration Review* 66, no. 6 (2006): 823–836.

60. N. Alexander Aquado and H. George Frederickson, "Gender and Careers in City Management: A Case Study of the Career Paths of One Department's MPA Graduates," *Journal of Women, Politics & Policy* 33, no. 1 (2012): 25–37.

61. Bowling, Kelleher, Jones, and Wright, "Cracked Ceilings"; Eisinger, "Black Employment in Municipal Jobs."

62. Stein, "Representative Local Government."

63. J. Edward Kellough, "Integration in the Public Workplace: Determinants of Minority and Female Employment in Federal Agencies," *Public Administration Review* 50, no. 5 (1990): 557–566.

64. Christopher Cornwell and J. Edward Kellough, "Women and Minorities in Federal Government Agencies: Examining New Evidence from Panel Data," *Public Administration Review* 54, no. 3 (1994): 265–270.

65. Bradbury and Kellough, "Representative Bureaucracy."

66. Kenneth J. Meier, Robert D. Wrinkle, and J. L. Polinard, "Representative Bureaucracy and Distributional Equity: Addressing the Hard Question," *Journal of Politics* 61, no. 4 (1999): 1025–1039; Robert Aaron and Glen Powell, "Feedback Practices as a Function of Teacher and Public Race during Reading Group Instruction," *Journal of Negro Education* 51, no 1 (1982): 50–59.

67. John J. Hindera, "Representative Bureaucracy: Further Evidence of Active Representation in the EEOC District Offices," *Journal of Public Administration Research and Theory* 3, no. 3 (1993): 415–429; Sally Coleman Selden, "Passive and Active Representation in the Farmers Home Administration," *American Review of Public Administration* 27, no. 1 (1997): 22–42; Sally Coleman Selden, Jeffery L. Brudney, and J. Edward Kellough, "Bureaucracy as a Representative Institution: Toward a Reconciliation of Bureaucratic Government and Democratic Theory," *American Journal of Political Science* 42, no. 3 (1998): 717–744.

68. Jessica E. Sowa and Sally Coleman Selden, "Administrative Discretion and Active Representation: An Expansion of the Theory of Representative Bureaucracy," *Public Administration Review* 63, no. 6 (2003): 700–710.

69. Hindera, "Representative Bureaucracy."

70. Gregory S. Thielemann and Joseph Stewart Jr., "A Demand-Side Perspective on the Importance of Representative Bureaucracy: AIDS, Ethnicity, Gender, and Sexual Orientation," *Public Administration Review* 56, no. 2 (1996): 168–173.

71. Vicky Wilkins and Brian Williams, "Representing Blue: Representative Bureaucracy and Racial Profiling in the Latino Community," *Administration & Society* 40, no. 8 (2009): 775–798.

72. Dolan, "Representative Bureaucracy."

73. Thomas S. Dee, "A Teacher Like Me: Does Race, Ethnicity, or Gender Matter?" *American Economic Review* 95, no. 1 (2005): 158–165; Jason A. Grissom, Jill Nicholson-Crotty, and Sean Nicholson-Crotty, "Race, Region, and Representative Bureaucracy," *Public Administration Review* 69, no. 5 (2009): 911–919.

74. Thielemann and Stewart, "A Demand-Side Perspective on the Importance of Representative Bureaucracy."

75. Vicky M. Wilkins and Lael R. Keiser, "Linking Passive and Active Representation by Gender: The Case of Child Support Agencies," *Journal of Public Administration Research and Theory* 16, no. 1 (2006): 87, 102–167.

76. Julie Dolan, "Representative Bureaucracy in the Federal Executive: Gender and Spending Priorities," *Journal of Public Administration Research and Theory* 12, no. 3 (2002): 353–375.

77. Selden, "Passive and Active Representation."

78. Sergio Fernandez, Deanna Malatesta, and Craig R. Smith, "Race, Gender, and Government Contracting: Different Explanations or New Prospects for Theory?" *Public Administration Review* 73, no. 1 (2013): 109–120.

79. Hindera, "Representative Bureaucracy."

80. Selden, "Passive and Active Representation."

81. Kenneth J. Meier and Joseph Stewart Jr., "The Impact of Representative Bureaucracies: Educational Systems and Public Policies," *American Review of Public Administration* 22, no. 3 (1992): 157–171.

82. Dee, "Teachers, Race, and Student Achievement."

83. Luis Ricardo Fraga, Kenneth J. Meier, and Robert E. England, "Hispanic Americans and Educational-Policy: Limits to Equal Access," *Journal of Politics* 48, no. 4 (1986): 850–876.

84. Aaron and Powell, "Feedback Practices."

85. Meier, Wrinkle, and Polinard, "Representative Bureaucracy"; David W. Pitts, "Representative Bureaucracy, Ethnicity and Public Schools: Examining the Link between Representation and Performance," *Administration & Society* 39, no. 4 (2007): 497–526; Kenneth J. Meier, "Latinos and Representative Bureaucracy: Testing the Thompson and Henderson Hypotheses," *Journal of Public Administration Search and Theory* 3, no. 4 (1993): 393–414.

86. Pitts, "Representative Bureaucracy, Ethnicity."

87. Dee, "Teachers, Race, and Student Achievement"; Dee, "A Teacher Like Me"; Rene R. Rocha and Daniel P. Hawes, "Racial Diversity, Representative Bureaucracy, and Equity in Multiracial School Districts," *Social Science Quarterly* 90, no. 2 (2009): 326–344; Meier, "Latinos and Representative Bureaucracy"; Kenneth J. Meier, Joseph Stewart Jr., and Robert E. England, "The Politics of Bureaucratic Discretion: Educational Access as an Urban Service," *American Journal of Political Science* 35, no. 1 (1991): 155–177.

88. Lael R. Keiser, Vicky M. Wilkins, and Kenneth J. Meier, "Lipstick and Logarithms: Gender, Institutional Context, and Representative Bureaucracy," *American Political Science Review* 96, no. 3 (2002): 553–564.

89. Danielle Atkins and Vicky M. Wilkins, "Going Beyond Reading, Writing, and Arithmetic: The Effects of Teacher Representation on Teen Pregnancy Rates," *Journal of Public Administration Research and Theory*. 23, no. 4 (2013): 771–790.

90. Pitts, "Representative Bureaucracy."

91. Meier, Wrinkle, and Polinard, "Representative Bureaucracy."

92. Rocha and Hawes, "Racial Diversity."

93. Meier and Stewart, "The Impact of Representative Bureaucracies."

94. Pitts, "Representative Bureaucracy."

95. Stewart, England, and Meier, "Black Representation in Urban School Districts."

96. Jason A. Grissom and Lael Keiser, "A Supervisor Like Me: Race, Representation, and the Satisfaction and Turnover Decisions of Public Sector Employees," *Journal of Policy Analysis and Management* 30, no. 3 (2011): 557–580.

97. Kenneth J. Meier and Kevin B. Smith, "Representative Democracy and Representative Bureaucracy: Examining the Top-Down and Bottom-Up Linkages," *Social Science Quarterly* 75, no. 4 (1994): 790–803.

98. Mark Bradbury and J. Edward Kellough, "Representative Bureaucracy: Assessing the Evidence on Active Representation," *American Review of Public Administration* 41, no. 2 (2011): 157–167.

99. Billy R. Close and Patrick L. Mason, "After the Traffic Stops: Officer Characteristics and Enforcement Actions," *Topics in Economic Analysis & Policy* 6, no. 1 (2006) 1–43; Stacia Gilliard-Mathews, Brian R. Kowalski, and Richard Lundman, "Officer Race and Citizen-Reported Traffic Ticket Decisions by Police in 1999 and 2002," *Policy Quarterly* 11, no. 2 (2008): 2002–2019.

100. Meier and Nicholson-Crotty, "Gender, Representative Bureaucracy, and Law Enforcement."

101. Robert A. Brown and James Frank, "Race and Officer Decision Making: Examining Differences in Arrest Outcomes between Black and White Officers," *Justice Quarterly* 23, no. 1 (2006): 96–126.

102. Bradbury and Kellough, "Representative Bureaucracy."

103. Ivan Y. Sun and Brian K. Payne, "Racial Differences in Resolving Conflicts: A Comparison between Black and White Police Officers," *Crime & Delinquency* 50, no. 4 (2004): 516–541.

104. Nick A. Theobald and Donald P. Haider-Markel, "Race, Bureaucracy, and Symbolic Representation: Interactions between Citizens and Police," *Journal of Public Administration Research and Theory* 19, no. 2 (2009): 409–426.

105. Yongbeom Hur, "Racial Diversity, Is It a Blessing to an Organization? Examining Its Organizational Consequences

in Municipal Police Departments," *International Review of Administrative Sciences* 79, no. 1 (2013): 149–164.

106. Wilkins and Williams, "Representing Blue: Representative Bureaucracy."

107. Meier, "Latinos and Representative Bureaucracy."

Chapter 8

1. Josh Earnest, "President Obama Supports Same-Sex Marriage," May 10, 2012, https://www.whitehouse.gov/blog/2012/05/10/obama-supports-same-sex-marriage.

2. Jo Becker, "How the President Got to 'I Do' on Same-Sex Marriage," *New York Times,* April 16, 2016, http://www.nytimes.com/2014/04/20/magazine/how-the-president-got-to-i-do-on-same-sex-marriage.html.

3. Benjamin I. Page and Robert Y. Shapiro, "Effects of Public Opinion on Policy," *American Political Science Review* 77, no. 1 (1983): 175–190.

4. Jeffrey R. Lax and Justin H. Phillips, "The Democratic Deficit in the States," *American Journal of Political Science* 56, no. 1 (2012): 148–166; Jeffrey Lax and Justin H. Phillips, "Gay Rights in the States: Public Opinion and Policy Responsiveness," *American Political Science Review* 103, no. 3 (2009): 367–386.

5. https://gssdataexplorer.norc.org.

6. Christopher Tarman and David O. Sears, "The Conceptualization and Measurement of Symbolic Racism," *Journal of Politics* 67, no. 3 (2005): 733.

7. Tarman and Sears, "The Conceptualization and Measurement of Symbolic Racism," 738.

8. The question asked: "Are you in favor of desegregation, strict segregation, or something in between?" http://www.electionstudies.org/nesguide/toptable/tab4b_3.htm.

9. Respondents were asked how strongly they agreed with the following statement: "White people have a right to keep (Negroes/Blacks/African-Americans) out of their neighborhoods if they want to, and (Negroes/Blacks/African-Americans) should respect that right." https://gssdataexplorer.norc.org.

10. https://gssdataexplorer.norc.org.

11. Janet K. Swim, Kathryn J. Aikin, Wayne S. Hall, and Barbara A. Hunter, "Sexism and Racism: Old Fashioned and Modern Prejudices," *Journal of Personality and Social Psychology* 68, no. 2 (1995): 199, 214.

12. Swim, Aikin, Hall, and Hunter, "Sexism and Racism," 200.

13. Swim, Aikin, Hall, and Hunter, "Sexism and Racism."

14. Gallup, "Gay and Lesbian Rights," October 14, 2014, http://www.gallup.com/poll/1651/Gay-Lesbian-Rights.aspx.

15. Jeffrey M. Jones, "More Americans See Gay, Lesbian Orientation as Birth Factor by 47% to 33%, Americans Say It Is Inherent Rather Than Product of Environment," May 16, 2013, http://www.gallup.com/poll/162569/americans-gay-lesbian-orientation-birth-factor.aspx.

16. Gregory B. Lewis, "Does Believing Homosexuality Is Innate Increase Support for Gay Rights?" *Policy Studies Journal* 37, no. 4 (2009): 669–693; Donald D. Haider-Markel and Mark R. Joslyn, "Beliefs about the Origin of Homosexuality and Support for Gay Rights: An Empirical Test of Attribution Theory," *Public Opinion Quarterly* 72, no. 2 (2008): 291–310.

17. Lewis, "Does Believing Homosexuality." Attribution theory would also fail to explain why white Americans did not give rights to blacks, since race is innate.

18. Aaron T. Norton and Gregory Herek, "Heterosexuals' Attitudes toward Transgender Peoples," *Sex Roles* 68, no. 1 (2013): 738–753.

19. There were some wording changes over the years, such as using the term *Negro* instead of *black*, and in 1980 the phrase "even if it means giving them preferential treatment" was used; http://www.electionstudies.org/nesguide/toptable/tab4b_4.htm.

20. There were some wording changes over the years, such as using the term *Negro* instead of *black*, and after 1986 the following phrase was added: "or is this not the federal government's business?" and in other years the phrase "or should the government in Washington leave these matters to the states and local communities?" was added. http://www.electionstudies.org/nesguide/toptable/tab4b8.htm.

21. https://gssdataexplorer.norc.org.

22. https://gssdataexplorer.norc.org.

23. The specific question asked: "What do you think the chances are these days that a white person won't get a job or promotion while an equally or less qualified black person gets one instead? Is this very likely, somewhat likely, or not very likely to happen these days? https://gssdataexplorer.norc.org.

24. These figures were calculated by author.

25. Gallup, "Gay and Lesbian Rights."

26. Gallup, "Gay and Lesbian Rights."

27. Public Religion Research Institute, "Strong Majorities of Americans Favor Rights and Legal Protections for Transgender People," October 3, 2011, http://publicreligion.org/research/2011/11/american-attitudes-towards-transgender-people/#.VVN8i9pVikp.

28. Donald D. Haider-Markel, "Morality Policy and Individual-Level Political Behavior: The Case of Legislative Voting on Lesbian and Gay Issues," *Policy Studies Journal* 27, no. 4 (1999): 735–749.

29. Lydia Saad, "Americans More Pro-Immigration Than in Past," July 11, 2013, http://www.gallup.com/poll/163457/americans-pro-immigration-past.aspx.

108. John J. Hindera and Cheryl D. Young, "Representative Bureaucracy: The Theoretical Implications of Statistical Interaction," *Political Research Quarterly* 51, no. 3 (1998): 655–671.

30. Saad, "Americans More Pro-Immigration."

31. Pew Research Center for People and the Press, "Broad Public Support for Legal Status for Undocumented Immigrants," June 4, 2015, http://www.people-press.org/files/2015/06/6-4-15-Immigration-release.pdf, accessed August 28, 2015.

32. Pew Research Center for the People and the Press, "Broad Public Support."

33. Rich Morin, "Study: Polls May Underestimate Anti-Gay Sentiment and Size of Gay, Lesbian Population," October 9, 2013, http://www.pewresearch.org/fact-tank/2013/10/09/study-polls-may-underestimate-anti-gay-sentiment-and-size-of-gay-lesbian-population/.

34. James H. Kuklinski, Michael D. Cobb, and Martin Gilens, "Racial Attitudes and the New South," *Journal of Politics* 59, no. 2 (1997): 323–349.

35. Kuklinski, Cobb, and Gilens, "Racial Attitudes and the New South"; David P. Redlawsk, Caroline J. Tolbert, and William Franko, "Voters, Emotions, and Race in 2008: Obama as the First Black President," *Political Research Quarterly* 63, no. 4 (2010): 875–889; Alexander L. Janus, "The Influence of Social Desirability Pressure on Expressed Immigration Attitudes," *Social Science Quarterly* 91, no. 4 (2010): 928–946; Matthew J. Steb, Barbara Burrell, Brian Frederick, and Michael J. Genovese, "Social Desirability Effects and Support for a Female American President," *Public Opinion Quarterly* 72, no. 1 (2008): 76–89.

36. Stanley Feldman, "Values, Ideology, and the Structure of Political Attitudes," in *Oxford Handbook of Political Psychology,* ed. David O. Sears, Leonie Huddy, and Robert Jervis (New York: Oxford University Press, 2003), 481; Carroll J. Glynn, Susan Herbst, Garrett J. O'Keefe, and Robert Y. Shapiro, *Public Opinion* (Boulder, CO: Westview, 1999), 105.

37. Glynn, Herbst, O'Keefe, and Shapiro, *Public Opinion,* 104.

38. Glynn, Herbst, O'Keefe, and Shapiro, *Public Opinion,* 105.

39. Special Eurobarometer 393: "Discrimination in the EU in 2012," November 2012, http://ec.europa.eu/public_opinion/archives/ebs/ebs_393_en.pdf.

40. Special Eurobarometer 393: "Discrimination," 28.

41. Special Eurobarometer 393: "Discrimination," 58.

42. Special Eurobarometer 393: "Discrimination," 33.

43. Special Eurobarometer 393: "Discrimination," 60.

44. Special Eurobarometer 393: "Discrimination," 90.

45. Special Eurobarometer 393: "Discrimination," 79.

46. Special Eurobarometer 393: "Discrimination," 80.

47. Pew Center's Religion and Public Life Project, "Changing Attitudes on Gay Marriage," September 24, 2014, http://features.pewforum.org/same-sex-marriage-attitudes/index.php.

48. Pew Research Center for People and the Press, "Most Say Illegal Immigrants Should Be Allowed to Stay, But Citizenship Is More Divisive," March 28, 2013, http://www.people-press.org/2013/03/28/most-say-illegal-immigrants-should-be-allowed-to-stay-but-citizenship-is-more-divisive/.

49. Pew Research Center for People and the Press. "Trends in Political Values and Core Beliefs 1987–2007," March 22, 2007, http://www.people-press.org/files/legacy-pdf/312.pdf.

50. http://www.electionstudies.org/nesguide/2ndtable/t4b_4_1.htm.

51. http://www.electionstudies.org/nesguide/2ndtable/t4b_4_1.htm.

52. Pew Research Center for People and the Press, "Most Say Illegal Immigrants."

53. Ravi K. Perry and Yasmiyn A. Irizarry, "Challenging the Black Church Narrative: Race, Class, and Homosexual Attitudes," *Journal of Homosexuality* (Forthcoming).

54. Perry and Irizarry, "Challenging the Black Church."

55. Paul R. Brewer, *Value War: Public Opinion and the Politics of Gay Rights* (Lanham, MD: Rowman & Littlefield, 2008), 28.

56. Mark Hugo Lopez and Danielle Cuddington, "Latinos' Changing Views of Same-Sex Marriage," June 19, 2013, http://www.pewresearch.org/fact-tank/2013/06/19/latinos-changing-views-of-same-sex-marriage/.

57. For example, see Brewer, *Value War,* chap. 2 and 3.

58. Pew Research Center for People and the Press, "Trends in Political Values."

59. Sara Goo, "In Your Words: Views of Same-Sex Marriage, Homosexuality," Pew Research Center, June 6, 2013, http://www.pewresearch.org/fact-tank/2013/06/06/in-your-words-views-of-same-sex-marriage-homosexuality/.

60. Pew Research Center for People and the Press, "Most Say Illegal Immigrants."

61. Eric Leon McDaniel, Irfan Nooruddin, and Allyson Faith Shortle, "Divine Boundaries: How Religion Shapes Citizens' Attitudes toward Immigrants," *American Politics Research* 39, no. 1 (2011): 205–233.

62. Pew Research Center for People and the Press, "In Gay Marriage Debate, Both Supporters and Opponents See Legal Recognition as Inevitable," June 6, 2013, http://www.people-press.org/2013/06/06/in-gay-marriage-debate-both-supporters-and-opponents-see-legal-recognition-as-inevitable/.

63. Pew Research Center for People and the Press, "Most Say Illegal Immigrants."

64. This was calculated by author using 2012 GSS data. The question asked: "Some people say that because of past discrimination, blacks should be given preference in hiring and promotion. Others say that such preference in hiring and promotion of blacks is wrong because it discriminates against whites. What about your opinion—are you for or against preferential hiring and promotion of blacks? Then were asked, "Do you favor/oppose preference in hiring and promotion strongly or not strongly?"

65. Angus Campbell, Philip E. Converse, Warren E. Miller, and Donald E. Stokes, *The American Voter* (New York: Wiley, 1960).

66. Morris Fiorina, *Retrospective Voting in American National Elections* (New Haven, CT: Yale University Press, 1981).

67. http://www.electionstudies.org/nesguide/2ndtable/t4b_4_1.htm.

68. Pew Research Center's Religion and Public Life Project, "Changing Attitudes on Gay Marriage."

69. Pew Research Center for People and the Press. "Trends in Political Values," 35.

70. Pew Research Center for People and the Press, "Most Say Illegal Immigrants."

71. http://www.electionstudies.org/nesguide/2ndtable/t4b_4_1.htm.

72. Pew Research Center's Religion and Public Life Project, "Changing Attitudes on Gay Marriage."

73. Gordon W. Allport, *The Nature of Prejudice* (Cambridge, MA: Perseus Books, 1954); Jay Barth, L. Marvin Overby, and Scott H. Huffman, "Community Context, Personal Contact, and Support for an Anti-Gay Rights Referendum," *Political Research Quarterly* 62, no. 2 (2009): 355–365; L. Marvin Overby and Jay Barth, "Contact, Community Context, and Public Attitudes toward Gay Men and Lesbians," *Polity* 34, no. 3 (2002): 434–456; Gregory M. Herek and Eric K. Glunt, "Interpersonal Contact and Heterosexuals' Attitudes toward Gay Men: Results from a National Survey," *Journal of Sex Research* 30, no. 3 (1993): 239–244; Lee Singleman and Susan Welch, "The Contact Hypothesis Revisited: Black White Interaction and Positive Racial Attitudes," *Social Forces* 71, no. 3 (1993): 781–795; Robert M. Stein, Stephanie Shirley Post, and Allison I. Rinden, "Reconciling Context and Contact Effects on Racial Attitudes," *Political Research Quarterly* 53, no. 2 (2000): 285–303.

74. Goo, "In Your Words."

75. In the responses, African American respondents were removed from analysis about affirmative action, Hispanics were removed when looking at immigration, and individuals who had had sex with someone of the same sex in the past five years were removed when examining same-sex marriage.

76. Susan Welch, Lee Sigelman, Timothy Bledsoe, and Michael Combs, *Race and Place: Race Relations in an American City* (New York: Cambridge University Press, 2001).

77. Brewer, *Value War*.

78. V. O. Key Jr., *Southern Politics in the State and Nation* (Knoxville: University of Tennessee Press, 1949).

79. H. M. Blalock Jr., "Per Cent Non-White and Discrimination in the South," *American Sociological Review* 22, no. 6 (1957): 677–682; H. M. Blalock Jr., "Economic Discrimination and Negro Increase," *American Sociological Review* 21, no. 5 (1956): 584–588; Caroline J. Tolbert and John A. Grummel, "Revisiting the Racial Threat Hypothesis: White Voter Support for California's Proposition 209," *State Politics and Policy Quarterly* 3, no. 2 (2003): 183–202; Michael W. Giles, "Percent Black and Racial Hostility: An Old Assumption Reexamined," *Social Science Quarterly* 58, no. 3 (1977): 412–417; Michael W. Giles and Kaenan Hertz, "Racial Threat and Partisan Identification," *American Political Science Review* 88, no. 2 (1994): 317–326.

80. Tolbert and Grummel, "Revisiting the Racial Threat."

81. D. Stephen Voss, "Beyond Racial Threat: Failure of an Old Hypothesis in the New South," *Journal of Politics* 58, no. 4 (1996): 1156–1170; N. Susan Gaines and James C. Garand, "Morality, Equality, or Locality: Analyzing the Determinants of Support for Same-Sex Marriage," *Political Research Quarterly* 63, no. 3 (2010): 553–567; Michael W. Giles and Melanie A. Buckner, "David Duke and Black Threat: An Old Hypothesis Revisited," *Journal of Politics*. 55, no. 3 (1993): 702–713.

82. Voss, "Beyond Racial Threat"; Giles and Buckner, "David Duke and Black Threat"; Michael W. Giles and Melanie A. Buckner, "Beyond Racial Threat: Failure of an Old Hypothesis in the New South: Comment," *Journal of Politics* 58, no. 4 (1996): 1171–1180.

83. Michael W. Giles and Kaenan Hertz, "Racial Threat and Partisan Identification," *The American Political Science Review* 88, no. 2 (1994): 317–326; Key, *Southern Politics*.

84. J. Eric Oliver and Janelle Wong, "Intergroup Prejudice in Multiethnic Settings," *American Journal of Political Science* 47, no. 4 (2003): 567–582.

85. Rene R. Rocha and Rodolfo Espino, "Racial Threat, Residential Segregation, and the Policy Attitudes of Anglos," *Political Research Quarterly* 62, no. 2 (2009): 415–426.

86. Gary Mucciaroni, *Same Sex, Different Politics: Success and Failure in the Struggles over Gay Rights* (Chicago: University of Chicago Press, 2008).

87. Brewer, *Value War*, 70.

88. John Zaller, *The Nature and Origins of Mass Opinion* (New York: Cambridge University Press, 1992).

89. Brewer, *Value War*.

90. Rebecca J. Kreitzer, Allison J. Hamilton, and Caroline J. Tolbert, "Does Policy Adoption Change Opinions on Minority Rights? The Effects of Legalizing Same-Sex Marriage," *Political Research Quarterly* 67, no. 4 (2014): 795–808.

Chapter 9

1. David E. Wilkins and Heidi K. Stark, *American Indian Politics and the American Political System,* 3rd ed. (Lanham, MD: Rowman & Littlefield, 2011), 141.

2. Wilkins and Stark, *American Indian Politics,* 141–142.

3. Wilkins and Stark, *American Indian Politics,* 142.

4. National Indian Gaming Commission, http://www.nigc.gov/LinkClick.aspx?fileticket=63DH1pii2Z4%3d&tabid=67; Randall K. Q. Akee and Jonathan B. Taylor,

Social and Economic Change on American Indian Reservations: A Databook of the US Censuses and the American Community Survey 1990–2010 (Sarasota, FL: Taylor Policy, Inc., 2014).

5. National Indian Gaming Commission.

6. Jonathan B. Taylor and Joseph P. Kalt, *American Indians on Reservations: A Databook of Socioeconomic Change between 1990 and 2000 Censuses* (Cambridge, MA: Harvard Project on American Indian Economic Development), January 2005, http://www.ksg.harvard.edu/hpaied.

7. https://www.opensecrets.org/industries/totals.php?cycle=2014&ind=G6550.

8. https://www.opensecrets.org/industries/indus.php?cycle=2014&ind=G6550.

9. https://www.opensecrets.org/industries/background.php?cycle=2014&ind=G6550.

10. Daniel McCool, Susan M. Olson, and Jennifer L. Robinson, *Native Vote: American Indians, the Voting Rights Act, and the Right to Vote* (New York: Cambridge University Press, 2007), chap. 8.

11. Wilkins and Stark, *American Indian Politics,* 169–170.

12. Sidney Verba, Kay Lehman Schlozman, and Henry E. Brady, *Voice and Equality: Civic Voluntarism in American Politics* (Cambridge, MA: Harvard University Press, 1995).

13. These were all listed as swing states by *Politico, The New York Times,* and *CNN.* Other states sometimes listed were North Carolina and Nevada.

14. This includes just those who identified as African American alone, not with another race as well. http://quickfacts.census.gov/qfd/states/00000.html.

15. This figure is for those who identified as Hispanic alone and not another race or ethnicity. http://quickfacts.census.gov/qfd/states/00000.html.

16. This figure is for those who identified as Asian American alone and not with another race. http://quickfacts.census.gov/qfd/states/00000.html.

17. These figures do not include Native Hawaiians or other Pacific Islanders. Collectively, this group is only about 0.2% of the population.

18. These figures are based on 2012 census estimates. http://quickfacts.census.gov/qfd/index.html.

19. Elizabeth M. Hoeffel, Sonya Rastogi, Myong Ouk Kim, and Hasan Shahid, "The Asian Population: 2010: 2010 Census Briefs," March 2012, http://www.census.gov/prod/cen2010/briefs/c2010br-11.pdf, 4; Sharon R. Ennis, Merarys Rios-Vergas, and Nora G. Albert, "Hispanic Population: Census Brief: 2010," May 2011, http://www.census.gov/prod/cen2010/briefs/c2010br-04.pdf.

20. Anna Brown, "U.S. Hispanic and Asian Populations Growing, but for Different Reasons," June 26, 2014, http://www.pewresearch.org/fact-tank/2014/06/26/u-s-hispanic-and-asian-populations-growing-but-for-different-reasons/

21. Brown, "U.S. Hispanic and Asian Populations."

22. Lindsay M. Howden and Julie A. Meyer, "Age and Sex Composition: 2010: 2010 Census Briefs," May 2011, http://www.census.gov/prod/cen2010/briefs/c2010br-03.pdf.

23. "Life Expectancy Racial Gap Shrinks, Study Shows," *Huffington Post,* August 5, 2012, http://www.huffingtonpost.com/2012/06/05/life-expectancy-racial-gap-shrinks-study_n_1571991.html.

24. http://www.pewhispanic.org/files/2012/02/Statistical-Portrait-of-Hispanics-in-the-United-States-2010_Apr-3.pdf.

25. Howden and Meyer, "Age and Sex Composition: 2010."

26. Calculated by author from Howden and Meyer, "Age and Sex Composition: 2010: 2010 Census Briefs," May 2011, http://www.census.gov/prod/cen2010/briefs/c2010br-03.pdf. Table 3.

27. Gary Gates and Frank Newport, "LGBT Percentage Highest in D.C., Lowest in North Dakota," February 15, 2013, http://www.gallup.com/poll/160517/lgbt-percentage-highest-lowest-north-dakota.aspx; Gary J. Gates, "How Many People Are Lesbian, Gay, Bisexual and Transgender?" Los Angeles, CA: The Williams Institute at UCLA School of Law, April 2011, http://williamsinstitute.law.ucla.edu/research/census-lgbt-demographics-studies/how-many-people-are-lesbian-gay-bisexual-and-transgender/.

28. Gates, "How Many People."

29. The question asked: "Do you, personally, identify as lesbian, gay, bisexual or transgender?" The tracking poll interviewed 206,186 individuals in 2012, so even though LGBT only made up 3.5% of those interviewed, there were still enough LGBT to generalize their attitudes and traits.

30. Rich Morin, "Study: Polls May Underestimate Anti-Gay Sentiment and Size of Gay, Lesbian Population," October 9, 2013, http://www.pewresearch.org/fact-tank/2013/10/09/study-polls-may-underestimate-anti-gay-sentiment-and-size-of-gay-lesbian-population/.

31. In the question on whether they were attracted to the same sex, the differences were 14% to 15%.

32. Gates and Newport, "LGBT Percentage."

33. Gates and Newport, "LGBT Percentage."

34. Gary J. Gates, "LGBT Adult Immigrants in the United States," The Williams Institute, March 2013, http://williamsinstitute.law.ucla.edu/wp-content/uploads/LGBTImmigrants-Gates-Mar-2013.pdf.

35. Gates, "LGBT Adult Immigrants."

36. http://www.census.gov/population/race/data/ppl-ba12.html, Table 7.

37. http://www.census.gov/population/race/data/ppl-ba12.html, Table 7.

38. Pew Research Center for People and the Press, "Rise of Asian Americans," April 4, 2013, http://www.pewsocialtrends.org/files/2013/04/Asian-Americans-new-full-report-04-2013.pdf, 1.

39. Pew Research Center for People and the Press, "Rise of Asian Americans," 24.

40. Pew Research Center for People and the Press, "Rise of Asian Americans," 10.

41. Pew Research Center for People and the Press, "Rise of Asian Americans," 24.

42. Anna Brown and Eileen Patten, "Statistical Portrait of Hispanics in the U.S. 2012," April 29, 2014, http://www.pewhispanic.org/2014/04/29/statistical-portrait-of-hispanics-in-the-united-states-2012/, Table 4.

43. Brown and Patten, "Statistical Portrait of Hispanics," Table 4.

44. Pew Hispanic Center, "The Path Not Taken: Two-thirds of Legal Mexican Immigrants Are Not U.S. Citizens," February 4, 2013, http://www.pewhispanic.org/files/2013/02/Naturalizations_Jan_2013_FINAL.pdf.

45. http://www.census.gov/population/race/data/ppl-ba12.html, Table 1; http://www.pewhispanic.org/2013/06/19/hispanics-of-honduran-origin-in-the-united-states-2011/.

46. http://www.census.gov/population/race/data/ppl-aa12.html, Table 1.

47. One exception is that Cubans are older; only 18% are under eighteen years old. http://www.census.gov/population/hispanic/data/2012.html, table 3; http://www.census.gov/population/hispanic/data/2012.html, Table 1.

48. http://www.census.gov/population/www/cen2000/briefs/phc-t9/index.html, Table 1.

49. Howden and Meyer, "Age and Sex Composition: 2010."

50. Pew Research Center for People and the Press, "A Survey of LGBT Americans," 4.

51. Pew Research Center for People and the Press, "A Survey of LGBT Americans," 45.

52. http://www.pewhispanic.org/files/2014/04/FINAL_Statistical-Portrait-of-Hispanics-in-the-United-States-2012.pdf, Table 9.

53. http://www.pewhispanic.org/files/2014/04/FINAL_Statistical-Portrait-of-Hispanics-in-the-United-States-2012.pdf, Table 9.

54. http://www.pewhispanic.org/files/2014/04/FINAL_Statistical-Portrait-of-Hispanics-in-the-United-States-2012.pdf, Table 9.

55. Calculated by author from http://census.gov/hhes/www/socdemo/voting/publications/p20/2012/tables.html.

56. Sidney Verba and Norman H. Nie, *Participation in America: Political Democracy and Social Equality* (Chicago: University of Chicago Press, 1972).

57. Verba and Nie, *Participation in America.*

58. Verba, Schlozman, and Brady, *Voice and Equality.*

59. U.S. Census, "Table 616. Employed Civilians by Occupation, Sex, Race and Hispanic Origin: 2010," 2012, https://www.census.gov/compendia/statab/2012/tables/12s0616.pdf.

60. U.S. Census, "Table 616."

61. U.S. Census, "Table 616."

62. U.S. Census, "Table 616."

63. http://www.census.gov/hhes/www/income/data/historical/people/index.html.

64. Akee and Taylor, "Social and Economic Change," 33.

65. http://factfinder.census.gov/faces/tableservices/jsf/pages/productview.xhtml?src=bkmk.

66. Akee and Taylor, "Social and Economic Change," 35. n.

67. Akee and Taylor, "Social and Economic Change," 56–57; http://factfinder.census.gov/faces/tableservices/jsf/pages/productview.xhtml?src=bkmk.

68. Gary J. Gates and Frank Newport, "Special Report: 3.4% of U.S. Identify as LGBT," October 18, 2012, http://www.gallup.com/poll/158066/special-report-adults-identify-lgbt.aspx.

69. Pew Research Center for People and the Press, "A Survey of LGBT Americans"; but see Gates and Newport, "Special Report."

70. Pew Research Center for People and the Press, "A Survey of LGBT Americans," 4.

71. Gary Gates and Frank Newport, "LGBT Americans Skew Democratic, Largely Support Obama," October 18, 2012, http://www.gallup.com/poll/158102/lgbt-americans-skew-democratic-largely-support-obama.aspx.

72. Gates and Newport, "Special Report."

73. W. V. Lee Badgett, Laura E. Durso, and Alyssa Schneebaum, "New Patterns of Poverty in the Lesbian, Gay, and Bisexual Community," June 2013, http://williamsinstitute.law.ucla.edu/wp-content/uploads/LGB-Poverty-Update-Jun-2013.pdf.

74. http://epp.eurostat.ec.europa.eu/statistics_explained/index.php/Gender_pay_gap_statistics#Further_Eurostat_information, accessed September 30, 2014.

75. http://epp.eurostat.ec.europa.eu/statistics_explained/index.php/Gender_pay_gap_statistics#Further_Eurostat_information, accessed September 30, 2014.

76. http://epp.eurostat.ec.europa.eu/statistics_explained/index.php/Gender_pay_gap_statistics#Further_Eurostat_information, accessed September 30, 2014.

77. http://epp.eurostat.ec.europa.eu/statistics_explained/index.php/Gender_pay_gap_statistics#Further_Eurostat_information, accessed September 30, 2014.

78. Eurostat European Commission, "Indicators of European Integration: A Pilot Study," 2011, http://epp.eurostat.ec.europa.eu/cache/ITY_OFFPUB/KS-RA-11-009/EN/KS-RA-11-009-EN.PDF, accessed September 30, 2014.

79. "Eurostat European Commission, "Indicators of European Integration," Table 4.

80. "Eurostat European Commission, "Indicators of European Integration," Table 4.

81. Verba, Schlozman, and Brady, *Voice and Equality.*

82. Janelle Wong, S. Karthick Ramakrishnan, Taeku Lee, and Jane Junn, *Asian American Political Participation: Emerging Constituents and Their Political Identities* (New York: Russell Sage Foundation, 2011).

83. Bureau of Labor Statistics, "Economic News Release: Volunteering in the United States, 2014," February 25, 2015, http://www.bls.gov/news.release/volun.nr0.htm, Table A. Volunteers were people who did unpaid work through or for an organization. The survey was a supplement to the monthly 60,000 household survey.

84. Bureau of Labor Statistics, "Economic News Release: Table 2: Volunteers by Annual Hours of Volunteer Activities and Selected Characteristics, September 2014," February 25, 2015, http://www.bls.gov/news.release/volun.t02.htm.

85. Bureau of Labor Statistics, "Economic News Release: Volunteering in the United States, 2014," Table A.

86. Bureau of Labor Statistics, "Economic News Release: Volunteering in the United States, 2014," Table A.

87. The exact wording was "In the past month, did you do any volunteer activity through organizations, that is donate your time and energy not for pay?" These figures were calculated by the author.

88. See Note 87.

89. Pew Research Center for People and the Press, "Rise of Asian Americans."

90. Pew Research Center, "The Shifting Religious Identity of Latinos in the United States: Nearly One in Four Are Former Catholics," May 7, 2014, http://www.pewforum.org/files/2014/05/Latinos-Religion-07-22-full-report.pdf, 19.

91. Wong, Ramakrishnan, Lee, and Junn, *Asian American Political Participation*.

92. Pew Research Center, "The Shifting Religious Identity," 46.

93. Calculated by author using 2012 GSS data.

94. Pew Research Center, "A Survey of LGBT Americans."

95. Pew Research Center, "A Survey of LGBT Americans," 95.

96. Pew Research Center, "A Survey of LGBT Americans," 13–14.

97. Tristan Ahtone, "Paying Attention to the Native American Vote: Votes of Native Americans Could Impact Several Battleground States," *PBS Frontline World*, November 4, 2008, http://www.pbs.org/frontline world/election2008/2008/11/paying-attention-to-the-n.html.

Chapter 10

1. Sonia Johnson, *From Housewife to Heretic* (Garden City, NY: Doubleday, 1981): 89.

2. Johnson, *Housewife to Heretic*, 106.

3. Johnson, *Housewife to Heretic*, chap. 5.

4. Deborah J. Schildkraut, "Which Birds of a Feather Flock Together? Assessing Attitudes about Descriptive Representation among Latinos and Asian Americans," *American Politics Research* 41, no. 4 (2012): 706.

5. Regina Branton, "Latino Attitudes toward Various Areas of Public Policy: Importance of Acculturation," *Political Research Quarterly* 60, no. 2 (2007): 293–303.

6. Atiya Kai Stokes-Brown, "Racial Identity and Latino Vote Choice," *American Politics Research* 34, no. 5 (2006): 627–652; Schildkraut, "Which Birds of a Feather."

7. Gabriel R. Sanchez, "The Role of Group Consciousness in Political Participation among Latinos in the United States," *American Politics Research* 34, no. 4 (2006): 439.

8. Calculated by author from census data presented at https://www.census.gov/population/foreign/files/cps2012/2012T4.pdf, Table 4.1.

9. Camille Ryan, "Language Use in the United States: 2011," August 2013, http://www.census.gov/prod/2013pubs/acs-22.pdf.

10. Gary, J. Gates, "LGBT Adult Immigrants in the United States," The Williams Institute, March 2013, http://williamsinstitute.law.ucla.edu/wp-content/uploads/LGBTImmigrants-Gates-Mar-2013.pdf.

11. Ryan, "Language Use in the United States."

12. Elizabeth M. Grieco, "Race and Hispanic Origin of the Foreign-Born Population in the United States: 2007. American Community Survey Report," January 2010, http://www.census.gov/prod/2010pubs/acs-11.pdf.

13. Calculated by author. The question asked: "Overall, do you think of yourself as a typical American or very different from the typical American?"

14. Pew Research Center for People and the Press, "Rise of Asian Americans," April 4, 2013, http://www.pewsocialtrends.org/files/2013/04/Asian-Americans-new-full-report-04-2013.pdf.

15. Pew Research Center for People and the Press, "Rise of Asian Americans," 10.

16. Calculated by author.

17. Calculated by author from the Pew Research Center's 2012 National Survey of Latinos.

18. Anna Brown and Eileen Patton, "Statistical Portrait of Hispanics in the United States, 2012," April 19, 2014, http://www.pewhispanic.org/2014/04/29/statistical-portrait-of-hispanics-in-the-united-states-2012/, Table 20.

19. Brown and Patten, "Statistical Portrait of Hispanics," Table 20.

20. Calculated by author from the Pew Research Center's 2012 National Survey of Latinos.

21. Julie Siebens and Tiffany Julian, "Native North American Languages Spoken at Home in the United States and Puerto Rico: 2006–2010," December 2011, https://www.census.gov/prod/2011pubs/acsbr10-10.pdf.

22. David E. Wilkins and Heidi K. Stark, *American Indian Politics and the American Political System,* 3rd ed. (Lanham, MD: Rowman & Littlefield, 2011): 172–173.

23. Michael C. Dawson, *Behind the Mule: Race and Class in African-American Politics* (Princeton, NJ: Princeton University Press, 1994); Sharon D. Wright Austin, Richard T. Middleton, and Rachel Yon, "The Effects of Racial Group

Consciousness on the Political Participation of African Americans and Black Ethnics in Miami-Dade County, Florida," *Political Research Quarterly* 65, no. 3 (2011): 629–641; Gabriel R. Sanchez, "The Role of Group Consciousness"; Zulema Valdez, "Political Participation among Latinos in the United States: The Effect of Group Identity and Consciousness," *Social Science Quarterly* 91, no. 2 (2011): 466–482; Patricia Gurin, "Women's Gender Consciousness," *Public Opinion Quarterly* 49, no. 1 (1985): 143–163; Clyde Wilcox, "Racial and Gender Consciousness among African-American Women: Sources and Consequences," *Women & Politics* 17, no. 1 (1997): 73–94; Dennis Chong and Reuel Roger, "Racial Solidarity and Political Participation," *Political Behavior* 27, no. 4 (2005): 347–374.

24. Natalie Masuoka, "Together They Become One: Examining the Predictors of Panethnic Consciousness among Asian Americans and Latinos," *Social Science Quarterly* 87, no. 5 (2006): 993–1011; Dawson, *Behind the Mule*.

25. Masuoka, "Together They Become One"; Dawson, *Behind the Mule*.

26. Wright, Middleton, and Yon, "The Effects of Racial Group Consciousness."

27. Valdez, "Political Participation among Latinos."

28. Valdez, "Political Participation among Latinos."

29. Sylvia Manzano and Gabriel R. Sanchez, "Take One for the Team? Limits of Shared Ethnicity and Candidate Preferences," *Political Research Quarterly*, 63 no. 3 (2010): 568–580; Stokes-Brown, "Racial Identity and Latino"; Dawson, *Behind the Mule*; Bryan O. Jackson, "The Effects of Racial Group Consciousness on Political Mobilization in American Cities," *Western Political Quarterly* 40, no. 4 (1987): 631–646; Matt A. Barreto, *Ethnic Cues: The Role of Shared Ethnicity in Latino Political Participation* (Ann Arbor: University of Michigan Press, 2010).

30. Schildkraut, "Which Birds of a Feather."

31. Wright, Middleton, and Yon, "The Effects of Racial Group Consciousness"; Atiya Kai Stokes, "Latino Group Consciousness and Political Participation," *American Politics Research* 31, no. 4 (2003): 361–378; Janelle S. Wong, Pei-Te Lien, and Margaret Conway, "Group-Based Resources and Political Participation among Asian Americans," *American Politics Research* 33, no. 4 (2006): 545–576; Janelle Wong, S. Karthick Ramakrishnan, Taeku Lee, and Jane Junn, *Asian American Political Participation: Emerging Constituents and Their Political Identities* (New York: Russell Sage Foundation, 2011).

32. Wong, Lien, and Conway "Group-Based Resources"; Wong, Ramakrishnan, Lee, and Junn, *Asian American Political Participation*.

33. Melinda S. Jackson, "Priming the Sleeping Giant: The Dynamics of Latino Political Identity and Vote Choice," *Political Psychology* 32, no. 4 (2011): 691–716.

34. This definition is based on one of the initial uses of priming in the political science literature: Shanto Iyengar, Mark D. Peters, and Donald R. Kinder, "Experimental Demonstrations of the 'Not-So-Minimal' Consequences of Television News Programs," *American Political Science Review* 76, no. 4 (1982): 848–858.

35. Melissa R. Michelson, "The Corrosive Effect of Acculturation: How Mexican Americans Lose Political Trust," *Social Science Quarterly* 84, no. 4 (2003): 917–930; John A. Garcia and Gabriel Sanchez, "Electoral Politics," in *Latino Americans and Political Participation*, ed. Sharon A. Navarro and Armando Xavier Mehia (Santa Barbara, CA: ABC-CLIO, 2004).

36. Deborah J. Schildkraut, "The Rise and Fall of Political Engagement among Latinos: The Role of Identity and Perceptions of Discrimination," *Political Behavior* 27, no. 3 (2005): 285–312.

37. Wong, Ramakrishnan, Lee, and Junn, *Asian American Political Participation*.

38. Schildkraut, "The Rise and Fall of Political Engagement."

39. Valdez, "Political Participation among Latinos."

40. Sue Tolleson-Rinehart, *Gender Consciousness and Politics* (New York: Routledge, 1992), 32.

41. Clyde Wilcox, "Racial and Gender Consciousness among African-American Women: Sources and Consequences," *Women & Politics* 17, no. 1 (1997): 74.

42. Tolleson-Rinehart, *Gender Consciousness and Politics*; Pamela Johnston Conover, "Feminists and the Gender Gap," *Journal of Politics* 50, no. 4 (1988): 985–1010; Lauren E. Duncan, "Motivation for Collective Action: Group Consciousness as Mediator of Personality, Life Experiences, and Women's Rights Activism," *Political Psychology* 20, no. 3 (1999): 611–635.

43. Duncan, "Motivation for Collective Action."

44. Gurin, "Women's Gender Consciousness."

45. Gurin, "Women's Gender Consciousness."

46. Donna Henderson-King and Natalya Zhermer, "Feminist Consciousness among Russians and Americans," *Sex Roles* 48, no. 3/4 (2003): 143–155.

47. Henderson-King and Zhermer, "Feminist Consciousness among Russians," 149.

48. Evelyn M. Simien, "Race, Gender, and Linked Fate," *Journal of Black Studies* 35, no. 5 (2005): 529–550; Evelyn M. Simien and Rosalee A. Clawson, "The Intersection of Race and Gender: An Examination of Black Feminist Consciousness, Race Consciousness, and Policy Attitudes," *Social Science Quarterly* 85, no. 3 (2004): 793–810; Claudine Gay and Katherine Tate, "Doubly Bound: The Impact of Gender and Race on the Politics of Black Women," *Political Psychology* 19, no. 1 (1998): 169–184.

49. Simien and Clawson, "The Intersection of Race and Gender"; Gay and Tate, "Doubly Bound"; Wilcox, "Racial and Gender Consciousness."

50. Wilcox, "Racial and Gender Consciousness."

51. Egan, Patrick J., "Group Cohesion without Group Mobilization: The Case of Lesbians, Gays and Bisexuals," *British Journal of Political Science* 42, no. 3 (2012): 597–616.

52. Pew Research Center for People and the Press, "A Survey of LGBT Americans: Attitudes, Experiences and Values in Changing Times," June 13, 2013, 1, http://www.pewsocialtrends.org/files/2013/06/SDT_LGBT-Americans_06-2013.pdf.

53. Pew Research Center for People and the Press, "A Survey of LGBT Americans," 39–40.

54. Jaime M. Grant, Lisa A. Motter, and Justin Tanis, "Injustice at Every Turn: A Report of the National Transgender Discrimination Survey," 2011, http://www.thetaskforce.org/downloads/reports/reports/ntds_full.pdf.

55. Grant, Motter, and Tanis, "Injustice at Every Turn," 2–6.

56. Grant, Motter, and Tanis, "Injustice at Every Turn," 2.

57. Calculated by author.

58. http://www.docstoc.com/docs/4392626/Center-for-the-Advancement-of-Women-Progress-and-Perils.

59. Pew Research Center for People and the Press, "Rise of Asian Americans," 12.

60. Pew Research Center for People and the Press, "Rise of Asian Americans," 11.

61. Calculated by author from the Pew Research Center's 2012 Survey of Asian Americans.

62. Mark Hugo Lopez, Rich Morin, and Paul Taylor, "Illegal Immigration Backlash Worries, Divides Latinos," October 28, 2010, http://www.pewhispanic.org/files/reports/128.pdf. The question asked: "In general, do you think discrimination against Latinos is a major problem, a minor problem, or not a problem preventing Latinos in general from succeeding in America?"

63. Mark Lopez, "Three-fourths of Hispanics Say Their Community Needs a Leader," October 22, 2013, 13, http://www.pewhispanic.org/files/2013/10/National_Latino_Leader_10-2013_FINAL.pdf.

64. Lopez, Morin, and Taylor, "Illegal Immigration Backlash." The question asked: "During the past five years, have you, a family member or close friend experienced discrimination because of your racial or ethnic background, or not?"

65. Calculated by author from 2012 GSS.

66. Carroll Doherty, "For African Americans Discrimination Is Not Dead," June 28, 2013, http://www.pewresearch.org/fact-tank/2013/06/28/for-african-americans-discrimination-is-not-dead/. The question asked: "How much discrimination is there against African Americans?"

67. Pew Research Center, The question asked: "During the past 12 months, have you personally experienced discrimination or been treated unfairly because of your race or ethnic background, or not?"

68. Pew Research Center for People and the Press, "A Survey of LGBT Americans." The specific question asked: "How important, if at all, is being [INSERT ID, e.g. lesbian] to your overall identity? Would you say it is extremely, very, somewhat, not too, not at all?"

69. Calculated by author.

70. Calculated by author.

71. All the figures for this paragraph were calculated by the author using the Pew Research Center 2012 Survey of Asian Americans. For the identity question, numbers do not equal 100% since a few indicated "it depends."

72. The question asked: "People sometimes use different terms to describe themselves. In general which one of the following terms do you use to describe yourself most often?" Lopez, "Three-fourths of Hispanics," 15.

73. Lopez, "Three-fourths of Hispanics," 24

74. Calculated by author using Pew Research Center's 2011 National Survey of Latinos.

75. Calculated by author.

76. Quoted in Paula D. McClain and Joseph Stewart Jr., *Can We All Get Along? Racial and Ethnic Minorities in American Politics* (Boulder, CO: Westview Press, 2014), 78.

77. Calculated by author.

78. These data were calculated by the author using 2012 GSS survey.

79. Calculated by author using ANES data.

80. Michael Martinez, Stephanie Elam, and Erica Henry, "Unwritten Rules for Raising Black Sons," *CNN*, August 21, 2014, http://www.cnn.com/2014/08/15/living/parenting-black-sons-ferguson-missouri/.

81. Pete K. Hatemi, Sarah E. Medland, and Lindon J. Eaves, "Do Genes Contribute to the 'Gender Gap'" *Journal of Politics* 71, no. 1 (2009): 262–276.

82. Dawson, *Behind the Mule*; Wright Austin, Middleton, and Yon, "The Effects of Racial Group Consciousness"; Wilcox, "Racial and Gender Consciousness."

83. These figures were calculated by the author. For whites and blacks, 2012 GSS data were used, for Hispanics, the Pew Research Center's 2012 National Survey of Latinos was used, and for Asian Americans Pew Research Center 2012 Survey of Asian Americans was used.

84. Calculated by the author using the 2012 GSS. This included several different Baptist churches.

85. Pew Research Center, "The Shifting Religious Identity of Latinos in the United States: Nearly One in Four Are Former Catholics," May 7, 2014, 5, http://www.pewforum.org/files/2014/05/Latinos-Religion-07-22-full-report.pdf.

86. Pew Research Center, "The Shifting Religious Identity of Latinos."

87. Pew Research Center for People and the Press, "Rise of Asian Americans."

88. Barry A. Kosmin, Egon Mayer, and Ariela Keysar, "American Religious Identification Survey 2001," City University of New York, http://www.gc.cuny.edu/CUNY_GC/media/CUNY-Graduate-Center/PDF/ARIS/ARIS-PDF-version.pdf.

89. Calculated by author using 2012 GSS.

90. Pew Research Center for People and the Press, "A Survey of LGBT Americans."

91. Lydia Saad, "Public Opinion about Abortion—An In-depth Review," Gallup, January 22, 2002, http://www.gallup.com/poll/9904/public-opinion-about-abortion-indepth-review.aspx; Pew Research Center, "Changing

Attitudes on Gay Marriage" September 24, 2014, http://www.pewforum.org/2014/09/24/graphics-slideshow-changing-attitudes-on-gay-marriage/.

92. Gary Gates and Frank Newport, "LGBT Americans Skew Democratic, Largely Support Obama," October 18, 2012, http://www.gallup.com/poll/158102/lgbt-americans-skew-democratic-largely-support-obama.aspx.

93. Calculated by author from the Pew Research Center for People and the Press, "Rise of Asian Americans."

94. Calculated by author using 2012 GSS.

95. McClain and Stewart, *Can We All Get Along?*

96. Pew Research Center, "Political Polarization in the American Public: How Increasing Ideological Uniformity and Partisan Antipathy Affect Politics, Compromise and Everyday Life," June 21, 2014, http://www.people-press.org/2014/06/12/political-polarization-in-the-american-public/.

97. Percentages do not add up to 100% because 1.7% of women and 4.1% of men said they identified with another party.

98. Pew Research Center for People and the Press, "A Survey of LGBT Americans."

99. Pew Research Center for People and the Press, "A Survey of LGBT Americans," 104.

100. The 2012 GSS data were used for African Americans, whites, and other races.

101. The percentages do not add to 100% because a few people identify with another party: 3.3% of whites, 1.3% of African Americans, and 1.0% of Other.

102. Calculated by author using the Pew Research Center 2012 National Survey of Latinos. Independent-leaning partisans were included but those who did not answer were not included in the percentages.

103. Calculated by author using the Pew Research Center for People and the Press, "Rise of Asian Americans." Independents who lean toward one of the parties were included as partisans, and those who did not answer or listed a different party were not included.

104. Wong, Ramakrishnan, Lee, and Junn, *Asian American Political Participation.*

105. Stephen Cornell and Joseph P. Kalt, "American Indian Self Determination: The Political Economy of a Policy That Works" (Faculty Research Working Paper Series), Harvard University, John F. Kennedy School of Government, RWP10-043, November 2010, file:///C:/Users/rherric/Downloads/RWP10-043_Cornell_Kalt%20(1).pdf.

106. Wilkins and Stark, *American Indian Politics,* 179–180.

107. http://www.cnn.com/election/2012/results/race/president.

108. Gary Gates, "LGBT Vote 2012," http://williamsinstitute.law.ucla.edu/wp-content/uploads/Gate-LGBT-Vote-Nov-2012.pdf.

109. McClain and Stewart, *Can We All Get Along?* 129.

110. Figure from research by Native Votes Washington as reported by Wilkins and Stark, *American Indian Politics,* 184.

111. Pew Research Center for People and the Press, "Rise of Asian Americans."

112. Calculated by author using Pew Research Center's 2011 National Survey of Latinos.

113. Stokes-Brown, "Racial Identity and Latino Vote Choice"; Valdez, "Political Participation among Latinos."

114. These figures were calculated by author.

Chapter 11

1. Gregory A. Allen, "Campaigns Targeting Hispanics, but with Tight Focus," *NPR,* October 2, 2012, 1–3, http://www.npr.org/2012/10/02/162173953/campaigns-targeting-hispanics-but-with-tight-focus.

2. Elise Foley, "Barack Obama Speaks Spanish, Touts Support for 'Dreamers' in New Ad," *Huffington Post,* October 9, 2012, http://www.huffingtonpost.com/2012/10/09/barack-obama-spanish-dreamer_n_1951678.html, accessed October 3, 2014.

3. http://americasvoice.org/blog/americas-voice-translates-new-romney-spanish-language-ad/, accessed October 2, 2014.

4. Elizabeth Llorente and Bryan Llenas, "The Conventions: Republicans, Democrats Make Push for Latino Voters," *Fox News Latino,* August 23, 2012; http://latino.foxnews.com/latino/politics/2012/08/23/rnc-and-dnc-conventions-what-is-at-stake-with-latino-voters/.

5. Sidney Verba and Norman H. Nie, *Participation in America: Political Democracy and Social Equality* (Chicago: University of Chicago Press, 1972).

6. Lawrence Bobo and Franklin Gilliam, "Race, Sociopolitical Participation and Black Empowerment," *American Political Science Review* 84, no. 2 (1990): 377–393.

7. Lester K. Spence and Harwood McClerking, "Context, Black Empowerment, and African American Political Participation," *American Politics Research* 38, no. 5 (2010): 909–930.

8. Kenny J. Whitby, "The Effects of Black Descriptive Representation on Black Electoral Turnout in the 2004 Elections," *Social Science Quarterly* 88, no. 4 (2007): 1010–1023; Rene R. Rocha, Caroline Tolbert, Daniel C. Bowen, and Christopher Clark, "Race and Turnout: Does Descriptive Representation in State Legislatures Increase Minority Voting?" *Political Research Quarterly* 63, no. 4 (2010): 890–907.

9. For example see, Claudine Gay, "The Effect of Black Congressional Representation on Political Participation,"

American Political Science Review 95, no. 3 (2001): 589–602.

10. Benjamin J. Deufel and Orit Kedar, "Race and Turnout in U.S. Elections Exposing Hidden Effects," *Public Opinion Quarterly* 74, no. 2 (2010): 286–318.

11. Seth C. McKee, M. V. Hood III, and David D. Hill, "Achieving Validation: Barack Obama and Black Turnout in 2008," *State Politics and Policy Quarterly* 12, no. 1 (2012): 3–22.

12. McKee, Hood, and Hill, "Achieving Validation," 11.

13. Information for this Spotlight comes from Rafael López Pintor, Maria Gratschew, and Kate Sullivan, "Voter Turnout Rates from a Comparative Perspective," http://www.idea.int/publications/vt/upload/Voter%20turnout.pdf, accessed October 3, 2014; Joni Seager, *The Penguin Atlas of Women in the World,* 4th ed. (New York: Penguin Books, 2008).

14. López Pintor, Gratschew, and Sullivan, "Voter Turnout Rates."

15. J. Kevin Corder and Christina Wolbrecht, "Political Context and the Turnout of New Women Voters after Suffrage," *Journal of Politics* 68, no. 1 (2006): 34–49.

16. Pew Research Center for People and the Press, "A Survey of LGBT Americans: Attitudes, Experiences and Values in Changing Times," June 13, 2013, 112, http://www.pewsocialtrends.org/files/2013/06/SDT_LGBT-Americans_06-2013.pdf.

17. Gary J. Gates and Frank Newport, "LGBT Americans Skew Democratic, Largely Support Obama: Conservative LGBT Individuals Tend to Be Older, White and More Religious," October 18, 2012, http://www.gallup.com/poll/158102/lgbt-americans-skew-democratic-largely-support-obama.aspx.

18. Gary J. Gates, "LGBT Votes 2012," November 2012, http://williamsinstitute.law.ucla.edu/research/census-lgbt-demographics-studies/lgbt-vote-2012/.

19. Figures for voting age population come from Paula D. McClain and Joseph Stewart Jr., *Can We All Get Along? Racial and Ethnic Minorities in American Politics* (Boulder, CO: Westview, 2014), 103.

20. Calculated by author from http://www.census.gov/hhes/www/socdemo/voting/publications/p20/2012/tables.html.

21. Calculated by author from http://www.census.gov/hhes/www/socdemo/voting/publications/p20/2012/tables.html.

22. http://www.census.gov/hhes/www/socdemo/voting/publications/p20/2012/tables.html.

23. http://www.census.gov/hhes/www/socdemo/voting/publications/p20/2012/tables.html.

24. Thom File, "The Diversifying Electorate—Voting Rates by Race and Hispanic Origin in 2012 (and Other Recent Elections)," May 2013, http://www.census.gov/prod/2013pubs/p20-568.pdf.

25. Janelle Wong, S. Karthick Ramakrishnan, Taeku Lee, and Jane Junn, *Asian American Political Participation: Emerging Constituents and Their Political Identities* (New York: Russell Sage Foundation, 2011); John A. Garcia and Gabriel Sanchez, "Electoral Politics," in *Latino Americans and Political Participation,* ed. Sharon A. Navarro and Armando Xavier Mejia (Santa Barbara, CA: ABC-CLIO, 2004).

26. http://www.census.gov/hhes/www/socdemo/voting/publications/p20/2012/tables.html, table 2.

27. Jerry D. Stubben, *Native Americans and Political Participation: A Reference Handbook* (Santa Barbara, CA: ABC-CLIO, 2006).

28. Laughlin McDonald, *American Indians and the Fight for Equal Rights* (Norman: University of Oklahoma Press: 2010), chap. 9.

29. Dennis Chong and Reuel Roger, "Racial Solidarity and Political Participation," *Political Behavior* 27, no. 4 (2005): 347–374; Janelle S. Wong, Pei-Te Lien, and M. Margaret Conway, "Group-Based Resources and Political Participation among Asian Americans," *American Politics Research* 33, no. 4 (2006): 545–576; Verba and Nie, *Participation in America;* Garcia and Sanchez, "Electoral Politics"; Wong et al., *Asian American Political Participation.*

30. Sidney Verba, Kay Lehman Schlozman, and Henry E. Brady, *Voice and Equality: Civic Voluntarism in American Politics* (Cambridge MA: Harvard University Press, 1995).

31. Verba, Schlozman, and Brady, *Voice and Equality,* 233.

32. Verba, Schlozman, and Brady, *Voice and Equality,* 254.

33. Calculated by author using Karthick Ramakrishnan, Jane Junn, Taeku Lee, and Janelle Wong, "National Asian American Survey," 2008.ICPSR31481-v2. Ann Arbor, MI: Inter-university Consortium for Political and Social Research [distributor], 2012-07-19. http://doi.org/10.3886/ICPSR31481.v2.

34. Calculated by author using Ramakrishnan, Junn, Lee, and Wong, "National Asian American Survey."

35. Wong, Ramakrishnan, Lee, and Junn, *Asian American Political Participation.*

36. Pew Research Center for People and the Press, "A Survey of LGBT," 86.

37. Pew Research Center for People and the Press, "A Survey of LGBT," 87.

38. Pew Research Center for People and the Press, "A Survey of LGBT," 87.

39. http://www.pewsocialtrends.org/files/2013/06/SDT_LGBT-Americans_Topline.pdf.

40. http://www.pewsocialtrends.org/files/2013/06/SDT_LGBT-Americans_Topline.pdf.

41. http://www.pewsocialtrends.org/files/2013/06/SDT_LGBT-Americans_Topline.pdf.

42. http://www.pewsocialtrends.org/files/2013/06/SDT_LGBT-Americans_Topline.pdf.

43. http://www.pewsocialtrends.org/files/2013/06/SDT_LGBT-Americans_Topline.pdf.

44. Pew Research Center for People and the Press, "A Survey of LGBT," 87.

45. Verba and Nie, *Participation in America*.

46. Verba, Schlozman, and Brady, *Voice and Equality*.

47. Verba and Nie, *Participation in America*; Verba, Schlozman, and Brady, *Voice and Equality*; Wong, Ramakrishnan, Lee, and Junn, *Asian American Political Participation*; Garcia and Sanchez, "Electoral Politics."

48. Verba and Nie, *Participation in America*.

49. See, for example, Verba, Schlozman, and Brady, *Voice and Equality*.

50. The 2012 figures were calculated by the author, and 2008 and 2004 data come from ANES, http://electionstudies.org/nesguide/2ndtable/t6c_1a_1.htm.

51. These figures were calculated by the author.

52. Wong, Ramakrishnan, Lee, and Junn, *Asian American Political Participation*.

53. Verba, Schlozman, and Brady, *Voice and Equality*.

54. Anthony Downs, *An Economic Theory of Democracy* (New York: Harper and Row, 1957).

55. Mancur Olson, *The Logic of Collective Action: Public Goods and the Theory of Groups* (Cambridge, MA: Harvard University Press, 1965).

56. Verba, Schlozman, and Brady, *Voice and Equality*.

57. The specific language read before the statement was: "Now I am going to read you another series of statements on some different topics. For each statement, please tell me if you completely agree with it, mostly agree with it, mostly disagree with it or completely disagree with it. The first one is... Do you completely agree, mostly agree, mostly disagree, or completely disagree?"

58. These were calculated by the author.

59. Pew Research Center for People and the Press, "A Survey of LGBT Americans," 112.

60. Pew Research Center for People and the Press, "A Survey of LGBT Americans," 122.

61. Garcia and Sanchez, "Electoral Politics."

62. Zoltan Hajnal, "Who Loses in American Democracy? A Count of Votes Demonstrates the Limited Representation of African Americans," *American Political Science Review* 103, no. 1 (2009): 37–56.

63. Hajnal, "Who Loses in American Democracy?" 45.

64. Hajnal, "Who Loses in American Democracy?"

65. Matt A. Barreto, Gary M. Segura, and Nathan D. Woods, "The Mobilizing Effect of Majority-Minority Districts on Latino Turnout," *American Political Science Review* 98, no. 1 (2004): 65–75.

66. Wong, Ramakrishnan, Lee, and Junn, *Asian American Political Participation*.

67. Danny Hayes and Seth McKee, "The Intersection of Redistricting, Race, and Participation," *American Journal of Political Science* 56, no. 1 (2012): 115–130.

68. Matt A. Barreto, *Ethnic Cues: The Role of Shared Ethnicity in Latino Political Participation* (Ann Arbor: University of Michigan Press, 2010).

69. Seung-Jin Jang, "Get Out on Behalf of Your Group: Electoral Participation of Latino and Asian Americans," *Political Behavior* 31, no. 4 (2009): 516.

70. Jang, "Get Out on Behalf."

71. Jennifer L. Merolla, Adrian D. Pantoja, Ivy A. M. Cargile, and Juana Mora, "From Coverage to Action: The Immigration Debate and Its Effects on Participation," *Political Research Quarterly* 66, no. 2 (2013): 322–335.

72. Wong, Ramakrishnan, Lee, and Junn, *Asian American Political Participation*; Garcia and Sanchez, "Electoral Politics,"

73. Wong, Ramakrishnan, Lee, and Junn, *Asian American Political Participation*.

74. Garcia and Sanchez, "Electoral Politics"; Wong, Ramakrishnan, Lee, and Junn, *Asian American Political Participation*.

75. Carol A. Cassel, "Hispanic Turnout: Estimates from Validated Voting Data," *Political Research Quarterly* 55, no. 2 (2002): 391–408.

76. Maria-Elena D. Diaz, "Asian Embeddedness and Political Participation: Social Integration and Asian-American Voting Behavior in the 2000 Presidential Election," *Sociological Perspectives* 55, no. 1 (2012): 141–166.

77. Wong, Ramakrishnan, Lee, and Junn, *Asian American Political Participation*; Diaz, "Asian Embeddedness."

78. Diaz, "Asian Embeddedness."

79. Wong, Ramakrishnan, Lee, and Junn, *Asian American Political Participation*.

80. Eric Swank and Breanne Fahs, "Predicting Electoral Activism among Gays and Lesbians in the United States," *Journal of Applied Social Psychology* 43, no. 7 (2013): 1382–1393.

81. U.S. Census Bureau, Current Population Survey November 2012, https://www.census.gov/hhes/www/socdemo/voting/publications/p20/2012/tables.html, Table 10.

82. File, "The Diversifying Electorate," 5.

83. File, "The Diversifying Electorate," 5.

84. Gates, "LGBT Votes 2012," November 2012, http://williamsinstitute.law.ucla.edu/research/census-lgbt-demographics-studies/lgbt-vote-2012/.

85. McClain and Stewart, *Can We All Get Along?* 101–102.

86. McClain and Stewart, *Can We All Get Along?* 102.

87. Daniel McCool, Susan M. Olson, and Jennifer L. Robinson, *Native Vote: American Indians, the Voting Rights Act, and the Right to Vote* (New York: Cambridge University Press 2007), 177.

88. Stubben, *Native Americans*.

89. McCool, Olson, and Robinson, *Native Vote*, chap. 8.

90. Allen, "Campaigns Targeting Hispanics."

91. Allen, "Campaigns Targeting Hispanics."

92. Nia-Malika Henderson, "Mitt Romney Reaches Out to Black Voters," *Washington Post*, July 10, 2012, http://www.washingtonpost.com/politics/mitt-romney-to-address-naacp/2012/07/10/gJQA5UbUbW_story.html.

93. Henderson, "Mitt Romney Reaches Out."

94. Devin Dwyer, "Obama Targets Black Voters in New Campaign," February 1, 2012, http://abcnews.go.com/blogs/politics/2012/02/obama-targets-black-voters-in-new-campaign/.

95. Debbie Siegelbaum, "Overlooked Asian-American Votes Could Tip Scales in November Election," *The Hill*, June 27, 2012, http://thehill.com/homenews/campaign/234957-overlooked-asian-american-voters-could-tip-scales-in-november-election.

96. Jonathan Salant, "War on Women Is 2012 Democratic Rallying Theme against Republicans," *Bloomberg*, June 8, 2011, http://www.bloomberg.com/news/2011-06-08/war-on-women-is-2012-democratic-rallying-theme-against-republicans.html; Laurie Kellman, "Single Women Voters: Democrats, Republicans Woo Unmarried Ladies," *Huffington Post*, March 27, 2012, http://www.huffingtonpost.com/2012/03/27/single-women-voters-democrats-republicans_n_1383394.html.

97. Llorente and Llenas, "The Conventions"; Ryan Grim and Nate Willis, "Republican Convention 2012 Speakers: A Disproportionate Parade of Diversity," *Huffington Post*, August 29, 2012, http://www.huffingtonpost.com/2012/08/29/republican-convention-2012_n_1837981.html.

98. Rosalind Helderman and Jon Cohen, "As Republican Convention Emphasizes Diversity, Racial Incidents Intrude," *Washington Post*, August 29, 2012, http://www.washingtonpost.com/politics/2012/08/29/b9023a52-f1ec-11e1-892d-bc92fee603a7_story.html; Grim and Willis, "Republican Convention 2012 Speakers."

99. Zach Ford, "Democratic Convention Speakers Celebrate LGBT People and Equality," *Think Progress*, September 5, 2012, http://thinkprogress.org/lgbt/2012/09/05/796501/democratic-convention-speakers-celebrate-lgbt-people-and-equality/.

100. McCool, Olson, and Robinson, *Native Vote*, chap. 8.

101. McDonald, *American Indians and the Fight for Equal Rights*, chap. 9.

Chapter 12

1. Helene Whitson, "The San Francisco State Strike Collection: Introductory Essay," San Francisco State University, http://www.library.sfsu.edu/about/collections/strike/essay.html.

2. The outline of events for the strike comes from the San Francisco State Strike Collection: Chronology of Events, http://www.library.sfsu.edu/about/collections/strike/chronology.html.

3. Craig A. Rimmerman, *The Lesbian and Gay Movements: Assimilation or Liberation?* (Boulder, CO: Westview, 2014); Kenneth D. Wald, "The Context of Gay Politics," in *The Politics of Gay Rights*, ed. Craig A. Rimmerman, Kenneth D. Wald, and Clyde Wilcox (Chicago: University of Chicago Press, 2000), 1–30.

4. Rimmerman, *The Lesbian and Gay Movements.*

5. Rimmerman, *The Lesbian and Gay Movements*, 5.

6. John A. Salmond, *My Mind Set on Freedom: A History of the Civil Rights Movement, 1954–1968* (Chicago: Ivan R. Dee, 1997).

7. While this is the standard view of events, it is likely that Parks refused to give up her seat as a means to create the action.

8. The whole paragraph is based on Salmond, *My Mind Set on Freedom.*

9. Salmond, *My Mind Set on Freedom.*

10. Salmond, *My Mind Set on Freedom*, 93.

11. Civil rights were not part of the Kennedy administration's agenda, which saw the Freedom Rides and similar actions as a distraction and an embarrassment abroad. Robert Kennedy encouraged the movement to work on voter registration, since he mistakenly thought it would be less confrontational (Salmond, *My Mind Set on Freedom*, 94).

12. Salmond, *My Mind Set on Freedom*, 100.

13. Salmond, *My Mind Set on Freedom*, 72; Dennis Chong, *Collective Action and the Civil Rights Movement* (Chicago: University of Chicago Press, 1991), chap. 9.

14. http://abacus.bates.edu/admin/offices/dos/mlk/letter.html.

15. http://ellabakercenter.org/about/who-was-ella-baker, accessed October 6, 2014.

16. Sherly Gay Stolberg, "Still Marching on Washington 50 Years Later," *New York Times*, August 13, 2013, http://www.nytimes.com/2013/08/14/us/politics/50-years-later-fighting-the-same-civil-rights-battle.html?pagewanted=all&_r=0, http://johnlewis.house.gov/john-lewis/biography, accessed October 6, 2014.

17. Sandra L Barnes, "Malcolm X (1925–1965)," in *Encyclopedia of Racism in the United States,* vol. 2, ed. Pyong Gap Min (Westport, CT: Greenwood Press, 2005), 371.

18. http://www.apri.org/ht/d/sp/i/225, accessed October 5, 2014.

19. Etsuko Maruoka-Ng, "Randolph, A. Philip (1889–1979)," in *Encyclopedia of Racism in the United States,* vol. 2, ed. Pyong Gap Min (Westport, CT: Greenwood Press 2005), 516.

20. Steve Hendrix, "Bayard Rustin, Organizer of the March on Washington, Was Crucial to the Movement," *Washington Post*, August 17, 2011, http://www.washingtonpost.com/lifestyle/style/bayard-rustin-organizer-of-the-march-on-washington-was-crucial-to-the-movement/2011/08/17/gIQA0oZ7UJ_story.html; http://www.biography.com/people/bayard-rustin-9467932#synopsis, accessed October 6, 2014.

21. Salmond, *My Mind Set on Freedom*, 65.

22. Carlos Munoz Jr., *Youth, Identity and Power: The Chicano Movement* (New York: Verso, 1989), 15–16.

23. Munoz, *Youth, Identity and Power.*

24. http://www.latinamericanstudies.org/latinos/joaquin. htm. "Yo Soy Joaquin" is reprinted with permission from the publisher of *Message to Aztlan* by Rodolfo "Corky" Gonzales (© 2001 Arte Público Press - University of Houston).

25. Munoz, *Youth, Identity and Power.*

26. Quoted in Munoz, *Youth, Identity and Power,* 77–78.

27. Aztlan is the home of the Aztecs, and thought to comprise northern Mexico and the Southwestern United States.

28. Don-Ho Cho, "El Teatro Campensino," in *Encyclopedia of Racism in the United States,* vol. 1, ed. Pyong Gap Min (Westport, CT: Greenwood Press, 2005), 201; Rose Kim, "Chavez, Cesar (1927–1993)," in *Encyclopedia of Racism in the United States,* vol. 1, ed. Pyong Gap Min (Westport, CT: Greenwood Press, 2005), 112–113; http://www.biography.com/people/ cesar-chavez-9245781, accessed October 5, 2014.

29. Dong-Ho Cho, "Gonzales, Rodolfo."

30. http://www.escuelatlatelolco.org/Corky.html, accessed October 6, 2014; Dong-Ho Cho, "Gonzales, Rodolfo 'Corky' (1928-)," in *Encyclopedia of Racism in the United States,* vol. 1, ed. Pyong Gap Min (Westport, CT: Greenwood Press, 2005), 244.

31. http://www.biography.com/people/dolores-huerta- 188850#early-life-and-career, accessed October 6, 2014; http://www.nwhm.org/education-resources/biography/biog- raphies/dolores-fernandez-huerta/, accessed October 6, 2014.

32. David E. Wilkins and Heidi K. Stark, *American Indian Politics and the American Political System,* 3rd ed. (Lanham, MD: Rowman & Littlefield, 2011), 204.

33. Wilkins and Stark. *American Indian Politics,* 189.

34. Gabriel Chrisman, "The Fish-in Protests at Franks Landing," University of Washington Department of Edu- cation, Seattle Civil Rights and Labor History Project, http://depts.washington.edu/civilr/fish-ins.htm.

35. Chrisman, "The Fish-in Protests at Franks Landing."

36. Wilkins and Stark, *American Indian Politics,* 206.

37. Christine K. Gray, *The Tribal Moment in American Politics* (Lanham, MD: AltaMira Press, 2013), 187–189.

38. Gray, *The Tribal Moment in American Politics,* 189.

39. Wilkins and Stark, *American Indian Politics,* 207.

40. Gale Courey Toensing, "Dennis Banks on the AIM Era: I Regret It Ended Too Soon," *Indian Country Today,* April 25, 2013, http://indiancountrytodaymedianetwork. com/2013/04/25/dennis-banks-aim-era-i-regret-it-ended- too-soon-149019, accessed October 7, 2014; http://www .encyclopedia.com/topic/Dennis_J._Banks.aspx, accessed October 7, 2014.

41. Robert D. McFadden, "Russell Means, Who Clashed with Law as He Fought for Indians, Is Dead at 72," *New York Times,* October 22, 2012, http://www.nytimes. com/2012/10/23/us/russell-means-american-indian-activist- dies-at-72.html?pagewanted=all&_r=0, accessed October 7, 2014.

42. William Wei, *The Asian American Movement* (Philadelphia, PA: Temple University Press, 1993), chap. 1.

43. Wei, *The Asian American Movement,* 1.

44. Wei, *The Asian American Movement.*

45. Julie Dolan, Melissa Deckman, and Michele L. Swers, *Women and Politics: Paths to Power and Political Influ- ence* (Upper Saddle River, NJ: Pearson/Prentice Hall, 2011).

46. Judith Lorber, *Gender Inequality: Feminist Theories and Politics,* 3rd ed. (Los Angeles, CA: Roxbury, 2005).

47. Nancy E. McGlen and Karen O'Connor, *Women, Politics, and American Society* (Upper Saddle River, NJ: Pearson/ Prentice Hall, 1998), 120–121.

48. Dolan, Deckman, and Swers, *Women and Politics.*

49. Lynne E. Ford, *Women & Politics: The Pursuit of Equality,* 3rd ed. (Boston, MA: Wadsworth, 2011), 61.

50. Dolan, Deckman, and Swers, *Women and Politics,* 27.

51. Ford, *Women & Politics,* 65.

52. Sarah Hepola, "Gloria Steinem, A Woman Like No Other," *New York Times,* March 16, 2012, http://www.nytimes .com/2012/03/18/fashion/in-the-womans-movement-who- will-replace-gloria-steinem.html?pagewanted=all&_r=0, accessed October 9, 2014; http://www.biography.com/ people/gloria-steinem-9493491, accessed October 9, 2014.

53. Larry Schwartz, "Billie Jean Won for All Women," *ESPN,* https://espn.go.com/sportscentury/features/00016060. html, accessed October 9, 2014.

54. http://www.biography.com/people/betty-friedan- 9302633#early-life-and-career, accessed October 9, 2014.

55. Much of the information for this Spotlight comes from http://www.biography.com/people/susan-b-anthony- 194905#synopsis.

56. Wei, *The Asian American Movement,* 76.

57. John D'Emilio, "Cycles of Change, Questions of Strategy: The Gay and Lesbian Movement after Fifty Years," in *The Politics of Gay Rights,* ed. Craig A. Rimmerman, Kenneth D. Wald, and Clyde Wilcox (Chicago: University of Chicago Press), 31–53.

58. Ashley Currier, *Out in Africa: LGBT organizing in Namibia and South Africa* (Minneapolis, MN: University of Minnesota Press, 2012), quoted on p. 46.

59. D'Emilio, "Cycles of Change," 35.

60. D'Emilio, "Cycles of Change," 36–37.

61. http://www.cdc.gov/mmwr/preview/mmwrhtml/ mm6021a2.htm.

62. Craig A. Rimmerman, "Beyond Political Mainstream- ing: Reflections on Lesbian and Gay Organizations and the Grassroots," in *The Politics of Gay Rights,* ed. Craig A. Rimmerman, Kenneth D. Wald, and Clyde Wilcox (Chicago: University of Chicago Press): 54–78; Rimmerman, *The Lesbian and Gay Movements.*

63. http://www.freedomtomarry.org/pages/about-us.

64. http://www.ncsl.org/research/human-services/same- sex-marriage-laws.aspx, November 20, 2014, accessed December 8, 2014.

65. Rimmerman, *The Lesbian and Gay Movements.*

66. Rimmerman, *The Lesbian and Gay Movements.*

67. For a discussion of these concerns, see Thomas Keck, "Beyond Backlash: Assessing the Impact of Judicial Decisions on LGBT Rights," *Law and Society Review* 43, no. 1 (2009): 151–186.

68. Rimmerman, *The Lesbian and Gay Movements.*

69. Pew Research Center for People and the Press, "A Survey of LGBT Americans: Attitudes, Experiences and Values in Changing Times," June 13, 2013, http://www.pewsocialtrends.org/files/2013/06/SDT_LGBT-Americans_06-2013.pdf, 88.

70. David E. Newton, *Gay and Lesbian Rights,* 2nd ed. (Santa Barbara, CA: ABC-CLIO, 2009), 162–163.

71. Jesse Green, "4000 Pages and Counting," *New York Magazine,* December 27, 2009, http://nymag.com/news/features/62887/, accessed October 6, 2014.

72. Newton, *Gay and Lesbian Rights,* 156–157.

73. Mancur Olson, *The Logic of Collective Action: Public Goods and the Theory of Groups* (Cambridge, MA: Harvard University Press, 1965); Chong, *Collective Action.*

74. Chong, *Collective Action.*

75. Chong, *Collective Action.*

76. Two key resource mobilization sources are Charles Tilly, *From Mobilization to Revolution* (Reading, MA: Addison-Wesley, 1978); John D. McCarthy and Mayer N. Zald, *The Trend of Social Movements* (Morristown, NJ: General Learning Press, 1973).

77. James W. Button, Barbara A. Rienzo, and Kenneth D. Wald, "The Politics of Gay Rights at the Local and State Level" in *The Politics of Gay Rights,* ed. Craig A Rimmerman, Kenneth D. Wald, and Clyde Wilcox (Chicago: University of Chicago Press, 2000), 281.

78. Ellen Ann Andersen, *Out of the Closets & into the Courts: Legal Opportunity Structure and Gay Rights Litigation* (Ann Arbor: University of Michigan Press 2005), 4–5.

79. Suzanne Staggenborg, "The Consequences of Professionalization and Formalization in the Pro-Choice Movement," *American Sociological Review* 54, no. 4 (1988): 585–606.

80. Gary Mucciaroni, *Same Sex, Different Politics: Success and Failure in the Struggles over Gay Rights* (Chicago: University of Chicago Press, 2008), 46.

81. Some of the key researchers focusing on political opportunity structures are Peter K. Eisenger, "The Conditions of Protest Behavior in American Cities," *American Political Science Review* 67, no. 1 (1973): 11–28, Sidney Tarrow, *Power in Movement: Social Movements, Collective Action, and Politics* (Cambridge: Cambridge University Press, 1994); Doug McAdams, *Political Process and the Development of Black Insurgence, 1930-1954* (Chicago: University of Chicago Press, 1982).

82. Andersen, *Out of the Closets.*

83. Andersen, *Out of the Closets,* 7.

84. Andersen, *Out of the Closets,* 8.

85. Ann N. Costain, Richard Braustein, and Heidi Berggren, "Frames and the Women's Movement," in *Women,*

86. Costain, Braustein, and Berggren, "Frames and the Women's Movement."

87. Paul R. Brewer, *Value War: Public Opinion and the Politics of Gay Rights* (Lanham, MD: Rowman & Littlefield, 2008).

88. Costain, Braustein, and Berggren, "Frames and the Women's Movement."

89. Paul R. Brewer, *Value War.*

90. Andersen, *Out of the Closets.*

91. Much of the information on the NAACP comes from its webpage: http://www.naacp.org.

92. Much of the information on the Urban League comes from its webpage: http://nul.iamempowered.com.

93. Much of the information on SCLC comes from its webpage: http://sclcnational.org.

94. Much of the information on CORE comes from its webpage: http://core-online.org/.

95. Janell Ross, "How Black Lives Matter Moved from a Hashtag to a Real Political Force," *Washington Post,* August 19, 2015, http://www.washingtonpost.com/news/the-fix/wp/2015/08/19/how-black-lives-matter-moved-from-a-hashtag-to-a-real-political-force/, accessed September 2, 2015.

96. Much of the information on the LULAC comes from its webpage: http://lulac.org/about/mission/.

97. Much of the information on NCLR comes from its webpage: http://www.nclr.org/.

98. Much of the information on UFW comes from its webpage: http://www.ufw.org/.

99. Much of the information on USHCC comes from its webpage: http://ushcc.com/.

100. Much of the information on SVREP comes from its webpage: http://svrep.org/.

101. Much of the information on NAAPAE comes from its webpage: http://www.naapae.net/.

102. Much of the information on LEAP comes from its webpage: http://leap.org/.

103. Much of the information on APALANET comes from its webpage: http://apalanet.org/about/.

104. http://apalanet.org/about/.

105. Much of the information on NCAI comes from its webpage: http://www.ncai.org/about-ncai/mission-history.

106. Wilkins and Stark, *American Indian Politics,* 194.

107. Wilkins and Stark, *American Indian Politics,* 191.

108. Much of the information on AIM comes from its webpage: http://www.aimovement.org/ggc/index.html.

109. Wilkins and Stark, *American Indian Politics,* 197.

110. Much of the information on NARF comes from its webpage: http://www.narf.org/.

111. Wilkins and Stark, *American Indian Politics,* 199.

112. Niraj Chokshi, "Alaska Natives Secure a Voting Rights Victory in Court," *Washington Post,* September 5, 2014,

http://www.washingtonpost.com/blogs/govbeat/wp/2014/09/05/alaska-natives-secure-a-voting-rights-victory-in-court/?wpisrc=nl_pmpol&wpmm=1).

113. Wilkins and Stark, *American Indian Politics,* 199.

114. Much of the information on the NOW comes from its webpage: http://www.now.org.

115. Much of the information on the Feminist Majority comes from its webpage: http://www.feminist.org/welcome/mandp.asp.

116. Ailsa Chang, "From Humble Beginnings a Powerhouse Fundraising Class Emerges," *NPR,* May 6, 2014, http://www.npr.org/2014/05/06/310134589/from-humble-beginnings-a-powerhouse-fundraising-class-emerges and http://www.emilyslist.org.

117. http://www.opensecrets.org/orgs/summary.php?id=d000000113.

118. Much of the information on CWFA comes from its webpage: http://www.cwfa.org.

119. Lori Arnold, "Beverly LaHaye Marks Three Decades of Promoting Traditional Values through CWA," *Christian Examiner,* December 6, 2009, http://www.christianexaminer.com/Articles/Articles%20Dec09/Art_Dec09_06.html.

120. http://www.eagleforum.org/misc/descript.html.

121. Much of the information on the Eagle Forum comes from its webpage: http://www.eagleforum.org/misc/descript.html.

122. https://www.opensecrets.org/orgs/summary.php?id=D000000586.

123. Much of the information on WISH List comes from its webpage: http://www.thewishlist.org/.

124. Susan B. Anthony List webpage: http://www.sba-list.org/about-sba-list/our-mission.

125. https://www.opensecrets.org/orgs/summary.php?id=D000029292.

126. http://www.HRC.org.

127. https://www.opensecrets.org/outsidespending/nonprof_contrib_summ.php?id=521243457.

128. https://www.opensecrets.org/lobby/clientsum.php?id=D000000158&year=2014.

129. https://www.opensecrets.org/outsidespending/detail.php?cmte=Human+Rights+Campaign&cycle=2014.

130. https://www.opensecrets.org/outsidespending/detail.php?cmte=Human+Rights+Campaign&cycle=2014.

131. Much of the information for the Task Force comes from its webpage: http://www.thetaskforce.org/about/mission-history.html.

132. http://www.victoryfund.org.

133. Much of the information for the Victory Fund comes from its webpage: https://www.victoryfund.org/our-results/financial-information.

134. Much of the information for the National Center for Transgender Equality comes from its webpage: http://transequality.org/About/about.html.

135. Much of the information for the Focus on the Family comes from its webpage: http://www.focusonthefamily.com/.

136. https://www.opensecrets.org/orgs/summary.php?id=D000025863&cycle=2014.

137. Much of the information for the Log Cabin Republicans comes from its webpage: http://www.logcabin.org/.

Chapter 13

1. Juliet Williams, "California Affirmative Action Bill Sparks Pushback from Asian Americans," *Huffington Post,* April 23, 2014, http://www.huffingtonpost.com/2014/04/23/california-affirmative-action_n_5197690.html.

2. Josie Huang, "Sca5: A Political Coming of Age Story for Chinese Americans," March 21, 2014, http://www.scpr.org/blogs/multiamerican/2014/03/21/16152/sca-5-chinese-americans-immigrants-asian-americans/.

3. Quoted in Williams, "California Affirmative Action."

4. http://80-20initiative.blogspot.com/2014_02_01_archive.html.

5. Williams, "California Affirmative Action."

6. http://www.scpr.org/blogs/multiamerican/2014/03/21/16152/sca-5-chinese-americans-immigrants-asian-americans/.

7. Jeffrey M. Jones, "Americans Rate Racial and Ethnic Relations in U.S. Positively: View Black-Hispanic Relations Least Positively," July 17, 2013, http://www.gallup.com/poll/163535/americans-rate-racial-ethnic-relations-positively.aspx.

8. Paula D. McClain and Albert K. Karnig, "Black and Hispanic Socioeconomic and Political Competition," *American Political Science Review* 84, no. 2 (1990): 535–545; Paula D. McClain, "The Changing Dynamics of Urban Politics: Black and Hispanic Municipal Employment—Is There Competition?" *Journal of Politics* 55, no. 2 (1993): 399–414.

9. McClain and Karnig, "Black and Hispanic Socioeconomic"; Paula D. McClain and Steven C. Tauber, "Black and Latino Socioeconomic and Political Competition: Has a Decade Made a Difference?" *American Politics Quarterly* 26, no. 2 (1998): 237–252.

10. McClain and Karnig, "Black and Hispanic Socioeconomic"; McClain and Tauber, "Black and Latino Socioeconomic"; Kenneth J. Meier, Paula D. McClain, J. L. Polinard, and Robert D. Wrinkle, "Divided or Together? Conflict and Cooperation between African-Americans and Latinos," *Political Research Quarterly* 57, no. 3 (2004): 399–409.

11. Kenneth J. Meier and Joseph Stewart Jr., "Cooperation and Conflict in Multiracial School Districts," *Journal of Political Science* 53, no. 4 (1991): 1124–1133; Michael W. Giles and Arthur Evans, "The Power Approach to Intergroup Hostility," *Journal of Conflict Resolution* 30, no. 3 (1986): 469–486; Rene R. Rocha, "Black-Brown Coalitions in Local School Board Elections," *Political Research Quarterly* 60, no. 2 (2007): 315–327.

12. Karen M. Kaufmann, "Black and Latino Voters in Denver: Responses to Each Other's Political Leadership," *Political Science Quarterly* 118, no. 1 (2013): 107–125.

13. Rodney E. Hero and Robert Preuhs, "Beyond (the Scope of) Conflict: National Black and Latino Advocacy Group Relations in the Congressional and Legal Arenas," *Perspective of Politics* 7, no. 3 (2009): 501–517.

14. Byran O. Jackson, Elisabeth R. Gerber, and Bruce E. Cain, "Coalitional Prospects in a Multi-Racial Society: African-American Attitudes towards Other Minority Groups," *Political Research Quarterly* 47, no. 2 (1994): 277–294.

15. Paula D. McClain, Niambi M. Carter, Victoria M. DeFrancesco Soto, Monique L. Lyle, Jeffrey D. Grynaviski, Shayla C. Nunnally, Thomas J. Scotto, J. Alan Kendrick, Gerald F. Lackey, and Kendra Davenport Cotton, "Racial Distancing in a Southern City: Latino Immigrants' Views of Black Americans," *Journal of Politics* 68, no. 3 (2006): 571–584; Karen M. Kaufmann, "Cracks in the Rainbow: Group Commonality as a Basis for Latino and African-American Political Coalitions," *Political Research Quarterly* 56, no. 2 (2003): 199–210.

16. Kaufmann, "Cracks in the Rainbow."

17. Jackson, Gerber, and Cain, "Coalitional Prospects."

18. Kaufmann, "Cracks in the Rainbow"; Jackson, Gerber, and Cain, "Coalitional Prospects"; James Dyer, Arnold Vedlitz, and Stephen Worchel, "Social Distance among Racial and Ethnic Groups in Texas: Some Demographic Correlates," *Social Science Quarterly* 70, no. 3 (1989): 607–616; Nancy Horak Randall and Spencer Delbridge, "Perceptions of Social Distance in an Ethnically Fluid Community," *Sociological Spectrum: MidSouth Sociological Association* 25, no. 1 (2005): 103–122; McClain et al., "Racial Distancing in a Southern City."

19. Dyer, Vedlitz, and Worchel, "Social Distance among Racial"; Randall and Delbridge, "Perceptions of Social Distance."

20. Frustration-aggression approach is defined as "displaced aggression onto a weak target" (Dyer, Vedlitz, and Worchel, "Social Distance among Racial," 608).

21. Randall and Delbridge, "Perceptions of Social Distance."

22. Gabriel R. Sanchez, "Latino Group Consciousness and Perceptions of Commonality with African Americans," *Social Science Quarterly* 89, no. 2 (2008): 428–444; Kaufman, "Cracks in the Rainbow"; McClain et al., "Racial Distancing in a Southern City."

23. Kaufman, "Cracks in the Rainbow"; Sanchez, "Latino Group Consciousness."

24. Sanchez, "Latino Group Consciousness."

25. McClain et al., "Racial Distancing in a Southern City."

26. Kevin Wallsten and Tatishe M. Nteta, "Something in Common? Elite Messages, Partisanship, and Latino Perceptions of Commonality with African Americans," *Du Bois Review* 9, no. 2 (2012): 355–374.

27. Sanchez, "Latino Group Consciousness"; Kaufman, "Cracks in the Rainbow"; Randall and Delbridge, "Perceptions of Social Distance"; Jackson, Gerber, and Cain, "Coalitional Prospects"; Dyer, Vedlitz, and Worchel, "Social Distance among Racial"; McClain et al., "Racial Distancing in a Southern City."

28. Samuel L. Gaertner, John F. Dovidio, Phyllis A. Anastasio, Betty A. Bachman, and Mary C. Rust, "The Common Ingroup Identity Model: Recategorization and the Reduction of Intergroup Bias," *European Review of Social Psychology*, 4, no. 1 (1993): 1–26, DOI: 10.1080/14792779343000004.

29. For example, see Maureen A. Craig, Tracy DeHart, Jennifer A. Richeson, and Luke Fiedorowicz, "Do unto Others as Others Have Done unto You? Perceiving Sexism Influences Women's Evaluations of Stigmatized Racial Groups," *Personality and Social Psychology Bulletin* 38, no. 9 (2012): 1107–1119.

30. Kaufman, "Cracks in the Rainbow."

31. Sanchez, "Latino Group Consciousness"; Maureen A. Craig and Jennifer A. Richeson, "Coalition or Derogation? How Perceived Discrimination Influences Intraminority Intergroup Relations," *Journal of Personality and Social Psychology* 102, no. 4 (2012): 759–777.

32. Craig et al., "Do unto Others"; Dyer, Vedlitz, and Worchel, "Social Distance among Racial."

33. Claudine Gay, "Seeing Difference: The Effect of Economic Disparity on Black Attitudes toward Latinos," *American Journal of Political Science* 50, no. 4 (2006): 982–997.

34. McCain et al., "Racial Distancing in a Southern City."

35. J. Eric Oliver and Janelle Wong, "Intergroup Prejudice in Multiethnic Settings," *American Journal of Political Science* 47, no. 4 (2003): 567–582.

36. Shang E. Ha, "The Consequences of Multiracial Contexts on Public Attitudes toward Immigration," *Political Research Quarterly* 63, no. 1 (2008): 29–42.

37. Gay, "Seeing Difference."

38. Lawrence Bobo and Vincent Hutchings, "Perceptions of Racial Group Competition: Extending Blumer's Theory of Group Position to a Multiracial Social Context," *American Sociological Review* 61, no. 6 (1996): 951–972.

39. Bobo and Hutchings, "Perceptions of Racial Group."

40. Rocha, "Black-Brown Coalitions."

41. Jason P. Casellas, "Coalitions in the House? The Election of Minorities to State Legislatures and Congress," *Political Research Quarterly* 62, no. 1 (2009): 120–131.

42. Irwin L. Morris, "African American Voting on Proposition 187: Rethinking the Prevalence of Interminority Conflict," *Political Research Quarterly* 53, no. 1 (2000): 86.

43. Craig A. Rimmerman, *The Lesbian and Gay Movements: Assimilation or Liberation?* (Boulder, CO: Westview, 2014), 134.

44. Rene R. Rocha, "Black-Brown Coalitions in Local School Board Elections," *Political Research Quarterly* 60, no. 2 (2007): 315–327.

45. Karen M. Kaufmann, "Black and Latino Voters in Denver: Responses to Each Other's Political Leadership," *Political Science Quarterly* 118, no. 1 (2003): 107–125.

46. Hero, and Preuhs, "Black–Latino Relations."

47. Rimmerman, *The Lesbian and Gay Movements*, 24.

48. Eric Gonzalez Juenke and Robert R. Preuhs, "Irreplaceable Legislators? Rethinking Minority Representatives in the New Century," *American Journal of Political Science* 56, no. 3 (2012): 705–715; Katherine Tate, *Black Faces in the Mirror: African Americans and Their Representatives in the U.S. Congress* (Princeton, NJ: Princeton University Press, 2003), chap. 4; Susan Welch, "Are Women More Liberal Than Men in the U.S. Congress?" *Legislative Studies Quarterly* 10, no. 1 (1985): 125–134.

49. For example, see Edith Barrett, "The Policy Priorities of African American Women in State Legislatures," *Legislative Studies Quarterly* 20, no. 2 (1995): 223–247; Rodney E. Hero and Robert R. Preuhs, "Black-Latino Relations in U.S. National Politics: Evidence and the Role of Institutions," *Politics, Groups, and Identities* 1, no. 2 (2013): 251–259; Luis Ricardo Fraga, Linda Lopez, Valerie Martinez-Ebers, and Ricardo Ramirez, "Gender and Ethnicity: Patterns of Electoral Success and Legislative Advocacy among Latina and Latino State Officials in Four States," *Journal of Women, Politics & Policy* 28, no. 3–4 (2006): 121–145; William C. Ellis and Walter C. Wilson, "Minority Chairs and Congressional Attention to Minority Issues: The Effect of Descriptive Representation in Positions of Institutional Power," *Social Science Quarterly* 94, no. 5 (2013): 1207–1221.

50. To find out what how each score card was scored, see the following webpages: http://naacp.3cdn.net/cb0f6053dfa585f0ff_dom6vrdc6.pdf; http://hrc-assets.s3-website-us-east-1.amazonaws.com//files/assets/resources/112thCongressionalScorecard_2012.pdf#__utma=149406063.212690201.1355933003.1409110942.1409190806.41&__utmb=149406063.1.10.1409190806&__utmc=149406063&__utmx=-&__utmz=14940606 3.1409190806.41.4.utmcsr=yahoolutmccn=(organic)lut mcmd=organiclutmctr=hrc%20scorecard%20112th%20 congress&__utmv=-&__utmk=167678398; http://www

.aauwaction.org/wp-content/uploads/2012/09/CVR2012 .pdf; and http://www.immigrationscores.com/.

51. Fraga, Lopez, Martinez-Ebers, and Ramirez, "Gender and Ethnicity."

52. CQ Roll Call, "Updated Guide to the New Congress," November 5, 2014, http://info.cqrollcall.com; Paula D. McClain and Joseph Stewart, *Can't We All Just Get Along? Racial and Ethnic Minorities in American Politics* (Boulder, CO: Westview, 2014); Norman J. Ornstein, Thomas E. Mann, Michael J. Malbin, Andrew Rugg, and Raffaela Wakeman, "Vital Statistics on Congress Data on the U.S. Congress: A Joint Effort from Brookings and the American Enterprise Institute," July 2013, http://www.brookings.edu/research/reports/2013/07/vital-statistics-congress-mann-ornstein, Tables 1-16 to 1-19.

53. William H. Flanigan, Nancy H. Zingale, Elizabeth A. Theiss-Morse, and Michael W. Wagner, *Political Behavior of the American Electorate*, 13th ed. (Washington, DC: CQ Press, 2014), 84.

54. Pew Research Center, "Muslim Americans: Middle Class and Mostly Mainstream," May 22, 2007, http://pew research.org/files/old-assets/pdf/muslim-americans.pdf, 9.

55. Pew Research Center, "Muslim Americans: No Signs in Growth of Alienation or Support for Extremism," August 2011, http://people-press.org/files/2011/08/muslim-american-report.pdf.

56. Pew Research Center, "Muslim Americans: No Signs," 8.

57. Pew Research Center, "Muslim Americans: No Signs," 16.

58. Pew Research Center, "Muslim Americans: No Signs," 65.

59. Pew Research Center, "Muslim Americans: No Signs," 6.

60. Pew Research Center, "Muslim Americans: No Signs," 7.

61. Pew Research Center, "Muslim Americans: No Signs," 46.

62. Joel S. Fetzer and J. Chistropher Soper, *Muslims and the State in Britain, France, and Germany* (New York: Cambridge University Press, 2005), 1.

63. "Muslims in Europe: Country Guide," *BBC*, December 23, 2005, http://news.bbc.co.uk/2/hi/europe/4385768.stm.

64. "Muslims in Europe: Country Guide."

65. Fetzer and Soper, *Muslims and the State*, 3

66. "France's Veil Ban Goes into Effect," April 10, 2011, http://www.voanews.com/content/frances-veil-ban-goes-into-effect-on-monday-119587889/137809.html.

67. Bruce Stokes and Russ Oates, "A Fragile Rebound for EU Image on Eve of European Parliament Elections: EU Favorability Rises, but Majorities Say Their Voice Is Not Heard in Brussels," May 12, 2014, http://www.pewglobal.org/2014/05/12/chapter-4-views-of-roma-muslims-jews/.

68. Pew Research Center, "Few Signs of Backlash from Western Europeans: Muslims in Europe: Economic Worries Top Concerns about Religious and Cultural Identity," July 6, 2006, http://www.pewglobal.org/files/pdf/7-6-06.pdf.

69. Pew Research Center, "Few Signs of Backlash."

70. Fetzer and Soper, *Muslims and the State*, chap. 1.

71. Soeren Kern, "Muslim Voters Change Europe," May 17, 2012, http://www.gatestoneinstitute.org/3064/muslim-voters-europe.

72. Euro-Islam.info, "Muslims in European Politics," no date, http://www.euro-islam.info/key-issues/political-representation/.

73. Euro-Islam.info, "Muslims in European Politics," no date, http://www.euro-islam.info/key-issues/political-representation/.

74. Pew Research Center, "Muslim Americans: No Signs," 53.

75. Pew Research Center, "Muslim Americans: No Signs," 53.

76. Pew Research Center, "Muslim Americans: No Signs," 56.

77. Pew Research Center, "Muslim Americans: No Signs," 61.

78. Pew Research Center, "Muslim Americans: No Signs," 63.

79. Pew Research Center, "Muslim Americans: No Signs," 73.

80. Arab American Institute, "Americans' Attitudes toward Arabs and Muslims," July 29, 2014. http://b.3cdn.net/aai/3e05a493869e6b44b0_76m6iyjon.pdf.

81. http://muslimmedianetwork.com/mmn/?p=3257.

82. Jeffrey M. Jones, "Atheists, Muslims See Most Bias as Presidential Candidates: Two-thirds Would Vote for Gay or Lesbian," June 21, 2012, http://www.gallup.com/poll/155285/Atheists-Muslims-Bias-Presidential-Candidates.aspx.

83. As with most terms of any importance, there are debates about what it means to be an atheist. Instead of engaging in those religious debates, I will rely on self-reports.

84. Nick Wing, "Here Are All the Atheists in Congress," *Huffington Post*, September 19, 2013, http://www.huffingtonpost.com/2013/09/19/atheists-in-congress_n_3944108.html.

85. Michael Lipka, "5 Facts about Atheists," October 23, 2013, http://www.pewresearch.org/fact-tank/2013/10/23/5-facts-about-atheists/.

86. Jeffrey M. Jones, "Atheists, Muslims See Most Bias."

87. Wing, "Here Are All the Atheists."

88. http://freethoughtequality.org/.

89. https://www.opensecrets.org/pacs/lookup2.php?strID=C00545202.

90. Caroline Fairchild and Jillian Berman, "How 7 Occupy Wall Street Issues Stack Up 2 Years Later," *Huffington Post*, September 17, 2013, http://www.huffingtonpost.com/2013/09/17/occupy-wall-street-issues_n_3937483.html.

91. Fairchild and Berman, "How 7 Occupy Wall Street."

92. Chad Stone, Danilo Trisi, Arloc Serman, and William Chen, "A Guide to Statistics on Historical Trends in Income Inequality," April 17, 2014, http://www.cbpp.org/cms/index.cfm?fa=view&id=3629.

93. Stone, Trisi, Serman, and Chen, "A Guide to Statistics."

94. Stone, Trisi, Serman, and Chen, "A Guide to Statistics."

95. http://www.census.gov/hhes/www/poverty/about/overview/index.html.

96. http://www.opensecrets.org/pfds/.

97. http://www.nytimes.com/1992/02/05/us/bush-encounters-the-supermarket-amazed.html.

98. Lucy Madison, "Fact-checking Romney's 47% Comment," September 25, 2012, *CBS News*, http://www.cbsnews.com/news/fact-checking-romneys-47-percent-comment/, accessed December 7, 2014.

99. Emily Thomas, "Hillary Clinton: 'We Were Dead Broke upon Leaving the White House,'" *Huffington Post*, June 9, 2014, http://www.huffingtonpost.com/2014/06/09/clintons-broke-white-house_n_5474015.html.

100. http://www.electionstudies.org/nesguide/2ndtable/t6a_1_1.htm.

101. http://www.electionstudies.org/nesguide/2ndtable/t9a_1_1.htm.

102. http://www.electionstudies.org/nesguide/2ndtable/t9b_1_1.htm.

103. http://www.electionstudies.org/nesguide/2ndtable/t5a_1_1.htm.

104. http://www.electionstudies.org/nesguide/2ndtable/t5b_3_1.htm.

105. http://www.electionstudies.org/nesguide/2ndtable/t5b_1_1.htm.

106. http://www.electionstudies.org/nesguide/2ndtable/t6c_1a_1.htm.

107. Frederick Burkhardt and Sydney Smith, eds., *The Correspondence of Charles Darwin* (New York: Cambridge University Press, 1990), 438.

108. Jim Endersby, "Lumpers and Splitters: Darwin, Hooker and the Search for Order," *Science* 362, no. 5959 (2009): 1496–1499, http://www.sciencemag.org/content/326/5959/1496.full#ref-14.